TEXAS

ATCHISON, STEVE
443-2857

FIFTH EDITION

TEXAS
The Lone Star State

Rupert N. Richardson

Ernest Wallace

Adrian Anderson
LAMAR UNIVERSITY

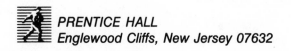
PRENTICE HALL
Englewood Cliffs, New Jersey 07632

Library of Congress Cataloging-in-Publication Data

RICHARDSON, RUPERT NORVAL, [DATE]
    Texas, the Lone Star State.

    Bibliography: p.
    Includes index.
    I. Texas—History. I. Wallace, Ernest.
II. Anderson, Adrian N. III. Title. IV. Title:
Lone Star State.
F386.R52   1988   976.4   87-25492
ISBN 0-13-912452-7

Editorial/production supervision: *Edith Riker*
Cover design: *Lundgren Graphics*
Manufacturing buyer: *Ed O'Dougherty*

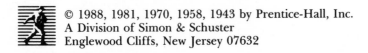 © 1988, 1981, 1970, 1958, 1943 by Prentice-Hall, Inc.
A Division of Simon & Schuster
Englewood Cliffs, New Jersey 07632

Printed in the United States of America

10 9 8 7 6 5 4 3 2 1

ISBN 0-13-912452-7   01

Prentice-Hall International (UK) Limited, *London*
Prentice-Hall of Australia Pty. Limited, *Sydney*
Prentice-Hall Canada Inc., *Toronto*
Prentice-Hall Hispanoamericana, S.A., *Mexico*
Prentice-Hall of India Private Limited, *New Delhi*
Prentice-Hall of Japan, Inc., *Tokyo*
Simon & Schuster Asia Pte. Ltd., *Singapore*
Editora Prentice-Hall do Brasil, Ltda., *Rio de Janeiro*

CONTENTS

PREFACE

Since the first edition of *Texas: The Lone Star State* appeared almost fifty years ago, much history has been made and much has been written. Texans have experienced the anxieties and agonies of wars and postwar adjustments; technological change has altered the way in which most of the population earns its livelihood; and most people of the state are accustomed to a life among suburbs and freeways. In recent years, minorities, racial and otherwise, have continued their search for equality, justice, power, and position, in many instances with considerable success.

Our understanding of the heritage of our state has also changed during these decades. The discovery of new information has sometimes led to the reexamination of past events and new conclusions. More often, however, it is an increased awareness of the contributions and role of minorities—women and other groups—which have been ignored or inadequately recognized in the past that has led to a new, and hopefully, a more complete and meaningful understanding of the past. Certainly, the preparation of this edition of *Texas: The Lone Star State* has been done with that goal in mind.

Notwithstanding the developments of the recent past, the history of Texas in many respects remains unchanged. It is replete with adventure and heroic action. The reader meets with self-denying priests and mail-fisted conquerors of Spain, with filibusters and *empresarios* from beyond the Mississippi, with frontiersmen from Tennessee and planters from Alabama. The Anglo-Americans vied with the Mexicans for supremacy until 1848 and took the country from the Indians by 1875. Thereafter came the struggle for law and order, the lusty cattle industry, the surge of land-hungry farmers seeking virgin soil, the rapid approach of railroads, and the discovery of oil fields. In recent times the challenge of space travel and the explosive growth of urban Texas have continued the tradition of adventure and progress.

In addition to the addition of new materials to bring the text up-to-date in this edition, many of the chapters which deal with the more distant past have been revised. Some of the earlier chapters have been rewritten; in several places the organization has been changed to present certain subjects more fully and clearly; and where new scholarship is available, it has been included to offer new insights and information. Considerable care has been taken to provide a comprehensive listing of recently published books and articles in the bibliographies at the end of each chapter.

In trying to provide a complete survey of the history and current state of Texas, *Texas: The Lone Star State* seeks to give a fair amount of space to certain less interesting but important affairs, without neglecting the more colorful and romantic. The general reader or the college student can easily follow chronologically in the main course of public affairs, breaking the sequence from time to time for a closer look at important movements and life and society in general. Those who prefer to follow the topical units will find the Table of Contents and the Index useful.

We are deeply grateful to the teachers, students, and general readers, whose criticism and constructive suggestions have helped greatly in the work of revision.

A.A.

CHAPTER ONE
THE COUNTRY AND ITS NATIVE PEOPLES

The name Texas comes from *Tejas*, meaning "friends" or "allies," a name applied by Spanish explorers and missionaries to an Indian confederacy, the Hasinai, that they found in this country. Although the name was given to the land very early in the era of Spanish activities and used consistently, the boundaries of the country that it identified changed many times during succeeding centuries. At first, it was applied only to the land of the Hasinai, but borders were adjusted several times during the period of Spanish rule and thereafter until the present boundaries were finally established in 1850. As the size of the country grew, so did its diversity. Today it is a land of contrast, a land of forests and plains, mountains and prairies, deserts and swamps.

People have long inhabited this great land. Relics found at various points over the state indicate the presence of prehistoric people in Texas many thousands of years ago. Much is unknown about these early peoples, but it is evident that their lifestyle changed over the centuries from one dependent upon hunting and foraging to a more complex one of domesticated animals and cultivated crops. In time, for one reason or another, these peoples disappeared and were replaced by the Indians who inhabited the land when European and African explorers made their way to Texas.

With cultures as diverse as the land they occupied, these peoples lived their lives in ways that were sometimes very similar but sometimes were very different.

THE COUNTRY

The distinctive shape that outlines Texas today evolved slowly over several centuries. The land of the Hasinai that originally was Texas included a considerable area of present-day Louisiana and only a portion of East Texas. Early in the eighteenth century, however, the borders of Texas were extended westward to include Spanish settlements that had been planted on the San Antonio River and Matagorda Bay. A definite boundary on the west was first fixed in 1746, when it was declared that the Medina River should separate Texas from the Spanish province of Nuevo Santander. In 1775 this western boundary was moved further west to the Nueces River, and in 1819 the eastern boundary was adjusted to be located in part on the Sabine River. During the time of the republic, ambitious Texans set the Rio Grande as the boundary, thus claiming about half of present New Mexico, a generous amount of present Colorado, and portions of present Oklahoma, Kansas, and Wyoming. As finally adjusted in 1850, a large part of the border of the state consists of natural boundaries, the Rio Grande, the Gulf of Mexico, and the Sabine and Red rivers. The remainder of the boundary consists of straight lines established by surveyors at one time or another in conformity with various treaties and agreements.

With its 267,339 square miles of territory, extending from the High Plains of the Texas Panhandle to the Gulf of Mexico, Texas is, except for Alaska, the largest state in the Union. One can travel eight hundred miles in a straight line within its borders. Texarkana, on the Arkansas border, is closer to Chicago than it is to El Paso, on the Rio Grande. The distance from Brownsville to Mexico City is over one hundred miles shorter than the distance to the city of Texline, a town on the northern fringe of the Texas Panhandle. Orange, on the Sabine River, is closer to the Atlantic, and El Paso, on the Rio Grande, is closer to the Pacific than the two cities are to each other.

The land enclosed by these great distances is not physiographically uniform, but rather it is made up of parts of at least three major physical divisions, namely the Atlantic-Gulf coastal plain, the Great Plains (Continental Interior Plain) of central North America, and the Rocky Mountain system (sometimes called the Western Interior Mountains and Basins Region). The fact that these physiographic areas join within the state means that there is variety and contrast in topography, climate, and

Texas contains a number of regions determined by geological makeup and the resultant physiographic forms. Grasses, timber, soils, and other natural resources have affected its history greatly. (Adapted from Stanley A. Arbingast, Lorrin G. Kennamer, and Michael E. Bonnie, *Atlas of Texas, Bureau of Business Research, The University of Texas at Austin, 1967.*)

resources. These areas are further divided into a number of natural regions, determined mainly by soil and climate.

The Gulf Coast Plain extends from the shore a little south of Corpus Christi to the Sabine River and inland for about one hundred to two hundred miles. Near the coast the land is low and marshy; inland it is well-drained, and there is much heavy soil with a great variety of vegetation. Its better clay and loam soils were once savannas affording excellent grazing, but they now are frequently farmland. There are a number of islands off the coast. These are generally long and narrow, the product of sand that has gradually built up from the bottom of the Gulf. Although Europeans were not quick to settle in this area, it has become one of the more populated areas of the state, including Houston and a host of smaller cities such as Beaumont, Port Arthur, and Corpus Christi. A combination of petroleum production and refining, chemical manufacturing, agriculture, and transportation facilities has provided opportunities and employment.

The natural region often called East Texas is sometimes named the Piney Woods or other names which emphasize one of the most distinctive characteristics of the land, the great, tall, stately pine trees. It is a country of forests and farmlands, of rolling hills and broad valleys. The pine lands are the western edge of the southern pine forest that extends eastward to the Atlantic Ocean. Although the original or virgin timber stand has long since been cut, replanting of forests has maintained a steady and valuable timber industry that, together with petroleum and agriculture, has made the area a prosperous land. In the western part of the region is an extensive area of sandy soils and post oak timber, extending far into Central Texas.

The Central Texas Prairies extend from the Colorado River in the vicinity of Austin northward to the Red River (and beyond into Oklahoma). The prairielands are broken by the Eastern Cross Timbers, a thin wedge of trees extending northward from the vicinity of Waco through the Dallas country to the Red River valley. East of this narrow belt of timber is the Blackland Prairie and to the west lies the Grand Prairie. Rich, black soils predominate, now largely cultivated except where they are too thin. Once this was the heart of cotton country, but insects and other problems have reduced the emphasis on cotton production, and more attention is now devoted to grain and livestock. It is one of the most heavily populated regions of the state. Dallas, Fort Worth, and Austin are the largest cities, but there are ten or so cities of lesser but substantial size.

The Cross Timbers, lying between Fort Worth and Abilene and extending from the vicinity of the Colorado River to the Red River and beyond, is a farming and stock-raising country. It produces peanuts, vegetables, dairy products, and poultry, grown on soils which range from belts of loose, blowing sand to black loams. Like most regions, it contains some petroleum and coal deposits, and at one time was the center of a major coal mining industry.

The Rolling Plains, or North Texas Plains belt, includes the Abilene, Vernon, and Wichita Falls country. It is separated from the High Plains to the west by the Caprock, a prominent limestone escarpment. Some of the Rolling Plains terrain is highly eroded; other areas consist of spacious prairies. There is some petroleum production, but agriculture—mainly cotton, wheat, grain sorghum, and cattle—is the foundation of the economy of most areas.

The High Plains is a part of a great plain that extends from Texas northward into Canada. Once an awesome sea of grass that was rarely broken by trees or anything else as far as the eye could see, the area is now frequently plowed into farmland. Cotton, maize, and several other crops are grown in large quantities, their production largely dependent on irrigation supplied by underground water supplies. Within the area have grown the cities of Amarillo, Lubbock, Plainview, and a score of thriving towns. In more recent years, declining water supplies have become a source of concern.

The Edwards Plateau, sometimes called the Hill Country, is a broken tableland, an extension of the Great Plains but eroded into rocky, hilly country. It is situated between the Rolling Plains and Cross Timbers on the north and the South Texas Plain on the south. In most places the soil is too shallow for farming. Widely known as a livestock region, its ranches produce cattle, sheep, goats, wool, and mohair. On the southern fringe of the region are located portions of Austin and San Antonio. Until recent times, the area was only thinly populated, for the sparse resources of the land produced only enough for a small population, but the development of water reservoirs and the attractiveness of both land and climate have drawn a large number of people since the end of World War II.

The South Texas Plain forms roughly a triangle, bounded by a point near Corpus Christi, westward by way of San Antonio to about Del Rio on the Rio Grande, and southward to the Gulf. It is a land of highly eroded localities, interspersed with prairies. Petroleum production is important, but there is considerable farming and livestock raising. A portion, irrigated from wells and the water of the Rio Grande and sometimes known as the Winter Garden, produces bountiful crops of citrus fruit, vegetables, and cotton. The Spanish and Mexican heritage of Texas is particularly evident in the people and cultures of the region. San Antonio, partially located in the South Texas Plain, is the largest city, but there are a number of other cities, especially along the Rio Grande.

The Basin and Mountain Region, lying mainly west of the Pecos River and sometimes called the Trans-Pecos, is the most diverse of the Texas regions. It is a country of deserts and mountains, of bitterly cold winters and searing hot summers, of splendor and harshness. It is primarily livestock country, for on the best soils and under favorable conditions, grass will grow. A scattering of irrigated areas adds to the diversity and the productivity of the area. There is some petroleum production, particularly natural gas from wells that extend deep into the earth, and from time to time, a number of mines have operated. Except for the area on the Rio Grande around El Paso, which accounts for most of the population of the region, it was the last area of Texas to be settled and populated by peoples other than Indians.

THE RIVERS 13 major

Although there are many streams, bayous, and creeks (altogether about 4,000) in Texas, there are only thirteen major rivers. Most of these flow from the northwest to the south and east, and all but two empty into the

Gulf of Mexico or other Texas rivers. In most instances, the Spanish named the rivers and mapped their courses. Very important in the lives of the native peoples, the rivers have continued to play a major role in the settlement of the land and the development of towns and cities.

Three rivers make up parts of the boundary of Texas. The Sabine (named after the Spanish word for "cypress") is formed by three streams that begin in Collin and Hunt counties. A relatively large, if not very long, river, it forms a part of the eastern boundary of the state. The Red River is an exceptionally long stream, beginning in New Mexico and traveling 1,360 miles. After flowing across Texas, it forms a portion of the boundary between Oklahoma and Texas. In its upper reaches, the Red River divides into several branches, giving rise to several boundary controversies in times past. The Rio Grande is the other stream to form a part of the Texas border. Not quite as long as the Red River, the Rio Grande begins in Colorado, flows across New Mexico, and then forms the boundary between Texas and Mexico.

There are three major rivers whose location is largely confined to East Texas. The Trinity River, which begins in Dallas County, travels in a relatively southern course to empty into Galveston Bay. Since the Trinity normally contains a large amount of water, its use for navigation purposes has been frequently suggested. However, only the lower reaches of the river have ordinarily been navigable for commercial purposes. The Neches is truly an East Texas river, beginning and traveling through East Texas until it empties into Sabine Lake and ultimately the Gulf of Mexico. It was near the Neches that the first Spanish settlements in East Texas were located. Carrying a large volume of water, it was used by steamboats for a time during the nineteenth century, and today forms a channel for seagoing ship traffic as far north as Beaumont. One of the shorter Texas rivers, the San Jacinto, begins in Harris County and enters Galveston Bay. In the story of nineteenth century Texas, it is almost always associated with the battle that ended the Texas Revolution. Today, it is an important part of the water complex that forms the Houston Ship Channel to make Houston one of the major ports in the nation.

There are two major rivers that make their way from northwestern Texas southeastward through the center of the state to the Gulf of Mexico. The Brazos River, which extends for 840 miles from Stonewall County near the edge of the High Plains, finally enters the Gulf of Mexico near present-day Freeport. Since much of the land on either side of the river is fertile soil, particularly suitable for cotton production, the Brazos River Valley attracted many settlers during the period of Mexican rule and is associated with many of the events of the Texas Revolution. The Colorado River begins in canyons cut into the edge of the High Plains and travels for about 600 miles before it enters Matagorda Bay. The river and its tributaries provided many of the favorite campgrounds of the Comanches and their allies, and a number of the Indian battles fought in the nineteenth century took place on or near the Colorado.

Four rivers have their beginning in the central and west central portion of the state and flow southeastward toward the Gulf. The Nueces River, which begins in Edwards County, enters the Gulf of Mexico near Corpus Christi. At one time it formed a part of the western boundary of the Spanish province of Texas, and later was a dividing point between Coahuila and Texas during the period of Mexican rule. The Guadalupe River, which is formed in Kerr County, flows some 250 miles before emptying into the Gulf of Mexico. On its banks was fought the first land battle of the Texas Revolution. Beginning in the city of San Antonio, the San Antonio River is one of the shorter but more beautiful rivers in the state. Its attractions captured the interest of the Spanish early in their settlement of Texas, and soon thereafter the city of San Antonio was founded. Only 180 miles long, it empties into the Guadalupe River. The Lavaca River, even shorter, begins in Lavaca County and empties into Matagorda Bay. Somewhere near its banks, the explorer La Salle established the post of Fort St. Louis and claimed the land of Texas for France.

The Canadian River, which begins in New Mexico and empties into the Arkansas River, is an unusual Texas river in that during its course across Texas it does not flow to the southeast but rather to the northeast. Flowing across the Panhandle, the Canadian is characterized by steep-sided gorges and treacherous quicksands. It was near this river that the Battle of Adobe Walls was fought in 1874, beginning the final major Indian war in Texas.

THE CLIMATE

Although Texas generally has a mild climate, it is a land of contrast and change where matters of weather are concerned. The climate is determined in large measure by prevailing winds that affect both temperatures and rainfall and by latitude, or the distance Texas lies from the equator. Considering the size of the state, it is not surprising that climatic conditions can vary considerably from one extreme to the other in the same day.

The prevailing winds that tend to blow from the southwest to the northeast have a particularly significant effect on the rainfall of the state. The winds that blow over the waters of the Gulf of Mexico sweep up large amounts of moisture that is subsequently deposited as rainfall in East Texas. The winds from the southwest that sweep across western areas of the state have traveled over the desert areas of northern Mexico and bring little rainfall. Consequently, the rainfall pattern in Texas drops from very high—fifty or more inches per year in East Texas—to as little as eight inches per year in far West Texas.

Temperatures in Texas likewise vary significantly. Summertime in Texas is generally hot, no matter where it is, with temperatures along the Rio Grande and in North-Central Texas sometimes exceeding 100° Fahrenheit. During the winter months, however, the temperature may vary considerably. In southern areas, the temperatures are generally mild, freezing temperatures are rare, and the growing season in some areas may exceed three hundred days each year. In the northwestern areas, winters are more severe, with accumulations of ice and snow not unusual but seldom lasting for more than a few days.

PREHISTORIC PEOPLES

Discoveries during the last half-century, some in Texas, indicate that humans have been in America much longer than had been previously believed. In the Trinity River gravel beds near Malakoff and Trinidad, three stone images were found that may be 30,000 or more years old, but the evidence is too scanty to warrant certainty. The evidence of human life in Texas at least ten or twelve thousand years ago, however, seems convincing. As recently as 1982, archaeologists discovered intact near Leander, Texas, the remarkably well-preserved skeleton of a woman who lived perhaps 10,000 years ago. Near this "Leanderthal" woman were discovered arrow points of very ancient origin and a grinding stone that may in time tell more about these ancient Texans.

Other sites that indicate the presence of these Paleo-Americans are those near Abilene, Midland, and Plainview, Texas, and Clovis, New Mexico—all in the plains country, principally the High Plains, or as it is sometimes called, the Llano Estacado. The people represented in these discoveries are sometimes designated as belonging to the Llano Culture. In this region the Paleo-Americans hunted, and at least occasionally killed in numbers, a species of elephant now extinct. Their spear and dart points, known as Clovis fluted points, were widely distributed. Estimates, based on radioactivity measurements of artifacts, suggest that the Llano people lived some twelve thousand years ago.

Somewhat later than the Llano Culture was the Folsom Culture, named after a town in northeastern New Mexico. Highly finished projectile points, characterized by longitudinal flutes or channels in the blade faces and apparently used in hunting huge bison, were found near Folsom. Similar fluted points imbedded in bison skeletons have been found in excavations near Lubbock and Plainview. Dating with radiocarbon tests indicate that these tools and skeletons of perhaps one hundred bison have been there for about nine thousand years.

About 5000 B.C., either the Paleo-American culture gave way to another culture, or the way of life of these people changed. Perhaps the ending of the ice age and the disappearance of the elephants, the great bisons, and other animals that they had hunted were factors in the change. Also, other peoples may have migrated to America during the centuries following 5000 B.C. These changes brought in the Archaic peoples. They were hunters and gatherers, but instead of a few well-made stone implements, they had a great variety of stone points and tools. At least twenty-seven types of dart points have been found in the Edwards Plateau. They also used polished stones; pestles and mortars indicate that they relied more on seeds than did their predecessors. In time these peoples domesticated the dog, adopted the practice of growing corn (sometime after 2500 B.C.), eventually learned the craft of pottery making, and began building more substantial abodes. In many respects their way of life did not differ significantly from that of some Indian tribes living in Texas at the time of the arrival of the first Europeans.

In pictographs like these at Paint Rock, Indians recorded the significant events of their lives. (Texas Highway Department)

THE INDIANS

Texas lies within the three areas in which Indian civilization reached its highest development in North America. These were the Mayan civilization of Mexico and Central America, the Pueblo of the upper Rio Grande, and the Mound Builder of the Mississippi Valley. In a sense, Texas was a meeting place of these three cultures, but it appears that none of them was extensively established within its boundaries, and apparently none had a major influence on the development of Texas Indian culture. In fact, there was not a dominant Texas Indian culture. The ways of life of these peoples differed even more widely from region to region than do those of modern people.

Although differences were many, there were certain cultural practices common to most, if not all, Texas Indians. Family organization and religious beliefs in most instances were similar, whether the Indians were hunters of the plains or gardeners in the woodlands. Common to all was a basic belief in a supreme being or beings. Few, if any, were truly monotheistic (believing only in one supreme being), but many tribes tended to accept the ideal of a creator or being who seemingly was of more significance than other deities. In one form or another, most incorporated into their religious beliefs a reverence for the various aspects or entities of nature—that is, the sun, moon, wind, rain, or other natural phenomenon. Among some tribes, the Kiowas, for example, elaborate religious ceremonies were held on regular schedules to honor and worship the deities that affected the health and well-being of the tribe. In other tribes, such as the Comanches, religion seems to have been far more of an individualistic matter, generally accepted by all but rarely the occasion for tribal activity. Members of virtually all tribes believed in the supernatural power of healers called *shamans*, usually men but sometimes women, who could deal with matters of disease or injury through their ability to call upon the strength of tribal deities.

Similarly, the family was the basic social organization in virtually all Texas tribes. Ordinarily, the structure of the marriage was monogamous, but in most tribes there were situations where it was expected that a man might have more than one wife. Most of the time courtship practices involved the would-be suitor negotiating with the parents or family of the bride-to-be in an attempt to persuade them of the merits of the proposed alliance. However, occasionally a young man and a young woman would elope and establish a new family without parental approval but ordinarily without any punishment or unpleasant consequences. Marriage ceremonies were rare. Divorce was not unusual but ordinarily was arranged quickly and with little formality.

Within the family structure there was a clear and definite division of responsibilities. In some respects, it would appear that the women were treated unfairly, inasmuch as they usually were obligated to haul the wood, cook the meals, pack the belongings and carry them on the trail, put up the housing, and do virtually all of the menial work around the camp. In a few tribes, such as those of the Caddo and Wichita peoples, the men did some of the work in the fields, but this was rarely true in other tribes. Ordinarily, the men spent much of their time hunting and fishing and either making war or making preparations for war. However, hunting and fishing provided an essential part of the food supply, and survival in a world where conflict with other people was frequent and required the skills of the warrior perhaps justified the apparently unequal distribution of labor.

There was some sharing of responsibility in the rearing of children. Training of children began at a very early age. Young Comanches, for example, were taught the fundamental skills of horsemanship by the age of four. In most tribes, young men were trained to endure danger and hardships, while young women were taught to care for the needs of the family and the camp. Punishment of children was not unknown, but it was rare. Children were expected to learn through example, and apparently seldom violated family or tribal rules.

The first Europeans found many Indian tribes in Texas. There were the Caddoan peoples of eastern Texas; the Karankawas along the Gulf Coast; the Wichita and Tonkawa groups of tribes in Central Texas; the Coahuiltecans of South Texas and northern Mexico; and the Jumanos along the Rio Grande. Later there were the Apaches and Comanches of western Texas and the Coushattas, Alabamas, and Cherokees of eastern Texas; and there were still others. In some instances, certain of these Indian tribes were called by other names, and in some instances, the tribal name referred to several different groups, each bearing its own name.

Most of the Indians of East Texas belonged to the great Caddoan family and were included in two confederacies: the Caddo, located in Arkansas, Louisiana, and the part of Texas near present-day Texarkana; and the Hasinai, on the upper Angelina and Neches rivers. In the story of Texas the Hasinai confederacy is the more important of the two. It was in this confederacy that the Spaniards first established missions in the interior of Texas. Probably a dozen tribes belonged to the confederacy, the more important being the Nabedache, the Nacogdoche, the Hainai, the Nasoni, and the Neche. In about 1690, when the first Spanish missionaries arrived, these tribes together probably numbered from three thousand to five thousand persons. Each tribe had its own chiefs and tribal government but owed a measure of allegiance to the *caddi*, that is, the chief of the Hainai tribe and head chief of the confederacy. More powerful than the grand *caddi*, however, was the *chenesi*, or head priest, who kept the fire temple. The fire in it was never extinguished, and from it the fires of all the confederacy were lighted. In a custom unusual among other Indians, but not unknown in other tribes, women enjoyed some authority and status. In tribal government women sometimes held positions of responsibility, and both men and women shared the work in the fields.

The Caddoes lived in domelike houses, reinforced with stakes, thatched with twigs, daubed with mud, and covered with grass. These homes were located in hamlets of seven to 15 houses divided by woodlands and farms and situated near the bank of a river or stream. The furnishings within suggested beauty as well as comfort. In the houses were many-colored rugs, woven of reeds; beds, made of reeds resting on a framework of poles and covered with buffalo hides; reed baskets, filled with beans, acorns, and nuts; jars, filled with corn and covered over with ashes to keep out the weevils; and corn, shucked and hung where exposure to smoke would drive away the weevils. Each year these Indians kept enough seed for two years, lest one crop should be a total failure. Of course, a great part of their food was secured by hunting. Deer and bear were abundant, and hunting parties frequently visited the buffalo range, located about a hundred miles to the west.

Some Indians with cultures similar to that of the Caddoes did not settle in Texas until the nineteenth century. The Alabamas and the Coushattas located a small village on the Trinity River in 1807. Around 1820 in somewhat larger numbers, some members of the highly civilized Cherokee tribe occupied lands to the north of Nacogdoches. And there were small numbers of Indian immigrants from other tribes formerly located in the southeastern part of the United States.

Immediately to the south of the Caddoes in southeastern Texas and southwestern Louisiana were the Attacapans (or Attakapans). Composed of at least four distinct groups, the Attacapans were hunters who were comfortable in the marshy wetlands where they lived off small animals, fish, and wild fruits. In many respects their lifestyles were a mixture of the culture of the Caddo people to their north and the Karankawas who made their home further to the south along the Gulf Coast.

The habitat of the Karankawas extended along the Gulf Coast from about Trinity Bay on the north to Matagorda Bay on the south and inland as much as a hundred miles or more. There were several different groups of Karankawas, but by the early eighteenth century, four bands apparently accounted for a majority of the population of the tribe. The Karankawas were strong and tall and, according to early day European travelers, notable for their prowess as runners, hunters, and swimmers. Their diet was composed of food from the sea, small game, wild fruits and berries, and alligators. To protect themselves from the ever-present mosquitoes, they coated themselves with a mixture of shark, fish, and alligator oils, an effective but not very sweet-smelling insect repellent.

Although the first Europeans to encounter Karankawas were actually treated very well, the tribe soon gained a reputation as fierce and relentless enemies of European intruders. Adding to their fearsome reputation, there were also widely advertised reports of the practice of cannibalism. Actually, the cannibalism of the Karankawas was likely a ceremonial type similar to that practiced by a number of Indian tribes in Texas and elsewhere. Notwithstanding the fierce reputation of the Karankawas, the determined Spanish Catholic friars who came into their territory repeatedly attempted to convert the tribe to Christianity and the ways of the white man's life. A few eventually were converted, or at least lived for a time in or near Spanish missions, but most had little use for the restrictions of mission life.

To the north of the Karankawas and to the west of the Caddoes in South-Central Texas lived the Tonkawa. Perhaps somewhat more advanced than the Karankawas, they were primarily hunters and traders who lived in skin houses and when possible hunted the buffalo. They were alternately at peace and at war with the Spaniards during the eighteenth century, and their relations with the Hasinais in the east, the Wichitas and Comanches in the north, and the Apaches in the west were at best uncertain. In some respects, they were more similar to the plains Indians who lived to their west than they were to the Indians of the woodlands who lived to their east.

From the Arkansas River in Kansas southward to the vicinity of present-day Waco lived the Wichita tribes. Actually a confederacy of several bands with a common dialect, these Indians lived in dome-shaped grass and reed houses in permanent villages, grew a wide variety of crops, hunted the buffalo, and carried on extensive trading activities whenever possible. Of these tribes, the Wichita proper (sometimes identified as the Taovayas or Tawehash) lived along the Red River and during the nineteenth century, became widely known for their talented horsemanship and energetic efforts to take horses belonging to other tribes and white settlers. The Tawakoni and Waco tribes lived in North-Central Texas until the remnants of the tribes were expelled in 1859. In some respects, the Wichita people lived much like their Caddoan kinspeople to the east; in other respects, they were like the Indians of the plains. They farmed to a limited extent and from time to time made hunting trips westward onto the plains. A proud people, they were not as warlike as some tribes, but when involved in warfare, they were a formidable foe.

The Coahuiltecans of South Texas and northern Mexico were among the more primitive Indian groups in Texas. Somewhat the prisoners of one of the harshest environments in Texas, the Coahuiltecans followed a lifestyle adapted to living off of whatever resources were available. Accordingly, they included in their diet lizards, seeds, rodents, snakes, mesquite beans, deer, rabbits, cactus, and even dirt—an amazingly broad collection of foods. Their language was unrelated to that of any other Texas Indians, but it was very nearly identical to the language of a group of Indians found in California with similar cultural patterns. They were nomadic Indians,

Wichita grass covered arbor and houses, Anadarko, Oklahoma. The houses of the Hasinai and Caddo in East Texas were of similar construction. (From Earl H. Elam. "The History of the Wichita Indian Confederacy to 1868," Ph.D. dissertation; Lubbock, Texas, 1971, p. 58 By permission of the author.)

moving frequently in small bands while living in shelters made of sticks and leaves. Not especially warlike and located in the path of some of the early Spanish settlements north of the Rio Grande, the tribe was among those selected by priests for missionary efforts in the area around San Antonio.

One of the most mysterious (and confusing) of Texas Indian tribes was the Jumano tribe, which lived primarily along the big bend of the Rio Grande in the general vicinity of present-day Presidio. The mystery and confusion associated with the Jumanos lies in the fact that much is unknown and much of what is known is contradictory, probably because the tribe apparently traveled great distances and was found in unexpected places and because other tribes were on occasion mistakenly identified as Jumanos.

The Jumanos who lived along the Rio Grande were sedentary Indians with a comparatively advanced style of living. Their homes were made of sun-dried brick (adobe) with flat roofs and were located in villages. From gardens sometimes irrigated from the waters of the Rio Grande, they raised crops of vegetables and lived on a diet of fish, game, corn, beans, gourds, and prickly pear. Relatively friendly with the Europeans who came among them, they were logical candidates for Spanish missionary activities, but their locations seem to have prevented or delayed most such efforts.

Although the Rio Grande was apparently the primary habitat of the Jumanos, they were indefatigable travelers and traders. They traveled far enough to the east to make contact with the Caddoes of East Texas, and if Spanish explorers correctly identified them, lived at times in the Concho River country of West-Central Texas near present-day San Angelo and Ballinger. In the eighteenth century the tribe, or at least some of it, apparently joined forces with the Lipan Apaches and occasionally took part in Apache hunting and war parties.

Some of the more powerful Indian tribes in central and western Texas were not truly native Texans but migrants who came into the land about the time of or even after the arrival of the first Europeans and Africans. These were the Apaches, Comanches, Kiowas, and some of the Wichitas. The Apaches apparently made their way to Texas from the northern plains by way of New Mexico and the Texas Panhandle shortly before the Spaniards arrived. An aggressive people, they soon dominated the western part of the state from the Panhandle to the Rio Grande. When the Spanish explorer, Francisco Coronado, traveled the High Plains in 1541, he met a tribe he named the Querechos. These were probably Apaches. Within a short period of time, the Apaches acquired Spanish horses and firearms and presented a dangerous threat to any who dared to challenge them. In every sense a plains people, the Apaches were nomads who centered their lifestyle around the buffalo hunt, lived in skin teepees, and moved frequently from place to place.

Of the several bands of Apaches, the Lipans, the Natages, and the Mescalero seem to have located in Texas. More numerous than the other bands and dominating areas in or near Spanish settlements, the Lipans were frequently a source of concern to the Europeans who made their way into Texas. By the eighteenth century the Lipans were located on the Edwards Plateau to the north of San Antonio where they were a constant threat to Spanish settlements until driven from the region by the still more powerful Comanches. For a time they moved to the area between the Nueces River and the Rio Grande where they continued their warfare against the Spanish. Dwindling in numbers because of disease, they eventually migrated northwestward into the mountains of far west Texas where they joined their Mescalero kinsmen before eventually locating in present New Mexico.

By the eighteenth century the Great Plains of Texas and a part of adjacent territory were occupied by the Comanche Indians. They came from the north early in the century and drove a wedge between the Apache country in the west and the Caddoan country in the east. Their intrusion quickly extended as far south as the vicinity of present Austin and San Antonio. Shorter and stockier than many Indian peoples, the Comanches nevertheless were fearless warriors, unsurpassed in their skills on horseback and relentless in their warfare with other tribes and with the white man's civilization that threatened their way of life. Their life centered around the hunting of the buffalo and, after they acquired horses from the Spanish, their development of their skills in the use of the horse.

There were several Comanche tribes, or Comanche bands, with the status of independent tribes. Of these tribes or bands, the better known

Comanche camp in 1872. (Bureau of American Ethnology)

were the Penatekas, or Honey-eaters in the south, who drove the Apaches out of the Edwards Plateau in the mid-1700s; the Kotsotekas, or Buffalo-eaters, and Nokonies, who usually were found along the Red and Canadian rivers; the Yamparikas, or Root-eaters, who usually ranged along the Arkansas River; and the Kwahadis of the High Plains. The Penatekas lived in Texas and the other Comanche peoples either lived in Texas or visited it from time to time.

The Comanches were a nomadic people who never planted crops of any kind. Although each tribe or band regarded a given region as its home and always returned to it after its wanderings, the Comanches never remained for long in any one place. They would break camp on the slightest excuse or with no excuse at all. If a prominent person died, or if an epidemic caused several deaths at a certain camp, the site would be abandoned at once, and the Indians would never return there—a practice that, in spite of its obvious inconvenience, no doubt checked the ravages of disease.

The Kiowas were another plains people who migrated to Texas, probably about the same time as the Comanches and likely from the mountain areas of northern New Mexico. Since they arrived in Texas about the same time as the Comanches, who did not take a challenge to their territory lightly, war between the Comanche people and the Kiowas would seem to have been almost certain. However, the two tribes established an alliance that remained firm until the final days of Indian freedom on the High Plains. Although the cultures of the two tribes were similar, there were differences that stood the test of time. The Comanches and Kiowas traveled together, hunted together, and fought together, but they maintained their separate tribal identities until the end.

Superb horsemen and warriors, the plains tribes harried the settlements of Texas and other northern Mexican provinces until the late years of the nineteenth century. Their fierce determination to protect their territory and their way of life was a barrier to the settlement of white people until the force of numbers and superior resources at last forced them to accept life on reservations in Indian Territory.

In most instances, however, it was not warfare but disease that doomed the existence of Texas Indians. From the time of the earliest Spanish settlements, the diseases of Europeans were a threat to the lives of Indian people, sometimes ravaging entire tribes. Smallpox was the most serious threat, but even lesser diseases of white people sometimes brought death in large numbers to the Indians. Before the end of the eighteenth century, disease had destroyed a large portion of the Caddoan peoples, the Karankawas, and many other tribes. Consequently, when finally defeated in their contest for the lands of Texas, it was generally only pitiful remnants of a proud people who made their way to the north across the Red River to settle in Indian Territory.

In the story of Texas the story of Indian people is worthy of study and understanding. Their way of life, their hopes and fears, their values and traditions are a part of the heritage of Texas. They knew and understood the land and perhaps appreciated the world around them more than the people who would replace them. For more than three centuries, moreover, they were of significant importance in determining the fate of the people who challenged them for the land. It was, in part, the hope of finding Indians whose treasures could be exploited that brought the early Spanish expeditions into Texas. A desire for trade with the natives was a great factor in bringing other adventurers, including the French, into the country. Of particular importance as a motive was the yearning of zealous priests who hoped to win over the natives to the Christian religion.

Indeed, the Indians more than the white people determined the nature of frontier institutions. From them white people learned of crops and effective means of tillage; of foods, their preparation and preservation; and of wild game, their habits and the methods for hunting them. If the Indians were friendly, the white people explored and settled the country rapidly; if they were docile, it was easy to exploit or, at least, to ignore their rights. If the Indians were organized in weak and fragmentary tribes, the whites easily drove them away; but if they were powerful and warlike, they retarded the advance of the intruders for decades, and even for centuries. Furthermore, the Indian largely determined the type of warfare that was carried out. The Caddo of the timber, the Comanche of the plain, and the Apache of the mountain all had different tactics, and the Euro-Americans had to meet them in a fashion suited to the condition that prevailed.

Although the Spaniards, who approached from the west and south, and the Anglo-Americans, who came from the east, had already developed pioneering institutions before they reached Texas, these institutions proved unsatisfactory in certain important respects. For instance, the Spanish mission system, which attempted to convert Indian peoples to Christianity, was designed for compact pueblos or for Indians brought together in colonies and often already accustomed to domination by other people. It failed among the Caddoes of eastern Texas, who lived in scattered hamlets and refused to move to missions and accept the restrictions of another way of life. It failed even more miserably when attempted with the freedom-loving nomads of the west. Similarly, the Anglo-Americans, who had learned to meet Indians who fought on foot, had to develop new tactics for coping with the mounted Indians of the plains who struck on horseback, fought, and retreated with the advantages of surprise and swiftness. For good reason then, the story of Texas for almost four centuries after the first Spaniards trod the land is the story of both white people and Indians.

SELECTED BIBLIOGRAPHY

Important bibliographies pertaining to Texas are John H. Jenkins, *Basic Texas Books* (Austin, Jenkins Publishing Company, 1983); Thomas W. Streeter, *Bibliography of Texas, 1795–1845* (2 vols., Cambridge, Mass., 1956); E. W. Winkler, *Check List of Texas Imprints, 1846–1876* (Austin, 1949); E. W. Winkler and Llerena Friend, *Check List of Texas Imprints, 1861–1876* (Austin, 1963); Seymour V. Connor, "A Preliminary Guide to Archives of Texas," *Southwestern Historical Quarterly*, LX, 255–334; Chester V. Kielman, *University of Texas Archives* (Austin, 1967).

It is well to be acquainted with *Resources of Texas Libraries* by Edward G. Holley and Donald D. Hendrick (Austin, 1968). The most comprehensive work on the history of Texas is the *Handbook of Texas*, edited by Walter Prescott Webb and H. Bailey Carroll (vols. I and II, Austin, 1952), and Eldon S. Branda (vol. III, Austin, 1977). *The Texas Almanac*, published biennially by the *Dallas News*, is a dependable reference.

The greatest collection of writings on Texas history is the *Quarterly of the Texas State Historical Association* (I–XV, Austin) from 1897 to 1912; and its successor, the *Southwestern Historical Quarterly*, beginning in July 1912. Much Texas material may be found also in the *Mississippi Valley Historical Review* (and its successor, the *Journal of American History*) from 1914; the *Journal of Southern History* from 1934; the *Southwestern Social Science Quarterly* from 1920; the *American West* from 1963; and *Texana*, a quarterly journal of Texas history published since 1962 in Waco. Some regional publications contain a great deal of Texas history: the *East Texas Historical Journal* from 1963; *Texas Gulf Coast Historical Publications* from 1957; the *Panhandle-Plains Historical Review* from 1927; and the *West Texas Historical Association Year Book* from 1925.

Good basic references on Texas geography are Terry G. Jordan et al., *Texas: A Geography* (Boulder, 1984); Stanley A. Arbingast et al., *Atlas of Texas* (Austin, 1976); and William C. Pool, *A Historical Atlas of Texas* (Austin, 1975).

Also useful are Harry C. Oberholser, *The Bird Life of Texas* (2 vols., Austin, 1974); Walter Keene Ferguson, *Geology and Politics in Texas, 1845–1909* (Austin, 1969); Jim Bones and John Graves, *Texas Heartland: A Hill Country Year* (College Station, 1975); Pauline Robertson, *Panhandle Pilgrimage* (Austin, 1978); and Terry Jordan, "Pioneer Evaluation of Vegetation in Frontier Texas," *Southwestern Historical Quarterly*, LXXVI, 233–254. Older but valuable are Elmer H. Johnson, *The Natural Regions of Texas* (University of Texas *Bulletin*, no. 3113, Austin, 1931); Frederick W. Simonds, *The Geography of Texas* (Boston, 1914); W. T. Carter, *The Soils of Texas* (College Station, Tex., 1931); W. A. Silveus, *Texas Grasses* (San Antonio, 1933); and Roy Bedicheck, *Adventures with a Texas Naturalist* (New York, 1947).

A basic source for Texas archeology is Dee Ann Suhm and Alex D. Krieger, *An Introductory Handbook of Texas Archeology*, Texas Archeological Society *Bulletin*, XXV (Austin, 1954). Useful also is E. H. Sellards, *Early Man in America: A Study in Pre-History* (Austin, 1952); T. N. Campbell, "A List of Radiocarbon Dates from Archeological Sites in Texas," *Bulletin of the Texas Archeological Society*, 1959, 311–

320; and Jane Holden Kelley, "Comments on the Archeology of the Llano Estacado," *Bulletin of the Texas Archeological Society*, 1964, 1–17. An authoritative book on archeology and Indians, containing a comprehensive bibliography, is *The Indians of Texas* by W. W. Newcomb, Jr. (Austin, 1961). Rich in source material is Dorman H. Winfrey and James M. Day (eds.), *The Indian Papers of Texas and the Southwest, 1825–1916* (5 vols., Austin, 1966). Some histories of Indian tribes are: Mildred P. Mayhall, *The Kiowas* (Norman, Okla., 1962); Rupert N. Richardson, *The Comanche Barrier to South Plains Settlement* (Glendale, Calif., 1933); Ernest Wallace and E. A. Hoebel, *The Comanches, Lords of the South Plains* (Norman, Okla., 1952); and Charles L. Sonnichsen, *The Mescalero Apaches* (Norman, Okla., 1973).

CHAPTER TWO
EXPLORATION
AND OCCUPATION
1519–1763

In October 1492 Christopher Columbus and the crew of his three small ships sighted land, an island in the Bahamas off the coast of Florida. While searching for a new way to the Far East, Columbus had opened the door to a new world, the Americas. From bases soon founded on the islands of the Caribbean Sea other Spaniards quickly moved to the mainland of Central and North America and explored the regions bordering on the Gulf of Mexico. In 1519 Hernando Cortez defeated the Aztecs in the Central Valley of Mexico, occupied their principal city, and confiscated their rich supplies of gold and silver. Renaming the Aztec capital Mexico City, the Spanish made it the center of their new empire in the Americas, New Spain.

From the earliest days of New Spain, Texas was a part of the empire. Within fifty years, expeditions had explored the distant corners of the region. Although settlement in Texas would be delayed for more than a century, the challenge of French intruders on the coast would eventually bring not only more exploration but occupation.

SPANISH EXPLORATION

In the same year that Cortez defeated the Aztecs, a Spanish expedition explored the coast of Texas. Commissioned by the governor of Jamaica,

Cortez (mumen + Uytees)

1519 Alonso Álvarez de Piñeda in 1519 mapped the coast of the Gulf of Mexico from Florida to Vera Cruz. Piñeda spent forty days at the mouth of the "River of Palms," perhaps the Rio Grande, and recommended that a settlement be planted there.

Piñeda's recommendation was not heeded at the time, but more Spaniards would soon explore the interior. Alvar Nuñez Cabeza de Vaca and three companions, survivors of the ill-fated Pánfilo de Narváez expedition, were destined to be the first Europeans to spend a significant amount of *1528* time in Texas. The Narváez expedition landed in Florida in 1528. After failing to find rumored riches, the 242 stranded survivors in five overcrowded boats tried to reach Panuco on the eastern coast of Mexico by sailing westward along the coast. The party was shipwrecked in November, apparently on Galveston Island, and only a few escaped from the sea. After nearly six years of servitude to the Indians, four survivors, including De Vaca and a black man named Estevanico, managed to escaped into the interior. Thence, after wandering many hundreds of miles, probably near present-day San Antonio and Presidio, they arrived on May 18, 1536, at the northern outpost of Culiacán, near the Gulf of California in western Mexico.

The tales related by De Vaca created great excitement in Mexico City. Although he had not seen them, he had heard from the Indians of large cities in the north, where there was gold and silver in abundance. These, Spaniards believed, must be the fabulous Seven Cities of Cibola, long *Estevanico the moor* promised in the tales of Spanish folklore. Viceroy Antonio de Mendoza quickly dispatched Fray Marcos de Niza, with Estevanico, to find the fabled cities. When Fray Marcos reported that he had indeed seen from afar a great city (Estevanico had fallen to Indian spears and arrows), Mendoza then commissioned Francisco Vásquez de Coronado, governor of the province of Nueva Galicia, to penetrate the mysterious north country. Starting from Compostela in western Mexico in February 1540, Coronado had in his command three hundred horsemen, seventy footmen, and more than one thousand Indians.

Instead of the splendid Seven Cities of Cibola, Coronado found, near the present Arizona-New Mexico line, only humble pueblos inhabited by hostile Indians. Nor did he find anything precious at Tiguex on the Rio Grande, a few miles north of present Albuquerque, where he spent the winter of 1540-1541. When spring came, he set out in search of Quivira, a gilded land that an Indian slave told him lay somewhere to the east. He spent many days wandering over the treeless and level plains of Texas and probably crossed Palo Duro Canyon, located near present Amarillo. After 77 days of marching across a land where he had seen "nothing but cows and the sky," he found Quivira—several Wichita Indian villages of grass houses in central Kansas. The chief wore a copper plate around his neck, but there was no gold. Thoroughly discouraged, Coronado returned by way of Tiguex to Mexico to make his report to his king, Charles I of Spain.

Coronado

While Coronado was searching the southwestern lands of present-day United States, another Spaniard, Hernando de Soto, with about 600 men was exploring the region north of the Gulf of Mexico with no better success. After DeSoto's death at the Mississippi River in May 1542, the expedition under the command of Luis de Moscoso de Alvarado entered Texas. Passing through the piney woods of the Tejas Indians in eastern Texas, it marched probably as far west as the Brazos River. Unable to get in touch with Coronado, of whom they had heard from the Indians, and beset by a lack of food and unfriendly natives, Moscoso and his followers returned to the Mississippi River. Here they built seven crude boats and on July 3, 1543, began floating downstream. Eleven weeks later, after caulking their boats with cakes of tar taken from Texas beaches, the 311 survivors reached Panuco.

1542

Mexico

Although the Coronado and DeSoto-Moscoso expeditions strengthened the claim of Spain to the land that included present-day Texas, the immediate effect of their efforts was to delay Spanish activity in the area. Coronado did not consider the country he had explored to be of sufficient value to warrant its being occupied by the Spanish. There were no precious metals, and the natives were either nomads who lived in lodges made of skin or semisedentary barbarians who lived miserably in little villages. The report of the DeSoto-Moscoso survivors supported his conclusion. Therefore, for many decades thereafter, the Spaniards gave little thought to the region now known as Texas, except for an occasional venture originating from Spanish settlements in New Mexico.

Notwithstanding the report of Coronado, the Spanish continued to be interested in the lands along the Rio Grande, especially the upper reaches of the river of present-day New Mexico. In most instances, settlements in this area were in the form of missions, a religious settlement operated by Catholic priests primarily for the purpose of teaching religion to surrounding Indians. By 1563 the frontier of New Spain had been extended to Santa Barbara on the headwaters of the Conchos, a stream that flows northward into the Rio Grande. In 1598 Juan de Oñate established a Spanish settlement on the Rio Grande a few miles north of present-day Santa Fe. Three years later, while searching for Coronado's Quivira, Oñate led an expedition across the Panhandle of Texas. In 1609 Santa Fe had its beginning, and soon several missions were scattered along the upper Rio Grande. From one of these Father Juan de Salas in 1629 accompanied some visiting Jumano Indians southeastward nearly 300 miles into Texas, perhaps to the Pecos or Concho (a tributary of the Colorado) River.

1563

San Angelo

1598

1609

Blue Lady

In the early 1650s two other expeditions from New Mexico visited and traded with the Jumanos in the same area. A mission was founded on the site of modern Juarez in 1659, and in 1680 the Spanish established a pueblo and Mission Corpus Christi de la Isleta on the site of present-day Ysleta (near present El Paso). This was the first permanent European settlement within the present boundaries of Texas.

1659

1680

Temp

From it an effort was made to establish a settlement in the Hill Country of central West Texas. Led by Father Nicolás López and Captain Domínguez de Mendoza, an expedition of 30 soldiers and two priests in 1683 went by way of present Presidio and Horsehead Crossing (near McCamey) on the Pecos River to a site probably on the San Saba River west of present-day Menard. They built a combination chapel and fort, named it San Clemente, gathered an abundant number of buffalo hides, and baptized many Indians. But Apache Indians threatened the settlement, and Mendoza and Lopez returned to Mexico to seek permission to locate a stronger mission among the Jumanos. The petition was never granted. Reports of a French settlement on the Gulf Coast in Texas had reached New Spain, a flagrant violation of Spanish claims. These intruders had to be found and expelled, and toward that end the best efforts of New Spain were directed.

FRENCH INTRUSION: LA SALLE

The Frenchman whose settlement in Texas provoked Spain's ire was Robert Cavelier, Sieur de La Salle, a trader from the French colony of Quebec (Canada). In 1682 La Salle had descended the Mississippi to its mouth and claimed for his king, Louis XIV, all of the country that it drained, even "to the mouth of the River of Palms" (Rio Grande). Returning to France, La Salle obtained from Louis XIV a commission to found a colony at the mouth of the Mississippi. The colony was expected to control trade along the river and to extend trading opportunities into the rich mining area of northern Mexico. On August 1, 1684, he set sail with 280 persons in four ships to carry out his plan. Missing the mouth of the Mississippi, La Salle landed at Matagorda Bay on the Texas coast in February 1685. He erected a crude stockade, Fort St. Louis, on Garcitas Creek, in the vicinity of present-day Vanderbilt, and set out to explore the country. After a six-month journey to the south and west, he returned (with only eight of the 30 men who had started) to find that he was stranded. Not one of his four ships was left. Two were wrecked, one had been destroyed by the Spanish, and the fourth had sailed away. Furthermore, the first crop had failed, the supplies were gone, the Karankawa were making life unsafe, and only 45 people were still alive. La Salle thus determined to find the Mississippi and go to Canada for help.

But La Salle never reached Canada. He made a fruitless journey to the east, perhaps as far as to the Sabine River, and then launched a third expedition northeastward into the piney woods. There, somewhere between present-day Navasota and Jacksonville, some of his own men assassinated him. Six survivors of the settlement who were not involved in the conspiracy finally made their way to Canada. Meanwhile, Fort St. Louis had been destroyed and its inhabitants had been slain by or had gone to live with the Indians.

Two years later the Spanish finally located the ruins of Fort St. Louis. Through French pirates whom they happened to capture, the Spaniards learned of La Salle's settlement soon after it was founded. Several expeditions by both land and sea, however, failed to discover the intruders. At last, on his fourth expedition into Texas, Governor Alonso de León of the province of Coahuila reached the ruins of Fort St. Louis on April 22, 1689. Afterward, De León found two of La Salle's men living among the Indians and from them learned the sad history of the colony.

THE FIRST MISSIONS IN EAST TEXAS

Although fate had removed the French menace from the Gulf Coast, thoughtful Spaniards realized that Spain's claim to the region would always be disputed until they occupied it. On his return to Mexico, De León sent to the viceroy a glowing report of the country of the Tejas. The land was fertile; the climate was desirable; and the natives were friendly and civilized. Spain should occupy the country at once. Father Damian Massanet, who had accompanied De León and had visited with a Tejas chief, was even more eager for the Spaniards to move into the region. He had promised the Tejas chief that he would return. Thus, the priest and the soldier made a joint petition asking the viceroy, the Count of Galve, to authorize and support a missionary expedition to the Tejas.

Their petition having been officially approved, Father Massanet, accompanied by three other priests, and De León, with a military escort of more than a hundred soldiers, set out from Monclova for Texas in late March 1690. The Tejas chief, with a welcoming party of 14 Indians, met them at the Trinity, and on May 22, 1690, they arrived at the principal village of the Nabedache, one of the tribes of the Hasinai (Caddo) Confederacy. Fields of corn, beans, and melons and a welcoming feast of tamales and mush gave new confidence to the Spanish. Twelve days later the priests celebrated mass and sang *Te Deum Laudamus* (a song of praise) in the first mission in the land of the Tejas—San Francisco de los Tejas, located a few miles west of the Neches River, near the present-day village of Weches in Houston County. On the next day De León and Father Massanet began their homeward trek, leaving behind three priests and three soldiers to man this remote post against further French intrusion.

Although a second mission, Santisimo Nombre de Maria, was founded a few miles from San Francisco de los Tejas, the settlement in the land of the Tejas did not flourish. When Governor Domingo Terán de los Rios of the new province of Coahuila and Texas and Father Massanet visited the area in 1691, they found affairs at the mission going badly. An epidemic had killed many of the Indians; a priest had died; drought had destroyed the crops; and the Indians had grown first indifferent, then hostile. In January 1692 Santa Maria was abandoned, and an extended search of the region revealed no sign of any French activity. More supplies were sent, but by 1693 Spanish officials, including even the indomitable Massanet, had concluded that East Texas should be abandoned. On October 25, 1693, even before word had been received authorizing the abandonment of the place, Spanish priests set fire to their mission and stole away.

These efforts had not been altogether in vain. They had acquainted the Spaniards with the geography and the Indians of Texas, and their failure proved that missions in that country could not succeed unless sustained by presidios (forts) and settlements.

OCCUPATION OF EAST TEXAS

Although the administrators of New Spain had abandoned the Tejas country, the priests and the captains of the frontier did not forget the land of sturdy oaks and stately pines. One of the priests, Father Francisco Hidalgo, spent most of his time in a settlement near the west bank of the Rio Grande, San Juan Bautista (near present Eagle Pass), hoping anxiously for an opportunity to return to Texas. The dedicated missionary had to wait for many years until the threat from the French reappeared.

After a delay of more than a decade, the French returned to the Gulf Coast, establishing a post at Biloxi in April 1699 and one at Mobile three years later. Family ties in Europe between the thrones of Spain and France led the Spanish government to accept French occupation of the Mississippi Valley (Louisiana), but while relations between the two nations were cordial for a time, the Spaniards were reluctant to go to the extent of opening their doors to trade with the French. Nevertheless, the governor of Louisiana, Antoine de la Mothe Cadillac, was determined to find a way to trade with the Spanish. The opportunity arose when Cadillac received a strange letter from Father Hidalgo of Mission San Juan Bautista. Hidalgo suggested that the French help with the missionary work among the Indians of East Texas. Cadillac saw in the invitation a possible opportunity for the expansion of trade. Accordingly, he commissioned the Canadian-born Captain Luis Juchereau de St. Denis to go to the country of the Tejas, find Father Hidalgo, and inaugurate a trading program with the Spaniards on the northern frontier of Mexico. St. Denis was a successful trader and commander of a military post, who had been in Louisiana since 1699 and was fluent in Spanish and several Indian languages. With a large amount of trade goods, he proceeded to a village of the Natchitoches on the Red River. In October 1713 he built a storehouse at what became the French post of Natchitoches and then traded leisurely with several Indian tribes and inquired among the Tejas about Father Hidalgo. During the next summer he made his way with a small party across Texas to San Juan Bautista on the Rio Grande, arriving there on July 18, 1714.

St. Denis's coming excited and alarmed the Spaniards. There were positive orders, without exceptions, against the introduction of foreign goods or the admission of foreigners into New Spain. Both St. Denis and Father Hidalgo were called to Mexico City for explanations. They fared well, nevertheless. The Frenchman had managed to win a promise of marriage from Manuela Sánchez, the granddaughter of the commander of the presidio at San Juan Bautista, Captain Diego Ramón. When the Spanish viceroy decided to reestablish missions in East Texas, St. Denis obtained a contract to serve as a guide in the venture. And Father Hidalgo received permission to return to the Tejas. Thus, the threat of the French once more spurred the Spaniards to action, but this time there would be more priests as well as presidios and civil settlements.

Traveling with his new bride, St. Denis guided a sizeable Spanish expedition into the country of the Tejas in June 1716. The expedition, commanded by Captain Domingo Ramón who was the son of the commander at San Juan Bautista, included 25 soldiers, 30 civilian men and married women, nine priests, St. Denis, and two other Frenchmen. The reception by the Hasinai, like that accorded to De León and Massanet more than a quarter of a century before, was most cordial.

Before the year ended, the Spaniards had established six missions, five extending in a line from the Neches River eastward to a point almost within cannon shot of the French outpost of Natchitoches on the Red River. Renamed Nuestro Padre San Francisco de los Tejas, the San Francisco mission of 1690 was reestablished on July 3, 1716, with Father Hidalgo in charge. During the next few days three other missions were established: Nuestra Señora de la Purisima Concepción among the Hasinai on the Angelina River about 15 miles west of the present city of Nacogdoches, Nuestra Señora de Guadalupe de los Nacogdoches at Nacogdoches, and San José de los Nazonis near the north line of Nacogdoches County and two and one-half miles north of the present village of Cushing. To offset French influence (but at the suggestion of St. Denis, who wanted the missions at sites suitable for French trade), Ramón in December 1716 founded San Miguel de Linares de los Adaes at the site of modern Robeline, Louisiana. Then, before the end of the year, he established Nuestra Señora de los Dolores among the Ais Indians, at modern San Augustine, Texas. As quarters for his soldiers, Ramón built Presidio Nuestra Señora de los Dolores de los Tejas on the east bank of the Neches River, across from the Tejas mission.

The settlements in East Texas soon led to the establishment of another on the San Antonio River between the Rio Grande and the land of

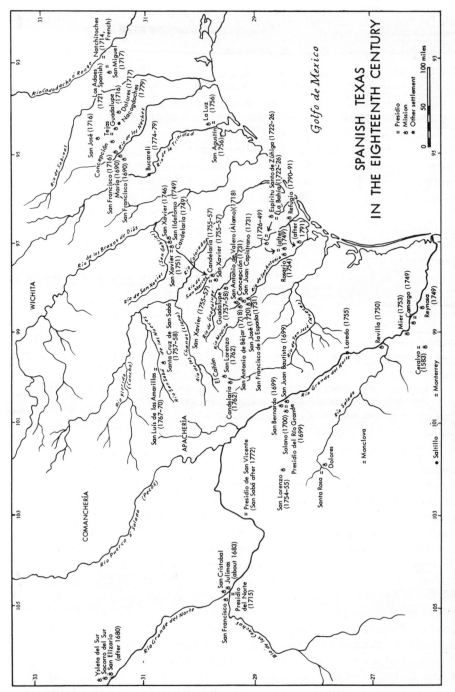

SPANISH TEXAS
IN THE EIGHTEENTH CENTURY

= Presidio
ᵟ Mission
• Other settlement

0   50   100 miles

(From Robert S. Weddle, The San Saba Mission, Spanish Pivot in Texas, Austin, 1964, p. 4. By permission of the author and publisher, the University of Texas Press.)

28

Mission San José y San Miguel de Aguayo, founded in 1720 for the Zacatecan brotherhood in San Antonio, was the center of Spanish mission efforts in Texas. (Texas Highway Department)

the Tejas. Father Antonio de Buenaventura Olivares, who had done missionary work among some Indians along the river, had petitioned for a mission in that area. Moreover, the long distance between San Juan Bautista and East Texas made the need for a midway resting point imperative. Thus, the petition of Olivares and the need for supplies and reinforcements in East Texas resulted in the founding of present-day San Antonio. Martín de Alarcón, governor of Coahuila and Texas, on May 1, 1718, founded Mission San Antonio de Valero (its chapel later becoming known as the Alamo), which was entrusted to Olivares, and on May 5, about one mile to the north, established Presidio San Antonio de Bexar. The ten families that settled around the presidio constituted the Villa de Bexar, a village destined to become the most important Spanish settlement in Texas.

The halfway post was established none too soon. The Spaniards in East Texas were desperately in need of supplies, the Indians were refusing to accept mission life, and France and Spain were now at war. The French in Louisiana learned of the war long before the news reached the Spaniards in Mexico. A French corporal with six soldiers from Natchitoches in June 1719 captured the Adaes mission and the two residents present, a soldier and a lay brother. However, in the confusion caused by the squawking of excited chickens, the lay brother escaped and fled hurriedly to the Dolores mission, where he reported that the French were invading with a large force. Thereupon, the residents of Dolores rushed to the presidio where Captain Ramón was still in command. Ramón decided that the Spaniards should again abandon East Texas, and in October the caravan of motley refugees straggled into San Antonio. The French "invasion," or "Chicken War," had revealed that the Spaniards' claim to the country of the Tejas was not yet secure.

Alarmed, angry, and somewhat embarrassed, the viceroy was convinced that vigorous action was needed. He appointed the Marquis de San Miguel de Aguayo, a wealthy citizen of Coahuila who had offered to drive the French out of Texas at his own expense, to be governor and captain-general of the provinces of Coahuila and Texas. Aguayo was charged with the task of recruiting a force, driving the French from Texas, and reestablishing the missions in East Texas. In the early spring of 1721 Aguayo set out for Texas with 500 men, 5,000 horses and mules, and large herds of cattle and sheep. At San Antonio he found that some refugee priests from East Texas had dedicated a new mission, San José y San Miguel de Aguayo. Located on the San Antonio River about five miles from San Antonio de Valero, this soon became the most successful mission in Texas. Accompanied from San Antonio by the friars who had fled from East Texas in 1719, Aguayo reached the Tejas country in mid-July. The Indians there were friendly and welcomed the Spanish with evident delight.

St. Denis, who was now commander at Natchitoches, informed Aguayo that, inasmuch as France and Spain had made peace, he would withdraw the French forces to Natchitoches. Aguayo reestablished all the abandoned missions (San Francisco a few miles farther east and renamed San Francisco de los Neches) and turned them over to the churchmen with impressive ceremonies. Then, in spite of St. Denis's protests, he established at Los Adaes, in the autumn of 1721, the presidio of Nuestra Señora del Pilár and left in charge a garrison of a hundred men, equipped with six brass fieldpieces and plenty of powder and shot. This place, with its garrison, mission, and small civil settlement, became the capital of the newly-created province of Texas.

In the spring of 1722 Aguayo went to the site of La Salle's Fort St. Louis and directed the construction of a mission, Nuestra Señora del Espíritu Santo Zuñiga, and a presidio, Nuestra Señora de Loreto, commonly called La Bahía. When he returned to Coahuila, Aguayo left behind 269 soldiers, quartered in presidios at San Antonio, on the Angelina, at Los Adaes, and at La Bahía. Each of the four presidios marked a mission center

Mission and (restored) Presidio La Bahia, Goliad. Before he withdrew from the Presidio in one of the bloodiest battles in Texas history, James Fannin buried the ancient hand-poured cannon (shown below) to prevent its being taken by the Mexicans. On the prairie a few miles away, Fannin's force of some four hundred troops was captured and later shot by Mexican firing squads. (Texas Highway Department)

and altogether they guarded nine missions. As a result of the Aguayo expedition, Spain's claim to Texas was never again seriously challenged by the French.

But the complete and adequate establishment left by Aguayo did not mean the end of French activity. In search of economy, the viceroy of New Spain, the Marquis de Casafuerte, in 1727 reduced the number of soldiers at Los Adaes from 100 to 60, and the presidio on the Angelina River was abolished. The abandonment of the presidio led to the removal of three missions, San Francisco, Concepción, and San José, in 1730 to the Colorado River and in the following year to San Antonio. As Spanish influence declined, French influence increased.

Nevertheless, Franco-Spanish relations on the border of Texas remained generally quiet and peaceful until 1762. Representatives of both nations accepted in practice the Arroyo Hondo, a small stream running between Los Adaes and Natchitoches, as the dividing line between the two empires. In the contest for the Indian trade, the French were more successful. By means of a trading post on the Red River near present Texarkana, the French controlled the trade of the Caddo tribes in the vicinity. Likewise, they appropriated the trade of the Wichita and Tawakoni in northern Texas and of the Tonkawa farther south. Farther west on the Red River by 1750 the French were trading with the Taovayas near the present town of Nocona.

EFFORTS AT EXPANSION

As early as 1730 French traders from Louisiana crossed the Sabine River and traded among the Orcoquizac on the Texas coast near the Trinity River. To meet the French challenge, the Spaniards in 1756 established the presidio of San Agustin de Ahumada and a mission, Nuestra Señora de la Luz del Orcoquisac, near the mouth of the Trinity in the general vicinity of modern Anahuac. Commonly called El Orcoquisac, the settlement never flourished and lasted only about fifteen years.

The Spanish occupation of the Gulf region along the lower Trinity River in 1756 was, in a way, only one part of a general program of expansion in practically all of northern New Spain. In Texas, the expansion movement got under way about 1745 and continued, with various interruptions, until the cession of Louisiana to Spain by France in 1762. In addition to the establishment of the post at the mouth of the Trinity, there were three other areas of expansion activity: in Nuevo Santander, on the lower Rio Grande; on the San Gabriel River, northeast of San Antonio; and on the San Saba and upper Nueces rivers, northwest of San Antonio.

In their northward advance in New Spain, the Spaniards had bypassed the vast coastal area extending from Tampico on the Mexico coast to the La Bahía post and inland toward San Antonio, San Juan Bautista, Monterrey, and Monclova. The task of subduing the Indians and colonizing this region, which extended as much as 300 miles in some directions, was assigned in 1746 to José de Escandón, a veteran Indian fighter. In 1749 Escandón entered the region, which had been renamed Nuevo Santander, with more than 3000 settlers, soldiers, and priests. By 1755 he had placed almost 6,000 people in 23 settlements, two of which, Dolores and Laredo, were north of the Rio Grande in present Texas. Dolores, in present Zapata County, was soon abandoned, but Laredo's population grew quite rapidly. Meanwhile, Franciscan missionaries had founded 15 missions. Of later significance, most of the land between the Rio Grande and the Nueces River was either granted to or appropriated by Spanish ranchers who lived south of the Rio Grande.

Modern Goliad also had its beginning with Escandón. In 1726 Mission La Bahía del Espíritu Santo de Zuñiga and Presidio Nuestra Señora de Loreto, which had been founded by Aguayo, were moved to the Guadalupe River in the vicinity of present-day Victoria. Because of the unhealthy climate and the inability to irrigate the surrounding lands, Escandón had the mission and presidio moved to the San Antonio River at the present site of Goliad. Although many miles in the interior, the new establishment continued to be known simply as La Bahía. In 1754 Mission Nuestra Señora del Rosario was founded for the Karankawas, about three miles to the southwest. Around these establishments, which were under the jurisdiction of the province of Nuevo Santander until 1755 when the boundary of Texas was reset at the Nueces River, grew up one of the three principal settlements in Spanish Texas, La Bahía, or Goliad.

Simultaneously, 150 miles northeast of San Antonio, other Spaniards were attempting, less successfully, to expand the mission system. Along the San Gabriel River, called San Xavier by the Spanish, near modern Rockdale, lived the Tonkawas and a conglomeration of other small tribes and remnants of tribes, referred to as *Rancheria Grande*. Harassed by both the Apaches and the Comanches, in 1745 the Tonkawas asked the Spaniards to send missionaries and soldiers to the San Gabriel. Between 1748, when the viceroy gave the authorization, and 1751, the Spanish established along the San Gabriel, in the vicinity of the present towns of Rockdale and San Gabriel, three Franciscan missions (San Francisco Xavier de Horcasitas, San Ildefonso, and Nuestra Señora de la Candelaria) and Presidio San Francisco Xavier, all generally referred to as San Xavier. They were never free of turmoil and strife. Unfaithful Indians, smallpox, measles, drought, hostile Apaches, and illegal French traders accounted for only part of the troubles. Constant friction between the presidial commander and the priests culminated in the murder of one of the priests. The presidial commander was charged but never convicted. In the confusion one mission was abandoned, and in the summer of 1755 the new military commander, without authorization, moved the establishment to the upper San Marcos River. Mission San Francisco Xavier, however, was temporarily relocated on the Guadalupe River near present-day New Braunfels, and early in 1757 the entire properties of the San Xavier mission were transferred to a new mission to be established on the San Saba River.

The San Xavier enterprise was followed by the most ambitious and the most ill-fated mission extension program undertaken by the Spaniards in Texas—the San Sabá post for the Lipan Apaches. Lipan hostility toward the Spaniards was a matter of long standing, but in 1745 the Lipans, hard pressed by the Comanches to the north, were in San Antonio asking for a mission. Four years later the Spanish and the Lipans negotiated a peace treaty, but a mission subsequently built for the tribe in Coahuila was unsuccessful. A wealthy mine owner and philanthropist, Don Pedro Romero de Terreros, offered to finance a mission for three years for the Apaches in the area around the San Saba River, a tributary of the Colorado River and certainly more in the heart of Apache country. Terreros required that his cousin, Father Alonso de Terreros, be placed in charge, that the government bear all military expenses, that the mission's expenses be assumed by the government after three years, and that he would have a monopoly over the mining rights in the area. On May 18, 1756, the viceroy ordered the establishment of a post in accordance with these terms.

In the spring of 1757 Colonel Diego Ortiz Parilla, in command of nearly 100 soldiers, 237 Indian servants, women, and children, and six Franciscan priests headed by Father Terreros, founded Mission San Sabá de la Santa Cruz, Presidio San Luis de las Amarillas, and a civil settlement on the San Saba River, near present-day Menard. The Apaches came in swarms but never found it convenient to stay. The alliance of the Spaniards with the Apaches had antagonized the Comanches and their Wichita allies, who with an estimated 600 to 2,000 warriors, attacked the mission in March 1758, killing ten persons, among them Father Terreros and another priest. In another attack the next year, the hostile Indians killed 19 persons. In retaliation, Colonel Parilla in January 1759 started out with a mixed force of 500, consisting of presidial troops, mission Indians, and Apache warriors. North of the Brazos River the expedition defeated a band of Tonkawas, and then continued northward to the Taovayas village near the present Spanish Fort on the Red River. To their amazement, the Spaniards found the Comanches and their Wichita allies entrenched behind a stockade fortification, over which flew a French flag. There, on October 7, Parilla was beaten by the hostile Indians and hurriedly retreated to San Saba, leaving behind the cannon that had been ineffective in the battle. Spain had suffered the most humiliating defeat at the hands of Indians in the entire history of Texas.

The mission on the San Saba was never rebuilt. Missionary activities on behalf of the Apaches were transferred to the upper Nueces River, near present-day Barksdale, where two missions, San Lorenzo de la Santa Cruz and Nuestra Señora de la Candelaria del Cañon, were established in 1762. For a while these missions prospered, but they were never given any support by the government and were abandoned seven years later. The presidio at San Saba was strengthened and maintained until 1769.

Thus, Spain's efforts at expansion in Texas, except at Goliad and Laredo, were failures. El Orcoquisac, placed at the mouth of the Trinity to expel French intruders, may have been of some value, but it never developed into a civil settlement or even a mission center of any consequence. The mission efforts on the San Xavier and the San Saba ended in calamity.

LIFE IN SPANISH TEXAS: THE MISSIONS

In the settlement of Texas, Spaniards used three institutions: missions, presidios, and civil settlements. Of these, the mission was the most preferred method. The Spanish mission system as it was introduced in Texas was developed in the Central Valley of Mexico, where the Europeans found the Indians living in relatively compact and permanent pueblos. The purpose of the mission was threefold: first, to convert the Indians to Christianity (Catholicism); second, to teach them the habits and customs of Spanish life and make them creditable and self-sustaining subjects of the king; and third, to extend the influence of Spain and to hold the territory in its vicinity against all intruders.

The mission belonged both to the church and the state. Indeed, the missionaries were employees of the king. Although they were selected by the evangelical colleges (divisions of a Catholic religious order), their stipends—generally 450 pesos a year—were paid out of the royal treasury, and their appointments had to be approved by the viceroy. The stipends were not used as salaries for the missionaries but by the college to maintain the mission. New missions could not be established without viceregal assent, and the undertaking was a function of both church and state. The government bore the initial expense of founding a mission, and the evangelical colleges maintained it. A mission was generally maintained for about ten years, after which time it was secularized; that is, its lands and property were distributed among the neophytes (religious converts) and its church taken over by the secular clergy. The time limit was not enforced, however, and in Texas the most successful missions continued in operation for many decades.

The missionaries who served in Texas belonged to the Franciscan order, nearly all sent either by the College (seminary) of Santa Cruz de Querétaro, established at Querétaro in 1683, or by the College of Nuestra Señora de Guadalupe de Zacatecas, founded at Zacatecas in 1707.

The last mission established in Texas was near the coast. In 1793 Nuestra Señora del Refugio was located at the junction of the Guadalupe and San Antonio rivers. Two years later it was moved to a better site in the vicinity of Refugio, but its faithful Zacatecan padres were no more successful than their predecessors had been in converting and changing the habits of the Karankawas and their neighbors.

It was at San Antonio that Spanish mission activity attained its highest success. According to reports of competent authorities in 1749, 1768, and 1781, San Jose was the most successful. Indeed, in 1768 Father José Gaspar de Solís, inspector of the Zacatecan missions, recorded that "it is so pretty and well arranged both in a material and a spiritual way that I have no voice, words, or figures to describe its beauty."

The establishment consisted of a square, approximately 204 yards on each side, enclosed by a stone wall with towers in two opposite corners. Against the wall were 84 quarters built of stone, each supplied with a small kitchen and loopholes for defense. Other structures of stone and mortar inside the enclosure included the church, friary, offices, refectory, an arch granary, a workshop for spinning and weaving cotton and woolen cloth,

The Rose Window of the Mission San José y San Miguel de Aguayo is renowned as a masterpiece of art. (Texas Highway Department)

1768

shops for carpentry, iron work, and tailoring, and a lime kiln. The present church, started in 1768 and large enough to accommodate 2000 persons, with its vaulted roof and its famous Rose Window, is reputed to be the finest mission architecture in New Spain. Outside the walls, there was a mill and an irrigation ditch so large that it "seemed to flow like a small river," which ran from the river by the houses to the fields fenced in for more than a league. There Indians grew corn, brown beans, lentils, melons, peaches (some a pound in weight!), sweet and Irish potatoes, sugar cane, and cotton. So abundant were the crops that the mission, with more than 350 Indians in 1768, supplied in part the presidios at San Antonio, La Bahía, San Sabá, El Orcoquisac, and Los Adaes. The Indians were described as energetic, skilled, and versatile laborers who worked even without supervision. They maintained their own guard and patrol for the defense of the establishment and had their own government with much the same officers and courts as a Spanish pueblo.

Unfortunately, not all Indians accepted mission life as well as those at San José. Reports from other missions frequently complained of Indians who ran away or who pretended to be sick in order to avoid work. Smallpox and other diseases were constant threats, but the priests felt sure that illness was not always the problem.

A typical day for the mission Indians was rather routine. It began with a religious service at dawn followed by 30 minutes or an hour of instruction in the catechism; breakfast; then work in the fields or the shops, or more frequently for the women, work on the looms, at the pottery wheel, or in the kitchen; and school for the children. All work and instruction were under the direction and personal supervision of the priests, or of the soldiers assigned to the mission for such purposes. In the evening all gathered in front of the church for another hour of instruction and the rosary.

Some missions enjoyed comparative prosperity, and reports indicate that in San Antonio, at least, the padres did effective work. An inspector in 1745 reported 2,441 baptisms since 1718. At the time of the report 885 Indians, most of whom had been baptized, were living in the missions. They had more than 5,000 head of cattle, about half that many sheep, and large herds of goats and horses. The mission produced annually about 8,000 bushels of corn and quantities of beans, melons, watermelons, sweet potatoes, and cotton.

Life for the religious, however, was hard indeed when the governor or the presidial officials were hostile toward them, a condition that occasionally prevailed. The most serious quarrel of this kind was with the Governor Franquis de Lugo (1736–37), who seems to have used every device within his power to annoy the missionaries and discredit them with the Indians and the populace of San Antonio. The priests appealed to the viceroy. Franquis de Lugo was reprimanded and later removed, but before they were rid of his presence many of the Indians had fled, and the whole mission field was demoralized.

Soon after Father De Solís made his inspection, the missions began a decline that continued until the close of the Spanish era. There were only nine missionaries active in 1785. Some missionary work continued at San Antonio until 1823, and Mission Refugio continued until 1830.

POLITICAL AND MILITARY AFFAIRS

The political system of Texas was similar to that of the other provinces in New Spain. It was subject directly to the viceroy, who in turn referred important matters to advisors such as the fiscal of the Royal Audiencia and to the *auditor de guerra*. In important cases, before a final decision was made, a *junta*, or general council, composed of various dignitaries might be called together. All important decisions of the viceroy were subject to royal approval, and except in emergencies, policies of great consequence were not adopted until the king approved them. In 1776, in search of economy, efficiency, and more protection on the frontier, the Interior (northern) Provinces, or *Provincias Internas*, were organized under a commandant general who was responsible to the king and practically independent of the viceroy.

Except for the *villa* of San Fernando de Beẋar, which had self-government in some measure, the government of Texas was almost wholly military. At the head of the administration was a governor appointed by the crown. He commanded the army and the militia of the province and had the authority to grant land titles, issue licenses, hear appeals from the alcalde court, supervise fiscal matters, and administer and execute laws and decrees. The terms of the governors varied in length, but the average term was about four years. Inspectors from time to time checked on the governors, and at the end of their term a *residencia* or investigation of their administration was made.

Military life in Texas, especially for the ordinary soldier, was frequently unpleasant. Discipline was harsh, sometimes cruel; the daily routine was boring; and campaigns against the Indians were dangerous. Although the buildings of the presidios at La Bahía and San Antonio were generally well-maintained, elsewhere the forts often received little attention. Evidently the presidios were badly managed. The common soldiers received about 450 pesos a year out of which they had to purchase their equipment and maintain themselves and their families. They spent a great deal of time working on the private estates of the officers. The captain of a presidio served as the merchant of the post, sometimes charging the soldiers exorbitant prices for their supplies, in spite of regulations intended to prevent that abuse. Probably the case of Governor Martos y Navarrette (1759-1767), who was charged with making $80,000 in profits on goods sold to soldiers at Los Adaes, is too extreme to be typical, but it suggests the weaknesses in the system. No doubt this graft greatly lowered the efficiency of the commands. In 1737 Governor Franquis de Lugo reprimanded Captain Gabriel Costales at La Bahía for failure to pay and to supply his men adequately, alleging that certain soldiers came to San Antonio from La Bahia practically naked, their arms out of order, and their horses so poor that they were a disgrace.

LIFE IN THE CIVIL SETTLEMENTS

The first civil settlement in Texas was established in San Antonio in 1718. It consisted of ten families under the protection of a military guard and was called Villa de Bexar. In 1731 55 persons, most of them from the Canary Islands, were moved to San Antonio and located at public expense. The place was now called San Fernando de Bexar. The settlement grew slowly. The population in 1770 was about 800, but this number may not have included persons living on ranches in the vicinity. Enjoying some rights of self-government, landowners elected an *ayuntamiento*, or council, and there was an *alcalde* who combined the responsibilities of mayor, sheriff, and justice of the peace. In 1770 San Antonio became the de facto capital, and after abandonment of Los Adaes three years later, it was officially the seat of government in the province.

The only other civil settlements in Spanish Texas worthy of notice were Goliad, Nacogdoches, and Adaes. After the La Bahía mission and presidio moved to the site of Goliad in 1749, a settlement and important ranching interests developed in the area. The population of the community in 1782 was 512. Likewise, in the late years of the eighteenth century, Nacogdoches experienced considerable growth. A commissary for Indian trade was established, and there was a flourishing but illicit trade with Louisiana. A census in 1790 showed a population of 480. Los Adaes, the capital of Texas from 1722 to 1773, was always a small struggling settlement.

From the early beginnings, even in the early days of exploration, Texas was never exclusively a man's world. Wives accompanied their soldier husbands on some of the first expeditions as they crossed the plains and explored the forests. Families were a part of the second effort to establish a settlement in East Texas in 1716, and more soon followed. Census figures vary somewhat, but all reports indicate that the population of Texas by 1780 was about 45 percent female and 55 percent male, with about one-fourth to one-third of it composed of children. Most men and women were married, but possibly reflecting the difficulties of life on the frontier, widows and widowers accounted for about ten percent of the population.

The basic economy of the civilian population of Spanish Texas was livestock and farming. Livestock ran unattended, with innumerable wild cattle free for the taking; the fertile soils produced good crops; and the countryside and streams contained an abundance of wild game, edible plants, and fish. The ranching industry of Texas developed during these years. Cattle thrived and after markets opened in Louisiana, constituted the principal revenue. Ranchers adopted the practices of roundups, roping, branding, and driving cattle to market. By 1803 an estimated 15,000 head of cattle were annually driven to markets in Louisiana. Despite orders to the contrary, smuggling flourished between East Texas and the French after 1716, and apparently much of the revenue derived from the sale of cattle was used to purchase goods, which were considerably cheaper than those brought overland from Vera Cruz. Spanish settlers also tried to raise sheep, but predatory animals and the wet woodlands of East Texas generally led to failure.

Despite the importance of ranching, most people were farmers. Corn was the staple crop. Other crops included beans, chiles, sugar cane, pumpkins, melons, and gourds. Obviously, not all people were ranchers and farmers. In San Antonio in 1795 approximately one-third of the workers were servants, merchants, tailors, cobblers, teamsters, blacksmiths, and fishermen. There was no lawyer and only one physician listed on the census roll.

Religious and educational opportunities were limited, simple, and often not available. The number of clergymen was never large. Not until 1750 did San Antonio get a church, and then only by royal aid. Yet, as a result of the few faithful missionaries (only nine in 1785), the people remained devout adherents to their Catholic heritage. The first school, which opened in San Antonio in 1789, was short-lived. In 1803 the governor of Texas received orders to see that a school was established near each settlement or presidio, that each boy under 12 was in school, and that each parent paid monthly tuition in the amount of one-fourth peso. Schools were opened soon thereafter in San Antonio and in La Bahía, but the lieutenant governor at Nacogdoches responded that most of the boys there lived on scattered ranches and that consequently it would be impossible to enroll a sufficient number for the teacher to make a living.

Illness and death were not strangers to most households. Outbreaks of the dreaded smallpox and cholera were periodic, and the major remedy was prayer. Although local officials imposed sanitary regulations, there was no pharmacist or civilian physician, and only one hospital (a military one) was ever established.

The behavior and social activities of the people were carefully regulated. Treason, slander of any member of the royal family, murder, arson, or major theft was punishable by death. Whipping, loss of all or half of one's property, or eight to ten years in the galleys was the penalty for robbery or the abuse of a holy person. In matters less serious, there was an abundance of rules. Travel without a passport was forbidden; men under the age of 25 could not marry without parental consent; a man and a woman were forbidden to ride on the same horse. Indeed, there was even a regulation against burning trash.

Yet, notwithstanding such drastic penalties and petty regulations, life was not always a matter of toil and trouble for the civilian Spaniards of Texas. They found time for relaxation and enjoyed several kinds of entertainment. Dancing and the fandangos on the public square (although at times such dances were illegal) were popular, and horse racing, even on religious holidays when participation might bring punishment in the form of 25 lashes, attracted many.

Although never large, the civilian population of Texas nevertheless played a major role in making the hold of Spain more secure. Only where there were farms and ranches and towns did the Spanish culture make itself evident and permanent.

SELECTED BIBLIOGRAPHY

A satisfactory bibliography on Spanish Texas for the material available at the time it was published is Henry R. Wagner, *The Spanish Southwest, 1542–1794; An Annotated Bibliography* (Berkeley, Calif., 1924). The history of Texas in its relation to that of the rest of New Spain is dealt with in H. E. Bolton and Thomas M. Marshall, *The Colonization of North America, 1492–1783* (New York, 1921); H. E. Bolton, *The Spanish Borderlands* (New Haven, 1921); Edward G. Bourne, *Spain in America* (New York, 1904). Of the older histories of Texas, the most satisfactory for the Spanish period are H. H. Bancroft, *History of the North Mexican States and Texas* (2 vols., San Francisco, 1884 and 1889); and Henderson Yoakum, *History of Texas* (2 vols., New York, 1855). A comprehensive history of early Texas is C. E. Castañeda's *Our Catholic Heritage in Texas 1519–1936* (7 vols., Austin, 1936–1958). Some recently published, shorter accounts of the history of Spain in Texas are Odie B. Faulk, *A Successful Failure* (Austin, 1965); O. B. Faulk, *The Last Years of Spanish Texas* (The Hague, 1964); Elizabeth A. H. Johns, *Storms Brewed in Other Men's Worlds* (College Station, 1975); Hodding Carter, *Doomed Road of Empire: The Spanish Trail of Conquest* (New York, 1963). David J. Weber, *New Spain's Northern Frontier: Essays on Spain in the American West, 1540–1821* (Albuquerque, 1979) is especially valuable.

A voluminous amount of Spanish source material is available. The best source of primary material is the Béxar Archives, located at the University of Texas. The best collection of translated sources is Charles W. Hackett (ed. and trans.), *Pichardo's Treatise on the Limits of Louisiana and Texas* (4 vols., Austin, 1931–1947). Other useful sources include Juan Agustín Morfi, *History of Texas, 1673–1679* (2 vols., Albuquerque, N.M., 1935); E. Wallace and D. M. Vigness (eds.), *Documents of Texas History; Documentos para la Historia Eclesiástica y Civil de la Provincia de Texas o Nueves Philipinas, 1720–1779* (Madrid, 1961).

There is an abundance of material on early explorers. General accounts are H. E. Bolton (ed.), *Spanish Exploration in the Southwest, 1542–1706* (New York, 1925 and 1959); F. W. Hodge and T. H. Lewis (eds.), *The Spanish Explorers in the Southern United States, 1528–1543* (New York, 1907 and 1959). See also Harbert Davenport and Joseph K. Wells, "The First Europeans in Texas, 1528–1536" (Cabeza de Vaca), *Southwestern Historical Quarterly*, XXII, 111–42, 205–259; Morris Bishop, *The Odyssey of Cabeza de Vaca* (New York, 1933); G. P. Winship, "The Coronado Expedition, 1540–1542," *Fourteenth Annual Report of the Bureau of American Ethnology, 1892–1893*, I, 329–637 (Washington, D.C., 1896); C. W. Hackett (ed.), *Historical Documents Relating to New Mexico, Nueva Vizcaya, and Approaches Thereto to 1773* (2 vols., Washington, D.C., 1923–1926); H. E. Bolton, *Coronado, Knight of Pueblos and Plains* (New York, 1949); David Donoghue, "The Route of the Coronado Expedition in Texas," *Southwestern Historical Quarterly*, XXXII, 181–92; W. C. Holden, "Coronado's Route across the Staked Plains," *West Texas Historical Association Year Book*, XX, 3–20; Francis Parkman, *LaSalle and the Discovery of the Great West* (Boston, 1893); Rex W. Strickland, "Moscoso's Journey through Texas," J. W. Williams, "Moscoso's Trail in Texas," and Albert Woldert, "The Expedition of Luis de Moscoso in Texas," *Southwestern Historical Quarterly*, XLVI, 109–66; Robert S. Weddle, "Spanish Search for a French Fort: A Path to Danger and Discovery," *American West*, XX, 26–34.

The best available material on the history of early missions and presidios is C. E. Castañeda, *Our Catholic Heritage in Texas*; Robert C. Clark, *The Beginnings of Texas, 1684–1718* (Austin, 1907); C. L. Sonnichsen, *Pass of the North: Four Centuries on the Rio Grande* (El Paso, 1968); H. E. Bolton, "The Location of LaSalle's Colony on the Gulf of Mexico," *Southwestern Historical Quarterly*, XXVII, 171–89; George L. Crocket, *Two Centuries in East Texas* (Dallas, 1932); Walter F. McCaleb, *Spanish Missions of Texas* (San Antonio, 1954); E. W. Cole, "LaSalle in Texas," *Southwestern Historical Quarterly*, XLIX, 473–500; Robert S. Weddle, *San Juan Bautista: Gateway to Spanish Texas* (Austin, 1968); R. S. Weddle, *The San Sabá Mission: Spanish Pivot in Texas* (Austin, 1964); Lesley B. Simpson (ed.), *The San Sabá Papers: A Documentary Account of the Founding and Destruction of the San Sabá Mission* (San Francisco, 1959); B. W. Aston, "Evolution of Nuevo Santander, 1746–1821" (unpublished thesis, Texas Tech University, Lubbock, 1964); James Day and others, *Six Missions of Texas* (Waco, 1965); Kathryn N. O'Connor, *The Presidio La Bahía del Espíritu Santo de Zuñiga, 1821–1846* (Austin, 1966).

On border relations and efforts at expansion, two scholarly studies by H. E. Bolton are *Texas in the Middle Eighteenth Century* (Berkeley, Calif., 1915) and *Athanase de Mézières and the Louisiana-Texas Frontier, 1768–1780* (2 vols., Cleveland, 1914). Useful also are C. W. Hackett, "Policy of the Spanish Crown Regarding French Encroachments from Louisiana, 1721–1762," in *New Spain and the Anglo-American West* (Los Angeles, 1932); William E. Dunn, "Missionary Activities among the Eastern Apaches . . . ," *Quarterly of the Texas State Historical Association*, XV, 186–200; I. J. Cox, "The Louisiana-Texas Frontier," *ibid.*, X, 1–75; XVII, 1–42, 140–187; W. E. Dunn, "The Apache Mission on the San Saba River . . . ," *ibid.*, XVII, 379–414; Ralph A. Smith (ed. and trans.), "Account of the Journey of Bénard de la Harpe: Discovery Made by Him of Several Nations Situated in the West," *ibid.*, LXII, 75–86, 246–259, 371–385, 525–541.

On the Spanish political and military administration, the best source is H. E. Bolton, *Texas in the Middle Eighteenth Century*. See also M. A. Hatcher, "The Municipal Government of San Fernando de Béxar, 1730–1800," *Quarterly of the Texas State*

Historical Association, VIII, 277–352; F. C. Chabot, *San Antonio and Its Beginnings*; Sidney B. Brinckerhoff and O. B. Faulk, *Lancers for the King; A Study of the Frontier Military System of Northern New Spain, with a Translation of the Royal Regulations of 1772* (Phoenix, 1965); B. E. Bobb, *The Viceregency of Antonio Mariá Bucareli in New Spain, 1771–1779* (Austin, 1962); Nettie Lee Benson, "Texas Failure to Send a Deputy to the Spanish Cortes, 1810–1812," *Southwestern Historical Quarterly*, LXIV, 14–35; Virginia Taylor (ed. and trans.), *Letters of Antonio Martínez, Last Governor of Texas, 1817–1822* (Austin, 1957); Felix D. Alamaraz, Jr., *Tragic Cavalier: Governor Manuel Salcedo of Texas, 1808–1813* (Austin, 1971); E. Wallace and D. M. Vigness (eds.), *Documents of Texas History*; D. M. Vigness, *The Revolutionary Decades*; O. B. Faulk, *The Last Years of Spanish Texas, 1778–1821*.

For a description of various missions, see C. E. Castañeda, *Our Catholic Heritage*, vol. IV; H. E. Bolton, *Texas in the Middle Eighteenth Century; F. C. Chabot, San Antonio and Its Beginnings, 1691–1731*; Margaret K. Kress (trans; introduction by M. A. Hatcher), "Diary of a Visit of Inspection of the Texas Missions Made by Fray Gaspar José de Solís in the Year 1767–'68," *Southwestern Historical Quarterly*, XXXV, 28–76; W. E. Dunn, "The Founding of Nuestra Señora del Refugio, the Last Spanish Mission in Texas," *ibid.*, XXV, 174–184; E. M. Schiwetz (historical notes by Robert S. Weddle), *Six Spanish Missions of Texas: A Portfolio of Paintings* (Austin, 1967); William H. Oberste, *History of Refugio Mission* (Refugio, 1942); K. S. O'Connor, *The Presidio La Bahía del Espíritu Santo Zuñiga, 1821–1846*; Billie Persons, "Secular Life in the San Antonio Missions," *Southwestern Historical Quarterly*, LXII, 45–62; E. Wallace and D. M. Vigness (eds.), *Documents of Texas History*; Mattie Austin Hatcher (trans.), "A Description of Mission Life," in E. C. Barker (ed.), *Readings in Texas History* (Dallas, 1929); Marion A. Habig, *The Alamo Chain of Missions* (Chicago, 1968); James Day and others, *Six Missions of Texas*.

Many writings about Spanish Texas contain references to the economic and social life of the settlers, but the best study is Oakah L. Jones, *Los Paisanos: Spanish Settlers on the Northern Frontier of New Spain* (Norman, Okla., 1979). Other excellent, though shorter or more specialized accounts are O. B. Faulk, *A Successful Failure*; Fane Downs, "The History of Mexicans in Texas" (unpublished dissertation, Texas Tech University, Lubbock, 1970); I. J. Cox, "Educational Efforts in San Fernando de Béxar," *Quarterly of the Texas State Historical Association*, VI, 27–63; F. C. Chabot, *San Antonio and Its Beginnings*; Sandra L. Myres, *The Ranch in Spanish Texas* (El Paso, 1969). See also Benedict Leutenegger (trans.), "Memorial of Father Benito Fernandez Concerning the Canary Islanders, 1741," *Southwestern Historical Quarterly*, LXXII, 265–296.

CHAPTER THREE
SPANISH TEXAS
1763–1821

The last years of Spanish Texas were years of frequent change and often years of turmoil and violence. With the acquisition of Louisiana by Spain in 1762, Texas was no longer on the border of New Spain, and the maintenance of settlements in East Texas was no longer regarded as necessary or prudent. But the loss of Louisiana in 1800 and its subsequent purchase by the United States brought an immediate renewal of Spanish interest in Texas and a quarrel over the eastern boundary that almost led to war. The outbreak of the Mexican Revolution in 1810 led to violence and invasions, and there was unrest in the land until the final triumph of the revolution. Meanwhile, a trickle of Anglo-Americans entered Texas, and more significantly, the way was opened for many more.

ADJUSTMENTS FOLLOWING THE ACQUISITION OF LOUISIANA

The Seven Years' War resulted in major changes in Spanish policy in Texas. The Seven Years' War (known to Americans as the French and Indian War), which began in 1754 between France and England, soon developed into a major world conflict. Spain, a belated ally of France, was eventually on the losing side, but before the war ended, France ceded western Louisiana to Spain. By the Treaty of Paris of 1763, Spain ceded Florida to England but was permitted to keep western Louisiana.

Acquisition of Louisiana was not without its problems. Louisiana had cost France "eight hundred thousand *livres* a year, without yielding a *sou* in return," and it was to prove no less a burden to Spain. It was a vast domain, which the declining Spanish Empire did not have the resources to defend and develop. On the northeast border, the aggressive English along the Mississippi, rather than the tolerant French along the Red River, were now Spain's neighbors. Twenty years later the Republic of the United States had its beginning, and its frontier people were even more restless than they had been as British subjects. Internal troubles in New Spain (Mexico) were even more threatening than external dangers. In Texas and other northern provinces hordes of Indians were becoming more and more destructive.

Drastic reforms and energetic measures were necessary to meet such problems. Fortunately for Spain, the king at this time was Charles III, one of the ablest men of the Bourbon line. Among the various officials whom he sent to America to carry out his reforms was the Marqués de Rubí, appointed inspector of the northern frontier. Rubí set out in 1766 to explore the frontier from the Gulf of California to Louisiana. Entering Texas during the summer of 1767, he visited El Cañon, San Sabá, San Antonio, Nacogdoches, Los Ais, Los Adaes, San Augustín de Ahumada (Orcoquisac), and La Bahía. At the end of his journey in Mexico City, Rubí had traveled about 7,000 miles in less than three years. The inspector confirmed what Spanish frontier officers had long been trying to impress on their superiors. The far-flung posts could not be maintained with the resources available. His very comprehensive and informative reports brought forth on September 10, 1772, a royal order, "Regulation for the Presidios," which substantially followed his recommendations.

In short, as it applied to Texas, the new regulation called for:

(1) the abandonment of all missions and presidios except San Antonio and La Bahía;

(2) the strengthening of San Antonio de Beẍar by moving to it settlers from East Texas; and

(3) the inauguration of a new Indian program calling for friendly relations with the Comanches and Wichitas and a war of extermination against the Apaches.

Thus, Spain had decided to give up not only all attempts to occupy the country north of the San Antonio but also to abandon, except San Antonio and La Bahía, all its establishments in Texas.

It did not take a royal order to bring about the abandonment of San Sabá and El Cañon; the Comanches forced that in 1769. Two years later the presidio at Orcoquisac was abandoned, and shortly thereafter the missionaries left their post in that vicinity. These readjustments took place before the new regulation went into effect.

The abandonment of the East Texas settlements, however, was a different matter. These settlers were removed, not because of the problem of maintaining them, but because they were no longer needed as a barrier against French aggression and could be used to strengthen San Antonio. Baron Juan María de Ripperdá, governor of Texas, supervised the cruel removal, a task not to his liking. In the summer of 1773 the missions were abandoned, and more than 500 persons were torn away from their homes and forced to leave behind their growing crops and even their livestock.

Dissatisfied with San Antonio, because of the poor land on which they were located and the Comanche raids on their livestock, the East Texans petitioned to return to Los Ais, where their leader, Antonio Gil y Barbo (Ybarbo), had a ranch. Ripperdá endorsed their petition, but the viceroy consented for them to return no closer to Natchitoches than one hundred leagues. In modern Madison County, where the Nacogdoches road crossed the Trinity River, the refugees in August 1774 laid out the settlement of Bucareli. Three years later Bucareli was the home of 347 persons. Plagued by floods and raids by Comanche Indians, they again moved in 1779, this time without permission, to Nacogdoches. The authorities reluctantly gave their approval, and eventually some settlers scattered to their former homes.

Another part of the new regulation called for the pacification of the northern tribes and a war of "reduction or destruction" against the Apaches. The Spaniards were wise enough to adopt in part the French system in dealing with Indian affairs and to employ Frenchmen to deal with the Indians. The plan adopted was substantially what Rubí had recommended. The guiding genius in this arrangement was Athanase de Mézières, who was appointed lieutenant governor of the Natchitoches district in 1769. De Mézières, a man of unusual ability who was fluent in several Indian languages, French, Spanish, and Latin, had been seasoned by thirty years of service in Louisiana as a soldier, planter, and Indian trader. By 1771 he had made peace with the Wichitas. In the summer of 1772 he visited the Tawakoni villages (near present-day Waco) and made contact with the Taovayas. Two years later J. Gaignard, a trader from Natchitoches, signed a treaty with a Comanche band, possibly the Nokoni, but the other Comanche bands continued to harass San Antonio. For several more years De Mézières worked with Ripperdá on plans to get the northern tribes to join the Spaniards in a campaign against the Apaches, but he died before achieving his goal.

De Mézières's task of pacifying the northern tribes was never completed. A united campaign against the Apaches was never waged, although Comanche war parties occasionally joined the Spaniards on expeditions against the hated Apaches. The military strength of the province was rarely sufficient to cope with the many hostile Indians. With less than two hundred troops to divide among three or four presidios or outposts, to furnish escorts for traveling parties, and to supply guards for the various missions, there was never enough soldiers. A peace treaty with the Apaches in 1749 and subsequent treaties with the Comanches in 1774 and 1785 in each instance brought only a temporary respite.

Baron Ripperdá, who came to San Antonio as governor in 1770, sent to his superiors dramatic accounts of the plight of that place and urgent pleas for more troops. Additional troops were sent, but Ripperdá never felt secure. His successor, Domingo Cabello, in 1789 wrote Teodoro de Croix, commandant of the *Provincias Internas*,: "There is not an instant by day or night when reports do not arrive from all these ranches of barbarities and disorder falling on us. Totally unprotected as we are, they will result in the absolute destruction and loss of this province." In 1792 Governor Manuel Muñoz complained that peace agreements and presents did not stop Comanche raids and that Apache depredations were chronic. The Indians accepted the gifts but did not stop their marauding expeditions.

Fear of foreign intruders and pressing military needs led to several extensive explorations of Texas and New Mexico in the 1780s. The Spanish hoped to influence the Comanche and Wichitas to serve as a barrier against Anglo-American intrusion, and sought out desirable travel routes linking San Antonio, Santa Fe, and Natchitoches. Pedro (Pierre) Vial, a French trader employed by the Spanish governor, in the winter of 1786-1787 traveled from San Antonio by way of present Brownwood, thence to the Tawakoni village near Waco, and by way of present Spanish Fort on the Red River to Santa Fe.

Not satisfied with Vial's report, Governor Fernando de la Concha of New Mexico sent out another expedition. In the summer and fall of 1787, Corporal José Mares traveled eastward across the plains to a point near present Quanah and the Taovayas villages near Spanish Fort and then southward by present-day Jacksboro to San Antonio. On his return trip, he went near the sites of present Coleman and Abilene and then across the plains to Santa Fe. This journey was the shortest route of the three, but even so, he traveled a distance of more than 800 miles. Subsequently, Vial in 1788 and 1789 traveled eastward from Santa Fe across the plains, then by way of the Red River to present Gainesville and Greenville to Natchitoches, and then to San Antonio by way of the site of San Augustine and Nacogdoches. After a brief stop, the tireless explorer returned to Santa Fe by a route similar to one used by Mares in the preceding year.

No more explorations were made for a time, but the hope of a satisfactory route to Santa Fe from points in the province of Texas did not die easily. In 1808 Don Francisco Amangual with the aid of Comanche guides was able to go from San Antonio to Santa Fe with two hundred troops. Spanish officials were concerned about the exploring expedition of Lieutenant Zebulon Pike of the United States Army into Spanish Texas two years earlier. They wanted to impress both the Americans and the Comanche Indians with the power and mobility of the Spanish military. Amangual's route, which went by way of the old San Saba post, thence to present-day San Angelo and along the eastern side of the Caprock before turning west across the plains by way of present Amarillo, was no more satisfactory than were earlier routes.

In no way did these ambitious efforts meet the goals of the Spaniards. The explorers learned much about the land, and the journeys, which were filled with hardships of all kinds, amply demonstrated their courage and resourcefulness. But the Indians of the north were apparently less than impressed, and there was little to indicate that the expeditions affected either Anglo-Americans or the United States government. Moreover, the explorations demonstrated the impracticality of a route from San Antonio to Santa Fe and suggested that a route between Natchitoches and Santa Fe was only a marginal possibility. The inhospitality of the plains and the hostility of the Comanches were too much of a barrier.

SPAIN, TEXAS, AND THE UNITED STATES

Spanish policy in Texas changed again after 1803. The occasion for the change occurred when Napoleon of France, hoping for a renewed French empire in America, forced Spain to return Louisiana to France in 1800. Then, after his dream of an American empire faded, in 1803 he sold Louisiana to the United States for approximately $15 million. Texas was once again on the border of New Spain, and an indefinite boundary separated it from the land-hungry Americans. To meet the new situation Spain adopted a threefold imperial policy; first, to hold the territory with its ancient boundaries unimpaired; second, to increase its garrisons and colonize the territory with loyal Spanish subjects; and third, to keep out Anglo-American intruders.

A controversy over the western boundary of Louisiana seemed inevitable. The purchase treaty, rather than naming specific boundaries, provided for the transfer of the territory as it had been prior to its cession to Spain in 1762. President Thomas Jefferson, on the basis of the French claim, held that the territory extended to the Rio Grande, while the Spaniards, with more justification, contended that it did not extend west of the Red River. The Spaniards placed additional troops in Texas, including detachments at the old post El Orcoquisac at the mouth of the Trinity and at points east of the Sabine, and thwarted efforts of the United States to explore the disputed territory. The Thomas Freeman expedition, sent up the Red River in 1806, was stopped at a point near the western boundary of the present state of Arkansas, and Zebulon Pike, who succeeded in reaching the upper waters of the Rio Grande, was captured by a Spanish force.

The United States, on the other hand, sent troops into Louisiana, drove the Spanish troops from Los Adaes, and made preparations for war. Strained relations between the two countries were aggravated by the report that Aaron Burr, formerly Vice-President of the United States, was planning to lead a filibustering expedition into Texas or some other Spanish province. Burr's force disintegrated, however, before it reached New Orleans. When Wilkinson, who is believed to have been both in league with Burr and in the secret pay of Spain, realized that the Burr expedition was a failure, he hurriedly abandoned the project and hastened to prove his determination to protect the frontier.

Fortunately, a clash of arms was avoided. In November, 1806, Wilkinson, in command of the United States forces, made with General Simón Herrera, in command of Spanish troops on the border, what is known as the Neutral Ground Agreement. This provided that the Spaniards should remain west of the Sabine River and the Americans east of the Arroyo Hondo until their respective governments had reached a settlement. Although it was unofficial, leaders of both nations honored the understanding until the question could be resolved in a more formal way. The agreement avoided war, but unfortunately the absence of law made the area between the two boundaries a haven for an assortment of outlaws and thieves. In later years there were many who believed that much of the lawlessness that sometimes occurred in East Texas had its roots in the ungoverned lands of the Neutral Ground Agreement.

The diplomatic question concerning the western boundary of the Louisiana purchase continued to be an issue, however, and was linked to the claims of the United States to West Florida. Negotiations were discontinued in 1807 and were not resumed until ten years later. At last, the Adams-Onís, or Florida Purchase, Treaty was signed in 1819 and became effective two years later. By that agreement the United States acquired Florida from Spain and gave up its shadowy claim to Texas. Also, the Louisiana-Texas boundary was fixed as follows: the west bank of the Sabine River from the Gulf to the thirty-second parallel, north to the Red River, along the south bank of that stream to the one hundredth meridian, north to the Arkansas River, along the south or west bank of that stream to its source, north to the forty-second parallel, and along that parallel to the Pacific Ocean.

THE FIRST ANGLO-AMERICANS IN TEXAS

In the late eighteenth and early nineteenth century a few Anglo-Americans began to make their way into Texas. Generally, these people were of two kinds—sober, hardworking citizens who were looking for an opportunity to build a new life, or adventurers who in some way or another had political ambitions. Until almost the end of Spanish rule, official policy frowned on both types, but often the respectable citizens were accepted and even made welcome. For example, William Barr was an Irishman who had lived in the United States. Together with Peter Davenport from Philadelphia, they formed a company that traded with the Indians and Spanish soldiers in East Texas.

A larger group of Anglo-Americans peacefully and permanently settled in northeast Texas in present-day Red River County. Because of the uncertainty of the western limits of Louisiana Territory, they settled at sites that a later boundary survey placed in Texas. The first arrivals were Indian traders, but in 1815 William Lawrence and William Hensley settled on the Red River, north of present-day Clarksville, at a site they named Jonesborough, for a trader already there. The next year more settlers built their cabins at Pecan Point, about thirty miles downstream at the junction of Pecan Bayou and the Red River. Within two years twelve families and several traders were there.

As Spanish rule came to an end, confusion over the location of the Jonesborough and Pecan Point settlements increased. In 1820 the newly created Territory of Arkansas claimed the area and named it Miller County, and more settlers flooded in. But in subsequent years, perhaps to take advantage of Mexico's liberal policies, many settlers applied to the government of Mexico for land titles. Actually, the settlement was without question, at least after the negotiation of the Adams-Onís Treaty, in Spanish territory. It seems clear, however, that the original settlers of Miller County came in good faith with no intention of locating on Spanish soil.

From the viewpoint of Spanish officials, however, the tolerant attitude displayed toward Anglo-Americans who were respectable citizens could not be extended to Anglo-American adventurers, or "filibusters," who almost certainly were not working in the interest of Spain. Many of these were traders from Louisiana who appropriated much of the Indian trade and who offered a market for horses that the Indians stole from the Spanish posts. Some of these traders openly defied the authority of Spain. The best known was Philip Nolan, whose career is partly shrouded in mystery.

Nolan came to Texas as a trader as early as 1791 and with the permission of Spanish officials took horses out of the country. On one trip he drove out thirteen hundred; on another he rounded up about two thousand. The Spaniards became suspicious of his motive, and when he returned in the autumn of 1800 with a party of 17 armed followers, they sent a force of about a hundred soldiers to arrest him. In the fight that ensued near the present-day city of Waco on March 22, 1801, Nolan was killed. His followers were imprisoned in Mexico and later cast dice to see who of the nine survivors would die to satisfy the decree of the Spanish monarch. One of the survivors was Peter Ellis Bean, who would play an important role in East Texas affairs for many years.

The true extent of Nolan's intentions will never be known. Perhaps he was a merely an aggressive Anglo-American horse trader whose importance in the story of Texas has been romantically exaggerated over the years. On the other hand, some evidence indicates that Nolan was planning a more ambitious expedition against Texas. To a degree, Nolan was at the time and has since been judged by his association with General James Wilkinson. Nolan was a bookkeeper for, and protege of, Wilkinson, commander of the United States forces in Louisiana, whose capacity for double dealing has seldom, if ever, been surpassed in American history. The obscurity of Nolan's plans, however, would not be true in the case of filibusters to come. As revolution broke out in Mexico in 1810, more adventurers would make their way into Texas with definite and obvious purpose in mind.

THE MEXICAN REVOLUTION BEGINS

At the town of Dolores (about 200 miles northwest of Mexico City) on September 16, 1810, the priest Miguel Hidalgo, representing the poorer people of Mexico, raised the cry of revolt against the Spanish government. The examples of revolutions in the United States and in France had attracted the attention of Spanish colonials, and gradually the ideals of liberty, equality, and fraternity spread over most of the empire held by Spain in America. In Mexico where a small group of criollos (people of Spanish blood born in Mexico) dominated a great mass of desperately poor people, either *mestizos* (of mixed Spanish and Indian blood) or Indians, the situation was ripe for violence and revolution. Thus, Hidalgo's *Grito de Dolores*, a cry to rise and overthrow the Spanish rulers, launched a movement that would never die until independence was finally achieved. From Dolores, Hidalgo with a few soldiers and a straggling horde of Indians moved to Guanajuato, captured and sacked it, and set up a government. Soon the city of Guadalajara fell to the revolutionaries, and the provinces of Nuevo Santander and Coahuila were added to their territory.

The people of Texas at first declared their loyalty to the King but soon became indifferent and critical. Then, on January 22, 1811, Juan Bautista de las Casas, a resident of San Antonio and a former militia captain, along with a few fellow conspirators, seized without a struggle Simon Herrera, commander of the troops, Governor Manuel María de Salcedo, and other officials at San Antonio. Las Casas then proclaimed himself governor of Texas. After his delegations, with equal ease, had taken possession of Goliad and Nacogdoches, he notified Hidalgo of his success. The season of his power was short. On March 2, the loyalists, led by Juan

Manuel Zambrano, Erasmo Seguín, and Francisco Ruiz, captured Las Casas. In July they instituted royal rule and shortly thereafter executed Las Casas.

Although Hidalgo had already been captured and put to death (March 1811), the revolution went on under other leaders. Soon an invasion force was making its way into Texas from the United States. Bernardo Gutiérrez de Lara, a wealthy citizen of the city of Revilla (now Guerrero), was responsible. Gutiérrez went to the United States in 1811 as the envoy of the revolutionists. He was not officially recognized by the United States government, but some officials and other persons encouraged him in his search for assistance in the organization of a filibustering force to invade Texas. Moreover, reports from Texas assured him that the province would revolt on the approach of an invading army. Gutiérrez persuaded Augustus W. Magee to resign his commission in the United States Army, to join him, and to recruit the nucleus of an army. Magee was an adroit young officer who had made a good record on the Louisiana-Texas frontier but who was dissatisfied at not being promoted. Gutiérrez was named commander in chief, but Magee was the actual military commander.

Starting from Natchitoches with a conglomerate array of more than one hundred Anglo-Americans, Frenchmen, Mexican revolutionists, and Indian allies, Magee occupied with ease Nacogdoches in mid-August 1812. The Gutiérrez propaganda pamphlets, letters, and broadsides had smoothed the way. The Spanish soldiers deserted or fled, and the people drove away their officers and went out in a procession to greet the liberators. Gutiérrez followed the army to Nacogdoches and renewed his propaganda. In November the army laid siege to La Bahía. There Magee died, perhaps from illness, although some believed his death to be suicide. Meanwhile, the offensive was stalled until February 1813, when the Spaniards withdrew to San Antonio. In March Samuel Kemper, who had succeeded Magee, renewed the advance. After defeating a Spanish army of twelve hundred men commanded by Simón Herrera, the invaders occupied San Antonio on April 1, 1813. Five days later Gutiérrez issued a "Declaration of Independence of the State of Texas," a worthy document written according to the best traditions of liberalism.

But with victory came dissension. On April 17 Gutiérrez proclaimed a constitution that provided for a centralized government, rather than the republican form expected by the Anglo-Americans. The constitution provided for a governor and a *junta* with dictatorial powers. Also, by declaring that the "State of Texas" formed "a part of the Mexican Republic to which it remains inviolably joined," the instrument destroyed the hopes of the Americans that Texas would become a dependency of the United States. The execution of Governor Salcedo, General Herrera, and twelve other Spanish officers, apparently with the approval of Gutiérrez, disgusted and alarmed many members of the expedition.

Although some Americans left for the United States, others replaced Gutiérrez with José Alvarez de Toledo, a revolutionist from Spain, who promised a more independent and liberal government for Texas. Gutiérrez left a few days afterwards for exile in the United States, but the days of his insurrection were numbered. Torn by dissension in their ranks, the heterogeneous collection of 1,400 Americans, Mexicans, and Indians at San Antonio were no match for the 1,830 troops that Joaquín de Arredondo, commandant general of the Eastern Interior Provinces, brought against them. On the Medina River west of San Antonio, on August 18, 1813, the revolutionists were put to rout. Most of the Americans were slain; those lucky enough to escape fled to the United States. Thus the Mexican state of Texas came to an end after a troubled career of four months.

Arredondo followed up his victory with a purge calculated to rid Texas of all Anglo-Americans and others believed to be disloyal to Spain. Rebels were shot, their property confiscated, and their wives and daughters imprisoned and forced to do labor for the loyalist army. So thoroughly did he do his work that the province was virtually depopulated, save for the settlement at Bexar. Indeed, he was unable to put into effect the new liberal Spanish Constitution of 1812 because there were not enough suitable persons to fill the offices! No serious effort was again made to populate Texas until 1820, and meanwhile the officials forbade any trade with Louisiana.

But the rich lands of Texas constituted an invitation that offset the harshest decrees of the Spanish government. In 1818 the military had to drive away a band of about 120 Napoleonic sympathizers who, under a Frenchman named Charles Lallemand, had settled on the lower Trinity River. The next year a more serious threat to Spanish sovereignty appeared under the leadership of James Long. Long, a merchant of Natchez who married a niece of General Wilkinson, was angry over the terms of the Adams-Onis Treaty. Like many Americans on the southern frontier, he believed that the terms of the treaty, which acknowledged Spain's claim to Texas, represented the "surrender of Texas." At a meeting in Natchez, plans were formulated for driving out of Texas the few royalist troops, organizing a liberal government, and attracting immigrants by the offer of generous land grants. Under Long's leadership the party set out in June for Nacogdoches, gaining recruits as it advanced until it had three hundred men, among them Bernardo Gutiérrez. Shortly after their arrival at Nacogdoches on June 23, 1819, the invaders established a civil government, adopted a declaration of independence, and invited immigrants to share with them the blessings of liberty.

To hold various outposts, Long divided his forces and left for Galveston Island to enlist the aid of Jean Lafitte. For several years Galveston had served as the headquarters for various adventurers or buccaneers, including Colonel Henry Perry, a survivor of the Gutiérrez-Magee expedi-

Jane Long, wife of Filibuster James Long, became one of the best-known and most beloved women in nineteenth-century Texas. When her husband was arrested and carried to Mexico City, Jane Long, with only her baby, two-year-old daughter, and a black girl, waited at Bolivar Point on Galveston Bay throughout the winter of 1821–1822 for the return of her husband. After receiving word that he had been assassinated, she returned to Mississippi but later settled in Austin's colony. (Southwest Collection, Texas Tech University)

tion, and Luis Aury, who held a naval commission from the Mexican revolutionists, and Lafitte. Lafitte's tenure dated from April 1817, when he set up his "republic" on the island and made it the headquarters for his privateering activities. Long failed on his mission, and during his absence a Spanish force captured a part of his men and put others to flight. Long then made his way to New Orleans, only to return again with his family and another group of adventurers in 1820. Traveling by sea, he established his headquarters at Point Bolivar on Galveston Bay, where he remained for several months. Finally he made his way down the coast with about fifty men and eventually reached La Bahía on October 4, 1821, there to be warmly received as a revolutionary. Mexico, however, had already won its independence, and a few days later Long was sent to Mexico City. About six months later a Mexican soldier shot and killed him, perhaps accidentally, but possibly as a way of removing a potential threat to the new nation.

THE BEGINNING OF ANGLO-AMERICAN COLONIZATION

Although Spanish officials had little use for filibusters such as James Long, in these fading years of empire, Spanish policy was in the process of changing to accept, even to encourage, Anglo-American immigration on a large scale. The Anglo-American settlement in Miller County was unrecognized, perhaps even unknown for sometime. But in September 1820, the *Cortes* (ruling council) of Spain issued a decree opening all Spanish dominions to

Moses Austin. In 1820, when hard times came to Potosi, Missouri, which Austin had founded in 1798, he went to Texas and obtained the governor's permission to settle three hundred families there. (E C. Barker History Center, University of Texas)

any foreigners who would respect the constitution and laws of the monarch. News of the opportunity spread quickly, even to the western borders of the United States, and there were those who were eager to take advantage of it.

Among them was 59-year-old Moses Austin, Connecticut born and seasoned by many years of business experience in Virginia and on the Missouri frontier. On December 23, 1820, Austin appeared before Governor Antonio de Martínez in San Antonio and asked permission to establish in Texas a colony of three hundred families. Austin had moved to Spanish Missouri in 1798, and he now came, he said, as a former Spanish subject who wished to renew his allegiance to the king. The role that Austin sought was that of an *empresario*. He petitioned for a contract to recruit settlers, bring them to Texas, build a settlement, and divide out the land within the terms and boundaries to be specified in the contract.

Perhaps it was only through chance that Austin succeeded in securing an approval of his petition. Governor Martínez was doubtful, but an old friend of Austin, the Baron de Bastrop, supported the application of the petitioner. Bastrop, a man of uncertain origins with a self-assumed title, was nonetheless an influential citizen in San Antonio. Consequently, Martínez finally endorsed the application and on January 17, 1821, a board of superior officers, known as the provincial deputation, approved it. Somewhat surprisingly, Joaquín de Arredondo, military commandant of the area including Texas and a man who cared little for Anglo-Americans, agreed to the contract.

Moses Austin died soon after his return to Missouri, and it was left to the son to complete the task begun by the father. Although only 27 years old, Stephen F. Austin was already a man of rich experience. He was well-educated. He had served five years in the legislature of the Missouri Territory, had been appointed district judge in the territory of Arkansas, and had engaged in a variety of business undertakings. In addition, he had operated a farm in Missouri, had served as a federal territorial judge in Arkansas, and had studied law in New Orleans. More important, he was as Professor Eugene C. Barker, his biographer, states, "patient; methodical; energetic; and fair-spoken; and acquainted from childhood with the characteristic social types that mingled on the southwestern border."

With a small party Austin went to San Antonio in the summer of 1821. There Governor Martínez received him cordially, recognized him as the heir to his father's commission, and authorized him to explore the country and to make other arrangements for his colony. News about the project had already traveled far, and on his return to Natchitoches, Louisiana, he found nearly a hundred letters from persons who were interested. Some settlers were soon on their way, but the fate of the new colony soon appeared to be in doubt, even before it was truly established. After years of hardship, the struggle for independence had succeeded. Spanish rule was at an end; Texas was now a part of the new nation of Mexico; and the validity of Spanish contracts such as that held by Austin was now in question.

A NEW NATION: MEXICO

For a time after the death of Hidalgo in 1811, Spanish officials were able to suppress the Mexican rebellion. The upper classes, that is the criollos and wealthy mestizos, did not support it, neither did the clergy nor the merchants. Yet, the death of Hidalgo did not bring an end to the insurrection. The flames of rebellion were beaten out, but the smoldering embers of discontent remained. After a time, events in Europe brought new support to the revolutionary cause when Napoleon of France installed his brother on the throne of Spain. Even some of the Mexican clergy, staunch supporters of monarchy, were alienated because they knew that Napoleon was disposed to take many liberties with the church.

Although the revolution continued under the leadership of José María Morelos until his execution in the fall of 1815 and thereafter under Vicente Guerrero, it did not go well. Indeed, at the end of the great European wars in 1815, it seemed that the royal government would suppress the rebels entirely. In 1819 Viceroy Juan Ruiz Apodaca reported to the king that no additional troops were necessary. Ironically, his judgment was made at the very time when events were happening that would give new life to the rebel cause. In Spain a liberal insurrection forced King Ferdinand to restore a liberal framework of government, the Constitution of 1812. This move antagonized and threatened the privileged classes in Mexico, especially the clergy, who resented certain anticlerical policies of the new government. Spain had become too liberal for New Spain. —

Thus a strange combination of privilege and poverty combined to overthrow royal rule. The key to the covenant was Agustín de Iturbide, a criollo army officer whose loyalties were not very reliable. Iturbide persuaded the viceroy to place him in charge of a 2,500 man army to defeat the rebels, but when Iturbide marched, he did so not to fight but to negotiate an agreement with Guerrero, the liberal leader. The agreement, known as the *Plan de Iguala*, was proclaimed on February 24, 1821. The plan declared that New Spain was an independent, moderate, constitutional monarchy, guaranteed it the Catholic religion, and proclaimed racial equality. In August, Juan O'Donoju, the last viceroy, recognized the independence of Mexico, and on September 27 Iturbide entered Mexico City. Thus, through an unusual combination of liberals and conservatives, the independence of Mexico was attained.

FAILURE AND LEGACY

In the measurements of population and settlements, Spain's three centuries of rule in Texas could hardly be termed a success. Notwithstanding all its efforts, Spain had in Texas, at the time the United States acquired Louisiana, only the settlements of San Antonio, Goliad, and Nacogdoches. San Antonio, consisting of five missions, the settlement of Bexar, and the *villa* of San Fernando, had a population of about 2,500. About 1,200 persons lived in Goliad and about 500 in Nacogdoches. Faced with the threat of Anglo-American aggression, Spain renewed its efforts to populate the province. In 1805 it established the *villa* of Salcedo on the Trinity River, opposite the ruins of Bucareli, and the *villa* of San Marcos, eight miles above the site of present-day Gonzales. But in 1809 when there were only 16 persons living in Salcedo and 82 in San Marcos, the entire population of Texas was estimated at only 4,155 persons, more than 1,000 of whom were soldiers. The invasions and reprisals associated with the outbreak of revolution in 1810 brought more soldiers, but significantly reduced the number of settlers.

The causes of the comparative failure of Spain in Texas were partly within and partly beyond its control. Its exclusive commercial policy, which prohibited trade even between the different parts of its dominions, was certainly a retarding factor. Strict and tyrannical methods of government, strangely mixed with laxity and tolerance of graft, were also causes of failure. Certain unfavorable conditions, chief of which was the hostility of nomadic Indian tribes, were beyond its control. Yet Spain might have changed its pioneering institutions—the *villa*, the presidio, and the mission—to meet the conditions peculiar to the northern frontier in a better way.

In general it may be said that Spain suffered most because of a lack of realism in its policies and the stubborn adherence to tradition in administration. For instance, it held doggedly to the notion that the pueblo type of mission was suited to Texas, although it soon proved of little value except along the Rio Grande and in the vicinity of San Antonio. It adhered rigidly to the high ideal that Indians should not have firearms and thereby compelled them to trade with its rivals. It never gave up the theory that, since Texas was an extension of New Spain, the province should trade with New Spain only; thus it impoverished its settlements and caused people of enterprise to violate the law. Notwithstanding abundant evidence that conditions were otherwise, Spain clung to the fiction that poorly paid captains of isolated posts would be scrupulously honest, would sell supplies to their soldiers at fair prices, would keep their men employed in the public service, and would not use them for their own gain. The fact that occasional rigid inspections were made and that sometimes the guilty were punished did not ensure honesty.

Spain's achievements in Texas must not be despised, however. It held Texas against all contenders until its empire in America collapsed and left upon it an imprint that will endure throughout the ages. Many streams and towns bear Spanish names. In almost every section there are land titles that go back to Spanish grants. The law shows Spanish influence, particularly that pertaining to the property rights of women. Fortunately, a few specimens of Spanish architecture still remain. In San Antonio some of the chapels of the old missions have withstood almost two centuries of assault by the elements and the occasional ravages of unfriendly hands. Their stateliness and gentle beauty command a reverent interest. They are worthy monuments to the idealism of the Spanish and fitting symbols of immortality in a transitory world.

SELECTED BIBLIOGRAPHY

The most useful reference for the period is the *Handbook of Texas*. The general accounts mentioned in the preceding bibliography also apply to this chapter. The best sources on the readjustment following the acquisition of Louisiana by Spain are H. E. Bolton, *Texas in the Middle Eighteenth Century*; H. E. Bolton, *Athanase de Mézières*; C. E. Castañeda, *Our Catholic Heritage in Texas, 1519–1936*, vol. IV; O. B. Faulk, *A Successful Failure*; Noel M. Loomis and A. P. Nasater, *Pedro Vial and the Roads to Santa Fé* (Norman, Okla., 1967). See also E. Wallace and D. M. Vigness (eds.), *Documents of Texas History*; H. E. Bolton, "The Spanish Abandonment and

Reoccupation of East Texas, 1773–1779," *Quarterly of the Texas State Historical Association*, IX, 67–137; A. B. Thomas (ed. and trans.), *Teodoro de Croix and the Northern Frontier of New Spain*, 1776–1783 (Norman, Okla., 1941); E. A. H. John, *Storms Brewed in Other Men's Worlds*; Elizabeth Ann Harper, "The Taovayas Indians in Frontier Trade and Diplomacy, 1769–1779," *Southwestern Historical Quarterly*, LVII, 181–201.

For the last years of Spain in Texas, the best scholarly studies are M. A. Hatcher, *The Opening of Texas to Foreign Settlement, 1801–1821* (University of Texas Bulletin, no. 2714; Austin, 1927); O. B. Faulk, *The Last Years of Spanish Texas;* D. M. Vigness, *The Revolutionary Decades* (Austin, 1965); N. L. Benson (ed. and trans.), "A Governor's Report on Texas in 1809," *Southwestern Historical Quarterly*, LXXI, 603–615; L. Friend, "Old Spanish Fort," *West Texas Historical Association Year Book*, XVI, 3–27; Kathryn Garrett, "Dr. John Sibley and the Louisiana-Texas Frontier, 1803–1814," *Southwestern Historical Quarterly*, XLVIII, XLIX; Harris G. Warren, *The Sword Was Their Passport* (Baton Rouge, 1943). Texas-Louisiana relations of that period are dealt with in Thomas M. Marshall, *A History of the Western Boundary of the Louisiana Purchase, 1819–1841* (Berkeley, Calif., 1914). See also Felix D. Almaraz, Jr., *The Crossroad of Empire: The Church and State on the Rio Grande Frontier of Coahuila and Texas, 1700–1821* (San Antonio, 1979); and Dan Flores, "Rendezvous at Spanish Bluff: Jefferson's Red River Exploration," *Red River Valley Historical Review*, IX, 4–26.

On the filibusters, see the general references previously cited and also: K. Garrett, *Green Flag over Texas* (Austin, 1969); D. M. Vigness, *The Revolutionary Decades*; H. S. Thrall, *Pictorial History of Texas* (St. Louis, 1879); M. A. Hatcher, "Joaquin de Arredondo's Report of the Battle of the Medina . . . ," *Quarterly of the Texas State Historical Association*, XI, 220–36; K. Garrett, "The First Constitution of Texas, April 17, 1813," *Southwestern Historical Quarterly*, XL, 290–308; Lois Garvèr, "Benjamin Rush Milam," *ibid.*, XXXVIII, 79–121; Henry P. Walker (ed.), "William McLane's Narrative of the Magee-Gutiérrez Expedition of 1812–1813," *ibid.*, LXVI, 234–51, 457–79, 569–88; James C. Milligan, "José Bernardo Gutiérrez de Lara, 1811–1841" (unpublished dissertation, Texas Tech University, Lubbock, 1975); E. Wallace and D. M. Vigness (eds.), *Documents of Texas History*; Ted Schwarz, *Forgotten Battlefield of the First Texas Revolution: The Battle of Medina, August 18, 1813* (Austin, 1985).

CHAPTER FOUR
TEXAS UNDER
MEXICAN RULE

For the people of Mexico in general and of Texas in particular, the end of Spanish rule was much more of a beginning than it was an end. In the new nation the uneasy alliance of conservative *ricos*, middle-class *criollos*, and liberal *pobres* soon and predictably fell apart. The knowledge necessary to establish a stable and free government was not lacking, but the necessary experience and consensus was. Consequently, in their first decade of freedom the people of Mexico would change their basic framework of government twice and their leaders several times more.

Although the uncertainties of national leadership affected the events and people of Texas, the first years of Mexican rule were nonetheless a time of growth and development. Mexican policy for a time continued to allow, even to encourage, Anglo-American immigration, and thousands of settlers made their way into Texas. They cleared their lands, built roads, laid out new towns, and expanded older ones. But even in these early years, there were indications that some Mexican leaders questioned the wisdom of an open door to Texas. A decree in 1830 slowed the stream of Anglo-American immigrants, but the more determined ones continued to make their way westward across the Sabine, and settlers from other nations added to their numbers.

THE EMPIRE OF MEXICO

Three hundred years of autocratic rule and 11 years of the war for independence combined to create a situation wherein the leaders of Mexico would have a difficult time establishing a stable government. The army, conservative and fearful of popular rule, had made independence possible, but remained suspicious of most civilian leaders. There were conflicts between monarchists and those who wanted to create a republic. There were anticlerics who wanted to break, or at least to severely curtail the power of the church, but others who continued to advocate clerical privilege. There were liberals and there were conservatives. And there were federalists who wished to distribute political power among a pattern of states and centralists who believed that stability and order demanded that power be exercised by a narrow elite. Most of the population of Mexico knew little about these issues, but those in power or who had hopes of power were strongly committed to positions on one side or another. Although the resulting conflict affected all of Mexico, Texans, dependent on government immigration policies, were particularly sensitive to it.

Conservatism and monarchy won an early triumph. Appointed a temporary presiding officer, Agustín Iturbide manipulated people and events to create a monarchy patterned after that of the European nobility. With much pomp and ceremony he was named Agustín I, blessed by the Bishop of Guadalajara, and crowned emperor for life. In reality his power was based primarily on military support, and when that faded after only a few months, the empire would end.

THE OLD THREE HUNDRED

Anglo-American immigration into Texas in significant numbers began during the empire of Iturbide. During the winter of 1821–1822 the first settlers of Austin's colony arrived in Texas. The first was Andrew Robinson, who arrived at the Brazos in November 1821 and would eventually establish and operate a ferry at the settlement of Washington on the Brazos. Two or three days later the three Kuykendall brothers and their families joined the Robinsons, and soon there were others who located settlements near the site of present Independence. Robert and Joseph Kuykendall and Daniel Gilliland located on the Colorado near present-day Columbus at Christmas time, and not long afterwards, Jared E. Groce, planter, lumberman, and capitalist of Alabama, arrived with his fifty wagons and ninety slaves and settled on the east side of the Brazos near the site of Hempstead. By March 1822 fifty people on the Brazos and one hundred on the Colorado were building houses and planting corn.

Meanwhile, with the aid of his New Orleans partner, Joseph H. Hawkins, Austin had purchased the schooner *Lively* and had sent it to Texas with eighteen settlers and essential supplies. He returned to Texas in the fall of 1821 by way of Natchitoches and Nacogdoches in route to the mouth of the Colorado River where he expected to meet the *Lively*. He suffered a heavy financial loss and was greatly disturbed when the *Lively* failed to show. Later he learned that it had landed by mistake at the mouth of the Brazos and that most of the immigrants on board, discouraged that Austin did not meet them, had returned with the ship to New Orleans.

Despairing of making contact with the *Lively,* Austin went to San Antonio in March 1822 to report to the governor on his progress. There he learned of the success of the Mexico revolution. Governor Martínez, near the end of his power, informed him that the officials at Monterrey had refused to recognize his authority to introduce settlers under his father's grant, that the new government of the Mexican nation was considering a colonization policy for Texas and the Californias, and that he should go to Mexico City to look after his interests. Austin, without delay, set out for Mexico City.

At the capital, where he arrived on April 29, 1822, Austin found a complex and unstable political situation. He patiently and methodically set to work to secure the approval of the contract, but many weeks would pass before he would succeed. While Iturbide maneuvered first to acquire and then to consolidate power, Austin used his time to good advantage. He mastered the rudiments of the Spanish language, learned much about some of the cardinal principles of Mexican politics, and talked with most of Iturbide's handpicked junta about the possibility of a general colonization law that would open the way for the approval of his grant. He met a number of other Anglo-Americans who were in Mexico City for the same or similar purpose. Finally, his efforts were rewarded with the passage of the Imperial Colonization Law on January 4, 1823.

Iturbide's power had begun to wane, however, and Austin dared not leave the capital lest a new government undo all that had been accomplished. On March 19 Iturbide abdicated, but the new leaders acted favorably on Austin's petition. The Congress, which Iturbide had abolished, was restored and approved a contract for Austin issued in accordance with the terms of the Imperial Colonization Law. A new executive committee approved it on April 14, 1823. The boundaries of the colony were not immediately defined, but in 1824 they were tentatively located for judicial purposes as extending from the seashore to the San Antonio-Nacogdoches Road and from the Lavaca River to the San Jacinto River. At the same time that Congress awarded Austin a contract, it also voided the Imperial Colonization Law, thereby making Austin the only person to receive a grant under its terms. Under the terms of the contract Austin was responsible for the government of the colony, and four days after its approval he left Mexico City for Monterrey to consult with the commandant general of the Eastern Interior Provinces regarding the details of this responsibility.

It was not until early August 1823 that Austin, accompanied by Baron de Bastrop, the commissioner empowered to grant land titles, arrived in the colony. Conditions were critical. A drought in 1822, hostile Indians in the area, and Austin's long absence had caused a number of people to return to the United States. The crisis ended, however, when Austin assured the colonists that his contract had been validated and Bastrop began issuing land titles.

The seat of government was established on the Brazos River at the Atascosito crossing and was christened by the governor as San Felipe de Austin. By the close of the summer of 1824 when he was called away, Bastrop had issued 272 titles. Eventually the total number of families would number 297 (including several single men who formed partnerships as "families" to secure a larger grant of land). The "Old Three Hundred," as these settlers came to be known, selected the rich plantation lands along the Brazos, Colorado, and Bernard rivers, from the vicinity of present-day Navasota, Brenham, and La Grange to the coast.

The terms of the Imperial Colonization Law were indeed generous. Each family was to receive one *labor* (177 acres) if engaged in farming, and a *sitio* (a square league or about 4,428 acres) for stock raising. Of course, most of the colonists preferred to be classed as stock raisers, and only about 20 titles called for less than a *sitio*. Special grants were made to a few men as compensation for substantial improvements such as mills. Jared E. Groce, the owner of many slaves, received ten *sitios*. Austin, as *empresario*, received about twenty-two *sitios*. The law required that the land be occupied and improved within two years after the receipt of the deed, that colonists profess the Catholic religion, that for six years they be exempt from the payment of tithes and duties on imports, and that children of slaves born in the empire be freed at the age of fourteen.

THE REPUBLIC OF MEXICO

When the empire of Iturbide collapsed, there was general agreement that the new government to be created would be in the form of a republic. But there was not agreement as to the organization of the new republic. Some, primarily wealthy landowners (*hacendados*), army officers, and clergy, advocated a centralist form, while others, primarily *criollos* and *mestizos* of a liberal belief, favored a federalist form. Centralists argued that Mexico did not have the strength or experience necessary if power were to be divided between a central government and a number of states. Federalists insisted that centralism would lead to dictatorship and that only a division of power among a collection of communities and states and the national government could protect democracy.

The federalists in some respects won the argument with the writing of the Constitution of 1824. Mexico was divided into nineteen states and four territories. The authority of the central government was divided among three branches, the judicial, the executive, and the legislative, and in many other respects, the Constitution of 1824 resembled the Constitution of the United States. Indeed, the Constitution of 1824 promised democracy, but it also contained provisions that threatened tyranny. Particularly dangerous if abused, and it would be, was a clause giving the president extraordinary powers in the event of an emergency, authority that amounted to the power of a dictator. Liberals were also concerned about provisions in the Constitution which gave special privileges to clergymen and to military officials. A clause of the Constitution established the Roman Catholic Church as the official religion of the nation. With the election of the moderate and honest Guadalupe Victoria to be the first president, the new republic was off to a promising beginning, but before his term ended, there would be armed insurrection and turmoil.

Texans participated in the organization of the new republic and in the formation of the state governments. Erasmo Seguín was a member of the Constituent Congress that wrote the Constitution of 1824. By a federal act of May 7, 1824, the two old Spanish provinces of Coahuila and Texas were united as one state until the population of Texas should become large enough for the maintenance of a separate government. When the legislature for the state of Coahuila and Texas was organized in Saltillo on August 15, 1824, Baron de Bastrop represented Texas. Under the constitution for the state of Coahuila and Texas, Texas was allotted one of the 12 deputies that made up the legislature. This number eventually was increased to three. In 1825 Texas was made a department within the state of Coahuila and Texas, to be presided over by a political chief who was appointed by and responsible to the governor. This officer, a kind of subgovernor, was to reside in Texas, watch over public tranquility, inflict punishments, command the local militia, see that the laws were enforced, and make reports to the governor. Later, Texas was divided into three departments, with headquarters and political chiefs in San Antonio, Nacogdoches, and San Felipe.

A NEW COLONIZATION PROGRAM

One of the laws of Congress passed early in the life of the new Republic was the National Colonization Law of August 18, 1824. By this act the government relegated to the states the administration of the public lands and authorized them to prescribe regulations for settlements, with only a few reservations. The most important of these were:

(1) that all state laws had to conform to the constitution then being framed;
(2) that, except by special approval of the federal executive, foreigners were not to settle within ten leagues of the coast or twenty leagues of the international boundary;
(3) that no person should hold more than eleven *sitios*;
(4) that no alien should receive a land grant;
(5) that "until after the year 1840, the general congress shall not prohibit the entrance of any foreigner, as a colonist, unless imperious circumstances should require it, with respect to individuals of a particular nation."

On March 24, 1825, the legislature of Coahuila and Texas passed the Coahuila-Texas Colonization Law. The law required immigrants to give satisfactory evidence of their Christian (Catholic) faith, morality, and good habits. Immigrants might receive titles to land individually or through an *empresario*. Each head of a family could receive, after the payment of a fee of $30.00, a *sitio* of land for $62.50 ($87.50 for irrigable land), payable in three annual installments beginning at the end of the fourth year, and he had to cultivate or occupy the land within six years. For his services an *empresario* was entitled to five *sitios* (approximately 22,140 acres) of grazing land and five *labors* (approximately 885 acres) of farming land for each one hundred families, up to eight hundred. *Empresario* contracts were to run six years and to be absolutely void if at least one hundred families had not been settled before the expiration of that time. Native-born Mexicans might purchase, for small fees, as much as eleven *sitios*. There were to be no essential changes in the law for a period of six years. Colonists were exempted from general taxation for ten years. The national tariff law of 1823, exempting colonists from payment of custom duties for a period of seven years, was applicable.

THE EXPANSION OF COLONIZATION

The adoption of the new colonization laws found many eager would-be *empresarios* prepared to apply for contracts. Moreover, Stephen Austin, who had largely fulfilled the terms of his "Old Three Hundred" contract, sought permission to bring in additional settlers. By almost any measure, Austin was the most successful of the *empresarios*. In 1825 he obtained a contract to settle an additional 500 families within the boundaries of his original grant. The "Little Colony," which he contracted in 1827 to settle 100 families, was on the east side of the Colorado River, immediately above his original grant. Bastrop became its principal town. The reserve zones of the national law did not apply to Austin's original settlers, and some had located within ten leagues of the coast. Austin subsequently petitioned for,

CHIEF COLONIZATION GRANTS

Miles

0   85

Austin's contract called for 300 families under the Imperial Colonization Law of April 14,1823. Three contracts under the state law, 1825, 1827, 1828, called for 900 additional families in the area of his first colony; and, with Sam M. Williams, he had a contract to settle 800 families north and west of his first colony. He located over 1500 families.

On April 15, 1825, Green DeWitt got a contract for 400 families to be located on the Guadalupe, San Marcos, and Lavaca rivers. He issued 166 titles. The Nashville Company, known by the name of its agent, Sterling C. Robertson, as Robertson's colony, secured a contract for 800 families in 1825. After the revolution it was allowed premium lands for 379 families.

David G. Burnet, Lorenzo de Zavala, and Joseph Vehlein secured colonization rights in 1826 for territory on the eastern border of Texas between the twenty-ninth and thirty-third parallels. These rights were transferred to the Galveston Bay & Texas Land Company, which issued, between Septermber 1834 and December 1835, titles to over 916 leagues.

On March 9, 1826, Arthur G. Wavell, an Englishman, secured a contract for 500 families to be located in northeast Texas. His associate, Benjamin R. Milam, located a number of families, but the United States contended that they were settled east of the boundary set by the treaty of 1819 with Spain, and the contractors never secured premium lands. Power and Hewetson granted almost 200 titles, McMullen and McGloin, 84. The Mexican *empresario,* De León, settled between 100 and 200 families.

and in 1828 received; permission to settle 300 additional families in this coastal reserve between the Lavaca and San Jacinto rivers. Thus, by 1828 Austin had signed four contracts to settle in Texas a total of 1,200 families. By then the population of his colonies was increasing rapidly. It was 2,021 in March 1828 and 4,248 in June 1830. Tabulations after his death indicate that the great *empresario* authorized a total of 1,540 grants to colonists.

In 1825 Green DeWitt, another Missourian and next to Austin the most successful of the *empresarios*, received a state contract to settle 400 families between the Lavaca River and a line two leagues west of and parallel to the Guadalupe River and between the San Antonio-Nacogdoches Road and the ten-league reserve adjacent to the coast. Gonzales, the main town, was located that same year, but after an attack by Comanche Indians in July 1826 the people moved to the lower Lavaca. Here their troubles did not end, for they were within the restricted zone and became involved in a quarrel with *Empresario* Martín de León. The following year they were ordered to leave. By the summer of 1828 they were back in Gonzales, where they were again harassed by the Comanches. At the expiration of DeWitt's contract on April 15, 1831, 166 titles had been issued to settlers, but the greater part of the land within his grant was still vacant.

Martín de León, whose contract was unique, had fair success as a colonizer. A native of and a rancher in the Spanish province of Nuevo Santander, De León, soon after visiting Texas in 1805, moved his operation to the vicinity of San Patricio. During the Mexican Revolution he cooperated with the republicans in San Antonio. In April 1824, after hearing of the Imperial Colonization Law, he obtained from the provincial delegation in San Antonio de Béxar a grant to settle an unspecified number of families (he stated that he had already recruited forty-one families) near the coast and between the Lavaca and Guadalupe rivers. The settlers were predominantly Mexican. Twelve families arrived that fall, and in October De León laid out the town of Guadalupe Victoria on the banks of the Guadalupe. The precise limits of the colony were not fixed, and this gave rise to a quarrel between De León and DeWitt, in part because some of DeWitt's settlers located within De León's grant and in part because some of De León's settlers located within DeWitt's grant. Nevertheless, in 1829 De León received permission to settle another 150 families in the area. When it was learned, however, that he intended to displace some of De Witt's colonists to enlarge his own colony, the second grant was cancelled. But Victoria continued to prosper and to grow, and by 1833 its population was over 200.

In addition to the concessions to Austin, DeWitt, and De León, the state of Coahuila and Texas made about twenty-two other contracts with *empresarios* under the law of March 24, 1825, calling in all for about eight thousand families. The great majority of these *empresarios* located no families or only a negligible number. Others were more successful, but their colonists, almost without exception, came during a later period of colonization.

THE FREDONIAN REBELLION

One of the early *empresario* grants led to a clash between Mexican officials and certain Anglo-American colonists in Texas. The dispute had its beginning in 1825 when Haden Edwards secured an *empresario* grant that permitted him to locate colonists in a large area of eastern Texas. Within the boundaries of the grant were (1) the descendants of settlers who had returned to Nacogdoches in 1779 with Gil Ybarbo, (2) a settlement of about thirty families on the San Jacinto that had been incorporated into Austin's first colony, (3) some who held or were entitled to grants, (4) a number of Anglo-American squatters, and (5) remnants of several Indian tribes. Edwards made an arbitrary ruling that all claimants must prove title or else pay him for their lands. This ruling alarmed and antagonized the settlers; many of them had been careless in seeing that their land titles were in order. The involvement of Edwards' son-in-law in an election dispute added to the conflict. Austin's advice to Edwards not to antagonize Mexican officials went unheeded, and Edwards' enemies took their cause to the higher officials. In response, on June 3, 1826, the president of Mexico ordered Edwards' expulsion, but it was not until October 20 that state officials transmitted the order cancelling Haden Edwards' contract and instructing him to leave the country.

On December 16, Benjamin Edwards, the brother of Haden, with between fifteen and thirty armed men rode into Nacogdoches and proclaimed the Republic of Fredonia. He was unable to generate any support from Anglo-Americans, however, and had no success in forming an alliance with the Cherokee Indians in the area. On learning of the approach of troops from San Antonio and militia from Austin's colony, the insurgents abandoned Nacogdoches and on January 31, 1827, crossed the Sabine into the United States. The rebellion was over. The Fredonian uprising, however, had a greater impact on Mexican sentiment than it deserved. Mexican officials concluded that the Fredonians had intended to add Texas to the United States and became increasingly suspicious of all Anglo-Americans.

THE LAW OF APRIL 6, 1830

Suspicions aroused by the Fredonian Rebellion and the very success of the colonization movement in Texas all but destroyed it. In 1828 General Manuel Mier y Terán, soldier, scholar, and statesman, was sent to survey the eastern boundary as defined in the Adams-Onís Treaty and to investigate the need for new military posts in Texas. His report, however, went far beyond these matters, for it presented a detailed description of conditions in Texas and recommendations for policy changes. What Terán saw in Texas alarmed him. He reported that Mexican influence diminished rapidly as he proceeded eastward. In Nacogdoches, the Mexican population was poor and a small number in comparison to the Anglo-Americans. The Anglo-Americans included slaveholders, honest laborers, criminals, and vagabonds and were taking the country. At Nacogdoches they maintained an English school; they were progressive but shrewd and unruly and demanded the privileges and rights guaranteed by the constitution. Mexico, Terán concluded, must act "now" or Texas "is lost forever." Terán proposed that the Mexican government should

(1) colonize Mexicans in Texas;
(2) colonize Swiss and Germans;
(3) encourage coastal trade between Texas and the rest of the republic; and
(4) place more troops in Texas, among them convict-soldiers who would become permanent settlers after their terms had expired.

Although Terán began his reports as early as June and July, 1828, political upheaval in Mexico City delayed action on his recommendations for almost two years. In September 1828, Gomez Pedraza, a conservative, was elected president, but a military uprising instigated by his opponent, Vicente Guerrero, prevented him from taking office. In the spring of 1829, Guerrero, a federalist, assumed the presidency and the authority to exercise dictatorial powers that Congress had given him. Although Guerrero's rise to power was hardly in the tradition of true democracy, he remained faithful to some liberal ideals, and on September 15, 1829, issued a proclamation ending slavery throughout the nation. The decree aroused little attention elsewhere in Mexico, but Texans protested vigorously and soon were excluded from its restrictions. Shortly thereafter, a centralist coup d'état deposed Guerrero and replaced him with Anastacio Bustamante. Bustamante posed as a defender of constitutional rule, but in reality his administration marked the return of conservatives to power and a move in the direction of military dictatorship.

Bustamante's government took steps to check Anglo-American influence in Texas. Lucas Alamán, minister of foreign relations, urged Congress to adopt Terán's proposals, and to go beyond them with the drastic Article 11, a part of which reads: "Citizens of foreign countries lying adjacent to the Mexican territory are prohibited from settling as colonists in the states or territories of the Republic adjoining such countries." In other words, no more immigrants from the United States could settle in Texas. The article, furthermore, declared suspended "all contracts not already completed and not in harmony with the law," and provided for the establishment of military posts by convict soldiers, for the settlement around these posts by the families of the soldiers and other Mexican colonists, and for the strict prohibition of any further introduction of slaves.

To the Mexican government, the law was a mandatory act to meet an emergency; to the colonists, however, the law seemed nothing less than a calamity. Austin succeeded in fending off the blow slightly, insofar as his colony and that of DeWitt were concerned, by an ingenious interpretation that permitted them to complete their quota of families without respect to the law. Thus, the population of Austin's settlements increased from 4,248 in June 1830 to 5,665 a year later. DeWitt's contract and one of Austin's soon expired by limitation, however; Austin's other contracts were soon filled, and in November of 1831, Austin had to admit that immigration of Anglo-Americans was totally prohibited. He and his secretary, Samuel M. Williams, then secured a grant to settle European and Mexican families, but in this they did not succeed. Meanwhile, Austin and others continued to maintain considerable pressure in an effort to secure the repeal of the Law of April 6, 1830. Eventually these efforts were rewarded when the prohibition against Anglo-American immigration was revoked, effective May 1, 1834.

THE CONTINUATION OF COLONIZATION

Although the Law of April 6, 1830, slowed the pace of immigration into Texas, it did not stop it. Immigrants who were not citizens of the United States were not barred by the law. In some instances, the law was simply disregarded or ignored; in other instances, efforts were made to evade its restrictions. On October 16, 1830, Lorenzo de Zavala, Joseph Vehlein, and David G. Burnet pooled their extensive grants in eastern Texas and assigned them to the Galveston Bay and Texas Land Company, a New York City-based organization. Although the company did not own any land and did not have the right to sell any, it advertised in a fashion similar to that used later by western railroad companies. It sublet huge blocks to subordinate contractors, and it sold scrip, amounting to nearly 7.5 million acres at prices of one to ten cents an acre, to prospective settlers and speculators, many of whom evidently believed that they were buying land. The scrip merely reserved the designated number of acres for the holder, who, before obtaining title to any land, still had to comply with all requirements of the Mexican colonization laws, which, at that time, did not permit persons from the United States to settle in Texas. Nevertheless, the company soon sent two groups of emigrants to Texas, but Mexican officials would not allow them to locate lands or to settle. Eventually, however, Mexican authorities finally recognized the company and allowed settlers to claim some lands. Between September 1834 and December 1835 a stream of immigrants claimed a total of 936 titles to land in the area north of Galveston Bay.

Another large contract involved the lands generally known as the Robertson Colony. This contract, first issued in 1825 through Robert Leftwich to the Texas Association of Nashville, controlled a huge block of land north and northwest of Austin's original grant and contained the right to settle eight hundred families. For various reasons, the company agent, Sterling C. Robertson, made very little progress toward settlement of the colony before the passage of the Law of April 6, 1830. In 1831 the territory was granted to Austin and his partner, Samuel M. Williams, who proposed to settle on it eight hundred Mexican and European families. Robertson vigorously resisted the cancellation of his contract and the transferral of it to Austin and Williams, and a legal and political conflict began that would not be resolved for decades. The governor, after examining Robertson's claim of having settled more than 100 families before the enactment of the Law of April 6, 1830, restored the colony to the Nashville Company (Robertson's group), but Austin and Williams regained the colony in May of the following year. By the time the revolution closed the land offices, more than 600 hundred families had located in the colony, and the towns of Nashville, Viesca, and Salado had been founded. In 1847, after Robertson's death, a Texas court ruled that his claim to the colony was valid and awarded his heirs premium land for 379 families.

Meanwhile, two Irish colonies, McMullen and McGloin and Power and Hewetson, were being settled in southern Texas. In August 1828 John McMullen and his son-in-law, James McGloin, both natives of Ireland but at the time merchants in Matamoros, Mexico, obtained a state contract to settle two hundred Irish families in a portion of the territory east of the Nueces River and immediately above the coastal reserve. The first group to arrive, 58 in late 1829, remained for a time at the Refugio mission but in October 1831 established Hibernia or San Patricio, the colony's principal town. The contract was voided by the Law of April 6, 1830, but in 1834 it was extended, and by the outbreak of the Texas Revolution, 84 land titles had been issued.

Although beset by misfortune, the other Irish colony was more successful. James Power, a native of Ireland, was engaged in business and mining in Mexico. James Hewetson, also a native of Ireland, settled in Saltillo and Monclova where he engaged in manufacturing, mining, and the mercantile business. In 1828, by special permission of both the national and the Coahuila-Texas governments, Power and Hewetson obtained a contract to settle two hundred families from Mexico and Ireland. Their lands included the ten-league coastal reserve between the Nueces and Guadalupe rivers, and (after a compromise with *Empresario* De León) a part of the former lands of the abandoned mission of Nuestra Señora del

Refugio. Power went to Ireland and in 1834 sailed for Texas with 350 immigrants, but enroute they contracted cholera. Seventy were left in New Orleans, some were buried at sea, and the survivors were forced to abandon their ship, losing all their supplies on the coast. In Texas others were stricken with the deadly plague. Refugio, on the site of the old mission by that name, became their central town, and by the time of the Texas Revolution, almost 200 land titles had been granted, many apparently to Anglo-Americans.

A third attempt to establish a colony of Europeans was a complete failure. John Charles Beales, a surgeon from England, and James Grant, a physician from Scotland, contracted in 1832 to settle eight hundred European families in the region between the Rio Grande and the Nueces River. The first colonists, including English, Germans, Mexicans, and Anglo-Americans, located the settlement of Dolores on Las Moras Creek near present-day Brackettville in March 1834. Another group of colonists came later, but crop failure, Indian hostility, and military campaigns of the Texas Revolution resulted in the abandonment of the colony.

COLONIZATION IN RETROSPECT

The Texas colonization era under Mexican rule ended legally with the closing of the land offices in November 1835. Later, an act of the Congress of the republic in June 1837 declared that all *empresario* contracts had ceased on the day of the declaration of independence, March 2, 1836. Much had happened in the preceding fifteen years. On the eve of revolution, the colonists were distributed from the Sabine to the Nueces, but an overwhelming majority were located east of the Guadalupe and south of the old road from San Antonio to Nacogdoches. Altogether, these settlers held about 3,500 land titles issued through the different *empresarios*, and there were a few who received grants directly from the Mexican government. Estimates of the total population vary. In 1834, the Mexican soldier and statesman, Juan N. Almonte, after a visit to Texas, placed the population at 24,700 including slaves, or at a little more than 20,000 for the Anglo-Americans and their slaves. Other estimates suggest that the population may have been more than 30,000.

Who were these people? Whence had they come and what were the forces that brought them? The evidence available indicates that they were, in the main, farmers and people of some means, although many had left behind them debts they could not pay. That they were honest and law abiding is evidenced by the small amount of crime committed in the colonies. The *empresarios* were required to see that lawless persons did not remain. Among the settlers, literacy was high for that time. Of more than 266 of Austin's "Old Three Hundred," only four could not write.

A surprising number of these immigrants were women. Most, of course, came in the company of their husbands and family, but some braved the dangers and hardships of the frontier alone. Austin's colonies in 1830 reported 20 widows, most of whom were responsible for the welfare of a number of children. No doubt, some of these women were widowed after their arrival in Texas, but sometimes widows and their children made their way into Texas to claim land and begin a new life.

Most Anglo-American settlers emigrated from southern states. Data kept by Austin for his colony show that the majority of his people came from Louisiana, Alabama, Arkansas, Tennessee, or Missouri, in the order named. A total of 699 registered from the trans-Appalachian states, as compared with a total of 107 from the Atlantic Seaboard. However, most adults living west of the mountains at that time had been born in the seaboard states.

A significant portion of the population were slaves (approximately ten percent), despite repeated efforts in Mexican law and policy to discourage the institution. The Imperial Colonization Law recognized slavery but forbade the slave trade and declared that slaves born in the empire should be free at the age of fourteen. The Coahuila-Texas constitution of 1827 recognized existing slavery and permitted the introduction of slaves for six months after its promulgation, but no person born thereafter could be a slave. Meanwhile, the Mexican government began to undo with its left hand what it had done with its right. It legalized the domestic slave trade by providing that a slave might "change" his or her master "if the new master would indemnify the old," and a state law of 1828 for all practical purposes legalized slave importation by recognizing labor "contracts made in foreign countries. . . ." Afterwards, upon entering Texas, most blacks were nominally servants under contract, but actually they were still slaves. After Guerrero's decree of 1829 abolishing slavery was nullified with respect to Texas, the Law of April 6, 1830 recognized existing slavery but prohibited the further introduction of slaves. An act of the state legislature in 1832 strengthened antislavery laws and limited to ten years the contracts with slaves and day laborers. Thus, by 1832, the introduction of slaves was positively barred, and peonage contracts were limited to ten years.

Although many slaves had been brought to Texas, their ratio to the free population declined in the later colonial years. In 1825 Austin's colony had 443 slaves and 1,347 free people. In 1834 Juan Almonte estimated the number of slaves in the Department of the Brazos (composed of Austin's colonies) as 1,000, out of a total population of about 10,000. No doubt, the uncertain status of the institution frequently caused anxiety and may have frightened away many prospective immigrants who were slaveholders.

These figures tell something about slavery in colonial Texas, but the description of her trip to Texas by a slave girl is perhaps more meaningful. As she later told the story, on her journey from New Orleans to Texas with a group of slaves, their owners "chained us together and marched us up near La Grange. . . . That was an awful time. . . . If one drank out of the stream, we all drank; when one got tired or sick, the rest had to drag and carry him." All slaves were blacks and most were located in the fertile valleys of the Trinity, Brazos, and Colorado rivers. Not all blacks were slaves, however. About 150 free blacks lived in Texas during the time of Mexican rule and under Mexican law enjoyed full legal and political rights.

Slaves came to Texas because they had little choice in the matter, but the forces that brought free people were varied and complex. They came to be with relatives and friends, to escape conflicts with the law or with some individuals, to drown their sorrows, to regain their health, or to satisfy their curiosity. They came because of the panic of 1819 and financial adversity. But above all, they came in search of land. Some wanted virgin soil to replace their eroded and worn-out farms, but the overwhelming majority came to get free or cheap land. Although there was an abundance of land in the public domain of the United States, a person could buy no less than 80 acres and was required to pay $1.25 per acre in cash. By comparison, in Texas the head of a family could obtain 4,428 acres of land in Austin's colony for only little more than the cost of 80 acres in the United States. The actual price of land in Texas varied from time to time and from place to place, but it would be fair to state that during the period of Mexican rule a *sitio* (4,428 acres) of land cost less than $150.00 (including fees), payable over a period of time.

GOVERNMENT IN MEXICAN TEXAS

The majority of the settlers in Mexican Texas were Anglo-Americans living in a country whose government, religion, customs, and attitudes differed greatly from those they had known before. Generally, they ran their own affairs with a minimum of interference from Mexican officials, and they modified Mexican institutions in many instances to conform to Anglo-American patterns. Thus government, especially government on the local level, became a peculiar mixture of Mexican institutions and Anglo-American practices.

The most important unit of local government was the municipality, which included one or more towns and adjacent territory. It might cover thousands of square miles. The *ayuntamiento*, or governing body of the municipality, had broad duties that suggest the combined functions of a modern city commission and a county commissioner's court. At its head was an *alcalde*, the chief executive officer, whose duties were similar to those of sheriff, judge, and mayor of a city. The *regidores*, like members of our own city commissions, had certain legislative powers as well as some administrative responsibilities. Each municipality had a *sindico* (an attorney and the state's representative), an *alguacil* (sheriff) appointed by the *alcalde*, and a secretary appointed by the *ayuntamiento*. Each subdivision of a municipality, known as a district or a precinct, had its *comisario*, a sort of *sub-alcalde*, generally thought of by Anglo-American colonists as a justice of the peace, and also a *sindico* for the district.

Local self-government began early when by order of the governor in November 1822, Austin's first colonists elected *alcaldes*. By 1828 the municipalities of Texas included Bexar, La Bahía or Goliad, Nacogdoches, and San Felipe, and by 1834 there was a total of thirteen. Municipal taxes were light and payable largely in kind, and for a number of years, colonists were exempted from state taxes, church tithes, and national customs duties.

The Anglo-Americans, with a love for legislating, passed many local laws but had little interest in enforcing them, primarily because the court system was most unsatisfactory. In all important cases the *alcalde* or *comisario* was required to send a record of the testimony to a higher official at Saltillo and wait for the return of his decision. Fortunately, there was very little crime in the colonies and most offenders seem to have been dealt with outside of the courts. Austin drove a number of undesirables from his colony; the *ayuntamientos* compelled some to leave; and occasionally the people persuaded certain ill-disposed persons that their health and happiness would be greater elsewhere. An act passed in 1834 provided for jury trials in both civil and criminal cases and for an appellate circuit court for Texas, but it never went into effect.

Into this pattern of government the *empresario* system was fitted. The duties of the *empresario* were numerous and trying. He had to deal not only with state and national governments that were sometimes unsympathetic but also with the Anglo-American pioneers who, though worthy and well-meaning, were prejudiced, stubborn, jealous of their freedom, and disposed to find fault with those in authority. Austin's burden was much greater than that of his fellow proprietors, for his colony was seven years old before regular constitutional government was established. He was responsible for selecting his colonists and their good character, and, although Bastrop, his land commissioner, actually issued the titles, for surveying the land and all business connected with obtaining and recording titles. At first, Austin was responsible for the government of the colony. Indeed, he was a lawgiver, for he wrote civil and criminal codes for the *alcaldes*, based on the Mexican laws but adapted to conditions in the colonies. He was commander in chief of the militia and responsible for defense and the maintenance of satisfactory relations with the Indians.

In addition, he had many informal obligations even more burdensome than those required by law. Prospective colonists expected entertainment at his home, and frequently he was called on to settle petty disputes. Many persons regarded him as a collecting agent; others expected him to

Stephen F. Austin, the Father of Texas, earned his title by his outstanding efforts as the greatest colonizer of the state. (University of Texas Library) Also shown, a replica of his home near Sealy. (Texas Highway Department)

make for them purchases and loans. With the establishment of constitutional government in 1828, the greater part of Austin's governmental responsibilities ceased, but there was no letup of the informal ones.

For Austin and the other early colonists, hostile Indians added to other perils. The Karankawas on the coast were always a threat. In the interior the Tonkawas were generally at peace, but along the Brazos River above the San Antonio Road, the Wacos and Tawakonis were periodically dangerous and always troublesome. In eastern Texas a few hundred Cherokees and Choctaws from east of the Mississippi and bands of indigenous sedentary Indians kept the colonists on the alert.

For defense against the Indians the colonists had to depend mainly on their own resources. The militia in Austin's first colony was first organized in 1822. From time to time new districts were created, until by the close of 1824, six companies had been organized. By 1830 the Indian menace of Austin's colony was a thing of the past. Bexar, Gonzales, and Goliad, however, did not fare as well as those to the east. In 1830 DeWitt wrote the governor that unless troops were sent to his colony, his settlements would be broken up. The settlers managed to hold out, although the fifteen troops and a six-pounder cannon sent the following year offered little help.

COLONIAL INSTITUTIONS

In Texas, as in other societies, religion was an important institution. By constitution and law, Roman Catholicism was the religion of Mexico, to the exclusion of any other. The Catholic faith was supposed to accompany Mexican citizenship, and heretics were subject to banishment and other punishment. Although he always stated these facts plainly to prospective colonists, Austin emphasized them less and less as his colony grew, and other proprietors apparently took much the same attitude. In fact, very few of the colonists were Catholics by faith, and not many were so even by name.

The people had more cause to complain of spiritual neglect and an indifferent public than of intolerance or persecution. Repeatedly, Austin petitioned the authorities to send a priest to his colony to christen children, legalize marriage contracts, and perform various other services that were expected in a Catholic country. Finally, in 1831 Father Michael Muldoon, an Irish priest, arrived. He was good-natured, loyal, and kind, but he did not always live up to the Anglo-American standards of piety for the ministry. Most of the settlers apparently had little interest in formal religion anyway. One observer, while praising them for the small amount of crime in Texas, added that, in respect to the gospel, conditions were "bad—bad! superlatively bad."

In spite of official opposition and the indifference of the colonists, the Protestants made considerable progress in colonial Texas. As early as 1820, Joseph E. Bays, a Baptist minister was preaching in Texas. William Stevenson, a Methodist who had preached at Pecan Point in the winter of 1818-1819, continued to preach despite warnings from Austin and others. Other missionaries came, and after the colonists drove out the Mexican garrisons in 1832, Protestant camp meetings became common. A few churches also were organized during this period. Presbyterians taught Sunday school in San Felipe, and John and Maria Kenney and Lydia Ann McHenry worked together to establish a Methodist church at New Caney in 1834. That same year, a state law, in violation of the constitution, afforded a measure of religious tolerance. It stated that no person should be molested on account of his or her religious or political opinions, provided he or she did not disturb the public order.

There was no system of public education in colonial Texas. A public school was established in San Antonio as early as 1746, and shortly after 1813 the Spaniards erected a building there to provide for seventy pupils. But when Colonel Almonte visited in 1834, he reported that the school in San Antonio had been discontinued, although there were schools in Nacogdoches, San Augustine, and Jonesborough. A small private school in Austin's colony was taught as early as 1833; Frances Trask opened a boarding school for girls on the site of Independence in 1834 and there were schools held for brief periods elsewhere. Education on a limited scale seems to have available for both boys and girls, although there were apparently more men teachers than women.

Although most Texans were farmers, trade and commerce was an important part of the colonial economy. San Felipe became a thriving town, but in 1830 it still had only one house not built of logs. By 1832 Brazoria was perhaps the leading shipping town, but soon it shared some of its trade with the new town of Matagorda, at the mouth of the Colorado. Galveston remained uninhabited during most of the colonial era. Nacogdoches, which had only thirty-six inhabitants in 1821, grew into a business center with stores well supplied with dry goods, notions, and foodstuffs. San Antonio, the most populous town throughout the entire period, did not grow as rapidly as some of the newer towns.

Two conditions hampered business severely; the lack of money or banking facilities and the absence of roads and other means of transportation. The account of George B. Erath, an Austrian-American, is typical. Erath traded clothes that he had brought from Germany for cattle and hogs, and he traded a horse for corn. His partner gave an ox for a sow valued at five dollars, a feather bed for three cows and calves, a gun for a mare, and another gun for a cow, calf, and yearling. The *ayuntamiento* permitted a person to pay two-thirds of a bill for local taxes in kind (settlers were generally exempt from state and national taxes), and gave an official stamp to bovine currency by stating that a cow and calf should be valued at ten dollars. Those unfortunate enough to have to borrow money found interest rates to be exorbitant.

Save for small quantities of salt, some horses, and occasional illicit purchases of tobacco, there seems to have been virtually no trade between Texas and the rest of Mexico. In 1821 on his first visit to Texas, Stephen F. Austin found a good trade already established between Natchitoches, Louisiana, and Goliad. Although Natchitoches continued to be a favorite trading post of Texans and most shipments into the colonies by land originated there, trade by sea with New Orleans increased throughout the period.

Inadequate ports constituted a great handicap to shipping. Galveston was not convenient to the principal settlements. Even small vessels had to be partly unloaded to cross a great sandbar in order to reach Brazoria and other points on the lower Brazos. Likewise, Matagorda Bay had its perils, and small schooners had difficulty in reaching either the mouth of the Lavaca or the town of Matagorda at the mouth of the Colorado.

Austin in 1829 stated that the chief possibilities for export from Texas were "cotton, beef, tallow, pork, lard, mules, etc." Almonte, whose data are the best extant but probably are little more than a collection of guesses, valued Texas exports for 1833 at $500,000. Of this, cotton made up $353,000; "furs" (probably hides of all kinds), $140,000; and cattle, $25,000. His estimate on cotton certainly is too high, but it may have been offset by miscellaneous items that he ignored and his failure to credit the Department of the Brazos with the shipment of cattle. The importation of goods for that year, Almonte said, amounted to $630,000.

It is well to remember that most families brought with them quantities of goods that are not considered in these estimates. These imports supplied approximately twenty thousand colonists with necessities and a few, a very few, with luxuries. The exports proved to be the great potential wealth of the land. Of great political importance, also, is the fact that these imported goods—almost wholly from the United States—kept alive the interest of the Anglo-Texans in the land of their birth.

SELECTED BIBLIOGRAPHY

Material on Texas colonization is comparatively abundant. Of the older accounts, the best is H. Yoakum, *History of Texas*. His text, along with some supplementary material, is reproduced in Dudley G. Wooten, *A Comprehensive History of Texas* (2 vols., Dallas, 1897). Other general accounts are William Kennedy, *Texas* (2nd ed., London, 1841; Fort Worth, 1925); H. H. Bancroft, *History of the North Mexican States and Texas*; John Henry Brown, *A History of Texas, 1685–1892* (2 vols., St. Louis, 1892–1893); Louis J. Wortham, *A History of Texas* (5 vols., Fort Worth, 1924); Clarence R. Wharton, *Texas under Many Flags* (5 vols., Chicago and New York, 1930); and H. S. Thrall, *Pictorial History of Texas*.

Of great value in understanding Spanish policy in this era is the work of David J. Weber, *The Mexican Frontier, 1821–1846: The American Southwest Under Mexico* (Albuquerque, 1982).

The most useful reference is the *Handbook of Texas*. Rich collections of source materials are E. C. Barker (ed.), *The Austin Papers* (3 vols.); vols. I and II were published as *The Annual Report of the American Historical Association*, 1919, II, and 1922, II (Washington, D.C., 1924 and 1928); vol. III (Austin, 1926); Malcolm D. McLean (ed.), *Papers Concerning Robertson's Colony in Texas* (13 vols., Fort Worth and Arlington, Tex., 1974–1986); E. Wallace and D. M. Vigness (eds.), *Documents of Texas History*; Juan N. Almonte, "Statistical Report on Texas," 1835 (trans. C. E. Castañeda), *Southwestern Historical Quarterly*, XXVIII, 177–222.

The most scholarly studies are E. C. Barker, *The Life of Stephen F. Austin* (Nashville and Dallas, 1925); E. C. Barker, *Mexico and Texas, 1821–1835* (Dallas, 1928); and D. M. Vigness, *The Revolutionary Decades*. For the decree of April 6, 1830, see Ohland Morton, *Terán and Texas* (Austin, 1948).

Articles on colonies and colonists are to be found in the *Quarterly of the Texas State Historical Association* (I–XV) and the *Southwestern Historical Quarterly* (XVI–). Among them are: "Journal of Stephen F. Austin on His First Trip to Texas, 1821," VII, 286–307; W. S. Lewis, "Adventures of the *Lively* Immigrants," III, 1–32; L. G. Bugbee, "What Became of the *Lively?*" III, 141–48; L. G. Bugbee, "The Old Three Hundred," I, 108–17; E. C. Barker, "Notes on the Colonization of Texas," XXVII, 108–119; Mary Virginia Henderson, "Minor Empresario Contracts for the Colonization of Texas, 1825–1834," XXXI, 295–324; XXXII, 1–28; Robert W. Amsler, "General Arthur G. Wavell: A Soldier of Fortune in Texas," LXIX, 1–21, 186–209; Andrew Forest Muir, "Humphrey Jackson, Alcalde of San Jacinto," LXVIII, 362–366; Charles A. Bacarisse, "The Union of Coahuila and Texas," LXI, 341–349; Henry W. Barton, "The Anglo-American Colonists under Mexican Militia Laws," LXV, 61–71; Roger N. Conger, "The Tomás de la Vega Eleven-League Grant on the Brazos," LXI, 371–382; Joseph W. McKnight, "Stephen Austin's Legalistic Concerns," LXXXIX, 239–68; John Wheat and Jesus De La Teja, "Bexar: Profile of a Tejano Community, 1820–1832," LXXXIX; Robert S. Martin, "Maps of an Empresario: Austin's Contribution to the Cartography of Texas," LXXXV, 381–400; and W. H. Timmons, "The El Paso Area in the Mexican Period, 1821–1848," LXXXIX, 1–28.

R. W. Strickland, "Miller County, Arkansas Territory, the Frontier That Men Forget," *Chronicles of Oklahoma*, XVIII, 12–34, 154–70; XIX, 37–54, is the best account available of the settlement of extreme northeast Texas. Excellent studies of the colonies in southern Texas include W. H. Oberste's comprehensive *Texas Irish Empresarios and Their Colonies* (Austin, 1953); Leroy P. Graf, "Colonizing Projects in Texas South of the Nueces, 1820–1845," *Southwestern Historical Quarterly*, L, 431–48; Carl Coke Rister, *Comanche Bondage* (Glendale, Calif., 1955), about Beale's colony; A. B. J. Hammett, *The Empresario Don Martín de León: The Richest Man in Texas* (Victoria, Tex., 1971).

On colonial institutions, there are in the *Southwestern Historical Quarterly:* E. C. Barker, "The Government of Austin's Colony, 1821–1831," XXI, 223–52; supplemented by the "Minutes of the *Ayuntamiento of San Felipe de Austin*, 1828–1832," XXI, 299–326, 395–423; XXII, 78–95, 180–96, 272–78, 353–59; XXIII, 69–77, 141–51, 214–23, 302–307; XXIV, 81–83, 154–66. Useful also is E. C. Barker, "The Influence of Slavery in the Colonization of Texas," *Southwestern Historical Quarterly*,

XXVIII, 1–33. J. H. Kuykendall, a colonist, gathered a series of interesting and valuable reminiscences of colonists; they are printed in the *Quarterly of the Texas State Historical Association* VI, 236–53, 311–30, and VII, 29–64; others, somewhat similar, are found in V, 12–18; XIII, 44–80; XIV, 24–73. Worthy of special mention are *Travel and Adventures in Texas in the 1820's: Being the Reminiscences of Mary Crownover Rabb* (Waco, Tex., 1962); and "Reminiscences of Mrs. Dilue Harris," *Quarterly of the Texas State Historical Association*, IV, 85–127, 155–89, 387, written in part from a journal kept by Mrs. Harris's father, Dr. Pleasant W. Rose. Noah Smithwick, *The Evolution of a State* (Austin, 1900), written when the author was ninety years old, is rich in detail and very accurate. The best descriptive book of Texas written by a contemporary is Mary Austin Holley, *Texas* (Baltimore, 1833; Lexington, Ky., 1836). Mrs. Holley's text is included in M. A. Hatcher, *Letters of an Early American Traveller: Mary Austin Holley. Her Life and Works, 1784–1846* (Dallas, 1933). For another biography of this remarkable observer of the Texas scene, see Rebecca Smith Lee, *Mary Austin Holley: A Biography* (Austin, 1962). Religion in early Texas is best discussed in W. S. Red, *The Texas Colonists and Religion, 1821–1836* (Austin, 1924).

CHAPTER FIVE
THE PRELUDE
TO REVOLUTION
1826–1835

"This is the most liberal and munificent Govt. on earth to emigra[n]ts—after being here one year you will oppose a change even to Uncle Sam—." Thus wrote Stephen F. Austin in 1829 to his sister and brother-in-law. As late as 1832, to his partner and boon companion, Samuel M. Williams, he wrote: "My standing motto—'Fidelity to Mexico'—ought to be in every man's mouth and repeated. . . ." Yet three years later, Austin, the most loyal of all of Mexico's adopted sons, was leading troops in rebellion against that government. This reversal in sentiment did not take place in one week, or even in one year, but was the natural reaction to ethnic and cultural differences and to a long chain of developments that all together led from fidelity through alienation to rebellion.

EARLY TROUBLES

Although conditions for immigration to Texas remained favorable for several more years, problems appeared early in the period of Mexican rule. The Fredonian Rebellion had little support among Anglo-American colonists, but Mexican officials were nonetheless more suspicious after the affair. Many Mexican officials linked inseparably the Fredonian affair with the effort of the United States to acquire, by purchase or otherwise, all or part of Texas. In 1825, President John Quincy Adams, who had often asserted that the Louisiana Purchase extended to the Rio Grande, inaugurated efforts to obtain for the United States a "more suitable" boundary. Joel R. Poinsett, envoy to Mexico, was authorized to offer one million dollars for the removal of the line to the Rio Grande. President Andrew Jackson raised Adams's offer to five million and continued the effort through Poinsett and Poinsett's successor, Anthony Butler. The only result was to aggravate Mexican suspicions concerning both the United States and the Anglo-American colonists.

In turn, a feeling of anxiety and suspicion was aroused among the colonists of Texas when President Guerrero proclaimed the emancipation of slavery on September 15, 1829. Upon receipt of the decree, the Mexican political chief at San Antonio petitioned and obtained an exemption for Texas, but the colonists, nevertheless, were left with a feeling that the future of slavery was uncertain.

THE DISTURBANCES OF 1831 AND 1832

Greater than the Fredonian rebellion, efforts of the United States to purchase Texas, or the emancipation proclamation in promoting ill feeling was the Law of April 6, 1830. It will be recalled that this law prohibited further colonization by people from the United States and provided for the collection of customs duties and for the garrisoning of troops in Texas. Lucas Alamán, who drafted the bill, feared that when the Americans became a preponderant majority they first would petition for changes or reforms, then create disturbances, and finally, by violence or diplomacy, take possession of the province. The law caused exactly what Alamán had hoped to prevent by it; out of it grew the chain of events that led from disturbances and petitions to rebellion and independence.

Although the provision of the Law of April 6, 1830, halting Anglo-American immigration caused much anxiety and unrest, the disturbances on the coast in 1831 and 1832 were actually the product of several complex issues. Colonists, who had been exempt from most Mexican custom duties, became subject to such taxes at about the same time as the Law of April 6, 1830 went into effect. State and national authorities who depended heavily on such taxes enforced their collection diligently. On the other hand, Anglo-Americans traditionally had little use for customs taxes and fees or the people who collected them.

Another problem centered around what was truly a conflict between state and national authority over the question of land titles and the right to issue such. But the most serious issue concerned the matter of military authority over civilians, a question on which Anglo-American and Mexican traditions had little in common. Adding to the explosiveness of the impending crisis was a more than adequate number of leaders on both sides who were prepared to respond to provocation with intemperance.

Ironically, two of the ranking Mexican officials involved were not Mexican-born, though both were Mexican citizens and loyal to their adopted country. The customs collector for ports east of the Colorado River, where the conflicts would occur, was George Fisher, a Serbian adventurer, once a citizen of the United States, and a citizen of Mexico since 1825. The military commander assigned to Anahuac on Trinity Bay was Colonel Juan Davis Bradburn. Bradburn, a native of Virginia, had been a liberal revolutionary in the war for Mexican independence but had turned more conservative and in the direction of centralism in later years. Although he knew many of the Anglo-Americans in Texas, he stood firmly in favor of the autocratic rule of the centralist, Anastacio Bustamante. Inasmuch as the state administration of Coahuila-Texas was identified with the federalist faction, a clash between state and national authority was not unlikely.

Trouble began early in 1831 when Bradburn arrested Francisco Madero, general land commissioner of Texas. Madero proposed to issue land titles to settlers, including those who had come independently of any *empresario*, and perhaps some colonists of the Galveston Bay and Texas Land Company. When Bradburn ordered Madero to desist, on the ground that the issuance of the titles would be in violation of the Law of April 6, 1830, Madero, arguing that he had been commissioned by both the state and federal governments to issue the titles, ignored the order. Never one to back down, Bradburn had Madero and his surveyor arrested. Eventually Madero was released, whereupon he issued a number of land titles, formed the new town of Liberty about thirty miles above Anahuac on the Trinity, and organized the town's *ayuntamiento*. Trouble, however, was only beginning. Bradburn's commanding officer, General Mier y Terán, moved the *ayuntamiento* of Liberty to Anahuac, thus arousing great resentment, and more disputes soon developed.

Meanwhile, George Fisher, the customs collector whose loyalties were somewhat more ambiguous than those of Bradburn, added another dimension to the conflict. Fisher, acting on the orders of General Mier y Terán, decreed that all ships leaving Texas from the mouth of the Brazos and certain other ports must clear through Anahuac. Since doing this sometimes required an overland journey of about two hundred miles or by sea a longer and more dangerous voyage, the order provoked strong protests. When in December 1831 some shippers ignored the order and ran by the guard on the lower Brazos, shots were exchanged, and one soldier was seriously wounded. A deputy collector was then placed at Brazoria, but the colonists remained unhappy.

Although the conflict over Fisher's orders and the question of customs regulations diminished somewhat in the spring of 1832, a long-standing dispute between Bradburn and Anahuac settlers over the question of slavery reached a crisis stage. When Bradburn gave asylum to two runaway slaves from Louisiana in the summer of 1831, settlers had charged him with using slave labor without compensation. Mier y Terán had determined that the controversy could only be decided by higher authorities in Mexico City and the United States, but it was not a time for careful investigation and thoughtful judgment. Bradburn's relations with area colonists grew steadily worse. When certain of them formed a vigilante group to intimidate Mexican soldiers who allegedly had committed crimes and gone unpunished, Bradburn arrested some of the leaders and held them for a time. Matters reached a climax when the owner of the slaves employed William Barret Travis, a young attorney newly arrived in Texas from Alabama, who demanded without success the return of the slaves. Attorneys Travis and Patrick Jack began to deliberately annoy Bradburn with mysterious messages about an armed force that was coming from Louisiana to recover the runaway slaves.

Bradburn arrested Travis, Jack, and eventually a number of others on charges of sedition, claiming the authority to do so on the grounds that the offense occurred on federal property subject to the jurisdiction of the military. Bradburn's explanation meant nothing to Anglo-Americans who had little experience with military rule over civilians, arrest without warrants, and trial without jury. To them, Bradburn's action was despotism, regardless of its legality under Mexican law.

The prolonged imprisonment of Travis and Jack brought the colonists to resistance. William H. Jack, brother of Patrick, having tried unsuccessfully to secure his brother's release, returned to San Felipe and called on his fellow colonists to join him in an attack on Bradburn. In early June men began to gather in Liberty, and soon John Austin (who may have been distantly related to Stephen F. Austin) from Brazoria arrived with 90 men. By June 10, Bradburn was besieged by 160 angry Texans. After some skirmishing and some negotiations, the colonists withdrew a few miles to Turtle Bayou and sent John Austin to Brazoria for a cannon with which to assault the fort.

Meanwhile, far to the south in central Mexico, Antonio López de Santa Anna, claiming to support liberalism and the Constitution of 1824, was leading a rebellion against President Bustamante. While waiting for Austin to return, the Texans on Turtle Bayou, aware of the insurrection, prepared a formal statement of the causes of their own rebellion against Bradburn, a loyal supporter of Bustamante. Thus, on June 13, in "The Turtle Bayou Resolutions," they asserted their loyalty to the constitution and to Santa Anna and the liberals. The resolutions were to serve them well.

Relief for the situation at Anahuac came from Nacogdoches. As soon as he learned of the matter, Colonel José de las Piedras, commander of the garrison in Nacogdoches, rushed to the troubled scene with some of his troops. Though not particularly sympathetic to the colonists, he feared a spread of the rebellion, and agreed to release the prisoners to civil authorities for trial, to replace Bradburn, to restore the *ayuntamiento* of Liberty, and to allow the settlers to petition for redress of their grievances. Bradburn soon resigned, the Texans dispersed, and most of the garrison declared for Santa Anna and sailed away.

The situation on the Brazos remained serious for a time. John Austin had returned to Brazoria, secured the cannon (also reinforcements of more than a hundred men), and started by boat for Anahuac. At Velasco at the mouth of the Brazos, Colonel Domingo de Ugartechea, commander of the fort there, tried to prevent his passage. In the ensuing battle ten Texans and five Mexicans were killed, but Ugartechea was forced to surrender the garrison and withdraw his troops to Matamoros.

The resistance spread rapidly, and the colonists were determined to drive every soldier from the settlements. In August settlers defeated Piedras and his troops in a bloody battle and forced them to abandon Texas. The post of Tenoxtitlan on the upper Brazos was also abandoned, leaving the eastern part of Texas completely free of Mexican troops, and on August 30 Ramón Músquiz, the political chief in San Antonio, tardily declared for Santa Anna.

Had it not been for the developments in Santa Anna's struggle for power that favored the Texans, these events would surely have brought severe retribution upon Texas. In early July in Matamoros, Colonel José Antonio Mexía was in command of the Santanista forces. Nearby was Colonel José Mariano Guerra in command of the Bustamante troops. When Mexía overhauled a ship carrying mail from Brazoria and learned of the disturbances in Texas, he proposed to Guerra that they declare a truce and pool their resources to save Texas for the Mexican confederation. Guerra agreed, and soon Mexía with about 400 soldiers was off for Texas. Fortunately for the colonists, he took along Stephen F. Austin, who had come by way of Matamoros on his return from the legislature in Saltillo. It is safe to conjecture that Austin spent many hours amplifying and emphasizing to Mexía what he had already written to the Mexican authorities in Texas. His argument was stated thus: "There is no insurrection of the Colonists against the Constitution and Government, neither do they entertain ideas endangering even remotely the integrity of the territory."

The colonists, who knew of the coming of the expedition, prepared for Mexía a most lavish reception. He was saluted at the mouth of the Brazos by a salvo of cannon, entertained in the home of John Austin, and assured by reception committees of the loyalty of the Texans. At Brazoria the general was given a dinner and ball; the crowd was "large, cheerful, and convivial," and drank many toasts to Santa Anna. Under such conditions there was nothing for Mexía to do but to return to Mexico. He could not make war on the people who were on his side of the contest and who were treating him like a king.

THE CONVENTIONS OF 1832 AND 1833

Although the insurrection of 1832 was eminently successful, the colonists were not willing to leave matters where they stood. They wanted reforms and some concessions from the Mexican government. Accordingly, on August 22, just a month after Mexía had sailed away, the *ayuntamiento* of San Felipe issued a call to the districts to send delegates to a convention to meet in San Felipe on October 1, 1832. Sixteen districts responded (not counting Goliad, whose delegation arrived too late for the proceedings) and sent 58 delegates. Stephen F. Austin was elected president. Several resolutions addressed to the federal and state governments were prepared and adopted; still others related to local affairs. In lengthy and urgent memorials, the convention petitioned the national government for the repeal of that part of the Law of April 6, 1830, prohibiting Anglo-American immigration, and for the admission of Texas as a state to the Mexican confederation. It also asked Congress to exempt the colonists from tariff duties on necessities for three years and to allow customs officers to be appointed by the *alcaldes* of the respective jurisdictions. It asked the state to issue land titles to settlers east of Austin's colony, to create additional *ayuntamientos* there, and to set aside land for school purposes. Locally, it provided for a committee, together with the *ayuntamiento* of Nacogdoches, to investigate the affairs of the Cherokees and other Indians in East Texas, and it approved a uniform plan for organizing the militia and suggested plans for defense against the Indians. The convention adjourned on October 6 and forwarded its petitions through the political chief in San Antonio.

The petitions were never officially presented to the Mexican officials. The governor instructed the political chief at San Antonio to remind the Texans that the convention was a violation of the constitution and the laws, and Austin believed that there was little chance of success without the support of Mexican officials in San Antonio. Moreover, Santa Anna, who had not yet assumed the presidency, frowned on the idea of unauthorized conventions.

Not intimidated, a Central Committee of Safety and Correspondence, organized in the Convention of 1832, issued a call for a second convention to meet in San Felipe on April 1. A larger number of discontented delegates was in attendance this time, evidenced by the selection of William H. Wharton, rather than Austin, as president of the convention. Only about one-third of the delegates had attended the first convention. The petitions were much the same as those prepared the previous year. The convention asked for the repeal of the anti-immigration law, adopted an exceptionally well-written memorial by David G. Burnet setting forth reasons why Texas should be a state separate from Coahuila, accepted a constitution drafted by a committee chaired by Sam Houston, who had come to Texas that year, and designated three delegates to carry the petition to Mexico City. Only one delegate, Stephen F. Austin, was able to make the journey.

AUSTIN'S JOURNEY TO MEXICO CITY

When Austin arrived in Mexico City on July 18, 1833, he found a confused, even chaotic, situation reminiscent of his visit eleven years earlier. Santa Anna, elected president in January 1833, had refused to take office and had designated Valentín Gómez Farías, the vice-president and a dedicated liberal, to act as president. Although Santa Anna had overthrown Bustamante and won the presidency on a platform calling for liberal reforms and the restoration of the Constitution of 1824, he was doubtful that the wealthy and powerful interests of Mexico would accept such a program.

Antonio López de Santa Anna. The reactionary dictatorship of this opportunistic general and politician provoked the Texas Revolution. His harsh treatment of the men of the Alamo and Goliad made his name hated in Texas. Defeated and captured by Sam Houston at San Jacinto, he nevertheless became president of Mexico twice again before his death in 1876. (Southwest Collection, Texas Tech University)

Thus, he decided to "recuperate his health at his estate" until Gómez Farías presented his reform program to Congress. If the proposed reforms proved popular, he could assume the presidency and claim the credit; if, on the contrary, they aroused strong opposition, he could assume the presidency and oppose them.

Austin conferred with Farías who, although suspicious of the intentions of the Texans, received him cordially. The ministry submitted to the house of deputies the petition asking for a state government. Then a cholera scourge caused all business in the capital to be suspended, and Austin, impatient at the delay, on October 1 told Farías bluntly that unless the government remedied "the evils which threaten that country [Texas] with ruin," the people of Texas would organize a state government without its approval. Farías took this statement as a threat; the two men quarreled, and Austin, while still in a huff, wrote the *ayuntamiento* in San Antonio, urging that body to take the initiative in a plan to organize a state government.

A little later the proprietor was reconciled to Farías, and on November 5 he had a conference with Santa Anna (now exercising the executive power) and his cabinet. He found Santa Anna sympathetic and friendly. The president would not approve separation from Coahuila, but he did assent to almost every other request. He agreed to the repeal of the prohibition on immigration; he would refer to the treasury office a request for better mail service and a modification of the tariff; and he promised to urge the state government to give Texas trial by jury.

Before he left the city on December 10, Austin actually witnessed the repeal of the law against immigration, which was to take effect six months later. On his way back to Texas he stopped on January 3, 1834, to see the commandant in Saltillo on a matter of business. There he was placed under arrest and then taken back to Mexico City. The cause was his letter of the preceding October to the *ayuntamiento* in San Antonio, written, as Austin said, "in a moment of irritation and impatience," suggesting that it take the initiative in the organization of a state government without waiting for the approval of the central government. The letter had found its way to the governor and finally back to Gómez Farías just after Austin had left Mexico City. It was the liberal federalist Farías who, acting on the recommendation of General Vicente Filisola, military commandant of the area which included Texas, ordered the arrest.

For some time Austin was kept *incommunicado* in the Prison of the Inquisition. He could get no trial, for no Mexican court would accept jurisdiction of his case. Two attorneys, Peter W. Grayson and Spencer H. Jack, were sent to his aid by the people of Texas, bearing many petitions for his release, but all they accomplished was to get him out of prison on bail on Christmas Day 1834. He was finally released through an amnesty law and left Mexico City in July 1835.

SANTA ANNA AND THE POLITICS OF MEXICO (1833–1835)

Born in Jalapa in 1794, Santa Anna became a cadet at the age of 15 and thereafter was a professional soldier. In the various contests over the supreme authority in Mexico before 1834, he consistently supported the constitution and popular government. Although frequently active in politics, he retired and remained out of the public eye for nearly two years when Bustamante came into power. But in January 1832 he prompted the garrison in Vera Cruz to start a revolt, soon became its leader, and finally forced Bustamante to capitulate. He was easily elected president for the term beginning April 1, 1833, but allowed Vice-President Farías to assume the powers of the office. There then followed a period most strange between April 1, 1833, and January 28, 1835, when these two men exchanged the presidency no less than seven times. Meanwhile, for a time the reforms to which both men were pledged were being carried out by Farías and a liberal congress. Church appointments were placed in the hands of the state; the clergy was forbidden to discuss political matters; forced collections of tithes were suspended; and plans were inaugurated to reduce the size and the influence of the army.

Obviously, the army, powerful clerics, wealthy *hacendados,* and other affluent interests did not permit these reforms to proceed without challenge. Quietly and surreptitiously they organized and found a leader in Santa Anna himself! The wily politician had permitted Farías to launch a trial balloon of liberalism, while he, in the eyes of the public, was a mere spectator. Seeing that the opposition was very powerful, he realized that, as its leader, he could make himself dictator. In April 1834 he returned to the capital and took over the supreme power from Farías. This time he repudiated liberalism, dissolved Congress, forced Farías into exile, dismissed all except one of Farías's cabinet, disbanded legislatures and *ayuntamientos,* declared void the laws against the privileges of the clergy, and in various other ways imitated Napoleon Bonaparte, whom he greatly admired.

A new framework of government based on authoritarian principles soon followed. The new and subservient congress supplemented and legalized what Santa Anna had done, and in October 1835 the Constitution of 1824 and federalism were replaced by the *Siete Leyes,* which provided for a centralized system of government. The new document converted the states into departments, ruled by a governor appointed by the president, and substituted an appointive council for each state legislature. The dictatorship of Santa Anna had been legalized—but in an illegal manner.

Federalists did not abandon their cause without resistance. In most states there were protests of one sort or another, and in some states, such as Zacatecas, California, Coahuila, and Texas, and eventually Yucatan there was open rebellion. Armed resistance in Zacatecas began over a decree that ordered the reduction of the number of militia to one soldier for every five hundred inhabitants and the surrender of excess arms. When the people of Zacatecas rose in rebellion, Santa Anna defeated 5,000 troops led by their governor, inflicted bloody reprisals, and permitted his soldiers to plunder the state capital.

AFFAIRS IN TEXAS AND COAHUILA (1833–1835)

When Colonel Juan Almonte, an investigator for Gómez Farías, visited Texas in the spring of 1834, he was pleased with what he found. The settlements were prospering, the colonists seemed content, and there was no evidence of unrest or disloyalty. There was good reason for these condi-

Map of Texas, 1835. (Southwest Collection, Texas Tech University)

tions. During 1833 and 1834 the state government was generous with Texas. The legislature repealed the law that had prohibited any but native-born Mexicans from engaging in retail merchandising. It divided Texas into three political departments, the capitals to be Bexar, San Felipe, and Nacogdoches. Texas was allowed three deputies out of the twelve that comprised the state legislature. The English language was recognized for official purposes, and religious toleration was granted. The court system, which had been the most constant object of complaint, was completely revised. A superior court was created for Texas and trial by jury was established. The new court proved defective, but it, like the other concessions, was an honest attempt to satisfy the colonists.

But even as these reforms were being adopted, trouble in state government was developing. The two principal sources of strife and agitation were the quarrel between Saltillo and Monclova over the location of the state capital and the squandering of the public lands of Texas through sales to speculators. Generally, except for the disturbances of 1832 when they declared for Santa Anna as a kind of afterthought, Texans had managed to avoid entanglements in Mexican politics. Beginning with 1834, however, this was no longer possible.

The quarrel over the state capital began in March 1833, when the legislature removed the seat of government from Saltillo in the southeastern corner of Coahuila to Monclova in the north. Later, a rival government was set up in Saltillo, but Santa Anna gave his nod to Monclova and the government remained there. In April 1835 the legislature criticized Santa Anna severely, and the dictator sent his brother-in-law, Martín Perfecto de Cós, to break up the state government. On the approach of the national forces Governor Agustín Viesca sought to transfer the government to Bexar but was arrested on his way by Cós's troops. Other state officers and a swarm of land speculators fled to Bexar. By August both the Saltillo and the Monclova factions accepted as governor Rafael Eca y Músquíz, who then moved the capital back to Saltillo.

Adding to the confusion and the chaos were the activities of land speculators whose greed seemed to know no limits. Speculation in Texas lands had been common ever since the passage of the state colonization law of 1825, which permitted a native Mexican to purchase as much as 11 *sitios* for a nominal sum. This speculation was eclipsed, however, by reckless and unwise, and perhaps dishonest, legislation in 1834 and 1835. Representatives John Durst, from Nacogdoches, and J. M. Carbajal, from San Antonio, were implicated in and probably profited from this business. An act of April 19, 1834, authorized the governor to dispose of as much as four hundred *sitios* of land for the purpose of maintaining the militia in defense against the Indians. Another law, that of March 14, 1835, empowered the governor to dispose of four hundred more sitios. The final act in this extravagant series was passed on April 7, 1835, authorizing the governor "to take of himself whatever measure he may think proper for securing the public tranquility. . . ." Apparently the governor thought the situation called for the frittering away of additional large blocks of land.

The operations of the partnership firm of Williams, Peebles, and Johnson are typical. In consideration for four hundred *sitios* of land they agreed to place and maintain in the field one thousand men for the defense of the state. Without supplying a single soldier, they issued to about 40 persons certificates calling for the entire 400 *sitios*. Later, the Texas convention of 1836 nullified some of these grants but validated others apparently no more meritorious.

Such activities alarmed and disgusted many Texans, and also confused the issue when Santa Anna discarded the constitution, established himself as a dictator, and began to act against those who challenged his power. The land speculators brought alarming reports to the effect that Santa Anna was planning to invade Texas, but most people believed that their talk was merely a cloud to screen their own bad conduct. One citizen responded to such warnings with "wolf, wolf. . . . What a pity. . . ." As late as midsummer of 1835, most Texans would have endorsed the statement of George Smythe, land commissioner in Nacogdoches, who wrote in May of that year that he was confident that there would be no war and added: "Come what may I am convinced that Texas must prosper. We pay no taxes, work no public roads, get our land at cost, and perform no public duties of any kind."

Yet there was a small but active war party, people who favored war and independence, and on the other extreme, a peace party, likewise small, active, and persistent. The great majority of Texans stood between these two extreme groups, indifferent at first but finding their complacent attitude more and more untenable. Developments during the summer of 1835 favored the war party.

SANTA ANNA FORCES THE ISSUE

The first violent action that led directly to revolution was associated with Anahuac, the seat of the disturbances of 1832. Indeed, the story of Texas during the summer of 1835 reads strangely like that of 1832. In January 1835 Santa Anna sent a small detachment of soldiers to Anahuac to enforce the collection of customs there and in Galveston. The collector at Velasco on the Brazos collected tonnage duties only, while the officers at Galveston and Anahuac, backed by the garrison, insisted on the payment of all duties. Andrew Briscoe, a merchant at Anahuac, and others became disgruntled and declared that no more duties should be collected at that port until collections were enforced equally throughout Texas. As a result of a misunderstanding, a Texan was wounded at Anahuac, and Briscoe and another citizen were imprisoned.

Meanwhile, General Cós, now military commandant of the area which included Texas, had heard of the threatening attitude of the people at Anahuac and had determined to reinforce the garrison. He wrote Captain Antonio Tenorio, its commander, to be resolute and of good cheer, that reinforcements were coming. It happened that the courier bearing Cós's letters and other communications in a similar vein stopped at San Felipe on June 21. There was much excitement in the community. The people knew of the breaking up of the state government and of the arrests of Governor Viesca and the citizens at Anahuac. Already excited over these events, the San Felipe war party seized and opened the courier's dispatches. Although there was strong opposition, the clique that favored drastic action met, elected J. B. Miller, political chief of the Department of the Brazos, chairman, and passed resolutions authorizing William B. Travis to collect a force and drive away the garrison at Anahuac. With some 25 or 30 men armed with rifles and a small cannon mounted on a pair of sawmill truck wheels, Travis appeared before the post and demanded its surrender. Without the firing of a weapon on either side, Tenorio on the morning of June 30 surrendered with 44 men. The prisoners were soon paroled.

This act of Travis and his band was looked upon with pronounced disfavor by the great majority of the people, and it was formally condemned by meetings in no less than seven communities. At a meeting on June 28 the people of Columbia emphatically denounced Travis' march to Anahuac as an act calculated to involve the citizens of Texas in a conflict with the central government. They pledged their loyalty to Mexico, and through a committee they asked the political chief to send to Cós assurances of the people's loyalty. More general gatherings in San Felipe on July 14 and 15 adopted resolutions of similar tenor, and J. B. Miller, as if to atone for his alignment with the radicals a few weeks earlier, wrote an apologetic letter to Cós. Then a conference of committees from Columbia, Mina (Bastrop), and San Felipe, meeting in San Felipe from July 17 to 21, sent representatives with conciliatory letters to Cós in Matamoros. The peace party was asserting itself. The agitators were on the defensive.

Cós was not in a compromising humor. He called for the arrest of Lorenzo de Zavala, a distinguished political refugee and enemy of Santa Anna, who had lately arrived in Texas. Then, at the suggestion of a member of the peace party, Colonel Ugartechea, commander at Bexar, sent to Cós a list of offenders: F. W. Johnson and Samuel Williams, who had been prominent in land speculation; Robert M. Williamson, the Patrick Henry of the Texas Revolution, commonly called "Three Legged Willie"; and William B. Travis. Cós insisted that the colonial officials arrest these men and turn them over to the military for trial. He refused to meet with the peace commissioners (who had gone as far as San Antonio on their way to confer with him) until this was done. To the Anglo-Americans, who believed that a person should be tried only by a jury composed of his or her peers, it was unthinkable to turn their fellow citizens over to the mercies of a Mexican military tribunal. Cós, who managed to secure and read copies of the various inflammatory speeches and utterances of the Texans, particularly a Fourth of July address by "Three Legged Willie" Williamson, became adamant. Thus did the season for conciliation pass.

In the American Revolution it was the committees of correspondence that began in Massachusetts in 1772 that kept the people in touch with developments and finally made possible organized resistance. Similar organizations existed during the Texas Revolution, and without them the colonists could not have been aroused to the point of resistance or have been organized with any degree of effectiveness. Mina (Bastrop) on the frontier led the communities by appointing on May 8, 1835, its Committee of Safety and Correspondence. Organizations in Gonzales and Viesca were formed a few days later. Before the end of the summer apparently every precinct had such an organization. Holding over from the convention of 1833 was the central committee that served as a guide and a clearing body for the local committee.

These committees were responsible for a decision to bring together representatives of the municipalities for a consultation. Apprehensive about the recent developments, on July 4 the Committee of Safety at Mina issued an address to the *ayuntamientos* of the Department of the Brazos, urging a consultation of the representatives of the several communities. Within ten days the *ayuntamientos* of Columbia and a citizens' meeting in San Felipe likewise had called for a consultation. It was the people of Columbia who actually called the general meeting. At a gathering of the citizens on August 15 with William H. Wharton, the staunch champion of action, presiding, the Committee of Safety and Correspondence was instructed to issue a call for a consultation of all Texans. Three days later the committee framed an address in which it asked that each jurisdiction elect and send five delegates to a consultation to be held in Washington on October 15. The tenor of its message is revealed in the sentence: "The only instructions which we would recommend to be given to our representatives is to secure peace if it is to be obtained on constitutional terms, and to prepare for war—if war is inevitable."

Some three weeks later Stephen F. Austin, free at last and home again, gave the consultation his approval. He accepted the chairmanship of the Central Committee of Safety of San Felipe and by common consent became the leader of the Texan cause. The news came that Cós was on his way to Bexar with reinforcements. This destroyed the last hope of peace, and on September 19 the central committee reinforced the call for a consultation and added: "War is our only resource. There is no other remedy. We must defend our rights ourselves and our country by force of arms."

WHY REVOLUTION?

A study of the causes of the Texan Revolution reveals striking resemblances to the American Revolution. Both can be traced to the disposition of the superior government to assert its authority after the colonists had learned to expect laxity and neglect. Customs duties and customs collectors played important parts in both stories. The Texans resented Mexican troops quartered among them, just as their forebears hated the British redcoats. But though there are many similarities, there are also many differences, particularly in the nature of the underlying causes that influenced and sometimes determined the course of events. That such underlying causes existed is certain; their identification, evaluation, and measurement cannot always be done with certainty.

To many Mexican authorities, and perhaps to the Mexican people, the revolution in Texas was the final drama in a conspiracy of United States officials and Anglo-American immigrants to foment rebellion in preparation for attaching Texas to the United States. Not without logic, the theory has survived and found acceptance in the historical writings of both countries. After all, Sam Houston, a hero of the revolution, and Andrew Jackson, President of the United States, were friends of long standing. The interest of the United States in the acquisition of Texas was clearly demonstrated by two efforts to purchase it, and many of the participants in the Texan cause were, in truth, recent arrivals from the United States, some arriving after the fighting began. The problem with the theory is the term "conspiracy," which suggests planning, preparation, collusion, and secrecy. There is scant evidence of such. Nevertheless, many in the United States wanted Texas (although many did not); many Texans wanted to be a part of their former country and welcomed the opportunity presented by the outbreak of rebellion.

Of all of the underlying causes of the revolution, slavery is the most difficult to evaluate and measure. A contemporary observer and abolitionist, Benjamin Lundy, viewed the revolution as the work of pro-slavery interests who wanted not only to preserve slavery in Texas but also to add Texas to the strength of the slave-holding South. Lundy's sincere convictions rested upon a certain amount of logic. Mexican policy contained in constitutions and laws threatened slavery; many, perhaps most Texans, supported slavery and were determined to retain the institution. However, this conflict of interests was not new in 1835; it was a conflict that had long existed. To attribute the outbreak of revolution in 1835 to slavery would seem to require additional evidence showing that circumstances had changed. In this respect, Lundy offered little. Nevertheless, the importance of slavery as a cause has remained a credible theory. Indeed, a recent writer observed that "violations of the Mexican law in regard to slavery eventually led" to the revolution.

Notwithstanding the exclusiveness of that rather simplistic explanation, there is some evidence to suggest that the conflict over slavery was becoming more critical by 1835. Although the proportion of slaves to free people migrating to Texas declined for a time, in the last year or two before the outbreak of rebellion, the number of slaves brought into the colonies apparently increased. Moreover, in the tension-filled days of the summer of 1835, Stephen Austin wrote that "Texas must be a slave country. It is no longer a matter of doubt." Alarmed by the impending arrival of Mexican troops, "Three Legged Willie" Williamson warned that the troops would "compel you to liberate your slaves." And there were others who sounded the call in defense of slavery in these final days before war.

The question is not truly one of whether or not slavery was a cause. It no doubt influenced the course of events. Rather, the question is one of evaluation and comparison. Just how significant was it in comparison to other influences? The answer to that question is not clear, and perhaps can be answered only through intuition.

Cultural and ethnic differences are another cause frequently suggested. Differences in religion, language, and government between the Mexican nation and the Anglo-American population of Texas were pronounced. Anglo-Americans were violently averse to the subordination of the civil to the military power and to any connection whatsoever of church and state. They came to Texas with a long heritage of successful experience in self-government. The first dispute at Anahuac in 1832 was a complex affair involving many different issues, but at the heart of it was a cultural conflict. Bradburn was likely correct in claiming that he acted within the law (though perhaps not always with wisdom), but Anglo-American settlers, regardless of the provisions of law and constitution, could not accept the idea of military authority over civilians. It is possible to exaggerate the extent of cultural differences. Religious restrictions were apparently more of an inconvenience than anything else; there were instances of intermarriage between the two peoples, and there were friendships and partnerships involving peoples from both cultures. But when conflict did occur, it was generally in a area where it was not easily resolved and in matters that often provoked violence and confrontation.

A final explanation places the responsibility for revolution on the failure of Mexico to establish a stable and democratic government, a failure that led to unpredictability, tyranny, and dictatorship. These were, indeed, chaotic years in Mexico. At the heart of the confusion was Santa Anna, whose lust for power was exceeded only by his capriciousness. His turn toward centralism and despotism brought revolution in many parts of Mexico, and, unfortunately for Mexican interests, disillusioned Stephen Austin, whose loyalty to Mexico up to this point was apparently both real and meaningful. Without reason for a basic faith that democratic government and tranquil prosperity was possible in the foreseeable future, the decision for rebellion, revolution, and ultimately independence was not an unexpected development.

All of the influences on the coming of the revolution must be judged while keeping in mind a sometimes overlooked fact. The Texan revolution did not occur easily or without opposition from within the Texas community. From the time of the first disturbances at Anahuac until long after the outbreak of fighting, there were substantial numbers of prominent Texans who opposed the strong stand taken against Mexican authority, albeit sometimes at a price. For their opposition to resistance in 1832, well-known Texans such as Samuel May Williams and Thomas Jefferson Chambers were hanged in effigy, and more than a score of residents in the Anahuac area were treated to a coat of tar and feathers. When Travis led his troops to Anahuac in the second disturbance in 1835, criticism of his action was widespread and strong. Even after the fighting was well under way, there were those who still hoped for a peaceful settlement. Generally, these opponents of insurgency were people of property, long-time residents of Texas, and sometimes tied financially to Mexican authorities. People of substance, their views were significant, and suggest that revolution in the face of their opposition was the product of exceptionally strong forces.

SELECTED BIBLIOGRAPHY

The general accounts cited in Chapter 4 are helpful, but the *Handbook of Texas* is the best single reference. The best accounts for this particular period are D. M. Vigness, *The Revolutionary Decades*; William C. Binkley, *The Texas Revolution* (Baton Rouge, La., 1952); and Frank W. Johnson, *A History of Texas and Texans* (E. C. Barker and E. W. Winkler, eds., 5 vols., Chicago and New York, 1914). Of the more intensive studies, the best are: E. C. Barker, *The Life of Stephen F. Austin*; E. C. Barker, *Mexico and Texas, 1821–1835*; E. C. Barker, "The Organization of the Texas Revolution," *Publications of the Southern History Association*, V, 1–26; E. C. Barker, "Public Opinion in Texas Preceding the Revolution," *Annual Report of the American Historical Association for 1911*, I, 217–28; O. Morton, "Life of General Don Manuel de Mier y Terán, As It Affected Texas-Mexican Relations," *Southwestern Historical Quarterly*, XLVI, 22–47, 239–54; XLVII, 29–47, 120–42, 256–67; XLVIII, 51–66, 193–218; Merton L. Dillon, "Benjamin Lundy in Texas," *Southwestern Historical Quarterly*, LXIII, 46–62; Llerena Friend, *Sam Houston, the Great Designer* (Austin, 1954); *The Texans* (Time-Life Books, 1975); Ohland Morton, *Terán and Texas: A Chapter in Texas-Mexican Relations*; E. C. Barker, "The Battle of Velasco," *Quarterly of the Texas State Historical Association*, VII, 326–328; Margaret Swett Henson, "Tory Sentiment in Anglo-Texan Public Opinion, 1832–1836," *Southwestern Historical Quarterly*, XC, 1–34; C. Alan Hutchinson, "General Jose Antonio Mexia and His Texas Interests," *ibid.*, LXXXII, 117–42; and Paul D. Lack, "Slavery and the Texas Revolution," *ibid.*, 181–202.

The most comprehensive collection of source material on the Texas Revolution has been compiled and edited by John H. Jenkins, *The Papers of the Texas*

Revolution, 1835–1836 (10 vols., Austin, 1973). Other source materials may be found in Robert E. Davis (ed.), *Diary of William Barret Travis, August 30, 1833, June 26, 1834* (Waco, Tex., 1966); E. C. Barker, *The Austin Papers;* C. A. Gulich, Katherine Elliott, and Harriet Smither (eds.), *The Papers of Mirabeau Bonaparte Lamar* (6 vols., Austin, 1921–1927); E. C. Barker, contributor of a series of important documents in the *Publications of the Southern History Association,* V, 451–76; VI, 33–40; VII, 25–31, 85–95, 200–206, 238–46; VIII, 1–22, 104–18, 343–62; IX, 87–98, 160–73, 225–33; and E. Wallace and D. M. Vigness (eds.), *Documents of Texas History.* For proceedings of the Texas convention, see H. P. N. Gammel (comp.), *Laws of Texas* (10 vols., Austin, 1898), I.

Accounts of the disturbances of the early 1830s are E. C. Barker, "Difficulties of a Mexican Revenue Officer in Texas," *Quarterly of the Texas State Historical Association,* IV, 190–202; Edna Rowe, "The Disturbances at Anahuac in 1832," *ibid.,* VI, 265–99; N. D. Labadie, "Narrative of the Anahuac, or Opening Campaign of the Texas Revolution," *Texas Almanac,* 1859, 30–36; Duncan W. Robinson, *Judge Robert McAlpin Williamson: Texas' Three-Legged Willie* (Austin, 1948); Forrest E. Ward, "Pre-Revolutionary Activity in Brazoria County," *Southwestern Historical Quarterly,* LXIV, 212–31; Boyce House, "An Incident at Velasco, 1832," *ibid.,* 92–95. However, these traditional views of the events should be balanced with the careful study of Margaret Swett Henson, *Juan Davis Bradburn: A Reappraisal of the Mexican Commander of Anahuac* (College Station, 1982).

Concerning the "OPQ" letters, see "Some Texas Correspondence," *Mississippi Valley Historical Review,* XI, 99–127. Almonte's report on Texas has been translated and edited by C. E. Castañeda in the *Southwestern Historical Quarterly,* XXVIII, 177–222. For affairs at the state capital, see E. C. Barker, "Land Speculation as a Cause of the Texas Revolution," *Quarterly of the Texas State Historical Association,* X, 76–95.

Concerning Santa Anna and national affairs, see Frank C. Hanighen, *Santa Anna: The Napoleon of the West* (New York, 1934); Wilfred H. Callcott, *Santa Anna* (Norman, Okla., 1936); H. H. Bancroft, *The History of Mexico* (6 vols., San Francisco, 1883–1888).

The best study of this particular period by a Mexican historian is Vito Alessio Robles, *Coahuila y Texas desde la consumación de la independencia hasta el tratado de paz de Guadalupe Hidalgo* (2 vols., Mexico, D.F., 1945–1946).

CHAPTER SIX
THE TEXAN REVOLUTION 1835–1836

The Texas Revolution, which began in the fall of 1835, was similar in many respects to other revolutions of modern times. There was uncertainty in the beginning about the goal of the revolution—whether the fighting was for independence or a more democratic government in Mexico. Throughout the affair, there was the usual dual theme of revolutions centering around the necessity to create an effective government while at the same time maintaining a successful military effort. As so often is the case in revolutions, the struggle involved civilians and brought both hardship and sorrow to a sizable part of the population. There were abundant examples of heroics and bravery on both sides, and regrettably, examples of cruelty and inhumanity.

In some respects, the Texan Revolution was unusual. It was short, lasting only about seven months in terms of military action. The eight battles generally involved small numbers of soldiers and, with only one or two exceptions, were astonishingly brief. Altogether, however, about 10,000 soldiers participated in the campaigns, most of them either untrained or possessing only limited military experience. Perhaps most unusual of all was the dramatic finale, a decisive victory for the Texan cause after weeks of retreat and defeat.

THE REVOLUTION BEGINS

The Consultation of delegates from the *ayuntamientos* had been called to meet on October 15, 1835, but the events outran the plans. In September General Martín Cós, angry over the opening of his official dispatches and refusal of the Texans to carry out the arrests that he had ordered, began embarking troops for Texas. Colonel Domingo de Ugartechea, commander of troops in San Antonio, sent five cavalrymen to Gonzales, seventy miles to the east and the farthest west of the Anglo-American towns, to get the six-pounder that had been provided to *Empresario* DeWitt about four years before for defense against the Indians. *Alcalde* Andrew Ponton hid the cannon, told the military authorities he had no authority to give it up, and sent out dispatches calling for aid. Meanwhile, some Texans were on their way to intercept General Cós, who with four hundred troops had landed at Copano near Goliad. Upon receipt of the news from Ponton, they turned aside to Gonzales. Ugartechea had already sent Lieutenant Francisco Castañeda with about 100 troops to seize the cannon. On September 29 the Mexican force encamped on the west bank of the Guadalupe River, a short distance above the town. Then, on October 2, Colonel J. H. Moore and about 160 Texans, with the disputed cannon loaded with chains and scrap iron and strung with a banner inscribed "COME AND TAKE IT," crossed the river and attacked the Mexican troops, killing one and forcing the others to retreat to San Antonio.

Not all the volunteers who had set out to intercept General Cós turned aside to Gonzales. One company from Matagorda under Captain George M. Collinsworth and joined by Benjamin R. Milam, who was returning from imprisonment in Mexico, captured Goliad and its approximately twenty-five defenders. Cós, with most of his troops, had already left Goliad for San Antonio, but the capture of Goliad and its well-supplied stores was significant. Moreover, Cós could no longer expect to obtain additional supplies and reinforcements by sea.

Meanwhile, more volunteers continued to arrive at Gonzales and raised the cry "On to San Antonio," but there was no organization and they could not agree on a commander. Fortunately, at the urgent request of a group of officers, Austin arrived and was unanimously selected. On October 12, the ragtag army, numbering about three hundred, started for San Antonio, where Cós had already arrived. With Ugartechea's command, Cós had at hand twelve hundred or more troops, well entrenched in strong positions. On October 28 James Bowie and James W. Fannin, Jr., while making a reconnaissance with ninety men, skirmished near Mission Purisima Concepción de Acuna with a Mexican cavalry force of about four hundred. The Texans reported the loss of one man, while claiming an enemy loss of sixty. Thereafter, the Texans, without heavy artillery, settled in for a siege, hoping that a lack of supplies would eventually bring the Mexican army to surrender.

Time passed slowly for the Texans laying siege to San Antonio. On November 25, Stephen Austin, named to a commission to seek aid in the United States, left. The volunteers who remained voted down a proposal to storm Cós's defenses, but four hundred pledged to remain and elected Edward Burleson their commander. On the next day, a skirmish known as the Grass Fight, occurred on the outskirts of town. When Erastus (Deaf) Smith returned to camp with word that a pack train was approaching the town, the colonists concluded that it was reinforcements and pay for the Mexican army. They set out to capture the train, only to meet a furious resistance from Mexican artillery sent out by Cós in rescue. The pack train turned out to be a foraging party sent to get grass for Mexican horses.

In some respects, the Grass Fight was a victory, for the Texans reported only two wounded and claimed the Mexican forces lost about 50 men, but the resolve of poorly clothed and inadequately fed Texans began to weaken in the winter cold. A few days later, the staff of officers decided to abandon the siege and go into winter quarters at Goliad. Before the withdrawal began, however, Ben Milam, who had learned from a Mexican deserter and some San Antonians that Mexican morale and supplies were low, defied the order to withdraw by calling out, "Who will go with old Ben Milam into San Antonio?" Three hundred men volunteered. Before

Benjamin Rusk (Ben) Milam, a native of Kentucky, had been a member of Dr. James Long's filibuster expedition into Texas in 1820 and an officer in the Mexican Army. Because of his opposition to Santa Anna's centralist government in Coahuila, he was captured by troops of General Martín Perfecto de Cós but escaped and in the fall of 1835 joined the Texas army at Goliad. On December 5, when the Texans were ready to give up the siege of General Cós at San Antonio (Béxar), Milam called for and led one group of volunteers that attacked the Mexicans. Two days later he was killed by a rifle ball, but on December 10 Cós capitulated. (Southwest Collection, Texas Tech University)

daylight on the morning of December 5, the Texas volunteers led by Milam began the attack.

Met with a concentration of artillery and small arms fire for three days (Milam was killed on the third day), the Texans finally resorted to a house-to-house assault. On December 9, Cós hoisted a white flag. Under the capitulation agreement, Cós gave to the Texans all the public property, money, arms, and supplies in San Antonio; in return, Cós and his men were permitted to return south of the Rio Grande after agreeing never again to oppose the restoration of the Constitution of 1824. About four hundred citizen soldiers had taken a town held by more than three times their number. The victory was not without a price. Overconfidence, stimulated by the victory, would contribute to many of the problems of the Texan cause in the months to come.

THE CONSULTATION

While these developments were taking place in the military field, the political scene had shifted several times. Texas had formed two temporary governments, and had organized a third that promised to be ineffective. Ironically, the first, which lasted only three weeks, is known as the Permanent Council. Organized on October 11, it consisted of the Committee of Public Safety in San Felipe joined by representatives from other communities. During its brief existence, the Permanent Council served well. It sent supplies and volunteers to the army in the field, commissioned privateers, established a postal system, ordered the land offices closed and surveying discontinued, authorized an agent to go to the United States and borrow money, and appealed to the citizens of the United States for men, money, and supplies. It kept the people of Texas informed about the revolution and spurred them to greater exertion.

The Consultation, the second governmental body of the revolution, was delayed because of the outbreak of hostilities and moved from Washington to San Felipe. When a quorum was finally reached on November 3, 55 delegates from 12 municipalities of the departments of the Brazos and Nacogdoches assembled. Branch T. Archer, a Brazoria delegate and former member of the Virginia assembly was elected president. An early issue in the meeting concerned the question of independence. A committee, composed of a delegate from each of the 12 municipalities, could not agree on whether the colonists were fighting for independence or for their rights under the Constitution of 1824. When the issue was returned to the full assembly, there was three days of "lengthy and animated" debate before the Consultation voted on November 6 for a "provisional government, upon the principles of 1824," and then 33 to 15 against a declaration of independence.

The declaration adopted was, however, a compromise between the majority and those who advocated immediate separation. It spoke of Santa Anna's tyranny and of the "natural rights" of the people of Texas, declared that the Texans were fighting to maintain the federal Constitution of 1824, and stated that they offered their assistance to all Mexicans who would join them in resisting military despotism. But the fifth article of the resolution suggests the possibility of more extreme action. The colonists, it stated, "hold it to be their right . . . to establish an independent government," but they would "continue faithful to the Mexican government so long as that nation is governed by the constitution and laws. . . ."

Another act of the body that constituted a definite step toward separation was the election of Branch Archer, William Wharton, and Stephen Austin as commissioners to the United States to obtain aid. The delegates must have known that their kinsmen east of the Sabine would not send men and money to Texas merely to have a part in an internal squabble of Mexican politics. In fact, the cause of the friends of the Constitution of 1824 was already lost. That instrument had been replaced on October 3 when the Mexican Congress, under the direction of Santa Anna, had adopted the *Siete Leyes*, which established an authoritarian system of centralist government.

The Consultation endorsed most of the work of the Permanent Council, adopted a plan for the creation of an army, elected Sam Houston commander in chief, and drew up a plan for a provisional government. The plan provided for a governor, a lieutenant-governor, and a general council to be composed of one member from each municipality. All officials were to be chosen from the members of the Consultation. The delegates voted to sustain the army, then in siege of Bexar, but declared that the volunteers were not obliged to submit to its control, thereby confessing the Consultation's weakness and transmitting to its successor an army over which it had no control. The Consultation finally adjourned on November 14, agreeing to reassemble on March 1, 1836, unless called sooner by the governor and council.

Although the Consultation performed very well in many matters, it made two serious mistakes. Despite the best of intentions, it deprived Texas of valuable services of its two most essential men. Austin, who should have been placed at the head of the provisional government, was sent away "in honorable exile" to the United States, and Houston was made a commander in chief without an army. Equally serious was the failure of the Consultation to delineate clearly the powers of the council and of the governor in the new provisional government. Henry Smith, who had served as political chief of the Department of the Brazos, was elected governor, and James W. Robinson of Nacogdoches was chosen lieutenant-governor. Smith sympathized with the aims of the war party; most members of the council tended to support the aims of the more moderate peace party.

THE FAILURE OF THE PROVISIONAL GOVERNMENT

For about a month the new provisional government worked creditably. It created and filled offices and completed the framework of the political structure, provided for the organization of a post office and a navy, and gave support to the army in the field. Internal discord, however, soon made it helpless. The crises came over a matter of policy. Like the Consultation, the council favored the Constitution of 1824 and cooperation with the Mexican liberals against Santa Anna. Thus, it approved a campaign against Matamoros, believing that its seizure would encourage the people there to resist Santa Anna. Governor Smith opposed the move, and after the council had repeatedly passed measures over his veto, he determined to cow it into submission or to dismiss it. On January 10, 1836, his message, vilifying certain members of the body in most intemperate language, was read to the council. Either the council should apologize for its evil ways, said the governor, and agree henceforth to cooperate with him or adjourn until the first of March. The council replied in language quite as severe as the governor's, declared the office of governor vacant, and inaugurated Lieutenant Governor Robinson as acting governor. Smith refused to deliver up the archives and continued to receive much mail addressed to the executive. The council could not secure a quorum after January 17, and thereafter, until a new convention assembled on March 1, the only

Henry Smith, who was one of the first to advocate Texas independence, was named governor of the Provisional State of Texas (of Mexico) by the Consultation in November 1835. (Southwest Collection, Texas Tech University)

semblance of government was Robinson and an advisory committee. Its results were negligible.

Although there were many fundamental differences between governor and council, the major controversy centered around the ill-advised and ill-fated effort to launch an invasion of Matamoros. The council was determined to carry out the invasion, despite the opposition of the governor and General Houston. It named Frank W. Johnson to head the campaign, and Johnson in turn named James Grant, an Englishman who was a citizen and landowner in Coahuila, to be commander in chief of the expedition. Grant was one of the most vocal and strongest supporters of the venture, but he had little military experience. What then followed was confusion that would have been comic had it not been a tragic waste of time and resources. Grant made his way to San Antonio, where he took four hundred of the Texas volunteers, most of the food and medical supplies, and virtually all of the munitions, leaving the commander of the garrison in San Antonio, J. C. Neill, complaining bitterly. Then, on January 3, Frank Johnson informed the council that he had decided the Matamoros campaign would be a mistake. Four days later the council named Colonel James Fannin, in command in Velasco, to raise volunteers and supplies and to invade Mexico. By then Johnson had changed his mind, and with the approval of the council, he left for Goliad to take command of the expedition.

Meanwhile, General Houston, who was trying to assemble the troops of the regular army in Goliad and Refugio and to keep Copano open, succeeded in persuading most of the volunteers with Johnson and Grant to abandon the Matamoros project. Johnson, nevertheless, informed Houston that the council had deposed Governor Smith and commissioned Fannin and himself to raise men and supplies and to take Matamoros. At that point, however, only a small number of volunteers for the project, no more than a scouting party, remained. These moved into the area around San Patricio to await reinforcements. Soon thereafter (February 2), Fannin landed at Copano with about two hundred men and moved inland by way of Refugio where he learned that Mexican troops were entering Texas. He thereupon decided against the Matamoros campaign, even though he eventually assembled about 450 volunteers. These troops would most assuredly have the opportunity to fight, but not in Matamoros.

In something of a huff, because the council had ignored the military government established by the Consultation by superseding the commander in chief with its own agents and plan of action, Houston took a furlough from the army until March 1. He then went to eastern Texas to carry out a previous order to negotiate a treaty with the Cherokee Indians. In the negotiations he was aided by William Goyens, a prominent black businessman of Nacogdoches, who served as an interpreter. On February 23, Houston signed a treaty that assured the Indians title to their lands in return for remaining at peace with the Texans.

While the Texans were arguing and debating in these weeks of indecision and confusion, Mexican armies were making their way northward to the Rio Grande. On October 27, 1835, President Santa Anna concluded at a meeting with his advisors that the Anglo-American colonists in Texas no longer wished to remain a part of Mexico and decided that he would personally lead an expedition against them. Then, in Saltillo on January 25, he held a grand review of the army, a dazzling spectacle. Having learned of the plans of the Texans to invade Mexico, he sent Colonel Jose Urrea with fifteen hundred cavalrymen to Matamoros with orders to march from there along the coast into Texas by way of Refugio and Goliad. He then proceeded to the Rio Grande, where he joined General Joaquin Ramirez y Sesma, who commanded his left flank with about fifteen hundred men. Santa Anna now had a total force of about six thousand men prepared to march into Texas.

THE ALAMO

In late December 1835, after Grant and Johnson stripped the garrison of men and supplies for the Matamoros expedition, J. C. Neill was left in command of the post at San Antonio with about one hundred poorly equipped men. The council was disposed to hold San Antonio at all costs, but on January 17 General Houston ordered James Bowie to take some

James (Jim) Bowie, born in Tennessee, at 19 moved to Louisiana and engaged in the illicit slave trade with Jean Lafitte. Migrating to Texas in 1828, in 1831 he married Ursula María de Veramendi, daughter of the vice-governor (governor 1832–1833) of Coahulia and Texas and engaged in business in Coahuila. In 1832 Bowie helped drive the Mexican troops from Texas and in 1835 joined the Texas volunteers and commanded the volunteers in San Antonio when William B. Travis arrived with a few regular army troops. Forced by illness to relinquish command to Travis, the bedridden Bowie was killed on March 6, 1836, when Santa Anna's troops stormed the Alamo. (Southwest Collection, Texas Tech University)

men to San Antonio, destroy the fortifications, and retreat to Gonzales, taking with him the cannon and as many supplies as possible. Once there, however, with about twenty-five men, Bowie decided to remain. In disregard of Houston's order, Governor Smith ordered Lieutenant Colonel William B. Travis, recruiting officer in San Felipe, to recruit 100 men and go to the relief of San Antonio. Travis, with only 29 men, reached San Antonio on February 3.

A few days later, Neill gave Travis command of the garrison and left for home because of illness in his family. The volunteers, however, refused to accept the arrangement and elected Bowie as their commander. Travis remained in command of the regulars. The stalemate was not for long; Bowie, already seriously ill, was compelled to leave the command to Travis.

A few other troops arrived, some already famous. James B. Bonham, a native of South Carolina, an Alabama lawyer, and the organizer of the Mobile Grays, left his company in Goliad to join his long-time friend, Travis. The most famous was David Crockett, ex-congressman from Tennessee, who with about a dozen of his "Tennessee boys" rode into San

The Alamo. The Texas revolutionaries took the town of San Antonio in December 1835 and three months later about 180 men led by Travis, Bowie, and Crockett died trying to hold the Alamo against Santa Anna's several thousand troops. Their heroic resistance made "Remember the Alamo" the rallying cry of the revolutionary army. (University of Texas Library)

Antonio unexpectedly on February 8. The new arrivals strengthened the determination of the men to ignore the orders to abandon the garrison.

Travis and his men occupied the building and grounds generally called the Alamo. It was the old Mission San Antonio de Valero, which had later been the home of a company from Alamo de Parras in Mexico. The walls of the mission were thick and twelve feet high; there was ample room for supplies of food; and there was plenty of water. Unfortunately, the size of the grounds required far more men for defense than Travis could muster, even with the several cannons that were available, and a portion of one wall was incomplete, protected only by a makeshift arrangement of sticks and dirt. Nevertheless, as Amelia Williams, historian of the Alamo has stated, "the place . . . seemed to cast some sort of spell over the Texas leaders." Travis wrote, "We consider death preferable to disgrace which would be the result of giving up the Post which has been so dearly won."

While Travis and his men prepared their defenses, Santa Anna's army made its way toward San Antonio. On February 16 the main army began crossing the Rio Grande with twenty-one cannons, eighteen hundred pack mules, thirty-three wagons and two hundred carts. They marched toward San Antonio, about 150 miles distant, in disregard of General Vicente Filisola's plea to march directly for San Felipe. Santa Anna, the self-styled "Napoleon of the West," wanted to avenge the defeat of Cós. The vanguard of the army reached San Antonio on February 23, to the great surprise of Travis, who did not expect it until after the grass was green and the weather warm.

When the Mexican army was first sighted on February 23, Travis sent two of his scouts to the *alcalde* of Gonzales with a plea for men and provisions. The men, he added, "are determined to defend the Alamo to the last." On the next day, while the Mexican artillery was bombarding the Alamo, he sent out a stirring appeal "To the People of Texas and All Americans in the World." In it he stated that "The enemy has demanded a surrender at discretion," but "*I shall never surrender or retreat . . . .* VICTORY OR DEATH." During the night of February 25, Juan Seguín, a prominent San Antonian, on Bowie's fast horse, rode through the Mexican sentries and raced for Gonzales with another urgent plea for aid.

To join the force barricaded in the Alamo indeed required a measure of courage. Bonham twice went out and twice came back. His return through the fire of the enemy at 11:00 a.m. on March 3, after it was evident that the Alamo was a deathtrap, should qualify him as a hero. And, there were others. Albert Martin and thirty-two men from Gonzales, in response to Travis's appeal and with courier John W. Smith as guide, slipped past the Mexican lines and into the Alamo at 3:00 a.m. on March 1. Unfortunately, the only detachment of troops that might have significantly altered the strength of the defense of the Alamo never arrived. Fannin started from Goliad for San Antonio on February 26 with most of his men but the next day returned to his fort.

On March 3 Travis sent out his last appeal for help, this one to the convention that he knew was scheduled to be in session in Washington on the Brazos. Although at least two hundred shells had fallen inside the works, the Texans had not lost a person, and their spirits were still high. It was better, Travis believed, to meet the enemy "here than to suffer a war of devastation to rage in our settlements." With this and a number of other notes, John W. Smith slipped out through the south wall. Travis hoped that the convention would issue a declaration of independence, but ironically he and other defenders of the Alamo officially died fighting for a federalist government under the Constitution of 1824, without knowing that such action had been taken.

On March 4 and 5 the Mexican cannons were moved closer and became more effective. Then, just before dawn on March 6, with the band playing *Deguello* (no quarter), Santa Anna took the fortress by storm, leaving only one defender alive. On the orders of Santa Anna the bodies of 182 Texans (183 according to a report by a Mexican officer) were stacked on layers of wood and burned. The Mexican dead, variously estimated from 600 to 1,600, were buried in the cemetery until it was filled, and the remainder were dumped into the river.

Although apparently only one Texan soldier (José María Guerrero, who convinced Santa Anna that he fought against his will) survived, there were several other survivors. Santa Anna ordered the release of some Mexican women and children who were in the Alamo. Mrs. Almaron Dickinson, the wife of a Texas officer killed in the battle, her daughter, and a black slave were also allowed to leave the scene. Those who perished in the struggle left a legacy of bravery and heroics. The defenders' courage and determination in the face of almost certain death were at the time and afterwards a source of inspiration. Not always recognized, but similarly worthy of admiration, was the courage and determination of the hundreds of Mexican soldiers who perished in the assault. In the face of deadly cannon and musket fire, they repeatedly attacked, while their comrades fell on all sides, until they overwhelmed the garrison and the guns fell silent.

Although the heroism of the Battle of the Alamo is obvious, an evaluation of the significance of the battle is not an easy task. It was, no doubt, a battle that Santa Anna did not need to fight and one that he should not have fought. If he had bypassed the garrison, marched on into the settlements to the east, and assumed control of the more populated areas of Texas, the outpost in San Antonio would have posed no threat. Its conquest, then, was a matter of ego, a matter of revenge, and the price was high. Had he ignored the fortress, he would have saved time and supplies, not to mention the lives of hundreds of his soldiers. His march to the east was delayed for several weeks, and the stand of Travis and his men became a cause and a battle cry for the Texans. On the other hand, there is little indication that Texans used the time purchased with the blood of the

Alamo to good advantage. The delay in part contributed to an opportunity for Houston to recruit and to train an army, but Santa Anna's decision to ignore the Texan commander's efforts was probably more meaningful.

After his victory at the Alamo, Santa Anna devised a three-column advance eastward through the settlements to complete the subjugation of Texas. In the south, General Urrea, reinforced by a detachment of about 600 troops from San Antonio, was to march by way of Victoria and Matagorda Bay to Brazoria and perhaps as far as Anahuac. General Antonio Gaona, with 725 men, was ordered to march to Nacogdoches by way of Bastrop and the upper crossing on Trinity River. The main army, with General Joaquin Ramirez y Sesma leading the advance, would proceed eastward by way of Gonzales and San Felipe. Santa Anna and General Vicente Filisola, next in command, left San Antonio on March 31 after the departure of the troops.

THE BIRTH OF THE REPUBLIC

The Texans who died at the Alamo did not know that they were fighting for independence from Mexico and for a newly created republic. On March 1, 1836, the contesting governors and council, impotent because of quarrels and bickering, were supplanted by a convention. Realizing that a reconvening of the Consultation would not be adequate to meet the emergency, the council had passed on December 14, 1835, over Governor Smith's veto, an act calling for the election of delegates to a convention "with ample, unlimited, or plenary powers as to the form of government to be adopted." The delegates, elected on February 1, convened on the morning of March 1 in Washington on the Brazos, a new town about thirty-five miles upstream from San Felipe. It was a dismal place, a visitor from Virginia recorded; the cold rain the night before had left the one street ankle-deep in mud, and the cotton cloth, stretched across the openings for windows in the unfinished building in which they met, only partially excluded the chilling wind.

The situation that confronted the delegates when they assembled that cold morning called for courage and statesmanship of the highest orders. Urrea's lancers were slashing their way toward Goliad, Santa Anna's legions were wearing out the garrison at the Alamo, and Travis was pleading for aid. There were no troops at Washington and none between Washington and San Antonio, 150 miles away. The life of every delegate was in danger; indeed all Texas was in peril and the outlook was well-nigh hopeless.

To meet this challenge, the voters of Texas had selected a group of able, even outstanding, delegates. Robert Potter and Samuel Carson had served in the Congress of the United States from South Carolina, and

Richard Ellis and Martin Parmer had helped to frame state constitutions before they came to Texas. Other men of less experience but of equal ability were Thomas J. Rusk, James Collinsworth, and George C. Childress. Colin McKinney, then seventy years old, but destined to outlive many of his colleagues, and James Gaines, who had known Texas since the days of Magee and Gutierrez, supplied such wisdom that comes only with age. One of the most distinguished and influential members was Lorenzo de Zavala, a former member of the Mexican Congress and a staunch opponent of Santa Anna's centralism. Sam Houston, a delegate from Refugio, was no doubt a valuable member, but he left the convention in less than a week to take command of the army. Of the fifty-nine delegates who attended the convention, fifty-two were from the United States. One was born in England, one in Mexico, one in Ireland, one in Canada, and one in Scotland. Two, José Antonio Navarro and José Francisco Ruiz, had been born in Texas.

On the first day the convention elected as president Richard Ellis of Pecan Point, and named H. S. Kimble as secretary. It selected a committee to be chaired by George C. Childress, who only recently had brought $5,000 from the citizens of Tennessee to aid the Texas cause, to draft a declaration of independence. On the next day, March 2, it adopted a declaration of independence written by Childress that followed the main features of the document written by Thomas Jefferson sixty years earlier.

The convention then began preparing a constitution for the new nation. The completed document, adopted at midnight on March 16, was a composite of excerpts from the constitutions of the United States and several states. There were some unique features, however. The term for the president was to be three years (the first constitutional president to serve two years only), and he was not to succeed himself; the president was not to lead armies in the field except with the consent of Congress; ministers of the gospel were not to hold office; each head of a family in Texas was to be granted a headright of a league and a *labor* of land; and the institution of slavery was legalized, but the African slave trade was considered piracy.

The convention also constituted itself the government of Texas and took steps to meet the emergency. Its most important work in that connection was the appointment on March 4 of Sam Houston as "Commander in Chief of all the land forces of the Texan Army, both regulars, volunteers, and militia, while in actual service." On Sunday, March 6, when Travis's last message arrived, the impetuous Robert Potter moved that the delegates adjourn and go to the relief of the Alamo, but after a long speech by Houston, who insisted that the establishment of a government should have priority, it was rejected. Houston then left the convention to rally a force to fight for the independence of the new nation. The last act of the convention, performed as the candles burned short on the night of March 16—

David G. Burnet was *ad interim* president of the Republic of Texas, March 16 to October 22, 1836, and vice-president, 1838–1841. A native of New Jersey, Burnet previously had commanded the launch that fired the first shot in the war for Venezuelan independence, had lived for almost two years with the Comanche Indians in West Texas while recovering from tuberculosis, and in 1826 had obtained an *empresario* grant in East Texas. In 1866 he was named to represent Texas in the United States Senate but was never seated. (Southwest Collection, Texas Tech University)

17, was the selection of an *ad interim* government to direct the infant republic until the constitution could be adopted and a regular government inaugurated. David G. Burnet was elected president; Lorenzo de Zavala, vice-president; Samuel P. Carson, secretary of state; Bailey Hardeman, secretary of the treasury; Thomas J. Rusk, secretary of war; Robert Potter, secretary of the navy; and David Thomas, attorney general. They were sworn in at 4:00 A.M.; a few hours later the convention adjourned.

THE WAR IN SOUTH TEXAS

While Santa Anna laid siege to the Alamo and delayed for about three weeks after victory and the convention delegates at Washington on the Brazos labored to create a new republic, General José Urrea on the southern front, with no more than one-fourth of the Mexican army under his command, moved from one victory to another. Leaving Matamoros on January 18, Urrea marched rapidly along the coastal road and on February 27 at San Patricio, on the Nueces River near present-day Corpus Christi, surprised Frank Johnson, who at the time had with him about 35 men. All the men were killed or captured, except Johnson and four or five of his companions, who managed to escape. Twenty miles further up the road, on March 2, Urrea destroyed James Grant and his scouting party of about 30 men and then continued toward Goliad.

At Goliad, Colonel Fannin continued to display the indecisiveness that he had shown in the past. Having failed to reinforce the Alamo, he had returned to Goliad where on March 14 he received an order from General Houston to fall back to Victoria. Unfortunately, he delayed in order to wait for the return of two detachments of troops, variously estimated from less than 100 to 180, under Amon B. King and William Ward. Neither King nor Ward returned, and the delay cost Fannin and most of his men their lives. King and his 33 men had been captured near Refugio and, except for some Germans, were shot on March 16. Ward and his men had escaped from Refugio but were surrounded and captured on March 22 near Victoria and were impounded with other prisoners at Goliad.

Fannin with his main force began his retreat on March 19, the day after Urrea, augmented by 600 troops from San Antonio, reached Goliad. That afternoon when a wagon loaded with ammunition broke down and the oxen needed to graze, Fannin camped on an open prairie, although another two or three miles would have brought him to timber and badly needed water at Coleto Creek. He was quickly surrounded by Urrea's cavalry. The Texans withstood the first attacks, but the next morning, when the main Mexican force arrived on the field with cannons, Fannin surrendered. Later, the survivors contended that they surrendered as prisoners of war to be treated in accordance with international policy, but the original document in the Mexican archives shows that they capitulated "subject to the disposition of the Supreme Government." In this battle the Texans had 9 killed, 51 wounded, and 234 captured; Urrea had at least 50 killed and 140 wounded, with some sources estimating more than 200 killed. The prisoners were returned to Goliad, kept in confinement for a week, and then, on orders of Santa Anna, about 350 (including Ward and 82 of his men) were shot, despite the protest of General Urrea. Two physicians, some nurses, several needed workmen, and about 28 who somehow or another managed to avoid death, were not executed. Some of the survivors owed their lives to Señora Francisca Alvarez, later remembered as the "Angel of Goliad."

RETREAT

By mid-March the settlers to the east of San Antonio were aware that Santa Anna's legions were marching in their direction and that there were few defenders to halt the advance. What hope there was depended on the efforts of General Sam Houston. From the convention in Washington on the Brazos, Houston went directly to Gonzales, where on his arrival on March 11 he found 374 men with less than two days' provisions, many without arms, and others without any ammunition. He immediately organized the First Regiment of Texas Volunteers with Edward Burleson in command. On the thirteenth he learned that General Joaquin Ramirez y Sesma with about 700 troops was marching toward Gonzales. Knowing that with his small, untrained, and poorly equipped force he could not defend the town, he had it burned and that night began his retreat. A rear guard shepherded the frightened settlers, who hurriedly abandoned their homes and fled eastward with the retreating army.

On the afternoon of March 17, Houston arrived at Burnam's (Burnham's) Ferry on the Colorado, near La Grange. By then he had about 600 men. After getting the refugees and the troops across, he destroyed the ferry and encamped a short distance downstream at Beason's Crossing, barely ahead of the arrival of units of the Mexican army on the west bank of the swollen river. Hounded by his own men to let them fight, Houston considered making a stand at the Colorado, but upon the arrival of news that Fannin had capitulated, he decided to withdraw to the Brazos. He realized that a victory over Sesma would not end the war and that a defeat would mean the total subjugation of Texas.

Ignoring the complaints of his unhappy soldiers, on March 26 Houston left for the Brazos, arriving late the next day at San Felipe, a village of 5 stores and 25 or 30 houses. Here, Captains Moseley Baker and Wiley Martin refused to retreat further. Houston thereupon assigned Baker with his company to guard the crossing at San Felipe and Martin to guard the crossing at Fort Bend, about 30 miles downstream. The

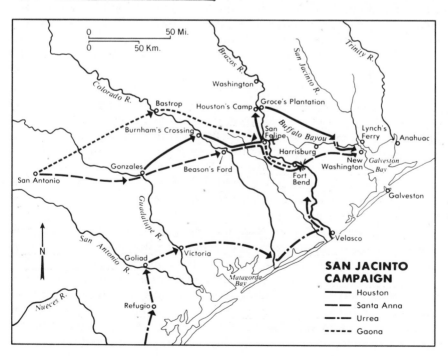

SAN JACINTO CAMPAIGN

——— Houston

– – – Santa Anna

–·– Urrea

····· Gaona

remainder of the troops sloshed upstream, less than 20 miles in three days, and camped on the west side of the Brazos across from the large plantation of Jared E. Groce. There, supplied with food and provisions from the rich larder of Groce's plantation, Houston remained for nearly two weeks, reorganizing and drilling the army.

Meanwhile, thousands of refugees fled eastward in advance of Santa Anna's soldiers. Probably as many as a thousand families lived along the Colorado and Brazos rivers along the paths of the armies. News of Houston's retreat, coupled with that of the fate of the Alamo and Goliad, carried eastward into the settlements by fleeing civilians and soldiers who left with or without leave to look after their families, created widespread fear. The incessant floods, mud, and cold weather, which also caused problems for Santa Anna and his troops, added to the misery of the Texans. The frontier began to fold back upon itself in an affair to be known as the "runaway scrape." Loading their wagons, oxcarts, or sleds, or taking such simple belongings as could be carried on horseback or even on foot, the people set out in a desperate rush to keep ahead of the Mexican army. Streams were swollen, ferries became jammed, epidemics prevailed, and the misery and suffering were indescribable.

Difficult for everyone, the retreat was perhaps the most difficult for the women who often had to assume responsibility for their families. Widow Angelina Peyton remembered that "Women led donkeys packed with a few household treasures, and her more precious treasures, her children." Mary Rabb reported being driven "out of ouer houses with ouer little ones to suffer with cold and hungry. . . ." Others recalled "horrible confusion" and "pitiful and distressing" scenes of river crossings. The strong Captain Moseley Baker wept at the sad sight he witnessed as the people trudged by his camp opposite San Felipe. In her reminiscences, Dilue Rose Harris states that there were five thousand people at Lynch's Ferry at the mouth of the San Jacinto when her family arrived there on April 10. But Texas women were accustomed to hardship, and they met the challenge. They helped to bury their dead, shared their grief, and cared for their children and those of others. Later, in describing the events of the revolution, Thomas Jefferson Rusk said "the women, with their little children around them, without means of defense or power to resist, faced danger and death with unflinching courage."

The government fled with the people. As the Mexican forces advanced, Texan headquarters were removed from Washington to Harrisburg (now within the city of Houston). Houston complained to the government for retreating, and Burnet in turn berated Houston. "The enemy are laughing you to scorn," he wrote, "you must fight them. You must retreat no farther. The country expects you to fight. The salvation of the country depends on you doing so." In commenting on his own conduct Houston wrote Rusk on March 29, "I consulted none—I held no councils-of-war. If I err, the blame is mine." Meanwhile, Burnet sent Secretary of State Carson to Fort Jessup, Louisiana, to appeal for aid to General Edmund P. Gaines, who commanded a strong force of United States troops.

In their march eastward Santa Anna's forces, suffering in much the same manner as the Texans, moved slowly. Having left General Filisola at the Colorado with a detachment of troops to help get the artillery and supplies across the swollen river, Santa Anna, with Sesma and a part of the army, on April 7 reached San Felipe, which Baker had burned. With the ferry destroyed and his slow rafts an easy target for Baker's riflemen on the opposite shore, Santa Anna was unable to cross. By going upstream Houston had left the government at Harrisburg and the lower settlements without any protection. Thus, Santa Anna decided first to lay waste that region and to deal with Houston later. Sending orders to Filisola, Urrea, and Gaona to march their commands to Fort Bend, near present-day Richmond, he moved downstream to the settlement with an advance detachment of Sesma's troops. When all the units arrived, he would have at his command a force of about 3,400, more than three times the size of Houston's. While at Fort Bend, he received word that Burnet and the *ad interim* government were only thirty miles away in Harrisburg. Upon arrival at Harrisburg on April 15 with a portion of his army, he learned that the Texas officials had moved to a location on Galveston Bay. Santa Anna then set the town of Harrisburg aflame, and marched toward Galveston Bay, only to find that Burnet and his cabinet had taken refuge on Galveston Island.

THE BATTLE OF SAN JACINTO

On April 12 a messenger from Fort Bend reached Houston's camp with word of Santa Anna's plans. This was the opportunity Houston wanted. With the aid of the steamboat *Yellowstone*, he moved his command across the river where it received the famous "Twin Sisters," two cannons donated by the people of Cincinnati, that would soon help win Texas independence. Houston then moved southeastward. Not far ahead the road forked, one leading to Louisiana, the other to Harrisburg. The men, especially Moseley Baker, who had rejoined the main command, threatened to mutiny if Houston took the road toward Louisiana. They were unaware, of course, that on the night before reaching the fork Houston wrote a friend that he was on his way to meet Santa Anna. Houston took the road to Harrisburg. On April 18, while he was camped near the ruins of the town, Deaf Smith, the faithful and effective scout, brought in a captured Mexican courier with dispatches that revealed more about Santa Anna's plans and movements. Houston thereupon crossed his army on rafts to the south side of

Buffalo Bayou, left his baggage and sick men with a small guard hidden in the woods, and during the next night proceeded with slightly more than nine hundred men across the wooden bridge over Vince's Bayou to Lynch's Ferry. Taking possession of the ferry, he pitched camp soon after dawn on April 20 with the bayou at his rear, the San Jacinto on his left, and open prairie on his front and right flank.

Until he reached Harrisburg, Houston apparently had no definite plan. His general plan had been to retreat eastward to gain the advantage of being nearer a source of supplies in the Texas settlements and in the United States, to draw the enemy farther and farther away from his base of supplies, and to avoid battle until the enemy made a mistake. On the afternoon of April 20, Santa Anna made a mistake. He camped where organized retreat was impossible.

A sharp skirmish occurred during the afternoon. Upon finding the Texans in control of the ferry, the surprised Mexicans hauled a cannon to some nearby timber and began firing at the Texans. During the action, Mirabeau B. Lamar, who had arrived only a few days before, performed with decision and courage, resulting in his appointment to the command of a unit of cavalry. That night, the Texans slept and the next morning, Thursday, April 21, had a good breakfast. In the hours of the early morning Santa Anna's forces received reinforcements when General Cós arrived with 542, or perhaps more, tired and hungry troops. Santa Anna, convinced that the Texans did not intend to attack, permitted all, except for a small guard, to eat and to retire to their tents for sleep and rest.

Houston prepared for battle. He sent Deaf Smith to destroy the bridge across Vince's Bayou, leaving neither army with an escape route. About noon, aware that the men were increasingly impatient, Houston told his officers to prepare for an attack. At 3:30 that afternoon, he formed his troops in a line that extended 1,000 yards along the edge of the woods. From left to right, the line order was the Second Regiment under Sidney Sherman, the First Regiment under Edward Burleson, artillery under George W. Hockley, a four-piece band, four companies of infantry under Henry Millard, and 61 cavalrymen under Lamar. The Texans moved quietly, hidden from view by a rise in the terrain, until they were within two hundred yards of the Mexican barricades. Then the "Twin Sisters" fired a blast of broken horseshoes and shrapnel directly into the Mexican camp; the four-piece band began playing an inappropriate popular love song, "Will You Come to the Bow'r I Have Shaded for You"; Colonel Sherman struck the enemy to his left; and the line, center and right, charged directly into the breastworks of the camp, shouting "Remember the Alamo!" and "Remember Goliad!" Many of the surprised Mexicans fled in panic. General Manuel Fernandez Castrillón, a brave and able officer, tried to rally the confused Mexican soldiers, but, despite General Rusk's efforts to save him, other Texans riddled him with bullets. Santa Anna and some of his

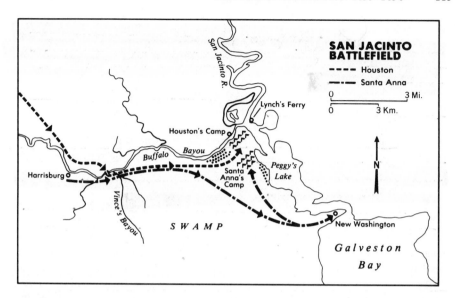

staff escaped into the woods, apparently hoping to reach his main army at Fort Bend.

The carnage at San Jacinto was indescribable. The battle, according to Houston's official report, lasted only eighteen minutes, but the pursuit, killing, and capture of the enemy continued much longer. The Texans, determined to exact full vengeance, could not be restrained. Arriving at the scene where a terrible slaughter was underway, an officer who ordered the men to stop was, according to Austin's nephew, met with a cocked rifle and flat refusal. According to Houston's official report four days later, 630 of the enemy were killed, 208 were wounded, and 730 were taken prisoner, including General Cós and Santa Anna, who were captured the next day. Of the Mexican force, which numbered around 1,400 at the beginning of the battle, only a few escaped. Nine Texans were killed and 34 wounded, including Houston whose right leg just above the ankle was shattered by shot in the midst of the action.

AFTER SAN JACINTO

The defeat of Santa Anna's forces saved the Texan cause for the time, but it did not immediately assure independence. There were about two thousand Mexican troops in Texas that might have to be reckoned with; and Houston was helpless and soon to take a steamer to New Orleans for the treatment of his ankle. The Texan army was, furthermore, almost as badly disorganized by victory as the Mexican army on the Brazos was by the reports of defeat and death. The Texas government faced several immediate problems: first, to restore order and establish among the people a sense of security and competence; second, to strengthen, supply, and keep control of the army; and third, to secure from Mexico the recognition of Texan independence, or at least to empty the country of Mexican troops.

Order and confidence returned gradually as the people learned of the completeness of the victory and observed that the government again was functioning. Many persons who had taken part in the "runaway scrape" went back to their homes at once. Government headquarters were moved from Galveston to Velasco where better quarters could be secured. The *Telegraph and Texas Register*, whose plant at Harrisburg had been destroyed, resumed publication in Columbia in August. On July 23, President Burnet issued a proclamation calling for a general election to be held on the first Monday in September to establish a constitutional government.

Although the gravest problem that confronted the *ad interim* government after San Jacinto was control of the army, the problem was inseparably linked with that of deciding what to do with the prisoner Santa Anna and arriving at some understanding with the Mexican forces still in Texas. Shortly after he had been brought to Houston's headquarters on April 22, the Mexican president entered into an armistice in consequence of which he wrote General Vicente Filisola, second in command, to retire with his troops to Bexar and to order Urrea to fall back to Victoria "pending some negotiations . . . by which the war is to cease forever." Even as Santa Anna wrote, the Mexican forces were in retreat, and the message did not overtake Filisola until April 28.

Shortly thereafter, in Velasco on May 14, Burnet negotiated two treaties with Santa Anna, one public and one secret. By the terms of the public treaty an end was declared to hostilities; the Mexican army was to retire at once beyond the Rio Grande, and all Texan prisoners were to be released by the Mexicans, the Texans agreeing to release a corresponding number of Mexican prisoners. The chief purpose of the secret treaty was to get from Santa Anna the pledge to use his influence on the Mexican government to secure the execution of the treaty already made and, also, to establish a permanent treaty whereby Mexico would acknowledge the independence of Texas, the boundary of which not to extend beyond the Rio Grande. The Texas government in turn pledged to release Santa Anna at once, giving him an escort to Vera Cruz.

There was widespread clamor that the dictator be put to death, but Burnet courageously determined to carry out the treaty and to return him to Mexico. On June 4, after General Santa Anna, his secretary Caro, and Colonel Almonte were aboard the schooner of war *Invincible*, a group of disgruntled and ambitious army officers flagrantly demonstrated their opposition. Led by General Thomas J. Green, newly arrived from the United States with a force of volunteers, they compelled Burnet, despite Santa Anna's protest, to remove the prisoners from the vessel and place them in confinement on land.

Developments during the next few weeks did not improve Santa Anna's position. Word came that the Mexican senate had annulled his treaty and had declared that the government would continue the war. Three Texan emissaries, sent to Matamoros under a flag of truce and bearing passports from Filisola to see if all prisoners had been released, were arrested and added to the Mexican prison rolls. On June 17, Rusk wrote from the army that Urrea was advancing on Goliad. Urrea's threat did not materialize, but several months would pass before President Houston finally resolved the problem of the captured dictator. Houston returned Santa Anna to Mexico by way of the United States.

Burnet's difficulties with insubordinate troops were not confined to volunteers in the seat of government. After the Battle of San Jacinto, Thomas J. Rusk reluctantly took command of the Texan army and followed the retreating Mexicans as far as Victoria. Word that Santa Anna was to be released provoked an army mass meeting and an insolent and threatening letter to Burnet. Thinking that army morale might be improved by a change of commanders, Burnet sent Mirabeau B. Lamar around July 1 to replace Rusk, but neither the men nor officers would accept Lamar. When a plan of the army officers to arrest and bring Rusk before the army for trial failed, Burnet sought to absorb the energies of the army by encouraging an expedition against Matamoros. This never materialized. He then sent word to agents in New Orleans to send no more short-term volunteers and passed the problem of the army on to his successor, Sam Houston.

AID FOR THE REVOLUTION

The expenditures of Texans in the cause of revolution were surprisingly small. Figures in the audits read more like those of a retail store than of the government of a sovereign state. Virtually every device for raising money known in that day was tried. Donations amounted to about $25,000. Treasury notes, issued in the total amount of $150,000, were almost worthless from the date of their issue. The most substantial receipts, about $100,000, came from loans negotiated in the United States by Commissioners Austin, Archer, and Wharton.

The revolution was financed largely by those who advanced supplies to the infant government on faith and by the troops who willingly served for little other compensation than the promise of land bounties. Many loyal persons pledged land, slaves, and other property to be sold for the benefit of the cause, but little money was raised in that way. Jane McManus offered to borrow money, with her land as security, to support the war effort. Other women manufactured cartridges and made clothing, donated livestock, and created more than one of the flags that flew over the ranks of the soldiers. Sometimes contributions added to the hardships of the settlers. Widow McElroy, who lost cattle and a wagon, appealed to President Burnet for compensation, for her family was in great need. Angelina Peyton, who failed to complete the proper forms, had trouble securing compensation for her oxen placed in the service of the army. Pamelia Mann, who allowed Houston to use her oxen while he traveled toward Nacogdoches, demanded their return when the general turned toward Harrisburg. Not usually intimidated, Houston apparently met his match and returned the animals. Altogether, loans and contributions such as these brought the government debt to $1.25 million by August 31, 1836.

War supplies came mainly from New Orleans. The firm of William Bryan and Company, Texan agents in that city, often used their own funds and impaired their private credit in the interests of the struggle. Also, the Texan merchant, Thomas F. McKinney, who declined the office of commissary general, worked faithfully in a private capacity toward supplying the troops, and to that end he spent large sums of his own money. The records show shipments of flour, rifles, powder, lead, clothing, and other necessary supplies for the army.

From east of the Sabine came men as well as supplies. As early as October 26, 1835, the Permanent Council addressed the citizens of the United States with an impassioned appeal to come to the aid of "suffering Texas." From New Orleans to Cincinnati friends of the colonists held meetings, raised funds, and sent out forces of volunteers of "armed emigrants." The chief recruiting stations were Louisville, Cincinnati, and New Orleans. Some of the best-known volunteer organizations were the two companies of "New Orleans Greys," in one of which were represented five foreign countries and 12 different states; the Georgia Battalion, composed of men from Georgia and Alabama and strengthened by recruits who joined them on the way to Texas; the "Mobile Grays," originally some 30 men under Captain David N. Burk; the Alabama "Red Rovers," almost 70 men under Captain Jack Shackelford, who arrived at Matagorda early in 1836; the "Mustangs," from Kentucky and Tennessee; and some 50 Tennesseans, among them David Crockett, who arrived in Nacogdoches on January 12, 1836. For most of these young Americans fate held a tragic ending. A majority of the men who had recently died in the Alamo had come from the United States, as was true of the forces of Johnson and Grant; and Fannin's men were, almost without exception, recent arrivals.

The most successful work in recruiting troops abroad for Texas was that of Thomas Jefferson Chambers. Authorized by the council to raise for Texas an "Army of the Reserve," Chambers in February 1836 proceeded to Natchez, Mississippi, and thence to points in Tennessee, Kentucky, and Ohio. Report of the victory at San Jacinto made it comparatively easy, both to secure volunteers and to raise the means to equip them. By December 1836 he had sent 1,915 well-equipped volunteers and, also, quantities of ammunition and other supplies. These forces arrived too late, however, to participate in the battles of the revolution.

Ironically, it was the colonists who lived in Texas before the revolution began who did the most effective fighting. It was they who drove the Mexicans out of Texas in 1835, and they constituted an overwhelming majority of Houston's army at San Jacinto. In no sense, however, were all of the Texans of Anglo-American heritage. Three Texans of Mexican heritage, Lorenzo de Zavala, José Francisco Ruiz, and José Antonio Navarro, signed the Declaration of Independence. Many others fought in the armies, including Juan Seguín, who commanded a cavalry unit. Black Texans also made their contributions. Greenbury Logan fought at Concepcion and San Antonio, and Samuel McCullough suffered a wound at Goliad in the early fighting of the revolution. Hendrick Arnold saw action at San Antonio and San Jacinto, and William Goyens was a valuable participant in negotiations to keep the Cherokees from joining the Mexican cause. There were others as well.

On occasion the black people of Texas still held in bondage contributed to the cause. Some of the information used by Houston on the eve of the Battle of Jacinto was provided by slaves who reported on the size and location of Mexican troops. A slave named Cary saw considerable service as a courier, and others provided supplies or served in some military capacity. Not all, however, supported the Texan cause. Mexican commanders sometimes promised freedom (and occasionally carried out their promise) to slaves who would join their forces, while in other instances, slaves took advantage of the confusion of war to seek and find freedom.

THE TEXAS NAVY

Although Gonzales is generally given the credit, the first battle in the revolution occurred at sea on September 1, 1835. The Mexican war schooner *Correo* fired upon the *San Felipe* bound for Victoria with a cargo of munitions. After a two-hour fight the *Correo* was captured and taken to New Orleans. Mexican war and transport ships continued to operate along the coast, and consequently, the provisional government on November 25 provided for the purchase of four schooners and for granting a letter of marque to privateers until the navy materialized. Meanwhile, the citizens in the coastal communities had bought and equipped the schooner *William Robbins*, which subsequently took the Mexican man-of-war *Bravo* and a prize it had just taken. Sentiment in the United States, however, was so strongly against privateering that the Texans had to discontinue the practice.

The Texas navy took form when, in January 1836, the Texas commissioners purchased four naval vessels: the 60-ton *William Robbins*, rechristened the *Liberty*; the 125-ton *Independence*, a former United States revenue cutter; the 125-ton *Invincible*, which had been built for the African slave trade; and the 125-ton, 8-gun *Brutus*, originally fitted as a privateer. About the same time, in March, President Burnet commissioned William A. Hurd to the rank of commodore and placed him in command of the fleet.

In cruising the coast and convoying shipments from New Orleans, the vessels rendered excellent service. The *Brutus* maintained a blockade along the Texas coast until it was lost in a storm in October 1837. The *Liberty* took as a prize the fine Mexican schooner *Pelicano*, filled with munitions for the Mexican army (packed in barrels of flour and apples). The *Invincible* took prizes along the coast until August 26, when it ran aground and was destroyed in Galveston harbor while engaged in a fight with two Mexican vessels. During the early months of 1836 the *Independence* captured a number of small Mexican vessels before sailing to New Orleans where its commander, Commodore Charles Hawkins, died. On its return, after a four-hour fight, it was captured in sight of Galveston.

As the Mexican army advanced in the spring of 1836, the Texas ships centered their activity on keeping the port of Galveston open, thereby allowing the Mexican forces uncontested use of the forts at the mouth of the Brazos and Copano Bay. Anticipating that the Mexicans might send troops through these ports, General Thomas J. Rusk ordered Major Issac W. Burton with a troop of thirty mounted men to patrol the coast. Sighting a Mexican vessel in Copano Bay, the unit on June 3 managed to decoy the captain and some crew members ashore, seize them, row out in their boat, and take the ship (loaded with supplies for the Mexican army) without resistance. Two weeks later, when two other ships load with supplies appeared, the "Horse Marines," as Burton and his rangers became known, managed to take both without a casualty.

Thus it was on the sea that the first and final battles of the revolution took place. Throughout the war, in conveying men and equipment, as well as preventing the free movement of troops and supplies by the enemy, the Texans were greatly aided by the navy. In fact, it seems safe to say that without the support rendered by the navy, the Texans would have had great difficulty winning the war.

SELECTED BIBLIOGRAPHY

A great deal has been written about the Texan Revolution. Of the older general histories, all cited at the beginning of the references for Chapter 4, good accounts may be had in J. H. Brown, H. H. Bancroft, W. Kennedy, H. Yoakum, D. G. Wooten (reprint of Yoakum's text), C. R. Wortham, and H. S. Thrall. Yoakum gives much source material. Thrall has many biographical sketches; Wortham devotes a volume to the revolution; Juan N. Almonte, *Noticia Estradistica. Sobre Tejas* (Mexico, 1835); Vicente Filisola, *Memoirs of the History of the War with Texas* (typescript trans. Verona Griffith, Library, Texas Tech University, Lubbock, Tex.; Mexico, 1848).

Of the newer general histories, two are superior: W. C. Binkley, *The Texas Revolution*; and D. M. Vigness, *The Revolutionary Decades*; two others of great value are Vito Alessio Robles, *Coahuila y Texas en la Epoca Colonial* (Mexico, 1938); and A. J. Houston, *Texas Independence* (Houston, 1938).

Several biographies are extremely valuable in connection with the revolution. The best is E. C. Barker, *The Life of Stephen F. Austin*. Others are L. Friend, *Sam Houston, the Great Designer*; Marquis James, *The Raven: A Biography of Sam Houston* (New York, 1929); E. Wallace, *Charles DeMorse, Pioneer Editor and Statesman* (Lubbock, Tex., 1943); Herbert P. Gambrell, *Mirabeau Bonaparte Lamar* (Dallas, 1934); Herbert P. Gambrell, *Anson Jones: The Last President of Texas* (New York, 1948); Mary Whatley Clarke, *David G. Burnet* (Austin, 1969); Herman Ehrenberg, *With Milam and Fannin* (trans. Charlotte Churchill and ed. Henry Smith; Austin, 1974); Hobart Huson, *Captain Phillip Dimmitt's Commandancy of Goliad* (Austin, 1974); Ernest C. Shearer, *Robert Potter, Remarkable North Carolinian and Texan* (Houston, 1951); Archie McDonald, *Travis* (Austin, 1976); W. N. Bate, *General Sidney Sherman: Texas Soldier, Statesman and Builder* (Waco, 1974); Cleburn Huston, *Deaf Smith, Incredible Spy* (Waco, 1973); Joseph Dawson, *José Antonio Navarro: Co-Creator of Texas* (Waco, 1969); J. A. Atkins, *David Crockett, the Man and the Legend* (Chapel Hill, N.C., 1956); John Henry Brown, *Life and Times of Henry Smith, the First American Governor of Texas* (Dallas, 1887); R. N. Richardson, and others, *Heroes of Texas* (Waco, 1964).

The source materials for the revolution are voluminous. The most comprehensive is John H. Jenkins (ed.), *The Papers of the Texas Revolution*. Other comprehensive collections are E. C. Barker (ed.), *The Austin Papers*; Amelia W. Williams and E. C. Barker (eds.), *The Writings of Sam Houston* (8 vols., Austin, 1938–1943); C. A. Gulick, Katherine Elliott, and Harriett Smithers (eds.), *The Papers of Mirabeau Bonaparte Lamar* (6 vols., Austin, 1921–1927); W. C. Binkley (ed.), *Official Correspondence of the Texan Revolution, 1835–1836* (2 vols., New York and London, 1936). Useful also is C. E. Castañeda (ed. and trans.), *The Mexican Side of the Texan Revolution* (Dallas, 1928); E. Wallace and D. M. Vigness (eds.), *Documents of Texas History*; John H. Jenkins (ed.), *Recollections of Early Texas: The Memoirs of John Holland Jenkins* (Austin, 1958).

Shorter studies dealing primarily with the early phase of the revolution include "General Austin's Order Book for the Campaign of 1835," *Quarterly of the Texas State Historical Association*, XI, 1–55; Fred H. Turner, "The Mejia Expedition," *ibid.*, VII, 1–28; E. C. Barker, "Proceedings of the Permanent Council," *ibid.*, IX, 287–88; E. C. Barker (ed.), "Journal of the Permanent Council," *ibid.*, VII, 249–78; E. C. Barker, "The Texan Declaration of Causes for Taking Up Arms against Mexico," *ibid.*, XV, 173–85; E. C. Barker, "The Tampico Expedition," *ibid.*, VI, 169–86; Ralph Steen, "Analysis of the Work of the General Council of Texas, 1835–1836," *Southwestern Historical Quarterly*, XL, 309–33; XLI, 225–40; E. C. Barker, "Don Carlos Barrett," *ibid.*, XX, 139–45; R. S. Lee, "The Publication of Austin's Louisville Address," *ibid.*, LXX, 424–42; Raymond Estep, "Lorenzo de Zavala and the Texas Revolution," *ibid.*, LVII, 322–35; Miles S. Bennett, "The Battle of Gonzales, the 'Lexington' of the Texas Revolution," *Quarterly of the Texas State Historical Association*, II, 313–16; E. C. Barker, "The Texas Revolutionary Army," *ibid.*, IX, 227–61; *The Texans* (Time-Life Books, 1975); Katherine Hart and Elizabeth Kemp (eds.), "E. M. Pease's Account of the Texas Revolution," *Southwestern Historical Quarterly*, LXVIII, 79–89.

On the war in the field, see: E. C. Barker, "The Texan Revolutionary Army,"

Quarterly of the Texas State Historical Association, IX, 227–61; E. C. Barker, "The San Jacinto Campaign," *ibid.*, IV, 237–345; John E. Roller, "Captain John Sowers Brooks," *ibid.*, IX, 157–209, contains letters from a soldier with Fannin; Ruby C. Smith, "James W. Fannin, Jr., in the Texas Revolution," *Southwestern Historical Quarterly*, XXIII, 79–90, 171–203, 271–84; Harbert Davenport, "Captain Jesus Cuellar, Texas Cavalry, Otherwise Comanche," *ibid.*, XX, 56–62; Amelia Williams, "A Critical Study of the Siege of the Alamo . . . ," *ibid.*, XXXVI, 251–87; XXXVII, 1–44, 79–115, 157–84, 237–312; James W. Pohl and Stephen Hardin, "The Military History of the Texas Revolution: An Overview," *ibid.*, LXXXIX, 269–308; Don Graham, "Remembering the Alamo: The Story of the Texas Revolution in Popular Culture," *ibid.*, LXXXIX, 35–66; M. L. Bonham, Jr., "James Butler Bonham: A Consistent Rebel," *ibid.*, XXXV, 124–36; H. Davenport, "The Men of Goliad," *ibid.*, XLIII, 1–41 (an interpretation of the entire Texan Revolution); H. M. Henderson, "A Critical Analysis of the San Jacinto Campaign," *ibid.*, LIX, 344–62; Jewel D. Scarborough, "The Georgia Battalion in the Texas Revolution: A Critical Study," *ibid.*, LXIII, 511–532; Thomas I. Miller, "Fannin's Men: Some Additions to Earlier Rosters," *ibid.*, LXI, 522–532; James Presley, "Santa Anna in Texas: A Mexican Viewpoint," *ibid.*, LXII, 489–512; Walter Lord, *A Time to Stand* (New York, 1961); Lon Tinkle, *Thirteen Days to Glory* (New York, 1958); Sam H. Dixon and Louis W. Kemp, *The Heroes of San Jacinto* (Houston, 1932).

For an account of the convention of 1836 see R. N. Richardson, "Framing the Constitution of the Republic of Texas," *Southwestern Historical Quarterly*, XXXI, 191–220; J. K. Greer, "The Committee of the Texas Declaration of Independence," *ibid.*, XXX, 239–51; XXI, 33–49, 130–49; Henderson Shuffler, "The Signing of Texas' Declaration of Independence: Myth and Reality," *ibid.*, LXV, 310–32; L. W. Kemp, *The Signers of the Texas Declaration of Independence* (Houston, 1944).

On developments after the Battle of San Jacinto, see W. C. Binkley, "Activities of the Texan Revolutionary Army after San Jacinto," *Journal of Southern History*, VI, 331–46.

Valuable for the period of the revolution as well as before and after is Fane Downs, "Tryels and Trubbles: Women in Early Nineteenth-Century Texas," *Southwestern Historical Quarterly*, XC, 35–56.

Concerning the attitude of President Jackson toward the Texan Revolution, two points of view are presented in E. C. Barker, "President Jackson and the Texas Revolution," *American Historical Review*, XII, 797–803; and R. C. Stenberg, "The Texas Schemes of Jackson and Houston, 1829–1836," *Southwestern Social Science Quarterly*, XV, 229–50.

J. E. Winston has published in the *Southwestern Historical Quarterly* a series of articles on aid from the United States. See XVI, 27–62, 277–83; XXI, 36–60; XVIII, 368–85; and XVII, 262–82. See also C. Elliott, "Alabama and the Texas Revolution," *ibid.*, IL, 316–28.

On the Texan navy, see Alex Dienst, "The Navy of the Republic of Texas," *Quarterly of the Texas State Historical Association*, XII, 165–203, 249–75; XIII, 1–43, 85–127; Jim Dan Hill, *The Texas Navy* (Chicago, 1937); George G. Haugh (ed.), "History of the Texas Navy," *Southwestern Historical Quarterly*, LXIII, 572–579.

CHAPTER SEVEN
THE REPUBLIC OF TEXAS 1836–1846

For ten years Texas existed as an independent republic. These were exciting, challenging years, often troubled with conflict and controversy but also filled with progress and accomplishment. In politics, the nation tended to align itself into factions either pro- or anti-Houston, a division that was in part a matter of politics and personalities but was also based on policy issues. Despite problems of money and Indian wars, immigrants continued to respond to a generous land policy and the population grew at an amazing pace.

In foreign affairs Texans managed to achieve a degree of success, although acceptance by other nations came slowly in some instances and not at all in others. Relations with Mexico were not good in the beginning and improved little, if at all. A minority of Texans firmly believed that the future of Texas as an independent nation was promising, but most hoped for annexation to the United States and rejoiced when that was finally accomplished.

THE ELECTION OF 1836

Even after the Texan victory at San Jacinto, the *ad interim* government had to cope with many critical problems. Consequently, President Burnet and his cabinet, without waiting until December as the convention had proposed, issued on July 23 a proclamation setting the first Monday of the following September as the date for an election. Three major issues were to be decided: first, ratification of the constitution; second, the election of the constitutional officers who would take office provided the voters approved the constitution; and third, whether the next government should seek annexation to the United States.

The ratification of the constitution and a favorable vote on annexation were unquestionably certain; thus the major interest in the election centered on the selection of a president. Since there were no political parties in Texas at the time, the candidates had to depend largely on their general popularity. Henry Smith, the first to announce for the presidency, sought to vindicate his policies as head of the provisional government. Austin entered the race at the solicitation of William Wharton, Branch Archer, and others. Despite his distinguished and unselfish service to Texas, Austin had become exceedingly unpopular. His early opposition to independence, his support of the government in saving Santa Anna from a firing squad, and the charge that he had not served Texas well while in the United States adversely affected his popularity.

It was soon evident that the third presidential candidate, Sam Houston, was the people's choice. Just 11 days before the election he formally accepted the nomination by numerous groups throughout the nation. In the election he received 5,110 votes, almost 80 percent of the total, Smith 743, and Austin, 587. Mirabeau B. Lamar was elected vice-president. The constitution was approved overwhelmingly. Only 233 voters were in favor of giving Congress the power to amend it, and only 93 voted against the mandate requiring the new president to negotiate for annexation to the United States.

HOUSTON'S FIRST ADMINISTRATION (1836–1838)

President Houston actually took office before his term began. *Ad interim* President Burnet convened the First Congress in Columbia on October 3, but there was a growing demand for Houston and Lamar to take office without waiting until the second Monday in December, as provided in the constitution. On October 22 Burnet resigned, and Houston took the oath of office as the first constitutionally elected president of the Republic of Texas. In his impromptu inaugural address, Houston spoke only briefly of his program, one based on his belief that Texas would soon be a part of the United States.

Houston's cabinet, which he claimed was selected "with a total disregard to personal preference" and "for the furtherance of the interests of the Country," was quickly determined. Austin, long the leader of con-

Columbia, the capital of Texas, 1836. (Southwest Collection, Texas Tech University)

servative Texans, was made secretary of state, and Henry Smith was appointed secretary of the treasury. Austin died about two months after taking office and was replaced by Dr. Robert Irion, a native of Tennessee. William Wharton was sent to represent the republic in Washington. James Collinsworth, a lawyer who nominated Houston to be commander in chief of the army in 1836, was appointed chief justice. The chief justice, acting

Sam Houston. Elected governor of Tennessee in 1827, Houston seemed to have a secure political future when two years later he resigned and moved to what is now Oklahoma, to rejoin the Cherokee Indians by whom he had been adopted in his youth. Houston came to Texas in 1833 and became a member of the conventions that declared Texas independent of Mexico and set up a provisional government. Criticized for retreating before the Mexicans, Houston regained popular favor when he defeated Santa Anna at San Jacinto in April 1836 and was elected the first president of the republic. (E. C. Barker History Center, University of Texas)

with the four district judges provided for in the law, constituted the supreme court.

The First Congress likewise quickly went about its work. It created 22 counties, corresponding in most cases to the Mexican municipalities (by 1845 there were 36). Each county was to have a court with a chief justice and two associate justices, elected by the county's justices of the peace. Congress also defined the limits of the republic with a law of December 19, 1836, setting the boundary at the center of the Rio Grande from its mouth to its source, north to the forty-second parallel, and east and south along the Adams-Onís Treaty line to the Gulf of Mexico. In response to threats of a Mexican invasion and to fear of hostile Indians, Congress in December authorized an army of 3,587 troops and 280 mounted rangers, a chain of forts and trading houses on the frontier, the enrollment of all able-bodied males between the ages of 21 and 50 in a militia organization, and the creation of a new navy.

Houston, however, was more interested in getting rid of the army than in increasing its size. The army, already insubordinate over the release of Santa Anna and commanders assigned to it, wanted to renew hostilities with Mexico with an invasion of Matamoros. Its morale did not improve when Houston named Thomas Rusk secretary of war. When Houston appointed Albert Sidney Johnston, a capable West Point officer, to take command, the army reaction was very nearly that of mutiny, as the soldiers rallied in support of their favorite, Felix Huston, a military adventurer. Huston challenged Johnston to a duel, wounded him, and retained the command. President Houston, however, solved the problem. In May 1837, while Huston was lobbying congressmen for authorization to lead a campaign into Mexico, the President furloughed or disbanded all but six hundred of the troops, offering free transportation to New Orleans to those who desired to return to the United States or two sections (1,280 acres) of land to those who would accept a discharge and settle in Texas. To offset the reduction in the strength of the army, Congress then provided for a corps of rangers eventually to be known as "Texas Rangers." Some names, famous for their daring, fearlessness, and heroism associated with this initial group included John Coffee ("Jack") Hays, Samuel H. Walker, Ben McCulloch, W. A. ("Bigfoot") Wallace, and John S. ("Rip") Ford.

Indian problems, which were primarily responsible for the organization of the ranger units, were indeed serious. Raids, mostly involving Comanche and Kiowas, threatened settlements on the frontier. In one of the raids, Comanches took one of their most famous captives, Cynthia Ann Parker, who later married a Comanche chief. In later years her son, Quanah Parker, was one of the great war chiefs of the Comanches. Ranger patrols in 1837 did not eliminate the raids of the kind which led to the captivity of Cynthia Ann Parker, but the problem was diminished.

First capital at Houston, 1837. (Southwest Collection, Texas Tech University)

A great part of Texas was once Comanche country. Pictured here is Quanah Parker, one of the last Comanche war chiefs and the son of Chief Nocona and Cynthia Ann Parker, a captive white woman. (Bureau of American Ethnology)

Another threatening situation concerned relations with the Cherokees in East Texas. The Cherokees began moving into Texas as early as 1819, settling on a vague grant given by the Spanish in the vicinity of Nacogdoches. During the Texas revolution, Sam Houston, by authority of the Consultation, negotiated with them a treaty providing for permanent title to their lands, in exchange for their promise to remain at peace during the war. When the senate, defying Houston's admonition, refused to ratify the treaty, the Cherokees and their associated tribes threatened to make trouble. Adding to the tension and confusion, Vicente Cordova, a Mexican citizen of Nacogdoches and an agent of the Mexican government, in the summer of 1838 led a band of nearly six hundred Mexicans and Kickapoo Indians in a rebellion near the Angelina River. The rebellion was of short duration, but Cordova and some of his Indian allies continued to pose a threat. Although the Cherokees were not involved in the affair, it generated a considerable amount of hostility toward all Indians in the area. Houston managed to preserve the rights of the Cherokees and a fragile peace for the balance of his term, but in no way did he achieve a permanent solution.

Money was another major problem of the Houston administration. Public expenses amounted to nearly $2 million, and income was a mere fraction of this amount. A tariff was the most productive tax. Tonnage dues and port fees, a direct property tax, poll taxes, business taxes, and land fees each added a little. Even when paid, the receipts were generally not in the form of specie and of limited value. The poverty of the government at times was embarrassing. For a period, Secretary of the Treasury Henry Smith could not attend to his duties because he had no stationery

President's mansion, Houston, 1837. (Southwest Collection, Texas Tech University)

and no funds with which to buy any. Houston could secure supplies for the army only by pledging his personal credit. Under such conditions the government turned to the use of paper money. Acts of 1837 led to the issue of $650,000 in promissory notes which held their value very well, but a succeeding issue soon depreciated to as little as sixty-five cents on the dollar.

Selecting a presidential candidate for the 1838 election proved difficult. Houston, restricted by the constitutional provision limiting the first president to two years, was not eligible to seek reelection. His supporters turned to others but without much success. Thomas J. Rusk refused to run. Peter W. Grayson, attorney general and commissioner to Washington, agreed to run, but while on an official mission to the United States, he took his own life. The Houston party then turned to 30-year-old James Collinsworth, a hero of the Battle of San Jacinto and chief justice of the supreme court, but in July 1838 he jumped from a boat in Galveston Bay and drowned, apparently a suicide victim. A few weeks before the election, the Houston group agreed to support Robert Wilson of Harrisburg, a promoter of the town of Houston and for a time a member of the senate. By this time it was clearly evident that Vice-President Lamar, a candidate but surely no Houston supporter, would be president. The vote for Lamar on November 16 was almost unanimous. David G. Burnet was elected vice-president.

LAMAR'S ADMINISTRATION (1838–1841)

In his inaugural address and first message to Congress, President Lamar promised an ambitious public program in keeping with his belief that Texas should remain an independent republic. Although some of his plans did not prove successful, others were adopted and of enduring value.

Lamar, who urged the enactment of the necessary laws, was a strong advocate of the development of public education. Accordingly, an act of January 20, 1839, provided that each country should be given three square leagues for primary schools and that fifty square leagues should be set aside for two colleges or universities. A year later a law provided additional lands for each county, and Congress also made land grants to several private institutions. Lands were cheap, and many years were to pass before Texas had even the semblance of a system of public education, but these laws, in large measure the responsibility of Lamar, laid the foundations.

A second piece of legislation to leave Lamar's trademark permanently on Texas was the Homestead Law. This measure, enacted on January 26, 1839, was the first legislation of its kind passed by any country that limited the seizure of property for debt. The property exemption, unknown in English common law, may have been influenced by Spanish law.

The location of a permanent capital for Texas was selected during the Lamar administration. The question concerning the seat of government

Mirabeau Buonaparte Lamar came to Texas from Georgia to join the revolutionaries in 1835 and took part in the Battle of San Jacinto. During his term as the second president of the republic (1838–1841), he secured foreign recognition of Texas's independence. He had hoped to make the republic self-sufficient, but his ill-advised expeditions to New Mexico left Texas in financial difficulties. (E. C. Barker History Center, University of Texas)

was carried over from Houston's regime. Columbia, the first location, was a temporary one for only a few months. In December 1836 Congress voted to move the seat of government to the new town of Houston in May 1837, with the stipulation that a permanent location would be designated by 1840. Prompted by Lamar, Congress in January 1839 authorized the appointment of a committee to select a site between the Colorado and Brazos rivers and north of the "Old San Antonio Road" and decided that it should be named for Stephen F. Austin. The commissioners chose a site near the small settlement of Waterloo on the Colorado River at the foot of the Balcones Escarpment. At that point they believed the roads linking the Red River with Matamoros and Santa Fe with Gulf of Mexico would intersect. In October 1839 President Lamar and his cabinet proceeded to the new capital. Four months later the town claimed a population of 856.

Upon assuming the presidency, Lamar immediately inaugurated a major change in Indian policy. Indians must either conform to Texas laws, leave the nation, or be exterminated. Secretary of War Albert Sidney Johnston, a majority of Congress, and many others agreed with him and urged an aggressive frontier policy. Actually, relations between Texan settlers and several Indian tribes were already critical. The Cherokees and associated tribes in eastern Texas had been put off with promises for too long; they were uneasy and unhappy. Farther west, the Wacos, Tawakonis, and Comanches, seeing settlers penetrate their hunting grounds deeper each season, were already on the warpath. Consequently, Lamar's administration was marked by the bloodiest Indian wars Texas had known.

The Cherokees were the first to be uprooted by Lamar's hostile Indian policy. Although the Cherokees remained at peace during Houston's term, other tribes made sporadic raids, and some settlers continued to believe that the Cherokees were conspiring with Mexican authorities. Papers taken from a party of marauders killed in a battle near Austin in May 1839 convinced Lamar and his cabinet that the tribe was in treasonable correspondence with the Mexicans. When the Cherokees defied Lamar's orders to leave peacefully and rejected a promise of compensation for their crops, an army of several hundred men marched into their country. In the Battle of the Neches on July 16, near the present city of Tyler, the Texans defeated several hundred Cherokee warriors led by Chief Bowles. Bowles, along with almost one hundred of his warriors, was killed, and the remainder were driven across the Red River into Indian Territory. The Shawnees and some other groups then abandoned the area, and the peaceful Alabama and Coushatta were moved to other lands in Texas.

The war with the Comanches was longer and more bloody. Disturbed by the westward advance of the Texans, some southern Comanches in 1838 asked for peace. President Houston, however, refused their demand for a boundary, and when Lamar became president, Comanche raids on the frontier were frequent. Congress promptly provided Lamar with punitive military forces, but the early campaigns were not rewarding. On February 14, 1839, J. H. Moore with three small companies of volunteers unsuccessfully attacked a Comanche village at Spring Creek in the valley of the San Saba. Later in the spring an Indian band of about three hundred, mostly Comanches, threatened another force of Texans with annihilation near present-day Belton.

Notwithstanding their victories, early in 1840 the southern Comanches requested a peace council. The offer was accepted, provided the Comanches would bring to the council in San Antonio all their white captives. On March 19, 1840, the Comanches, sixty-five men, women, and children, arrived for the council, bringing only one captive—Matilda Lockhart, a badly mutilated 15-year-old girl who had been captured near Gonzales in 1838. When the Texans, who had hidden troops in an adjacent room, attempted to take the Comanche warriors as hostages, a battle erupted in which 35 Indians were killed and 29 were taken prisoner. The Texans had 7 killed and 8 wounded. When they heard of the affair, known as the Council House Fight, other Comanches killed their prisoners. That summer they raided Victoria and destroyed Linnville near the town of Port Lavaca. As it moved homeward toward the plains, heavily loaded with booty, the raiding party was intercepted and defeated at Plum Creek near Lockhart on August 12 by a Texan force led by Edward Burleson, Felix Huston, and Ben McCulloch. Almost one hundred Comanches were killed but others escaped with most of their plunder. War was renewed in the autumn. In October Colonel J. H. Moore led an expedition in search of the elusive Comanches, and aided by Lipan Apaches, on October 23 surprised them and destroyed their village on the Colorado River, probably in the vicinity of present Ballinger. The Texans killed an estimated 130 Comanches and regained a large amount of the plunder and livestock taken on the Linnville raid. The Comanches thereupon withdrew far from the Texas frontier. By the end of 1840 Indian wars in Texas had practically ceased, but only until the end of the Republic.

The justice and humanity of Lamar's campaigns may be questioned but not their effectiveness. Lamar's Indian policy cost $2.5 million and the lives of several scores of white people and a larger number of Indians. However, his troops opened to settlers the rich Indian lands of eastern Texas, emptied the area of most of its Indians, and made the western frontier comparatively safe for advancing settlers for several years.

Lamar's financial program was not as successful. Financial affairs, not good under Houston, grew constantly worse during the Lamar administration. Tariff duties were reduced; other taxes were difficult to collect. Receipts for the three year period were $1,083,661, and expenditures were $4,855,213. The government sought a loan of $5 million, but determined efforts over several years resulted only in one loan of $457,380 from the Bank of the United States. Lamar proposed a gigantic Texas bank to be owned by the government, but Congress refused to approve his plan. Without more capital the establishment of the bank was impossible anyway.

The administration resorted to the expedient of paper money—in large amounts. When Lamar assumed office, there was outstanding more than $800,000 of treasury notes (paper money), already valued at eighty to eighty-five cents on the dollar. In 1839, 1840, and 1841 Congress authorized more notes, known as "red backs," amounting to $3,552,800. The value of these depended upon the confidence of the people, which apparently was very little. By November 1841 the "red backs" were quoted at twelve to fifteen cents on the dollar. Meanwhile, the public debt, approximately $2 million at the end of Houston's first term, rose to $7 million at the close of Lamar's term.

HOUSTON'S SECOND ADMINISTRATION (1841–1844)

By the end of the Lamar administration, voters were divided into two distinct camps: the administration group and the opposition led by Houston. It was natural, therefore, that Houston, who since the end of his presidential term had served in the house of representatives, should become the candidate to succeed Lamar. Administration forces supported David Burnet. There were issues such as public finances, Indian policies, and land policies, but issues were incidental. The campaign centered on gossip, scandal, and vituperation, which was of little credit to either side.

The race was not even close. Houston received 7,915 votes to Burnet's 3,616. Edward Burleson, perhaps as much of an independent as one could be, was elected vice-president.

As anticipated, the administration of Houston and a conservative Congress was in sharp contrast to Lamar's ambitious and costly programs. The Sixth Congress carried economy to the point of parsimony. Offices were abolished, the number of clerks was reduced, and salaries were lowered below a living wage. Military expeditions after 1841 were confined to the maintenance of a few companies of rangers. Total expenditures for Houston's term of three years was only a little more than $500,000. Only $200,000 of "exchequer bills" (paper money) were issued, but even though this was the only currency to be used in the payment of taxes, the money declined in value.

The frugality of the government was well-demonstrated in an effort to sell the Texas navy. When the navy continued to call for more money for needed repairs, the Congress in January 1843 solved the problem with a secret act ordering the sale of the four vessels. However, the people of Galveston were enthusiastic about the little fleet and sympathetic with its commander, Edwin W. Moore, who had been insubordinate, declared a pirate, and dishonorably discharged. By force certain citizens of Galveston prevented the auction of the four ships. After Texas became a part of the United States, the ships were transferred to the United States Navy.

Houston's pacific Indian policy, similar to that of his first administration, saved both money and lives. In September 1843 a treaty was signed at Bird's Fort with the Waco, Tawakoni, and other sedentary tribes. On October 8, 1844, near present-day Waco, President Houston and Chief Buffalo Hump for the Penateka Comanches signed the Treaty of Tehuacana Creek providing for trade and friendship. These treaties and Houston's peaceful policies reinforced Lamar's aggressive and successful military campaigns to preserve peace on the frontier.

Houston also brought peace to East Texas in the settlement of a feud between the "Regulators" and "Moderators." Almost as serious as the Indian problem, the feud had its beginnings as far back as the time of the Neutral Ground agreement. Killings started in 1840 in Shelby County but spread to neighboring counties. The Regulators, avowedly organized to suppress crime, were opposed by the Moderators, who claimed that the Regulators burned homes, forced families to leave their homes, and committed other excesses. Soon the opposing factions numbered about 150 each. President Houston ordered 600 militia men to the scene, and partly by force and partly by persuasion, reestablished peace in the area.

In 1844, Dr. Anson Jones, generally regarded as a Houston man and administration candidate, was elected president. Jones, a physician, member of Congress, and secretary of state, did not always support Houston's policies, but his election was viewed as a measure of Houston's popularity.

Although he denied any such connection, Vice-President Edward Burleson, who ran against Jones, was considered to be the candidate of the Lamar party. The vote was 7,037 for Jones to 5,668 for Burleson, with Jones winning in the east and Burleson carrying the west.

THE LAND POLICY OF THE REPUBLIC

Texans in the revolution had hardly returned to their homes from the army or from the "runaway scrape" before their kinspeople from east of the Sabine began to join them. In May 1837 the *Telegraph and Texas Register* stated that "crowds of enterprising emigrants are arriving on every vessel...." The following summer reports claimed that 6,000 immigrants crossed the Sabine on one ferry. Accounts indicate that in 1840 more immigrants arrived than had in any previous year and that the volume was sustained until the early part of 1842. Problems with Mexico in 1842 checked the flow sharply but by 1844 a veritable stream of homeseekers was arriving almost daily. Trains of immigrants gathered at the ferry crossings and had to wait for hours. The white population, estimated in 1836 at 34,470, had reached 102,961 by 1847; the slave population, estimated at 5,000 in 1836, had reached 38,753. Adding the 295 free blacks, the total population of Texas, except for Indians, was 142,009.

The liberal land policy of the republic and the Anglo-American lust for free or inexpensive virgin land was responsible for this phenomenal migration. The constitution specified that heads of families (blacks and Indians excepted) living in the republic on March 2, 1836, might receive free a First Class headright of a square league and a *labor* of land (4,605 acres) and that single men above seventeen years of age might receive one-third of a square league (1,476 acres). Congress later enacted measures that extended the land grants to others in smaller quantities. Laws created three additional categories of headrights, Second, Third, and Fourth Class, with the classification dependent upon the time of arrival in Texas, and amounts of land awarded accordingly. In no instance was the amount of land given under a headright less than 320 acres. Altogether, the republic granted 36,876,492 acres in headright certificates to reward those who aided in the struggle for independence or to encourage immigration.

Determined to make Texas a nation of homeowners, the lawmakers went even further. They enacted a limited homestead law in 1838 (preceding similar legislation in the United States by a quarter of a century). The following year they passed the Homestead Exemption Act, exempting from seizure for debt the home, 50 acres of land, and certain improvements. In 1845 Congress gave in a preemption act the opportunity for settlers living on vacant public lands an option to purchase (generally at fifty cents an acre) up to 320 acres. Ultimately, under the preemption and homestead laws Texas granted 4,847,136 acres. Additional lands were granted to permanently disabled veterans, to those who had participated in the Battle of San Jacinto, and to the heirs of the men who had fallen in the Alamo and in the Matamoros and Goliad campaigns. Even the soldiers who served after the end of the fighting were given lands.

The actual distribution of the land was done by a board of land commissioners in each county. The board validated the type or class of certificate, approved the claim of the applicant after the surveying of the proposed land, and certified the application to the General Land Office for the issuance of a land patent. The system, drawn partly from practices in southern states of the United States and Spanish and Mexican practices, cost little except for the modest fees charged to the applicants.

Although there were some forgeries and fraudulent claims, these were not the most unfortunate consequence of the land policies. The aim of the lawmakers to place the land in the possession of actual settlers was only partly attained. Inasmuch as many of the programs for acquiring land had no residence requirements, speculators went into the western areas far ahead of the settlements and surveyed and secured title to lands. Later, when *bona fide* settlers came, they found the best country already taken, sometimes as much as 10 to 30 years earlier.

CONTRACTS WITH IMMIGRANT AGENTS

In its eagerness for new citizens, the government of the republic turned to the use of contracts with immigrant agents, much like the *empresario* agreements under Mexican rule. Congress authorized these contracts with an act in February 1841 and a general colonization law on February 5, 1842. Most important were those made with W. S. Peters and Associates, afterwards known as the Texas Emigration and Land Company; Charles F. Mercer; Henri Castro; and with Fisher and Miller, afterwards transferred to the German Emigration Company. Although the contracts with these companies differed in certain details, they were alike in all essentials. Within a given area designated as "the colony," all unappropriated public land was closed to settlement by others until the proprietor had completed his contract or it had been declared forfeit. The contractor was allowed ten sections for each 100 families. He might also secure additional compensation from his colonists for surveying the land, erecting cabins, moving the colonists to Texas, and supplying certain necessities. The republic, and afterwards the state, retained alternate sections, and it was from the sale of these that it expected to secure revenue for the government.

Congress in February 1841 approved the request of a Louisville group, headed by W. S. Peters, for a grant on which to settle a colony of settlers from the United States. As finally amended, the contract with W. S.

Peters and Associates set aside for the colony more than 16,000 square miles, bounded on the north by the Red River, on the east by a line which ran south from the Red River to the vicinity of present-day Ennis, on the south by a line extending to the west to a point between present-day Cisco and Abilene, and on the west by a line extending to the north from that point to the Red River. The settlers, mostly nonslaveholders from the Ohio River Valley and Missouri, began arriving in 1841. They received Third Class headrights free (320 or 640 acres), without even any survey cost. Soon, however, the company was troubled by dissatisfied colonists, Texans who held certificates and wanted to locate in the area, and a government that seemingly changed its mind and wanted to terminate the contract. The attorney general in 1845 instituted proceedings to cancel the contract, giving rise to a considerable amount of subsequent legislation and litigation. By 1848, however, the company had introduced 2,205 families, located in the eastern portion of the grant.

Three *empresario* contracts were awarded under the general colonization law of 1842. One with Charles F. Mercer, signed just before Congress discontinued *empresario* contracts in early 1844, called for the location of families in a large area lying mainly south and east of Peters' colony and in that colony, subject to Peters' prior rights. Mercer and Associates met with difficulties similar to those that confronted Peters. A judicial decree declared the contract void in October 1848 because of the failure of Mercer to meet all of its requirements, but thereafter came more legislation and litigation.

Henri Castro, a Frenchman, was another and most energetic *empresario*. He advertised his colony extensively in Europe, and by March 1, 1843, about 300 colonists, mostly from the Rhine provinces of France, set out for Texas. The area assigned to him was the Indian-inhabited country between the Nueces and the Rio Grande. One tract was about 50 miles southwest of San Antonio and another in Starr County on the lower Rio Grande. Castro laid out the town of Castroville, the first permanent settlement between San Antonio and the Rio Grande, in September 1844, and by 1847 he had introduced 2,134 colonists.

The contract with Henry F. Fisher and Burchard Miller brought a large migration of Germans to Texas. In February 1842 and January 1844 Fisher and Miller contracted to locate six thousand colonists on a grant of three million acres lying between the Llano and Colorado rivers. Before introducing any settlers, however, they sold their grant to the *Adelsverein* (Society for the Protection of German Immigrants in Texas), organized in 1842 by a group of German noblemen for the purpose of promoting German immigration to Texas. With the founding of Industry in Austin County, a German settlement had been made in Texas as early as 1838, but the *Adelsverein* developed German immigration on a large scale. Its agent, Prince Carl of Solms-Braunfels who visited Texas in 1844, purchased for the society the Fisher and Miller lands, an extensive area north of San Antonio, and a tract on Matagorda Bay. Early in 1845 the society's first settlers established New Braunfels, named for the prince. During the next year the society founded Fredericksburg, about eighty miles north of New Braunfels but outside the Fisher and Miller grant. Indians, particularly the Penateka Comanches, threatened the settlement until 1847 when John O. Muesebach (Baron Ottfried Hans Freiherr von Muesebach, Solms-Braunfels' successor) exchanged presents worth three thousand dollars with the tribe for a treaty of peace. Fredericksburg grew rapidly; by 1850 its population was 754. Other settlements, such as Sisterdale, Boerne, and Comfort, were made, but many settlers avoided the area, still fearful of the Indians and unwilling to settle that far from the coast.

Perhaps the most interesting of the *empresario* proposals was one that was never approved. This was the proposal of the Franco-Texienne Company to introduce 8,000 French families and to establish 20 forts to form a barrier between the hostile Indians in the west and the Texas frontier. Even if all other problems could have been solved, the contract would have created a semiautonomous state on the border, thus threatening the unity of Texas. A bill to authorize the contract was introduced in January 1841. It passed the House of Representatives, perhaps because Congressman Sam Houston in one of his less prudent actions supported it, as did the French minister to Texas, Count Alphonse de Saligny. However, it was never considered by the Senate, probably because of opposition from President Lamar and David Burnet.

Although *empresario* projects enjoyed some success, the day of the *empresario* was near its end. It was no longer expedient to close from the general public thousands of square miles of public lands while an *empresario* appropriated the best lands. Predictably, persons holding land certificates opposed such colonization contracts in every way possible. Early in 1844 Congress passed (over Houston's veto) a bill repealing all laws authorizing colonization contracts and requiring the president to declare forfeited all that had not been complied with strictly.

THE EXTENSION OF SETTLEMENT

The frontier of Texas, which in 1836 lay approximately south and east of a line from San Antonio along the old road to Nacogdoches and extending north to the Red River, moved steadily westward each year thereafter. At first the most rapid advance was from the northeast corner where there was an abundance of timber, rich soil, good grass, and little fear of Mexican invasion. Moreover, the Red River after 1835, when a raft blocking navigation was removed, offered an outlet to the Gulf, sometimes on steamboats, during months of high water. From settlements such as Pecan Point and

Jonesborough on the Red River near Clarksville, settlers moved westward into Grayson County. From Bowie, Red River, and Lamar counties, they pushed southward into both the timbered country of Hopkins, Wood, and Van Zandt counties and the prairies of Hunt, Collin, and Kaufman. In 1844 Ben Anderson's store constituted the beginning of Greenville.

Meanwhile, the advance from the northeast had reached the upper Trinity. John Neely Bryan, a Tennessean, pitched his lonely cabin in 1841 near the three forks of the Trinity in Peters's Colony. Three years later his widely advertised town of Dallas had only two families and two small cabins. Peters's Colony headquarters at nearby Farmer's Branch was the larger settlement, but Dallas grew more rapidly after 1846 when it became the county seat.

While settlers were advancing from the northeast, settlers were likewise moving westward from the southeast along the lower Trinity, Brazos, and Colorado valleys. Parker's Fort near the Navasota River in Limestone County, which was established in 1834 but abandoned after a major Indian attack in 1836, was reoccupied shortly thereafter. Robertson County immediately to the south was organized in 1837; settlers began to locate in present-day Leon County in 1839; and by the close of 1846, Limestone, Navarro, and other counties in the vicinity had been formed.

Indian problems hindered the settlement of the valley of the Brazos. It was not until Houston's negotiation of a treaty with the tribes in the area in 1843 that white settlers were able to live even in partial security in Bell County. The Torrey Brothers and Associates' trading house was established in 1842 about eight miles southeast of the present-city of Waco. Two years later Neal McLennan settled not far away on the South Bosque, and in 1849 George B. Erath laid out the town of Waco. Three years afterwards, George Barnard established an Indian trading post farther up the Brazos River in present-day Hood County. Indian hostilities likewise delayed settlements along the Colorado River, but a few farmers had reached the vicinity of Austin when the town was laid out in 1839.

Fear of Mexican invasions as well as Indian depredations retarded the advance of settlements in southern Texas. For some time after the Mexican invasion of 1836, the counties of San Patricio, Victoria, Goliad, and Refugio were almost depopulated. However, in 1839 Henry L. Kinney and William Aubrey established a trading post in the vicinity of present-day Corpus Christi at the mouth of the Nueces River. The area between the Nueces and the Rio Grande was not organized into counties until sometime later.

By 1846, when a state government replaced that of the republic, the frontier line of settlement extended from Corpus Christi to San Antonio in the southwest, and northward through New Braunfels, Fredericksburg, Austin, Belton, Waco, Dallas, and Collin County to Preston on the Red River near the present city of Denison.

RELATIONS WITH THE UNITED STATES (1836–1839)

During the revolution and afterwards, relations with the United States were of particular concern to Texans. The Texas government sought aid—even intervention on its behalf—diplomatic recognition, and if possible, annexation by the United States at the earliest date possible. The first commissioners, Austin, Archer, and Wharton, were soon replaced by other representatives. James Collinsworth and Peter W. Grayson, the last representatives sent by the *ad interim* government, accomplished little, except to learn that President Andrew Jackson had sent an agent, Henry M. Morfit, to secure more information about affairs in Texas.

Houston, who considered the vote of September 1836 in favor of annexation a mandate, diligently pursued both annexation and diplomatic recognition. Santa Anna, still a prisoner, suggested that he be allowed to support the transfer of Texas to the United States in an interview with President Jackson. Despite the protests of Congress, Houston, who wanted to get his prisoner out of Texas, sent Santa Anna to Washington under escort. Jackson paid little attention to the Mexican leader and promptly sent him to Vera Cruz aboard an United States naval vessel.

Houston's commissioners in Washington, William H. Wharton, assisted by Memucan Hunt, found little encouragement. Morfit, Jackson's agent sent to Texas, reported unfavorably on affairs in the new nation, and the president's message to Congress in December, 1836, advocated delay in recognizing Texas independence. There was doubt as to the ability of Texas to maintain its independence, fear of offending Mexico, and belief that recognition would be regarded as a preliminary step toward annexation. Jackson, however, told Wharton that he would approve recognition if Congress would recommend it. Working diligently, Wharton and Hunt, with the aid of various supporters, persuaded Congress to appropriate expenses for a diplomatic agent to Texas whenever the President should deem it expedient. In his last official act, President Jackson appointed Alcee LaBranche *charge d'affaires* to the Republic of Texas.

Recognition now attained, Texas pressed for annexation, but Hunt's formal offer made on August 4, 1837, was firmly rejected. According to John Forsythe, the United States Secretary of State, treaty obligations with Mexico prevented the United States from entertaining the subject. A stream of memorials and petitions were submitted to the United States Congress in the fall of 1837, but opposition was very strong, particularly from anti-slavery forces, and no vote was ever taken. Shortly thereafter, Anson Jones, then representing Texas in Washington and acting under Houston's order, announced the "formal and absolute withdrawal" of the offer. The Texas Congress with President Lamar's sanction ratified the withdrawal on January 23, 1839. Annexation was not again an issue until 1843.

RECOGNITION BY EUROPEAN POWERS

In the summer of 1837 President Houston, convinced that the United States would not consider annexation and acting with the approval of Congress, opened diplomatic negotiations with the European powers. He sent Secretary of State J. Pinckney Henderson as minister plenipotentiary to Great Britain and France to secure recognition and negotiate commercial treaties. Lord Palmerston, British minister of foreign affairs, was disappointingly indifferent. England was opposed to slavery; British capitalists had millions invested in Mexican bonds; and England was not interested in aiding a nation that probably would soon join the United States. Henderson did, however, in 1838 secure a convention with Great Britain that provided for trade between Texas and that country.

France was more interested in a treaty of friendship with Texas. The French were involved in a war (the Pastry War) with Mexico; Texas had by this time withdrawn its offer of annexation to the United States; and Lamar, now president of the young republic, was firm in his determination to maintain an independent nation. Lamar's commissioner to France, James Hamilton, a former governor of South Carolina, was an experienced diplomat. Aided by Henderson, he signed a commercial treaty with France on September 25, 1839, but failed in his other mission, the negotiation of a much-needed loan. Thus, France was the first European nation to recognize the independence of Texas. Hamilton remained in Europe and on September 18, 1840, he signed a treaty with the Netherlands.

Meanwhile, Palmerston had changed his mind. In November 1840, he and Hamilton signed a treaty of commerce and navigation, a treaty obligating England to mediate with Mexico for Texas independence (Texas to assume, if successful, $5 million of Mexico's debt to British bondholders), and a treaty giving England great liberty in suppressing the foreign slave trade. The reluctance of the Texas Senate to agree to the third treaty delayed ratification, but the treaty was finally accepted in 1842.

RELATIONS WITH MEXICO

The Treaty of Velasco, signed on May 14, 1836 by President Burnet and Santa Anna, was almost immediately rejected by the Mexican Congress. At the same time, the Mexican government announced that it intended to subdue the rebellious Texans. President Houston, convinced that Mexico was too involved in internal difficulties to carry out the threat, took no steps to meet it. In large measure, he was correct. Relations with Mexico during the balance of his term could not be described as friendly; they were virtually nonexistent.

When Lamar became president in December 1838, the situation became more critical. Lamar in his first message to Congress stated: "If peace can only be obtained by the sword, let the sword do its work." However, he also sought peace with Mexico through diplomacy. To this end he sent three different agents to Mexico and solicited and secured the diplomatic aid of the United States and Great Britain. In some respects, the prospect for a diplomatic settlement seemed promising. Mexico was embroiled in a conflict with France, and Anastacio Bustamante, a weak leader but again in power, was struggling to overcome a federalist uprising in several northern Mexican states.

Lamar's first representative, Secretary of State Bernard Bee, traveled to Mexico in May 1839 with authority to offer the Mexican government as much as $5 million if it would recognize Texan independence and the Rio Grande as the boundary. Although supported by Richard Pakenham, the British minister to Mexico, Bee never got beyond Vera Cruz and accomplished nothing of consequence. The next representative sent to Mexico was James Treat, a British soldier of fortune. Bee met Treat, who claimed that he had information that his friend, Santa Anna, who was now back in power, wanted a treaty and that he could negotiate one. Influenced by Bee, Lamar sent Treat to Mexico City where he arrived in November 1839. Treat remained in Mexico City for ten months, engaged in unproductive negotiations that Mexican officials probably took part in only to keep the reactivated Texas navy away from their ports.

After Treat failed and Congress refused to respond to a recommendation for war to compel Mexico to recognize Texas, Lamar made one more effort at diplomacy. Encouraged by the prospect of help from Great Britain contained in the treaty of 1840, Lamar early in 1841 sent Secretary of State James Webb to Mexico. Although Great Britain did pressure the Mexican government, the Texas representative was not received officially and returned home to urge war measures immediately. Lamar entered into an agreement with the Mexican state of Yucatan, then in revolt against the central government, which enlisted the services of the Texas navy in the support of the revolutionaries. The alliance proved of little value. Shortly after it was made Yucatan renewed its allegiance to Mexico.

In the final year of his administration, Lamar took a bold step that replaced unproductive diplomacy with open hostilities. On the east side of the upper Rio Grande were a number of settlements that made up the Spanish province and later the Mexican territory of New Mexico. As defined by the Texas Congress, these settlements were within the boundaries of Texas. Believing reports that the hold of the Mexican government in this area was weak and that the people desired to be a part of Texas, President Lamar organized an expedition to go to Santa Fe, the largest and most important settlement of the upper Rio Grande Valley. Although Congress refused to authorize the venture, there were a number of merchants, soldiers, and adventurers who were eager to make the journey. Colonel Hugh McLeod commanded the military escort of 270 men; William G. Cooke, José Antonio Navarro, and Dr. Richard F. Brenham went along as commissioners of the Texas government. The commissioners were instructed to take possession of Santa Fe and to set up a government under the authority of Texas, but to use force only if convinced that the majority of the population favored Texas.

The story of the expedition, written by George Wilkins Kendall, editor of the New Orleans *Picayune*, was a tale of woe. Leaving Austin on June 19, 1841, the journey turned into a desperate experience with heat, hunger, hostile Indians, and unfriendly Mexicans. Misfortune dogged the trail of the party as it traveled thirteen hundred miles by way of present-day Wichita Falls and Quitaque, across the plains, and finally to New Mexico and Santa Fe. Exhausted and at the mercy of the Mexican forces who met them, the survivors were made prisoners and marched to Mexico City and thence to Perote and other prisons. Most were released in April 1842, but José Navarro was held until 1844.

Partly in retaliation for the Santa Fe expedition, Santa Anna sent an army into Texas in March 1842. A Mexican force of about 500 men, commanded by General Rafael Vásquez, took San Antonio, Goliad, and Refugio but retired after a day or two, having done little damage. The most unfortunate result was a panic in central Texas, resembling the "runaway scrape" of 1836. President Houston declared a public emergency and ordered the archives of the government moved to Houston. Some citizens of Austin, led by Mrs. Angelina Belle Eberly, a strong-minded hotel proprietor, obtained a cannon and refused to permit their removal, thus provoking the comical but grim "archive war."

Although many Texans prepared for war, Houston adopted a cautious approach. Militia forces rushed to San Antonio, and Houston sent to the United States for men, money, and supplies for the invasion of Mexico. But he delayed the assembling of Congress until June 27, because, as he stated in confidential communications, he could not "trust their wisdom" in the crisis. When Congress met, it voted for a declaration of war and appropriated ten million acres of land to meet the expense. Houston, obviously attempting to avoid a war if possible, pronounced this amount of support totally inadequate and vetoed the bill.

Houston's cautious policy was challenged a few months later, when a second Mexican army invaded Texas. General Adrian Woll, with about fourteen hundred men, held San Antonio for nine days. Again the militia was called out and gathered at San Antonio. The Texans encountered considerable resistance from the Mexican forces. A militia company from Fayette County, commanded by Captain Nicholas Dawson, suffered heavy losses. Thirty-six Texans in the company, among them Dawson, were killed, and fifteen more were captured. Finally forced to retreat on September 20, Woll took a number of prisoners with him on his march toward the Rio Grande, including officers, attorneys, the jury of a district court, and some of Dawson's men.

Responding to public demand for action, Houston ordered the organization of an expedition to ensure that Mexican forces had withdrawn from Texas. About the middle of November, 750 men under General Alexander Somervell started for Laredo. After occupying Laredo on December 8, a part of the force disbanded and returned home. The remainder then marched down the Rio Grande until December 19, when Somervell ordered them to return to Gonzales. About three hundred of the men refused to obey Somervell's orders, organized under Colonel W. S. Fisher, and on Christmas morning marched across the Rio Grande and occupied the Mexican village of Mier. After a desperate battle with a sizeable Mexican army under General Pedro Ampudia, they surrendered the day after Christmas. Then followed their march as prisoners toward Mexico City, a break for liberty, their recapture, and a drawing for black beans to determine which one-tenth of their number would be shot. The survivors were finally imprisoned in the dank Castle Perote with the men of the Texas Santa Fe expedition and the prisoners from San Antonio who had been taken by Woll. After many months of confinement they were released, primarily because of pressure from British and United States diplomats, and only after Santa Anna was overthrown and pushed into exile.

While resisting the popular clamor for war with Mexico, Houston was exerting every effort to secure peace and the recognition of independence. He urged the governments of Great Britain, France, and the United States to "require of Mexico either the recognition of the Independence of Texas, or to make war upon her according to the rules established and universally recognized by civilized nations." Waddy Thompson, the United States minister to Mexico, urged recognition and offered the services of his government in the interest of peace. Nothing of importance came directly from these efforts, except possibly the offer from Santa Anna in 1843 of peace if Texas would recognize Mexican sovereignty. Houston had no intention of accepting the offer, but he used it as an opportunity to bargain and to play for time. He proclaimed a truce on June 14, 1843, but an armistice signed the following February lasted only four months, ending when Texas and the United States began negotiations over annexation.

ANNEXATION ACHIEVED

If there was a positive result of the ill-fated Santa Fe and Mier expeditions, it was the rekindling of the interest of the people of the United States in Texas. At the same time, there were other influences at work to revive the subject of Texas annexation, which had been dormant since 1838. Houston reopened the issue with the United States as early as March 1842, but it was not until October 1843 that President John Tyler, perhaps motivated by fear of growing British influence in Texas, suggested negotiations. Houston agreed to negotiations on two conditions: The United States must place its armed forces in position to prevent invasion of Texas, and the negotiations must be kept secret. A. P. Upshur, Tyler's Secretary of State, refused to guarantee conditions, but his death shortly thereafter was followed by the appointment of John C. Calhoun to the office. Calhoun, fearful of aggressive British imperialism and eager to see the addition of more slaveholding territory to the United States, quickly assented to Houston's demands. On April 12, 1844, he and Isaac Van Zandt, the Texas minister in Washington, and J. Pinckney Henderson, a special Texas envoy in the negotiations, signed a treaty. The treaty provided for the annexation of Texas to the United States as a territory and for the United States to assume Texas' public debt. However, the United States Senate rejected the agreement on June 8. Anti-slavery forces in the United States opposed the addition of more slave territory; moreover, some senators were reluctant to make such an important decision on the eve of the national elections of 1844.

The question of the annexation of Texas became one of the major issues in the Presidential election of 1844. In the Democratic Party of the United States, Martin Van Buren, a leading candidate who refused to endorse annexation, lost the nomination to James K. Polk of Tennessee, an avowed expansionist who favored annexation. In the election Polk defeated Henry Clay, the Whig nominee, who opposed "immediate annexation."

The terms for annexation, however, were determined before Polk took office. In December, President Tyler, who would remain in the Presidency until March 4, 1845, told Congress that Polk's election was a mandate for immediate annexation and recommended that Congress take the necessary action. On February 28, 1845, Congress passed a joint resolution providing for annexation. The terms of the resolution were:

(1) Texas would enter the Union as a state if the terms of the resolution were approved by its delegates in an official convention;

(2) all questions concerning the international boundary were to be adjusted by the United States;

(3) Texas must cede to the United States its public property, including navy, posts, fortifications, and armaments;

(4) Texas would retain its public domain to be applied to its public debt;

(5) as many as four additional states, by the consent of Texas, might be formed out of its territory;

(6) slavery would be prohibited in any state formed out of the territory north of parallel 36 30'; and

(7) the President, should he prefer, could withhold the joint-resolution proposal and negotiate in its stead another treaty of annexation.

Tyler signed the joint resolution on March 1 and through his agent, Andrew Jackson Donelson, promptly submitted the offer to the Texan government. Newly inaugurated President James K. Polk urged that there be no delay, but for a time it appeared that President Anson Jones of Texas might provoke one. Great Britain and France opposed annexation. Accordingly Charles Elliot and Count de Saligny, representing Great Britain and France, respectively, persuaded President Jones on March 29 not to commit the government for ninety days. Meanwhile, Elliot would go to Mexico to secure a treaty guaranteeing Texan independence on the condition that the republic agree never to unite with the United States. On April 15 Jones called Congress to meet, but not until June 16.

Public sentiment for annexation, however, forced Jones to realize that he could not delay action. On May 5 he issued a call for a convention to meet in Austin on July 4. When Congress convened, he submitted to it both the proposal of annexation to the United States and the preliminary treaty with Mexico that Elliot had secured and rushed to Texas. Congress rejected the Mexican treaty, unanimously recommended the acceptance of the offer by the United States, approved President Jones's proclamation calling for the election of delegates to a convention, and adjourned. The convention met on July 4, adopted—with only one dissenting vote—an ordinance accepting the terms of annexation, and on August 27 completed a state constitution. On October 13, the voters approved annexation and ratified the constitution by a vote of 4,254 to 257 and 4,174 to 312, respectively. The constitution was accepted by the United States Congress, and President Polk on December 29, 1845, signed the act that made Texas a state of the United States.

At a special election on December 15 new state officials were chosen, and on February 19, 1846, at a ceremony in front of the Texas capitol, President Jones relinquished executive authority to Governor J. Pinckney Henderson. In concluding his address, Jones announced, "The final act in this great drama is now performed; the Republic of Texas is no more."

SELECTED BIBLIOGRAPHY

Of the older general histories that have been previously cited, good accounts of the Republic of Texas are included in H. H. Bancroft, J. H. Brown, W. Kennedy, H. Yoakum, H. S. Thrall, L. J. Wortham, and F. W. Johnson. The most useful reference is the *Handbook of Texas*. The best recent account is S. V. Connor, *Adventure in Glory* (Austin, 1965). Emphasizing certain phases are William R. Hogan, *The Texas Republic: A Social and Economic History* (Norman, Okla., 1946); Stanley Siegel, *Political History of the Texas Republic, 1836–1845* (Austin, 1956); Stephens B. Oates (ed.), *The Republic of Texas* (Palo Alto, Calif., 1968); John E. Weems, *Dream of Empire: A Human History of the Republic of Texas, 1836–1846* (New York, 1971); Joseph

Schmitz, *Texan Statecraft, 1836–1845* (San Antonio, 1941); E. T. Miller, *A Financial History of Texas* (Austin, 1916); Edward M. Neusinger, "The Monetary History of the Republic of Texas," *Southwestern Historical Quarterly*, LVII, 82–90; Anson Jones, *Memoranda and Official Correspondence Relating to the Republic of Texas, Its History and Annexation, Including a Brief Autobiography of the Author* (Chicago, 1966); W. P. Webb, *The Great Plains* (New York, 1931).

The best biographies of the period are those of Sam Houston, previously cited; A. K. Christian, "Mirabeau B. Lamar," *Southwestern Historical Quarterly*, XXIII, 153–70, 231–70; XXIV, 39–80, 87–139, 195–234, 317–24; H. P. Gambrell, *Mirabeau Bonaparte Lamar*; H. P. Gambrell, *Anson Jones*; John N. Cravens, *James Harper Star: Financier of the Republic of Texas* (Austin, 1950); Joe B. Frantz, *Gail Borden, Dairyman to a Nation* (Norman, Okla., 1951); and E. Wallace, *Charles DeMorse: Pioneer Editor and Statesman*. Useful also are John J. Linn, *Reminiscences of Fifty Years in Texas* (New York, 1883); and *A Biographical Directory of Texas Congresses and Conventions* (Austin, 1941).

On domestic affairs the following are useful: Charles P. Roland, *Albert Sidney Johnston: Soldier of Three Republics* (Austin, 1964); Mary A. Maverick, *Memoirs* (San Antonio, 1921); W. P. Webb, *The Texas Rangers* (Boston, 1935); J. Schmitz, *Texas Culture in the Days of the Republic, 1836–1846* (San Antonio, 1960); Tom Henderson Wells, *Commodore Moore and the Texas Navy* (Austin, 1960); E. W. Winkler, "The Seat of Government of Texas," *Quarterly of the Texas State Historical Association*, X, 140–171, 185–245; E. W. Winkler, "The Cherokee Indians in Texas," *ibid.*, VII, 94–165; Nancy N. Barker, *The French Legation in Texas*, vol. II: *Mission Miscarried* (Austin, 1973); D. H. Winfrey, "The Texan Archives War of 1842," *Southwestern Historical Quarterly*, LXIV, 171–84; G. F. Haugh (ed.), "History of the Texas Navy," *ibid.*, LXIII, 572–79; Anna Muckleroy, "The Indian Policy of the Republic of Texas," *ibid.*, XXV, 229–60; XXVI, 1–29, 128–148, 184–206; Jesse Guy Smith, *Heroes of the Saddlebags* (San Antonio, 1951); W. Eugene Hollon and Ruth L. Butler (eds.), *William Bollaert's Texas* (Norman, Okla., 1956); D. H. Winfrey (ed.), *Texas Indian Papers, 1825–1843* (Austin, 1959); D. H. Winfrey (ed.), *Texas Indian Papers, 1844–1845* (Austin, 1960); Earl H. Elam, "The History of the Wichita Indian Confederacy to 1868" (unpublished dissertation, Texas Tech University, Lubbock, 1971). See also Katherine J. Adams and George B. Wood, "Images of the Past: Imprints from the Republic of Texas," *Southwestern Historical Quarterly*, XC, 59–78; and John Edward Weems and Jane Weems, *Dream Empire—A Human History of the Republic of Texas* (College Station, 1986).

Sources and specialized studies relating to the land policy, immigration, *empresario* contracts, and extension of settlement are numerous. On these subjects, county and regional histories are essential, and indispensable to their effective use is H. B. Carroll, "Bibliography of Texas Counties," *Southwestern Historical Quarterly*, XLV, 74–98, 260–275, 343–361. Two good works of a regional nature are Lucy A. Erath (ed.), "Memories of Major Bernard Erath," *ibid.*, XXVI, 207–233, 255–280; XXVII, 27–51, 140–163; and James K. Greer, *Grand Prairie* (Dallas, 1935). The best studies on the land policy are A. S. Lang, *Financial History of the Public Lands in Texas* (Waco, 1932); and Thomas L. Miller, "Texas Land Grants to Veterans," *Southwestern Historical Quarterly*, XLIV, 342–437; Thomas L. Miller, *The Public Lands of Texas, 1519–1970* (Norman, Okla., 1972).

The best source of information on immigration to Texas is the United States census returns for 1850 and the Texas census of 1847, bound with *Laws Passed by the Second Legislature* (Houston, 1848). There is much information in E. E. Braman, *Braman's Information about Texas* (Philadelphia, 1857); and Jacob DeCordova, *Texas, Her Resources and Public Men* (Philadelphia, 1858). Barnes F. Lathrop's *Migration into East Texas, 1835–1860* (Austin, 1949) is an impressive study. B. M. Jones, "Health Seekers in Early Anglo-American Texas," *Southwestern Historical Quarterly*, LXIX, 287–299, shows that many of the immigrants came to Texas because of their health.

Studies dealing with colonizers, their settlers, and their lands include R. L. Biesele, *The History of the German Settlements in Texas, 1831–1861* (Austin, 1930); S. V. Connor, *The Peters Colony of Texas, A History and Biographical Sketches of the Early Settlers* (Austin, 1959); Irene M. King, *John O. Meusebach, German Colonizer in Texas* (Austin, 1967); Terry G. Jordan, *German Seed in Texas Soil: Immigrant Farmers in the Nineteenth Century* (Austin and London, 1966); S. V. Connor, "A Statistical Review of the Settlement of the Peters Colony, 1841–1848," *Southwestern Historical Quarterly*, LVII, 38–64; Nancy Eagleton, "The Mercer Colony in Texas, 1844–1883," *ibid.*, XXXIX, 275–291; XL, 35–57, 114–144; Julia N. Waugh, *Castroville and Henry Castro* (San Antonio, 1934); Bobby D. Weaver, *Castro's Colony: Empresario Development in Texas, 1842–1865* (College Station, 1985); and Feris A. Bass, Jr., and B. R. Brunson, *Fragile Empires: The Texas Correspondence of Samuel and James Morgan* (Austin, 1978).

On Lamar's efforts to extend the jurisdiction of Texas over Santa Fé, see W. C. Binkley, *The Expansionist Movement in Texas* (Berkeley, Calif., 1925); W. C. Binkley, "New Mexico and the Texan Santa Fé Expedition," *Southwestern Historical Quarterly*, XXVII, 85–107; George W. Kendall, *Narrative of the Texan Santa Fé Expedition* (London, 1845); H. Bailey Carroll, *The Texan Santa Fé Trail* (Canyon, Tex., 1951); N. Loomis, *The Texan-Santa Fé Pioneers* (Norman, Okla., 1958).

On foreign relations of the Republic of Texas, the most important source material is G. P. Garrison (ed.), *Texan Diplomatic Correspondence* (3 vols.), in *The Annual Report of the American Historical Association for 1907 and 1908* (2 vols., Washington, D.C., 1908 and 1911); a good survey is J. Schmitz, *Texan Statecraft*.

Definitive and impressive studies dealing with special phases of the subject include: E. D. Adams, *British Interests and Activities in Texas* (Baltimore, 1910); J. M. Nance, *After San Jacinto: The Texas-Mexican Frontier, 1836–1841* (Austin, 1963), a comprehensive study; J. M. Nance, *Attack and Counterattack: The Texas-Mexican Frontier, 1842* (Austin, 1964), another impressive study; J. H. Smith, *The Annexation of Texas* (New York, 1912). Some other specialized studies of significant value are: David M. Fletcher, *The Diplomacy of Annexation: Texas, Oregon, and the Mexican War* (Columbia, Mo., 1973); Milton Lindheim, *The Republic of the Rio Grande: Texas in Mexico, 1839–1840* (Waco, 1964); Thomas J. Green, *Journal of the Texan Expedition against Mier* (New York, 1845); Joseph D. McCutchan, *Mier Expedition Diary: A Texan Prisoner's Account* (ed. J. M. Nance, Austin, 1978); Ethel Z. Rather, "Recognition of the Republic of Texas by the United States," *Quarterly of the Texas State Historical Association*, XIII, 155–256; Annie Middleton, "Donelson's Mission to Texas in Behalf of Annexation," *Southwestern Historical Quarterly*, XXIV, 247–291; E. C. Barker, "The Annexation of Texas," *ibid.*, L, 49–74; Frederick Merk, *Slavery and the Annexation of Texas* (New York, 1972); Alfred J. Watkins and Arnold Fleischmann, "Annexation and Population Growth in Texas Cities," *Texas Business Review* (September 1978), pp. 173–178; Nancy N. Barker, "The Republic of Texas: A French View," *Southwestern Historical Quarterly*, LXXI, 181–193; L. B. Friend (ed.), "Sidelights and Supplements on the Perote Prisoners," *ibid.*, XLVIII, 366–374, 489–496; LXIX, 88–95, 224–230, 377–385, 516–524; Ralph A. Wooster, "Texas Military Operations against Mexico, 1842–1843," *ibid.*, LVII, 465–484; D. M. Vigness, "Relations of the Republic of Texas and the Republic of the Rio Grande," *ibid.*, LVII, 312–321; Josefina Vasquez, "The Texas Question in Mexican Politics, 1836–1845," *ibid.*, LXXXIX, 309–344; and John H. Schroeder, "Annexation or Independence: The Texas Issue in American Politics, 1836–1845," *ibid.*, LXXXIX, 137–164.

CHAPTER EIGHT
EARLY STATEHOOD
1846–1861

Between the time of the annexation of Texas to the United States and its secession to join the Confederacy, Texas was a part of the Union for a decade and a half. During these years, Texans took part in a war between Mexico and the United States, struggled with the national government over their western boundary, and paid off their public debt. Other problems, such as transportation, education, and Indian affairs were not resolved. The question of slavery grew more and more serious, threatening not only the harmony of the state but also the integrity of the nation.

Despite these problems, these were years of expansion and accomplishment. A new state government was installed; Texans constructed roads and public buildings; and extensive explorations opened the way into western areas and to points beyond. Meanwhile, the population continued to grow at a rapid rate as immigrants joined with thousands of land-hungry "old" Texans to push their settlements further westward in the state.

THE ESTABLISHMENT OF STATE GOVERNMENT

The Constitution of 1845, well-designed and well written, was the work of a group of exceptionally able men. Thomas Jefferson Rusk, president of the convention that wrote the document, had served the republic well in several capacities. Many of the other delegates were men of broad experience in public affairs. José Antonio Navarro, a member of the convention of 1836, was the only native Texan. Tennessee contributed eighteen members, Virginia eight, Georgia seven, Kentucky six, and North Carolina five.

The framers drew extensively from the Louisiana constitution, to some extent from the fundamental laws of other states, and from the Texas Constitution of 1836. The governor was to be chosen by the voters for a term of two years but was not eligible to serve more than four out of six years. Subject to the approval of the senate, the governor was to appoint the secretary of state, the attorney general, the three justices of the supreme court, and the district judges. The comptroller and treasurer were to be chosen by the legislature. Thus, of state officers, only the governor, lieutenant-governor, and members of the legislature were elected by the voters. In 1850, however, the constitution was amended to provide for the popular election of the attorney general, comptroller, and treasurer.

In some respects, the legislature resembled the congress of the republic. Representatives would serve two years and be apportioned according to the number of free inhabitants. Senators were to be apportioned on the basis of the number of qualified voters and would serve for four years. Unlike the republic, however, the legislature would meet biennially, rather than annually. The legislature could not incur debt in excess of $100,000; creation of corporations required a two-thirds vote; and property, under most circumstances, had to be taxed in proportion to its value. Married women were made secure in their right to own property, and property (two hundred acres or less) in a homestead was exempt from foreclosure for debt.

Officers of the new state were elected on December 15, 1845. J. Pinckney Henderson was chosen governor over Dr. James B. Miller by an overwhelming vote, and Albert C. Horton defeated N. H. Darnell for lieutenant governor by a slender majority. President Jones called the legislature to assemble in Austin on February 16, 1846, for the purpose of organizing a state government. Three days later in a formal ceremony Jones officially transferred the government to the newly elected state officials. Completing the major structure of the government, the first legislature shortly thereafter elected Thomas J. Rusk and Sam Houston to the United States Senate.

Changes and adjustments incident to the transition from republic to state consumed much of the effort of officers in Texas during Henderson's administration. The postal system was taken over by the United States, and arms, buildings, and other public property were transferred to the general government.

THE WAR WITH MEXICO

War between the United States and Mexico began shortly after the annexation of Texas. The causes, simply stated, were:

(1) the annexation of Texas,
(2) the desire of the United States to have a port in California,
(3) the inability or unwillingness of the Mexican government to settle claims by citizens of the United States,
(4) the instability of the Mexican government, and
(5) the location of the boundary.

On more than one occasion before annexation finally occurred, the Mexican government warned that the annexation of Texas by the United States would be regarded as a step toward war. When the joint-resolution establishing terms for annexation was adopted by Congress and approved by Tyler, Juan N. Almonte, the minister of the Santa Anna government in Washington, announced that Mexico would defend its rightful territory (Texas) by every means within its power and asked for Almonte's passport. Mexico's response to annexation, however, was not as simple as it appeared, primarily because the issue was mired in an almost indescribable entanglement of Mexican political intrigue. José Herrera, who replaced Santa Anna even before the adoption of the joint-resolution, was not particularly friendly toward the United States, but neither was he eager for war. Subsequently, the Mexican Congress in midsummer 1846 refused to declare war, and President Polk and his cabinet concluded that Herrera's government was seeking an amicable solution of the issues.

After determining that Herrera would accept an envoy from the United States who came with full powers to settle "the question" in dispute, President Polk in November 1845 sent John Slidell of Louisiana with full power to settle "all questions" in dispute. Slidell was instructed to buy as much of California and New Mexico as possible and to assume the claims of the United States against Mexico in return for Mexican recognition of the Rio Grande as the boundary between the two countries. The claims issue, which dated as far back as 1816, concerned the claims of United States citizens for debts owed to them by the Mexican government. The amount of the claims, officially estimated but exaggerated, amounted to $6,465,464 by December 1845. In 1843 Mexico had agreed to a program of payments, only to abandon it when the United States and Texas resumed negotiations over annexation.

The hope for a diplomatic solution through Slidell's mission quickly faded. When Slidell reached Mexico in December 1845, he was informed that Texas was the only question in dispute and that friendly relations could not be reestablished until Texas had been restored to Mexico. Although Mexican leaders were angry about Polk's efforts to purchase Mexican territory, their refusal to negotiate was also influenced by public demonstrations that threatened open rebellion if Herrera negotiated with Slidell. Early in 1846, centralists overthrew President Herrera and replaced him with a strong anti-American, Mariano Paredes. Slidell, acting on Polk's instructions, remained until March in an effort to negotiate with Paredes but with no success.

While diplomacy failed, the two nations moved closer to a military confrontation. In the summer of 1845, United States troops under the

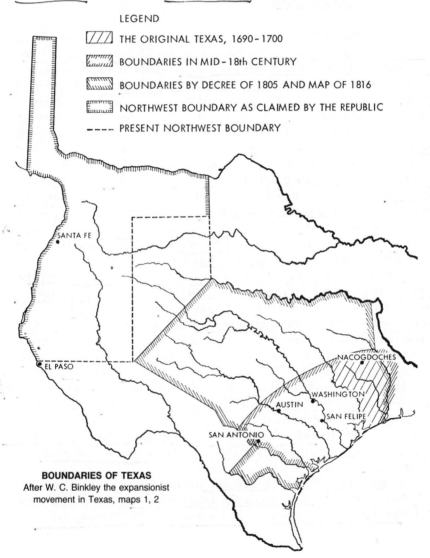

LEGEND

//// THE ORIGINAL TEXAS, 1690-1700

▨ BOUNDARIES IN MID-18th CENTURY

▨ BOUNDARIES BY DECREE OF 1805 AND MAP OF 1816

▨ NORTHWEST BOUNDARY AS CLAIMED BY THE REPUBLIC

- - - - PRESENT NORTHWEST BOUNDARY

SANTA FE

EL PASO

NACOGDOCHES

WASHINGTON

AUSTIN

SAN FELIPE

SAN ANTONIO

BOUNDARIES OF TEXAS
After W. C. Binkley the expansionist
movement in Texas, maps 1, 2

command of General Zachary Taylor established a post at the mouth of the Nueces River near present-day Corpus Christi. Mexican troops were concentrated at Matamoros but scattered along a series of posts on the south side of the Rio Grande. For about nine months there was no significant intrusion of troops from either country into the land between the Rio Grande and Nueces River.

The question of the boundary, implicit in the stationing of troops by both nations, was in fact a complicated question within a complex group of issues. The Nueces had been set by the Spaniards in 1775 as the boundary between Texas and the province of Nuevo Santander. Although it still contended that the Nueces was the boundary, in actual practice, Mexico, beginning with the capitulation of General Cós at San Antonio in December 1835, had adhered to the Rio Grande as the boundary. The Treaties of Velasco, never ratified by the Mexican government anyway, had not placed the boundary at the Rio Grande, only using the river as the limit beyond which Texas would not extend. However, the Republic of Texas by legislative act had designated the river as its southern and western boundary. The joint resolution, which stipulated the terms for Texas becoming a part of the United States, did little to clarify the matter, stating only that "all questions of boundary that may arise with other governments" were "subject to the adjustment by this government. . . ."

The question became a confrontation in March when Polk learned that Slidell would not be received. The President ordered General Taylor to move his troops to the Rio Grande. In early April Paredes stationed several thousand additional troops at Matamoros, and on April 12, General Pedro Ampudia, newly appointed commander of Mexican forces and more aggressive than his predecessor, delivered an ultimatum to the United States commander. Taylor must retire with his troops beyond the Nueces within twenty-four hours, or force of arms would decide the issue. On April 23 President Paredes proclaimed a "defensive" war against the United States, and on the next day Mexican troops crossed the Rio Grande and defeated a detachment of United States dragoons.

Meanwhile, Polk apparently had also decided on war. Writing in his diary on May 9, he confided that he had informed his cabinet that "we had ample cause of war, and that it was impossible that we could stand in *status quo,* or that I could remain silent much longer." That same day, he received news of the skirmish on the border. Before he learned of Taylor's victories on May 8 and 9 over a Mexican army at Palo Alto and Resaca de la Palma, President Polk and his cabinet decided to ask Congress for a declaration of war. Over the objections of Whigs, abolitionists, and others who questioned the necessity or desirability of war, Congress on May 13 declared war, responding to Polk's claim that Mexico had "shed American blood on American soil."

The war was unpopular with many citizens of the United States, but Texans supported it enthusiastically. Taylor immediately opened an offensive to drive the Mexican forces toward Monterrey. He asked Governor Henderson for two regiments of infantry and two of cavalry, and the legislature gave the governor a leave of absence to take command of the Texas troops who were mustered into the service of the United States. Before the end of May the Mexican troops had abandoned Matamoros to Taylor; on September 25 Taylor took possession of Monterrey; and on February 23 and 24, 1847, he defeated and put to flight a much larger force under Santa Anna (no longer President, but now a military commander) at Buena Vista. The Texans performed a key role both at Monterrey and at Buena Vista. At Buena Vista, Taylor's campaign ended, for it was doubted that an extended supply line across the deserts and mountains of northern Mexico could be maintained.

The United States won victory with the invasion and conquest of Mexico City. Polk sent another army, commanded by General Winfield Scott, to land at Vera Cruz and fight its way to Mexico City. Scott captured Mexico City in September 1847, and Santa Anna fled the country. In the fighting a number of Texans won distinction. One organization, that of John Coffee (Jack) Hays, made up largely of rangers, lawmen, and frontier Indian fighters and commanded by such men as Ben McCulloch, Samuel H. Walker, and John S. (Rip) Ford, attained renown. The Texas Rangers served as efficient scouts and as the advance units, and kept the supply lines open. Approximately five thousand Texans were in military service during the war.

John Coffee (Jack) Hays, a surveyor by profession, became captain of a Texas Ranger company in 1840. As colonel in command of the First Regiment, Texas Mounted Volunteers, during the Mexican War, he participated with distinction in the battles of Monterrey and Mexico City. (Southwest Collection, Texas Tech University)

In the Treaty of Guadalupe Hidalgo on February 2, 1848, which ended the war, Mexico accepted the Rio Grande as the boundary; in return, the United States agreed to assume the claims of its citizens against that nation up to $5 million. Mexico also ceded to the United States for a payment of $15 million the provinces of New Mexico and upper California.

THE TEXAS-NEW MEXICO BOUNDARY CONTROVERSY

The Treaty of Guadalupe Hidalgo ended the boundary controversy between Mexico and the United States, but opened the way for one between the state of Texas and the national government. During the republic Texas claimed lands extending to the Rio Grande, including a vast amount of territory never a part of Texas during Spanish or Mexican rule. Within this area were most of the principal settlements of New Mexico, scattered for the most part along the eastern side of the Rio Grande and including the prosperous community of Santa Fe.

Although Texas had failed in the Santa Fe expedition of 1841 to exercise sovereignty over the New Mexico lands, Texans continued after annexation to assert their claim. The justice of the claim was certainly debatable, but denial of it by the national government was at the very least inconsistent. Congress had declared war on Mexico in response to a presidential statement that "American blood had been shed on American soil"—north of the Rio Grande but most assuredly south of the Nueces. Nevertheless, even as the war was fought, it was clear that the claim of Texas to the Rio Grande was in jeopardy. In August, 1846, Stephen Kearny, in command of the Army of the West, occupied New Mexico and established a civil government there with the approval of his superiors and without regard to the claims of Texas. On June 4, 1847, Governor Henderson reminded Secretary of State James Buchanan of the Texan claims. Buchanan replied that the question would have to be settled by Congress, but he assured the governor that the temporary civil government would not affect the claim. Their fears thus quieted, the Texans awaited the outcome of the war and the signing of the peace treaty.

Ratification of the Treaty of Guadalupe Hidalgo on March 10, 1848, did not fulfill the expectations of Texans. In part, the obstacle to the claim of Texas to the territory east of the Rio Grande was raised by the question of slavery. During the war, the opposition of anti-slavery interests to the acquisition of any new slave territory was introduced in Congress by the Wilmot Proviso, which, if adopted, would have prohibited slavery in any territory acquired by the United States as a result of the war with Mexico. Although the proviso was not adopted, the issue remained, and pro- and anti-slavery interests aligned on opposite sides with little inclination to make concessions. If the boundaries claimed by Texas were permitted to stand, slave soil thus would extend at least as far westward as the Rio Grande. Divided, Congress found itself unable to pass any laws whatever concerning New Mexico.

The inhabitants of the upper Rio Grande Valley, sustained and encouraged by military officials on the scene, posed the other obstacle to the claims of Texas. Their opposition to being a part of Texas, evident during the republic, was made more clear when Texas on March 15, 1848, created Santa Fe County with boundaries including most of eastern New Mexico. Although the Texas government asked for support by the federal government and promptly sent Spruce M. Baird to Santa Fe to organize the new county and serve as judge, the military, certain civilian leaders, and an aroused public opposed him. Just before his arrival in November 1848, a convention was held in Santa Fe, and petitions were adopted asking that New Mexico be created a territory. On his arrival, Baird was informed by Colonel John M. Washington, commanding officer in Santa Fe, that he would sustain the government established in New Mexico by General Kearny "at every peril" until ordered to desist. Baird remained in the territory for a few months without accomplishing anything. Any hope of the Texans for an order overruling the federal officers in Santa Fe faded when Zachary Taylor assumed the Presidency on March 4, 1849. Taylor favored granting statehood to both California and New Mexico.

The situation, which became more tense with the passing of each month, was critical by the end of 1849. In November, Governor George T. Wood, who had succeeded Henderson as governor, suggested to the legislature that Texas assert its claim "with the whole power and resources of the state," but neither the governor nor the legislature took any decisive action. Peter Hansborough Bell, who defeated Wood's bid for reelection by pledging a more aggressive policy, shortly thereafter urged that the legislature send to New Mexico a force sufficient to maintain the authority of Texas. Meanwhile, the press and the public of Texas grew more restive.

While avoiding the use of military force, the legislature took action. On December 31, 1849, it designated new boundaries for Santa Fe county and created three additional counties to the south of it. Then, by authority of an act passed four days later, another commissioner, Robert S. Neighbors, was sent to organize the counties. He organized El Paso County without meeting resistance, but on arriving in New Mexico he found the majority of the people antagonistic and the military unsympathetic. Neighbors thereupon returned to Texas. His report to the governor, made public early in June 1850, caused great excitement. At mass meetings in Austin and other places there were protests, threats of secession, and proposals that the state assert its claim by military force. Governor Bell called a special session of the legislature to meet on August 12. When the legislature assembled, it heard the governor's message declaring that Texas must assert its rights "*at all hazards and to the last extremity*," and debated measures to organize the militia and send it into New Mexico.

Meanwhile, the people of New Mexico were busily at work organizing their own government. They adopted a constitution for their proposed state with boundaries so extended as to include most of the disputed territory and also some territory unquestionably Texan. Their work, however, was threatened by events in Washington. President Taylor, who supported their efforts, had died. Millard Fillmore, his successor, reinforced the army in New Mexico and stated flatly that he would send troops against the Texas militiamen if they attempted to occupy the region. However, Fillmore favored a settlement of the controversy through compromise measures that had been debated in Congress throughout the early months of 1850.

Beginning with one introduced by Senator Thomas Hart Benton of Missouri on January 16, 1850, Congress considered three different plans to resolve the dispute. In addition to Benton's proposal, there was one offered by Senator John Bell of Tennessee that would have divided Texas into three states, and another drafted by a committee engaged in trying to

Pearce Plan, 1850. (From *The Howling of the Coyotes: Reconstruction Efforts to Divide Texas,* by Ernest Wallace, published by Texas A&M University Press)

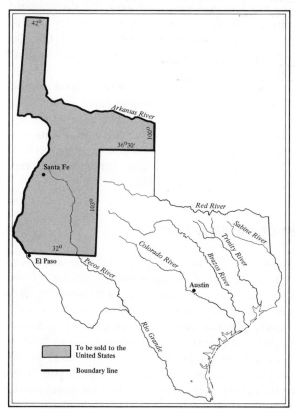

solve a number of different problems. Although each proposal was different, there were certain common elements in all: (1) boundary lines differed, but all limited the lands of Texas to a location south of 36 30' (the line established in the Missouri Compromise dividing slave and non-slave areas in the Louisiana Purchase); (2) all provided some sort of compensation for Texans, either money, or in the instance of Bell's proposal, added representation in Congress; (3) President Taylor opposed all of them; and (4) none of them passed.

A fourth proposal, one of a series of five laws known as the Compromise of 1850, finally passed. This bill, written by James A. Pearce of Maryland, was accepted by the Senate and passed by the House on September 6, 1850. It was supported by the Texas delegation and congressmen from both North and South. It fixed the northern and western boundary of Texas as it now stands, providing that it should begin at the intersection of 100th meridian and the parallel of 36 30', run west along that parallel to the 103rd meridian, follow that to the 32nd parallel, extend along that parallel to the Rio Grande, and follow that stream to its mouth. Texas was to renounce all claims to territory beyond the boundaries described, for which it would be paid $10 million. The bill also provided for the organization of the territory of New Mexico. A desire to resolve the dispute and ease the tensions tearing the nation apart was likely the primary motive behind much of the support for the measure, but there was another element involved. A group who held Texas bonds, anxious to ensure their claims, worked diligently on behalf of the bill.

Although there was considerable sentiment in Texas against accepting the proposition, a majority of the voters seemed to agree with the La Grange *Monument*, which announced that it was "doubtful whether ten years' trading would give Texas a better bargain that she can now make." At a special election the voters accepted the proposition by a majority of two to one, the legislature in special session approved it, and Governor Bell signed the act of acceptance on November 25, 1850.

SETTLEMENT OF THE DEBT OF THE REPUBLIC

The public debt of Texas, which developed during the republic and was to be paid with funds received in the boundary settlement, consisted of two major types of obligations, ordinary and revenue debt. The ordinary debt was created by the claims of participants in the Texas Revolution or suppliers of the Texas army, nearly all representing at most a hundred dollars each. The revenue debt consisted of principal and interest owed to holders of Republic of Texas securities. Under the terms of the boundary act, as interpreted by United States officers, the revenue debts were preferred obligations. To make sure that these were paid, the federal government retained $5 million in bonds, or half of the boundary settlement. The remainder was delivered to the state for payment of the ordinary claims. There were few problems involved in the payment of the ordinary debt, except for an occasional instance where the individual claimant had difficulty proving a claim. In fact, the state had $3.75 million left after these claims were paid.

The revenue debt, however, generated much controversy and ill will. The problems were twofold: payment was slow, and only a percentage of the debt was actually paid. Payment was delayed because some creditors neglected to file their claims, and the United States officials would not pay any claims until all were in. Final settlement was made by an act of February 28, 1855. By that time, the bonds held for Texas, with accrued interest, amounted to $6.5 million. Congress added to this amount $1,250,000 to reimburse Texas for damages resulting from Indian depredations in Texas since 1836. Altogether, there was a fund of $7,750,000 to be distributed among the creditors, but the revenue debt by this point with accumulated interest amounted to $10,078,703. Thus, when the fund was prorated among the creditors, each one received about 77 cents on the dollar. Many of the creditors objected, but the state contended that such scaling was equitable since the republic had not received full value for the obligations at the time they were issued.

The $3.75 million in bonds that remained after the ordinary debt had been paid was of great assistance to Texas. The greater part of it, $2 million, was set aside as an endowment for the public schools, and in turn loaned to railroads to aid construction. For six years, beginning in 1852, the state remitted to the counties nine-tenths of its taxes. The counties used the tax money for the construction of public buildings and various other purposes. Thus, Texas was able to endow its public schools, promote the construction of transportation facilities, construct buildings, and maintain all the while a very low tax rate.

THE POLITICS OF EARLY STATEHOOD

Although no permanent tradition was established, each of the first two governors of Texas served only one term. In fact, J. Pinckney Henderson, the first governor, only served a portion of a term. While he was absent commanding Texas troops during the Mexican War, Lieutenant Governor A. C. Horton served as governor until Henderson returned in November 1846. Henderson was succeeded on December 21, 1847, by George T. Wood, a Trinity River planter who had gained popularity as commander of volunteers in the Mexican War and whose vote for governor was substantially greater than that of his leading opponent, Dr. J. B. Miller. The most important public issues of the Wood administration were frontier defense, the public debt, and the controversy over the Rio Grande boundary. When Wood ran for reelection in 1849, he was defeated by Peter Hansborough

Bell, a veteran of San Jacinto and the war with Mexico. Wood attributed his defeat to inadequate support by Sam Houston, inasmuch as he was strongly opposed by anti-Houston forces, among them J. P. Henderson and William B. Ochiltree. Pro- and anti-Houston politics may have been a factor, but Bell's advocacy of a more aggressive policy in the boundary dispute may have also influenced the outcome.

The first administration of Peter Hansborough Bell, the first governor to be reelected, was a busy one. The settlement of the boundary dispute was only one of several issues. The state took steps to explore routes across Texas, and worked to secure the location of a line of military posts along the frontier. There was even a controversy over a futile effort to move the capital from Austin. When Bell ran for reelection in 1851, the growing importance of the slavery issue and Southern nationalism was evident. None of his opponents were in league with abolitionists, or even anti-slavery in their sympathies, but Bell was regarded as the most pro-Southern of them all and elected easily. His second term was occupied with the problems of paying of the public debt, controversies over the claims of certain emigrant agents, and the seemingly eternal question of frontier defense. A popular governor, Bell did not complete his second term. A few weeks before it expired, he resigned to fill a vacancy in Congress.

Several candidates entered the race for governor in 1853. W. B. Ochiltree, a Whig politician with a large personal following, was a popular candidate. Certain potential Democratic candidates, including M. T. Johnson and J. W. Henderson, fearful of the election of a Whig, withdrew

Peter H. Bell, a native of Virginia, fought at San Jacinto, was a Texas Ranger, and fought under General Zachary Taylor in the war with Mexico. He was governor of Texas from 1849 to 1853, and in the controversy that developed over the claims of Texas to the Rio Grande as its western boundary, he represented the state's interests with force and energy. (E. C. Barker History Center, University of Texas)

and urged their followers to support Elisha M. Pease. Pease, an "old" Texan especially popular in the southern and western part of the state, was elected.

Pease was an active and an able governor. His platform called for establishing a public school system, encouraging internal improvements (transportation facilities), and removing the Indians from Texas. The most important act of his administration was the school law of 1854. By its terms, the state set aside $2 million of the money received in the boundary settlement as a permanent endowment for public schools. Income from the fund was distributed each year on a per-capita basis to supplement the one-tenth of the annual revenue of the state which the constitution had reserved for schools. The legislature set aside $100,000 of the boundary settlement funds for the endowment of a university, but this later disappeared into the general revenue fund and was used for other purposes. The support of Pease and others for the building of railroads was evident in a program of loans and in a number of charters granted to railroads. Efforts to resolve Indian problems resulted in the establishment of three Indian reservations authorized by the legislature.

During the Pease years, conduct of political affairs along party lines became more important. Most Texas leaders and many other Texans, hail-

The Pease Mansion was bought by Elisha Marshall Pease, a New England Yankee who came to Texas in 1835 and settled in Bastrop (then called Mina). An outspoken advocate of independence, Pease was a member of the Committee of Safety in Mina and took part in the convention of 1836. Under his administration as governor (1853-1857) railroads were encouraged, taxes reduced, the state debt paid off, the state university planned, and a new capitol erected. A Unionist, Pease was appointed provisional governor again in 1867 but resigned because of disagreements over Reconstruction. (Texas Highway Department)

ing from other southern states, were supporters of the Democratic Party, although some were loyal to the opposition, the Whigs. However, the Whigs, regarded as the party that had opposed the annexation of Texas and the party of the elite, attracted few supporters. But during the republic, party affiliation meant almost nothing in Texas politics, and during the early years of statehood, it meant very little. Voters generally aligned themselves with the Houston or the anti-Houston leaders. As early as May 1846 an effort was made to organize the Democratic party, but without results. Both the Whigs and the Democrats held conventions from time to time, but the attendance was small. The Democratic convention in 1855 drew delegates from only twelve counties.

A new political party appeared in Texas in 1854, to challenge the complacent and disorganized Democrats. The new political organization, the American or Know-Nothing Party, was a secret and mysterious association, founded on the Atlantic Seaboard and based on nativist (anti-foreign) principles. It opposed foreigners holding office, was decidedly anti-Catholic, was strongly pro-Union, and grew rapidly as the Whig party disintegrated. In 1854 it elected a complete slate of officers in San Antonio. Its candidate was elected mayor of Galveston in the spring of 1855, and several newspapers seemingly joined the cause. In keeping with its penchant for secrecy, the party met in the guise of a river improvement association in a political convention in June, 1855, to organize and nominate political candidates. They nominated Lieutenant Governor D. C. Dickson for governor, formed a state organization with the respected R. E. B. Baylor as "grand president," and made plans to spread the party over the state. Party hopes were strengthened when Houston publicly expressed sympathy with aims of the organization.

In less than a week after the Know-Nothing convention, Democrats met in a second convention in Austin. They denounced all secret political factions and pledged support to Pease for governor and nominated H. R. Runnels in place of Dickson for lieutenant governor. Other Democratic contestants for governor were persuaded to withdraw, and a hard-fought campaign between Dickson and Pease followed. Pease won by a substantial majority, but the Know-Nothings managed to elect about 20 representatives and five senators to the state legislature.

The Know-Nothing party did not last, however. Growing conflict over slavery led to Texans to renew their loyalties to the Democrats, and many people found the secrecy and undemocratic policies of the Know-Nothings to be unacceptable. The disintegration of the Know-Nothing party was clearly evident by 1856, but the organization left its mark on Texas politics. The Democrats were forced to perfect their organization and to adopt the practice of nominating candidates by convention. When the Democrats convened to nominate candidates and select presidential electors, ninety-one out of ninety-nine counties were represented, and attendance at the convention in 1857 was even better. That convention named Hardin R. Runnels, a wealthy planter of Bowie County, as candidate for governor, and Francis R. Lubbock for lieutenant governor.

The development of politics along party lines, however, did not mean the disappearance of political battles between the factions of Houston and anti-Houston supporters. More and more the Houston group referred to themselves as Jackson Democrats or Unionists, while the opposition was often called Calhoun Democrats. Since 1836, Sam Houston had twice been president of the republic and thrice United States senator. Popular with many, he was also unpopular with others. The difference was in part a matter of personalities, but it also was a conflict over principles and policies. Houston antagonized proslavery leaders in 1848, by voting for the creation of the free-soil territory of Oregon and by refusing to sign South Carolina's John C. Calhoun's pro-slavery protest against what Calhoun termed the aggression of the free states. Houston's speeches in the debates in the controversy leading up to the Compromise of 1850 (which largely concerned slavery issues) created much excitement in 1849. It was, however, Houston's vote against the Kansas-Nebraska bill (the bill that opened to slavery certain lands in the Louisiana Purchase where slavery had been prohibited by the Missouri Compromise of 1820) in 1854 that created the most animosity toward him. His vote was regarded as treason by many southerners, and Democrats throughout Texas condemned him. His affiliation with the Know-Nothing movement in 1855 added to his unpopularity.

Apparently believing that the legislature would not again elect him to the United States Senate, Houston resigned from the senate to run for governor in the popular election of 1857. Accordingly, in May 1857, he announced for governor as an independent, running on his record as Jackson Democrat or Unionist. Although his opponent was Hardin Runnels, his most determined antagonist was Louis T. Wigfall (elected a United States Senator in 1858), a proslavery champion of states rights armed with extreme views and frantic energy. Whenever he could, Wigfall debated with Houston, and when Houston avoided debate, Wigfall and J. P. Henderson followed him and countered his arguments. Runnels and the Democratic ticket won a decisive victory. It was the only defeat in a major contest that Houston ever suffered.

The Runnels administration, 1857-1859, coincided with the final tension-filled years on the eve of the Civil War, filled with strife as the crisis over slavery moved toward a climax. Many issues claimed the attention of the state government, but of them, only the question of frontier defense received much notice as Texans and the remainder of the nation concentrated more and more on the growing rift between North and South.

EXPLORATIONS *Bill*

At the close of the Mexican War, Texas, west and north of a line through Denton, Dallas, Waco, Austin, Fredericksburg, San Antonio, Castroville, and Laredo, was an unknown Indian country. During the next twelve years, Texans and the United States Army explored and surveyed trails across the region in search of wagon, stage, and railroad routes.

Several explorations searched for practical routes between central Texas and El Paso. Hoping to open trade, a group of citizens of San Antonio persuaded John C. Hays to try to find a usable wagon road to El Paso. In the summer of 1848, the famed Texas Ranger traveled westward from San Antonio with a party of citizens and Texas Rangers by way of the Llano and Devils Rivers to a point beyond the Pecos River, where, lost and with supplies exhausted, he abandoned the venture and returned to San Antonio. The United States Army and citizens of Austin, who wanted to make their city a departure point for travelers to California, jointly sponsored the next effort to explore West Texas. In March 1849 Robert S. Neighbors, under military orders, and John S. (Rip) Ford, a Texas Ranger who represented citizens of Austin, set out with a party to find a practical wagon road between San Antonio and El Paso. They went by way of the Middle Concho, Horsehead Crossing on the Pecos River, and the Davis Mountains, and returned by way of Guadalupe Pass, the Pecos and Middle Concho Rivers, and Fredericksburg. About the same time Captain W. H. C. Whiting made an army reconnaissance to El Paso, returning by way of the Davis Mountains, Devils River, and the Las Moras River near present-day Brackettville. The army carried out more explorations to evaluate the practicality of these routes, and eventually an "upper" route and a "lower" route between central Texas and El Paso was determined. The "upper" led northward to Brady's Creek, westward to the Pecos at Horsehead Crossing, up the Pecos to the mouth of Delaware Creek near the present Texas-New Mexico line, and westward through Guadalupe Pass to El Paso. The "lower," used more extensively, followed a path westward from San Antonio to Fort Clark (now Brackettville), northwest to a point on the Pecos River near present-day Ozona, and then to El Paso by way of the Davis Mountains. Many emigrants, California bound, used the routes.

Meanwhile, the military was exploring and marking wagon roads across the northern part of the state. Captain Randolph B. Marcy in April 1849, escorted a party of immigrants to Santa Fe by following the Canadian River across the Texas Panhandle. On his return, Marcy passed through Guadalupe Pass, crossed the Pecos near the present town of Pecos, and moved eastward by way of the present towns of Colorado City, Stamford, Haskell, Newcastle, Jacksboro, Henrietta, and Preston, north of Sherman. A variation of Marcy's trail, which turned southwestward near the Clear Fork of the Brazos and then toward the west by way of the Middle Concho, was a major road to emigrants to California and other pioneers. A railroad survey, provided for by a congressional appropriation in 1853, substantially followed the Marcy Trail. Many years were to pass before the railroad was built, but the Southern Overland Mail Service that began operations in 1858 utilized a portion of the route.

In an attempt to solve transportation and supply problems in the arid regions of the west, the army experimented with camels. Secretary of War Jefferson Davis in 1856 and 1857, introduced seventy-five camels into Texas and headquartered them near present-day Kerrville. Camels were used as far west as California, but the camels were abandoned as a system of transportation before the Civil War and eventually vanished.

IMMIGRATION AND EXTENSION OF SETTLEMENT

Attracted by a liberal land policy, the crowds of immigrants who each year made their way to Texas during the republic increased after annexation. Indeed, the lure of cheap land in Texas was second only to that of gold in California. During 1845 newspapers in Missouri, Arkansas, and Louisiana abounded in news of settlers departing for Texas. There was a lull in 1846 and 1847 due to the Mexican War, but the news of the United States victory started the wave anew. One day in December 1848, 300 immigrants crossed the ferry at Washington on the Brazos, and during November 1849 more than 5,000 on their way to Texas crossed the Arkansas River at Little Rock. A year later, the editor of the *Northern Standard* at Clarksville wrote: "For the last two weeks scarcely a day has passed that a dozen or more movers' wagons has not passed through our town." Year after year, the numbers increased. In 1858 the editor of the *Standard* claimed that no fewer than fifty wagons of immigrants were passing through Clarksville each day. The census of 1850 showed 154,034 whites, 58,161 slaves, 397 free blacks, for a total of 212,592, or an increase of almost 50 percent since 1847. These figures increased threefold over the next decade. By 1860 the population had jumped to 604,215; of this number, 182,921 were blacks.

Almost three-fourths of the 1860 population had been born outside of Texas. A majority of the immigrants had come from the states of the Old South, Louisiana, Arkansas, and Missouri. Tennessee had contributed 42,265, more than any other state. Alabama was the next, with 34,193. The foreign-born, numbering 43,422, represented almost every country of Western Europe and Mexico. The Germans, numbering 20,553, made up the largest group of foreign born. German settlements were concentrated in western areas of central Texas. There they constituted a majority of the population in three counties in the San Antonio-Austin area and a substantial part in six other counties.

Mexican settlers, with 12,443, made up the second largest group of foreign-born, in 1860. The Mexican population was concentrated in the counties along the Rio Grande River and in South Texas where the counties of Nueces, Webb, Starr, and Cameron, created in 1848, in many ways reflected the influence of the Mexican culture and heritage. In an election return in Nueces County, thirty-seven of forty-four voters had Spanish surnames. Along the Rio Grande, far removed from most of the other Texas settlements, were a number of communities, including Laredo and Eagle Pass, whose populations were also largely Mexican. In 1850 this area and the counties of Cameron, Starr, and Webb had about thirteen thousand people. Higher up on the Rio Grande were several settlements, including Presidio and El Paso, with about four thousand persons.

Immigrants from Europe, other than the Germans, included French, Czechs, Poles, Swedes and Norwegians. La Réunion, a French colony, was established in 1855 near Dallas by followers of Victor Considerant, a socialist. The colonists, soon disenchanted with both the frontier and socialism, drifted away but generally remained somewhere in the state. The immigration of Czechs, which began during the republic, increased in the early statehood years, particularly after revolutions in Europe in 1848 brought more turmoil and tyranny into their lives. They settled in communities such as Cat Spring, New Ulm, New Bremen, Hostyn, and Fayetteville. From Poland came several hundred families in the 1850s to an area south of San Antonio where they founded the town of Panna Maria in Karnes County. A small Norwegian settlement was planted in Henderson County in 1845, but settlers from Scandinavia did not come in numbers until nearly a half-century later.

These immigrants, joined by other thousands of "old" Texans, advanced the frontier westward into the Western Cross Timbers. By 1849 the newly established towns of Sherman, Farmersville, Dallas, Waxahachie, Ennis, Waco, and Fredericksburg marked the western limits of white settlement. Villages sprang up near Fort Worth and Fort Croghan, but Indian hostility brought the rush to the frontier to a temporary halt in 1850 after the establishment of Gainesville, Belton, and Uvalde County.

The movement of military posts more than a hundred miles farther to the west in 1851 and 1852 opened the way for more settlements in Central and West Central Texas. Within two years, there were communities at Bandera, San Saba, Meridian, Gatesville, Cleburne, and Stephenville; and by the end of 1858 Comanche, Hamilton, Weatherford, Jacksboro, and Palo Pinto had been founded. On the eve of the Civil War, the frontier line of settlement extended from Henrietta on the north through Belknap, Palo Pinto, Brownwood, Llano, and Kerrville, to Uvalde.

THE INDIAN FRONTIER

Those Texans who believed that annexation to the United States would put an end to Indian depredations were soon disillusioned. The United States

Army added its strength to the services of state troops and the efforts of frontier citizens, but Indian raids and wars would continue for more than thirty years. Indian wars, in fact, actually increased in the years immediately following annexation. Although the primary responsibility for Indian defense properly rested with the federal government and the army, the outbreak of the Mexican War left Texas to defend its own frontiers. A treaty with the Penateka Comanches in 1846 did little to preserve peace, and defense was soon needed. Five companies of mounted Texas Rangers stationed along the frontier between the Trinity River and Castroville in 1846, proved insufficient, and during 1847 four additional companies were placed in service between San Antonio and the Rio Grande.

When the United States began withdrawing its troops from Mexico, it stationed seven companies of regulars in Texas to replace the state troops. A permanent line of defense made up of eight military posts between the Rio Grande and the Red River was established to block the movement of Indians into white settlements. From south to north these forts were Duncan at Eagle Pass; Inge, near Uvalde; Lincoln, 55 miles west of San Antonio; Martin Scott, at Fredericksburg; Croghan, near Burnet; Gates, on the Leon River; Graham, on the Brazos River; and Worth, at the present city of Fort Worth. The rapid advance of settlements rendered the line

Federal forts form Line of Defense, 1849.

obsolete within two years, and beginning in 1851, another line of seven forts was constructed generally along an irregular line about one hundred miles to the west. From north to south they were Belknap, at the present town of New Castle; Phantom Hill, 14 miles north of present-day Abilene; Chadbourne, on Oak Creek in present-day Coke County; McKavett, on the San Saba River about 24 miles above present-day Menard; Terrett, on the North Llano; Mason, at the present town of that name; and Clark, at present-day Brackettville. A third chain of forts, located along or near the Rio Grande, was built to protect the boundary lands where marauders of various types from both Mexico and the United States committed depredations on both sides of the border.

Although the effectiveness of military forces was often questioned and criticized, there is little doubt but that the army reduced the number of Indian raids. During 1853, for instance, there were 3,265 soldiers in Texas, the greatest at any prior to the Civil War. The frontier was comparatively tranquil. During the following year, after many troops had been withdrawn and the country between the Colorado and the Red Rivers was defended by only four small companies of infantry and two of dragoons, conditions became so bad that the army called on Governor Pease for state troops. At Fort Chadbourne there were only twenty men commanded by the post surgeon.

While relying on the army and force, the federal government also turned to the use of dedicated Indian agents and reservations to bring peace to the frontier. Two reservations were established in Texas in 1855. The state contributed the land, approximately 35,426 acres located at the junction of the Brazos and Clear Fork rivers near present-day Graham, for about a thousand survivors of the Caddo, Anadarko, Ioni, Waco, Tonkawa, Tawakoni, and other tribes. A second reservation, about 17,713 acres of state land on the Clear Fork in Throckmorton County, was set aside for the Penateka band of the Comanches. Only about half of the Penatekas could be persuaded to move onto the reservation. Some of the remainder united with other Comanche bands and became more troublesome than ever. Neither reservation could be termed a success in a permanent sense, but conditions on the frontier may have been improved temporarily. If so, much of the credit was due to the faithful Indian agents who worked under great handicaps to persuade Indians to move to the reservations and to protect them once this was accomplished. Of these, the most effective was Robert S. Neighbors, who had served the Republic of Texas as an Indian agent and afterwards continued in the service of the federal government for most of the years of early statehood.

Conditions near the Indian country improved greatly in 1856. In part the change seems to have been caused by the reservations, but the work of army troops and other forces deserve part of the credit, perhaps most of it. Among the officers of the United States Army, the Second Cavalry was a group of unusually talented men—Albert Sidney Johnston, Robert E. Lee, George H. Thomas, George Stoneman, and John B. Hood. When Johnston and a part of his regiment were ordered to Utah in 1857, depredations again became severe. During the following year both state and federal troops carried the war to the Indians. In April 1858, John S. (Rip) Ford led a force of 215 rangers and friendly Brazos Reservation Indians across the Red River into Indian Territory (present-day Oklahoma), and on May 12 decisively defeated a large band of Comanches in the Canadian River valley near the Texas-Oklahoma line. In September of the same year, Major Earl Van Dorn led a force of United States Cavalry from Texas against the Comanches in Indian Territory and in October defeated a band of Comanches and Wichitas near present-day Rush Springs, Oklahoma. About 125 friendly Indians from the Brazos Reservation under the command of Lawrence Sullivan Ross aided in this campaign. Later in the year Van Dorn carried his campaign even farther north and defeated another band of Comanches in southern Kansas.

Meanwhile, the reservation system of North-Central Texas came to an end. Despite the loyal aid of the Indians of the Brazos Reservation in the campaigns against the Comanches, people of the frontier, joined by many in the interior, charged that reservation Indians were raiding Texas settlements and demanded the dismantling of the reservations. Swarms of angry settlers repeatedly threatened the lives of the reservation people, and only the presence of federal troops prevented a massacre. In the late summer of 1859 the Indians of both reservations were moved across the Red River into the valley of the Washita River in Indian Territory. A much smaller reservation established in 1854 in Polk County by the state for the Alabama and Coushatta tribes was allowed to remain in existence, however.

The removal of the reservation Indians did not bring peace to the frontier. The northern Comanches and the Kiowas, aroused by the attacks from Texas, retaliated in the fall of 1859 with devastating raids. Although slavery dominated politics throughout the nation in 1859, the critical situation on the frontier was a major factor in the gubernatorial election that year. Houston, though not usually in favor of aggressive warfare against Indians, won over Hardin Runnels with a promise of strong measures. It was a time when neither the whites nor the Indians were in a mood for treaties.

After he took office, Houston acted promptly and decisively. By a series of orders he sent to the frontier by the end of March 1860 seven ranger companies, consisting of more than 500 men. Each frontier county was authorized to raise a company of up to 25 minutemen, and for a time that spring 23 such companies were available for service. Altogether, the state force numbered more than 1,000 men on active duty to reinforce the 2,651 federal troops in Texas, and there were 842 federal soldiers on their way to the state. The sizeable force of mounted troops temporarily caused the Indians to move away from the frontier. In May the minutemen were disbanded, but four companies of rangers scouted, sometimes in Indian Territory but without noteworthy success, for hostile Indians for nearly a year.

While most of the attention to frontier wars during early statehood was given to hostilities in northwestern areas, the lands of South Texas and especially along the lower Rio Grande were the scene of frequent raids and violence. Lawless men on both sides of the border and from the peoples of both nations committed crimes without regard to the boundary. Adding to the troubles of the land was the bitterness and anger of a sizeable portion of the population. Most of the people were of Mexican heritage, but Anglo Texans generally dominated the region. Moreover, many Mexican families had lost all or part of their lands, and even those who retained their property often complained of little protection from the law and unfair treatment.

There was an abundant number of outlaws and renegades who committed various crimes, but in time attention centered on the actions of Juan Nepomuceno Cortina. Cortina claimed to be the protector of the rights of Mexican peoples, and certainly he was a hero to a large part of that popula-

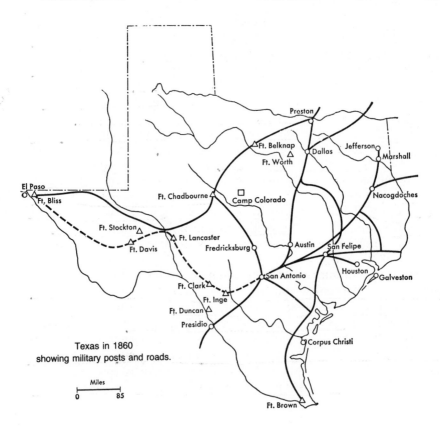

Texas in 1860
showing military posts and roads.

Miles
0   85

tion. Anglo Texans, however, generally viewed him as an outlaw who was responsible for much of the violence on both sides of the river. The owner of a ranch on the Rio Grande a few miles from Brownsville, Cortina took part in a bloody quarrel with the local sheriff whom he accused of mistreating one of his men. Cortina at that point retreated to his ranch and issued a proclamation announcing that he was a citizen of Texas defending the rights and property of the Mexican people of Texas. In the fall of 1859 he harassed Brownsville and the entire lower Rio Grande Valley. His fame and power grew, especially after he defeated a company of Texas Rangers sent from San Antonio, but he could not hold out against the overwhelming campaign organized to meet his challenge. Two companies of state troops, under the command of John S. Ford, went to the aid of a contingent of federal troops and after a lively campaign, Cortina was forced across the border into Mexico where he remained for some time.

Vigorous efforts in South Texas and on the northwestern frontier in 1859 and 1860 thus brought a measure of peace to the troubled frontier of Texas. However, Texas was on the eve of secession. There was to be no peace, on the frontier or elsewhere. Indeed the crisis on the frontier would soon return, and resolution of the problem of Indian wars would require many more years.

SELECTED BIBLIOGRAPHY

For a good bibliography on early statehood, see Ralph A. Wooster, "Early Texas Statehood: A Survey of Historical Writings," *Southwestern Historical Quarterly*, LXXVI, 121–141. For source material, see the *Houston Papers;* the *Handbook of Texas;* and E. Wallace and D. M. Vigness (eds.), *Documents of Texas History.*

The best general accounts of the period are S. V. Connor, *Adventure in Glory;* E. Wallace, *Texas in Turmoil* (Austin, 1965); O. M. Roberts, *A Political, Legislative, and Judicial History of Texas, 1845–1895,* in D. G. Wooten (ed.), *A Comprehensive History of Texas, 1685–1897* (2 vols., Dallas, 1898); and previously cited, older works by H. H. Bancroft, J. H. Brown, H. S. Thrall, F. W. Johnson, and L. J. Wortham.

Biographies that are essential for an understanding of the period include those of Sam Houston, previously cited; William Seale, *Sam Houston's Wife; A Biography of Margaret Lea Houston* (Norman, Okla., 1970); H. P. Gambrell, *Anson Jones*; Claude Elliott, *Leathercoat: The Life of James W. Throckmorton* (San Antonio, 1938); W. J. Hughes, *Rebellious Ranger: Rip Ford and the Old Southwest* (Norman, Okla., 1964); E. Wallace, *Charles DeMorse: Pioneer Editor and Statesman*; J. K. Greer, *Colonel Jack Hays* (New York, 1952); Ben H. Procter, *Not without Honor: The Life of John H. Reagan* (Austin, 1962); A. L. King, *Louis T. Wigfall: Southern Fire-eater* (Baton Rouge, 1970); and Elizabeth Silverhorne, *Ashbel Smith of Texas: Pioneer, Patriot, Statesman, 1805–1886* (College Station, 1982).

On the constitution of 1845, see a study by F. L. Paxson in *Southwestern Historical Quarterly*, XVIII, 386–398; and another by A. Middleton, *ibid.*, XXV, 26–62; also see *Debates of the Convention of 1845* (Houston, 1846).

For a background study of the war with Mexico, see Charles H. Harris, III,

Mexico Views Manifest Destiny, 1821–1846 (Albuquerque, N.M., 1976). For the war, several excellent studies are available, including: S. V. Connor and O. B. Faulk, *North America Divided: The Mexican War, 1846–1848* (New York, 1971); W. P. Webb, *The Texas Rangers*; John E. Weems, *To Conquer a Peace: The War between the United States and Mexico* (New York, 1974); N. W. Stephenson, *Texas and the Mexican War* (New Haven, Conn., 1921); Otis A. Singletary, *The Mexican War* (Chicago, 1960); Justin H. Smith, *The War with Mexico* (2 vols., New York, 1919); J. K. Greer, *Colonel Jack Hays*; Ernest C. Shearer, "The Carvajal Disturbances," *Southwestern Historical Quarterly*, LV, 201–230; H. W. Barton, "Five Texas Frontier Companies during the Mexican War," *ibid.*, LXVI, 17–30; E. Wallace, *Charles DeMorse: Pioneer Editor and Statesman;* Douglas W. Richmond, *Essays on the Mexican War* (College Station, 1986); and Tom Reilly, "Jane McManus Storms: Letters from the Mexican War, 1846–1848," *Southwestern Historical Quarterly*, LXXXV, 21–44.

The controversy over the Texas–New Mexico boundary and the settlement of the debt of the Republic of Texas are dealt with in W. C. Binkley, *The Expansionist Movement in Texas;* E. T. Miller, *A Financial History of Texas*; Holman Hamilton, *Prologue to Conflict: The Crisis and Compromise of 1850* (Lexington, Ky., 1964); Holman Hamilton, "Texas Bonds and Northern Profits: A Study in Compromise, Investment, and Lobby Influence," *Mississippi Valley Historical Review*, XLIII, 579–594; Kenneth F. Neighbours, "The Taylor-Neighbors Struggle over the Upper Rio Grande Region of Texas in 1850," *Southwestern Historical Quarterly*, LXI, 431–463; C. A. Bridges, "Texas and the Crisis of 1850" (unpublished manuscript, University of Texas Library, Austin); and S. V. Connor, *Adventure in Glory*.

On the politics of the era, besides the biographies and the general works mentioned above, there is F. B. Sexton, "J. Pinckney Henderson," *Quarterly of the Texas State Historical Association*, I, 187–203; Louis F. Blount, "A Brief Study of Thomas J. Rusk," *Southwestern Historical Quarterly*, XXXIV, 181–202, 271–292; Ralph A. Wooster, "Membership in Early Texas Legislatures, 1850–1860," *ibid.*, LXIX, 163–173; R. A. Wooster, "An Analysis of the Texas Know-Nothings," *ibid.*, LXX, 414–423; S. H. Sherman, "Governor George Thomas Wood," *ibid.*, XX, 260–268; Roy Sylvan Dunn, "The Knights of the KGC in Texas, 1860–1861," *ibid.*, LXX, 543–573; G. L. Crockett, *Two Centuries in East Texas;* E. W. Winkler (ed.), *Platforms of Political Parties in Texas* (Austin, 1916), indispensable to a study of Texas politics; Francis R. Lubbock (C. W. Raines, ed.), *Six Decades in Texas* (Austin, 1900); Norman G. Kittrell, *Governors Who Have Been, and Other Public Men of Texas* (Houston, 1921); James T. DeShields, *They Sat in High Places: The Presidents and Governors of Texas* (San Antonio, 1940). With special reference to education, see J. J. Lane, *History of Education in Texas* (Washington, D.C., 1903); Frederick Eby, *The Development of Education in Texas* (New York, 1925); and J. C. Jeffries, "Sketches of Old Baylor," *Southwestern Historical Quarterly*, LVI, 498–506.

For accounts of exploration, see Grant Foreman, *Marcy and the Gold Seekers* (Norman, Okla., 1936); "Marcy's Report on His Return from Santa Fé," *West Texas Historical Association Year Book*, I, 30–54; M. L. Crimmins, "Captain John Pope's Route to the Pacific," *Military Engineer* (March–April, 1931); W. J. Hughes, *Rebellious Ranger: Rip Ford and the Old Southwest*; W. Turrentine Jackson, *Wagon Roads West* (Berkeley, Calif., 1952); A. B. Bender, "Opening Routes across West Texas, 1848–1856," *Southwestern Historical Quarterly*, XXXVII, 116–135; W. H. Goetzman, "The United States–Mexican Boundary Survey, 1848–1853," *ibid.*,

LXII, 164–190; T. L. Connelly, "The American Camel Experiment: A Reappraisal," *ibid.*, LXIX, 442–462; E. B. Lammons, "Operation Camel: An Experiment in Animal Transportation in Texas, 1857–1860," *ibid.*, XLI, 20–49; W. H. Goetzman, *Army Exploration in the American West* (New Haven, Conn., 1959); and Chris Emmett, *Texas Camel Tales* (Austin, 1969).

For land policy, immigration, and the extension of settlements, most of the sources and studies cited under these subjects in the preceding chapter are also valuable for the period of early statehood. In addition, see W. C. Holden, *Alkali Trails* (Dallas, 1930); W. J. Hammond and Margaret F. Hammond, *La Réunion, a French Settlement in Texas* (Dallas, 1958); Ermance V. Rejebain, "La Reunion: The French Colony in Dallas County," *Southwestern Historical Quarterly*, XLIII, 472–478; H. R. Marsh, "The Czechs in Texas," *ibid.*, L, 236–240; Rondel V. Davidson, "Victor Considerant: Fourierist, Legislator, and Humanitarian" (unpublished dissertation, Texas Tech University, Lubbock, 1970); R. N. Richardson, *The Frontier of Northwest Texas, 1846–1876: Advance and Defense by the Pioneer Settlers of the Cross Timbers and Prairies* (Glendale, Calif., 1963); James Day, *Jacob de Cordova: Land Merchant of Texas* (Waco, 1962); B. P. Gallaway, "The Physical Barrier to Settlement in the Western Cross Timbers Frontier," *West Texas Historical Association Year Book*, XLII, 51–58; Mrs. William L. Cazneau (Cora Montgomery), *Eagle Pass or Life on the Border* (Austin, 1966); and W. H. Timmons, "American El Paso: The Formative Years, 1848–1854," *Southwestern Historical Quarterly*, LXXXVII, 1–36.

Of the large body of material dealing with the frontier and the Indians, the following are among the most useful: R. N. Richardson, *The Comanche Barrier*; W. P. Webb, *The Texas Rangers*; C. C. Rister, *The Southwestern Frontier* (Cleveland, 1928); D. H. Winfrey, *Texas Indian Papers, 1846–1859* (Austin, 1960); E. Wallace and E. A. Hoebel, *The Comanches*; W. C. Holden, "Frontier Defense, 1846–1860," *West Texas Historical Association Year Book*, VI, 35–64; Kenneth S. Neighbours, "Indian Exodus out of Texas in 1859," *ibid.*, XXXVI, 80–97; A. B. Bender, "The Texas Frontier," *Southwestern Historical Quarterly*, XXXVIII, 135–148; M. L. Crimmins (ed.), "Colonel J. K. F. Mansfield's Report on the Inspection of the Department of Texas in 1856," *ibid.*, LXII, 122–148, 215–257, 351–387; "W. G. Freeman's Report on the Eighth Military Department," *ibid.*, LII, 227–233; Lena Clara Koch, "The Federal Indian Policy in Texas, 1845–1860," *ibid.*, XXXVIII, 223–234, 259–286; XXIX, 19–35, 98–127; W. J. Hughes, " 'Rip' Ford's Indian Fight on the Canadian," *Panhandle-Plains Historical Review*, XXX, 1–26; J. K. Greer (ed.), *A Texas Ranger and Frontiersman: The Days of Buck Barry in Texas, 1845–1906* (Dallas, 1932); T. R. Havins, *Beyond the Cimarron: Major Earl Van Dorn in Comanche Land* (Brownwood, 1968); Kenneth F. Neighbours, *Robert Simpson Neighbors and the Texas Frontier* (Waco, 1975); Kenneth Neighbours, *Indian Exodus: Texas Indian Affairs* (Quanah, 1973); E. H. Elam, "The History of the Wichita Indian Confederacy to 1868"; Roger N. Conger and others, *Frontier Forts of Texas* (Waco, 1966).

CHAPTER NINE
PIONEER
INSTITUTIONS

By 1861 when the scourge of the Civil War ended all progress, the pattern of Texan civilization had been formed, and the state's cultural institutions had been established. In many respects they were like those of the Old South, from where a majority of the population had come, but there were many variations and a few distinct differences. Texas, in fact, belonged to both the Old South and the New West. Basic to the state's economy were the slaves and cotton of the South, but, whereas in the older states, the frontier was a thing of the past, in Texas it still affected all the people either directly or indirectly. Typical of the frontier, men outnumbered women, and in contrast to the Old South, the number of immigrants from Mexico and Europe was comparatively high.

Although most Texans were small subsistence farmers, owning few or no slaves, plantation owners and townspeople contributed more to the ideals and cultural institutions of the time. Of particular concern was the improvement of the primitive frontier transportation system. Otherwise, Texans worried about epidemics and disease and amused themselves in rather conventional fashion. Although they acquired a reputation for lawlessness, they also made more positive and longer-lasting achievements in such areas as education, literature and the arts, and religion.

THE PEOPLE

The customs and values of the Old South dominated pioneer institutions in some areas of the state, but the broad and diverse culture of antebellum Texas reflected the influence of people from many other parts of the world. Most made their homes on farms, but in 1860 foreigners constituted more than a third of the free population in five of the six largest towns. Whether on farms or in the cities, Europeans, Mexicans, and blacks all made their contributions.

German immigrants concentrated their numbers in the hill country of Central Texas, where they built strong, rugged homes often made of stone, but by 1860 one-fifth of the population of Houston, Galveston, and San Antonio were Germans. The townspeople were usually merchants or craftsmen, but some were known nationally for their achievements in science, medicine, and the arts. Immigrants from Poland, the Scandinavian nations, and other Western European countries added to the cultural mixture.

By 1860 the second largest group of foreign-born people living in Texas were the Mexican-Americans. The years following the revolution were often filled with bitter experiences for the Mexican people of Texas. Even though many had served in the revolutionary cause and some were notable leaders, prejudice and discrimination often characterized their treatment. Land titles were sometimes challenged. Most of the Mexican people who had lived around Nacogdoches for generations left their homes, and many who lived in South Texas lost their holdings.

Few returned to East Texas, but the Mexicans resumed their migration to South Texas in large numbers in the 1850s. Most lived off the land on farms and ranches, but some were attracted to the towns. Regardless of where they lived, most held proudly and with determination to the more essential parts of their cultural heritage—their religion, their language, their customs and tradition. Most were poor and lived simply in humble homes, but some were prominent and influential public figures. Santos Benavides, a mayor of Laredo, rose to the rank of general in the Civil War; José Navarro, a hero of the revolution, participated in the writing of the Constitution of 1845 and thereafter served in the Texas legislature.

Although most of the black people who made up one-third of the population of Texas in 1860 were slaves, some were free. Free blacks lived in Texas under Spanish rule with apparently some semblance of legal equality. More came under Mexican rule, and some won their freedom for their service in the revolution. In 1850 the census numbered 397 free blacks, but in 1860 the number decreased to 355. No doubt, the restrictions placed on free blacks in Texas discouraged growth in their numbers. In the republic, free blacks could not vote or own property. After statehood additional restrictions were imposed, especially with respect to punishments assessed for conviction of crimes.

Most free blacks were farmers or farm laborers and were quite poor, but a few were relatively well-to-do landowners, either with or without special legislative sanction. The most famous of them was William Goyens of Nacogdoches, although the Ashworth family of Jefferson County may have been more wealthy. Both owned slaves, as did two other black families.

OCCUPATIONS

Occupations of antebellum Texans included both the ordinary and the unusual. Merchants increased rapidly during the fifties, numbering 2,223 by 1860, while 3,541 persons found employment as domestic servants. Four Texans described themselves as "catchers of wild horses," a conventional occupation of the times. Less expected were four toymen, six daguerreotypists, three actors, forty-five artists, five clockmakers, and six dancing masters.

The professions were represented surprisingly well. In 1850 the town of Marshall, serving a wide area but with a relatively small population of 1,189, had 28 lawyers and 11 doctors. Certainly, there was no shortage of lawyers; the 428 located in Texas in 1850 doubled in number by 1860. Physicians, though often poorly trained, were likewise plentiful, their number increasing to 1,471 by 1860. But at the same time Texas had only 65 dentists, most of whom traveled from town to town to carry out their practice. There were 758 clergymen, but, as one might expect in a frontier society, only 8 architects.

Manufacturing and the crafts provided a living for some. The census of 1860 reported 3,449 persons employed in 983 manufacturing establishments. More than 400 worked in grist and saw mills, and an equal number of wheelwrights suggests the manufacture of wagons, carriages, and other vehicles. A plant in Houston manufactured hats; a factory in Harrison County produced textiles. In the crafts the 1,361 carpenters of 1850 doubled in number by 1860, and there were many brick and stone masons, blacksmiths, and saddle and harness makers.

By far the most common occupation was farming. In 1850 approximately 25,000 of the 43,000 persons who listed occupations called themselves farmers, and no doubt many others were similarly engaged. Farmers and farm laborers accounted for more than half of the 105,491 occupations of 1860. Appropriately, improved land in farms increased from 639,111 acres in 1850 to 2,650,781 acres ten years later, and during the same period the value of farms increased more than fivefold, reaching a total of about $88 million.

Early settlers of Comanche County in West-Central Texas: a representative group of sturdy ranchers, farmers, and an occasional lawyer, doctor, or preacher who probably migrated from counties in eastern Texas or directly from Tennessee, Alabama, Arkansas, or Louisiana during the period between 1854 (the year of the first settlement) and 1880. (E. C. Barker History Center, University of Texas)

For the marketplace, the most important crop was cotton. Except for occasional years when pests ravaged the crops, the output increased each year. It reached 58,072 bales in 1849–1850 and 431,463 a decade later. During the period of the republic, cotton farming had been confined to the river valley of the Coastal Plain and to eastern Texas from the upper Neches River northward, where there was limited production. By 1860 these regions still produced the great part of the crop, but cotton farming was being extended into Central Texas, even though the notion still prevailed that it was a bottomland crop not suited to the black prairies.

Although cotton was the money crop, in early Texas corn was indispensable. To a very large extent it sustained both the people and their animals. Reports claimed that an average yield in early years was 40 to 80 bushels to the acre and that as much as 110 bushels had been grown without the application of manure.

Other food crops included sweet potatoes, wheat, and sugar cane. Next to corn in importance were sweet potatoes, grown not only by the small subsistence farmer but also on the large plantations. Less abundant was wheat, not grown at all in southern Texas and a secondary crop elsewhere. During the period of low prices for cotton that followed the Panic of 1837, the planters near the coast turned to raising sugar cane. The industry grew until 1852, but because of occasional droughts and freezes it declined thereafter.

During this period there was some organized effort to improve farming. Agriculture societies were formed as early as 1843, but apparently their efforts were not long sustained. The first exposition known actually to have been held was the Corpus Christi Fair of 1852. At Dallas in 1858 the first recorded state fair in Texas was held. Formally chartered in 1886, it has become one of the leading annual exhibitions of the nation. Thomas Affleck, long active in the improvement of agriculture in the South, in 1858 established Glenblythe near Brenham as a model for Texas plantations.

Efforts to improve livestock breeds began at an early date. Purebred livestock was introduced during the Mexican regime; English-bred hogs, sheep, horses, and cattle were imported in 1840. In a land of horses, many were highly bred, some of racing stock. One stallion in the fifties was valued at $6,000. But cattle accounted for most of the value of Texas livestock, placed at $42,825,447 in 1860.

SLAVERY AND THE PLANTATION SYSTEM

In antebellum Texas, slavery and cotton cultivation expanded together; the largest cotton-producing counties contained the largest slave population. Slaveholders, only about one-third of the state's farmers, produced 90 percent of the cotton crop.

Estimated at 5,000 in 1836, the slave population increased at an accelerated pace after Texas became independent. The census of 1860 showed 182,566 slaves and 430,891 white persons. Since 1850 the slave population had increased 214 percent and the white population only 180 percent.

Slaves represented a substantial proportion of Texas capital. In 1850 the average value of a slave assessed for taxes was $362, while in 1860 this amount reached $672; the aggregate value of all slaves was about 20 percent greater than the value of the farms of Texas. On the market, field hands brought from $1,200 to $2,000 and "plow boys" from $1,000 to $1,500. Good hands could be hired out at from $200 to $300 for the year. Some enthusiasts contended that a good field hand who produced eight bales of cotton could pay for himself in a year.

Rapidly expanding agriculture created a demand for slaves that was never satisfied. Apparently most of the slaves were brought in by immigrants, and most sales were private transactions involving neighbors only. Yet dealers in Galveston and Houston kept on hand slaves of all ages and held regular auctions; in most communities there were sale or auction days. During the late 1850s there was considerable demand for the reopening of the African slave trade, a move supported by a number of prominent Texans and even by some church groups. The illicit African slave trade, meanwhile, brought in hundreds, perhaps thousands, through Galveston and other coastal points. Free blacks were sometimes enslaved, either through kidnapping or legal subterfuge.

Descriptions of slave life in Texas suggest that slaves could expect at best a life with basic necessities but few comforts and, at worst, a life of drudgery and brutality. Slave quarters on the plantation generally consisted of a one-room or a two-room cabin for each family, located along a street or around an empty square and near the overseer's house. The food of the slaves was much like that of the poorer whites; bacon and corn bread were the basis of the diet. Some, however, raised gardens and kept poultry. On the best plantations food was served from a common kitchen, especially during the planting and harvesting seasons. Clothing generally consisted of two suits each year, seldom made of homespun, for the planter considered ready-made articles more economical. Medical attention in most cases was perhaps as good as that available to sick white people. Religion was important in the life of many slaves. Some owners encouraged their slaves to attend and participate in services, and many were apparently eager to do so. However, some owners either discouraged or prevented involvement in religious activities.

For most slaves work was hard, monotonous, and never-ending drudgery. Working conditions on farms and plantations varied from owner to owner and depended on the season of the year, but there are reports of slaves working from four in the morning to nine at night. Sometimes there was little or no work on Sunday or perhaps even on Saturday, but at harvest time or in other busy seasons, the slaves might be in the fields every day of the week. The brutality of slave life was apparent in many ways, but the most common form was whipping. Owners were authorized by law to punish their slaves and seem to have usually done so through whipping. Slaves convicted of crimes were often whipped. For example, a slave in Hunt County charged with larceny in 1856 received seventy-six lashes at the instruction of the court. Owners accused of excessive cruelty could be charged in court, but instances where such charges were brought were rare and convictions even more rare.

In Texas as elsewhere, those in bondage longed for freedom. Slaves frequently ran away. Some returned voluntarily, but others were arrested and returned, while still others made their way to Mexico or to Indian Territory. It is estimated that more than four thousand escaped to Mexico. During the decade preceding the Civil War, there was growing uneasiness about slavery. Vigilance committees became common, and the punishment of slaves charged with disobedience became more severe.

Although most slaves worked on plantations, urban slavery expanded as Texas towns grew. By 1860 Houston and San Antonio each contained more than one thousand slaves, and smaller towns numbered slaves in the hundreds. Many of the urban slaves were household servants, but others worked in flour mills, sawmills, or other factories, while some were carpenters, blacksmiths, or skilled in other crafts.

Those who profited most from slavery, the planters, made up a small minority of the population. In 1860 there were 21,878 slaveowners in Texas, only 5.7 percent of all slaveowners in the nation. Only 2,163 of these owned 20 or more slaves, and only 54 owned 100 or more. More than half of all the slaveholders owned five or fewer. Only about ten percent of the slaveholders and less than five percent of all farmers operated on a scale large enough to necessitate hiring an overseer, thereby coming within the planter class.

The influence of the planters was, however, far out of proportion to their number. Nearly all were leaders in their communities, and many exercised statewide influence. More than any other group they stamped upon early Texas society its distinguishing characteristics.

A study of those planters with more than a hundred slaves revealed wide variations in wealth but several relatively consistent characteristics. Property holds of 47 great planters ranged from $60,000 to more than $600,000, cotton production from less than 250 bales to more than 800, and livestock holdings from $1,400 to more than $53,000. Although all but three were cotton planters, their agricultural practices were surprisingly diversified. Practically all owned cattle and hogs, about half of the group

The home the Houstons built in Huntsville, Texas in 1847. (C. C. Springfield, Huntsville)

raised sheep, every planter grew corn, more than three-fourths grew sweet potatoes, and a somewhat smaller proportion planted other food crops. The Texas plantation was far from self-sufficient, but it was likewise far from complete dependency on outside sources for many staple products.

The wealthier planters lived better than any other people of their day. They had food in great abundance and variety, and elaborate meals were frequently assembled from garden, woods, and stream, with hot breads, cakes, jellies, preserves, and rare delicacies from New Orleans. As they acquired more property, the planters replaced their log cabins with larger and better constructed buildings of cedar, walnut, or pine, and occasionally of brick. Many of these houses were built during the decade preceding the Civil War. Tastes varied from time to time, but a desire for luxuries remained constant. In 1831, cottonades and candle molds were in special demand; sideboards, tables, and jewelry were bought in quantity during the forties and fifties; and in 1848 one merchant apparently had difficulty in filling an order for a "Bathing Tub and Pea Fowl Brush."

LIFE ON THE FARMS

For most rural Texans the plantation system was something only to be observed and perhaps envied. For them their existence depended upon their own labor; their houses were simple, and their luxuries were few.

The houses built by country people were only slightly better than those of colonial times. Here and there was to be found a frame dwelling, well designed and carefully built, but the prevailing type in the middle of the century was still the log cabin. The double log cabin, or dog-run house, was the most popular. It consisted of two rooms under a continuous, gabled roof, separated by an open space or dog run. Commonly, a porch extended across the entire front. In addition to serving as a sleeping place for the dogs (and for overflow guests) and providing a space for family and friends to sit in during warm weather, the dog run and the porch served as catchalls for saddles, bridles, harnesses, chests, boxes, guns, and a dozen other things. The logs were hand-hewn and dovetailed at the corners. As the family grew, a lean-to might be added to the back of one or both rooms. Also a kitchen and perhaps a smokehouse might be built, but they were separate from the main house. Spaces between the logs were chinked with boards and daubed with clay or mortar. The roofs were of clapboards held securely in place by weight poles. Chimneys commonly were made of sticks, covered with mud. Floors, if any, were puncheon. While traveling in eastern Texas in 1855, Frederick Law Olmsted wrote of stopping for the night at a comparatively comfortable house, but he could "look out, as usual, at the stars between the logs." Traveler Rutherford B. Hayes, the future President of the United States, described a house he saw in Texas whose walls you "could throw a cat through at random." Olmsted frequently made note of houses having glass windows, but he mentioned them in such a way as to indicate that they were the exception rather than the rule. The Germans built better houses than the Anglo-Americans, frequently using stone in their construction. There was much building during the sixth decade of the century, and houses made of lumber became more common. Often such houses were flimsy, boxlike affairs, not as good as the sturdy log cabins they displaced.

For a country that might have produced fruits, vegetables, cereals, and honey in bountiful quantities, and where cattle were abundant, the diet of most early Texans was strangely monotonous. Even by 1860 many farm families lived as the earliest Texans did, almost wholly on salt pork, corn bread, and syrup. The most common vegetable was the sweet potato. Many people tasted fresh meat only occasionally, and a large percentage of them did not have milk and butter. Except in the northern counties, wheat bread was almost unknown in the poorer homes. Water was obtained from a nearby spring or stream or occasionally from a well or cistern.

Much of the burden of pioneer life was carried by the women of the family. To them fell the tiresome drudgery of washing and making clothes, making soap, taking care of the children, preparing and preserving food, taking care of the sick, and often looking after the livestock. In busy seasons and sometimes other times, many worked in the fields, chopping or picking cotton or doing whatever needed to be done. Education and cultural activities of the family, if any, were usually the responsibility of the women of the household. But, notwithstanding the heavy burden of everyday life, pioneer Texas women were active in community affairs, promoting the establishment of schools, starting Sunday schools, and encouraging the formation of churches.

The farm was substantially, though not totally, self-sufficient. Candles or lard-burning lamps supplied light. Ash hoppers and pork fat supplied materials for soap; corn was ground in steel hand mills; and cotton was carded, spun, and woven into cloth. Within less than five years one Texan recorded in his diary that he made a wheel, a coffin, a reel, a churn, a cradle, a bucket, a pump auger, an ox yoke, and a pair of shoes, in addition to working at the loom, hewing puncheons, and graining deerskins. Isaac Van Zandt, a man of distinction, made in emergencies a saddle, a pair of shoes, candles, and a baby's cradle. Toward the end of the period, however, imported manufactured cloth and ready-made clothing were rapidly supplanting homemade materials.

THE TOWNS

A person coming into Texas, direct from the Northern States might, perhaps, be suprised upon seeing many places called towns in Texas. He would, probably, as has been frequently the case, inquire, "where is the town?"

Thus did Melinda Rankin, a missionary from New England, comment on Texas municipalities in 1850. In truth, the state had no towns to spare. Galveston, with 4,177 inhabitants, was the largest. San Antonio, Houston, New Braunfels, and Marshall followed in the order named. No other towns had populations of as many as a thousand. Austin, long buffeted by hostile Indians and the threat of Mexican invasion, was the home of only 639 persons. Through trade with Mexico and growth as an army center, San Antonio had forged ahead, and by 1860 showed a total of 8,236 persons. Galveston moved to second place, Houston was third, and Austin fourth. Sixteen other towns, making twenty in all, are shown in the eighth census of 1860 to have had a population of 1,000 or more each.

Civic improvement came but slowly. Observers found Houston streets filled with "bottomless" mud and San Antonio streets almost impassable in bad weather. In 1857, however, Galveston paved its most traveled street with shells, and San Antonio spent twelve hundred dollars on street improvements and also built some bridges. About the same time San Antonio organized a "fire association" and in 1860 installed gas lights.

The best buildings in a town generally were the hotels. Dr. Ferdinand Roemer found the hotel in Houston "a rather pretentious two-story building," but the interior was so neglected as to remind him that he had reached the "borders of civilization." Service was poor and one was expected to occupy a room with several strangers. The pride of San Antonio was the Menger Hotel on Alamo Plaza, which opened in 1859. The building of fine-cut stone, two and one-half stories high, together with

The Texas capitol building, in Austin, 1853. It was destroyed by fire in November 1881. (Southwest Collection, Texas Tech University)

its carpets, decorations, and beautiful furniture cost $16,000. Only wealthy people and professional travelers patronized hotels; the rank and file put up at the wagon yards.

By 1860 one could purchase in the larger Texas towns almost any article to be had in the stores and warehouses in the East. Advertisements indicate that merchants kept in stock all kinds of farm machinery, carriages, wagons, building supplies, furniture, kitchen supplies, many kinds of cloth and clothing, jewelry, gold and silver plate, a large assortment of processed foods, ice, quantities of drugs and cosmetics, and liquors; indeed, an almost endless list of items. There were jobbers and wholesalers in Texas, but many merchants made their purchases in New Orleans or in other cities.

The scarcity of money and lack of banking facilities constituted a handicap for business during the period of the republic and early statehood, just as it had in colonial times. This condition was aggravated by the provision in the Constitution of 1845 prohibiting the chartering of banks. Although various firms carried out certain banking functions, only one bank was incorporated in Texas before the Civil War. This was the Bank of Commerce and Agriculture, opened in Galveston by McKinney and Williams in 1847, under an old charter of the state of Coahuila and Texas.

During the early years of the republic quantities of depreciated bank notes from the Unites States circulated in Texas, and the paper money issued by the Texan government was even less dependable. Promissory notes were sometimes used as money, with the most common hard money consisting of hammered Spanish dollars (old Spanish dollars with the royal effigy defaced) and Mexican dollars. Later the quality of bank notes brought in from the East improved.

TRANSPORTATION

"No one walks in Texas if the distance is more than a mile," said Dr. Ferdinand Roemer, who visited the country in 1846. Nevertheless, Texans found inadequate transportation facilities in the vast land to be one of their more difficult problems, one that for a long time retarded development in the state. Travelers and merchants depended on coastal and river traffic, roads, stage lines, and freight contractors. Railroad construction began in the fifties.

Invaluable for foreign and interstate traffic were the coastal outlets. The most serviceable ports were Galveston and Matagorda. Houston did considerable business through Buffalo Bayou; and Indianola, founded by Prince Carl of Solms-Braunfels in 1844, near the present Port Lavaca, came to be the principal port of West Texas. It was destroyed by a storm in 1875, rebuilt, and destroyed again in 1886.

Some areas relied on the rivers. The Brazos was navigable as far as Brazoria, and occasionally boats went even higher up the river. The Red River was navigable to Shreveport and under favorable conditions to Pecan Point and Jonesborough. Through Big Cypress Bayou, Caddo Lake, the Red River, and the Mississippi, Jefferson had water connection with New Orleans. In seasons of abundant rain small boats ascended the Sabine to Sabinetown near San Augustine; the lower Trinity would carry boats of shallow draft; and some cotton was shipped down the San Jacinto. Buffalo Bayou afforded good navigation to Houston. Because of a raft that closed its channel near the Gulf, the Colorado was useless for navigation.

The great majority of Texans depended on such roads as existed. The chief roads, or routes of travel that were called roads, were the old military road, from Red River through Dallas, Waco, and Austin; the old San Antonio–Nacogdoches Road, passing through Bastrop and Crockett; the road fron Indianola to San Antonio; and a road from Dallas and vicinity southward to Houston. The roads, which were bad even under favorable conditions, became impassable quagmires in wet weather. Olmsted, who entered Texas from the east, pronounced the road in Leon County "little better than a cowtrack." He described the road from Victoria to Lavaca as a "mere collection of straggling wagon ruts, extending for more than a quarter of a mile in width, from outside to outside, it being desirable in this part of the country, rather to avoid the road than follow it." Yet, all roads were not so nearly impassable. Rutherford B. Hayes, in the winter of 1848–1849, recorded in his diary, "Rode 14 miles on good dry roads on the banks of the Brazos [near Columbia]."

Freight contractors and stage lines provided public transportation. Using strong, heavy wagons of bois d'arc, "shaped like boats," with iron axles, wheels five and a half feet high, and tires six inches wide, freighters hauled loads averaging 7,000 pounds. These huge wagons, pulled by teams of ten to twenty mules or horses or from 20 to 30 oxen, sometimes moved in long trains, occasionally mixed with the smaller carts generally used by Mexican freighters. Freight rates varied with the weather and season, averaging about one cent per mile for each one hundred pounds, but more in bad weather.

Of the many vehicles used for public conveyances, the stage coach was the most popular. The quality of the coaches, at least on certain lines, was greatly improved during the fifties. Described as large, airy, and strong in contrast with the "ordinary hacks" used in the eastern states, they carried as many as nine passengers in the inside and a few on the outside. On the San Antonio–San Diego and the Southern Overland Mail Lines, the famous Concord coaches were used. Travel was nevertheless uncomfortable, sometimes dangerous, and usually expensive. Mud, high water, cold weather, Indian attacks, and robberies combined at times to make travel hazardous. The usual charge for a passenger was ten cents a mile, but some contractors doubled the charges in wet weather.

Interstate stage traffic was fast and dependable. In August 1857 a semimonthly mail and passenger service was opened between San Antonio and San Diego, California. The scheduled thirty-day trip cost $200; during the first year there was not a single failure to complete the journey. Still better service was that inaugurated in 1858 by the Southern Overland or Butterfield Mail Lines, which skirted the settlements of North Texas on its route from St. Louis and Memphis on the east to San Francisco on the west. Stages ran each way twice weekly and completed the journey of about 2,700 miles in 25 days or less.

Federal mail subsidies were largely responsible for the long stage lines. Mail contracts supplied the large expenditures necessary for stage stands, coaches, road repairs, and labor. Mail service otherwise was substantially improved by 1861, though it did not even approximate present-day standards. Wet mail and late mail were common causes of complaint, and post offices were scarce. Not until 1850, for instance, did San Antonio have one.

During the fifties the railroads began both to compete with and to feed the stage and freight lines. Late in 1852 construction on the first railroad line in Texas was begun in Harrisburg, nine miles south of Houston. It was the Buffalo Bayou, Brazos, and Colorado, commonly called the Harrisburg Railroad, and later a part of the Southern Pacific system. By 1855 it had been extended 32 miles, from Harrisburg on Buffalo Bayou to Richmond on the Brazos, and five years later it was built into Alleyton near the Colorado. Several other lines were built in the Houston area, and by 1860 there were railroads linking Victoria to Port Lavaca and Shreveport to Marshall. With a combination of rail and steamship service, passengers could travel between New Orleans and Galveston in twenty-two and a half hours.

With all its inconveniences, railroad travel was far superior to travel by other conveyances. Reflecting the contrast of the old and the new, the Harrisburg Railroad advertised in 1860, "The River Bottom and Wet Prairies are NOW BRIDGED, and what was (and is now on some routes) a journey of days is now performed in the same number of hours." Charges were five cents per mile for passengers and about one cent per mile for each hundred pounds of freight.

HEALTH

Early-day Texans claimed that their state was the most healthful in America; yet it seems to have been a place where doctors were fairly numerous. Most citizens, however, seem to have relied upon their own resources in times of illness, even though doctors were generally available in populated areas. Women, in particular, took care of the sick, some developing community-wide recognition for their skills. Childbirth usually occurred at home, sometimes with the assistance of a physician, but more often it was a community midwife who assisted in the delivery.

From time to time epidemics took a heavy toll. In the spring of 1833 cholera took 80 lives at Brazoria and nearly depopulated Velasco. The dreaded scourge returned in 1834, ravaging Nacogdoches and taking 91 lives in Goliad. Later cholera epidemics in 1849, 1850, and 1852 particularly endangered the slave population. In 1846 an epidemic, which may have been typhus, killed scores of people in New Braunfels and Fredericksburg and also many German immigrants in Indianola on their way to the settlements. Yellow fever appeared from time to time and, next to cholera, was the most dreaded disease. People suffered from many other ailments as well—chills and fever, inflammation of the eyes, summer complaints, rheumatism, biliousness, measles, whooping cough, and smallpox.

Although informed people associated cholera with filth, claims for nostrums and cures were far more extravagant than in our own day; and stores were filled with patent medicines ranging from cancer cures to cough remedies. One merchant said he believed the people used quinine in the same way they used cornmeal: They bought it and took it whether they were sick or not. Warning of an impending cholera epidemic, the San Antonio Board of Health in 1834 prescribed a cleanup campaign and also recommended a copper amulet be hung around the neck. Another prescription (almost 100 percent effective, it was claimed!) consisted of water from the boiled peyote cactus, a little lime, and a few drops of laudanum. Later "cures" were little, if any, more specific than those of earlier years. Brandy, cayenne pepper, and mustard were favorite remedies.

There was, however, some progress in medical science. Although it did not hold a second meeting for sixteen years, the state medical association was organized in 1853, with Dr. Ashbel Smith and Dr. J. W. Throckmorton among its more prominent members. In 1854 the distinguished surgeon Dr. Ferdinand Charles von Herff of San Antonio performed a major operation using chloroform.

AMUSEMENTS

The people of Texas brought to their new homes the traditional amusements of the Anglo-American frontier. Athletic contests in which trained teams participated were almost unknown, but there were house raisings, log rollings, shooting matches, bear hunts, wolf hunts, quilting bees, and a dozen other activities in which work, sport, and play were mixed. Dancing was popular in the country and in town, but the most active church people objected to it. Traveler Rutherford B. Hayes described a dance that began at two o'clock in the afternoon and lasted until half past four the next morning. Men and women came on horseback ten or fifteen miles through mud and rain.

Balls and formal dinners frequently were given in honor of some distinguished visitor or on some other special occasion. Apparently everybody joined in the patriotic celebrations on July 4 (Independence Day of the United States), March 2 (Texas Independence Day), and April 21 (the anniversary of the Battle of San Jacinto). Barbecues, patriotic songs, processions, and fervid oratory were the favorite forms of entertainment. Organizations, such as the Sunday School Union or the Sons of Temperance, sponsored and directed the programs on these occasions. Christmas and New Year's were times for dances, torchlight processions, and other amusements. Thanksgiving was celebrated on various dates, according to the proclamation of the President of the United States. The most

Colonel John S. "Rip" Ford, a South Carolinian by birth, came to Texas in 1836. In the course of a long career he practiced medicine in San Augustine, edited the *Texas Democrat* and later the *State Times* in Austin, and served in both the Congress of the Republic of Texas and the state senate. He attained renown as a ranger, defeating the Indians in two notable engagements, and as an officer in the Confederate army, commanding the troops that won the Battle of Palmito Ranch, the last land engagement of the war. His nickname "Rip" came from his practice during the war with Mexico of introducing death notices in his newspaper with "Rest in peace," which in the stress of battle became "R.I.P." (E. C. Barker History Center, University of Texas)

popular sport was horse racing, and every community had its racetrack. The track at Velasco was famous in Texas and well known in New Orleans.

Interest in cultural entertainment was creditable. Most towns had amateur theatrical organizations. As early as 1838 San Augustine had its "Thespian Corps." The distinguished lawyer W. B. Ochiltree was a member, and John Salmon "Rip" Ford, famous as an editor, soldier, and statesman, wrote a play for it. Houston and Galveston each had an active lyceum during the fifties. San Antonio, with its large German population, was a center for artists. The German Casino Association owned a fine building there that was used for theatrical performances, concerts, lectures, exhibits, and dramatic readings. In almost every community, literary societies sponsored debates on ponderous subjects; there were many lectures, both pay and free, and vocal and band concerts. Professional troupes gave performances in all the larger towns. A complete program consisted of a song, a dance, a farce, and a drama. Some of the farces were "Limerick Boy," "The Irish Tiger," and "The Widow's Victim." Among the dramas were "Cross of Gold," "The Maiden's Vow," and "William Tell."

CRIME, VICE, AND REFORM

Early Texas society, like that of our own day, presented many facets to observers. It could be clean and wholesome, base and immoral, or at some level between these two extremes, depending on the point of view of the person describing it.

At an early date Texas acquired a reputation for crime and lawlessness, a reputation not altogether undeserved. The high standards required of citizens by the *empresarios* were not maintained in later years, and many renegades drifted in. The *Houston Telegraph* of January 19, 1842, lists several homicides, and the editor states that they are so frequent as to "foster opprobrium upon the national character." Dueling continued, although the provision against it in the Constitution of 1845 reduced the practice.

As late as the republic (1836–1845), the criminal code was harsh, and several offenses were punishable by death. One rather notorious woman was sentenced to death for forgery, but President Lamar pardoned her. Whipping and branding were not infrequent. There was no penitentiary until 1849. Jails were small and crowded, and jail breaks were common. Law enforcement was lax, a condition that explains why vigilance committees occasionally used direct methods. In 1852 such an organization hanged twelve or more persons in the vicinity of San Antonio.

More common were lesser vices. Gambling was quite prevalent. Gamblers were held in low esteem, but public disapproval apparently was not strong enough to stop their operations. In 1842 the Harris County grand jury brought seventy-seven indictments for "playing at cards." The number found by grand juries after 1848 was decidedly smaller, but the decline was probably due more to greater laxity on the part of the officers than to any change in the habits of the people. Betting on horse races was very common, and occasionally men of some means lost all their property in a single day at the tracks. Drinking was widespread and drunkenness common. In some communities, at least, it was customary for candidates to set before voters an open barrel of whiskey. "Profaneness, gaming, and intemperance are prevailing vices against which we have to contend," wrote Martin Ruter, the Methodist missionary of Texas, in 1838.

Beyond a doubt, the temperance movement, which entered from the East shortly after annexation and enlisted the services of prominent churchmen, brought some change. The Sons of Temperance, a national organization opposing the use of alcohol, was organized in Texas in 1848 and in a little more than a year claimed three thousand members. During the following year it was stated that a majority of the members of the legislature belonged to it. Sam Houston, whose excessive drinking had often been a matter of public comment, had mended his ways and now worked in behalf of the organization. In 1851 a traveler found local organizations of the Sons in nearly every town and in many rural communities.

Meanwhile, there was some legislation on the subject of alcoholic drink. The republic had found it a troublesome subject and enacted laws requiring the licensing of dealers and a bond guaranteeing that they would keep orderly, reputable houses and prevent gambling and quarreling on their premises. A law in 1854 went much further. It permitted the electors of a county, by majority vote, to forbid the licensing of the sale of liquor in quantities of less than a quart, a provision aimed at the saloon. The champions of temperance were not satisfied with such a measure and, in a large convention in Huntsville, advocated a "thorough Maine Liquor Law" (prohibiting the sale of alcoholic beverages). Of the forty-one counties in which the subject was submitted to the voters, restriction of sale was adopted in thirty-five. The law was declared unconstitutional, however, and never went into effect.

EDUCATION

By 1850 there was a strong sentiment for a public school system. People generally were taking a greater interest in education; the agitation of the slavery question was producing an acute sectionalism; and proud Texans were loath to send their children to schools in the North. Even if the parent had to pay tuition, the state, they thought, should contribute funds to make the schools better. Earlier it was stated that in 1854 the legislature set aside $2 million in United States indemnity bonds for schools. The law provided for dividing the counties into school districts, but two years later this method of organization was abolished. Thereafter, any group of people might set up a school, employ a teacher, and draw from the state fund each child's money. The share for each child was pitifully small; it amounted to only 62 cents in 1854 and a dollar and a half the following year. Under the terms of the law it was not even necessary that the people of a community organize and start a public school in order to receive state funds. A parent might select a private school, pay his or her children's tuition, and at the end of the year receive from the county treasurer the amount of state *much* funds to which he or she was entitled. In fact, this was done in most cases, *c* with the result that only a few public schools were established.

Founded by Colonel R. T. P. Allen, the Bastrop Military Institute was incorporated in 1858 by a board of trustees elected by the Methodist Episcopal Church. The school offered preparatory and collegiate courses of study to such students as Joseph D. Sayers and Sam Houston, Jr. After being closed during the Civil War, Bastrop became the Texas Military Institute in 1868. (Texas Highway Department)

The most important institutions of learning in Texas before the Civil War were not a part of the public school system. Some were private, wholly under the control of one or two men or women. Frances Trask founded a boarding school in 1834; Lydia McHenry established one the next year; and there were others. Still others were community enterprises, and some were under the control of lodges or religious denominations. The Constitution of 1836 did not prohibit private or denominational schools from receiving public aid, and several of these early schools were given land grants by the republic. There was no classification and no uniformity of standards. Although with two or three exceptions their work was confined to elementary and secondary levels, they were called, indiscriminately, institutes, academies, colleges, and universities.

The churches regarded Christian education as an important church function, and they began to establish schools at a very early date. Martin Ruter, the Methodist missionary, had not been in Texas six months when he wrote: "My labor in Texas will be devoted to forming societies and circuits, establishing schools, and making arrangements for a college or university." Schools not under church control generally maintained religious environments. Most of the teachers were preachers. For instance, of the fourteen Presbyterian ministers who came to Texas as missionaries during the republic, nine engaged in teaching. As late as 1866, of the teachers who attended the Texas teachers' state convention, eighteen were ministers and seventeen laymen.

The first Protestant denominational school was Rutersville College (named for Martin Ruter), which was established by the Methodists near La Grange. Its preparatory and female departments were opened in January 1840 and its collegiate department for young men in 1841. It was chartered by the republic and endowed with four leagues of land. For a few years, the community was the leading school center in Texas, but in about 1850 the school began to decline rapidly. The University of San Augustine opened in 1842 with a grammar school, a female department, and a college, and for a few years was widely known. Perhaps the most prosperous and best-known school in its day was McKenzie College, founded near Clarksville in 1841. Like others of that day, the school simply grew up around a great teacher, in this case, J. W. P. McKenzie. For a period it had as many as three hundred boarding students.

Baylor University, a Baptist school chartered in Independence by the republic in 1845, attained a position of leadership at an early date. It granted 16 degrees in 1858 and 22 in 1859, more than all other schools in Texas combined. Waco University was founded in 1861. The two schools were consolidated as Baylor University and were located in Waco in 1886. The female department of Baylor University became Baylor Female College in 1866 and was moved to Belton in 1886.

From annexation to the beginning of the Civil War, the legislature granted charters to 117 schools and incorporated, in addition, 9 educational associations. There were 40 academies, 30 colleges, 27 institutes, 7 universities, 5 schools, 3 high schools, 2 seminaries, 1 collegiate institute, 1 orphan asylum, and 1 medical college. Of these, only 3 have survived with anything like a continuous history: Austin College, founded in 1849 in Huntsville through the influence of Dr. Daniel Baker and moved to Sherman in 1879, Ursuline Academy of San Antonio, and Ursuline Academy of Galveston.

Through their emphasis on discipline, as well as on the knowledge they dispensed, these old schools were great civilizing agencies. "Course of study full, instruction thorough and discipline strict," ran a typical advertisement of the fifties. "A strict discipline rigidly enforced," stated another. The curricula emphasized ancient and modern languages and philosophy. San Augustine University, however, required laboratory work in science and maintained a chemical laboratory and mineralogical cabinet. Even the simplest subjects were described in awe-inspiring terms. Surely, parents would be impressed and children terrified on reading that the city schools of Houston in 1841 were teaching "English, French, Spanish, and Latin, grammatically and etymologically, on the most approved and expeditious principles." Apparently, some of the teachers taught everything they had studied, and some, like the Reverend Marcus A. Montrose, graduate of Edinburgh, had had liberal training. At San Augustine University he taught mathematics, Latin, Greek, history, navigation, astronomy, rhetoric, logic, political economy, natural philosophy, chemistry, botany, and geology. In fact, for a period, he alone made up the faculty of the university, although he must have been assisted by some of the more advanced students.

Evidently a large majority of early-day Texas youths received their training either in their homes or in "old field schools," unknown beyond the confines of a single community. In spite of the handicaps that confronted teacher and pupil, such training must have been efficient. In 1850 a little less than 6 percent of the white men of Texas and 8 percent of the white women were illiterate. By 1860, illiteracy had decreased to less than 4 percent among the men and slightly more than 5 percent among the women.

Unlike most southern states, Texas did not have a law prohibiting the education of slaves. Few, however, were educated, and at the end of the Civil War, more than 95 percent were illiterate.

NEWSPAPERS, LITERATURE, AND ART

Newspapers in surprising numbers served the people of antebellum Texas. By 1840 no less than thirteen newspapers were being published, one or two of which were semiweeklies. The federal census of 1860 reports three daily, three triweekly, and sixty-five weekly newspapers, and three monthly publications. The circulation of the weekly papers was 90,615, a number sufficiently large to have reached practically every person in the state.

The most venerable publication was the *Telegraph*, revived in Columbia after the Texan Revolution and moved to Houston in 1837. A neighbor of the *Telegraph*, the *Daily News* of Galveston, started in 1842 as a "puny four-page sheet . . . born in a one-room, unpainted shack on the Strand" but lived to become the oldest business institution in Texas. Both the *Dallas News* and the *Galveston News* of our own day trace their lineage to this paper. The *State Gazette* of Austin, established in 1849, was edited from 1853 to 1861 by John Marshall, associated for a part of the time with William S. Oldham. Marshall and Oldham were brilliant, aggressive men, and their paper was noted for its opposition to Sam Houston. Beginning in 1842 Charles DeMorse, soldier, statesman, and editor, published in Clarksville the *Northern Standard*. Its files, unbroken until 1861 and renewed in 1865, constitute the richest source of information extant on early civilization in northeast Texas. Robert W. Laughery's *Texas Republican* in Marshall was well edited and influential. Worthy also were the *Weekly Herald* in Dallas and the *Chronicle* in Nacogdoches.

The newspapers of early Texas do not meet the standards of our own day. Apparently little or no use was made of such news-gathering agencies as the Associated Press, which was organized in 1848. Also, not until the late fifties was there sufficient telegraph mileage to distribute the news well. News from the outside generally came through New Orleans. Many social activities were ignored. It was not deemed good taste to print the names of women in newspapers, except under very unusual conditions. Yet, more clearly and fully than any other source, these papers describe for us the way of life of that era. They were, furthermore, replete with political news and sharp editorial comment on public affairs, and the people who read them were well informed on important current issues.

Texans who wanted to read beyond the offerings of newspapers could turn to other writings. Travel accounts were popular. Mary Austin Holley, a cousin of Stephen F. Austin, wrote down in vivid style her impressions of the new land. Her second work, more complete than the first, was published in 1836 as *Texas*. Matilda C. F. Houston, an English woman who visited about 1843, wrote *Texas and the Gulf of Mexico*, an informative account of the Galveston-Houston region. In 1849 a German scientist, Dr. Ferdinand Roemer, published *Texas*, a perceptive description of the frontier as it was at that time. A few years later came Frederick Law Olmsted, a landscape artist and engineer with broad interests. His *Journey through Texas* described the state as he saw it through critical eyes.

Other writers turned to history. George Wilkins Kendall, founder and associate editor of the New Orleans *Picayune*, who accompanied the Texan Santa Fe expedition of 1841, recorded in his history of the journey experiences that represented practically every element of adventure and

peril that could have befallen people on the southwestern frontier. William
Kennedy, an Englishman, published his *Texas* in 1841. Fourteen years
later, Henderson Yoakum brought forth *A History of Texas*, a truly remarkable study that received wide circulation.

Fiction, with adventure as a major theme, attracted the interest of a
few authors. Possibly the most successful was the Irishman Mayne Reid,
who wrote *Headless Horseman*, a tale based on a southwest Texas legend. In
poetry Mirabeau B. Lamar's "Daughter of Mendoza" was popular, as was
James Lytle's "Ranger's Song" and Reuben Potter's "Hymn of the Alamo."

Apparently, the number of books and magazines increased rapidly
during the fifties. The bookstore of Francis D. Allen of Galveston, for
instance, advertised books: "Standard, Classical, Scientific, Mechanical,
School, Historical Law, Medical, Theological, Agricultural, Poetical, Biographical, Voyages, Novels, etc." Richardson and Company sold ten thousand copies of the *Texas Almanac* for 1857, increased the output of the 1858
issue, and published 30,000 copies of the 1859 issue, featuring such items
as a biographical sketch of General Rusk and an account of the Texan
Revolution. In the census returns for 1850, twelve libraries were listed; the
returns for 1860 showed 132. Magazines that were read extensively were
Harper's, Blackwood's Edinburgh Review, Westminster Review, London Quarterly,
and *Godey's Lady's Book.*

Artists who recorded the scenes and people of antebellum Texas
numbered literally in the dozens. José Sanchez, a Mexican army officer
who visited Texas in 1828, did sketches of some of its scenes and people.
James Strange painted creditable portraits of the captives Santa Anna and
Juan Almonte. Some of the Germans who located in Texas in the 1850s
were artists of truly superior talent. Among these were Herman Lungkwitz
and Richard Petri. Lungkwitz was known more for his landscape scenes,
Petri for his Indians. Carl G. von Iwonski did portraits and groups of
people. In San Antonio, Louisa Heuser Wueste was another popular artist
who specialized in portraits.

A contemporary of the German artists, Frenchman Theodore Gentilz
of Castro's colony, painted the Indian peoples. Another French artist,
Eugenie Lavender, won acclaim at the French court before she came to
Texas in 1851. Best known of her work was *Saint Patrick,* in the cathedral in
Corpus Christi.

RELIGION

Of all the forces affecting early Texas society, none had a greater influence
than the churches. As previously stated, itinerant Protestant preachers
began their work during the colonial period. It was not until after Texas
had its independence, however, that a well-organized missionary program

was launched. Methodists and Baptists led the way; Presbyterians were not so numerous, but their influence was great, and other denominations were active.

When news of the defeat of Santa Anna reached the general conference of the Methodist Episcopal Church in session in Cincinnati, Ohio, in May 1836, church leaders were quick to realize that it meant the opening of a mission field rich with opportunities. Martin Ruter, already distinguished by years of service in the church, immediately volunteered as a missionary in Texas. Eighteen months later he crossed the Sabine at Gaines' Ferry and entered Texas. Two other Methodist missionaries had preceded him by a few days; the three worked feverishly, building churches, forming circuits, and organizing classes. In 1840, the Texas Conference was organized with 1,878 members and 25 local preachers. With 30,661 members and 224 traveling preachers, the Methodist church in 1860 was, by far, the strongest in Texas.

Since Baptists recognized the authority of the local congregation as superior to that of any other body in church matters, it was easy for them to establish churches under frontier conditions. There were preachers and deacons among the immigrants, and they frequently organized churches without the aid of a visiting missionary. The first church in Texas was the Pilgrim church, brought intact in 1834 by immigrants from Illinois under Daniel Parker. Another church was organized in Washington early in 1837, and at once it sent an appeal to organized Baptists in the United States to send missionaries. "Dear brethren, we ask you again," said the fervent Texans, "come over into Macedonia and help us!" Churches and associations were organized rapidly, and a state convention was formed in 1848. By 1860 there were approximately 500 Baptist churches in Texas. The denomination had 280 church buildings, as compared with 410 for the Methodists. Baptists, however, led all denominations in number of church publications.

Presbyterian mission work was begun in 1837 under the special patronage of the Synod of Mississippi. Joining the earlier missionaries in 1840 came Daniel Baker, whose name looms large in the annals of Texas. Already, Presbyterian churches had been established near Independence and in Houston, Austin, and Galveston. In 1857 the Presbyterians had 2,261 members in Texas and by 1860 had seventy-two church buildings.

Other churches were active. The Episcopal church sent R. M. Chapman of New York as a missionary to Texas in 1838, and by 1860 there were nineteen Episcopal church houses in Texas. The Christian church grew rapidly during the decade before the Civil War. In 1850 it owned only five buildings; ten years later it had thirty-nine. The Catholics maintained churches in Nacogdoches, San Augustine, and probably in other Texas communities continuously from colonial times. A Catholic church was established in Houston shortly after the Texas Revolution, and by 1860 there were thirty-three Catholic church buildings in the state.

The church people brought with them to Texas practices that had been developed in the United States and tried for a century—protracted meetings, basket meetings, and camp meetings. Sermons were usually long and fervent. Church women gave suppers, "refreshment parties," "fairs," and bazaars to raise money for the church. The Protestant leaders advocated a strict observance of Sunday but evidently did not succeed in bringing it about. Melinda Rankin complained that the day was ignored by many people, and in Crockett, Olmsted found all the stores open on Sunday and was told that it was the merchants' best day.

Sunday schools, which were maintained by the more active churches of all Protestant denominations, constituted powerful agencies for biblical and moral training as well as for enlarging the intellectual horizons of the people. Belinda McNair Fullinwider and her husband taught at a Sunday school in San Felipe as early as 1834. The best Sunday schools had libraries. The union school in Brownsville had one thousand volumes and another in Austin had thirteen hundred. It was stated that wherever a Sunday school was established, it generally was followed by Bible classes, temperance societies, and educational interests, and that it served as a "focus where all good influences have converged."

In the society of early days the churches were the greatest civilizing agencies. They brought the people together, clean and in their best apparel. At church the men exchanged greetings and talked on subjects ranging from the weather and crops to the political issues of the day. Here chatted farmers' wives and daughters, tired of drudgery and starved for companionship. The churches, moreover, set the moral standards for many of the people. They attacked immorality of every type; their leaders praised or condemned almost all conduct and every institution. It cannot be said that they always had their way on moral issues, but even the most reckless individual dared not ignore them.

The effectiveness of the early churches must be credited in large measure to the quality of their leaders, worthy and courageous men and women with a selfless devotion to duty. Some were educated, representing the highest culture of their day: Martin Ruter, who committed his church to the cause of education in Texas; Daniel Baker, founder of Austin College; and James Huckins, who wrote his sermons in a beautiful, forceful style. The majority had little schooling; they were people who brought spiritual comfort to the most destitute places. One of these, Noah Byars, the gunsmith in Washington on the Brazos who became a preacher, organized sixty churches in all.

Closely associated with the churches and next to them the most influential social agencies were the lodges. Freemasonry had barely been planted before the Texas Revolution uprooted it. With typical resilience the Masons reestablished their order within less than a year. The order was supported by many distinguished Texans, including Anson Jones and Sam Houston. By 1860, 252 lodges had been organized, one for practically every community, and the order numbered nearly ten thousand members. Children of poor Masons were provided assistance for attending schools, and the lodge maintained or sponsored a score or more schools. The Independent Order of Odd Fellows was introduced into Texas from Louisiana in 1838, chiefly through the efforts of Jacob De Cordova, publisher and land agent. It grew slowly at first, but there was rapid expansion in the fifties, and by 1860 there were 74 active lodges and more than 3,000 members. A noteworthy service for that age was the protection it offered members in the form of sick benefits and benefits for the orphans of deceased members.

SELECTED BIBLIOGRAPHY

Much has been written about Texan pioneers. Good general references are J. D. De Cordova, *Texas: Her Resources and Public Men*; the *Texas Almanac* (Galveston) from 1857 through 1862; C. C. Rister, *Southern Plainsmen* (Norman, Okla., 1938); W. Gard, *Rawhide Texas* (Norman, Okla., 1965); L. B. Friend, "The Texas of 1860," *Southwestern Historical Quarterly*, LXII, 1–17; Earl Fornell, *The Galveston Era* (Austin, 1961); and R. N. Richardson, *The Frontier of Northwest Texas, 1846–1876*.

For contemporary accounts, see Marilyn McAdams Sibley, *Travelers in Texas, 1761–1860* (Austin, 1967); and "Bishop Morris in Texas, 1841–1842," *East Texas Historical Journal*, III, 149–168; Gilbert J. Jordan, "W. Steinerts' View of Texas in 1849," *Southwestern Historical Quarterly*, LXXX, 57–78, 177–200, 283–301, 399–416; LXXXI, 45–72; Levi Lamoni Wight, *The Reminiscences and Civil War Letters of Levi Lamoni Wight: Life in a Mormon Splinter Colony on the Texas Frontier* (Davis Bitton, ed., Salt Lake City, 1970); Adolphus Sterne, *Hurrah for Texas! The Diary of Adolphus Sterne, 1838–1851* (Archie P. McDonald, ed., Waco, 1969); A. F. Muir (ed.), *Texas in 1837: An Anonymous Contemporary Narrative;* Mary Austin Holley, *The Texas Diary, 1835–1838* (J. P. Bryan, ed., Austin, 1967); R. S. Lee, *Mary Austin Holley: A Biography* (Austin, 1962); Frederick L. Olmsted, *A Journey through Texas* (1857; James Howard, ed., Austin, 1962); F. R. Lubbock, *Six Decades in Texas;* Charles Michael Gruener, "Rutherford B. Hayes' Horseback Ride through Texas," *Southwestern Historical Quarterly*, LXVIII, 352–360; and Melinda Rankin, *Texas in 1850* (Boston, 1950).

Some studies of life and institutions are W. R. Hogan, *The Texas Republic;* and his "Pamelia Mann, Texas Frontierswoman," *Southwest Review*, XX, 360–370; Kent Keeth, "Sankt Antonius: Germans in the Alamo City in the 1850's," *Southwestern Historical Quarterly*, LXXVI, 183–202; Susan Jackson, "Movin' on: Mobility through Houston in the 1850's," *Southwestern Historical Quarterly*, LXXXI, 251–282; Jane Dysart, "Mexican Women in San Antonio, 1830–1860: The Assimilation Process," *The Western Historical Quarterly*, VII, 365–373; J. B. Frantz, *Gail Borden;* W. P. Webb, "Christmas and New Year in Texas," *Southwestern Historical Quarterly*, XLIV, 357–379; J. W. Schmitz, *Texas Culture in the Days of the Republic, 1836–1846* (San Antonio, 1960); Dorothy Kendall Bracken and Maurine Whorton Redway, *Early Texas Homes* (Dallas, 1956); Kenneth W. Wheeler, *To Wear a City's Crown: The Beginnings of Urban*

Growth in Texas, 1836–1865 (Cambridge, Mass., 1968); Roy B. Broussard, *San Antonio during the Texas Republic: A City in Transition* (El Paso, 1968); Caroline Remy, "Hispanic-Mexican San Antonio, 1836–1861," *Southwestern Historical Quarterly*, LXXI, 564–570; A. F. Muir, "Intellectual Climate of Houston during the Period of the Republic," *ibid.*, LXII, 312–321; William Seale, *Texas Riverman* (Austin, 1966); and D. H. Winfrey, *Julian S. Devereux and Monte Verdi Plantation* (Waco, 1962).

Scholarly analysis of population characteristics may be found in three articles by R. A. Wooster: "Notes on Texas' Largest Slaveholders, 1860," *Southwestern Historical Quarterly*, LXV, 72–79; "Foreigners in the Principal Towns of Ante-Bellum Texas," *ibid.*, LXVI, 208–220; and "Wealthy Texans, 1860," *ibid.*, LXI, 163–180. See also Randolph B. Campbell and Richard G. Lowe, *Wealth and Power in Antebellum Texas* (College Station, 1977); "Slave Property and the Distribution of Wealth in Texas, 1860," *Journal of American History*, LXIII, 316–324; and "Wealthholding and Political Power in Antebellum Texas," *Southwestern Historical Quarterly*, LXXIX, 21–30.

For economic developments, see Robert L. Jones, "The First Iron Furnace in Texas," *Southwestern Historical Quarterly*, LXIII, 279–289; Charles H. Dillon, "The Arrival of the Telegraph in Texas," *ibid.*, LXIV, 200–211; and Randolph Campbell and Richard Lowe, "Some Economic Aspects of Antebellum Texas Agriculture," *Southwestern Historical Quarterly*, LXXXII, 351–378. William Seale emphasizes architecture in "San Augustine, in the Texas Republic," *Southwestern Historical Quarterly*, LXXII, 347–358. A. L. Carlson tells the history of Texas banking in the *Texas Monthly*, IV, 481–499, 615–641; V, 74–102. See also Mary Rena Green, *Sam Maverick, Texan, 1803–1870* (San Antonio, 1952). Transportation in early Texas has received considerable study. See Ralph Moody, *Stagecoach West* (New York, 1967) for a general treatment; also J. W. Williams, "The Butterfield Overland Mail Road across Texas," *Southwestern Historical Quarterly*, LXI, 1–19; and Emmie Giddings Mahon and Chester V. Kielman, "George H. Giddings and the San Antonio–San Diego Mail Line," *Southwestern Historical Quarterly*, XLI, 220–239. River travel is examined in Pamela Puryear and Nath Winfield, Jr., *Sandbars and Sternwheelers: Steam Navigation on the Brazos* (College Station, 1976), and Pat Kelley, *River of Lost Dreams: Navigation on the Rio Grande* (Lincoln, 1986). For railroads, good studies are C. S. Potts, *Railroad Transportation in Texas* (University of Texas Bulletin, no. 119; Austin, 1909); and S. G. Reed, *A History of Texas Railroads* (Houston, 1941). See also P. Briscoe, "The First Texas Railroad," *Quarterly of the Texas State Historical Association*, VII, 279–285; A. F. Muir, "Railroads Come to Houston, 1857–1861," *Southwestern Historical Quarterly*, LXIV, 42–63; and his "The Destiny of Buffalo Bayou," *ibid.*, LXVII, 19–22; and Eugene O. Porter, "Railroad Enterprise in the Republic of Texas," *ibid.*, LIX, 363–371.

On slavery and plantations, see Abigail Curlee, "The History of a Texas Slave Plantation, 1831–1863," *Southwestern Historical Quarterly*, XXVI, 79–127; and "A Glimpse of Life on Antebellum Slave Plantations in Texas," *Southwestern Historical Quarterly*, LXXVI, 361–383. General studies relating to slavery include Alwyn Barr, *Black Texans: A History of Negroes in Texas, 1528–1971* (Austin, 1973); Billy D. Ledbetter, "White over Black: Racial Attitudes in the Ante-Bellum Period," *Phylon*, XXXIV, 406–418; Karl E. Ashburn, "Slavery and Cotton Production in Texas," *Southwestern Social Science Quarterly*, XIV, 257–271; and E. Fornell, "Agitation in

Texas for Reopening the Slave Trade," *ibid.*, LX, 245–259. For studies of a more limited area, see Randolph Campbell, "Human Property: The Negro Slave in Harrison County, 1850–1860," *Southwestern Historical Quarterly*, LXXVI, 384–396; "Slaveholdings in Harrison County, 1850–1860: A Statistical Profile," *East Texas Historical Journal*, XI, 18–27; "Intermittent Slave Ownership: Texas as a Test Case," *Journal of Southern History*, LI, 15–30; and *A Southern Community in Crisis, Harrison County, Texas, 1850–1880* (Austin, 1983). See also Paul D. Lack, "Slavery and Vigilantism in Austin, Texas, 1840–1860," *Southwestern Historical Quarterly*, LXXXV, 1–20. M. L. Dillon ably presents the activities of an early abolitionist in Texas in *Benjamin Lundy and the Struggle for Negro Freedom*. Later effects of the slavery issue are discussed in Wesley Norton, "The Methodist Episcopal Church and the Civil Disturbances in North Texas in 1859 and 1860," *Southwestern Historical Quarterly*, LXVIII, 317–341. Legal aspects are considered in A. E. Keier Nash, "The Texas Supreme Court and Trial Rights of Blacks, 1845–1860," *Journal of American History*, LVIII, 623–642. Also see Ronnie C. Tyler (ed.), *The Slave Narratives of Texas* (Austin, 1974); and Elizabeth Silverhorne, *Plantation Life in Texas* (College Station, 1986).

Pioneer medicine is dealt with in George Plunkett Red, *The Medicine Man in Texas* (Houston, 1930); J. V. Haggard, "Epidemic Cholera in Texas, 1833–1834," *Southwestern Historical Quarterly*, XL, 216–230; P. I. Nixon, *A Century of Medicine in San Antonio* (San Antonio, 1936), *The Medical Story of Early Texas* (San Antonio, 1953), and *A History of the Texas Medical Association, 1853–1953* (Austin, 1954). See also Ashbel Smith, *Yellow Fever in Galveston* (Austin, 1951); B. M. Jones, *Health Seekers in the Southwest, 1817–1900* (Norman, Okla., 1967); and Paul J. Scheips, "Albert James Myer, an Army Doctor in Texas, 1854–1857," *Southwestern Historical Quarterly*, LXXXII, 1–24.

The best history of education in Texas remains F. Eby, *The Development of Education in Texas;* but see also C. E. Evans, *The Story of Texas Schools* (Austin, 1955); Mrs. Jonnie L. Wallis (ed.), *Sixty Years on the Brazos* (Los Angeles, 1930), an account of a schoolboy in old Washington; William M. Baker, *The Life and Labours of the Reverend Daniel Baker* (Philadelphia, 1859); F. B. Baillio, *A History of the Texas Press Association* (Dallas, 1916); Murl L. Webb, "Religious and Educational Efforts among Texas Indians in the 1850's," *Southwestern Historical Quarterly*, LXIX, 22–37; H. B. Carroll, *Masonic Influence on Education in the Republic of Texas* (Waco, 1960); James David Carter, *Masonry in Texas: Background, History, and Influence to 1846* (Waco, 1958); John C. English, "Wesleyan College of San Augustine," *East Texas Historical Journal*, III, 141–148; and James A. Tinsley, "Genesis of Higher Education in Texas," *Proceedings of the Philosophical Society of Texas* (1968). A glimpse of early schools may be had in Emily Jones Shelton, "Lizzie E. Johnson: A Cattle Queen of Texas," *Southwestern Historical Quarterly*, L, 349–366. See also Jefferson Davis Bragg, "Baylor University, 1851–1861," *ibid.*, XLIX, 37–65; and "Waco University," *ibid.*, LI, 213–224.

For studies on the arts see Pauline A. Pinckney, *Texas Artists of the Nineteenth Century* (Austin, 1967); William W. Newcomb, Jr., *German Artist on the Texas Frontier: Friedrich Richard Petri* (Austin, 1978); and "German Artist on the Pedernales," *Southwestern Historical Quarterly*, LXXXII, 149–172; and James McGuire, *Hermann Lungkwitz: Romantic Landscapist on the Texas Frontier* (Austin, 1983).

Valuable for information on newspapers is Marilyn McAdams Sibley, *Lone Star and State Gazettes: Texas Newspapers Before the Civil War (College Station, 1983).* On religion and the churches, see C. E. Castaneda, as listed in Chapter 2; and *The Historical Magazine of the Protestant Episcopal Church,* September, 1941; Macum Phelan, *A History of Early Methodism in Texas, 1817–1866* (Nashville, 1924); W. S. Red, *A History of the Presbyterian Church in Texas* (Austin, 1936); J. M. Carroll, *A History of Texas Baptists* (Dallas, 1923); L. R. Elliott (ed.), *Centennial Story of Texas Baptists* (Dallas, 1936); Mary Angela Fitzmorris, *Four Decades of Catholicism in Texas, 1820–1860* (Washington, D.C., 1926); G. L. Crocket, *Two Centuries in East Texas;* Stephen Daniel Eckstein, *History of the Churches of Christ in Texas, 1824–1950* (Austin, 1963); George H. Paschal, Jr., and Judith A. Benner, *A Hundred Years of Challenge and Change: A History of the Synod of Texas of the United Presbyterian Church in the U.S.A.* (San Antonio, 1968); R. Douglas Brackenridge, *Voice in the Wilderness: A History of the Cumberland Presbyterian Church in Texas* (San Antonio, 1968); and Carter E. Boren, *Religion on the Texas Frontier* (San Antonio, 1968).

CHAPTER TEN
SECESSION AND WAR
1860–1865

While Texans of the 1850s opened new lands, built new towns, and struggled to overcome the dangers of the frontier, the nation divided more and more into two well-defined camps. Citizens and leaders of North and South quarreled over many issues—state rights, distribution of western lands, the tariff—but it was the rancorous controversy over slavery that dominated public affairs. By 1856 pro-slavery southern extremists were threatening secession from the Union if an anti-slavery Republican were to be elected President. Mostly immigrants from southern states who were sympathetic to slavery, Texans generally supported the southern position. Although concerned about other matters, particularly frontier defense, they took part more and more in the conflict over slavery as the controversy intensified in the late 1850s.

When southern states began to secede from the Union after Republican Abraham Lincoln won the presidential election of 1860, Texas joined the secession movement. Secession led to war, and for four years Texas supported the Confederate cause. Few battles were fought within the state, but these were difficult years. Thousands of Texans served in the armies, while at home conflicts between Confederate and Union sympathizers generated distrust and sometimes violence. Indian raids ravaged the frontier, and life for those who remained at home was at best filled with toil and anxiety and sometimes with genuine hardship.

PRELUDE TO SECESSION

Most white Texans supported slavery, but some were unwilling to risk destruction of the Union. Consequently, the growing crisis in the 1850s over slavery brought dissension in Texas public affairs. Other issues demanded attention, however, and it was not until 1857 that the electorate became aligned in conservative and radical or Unionist and state rights groups. In that year the state rights faction gained control of the Democratic party. The Whig party was no more; gone also was the Know-Nothing organization, which had been basically Unionist. Henceforth the friends of the Union had no organization.

During the next two years the regular Democrats moved more and more toward the position of the extreme pro-slavery group east of the Mississippi. The legislature authorized the governor to send delegates to a Southern convention if it should be deemed expedient. John Marshall, chairman of the state Democratic committee, kept up a barrage of editorials in the *State Gazette* advocating the reopening of the African slave trade. The party convention of 1859 refused to endorse a proposal so extreme, but it applauded the decision of the Supreme Court in the *Dred Scott* case (holding that Congress could not legislate slavery out of the territories); and it nominated Hardin Runnels, a strong advocate of slavery, for reelection.

Against this organization, Houston, running as an independent on a platform endorsing the Constitution and promising allegiance to the Union, entered the contest for governor with all the strength of his personal popularity and skill as a campaigner. Ex-Governor Pease supported him, as also did J. W. Throckmorton, B. H. Epperson, and other old-time Whigs. Touring the state in a buggy, wearing an old linen duster, on hot days sometimes appearing without a shirt, the old warrior made a mighty appeal to the people. In this, his last political battle, he defeated Runnels by nearly 9,000 votes, 35,257 to 27,500. By a much narrower margin, Edward Clark, running with Houston as an independent, managed to defeat Francis Lubbock for lieutenant governor. No doubt various factors affected the results of the election. Houston's personal popularity weighed heavily, as did also the dissatisfaction of the people on the frontier who charged Runnels with neglecting to protect them. It is possible, however, that the state rights leaders had moved too rapidly for the majority of the voters.

Events thereafter strengthened the hands of the extreme pro-Southern faction. Abolitionist John Brown's raid on Harper's Ferry, Virginia, in October 1859 antagonized and alarmed people and may have accounted in part for the choice by the legislature of Louis T. Wigfall to represent Texas in the Senate. At the Democratic state convention at Galveston in early April 1860, the state rights leaders, having gained complete control, abandoned restraint. Texas as a sovereign state had the right, they stated, "to withdraw from the confederacy, and resume her place among the powers of the earth as a sovereign and independent nation." The platform deplored "the unnatural efforts of a sectional party at the North to carry on an 'irrepressible conflict' against the institution of slavery" and implied that the election of a Republican President would bring about a dissolution of the Union.

The strong pro-slavery views of the state Democratic party was evident in the actions of the national Democratic convention of 1860. The state party sent to the national convention, which met in April in Charleston, H. R. Runnels, Francis R. Lubbock, Guy M. Bryan, R. B. Hubbard, and Tom Ochiltree, all staunch champions of the slaveholder's cause. At that convention, when Stephen A. Douglas and the Northern Democrats insisted on a platform endorsing the theory of popular sovereignty in the territories, a moderate position, and denouncing the *Dred Scott* decision, the delegates from Texas and seven other Southern states withdrew.

Divided over the slavery issue, the Democrats held two more conventions and nominated two sets of presidential candidates. The Charleston convention adjourned to meet in Baltimore on June 18. In Baltimore, the Northern Democrats nominated Douglas for President and Herschel V. Johnson for Vice-President. The Southern Democrats then met in Richmond, chose as their candidates John C. Breckinridge of Kentucky and Joseph Lane of Oregon, and adopted a platform that supported the *Dred Scott* decision.

The Republican party encountered fewer problems. At its national convention, which met in Chicago on May 18, the Republican party adopted a resolution that slavery could not legally exist in a territory and selected Abraham Lincoln and Hannibal Hamlin as its nominees.

Since none of these tickets was to their liking, a group of pro-Union Southerners, including some of the large slaveholders, organized the Constitutional Unionist party. It was dedicated to the principle that secession would be ruinous to the South and that the only hope lay in fighting for Southern rights in the Union. In a convention held in Baltimore, Sam Houston received 57 votes as against 68.5 for John Bell of Tennessee for the party's presidential nomination. Bell was nominated on the second ballot, and Edward Everett was chosen as his running mate. Houston permitted his name to go before the country as "the People's candidate," but on August 18 he withdrew formally.

While politicians battled over nominations, public excitement in Texas reached the stage of hysteria. Severe fires, of incendiary origin, it was alleged, broke out in Dallas, Denton, Waxahachie, Kaufman, and various other points in North Texas. The fires were charged to abolitionists and linked with stories of slave uprisings, poisonings, and assassinations—generally exaggerated if not wholly unfounded. Vigilance committees sprang into action. In Dallas three blacks were hanged in the presence of a large crowd; three white men, presumably abolitionists, were hanged in

Fort Worth because they had been "tampering" with slaves. By 1860 a growing spirit of intolerance pervaded the entire state.

A secret order known as the Knights of the Golden Circle was introduced into Texas in 1860 and soon had established a number of local lodges or "castles." The plans of the organization seem to have been to make slavery more secure in the South, particularly by incorporating into the Union additional slave states from Mexican territory. Two poorly organized filibuster movements against Mexico in 1860 never got beyond the borders of Texas. The Knights did, however, supply organized forces that took an active part in the secession movement.

In the midst of such conflict and fear, the people made their decision at the polls. With the election of Republican Abraham Lincoln, the pro-Southern position suffered a humiliating defeat in the nation, but it won an overwhelming victory in the state. In Texas the Lincoln-Hamlin ticket was not placed on the ballot, and the Douglas-Johnson candidates received only 410 votes; 15,463 Texans voted for Bell and 47,548 for Breckinridge.

SECESSION

Lincoln's election alarmed many Texans who wanted to preserve the Union. The Unionists had no organization but among them were able men: Sam Houston, David G. Burnet, E. M. Pease, J. W. Throckmorton, John and George Hancock, E. J. Davis, and A. J. Hamilton. The burden of their argument was that the election of Lincoln, although unfortunate, did not warrant secession and that the South could better protect its interests in the Union than out of it. Houston wrote: "Mr. Lincoln has been constitutionally elected, and, much as I deprecate his success, no alternative is left me but to yield to the Constitution."

But each day the conservatives lost ground, and the radicals grew stronger. The Republican party had been born in opposition to the extension of slavery, and its leader, now the President-elect, had said publicly that slavery must ultimately be abolished. Some southern leaders had warned that Lincoln's election would mean the dissolution of the Union; to yield at this late date would, they argued, constitute a surrender of their rights. Rhetoric was often extreme and inflammatory. The editor of the *Navarro Express* wrote: "The North has gone overwhelmingly for Negro Equality and Southern Vassalage! Southern men, will you submit to the degradation?"

By early December Texans were moving toward secession. Various petitions, editorials, and letters directed at Governor Houston urged him to convene the legislature or call a convention. He refused to do either, whereupon the radicals took matters into their own hands. In Austin on December 3, a group of leaders, including George M. Flournoy, O. M.

Roberts of the Texas supreme court, Guy M. Bryan, W. S. Oldham, and John Marshall, drew up an address to the people of Texas. They called on the voters of each representative district to select, at an election to be held on January 8, two delegates to a state convention. Similar resolutions were adopted in several other meetings throughout the state. The elections were held, and the convention met as called on January 28, 1861. Meanwhile, on December 17 Houston had issued a call for the legislature to convene on January 21, 1861, in a special session. The legislature ignored Houston's claim that the recent election was illegal and authorized the convention to act for the people, subject only to the condition that the question of secession be submitted to the voters.

The convention acted quickly. With O. M. Roberts as president, it approved on the second day, by a vote of 152 to 6, a resolution stating: "It is the deliberate sense of this Convention that the State of Texas should separately secede from the Federal Union." A committee on Federal relations then drew up an ordinance of secession that declared that the ordinance of 1845 by which Texas had accepted annexation "is hereby repealed and annulled." The proposed ordinance was to be submitted to the voters on February 23, and, unless rejected by a majority of the votes cast, was to take effect on March 2, exactly twenty-five years after independence had been declared. The vote on the ordinance was taken at noon on February 1 in the presence of packed galleries. The scene had its dramatic incident. As the roll of delegates was called, only very infrequently was the response "No." Among those who voted thus was J. W. Throckmorton, who, while voting, violated the no-discussion rule. A hiss and applause followed, to which he made the memorable retort: "Mr. President, when the rabble hiss well may patriots tremble." The final vote was 166 to 8.

On the following day the convention drew up a "declaration of causes." It alleged that (1) the general government had administered the common territory of the Union in such a way as to exclude the Southern people from it; (2) because of the disloyalty of the people of the North and the "imbecility" of their government, incendiarism and outlawry were rampant in Kansas; (3) the United States had failed to protect Texas against Indian and Mexican bandits and had refused to reimburse it for expenditures made in defending itself; (4) the people of the North had become hostile to the Southern states and "their beneficent and patriarchal system of African slavery, preaching the debasing doctrine of the equality of all men, irrespective of race or color"; (5) the slaveholding states were now in a minority, unable to protect themselves against the fanatics of the North who preach a "higher law" than the Constitution; and finally, (6) the extremists of the North had elected as President and Vice-President "two men whose chief claims to such high positions are their approval of these long continued wrongs, and their pledges to continue them to the final consummation of these schemes for the ruin of the slave-holding states."

In South Carolina and certain other southern states the secession movement had moved more rapidly than it had in Texas. In Charleston on December 20, 1860, a special state convention had formally dissolved the union between South Carolina and the federal government. Soon Mississippi, Florida, Alabama, Georgia, and Louisiana followed; representatives of these commonwealths were about to form a government in Montgomery, Alabama. Technically, Texas could not act until the voters had spoken at the polls. Before it adjourned on February 5, the convention, nevertheless, sent seven delegates "in order that the views and interests of the people of Texas may be consulted with reference to the Constitution and provisional government that may be established by said convention."

The Texas convention adjourned to meet again on March 2, after the election. It left in session during the interim a powerful select group called the Committee on Public Safety. The legislature adjourned also, to convene again on March 18.

In the brief period available, many of the delegates took part in the campaign for the public vote on the ordinance of secession. Judge Roberts issued an appeal to the voters to support secession, and twenty thousand copies of the "Declaration of Causes" were distributed. In support of secession, state rights journals of long standing, such as the *Telegraph* (Houston), the *Galveston News*, *State Gazette* (Austin), and *Texas Republican* (Marshall), were soon joined by more conservative papers such as the *Dallas Herald*. The thin line of Unionists made a noble fight. Twenty-four opponents of secession, from the convention and the legislature, issued an address to the people of Texas urging that they oppose secession, at least until further efforts to reach a compromise. The speakers against secession, including Houston, Throckmorton, John Hancock, and others, had the editorial support of several newspapers, including the *Southern Intelligencer* (Austin), the *Bastrop Advertiser*, the *La Grange True Issue*, and the *Weekly Alamo Express*.

The secessionists amassed a vote of 46,129; their opponents, 14,697. Ten counties in the vicinity of Austin showed antisecession majorities, a fact to be attributed to the large German population, to several Unionist newspapers, and to the efforts of such leaders as Sam Houston, A. J. Hamilton, and John Hancock. Throckmorton and a few associates managed to carry seven counties in northern Texas, where there was a large immigrant population from the northern and border states. Angelina County in East Texas voted against secession for reasons that are not easily explained. With only a few exceptions, the heavy slaveholding counties yielded huge majorities for secession.

By their vote on February 23, the electors approved secession, but they had taken no action on joining the Confederate States of America. In the minds of most people, however, the two steps seem to have been inseparably linked. The convention reassembled on March 2. Three days later it

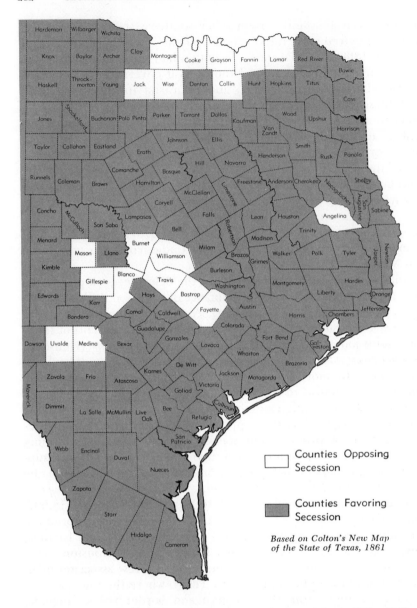

Counties Opposing Secession

Counties Favoring Secession

Based on Colton's New Map of the State of Texas, 1861

Counties voting against secession. From Ernest Wallace, *Texas in Turmoil,* Austin, 1965, p. 70. Reprinted with the permission and assistance of Steck-Vaughn Company, publisher.

"approved, ratified, and accepted" the provisional government of the Confederate States of America by a vote of 109 to 2 and directed the Texas delegates in Montgomery to apply for admission to that government. The application was not necessary; already the Confederate Congress had passed an act to admit Texas.

Shortly thereafter Houston was removed from office. When the convention called on him, along with other state officers, to take the oath of allegiance to the Confederacy, he insisted that it had no authority to join the Confederate States of America and defied it. Thereupon, the convention on March 16, 1861, declared the office of governor vacant and made Lieutenant Governor Edward Clark governor. President Lincoln offered to aid Houston if he would oppose the convention with force, but the governor, unwilling to bring on civil war, rejected the proposal. The convention ratified the constitution of the Confederacy on March 23 and three days later adjourned sine die.

While the convention was directing the course of secession, it also acted on military matters. Distributed along the frontier at twenty-one widely separated posts were about 2,700 Federal troops under the command of Major General D. E. Twiggs, with headquarters in San Antonio. Twiggs, a Georgian in sympathy with the South, in anticipation of the crisis asked his superiors for instructions, but no orders were given him. He submitted his resignation, but before he turned his command over to his successor, he was confronted with a critical situation. The Committee on Public Safety, acting under authority of the secession convention, demanded that he surrender to its representatives all public arms and munitions of war under his command. When Ben McCulloch, military commander representing the convention, led an armed force into San Antonio, Twiggs agreed to evacuate the 160 troops in San Antonio and surrender to representatives of the committee all federal property, on condition that the troops should retain their side arms, camp and garrison equipage, and the facilities of transportation, all to be delivered upon their arrival at the coast. On February 18 Twiggs agreed to the evacuation of all other forts in Texas under similar terms. Henry E. McCulloch received for the Texans the surrender of the northern posts, and John S. Ford took over the posts in the southern part of the state. Thus did the convention by a series of bold strokes and without the firing of a shot put out of action more than 10 percent of the regular army of the United States and acquire military supplies and other property valued at $3 million.

Elsewhere the course of secession was not as peaceful. At Fort Sumter, South Carolina, where Federal forces refused to evacuate their post, guns were fired on April 12, 1861. For the next four years troops of the Confederacy and of the Union would meet on the battlefields of the Civil War.

AT THE BATTLEFRONTS

Texas was a border state in the Confederacy, exposed to attack from the north, west, and south. In May 1861, the immediate threat of invasion from the north was removed when W. C. Young, a former sheriff and a resident of Cooke County, led a volunteer regiment of Texas cavalry across the Red River and took Forts Arbuckle, Cobb, and Washita without firing a shot, thereby making an invasion from the north unlikely.

The problem of protection from the Indian raids that had troubled Texas for a century and a half was not solved so easily. The Confederacy assigned a Texas regiment under John S. Ford the task of guarding the Rio Grande frontier from Fort Brown, near the Gulf Coast, to Fort Bliss, near the site of El Paso. During 1861, however, companies of minutemen bore the brunt of Indian warfare. Early in 1862 they were replaced by the Frontier Regiment, a state organization under James M. Norris. Norris established a chain of sixteen posts along the frontier from the Red River to the Rio Grande and a regular patrol along the line. The Frontier Regiment was reorganized in 1863, with J. E. McCord as commander. Since the patrols had not been successful, McCord replaced them with scouting expeditions in hope of surprising the Indians. In December 1863 the frontier defense system was again changed. The Frontier Regiment was transferred to Confederate service; a part of it, under the command of Colonel James Bourland, was assigned to defend the frontier along the Red River, and the remainder was sent to the Houston area. To offset the loss, the men in the frontier counties were enrolled in companies, and at least one-fourth were to be in the field at all times. Early in 1864 a total of 4,264 men were enrolled in these militia companies. Bourland's troops gave some aid, but most of the burden for frontier defense fell on the state troops. In the northern district, where the situation was the most critical, Governor Pendleton Murrah commissioned James W. Throckmorton as brigadier general and placed him in command. In October 1864, however, about 200 Comanches and Kiowas attacked settlements near Fort Belknap in Young County, killing 16 persons and capturing 7 others.

Hostilities on the frontier were never completely controlled. Because the troops and militia were unable to provide protection, groups of people along the frontier moved into stockades—"forting up," they called it. About 125 people northeast of present-day Albany joined together at "Fort Davis," one of the largest such places. During the last two years of the war, deserters added to the threat of hostile Indians by creating confusion on the frontier.

Ironically, a shameful blunder by the Texans resulted in the bloodiest battle with the Indians during the Civil War. In January 1864, at Dove Creek, a few miles south of the present San Angelo, 370 state troops, who attacked about 1,400 friendly Kickapoos migrating from Indian Territory to Mexico, were repulsed with heavy losses.

The most aggressive campaign in which Texans participated was an effort to occupy New Mexico. John R. Baylor, commander of a detachment of Texas troops, marched into New Mexico Territory and on August 1, 1861, issued a proclamation establishing the territory of Arizona, which was to comprise that part of New Mexico lying south of the thirty-fourth

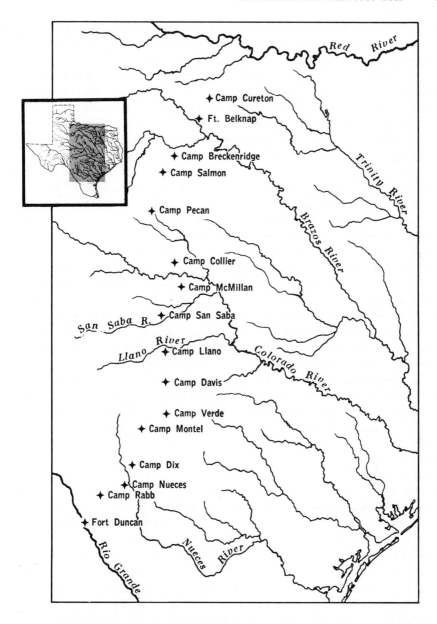

Texas military posts during the Civil War. From Ernest Wallace, *Texas in Turmoil*, Austin, 1965, p. 70. Reprinted with the permission and assistance of Steck-Vaughn Company, publisher.

parallel. Later, with Baylor as governor, a constitutional government was established, and for a short while Confederate troops occupied the country as far west as Tucson. Simultaneously, General H. H. Sibley, with three regiments of Texans, sought to drive the Federals out of New Mexico. He defeated a force of over 3,800 at Valverde on February 2, 1862, and took Albuquerque and Santa Fe. On March 28, however, at Glorietta Pass the Federals checked his advance and destroyed his supply train. As a result of this and other disasters, he was obliged to retire from the territory. When he returned to San Antonio in the summer of 1862 with the shattered remnant of his troops, the territorial government retreated with him. Thus ended the dream to extend the Confederacy to win control of a port on the Gulf of California and to control the gold and silver mines of the West.

Defense of the Texas coast was far more successful. In July 1861 the Federals extended their blockade to include Texas. Before a formidable enemy force, state and Confederate troops evacuated Galveston in October 1862. But John B. Magruder, fresh from campaigns east of the Mississippi and now in command of the Department of Texas, determined to recover the town. With two riverboats armored with cotton bales and 300 veterans of Sibley's New Mexico campaign serving as marines, he moved against it by sea. A land force was concentrated at Virginia Point, opposite Galveston. On January 1, 1863, the combined forces took Galveston with a loss of 26 killed and 117 wounded. The Federals suffered the loss of two warships and 414 men killed or captured. Four Federal gunboats made their escape.

Fighting also took place around Sabine Pass, the outlet for both the Sabine and the Neches rivers. In September 1862 a Federal blockade patrol forced the Confederates to abandon it. After retaking Galveston, the Confederates on January 21 reoccupied and fortified the post at Sabine Pass, Fort Griffin, as well as their limited means would permit. However, Union leaders Admiral David G. Farragut and General N. P. Banks planned for a major campaign against Texas that would begin with the retaking of Sabine Pass. Four gunboats and 23 transports, bearing about 5,000 troops for the initial landing, attacked Fort Griffin on September 8, 1863. To meet the formidable force, Lieutenant Dick Dowling had two small gunboats and a garrison of 46 men! Yet he disabled and captured two enemy craft, took about 350 prisoners, and turned back the entire expedition. His victory was a severe blow to the morale of the North and augmented doubts about the efficiency of the Federal navy.

Banks's next thrust was more successful. With a combined naval and land force of about seven thousand men, he moved against the lower Rio Grande, where the Confederate garrisons were pitiably weak. Beginning by taking the island of Brazos de Santiago off the mouth of the Rio Grande on November 1, 1863, seizures were extended to include Brownsville, Corpus Christi, Aransas Pass, Indianola, and other points, until Galveston and Sabine Pass were the only ports left to the Confederates.

In the spring of 1864 Banks made his last campaign against Texas. From Alexandria, Louisiana, 25,000 well-equipped veterans, sustained by a powerful flotilla of gunboats, moved up the Red River. Banks planned to unite this army with 15,000 men under General Frederick Steele, who was moving southward from Little Rock. It was expected that the combined forces would crush all opposition and extend their operations over all of northern Louisiana, southern Arkansas, and eastern Texas. The Confederate shops at Marshall and Henderson and the rich East Texas farm country constituted choice prizes. With a large part of his best troops drawn away to sustain the flagging Confederate cause in the East, General E. Kirby Smith, in command of the Trans-Mississippi Department, worked desperately to form an army to cope with Banks. Magruder in Texas sent him every man he could spare; and as the regiments hastened eastward, old men and beardless boys were enlisted to offset losses by death, disease, and desertion. With 8,000 cavalrymen, Sterling Price stopped Steele at Camden, Arkansas. Richard Taylor, in immediate command of the army that faced Banks, had a force made up largely of troops from Texas, Louisiana, Arkansas, and Missouri. On April 8, with 11,000 effective troops, he attacked and all but routed Banks' army at Mansfield, Louisiana, fifty miles below Shreveport, taking 2,500 prisoners. The Confederates were repulsed on the following day at Pleasant Hill, but Banks retreated to the east side of the Mississippi.

In the summer of 1864, the Confederate forces under John S. Ford recaptured Fort Brown and forced the Federals in South Texas to withdraw from the mainland. The last battle of the Civil War was fought in the valley in the spring of 1865 after Federal troops had heard that the war was over. On May 13 at Palmito Ranch near Brownsville, Ford with a force of 300 met and defeated two black regiments and a company of unmounted Texas (Union) cavalry. From the 111 prisoners he took in that engagement, Ford learned that General Robert E. Lee had surrendered more than a month before.

Even after Joseph E. Johnston had surrendered the last major Confederate army on April 18, 1865, Governor Murrah, General E. Kirby Smith, and other leaders insisted that the war be continued in the West. That was the decision on May 13 of the conference of the representatives of Trans-Mississippi states held in Marshall after Grant had insisted on the same terms of surrender that were granted to General Lee. Thereafter, Smith, Magruder, and Murrah made various unsuccessful efforts to secure more favorable terms. Meanwhile, the armies of the West melted away, and General Smith, left without an army, formally surrendered the Trans-Mississippi Department in Galveston on June 2.

SUPPLYING MEN

In Texas there was a tradition that young men should join the colors in an emergency, and as early as September 30, 1861, ten regiments of Texas troops had already been organized. It was thought at first that Texans would not be needed east of the Mississippi. Early in 1862, however, Governor Lubbock received a call for fifteen regiments of infantry, and volunteers, he stated in his memoirs, supplied these "in a few months." He thought Texas had about twenty thousand men in military service before conscription went into effect.

Soldiers served either in state military units or as Confederate troops, or sometimes in both types of service. The first Confederate conscription act was passed on April 16, 1862, applying to men from 18 to 35. In September of that year the age limit was raised to 45, and a later act extended the limits from 17 to 50. On December 25, 1861, the state provided for the enrollment and organization of the militia; an act of March 7, 1863, provided that the militia might be transferred into Confederate service for a period of not more than a year. A state act of May 28, 1864, provided for the transfer of state troops to Confederate service, except officers of the state government and privates not subject to the Confederate conscription laws.

Liberal exemptions allowed many to avoid military service. Officeholders, owners of large numbers of slaves, persons supposedly indispensable to the professions, agriculture, and industry, and certain Texans involved in frontier defense were exempt. The law, furthermore, permitted the hiring of substitutes. Beyond a doubt the exemption policy and the provision permitting a man to hire a substitute had a bad effect on the morale of the troops and the people behind the lines.

Texas contributed significantly to the Confederate military effort. It furnished one general (Albert Sidney Johnston), one lieutenant general (John Bell Hood), three major generals (S. B. Maxey, John A. Wharton, and Tom Green), 32 brigadier generals, and 97 colonels. It is impossible to determine the number of men who saw military service either as state or Confederate troops during the war. Even Governor Lubbock, who should be a dependable authority for the period when he was chief executive, gives figures that are difficult to reconcile. In February 1863 he stated that Texas had in actual service 68,500 men, including 6,500 state troops. His figures evidently included a number of duplications, particularly among those who volunteered for state duty and afterwards entered Confederate service. According to the census of 1860, white males in Texas between the ages of 18 and 45 numbered 92,145. Some 58,533 men were recruited in the cavalry alone. Probably two-thirds of those who served remained west of the Mississippi.

Texans fought on every battlefront, and a host of witnesses vouched for their valor. For mobility and heroic daring, the organization named after B. F. (Frank) Terry was unsurpassed; Ross's Texas Brigade fought well on both sides of the Mississippi; Hood's Texas Brigade broke the Federal lines in the Second Battle of Manassas and at Gaines' Mill, Virginia, and became a part of the first division of Longstreet's famous corps. Bravery, however, took its toll. Because of reporting difficulties and errors in records, the exact number of Texans killed and wounded in the Civil War is not known.

THE STATE AND THE CONFEDERACY

Party political activity did not cease, but it declined during the war. Unionists were obliged to keep their counsel in most areas, for secessionists were usually in control. No party nominations were made in 1861. In the race for governor, Francis Richard Lubbock, who had served as lieutenant governor during Runnels's administration, defeated Edward Clark, the incumbent, by only 124 votes. John M. Crockett, mayor of Dallas, was elected lieutenant governor. At the same election, congressmen were chosen to represent the state in Richmond. Louis T. Wigfall and W. S. Oldham were elected to the Confederate senate, and John H. Reagan accepted an appointment as postmaster general in President Jefferson Davis's cabinet.

State efforts during Lubbock's administration were centered on winning the war. The governor supported the Confederacy, and most legislation pertained to defense. A military board consisting of the governor, comptroller, and treasurer was authorized to dispose of the bonds of the United States held by Texas or to use other means in purchasing military supplies. Other acts suspended all laws for the collection of debts, validated bonds issued for military purposes, authorized special county taxes for war purposes, appropriated money for equipping troops, and authorized the receipt of Confederate notes and treasury warrants for taxes.

Confederate reverses, Lincoln's Emancipation Proclamation, and "signs of a latent dissatisfaction at the existing state of things if not a

John H. Reagan served Texas, the United States, and the Confederate States of America with distinction. He resigned as United States senator to accept the chairmanship of the first railroad commission of Texas in 1891. (University of Texas Library)

positive disloyalty to the Confederacy" caused Lubbock to call an extra session of the legislature for February 2, 1863. That body doubled taxes and appropriated $600,000 for the use of needy families of soldiers and $200,000 as a hospital fund for sick and wounded Texans in the Confederate armies.

In 1863 Lubbock entered the Confederate service and did not stand for reelection. The race soon became a contest between T. J. Chambers (candidate for the fourth time) and Pendleton Murrah, a Harrison County lawyer. Murrah, more emphatic than Chambers in his promise to support the Confederate cause in every way possible, defeated Chambers by a vote of 17,511 to 12,455. The total vote was only a little more than half that cast in the preceding election. F. S. Stockdale, who had helped draft the ordinance of secession, was elected lieutenant governor. The election results revealed no special dissatisfaction with the policies of the Confederate government in Richmond.

Every war governor proclaimed his loyalty to the Confederacy and his determination to work with it harmoniously. The Texas supreme court upheld the constitutionality of the Confederate conscription law. It declared constitutional the act abolishing substitution in the army, even though it violated the obligation of contract. But there were occasional problems. Brigadier General P. O. Hebert, a West Point valedictorian and former governor of Louisiana, succeeded Earl Van Dorn as commander of the Department of Texas. He created considerable resentment when in May 1862 he proclaimed martial law for the entire state in order to enforce the conscription law and allowed the Federals to occupy Galveston and Sabine Pass. He was replaced, however, in November by Brigadier General John B. Magruder. Magruder had some problems with state officials, particularly with Murrah, but fared better in his relations with the Texans.

The most serious clash of authority grew out of a Texas law of 1863, which provided for organizing into companies for defense all men of military age in frontier counties and for exempting them from conscription under the Confederate laws. The proposed exemption was in conflict with the Confederate constitution, but Murrah insisted on its enforcement. When General E. Kirby Smith, desperately in need of troops to repel Banks in Louisiana in the spring of 1864, called on Murrah through Magruder to send more men, the governor quibbled over certain relatively unimportant matters until it was too late for the state troops to be of service. In defense of Murrah it should be said that as the war progressed, the Trans-Mississippi states were thrown more and more on their own resources, and it was natural that he should hesitate to transfer men from state control to the Confederate authorities.

As the war proceeded, complaints of neglect of the West by the Confederate government became more emphatic. The governor of Arkansas stated in June 1862 that if the western states were not to be protected, the sooner they knew it the better. In response to the unrest, western leaders held two conferences. At the request of President Davis, Governor Lubbock and Governor Claiborne F. Jackson of the Confederate government of Missouri met in Marshall, Texas, in July 1862 and framed a request to the Richmond government for a commanding general for the Trans-Mississippi West, for money, and for arms and ammunition. The government in Richmond gave them a commanding general and a fiscal agency for the department.

E. Kirby Smith, commander of the Trans-Mississippi Department, called another conference of western state representatives in Marshall for August 15, 1863. The conference, presided over by Governor Lubbock, favored more friendly relations with the French (who under Emperor Maximilian were in control in Mexico), agreed on a plan of exchanging cotton for supplies in Mexico, suggested that Confederate notes be reissued for meeting military expenses, and recommended that in his department General Smith "assume at once and exercise the powers and prerogatives of the President of the Confederate States."

The sale of cotton, a matter considered by the second Marshall conference, was responsible for another conflict between state and Confederate authorities. Under the agreement reached at the conference, the Confederacy agreed to purchase half of the cotton held by growers with certificates redeemable in bonds, leaving the other half in the hands of the owners. However, the Texas Military Board proposed to transport all of a planter's cotton to the Rio Grande, pay for half of it with state bonds, and allow the planter to dispose of the other half as he wished. Obviously, the state program was in conflict with the national program and was more desirable from the standpoint of the planter, who would be able to sell the cotton that was retained for a tangible return. After considerable bickering took place, the Confederate Congress, through an act of February 6, 1864, seized control of the situation by prohibiting the exportation of cotton, tobacco, and certain other commodities, except under regulations made by the President. At a conference in July 1864 Governor Murrah and General E. Kirby Smith arrived at an understanding, and thereafter Murrah cooperated to the fullest extent.

The financial condition of the state during the war is difficult to describe accurately. Most of the transactions were made in depreciated Confederate currency and equally depreciated state treasury warrants. Net expenditures—that is, warrants actually paid by the treasurer from August 31, 1861, to June 8, 1865—amounted to $4,863,790.55, more than three-fourths of which was attributable to war expenses. Total net receipts for the same period were $8,161,298. About 40 percent of the receipts had been derived from a wide variety of taxes, 8 percent from the sale of bonds, 38 percent from profits on the penitentiary, and 14 percent from miscellaneous sources. In the treasury on August 1, 1865, was $3,368,510 (most of which was in the form of worthless money), and there was a debt of about $8,000,000. In its desperation the state government had used special trust monies, such as the school fund and the university fund, to the amount of almost $1,500,000. A commentary both on the confusion of the times and the poverty of the state is the fact that when certain persons looted the state treasury on the night of June 11, 1865, all they found of value was $5,000 in specie. Far greater than the burden of state taxes were Confederate taxes, which during the four years from 1861 through 1864 amounted in Texas to $37,486,854.

As the military activities of the war came to an end, state government in Texas ceased to function. After the surrender of the Confederate Trans-Mississippi Department, Generals E. Kirby Smith and John Magruder, Governor Pendleton Murrah, and many other prominent ex-Confederates fled to Mexico. Lieutenant Governor Fletcher S. Stockdale became governor but was unable to restore law and order.

CRITICS OF THE CONFEDERACY

Although the overwhelming majority of Texans were loyal to the Confederacy, Union sentiment in Texas was very strong in some areas. The rank and file of Union sympathizers may be classified into three groups: (1) those who, despite their Union sympathies, accepted the decision of the state electorate as binding upon them and heartily sustained the efforts of the Confederacy; (2) those who tried to remain neutral; and (3) those few who left the state or tried to do so. J. W. Throckmorton, who became a general in command of state troops, is, perhaps, the most widely known representative of the first class. Of those who remained neutral, the best known were Sam Houston, David G. Burnet, E. M. Pease, George W. Paschal, Morgan C. Hamilton, and Edward Degener. Also in this class belong many Germans in the settlements along the lower Brazos River and north of San Antonio, who, although never reconciled to secession, served the state and Confederacy as superb soldiers. A third group, headed by A. J. Hamilton, John Hancock, John L. Haynes, James P. Newcomb, and Edmund J. Davis, energetically served the Union.

Unionist sentiment was strongest along the lower Rio Grande, among the Germans, and in the northwestern counties. The lower Rio Grande area, where escape to Mexico was easy and whose Mexican population refused to support the Confederacy, became a site for many Unionist refugees and for the recruitment of volunteers for the United States Army. For protection against Indians and for avoiding conscription, German settlers in 1861 organized the militant Union Loyal League (five hundred members in Gillespie, Kerr, and Kendall counties) but later were forced to disband. A few Germans left the state, and one group of 65 on its way to

Mexico in August 1862 had 34 of it members killed by the Texas militia. Another group of 50 was hanged, and others were killed before German resistance in the western area was broken. In Colorado, Austin, and Fayette counties, Germans and some Anglo-Americans organized to resist the draft, but General Magruder declared martial law over the areas, arrested the leaders, and quelled open resistance.

Antiwar sentiment in the northwestern part of the state was also troublesome. There in 1862, a secret organization, popularly referred to as the Peace Party, was organized. The aims of its members were to avoid the draft, to provide a spy system for the Northern army, to desert during battle, if drafted, and to prepare the way for an invasion of North Texas by Federal troops. Spies visited its meetings, and soon the excited people were repeating in whispers reports that its leaders were planning arson, murder, and a general reign of terror. The Confederate military forces joined civilians in a grim campaign to destroy the movement in its infancy. About 150 men were arrested and tried in Gainesville by "people's courts," which were neither military nor constitutional. Some confessed; 40 were hanged, most of them on no other charge, it seems, than membership in the organization. The Wise County people's courts were more deliberate; only five men were hanged there. In Grayson County 40 men were arrested, but J. W. Throckmorton interceded with a plea for justice; a court of investigation reviewed their cases, and all but one were released.

Many outspoken critics of the war were arrested, in most cases by the military under laws that had suspended the writ of *habeas corpus.* Of such cases the best known is that of Dr. Richard R. Peebles, from near Hempstead, and four other prominent citizens who were arrested in October 1863 on charges of plotting treason against the Confederate government. Peebles and two associates were exiled to Mexico.

Numbers of Unionists managed to leave Texas early in the war, and many others made their way to Matamoros where they were rescued by Federal ships. Others hid themselves in isolated places, where soon they were joined by deserters from the state and Confederate forces.

By February 1863 the problem of desertion had become so serious that General Magruder was urging Governor Lubbock to aid him in suppressing it. Eight months later, Henry E. McCulloch, in command of the northern submilitary district, estimated that there were one thousand deserters in his territory and declared that he did not have sufficient troops to arrest them. He offered them special inducements to join the army and succeeded thus in enlisting three hundred, but he found that these "bush soldiers" had a weakness for returning to the brush! Soon deserters were so numerous in Wise, Denton, and neighboring counties that they intimidated loyal citizens. Sterner measures apparently brought about improvement in 1864, but during the last few weeks of the war conditions grew distinctly worse.

LIFE AT HOME DURING THE WAR

The war forced radical readjustments in farming. The demand for cotton declined and that for food crops increased. Newspapers urged the planting of more corn. There was some agitation for laws to compel changes in acreage to meet the emergency, but no such legislation was enacted. From time to time there was a shortage of farm labor, and the families of poor soldiers frequently found it difficult to work their farms. Crops were good during the years of the war, and except in a few isolated cases, no one suffered from lack of food. People soon learned to make various substitutions in food. The ashes of burnt corncobs served as baking soda; parched sweet potatoes, rye, and okra were substitutes for coffee. However, salt, an absolute necessity for livestock and the preservation of meat, became so scarce that a soldier's salary for a month would not buy a sack; the Grand Saline in Van Zandt County, the Brooks salines, and a few other sources supplied most of the state. The frontier people visited Ledbetter's Salt Works, near the site of Albany, the salt flats along the upper Brazos, and the salt lakes in the vicinity of El Paso.

There were never enough medicines, hospital supplies, and clothing. In 1864 a serious effort was made by the military authorities to encourage the growing of poppies for opium, and the press frequently called the attention of the public to shrubs and plants of medicinal value. Through ladies' aid associations loyal women did their best to supply bandages and other equipment for the wounded; much clothing also was contributed. Relief committees received donations and distributed funds and goods for the benefit of the wives and children of soldiers. In 1863 it was said that the citizens of Houston were contributing nearly $3,000 a week to this purpose. Women learned to make hats and fans out of shucks and straw; and the spinning wheel again came into use. The people took great pride in their self-sufficiency. Governor Lubbock was inaugurated in a homespun suit, and the "homespun dress that Southern ladies wear" became a theme of song and story. Indeed, the contribution of Texas women to the war effort went far beyond the wearing of homespun clothing. Their efforts provided desperately needed supplies for the armies, supported the families who remained at home, and maintained the production of the land.

The shortage of manufactured goods was a great handicap. An arsenal, which turned out a few cannon, and a cap and cartridge factory were established in Austin. Many corporations for the manufacture of goods were chartered, but most of them never reached production. The largest cloth factory was at the penitentiary in Huntsville. Iron foundries were opened near Jefferson and Rusk, and the tanning industry increased rapidly. Likewise, the output of wagons, ambulances, harnesses, and saddles increased sharply. By 1863 many newspapers were forced to suspend publication for want of paper.

As the Federal blockade became more effective, the flow of imports and exports to and from the South was reduced to an intermittent trickle. Cotton, the chief export commodity, was hauled to the Rio Grande over different routes and in such quantities that one observer declared that "the chaparral would be almost white in places from the lint detached from passing bales." In spite of the costs and hazards of the trade, men would undertake it, for cotton in 1862 at the Rio Grande brought from 20 to 72 cents per pound, and in 1864 the price in New York ranged from 72 cents to $1.90 per pound. On their return the cotton wagons brought sugar, coffee, cloth, nails, and sometimes medicines and military supplies.

Imported consumer goods were in great demand, but there never were enough to go around. After the arrival of a shipment, stores were more crowded than the present-day bargain counters on the morning of a special sale. Mrs. Maverick of San Antonio related that she "went and stood wedged up and swaying about till near 12," when, at last, she managed to get "one bolt of domestic cloth, one pr. shoes and 1 doz. candles for $180.00." Although that particular merchant's stock had cost $60,000 in specie, she expected it would be exhausted within a week. As the value of the currency declined and prices soared, there was much complaint about "unfair and unjust speculators."

Men of nonmilitary age and women made brave efforts to keep up the morale of their communities, in spite of the reports of Confederate reverses and the tragic news of sons and husbands that they received. There are accounts of Christmas celebrations as in ordinary times, of parties and receptions for returned soldiers, and of "war meetings" with stirring speeches and "dinner on the grounds." It was the zeal and courage of the people behind the lines, quite as much as the efforts of the men in the field, that sustained for four years the Confederate cause against overwhelming odds.

SELECTED BIBLIOGRAPHY

Good general accounts of Texas during the Civil War are in D. G. Wooten, F. W. Johnson, J. H. Brown, H. H. Bancroft, and E. Wallace, *Texas in Turmoil*, all previously cited. Two excellent but brief surveys of Texas in the Civil War are Allan C. Ashcraft, *Texas in the Civil War: A Resume History* (Austin, 1962); and Robert L. Kerby, *Kirby Smith's Confederacy: The Trans-Mississippi South, 1863–1865* (New York, 1972).

The chief sources for secession are E. W. Winkler (ed.), *Journal of the Secession Convention of Texas, 1861* (Austin, 1912); and *War of the Rebellion, Official Records, Union and Confederate Armies* (130 vols., Washington, D.C., 1880–1900). Accounts of some merit by participants, in addition to O. M. Roberts's in D. G. Wooten's work, are F. R. Lubbock, *Six Decades in Texas;* and E. L. Dohoney, *An Average American* (Paris, Tex., 1907). Good studies on secession are: Walter L. Buenger, *Slavery and the Union in Texas* (Austin, 1984); "Secession and the Texas German Community: Editor Lindheimer vs. Editor Flake," *Southwestern Historical Quarterly*, LXXXII, 377–402; "Texas and the Riddle of Secession," *ibid.*, LXXXVII, 151–182; and "Unionism on the Texas Frontier," *Arizona and the West*, XXII, 237–254; C. W. Ramsdell, *Reconstruction in Texas* (New York, 1910); C. W. Ramsdell, "The Frontier and Secession," reprinted from *Studies in Southern History and Politics* (New York, 1914); C. W. Ramsdell, *Behind the Lines in the Southern Confederacy* (Baton Rouge, 1944); A. L. King, *Louis T. Wigfall: Southern Fire-eater;* Laura W. Roper, "Frederick Law Olmstead and the Western Texas Free Soil Movement," *American Historical Review*, LIV, 58–65; C. Elliott, *Leathercoat: The Life of James W. Throckmorton;* Anna Irene Sandbo, "Beginnings of the Secession Movement in Texas," *Southwestern Historical Quarterly*, XVIII, 41–73; A. I. Sandbo, "The First Session of the Secession Convention of Texas," *ibid.*, 162–194; R. A. Wooster, "Analysis of the Membership of the Texas Secession Convention," *ibid.*, LXII, 322–335; C. A. Bridges, "The Knights of the Golden Circle," *ibid.*, XLIV, 287–302; Dunn, "The KGC in Texas, 1860–1861," *ibid.*, LXX, 543–573; C. Elliott, "Union Sentiment in Texas, 1861–1865," *ibid.*, L, 449–477; Frank H. Smyrl, "Unionism in Texas, 1856–1861," *ibid.*, LXVIII, 172–195; Floyd F. Ewing, "Origins of Union Sentiment on the West Texas Frontier," *West Texas Historical Association Year Book*, XXXII, 21–29; Floyd F. Ewing, "Unionist Sentiment on the Northwest Texas Frontier," *ibid.*, XXXIII, 58–70; Joe T. Timmons, "The Referendum in Texas on the Ordinance of Secession, February 23, 1861: The Vote," *East Texas Historical Journal*, XI, 12–28; and James Alex Baggett, "The Constitutional Union Party in Texas," *Southwestern Historical Quarterly*, LXXXII, 233–264.

Accounts of Texas troops in the war include Robert Lee Kerby, *The Confederate Invasion of New Mexico and Arizona, 1861–1862* (Los Angeles, 1958); B. F. Galloway (ed.), *The Dark Corner of the Confederacy* (Dubuque, Iowa, 1972); Harold Simpson (ed.), *Texas in the Civil War* (Hillsboro, 1965); C. P. Roland, *Albert Sidney Johnston: Soldier of Three Republics;* O. B. Faulk, *General Tom Green: Fightin' Texan;* W. J. Hughes, *Rebellious Ranger: Rip Ford and the Old Southwest;* Ludwell Johnson, *The Red River Campaign: Politics and Cotton in the Civil War* (Baltimore, 1958); E. Wallace, *Charles DeMorse: Pioneer Editor and Statesman;* C. Elliott, *Leathercoat: The Life of James W. Throckmorton;* Stephen B. Oates, *Confederate Cavalry West of the Mississippi River* (Austin, 1961); James L. Nichols, *The Confederate Quartermaster in the Trans-Mississippi* (Austin, 1964); J. B. Hood, *Advance and Retreat* (New Orleans, 1880); Victor M. Rose, *Ross' Texas Brigade* (Louisville, 1881); V. M. Rose, *The Life and Services of General Ben McCulloch* (Philadelphia, 1888; Austin, 1958); Walter P. Lane, *The Adventures and Recollections of General Walter P. Lane* (Marshall, 1887); August Santleben, *A Texas Pioneer* (New York, 1910), in the Union service; Xavier Blanchard DeBray, *A Sketch of the History of DeBray's (26th) Regiment of Texas Cavalry* (Waco, 1961); Harold B. Simpson (ed.), *Touched with Valor: Civil War Papers and Casualty Reports of Hood's Texas Brigade* (Hillsboro, 1964); Marcus J. Wright, *Texas in the War, 1861–1865* (Harold B. Simpson, ed., Hillsboro, 1965); W. H. Watford, "Confederate Western Ambitions," *Southwestern Historical Quarterly*, XLIV, 161–187; S. B. Oates, "Recruiting Confederate Cavalry in Texas," *ibid.*, LXIV, 463–477; Alwyn Barr, "Texas Coastal Defense, 1861–1865," *ibid.*, LXV, 1–31; A. Barr, "The Battle of Calcasieu Pass," *ibid.*, LXVI, 59–67; Ralph A. Wooster, "With the Confederate Cavalry in the West: The Civil War Experiences of Isaac Dunbar Affleck," *ibid.*, LXXXIII, 1–28; Ralph A. Wooster and Robert Wooster, " 'Rarin for a Fight': Texans in the Confederate Army," *ibid.*, LXXXIV, 387–426; Allen W. Jones, "Military Events in Texas during the Civil War, 1861–1865," *ibid.*, LXIV, 64–70; C. C. Jeffries, "The Character of Terry's Texas Rangers," *ibid.*, LXIV, 454–462; F. H. Smyrl, "Texans in the Union Army, 1861–1865," *ibid.*, LXV, 234–250; Charles C. Cumberland, "The Confederate Loss and Recapture of Galveston, 1862–1863," *ibid.*, LI, 109–130; E. C. Barker and Frank Vandiver, "Letters from the Confederate Medical Service in Texas, 1863–1865," *ibid.*, LV, 378–401, 459–474; Theophilus Noel, *Autobiography and Reminiscences* (Chicago, 1904); W. C. Holden, "Frontier Defense in Texas during the Civil War," *West Texas Historical Association Year Book*, IV, 16–31; Harry M. Henderson, *Texas in the Confederacy* (San Antonio, 1955); John P. Dyer, *The Gallant Hood* (New York, 1950); R. N. Richardson, *The Frontier of Northwest Texas;* Richard Taylor, *Destruction and Reconstruction* (Richard B. Harwell, ed., New York, 1955); and Don Alberts (ed.), *Rebels on the Rio Grande: The Civil War Journal of A. B. Peticolas* (Albuquerque, 1984).

For a scholarly account of two prominent Texans who served as officers in the Union Army, see Ronald N. Gray, "Edmund J. Davis: Radical Republican and Reconstruction Governor of Texas" (unpublished dissertation, Texas Tech University, Lubbock, 1976); and John L. Waller, *Colossal Hamilton of Texas: A Biography of Andrew Jackson Hamilton* (El Paso, 1968).

Phases of home life and public affairs during the Civil War are dealt with in Mrs. E. M. Loughery, *War and Reconstruction in Texas* (Austin, 1914); Thomas North, *Five Years in Texas* (Cincinnati, 1871); Grover C. Ramsey (comp.), *Confederate Postmasters in Texas, 1861–1865* (Waco, 1963); Alma D. King, "The Political Career of William Simpson Oldham," *Southwestern Historical Quarterly*, XXXIII, 112–133; C. W. Ramsdell, "The Texas State Military Board, 1862–1865," *ibid.*, XXVII, 253–275; Robert W. Shook, "The Battle of the Nueces, August 10, 1862," *ibid.*, LXVI, 31–42; Carland Elaine Crook, "Benjamin Théron and French Designs in Texas during the Civil War," *ibid.*, XLVIII, 432–454; Thomas L. Miller, "Texas Land Grants to Confederate Veterans and Widows," *ibid.*, LXIX, 59–65; Sam Acheson and Julie Ann Hudson O'Connell (eds.), "George Washington Diamond's Account of the Great Hanging at Gainesville, 1862," *ibid.*, LXVI, 331–414; Nancy Head Bowen, "A Political Labyrinth: Texas in the Civil War," *East Texas Historical Journal*, XI, 3–11; and Thomas Barrett, *The Great Hanging at Gainesville* (Austin, 1961).

Scores of county histories deal with certain phases of the war. Brief biographies of the governors of Texas may be found in J. T. DeShields, *They Sat in High Places; The Presidents and Governors of Texas*. Many excellent unpublished studies are available in the university libraries in Texas.

CHAPTER ELEVEN
RECONSTRUCTION
1865–1874

The decade following the end of the Civil War is generally called the Reconstruction period. These were difficult years for both the victors and the vanquished. The victorious North endeavored to assure the permanency of its major objectives in the war—the preservation of the Union, the abolition of slavery, and the establishment of government by and for all of the people. The war had preserved the Union, but restoration of the Southern states to a constitutional system of local and state government presented a host of difficult problems. Slavery was ended, but the political, economic, and social future of the former slaves who were now free people was uncertain and a matter of controversy. The war had promoted the cause of democracy, but restoration of order and civil government in the South sometimes involved military government, martial law, and voter disfranchisement. Four years of war left a heritage of violence and hatred that combined with racial prejudice to bring strife and trouble to the postwar years.

In addition to these challenges, Texas faced a few unique problems, particularly because of its isolation and vastness. By 1865 thousands of refugees, white and black, had entered Texas, and some contributed to the turbulence that followed the war. Furthermore, as the war ended, civil government ended, and for a time, anarchy prevailed. On the frontier,

Indian raids repeatedly threatened the lives and property of the settlers. And, while the end of slavery was proclaimed upon the arrival of Federal troops in Galveston, little was done to assure the welfare of the newly freed slave population.

PRESIDENTIAL RECONSTRUCTION

From the time Federal armies first conquered segments of the Confederacy, Northern leaders were divided over how reconstruction should be accomplished. President Lincoln held that secession was illegal and that reconstruction was thus the responsibility of the executive branch of the government. But some Republicans, termed "radicals," maintained that the Confederate states, by secession, had forfeited their statehood, and, since Congress alone had the power to admit new states, it also had the power to reconstruct. Radical Republicans generally favored a program that was much more strict than that of Lincoln, one which would promote the welfare of the newly freed population and the interest of the Republican party in the South.

Lincoln acted first. On December 8, 1863, he set forth his plan of reconstruction. Basically, the plan provided that when as many as ten percent of the number who had voted in 1860, with a few exceptions, took the oath of allegiance to the United States and accepted all official acts regarding slavery, they could establish a state government. In conformity with this plan, he accorded restoration to Tennessee, Louisiana, and Arkansas. ——

After Lincoln's death, President Andrew Johnson on May 29, 1865, prescribed in proclamations a process of reconstruction for the remaining Confederate states that was essentially the same as Lincoln's. The Amnesty Proclamation excluded 14 classes, including high-ranking military and civil officers and persons whose taxable property was worth over $20,000; the second proclamation provided for the reconstruction of civil government in North Carolina. During the next few weeks the President issued proclamations identical to the latter for each of the remaining six former Confederate states. On June 17 the Texas Proclamation was issued, in which Andrew Jackson (A. J.) Hamilton, a staunch Unionist and former congressman, was named provisional governor.

On June 2, the same day that General E. Kirby Smith formally surrendered, General Philip H. Sheridan assumed command of the Military Division of the Southwest, which included Texas, and established his headquarters in New Orleans. As soon as ships were available, he sent troops to Texas. On June 19, 1865, General Gordon Granger, with 1,800 troops, occupied Galveston and in the name of the President of the United States issued a proclamation that declared that the slaves were free; that all acts of the Texas government since secession were illegal; and that officers and men of the late Confederate army should be paroled.

By the end of the year an estimated 50,000 Federal troops were in Texas. Some were sent into the interior, but a larger number were concentrated along the Rio Grande to protect the Mexican border. The troops were supposed to restore the authority of the United States and to preserve order. They met with no organized resistance; in fact, a few commanders, including the colorful George A. Custer, who reached Austin with a detachment of troops in November 1865, became quite popular among the townfolk. Because of their small number, the great distances, and the confusion following the collapse of the Confederate armies, the troops were not able to eliminate lawlessness, but they had a salutary effect.

Governor Hamilton arrived in Galveston on July 21 and proceeded slowly to Austin. His reception was quite cordial. On August 9 he began establishing a new state government. He appointed James H. Bell, a former member of the Texas supreme court, as secretary of state and William Alexander as attorney general, both Union men. As rapidly as practicable, Union men, with a few exceptions, were appointed to the district, county, and precinct offices throughout the state. In keeping with President Johnson's plan of reconstruction, the governor called for an election, on January 8, 1866, of delegates to a constitutional convention to convene on February 7. Under the President's plan four conditions had to be met before he would accept the work of the convention: the abolition of slavery; the establishment of the civil status of the newly freed blacks; the repudia-

A native of Alabama, Andrew Jackson Hamilton moved to Texas in 1846, became a Unionist in the Civil War, and was appointed provisional governor of Texas in 1865. (Courtesy of Texas State Library)

tion of the ordinance of secession; and the repudiation of debts, both state and Confederate, incurred in behalf of the war.

When the convention assembled, two old factions, Unionists and secessionists, faced each other under new conditions. John Hancock, I. A. Paschal, and Edward Degener were sitting opposite such confirmed rebels as H. R. Runnels and O. M. Roberts. Between them was a group, larger than either, inclined to be conservative and to avoid any permanent alignment with the opposing factions. J. W. Throckmorton, a moderate who had been both a Unionist and a Confederate brigadier, was chosen president of the convention.

The convention spent much time in trying to decide what disposition to make of the ordinance of secession. Obviously, it was no longer in effect, but was it null and void from the date it was enacted, or did it become null and void as a result of the war? The question was never answered. By a vote of 55 to 21 the convention finally simply acknowledged the supremacy of the Constitution of the United States and declared void the ordinance of secession without reference to time.

The most important subject with which the convention dealt was the status of blacks. The questions of abolition and civil rights were combined in a single ordinance. The convention agreed that slavery no longer existed and that it could not be reestablished in Texas. However, it formally refused to approve the Thirteenth Amendment to the Constitution of the United States, claiming that it already had been ratified and declared in force. The convention also failed to grant to blacks equality before the law. After a sharp debate, it provided for their security in person and property, but it abridged their right to testify in court in cases in which blacks were not involved. Furthermore, it denied them the right to vote and to hold office. The new constitution thus failed to comply with the wishes of President Johnson, who wanted the right of suffrage extended to at least all adult black males who could read and write.

The convention was expected to repudiate the war debt; otherwise, it would be tantamount to recognition that secession and the war were legitimate. It went further and canceled all the state debts incurred during the war. This measure brought much criticism from the conservative press, for the state had incurred obligations in no way connected with carrying on the war. In defense of nullification it was pointed out that the debt had been acquired in violation of the Constitution of 1845 and that nearly all warrants were in the hands of speculators. Men of both parties voted for repudiation.

Before it adjourned, the convention approved all laws and all acts of officers of the Confederate state government not in violation of the Constitution of 1845 and without any direct relation to the war. The work of the convention was done through the passage of a series of ordinances. At first it delegated unto itself legislative and constituent power supreme and final;

but on March 27, after it had declared secession null and void, had canceled the war debt, and had fixed the status of freed slaves, it voted to submit to the electors amendments to the Constitution of 1845. Among the changes proposed was a plan to lengthen to four years the terms of most officers, to give constitutional status to county courts, and to provide for a possible division of the state.

An election to choose constitutional officers was held on June 25. The Unionists or radicals supported E. M. Pease for governor, and the conservatives stood behind J. W. Throckmorton. Although the contest was heated, the candidates did not differ as widely as their followers. Throckmorton upheld the reconstruction policy of President Johnson and opposed black suffrage in any form. Pease adopted a mild tone. He favored, as a matter of expediency, granting the right to vote to those who could read and write. His followers, however, charged the conservatives with disloyalty and with planning to drive the Union men from the state. Throckmorton received 49,277 votes to Pease's 12,168. By a comparatively close vote the amendments to the constitution were ratified.

Within a few weeks the newly elected government assumed office. Conspicuously conservative, the Eleventh Legislature convened on August 6, 1866. Three days later Governor Throckmorton and Lieutenant Governor G. W. Jones were inaugurated, and on August 20 President Johnson proclaimed the insurrection in Texas at an end.

The legislature had the task of naming two United States senators. By a decisive vote, it elected David G. Burnet, a Unionist in 1861 who had come out of retirement to denounce vehemently the radicals, and O. M. Roberts, who had been the president of the secession convention. Neither Burnet nor Roberts could take the test oath required of all United States officials by an act of July 2, 1862. Neither the senators-elect nor the three elected to the House of Representatives were seated (and Texas thus remained without representation in Congress). Then, following the suggestion of Governor Throckmorton, the legislators did not act on the Thirteenth Amendment to the Constitution of the United States and refused by an overwhelming vote to ratify the Fourteenth.

Evident in the laws passed by the legislature regarding the status of the newly freed black population was a belief that the freed slaves would become a new caste occupying a niche somewhere between that of slavery and freedom. Ignoring the warning of John H. Reagan that the radical Republicans were gaining control of the government and would demand racial equality in the South, legislators passed laws on the subject of apprenticeship, vagrancy, and labor contracts, all of which were calculated to keep at least some of the freed slaves in a state of peonage. Neither the apprentice nor the vagrancy acts met with strong opposition, but the labor law was especially offensive to champions of black rights. Its tenor may be judged by the provisions that laborers should not leave home without permission or have visitors during working hours and that they must be obedient and respectful. Although the "black codes," which had replaced the old "slave codes," were even more harsh in some other states, these laws, also to be considered "black codes," were harsh and unjust as well.

A federal agency, the Freedmen's Bureau, offered some protection against the black codes. The Freedmen's Bureau, created pursuant to an act of Congress of March 3, 1865, was clothed with the authority to take control of all affairs relating to freed slaves, refugees, and abandoned lands in the conquered states. In September of that year the bureau was set up in Texas under General E. M. Gregory, assistant commissioner. Gregory set to work with enthusiasm. Although he admonished the blacks to work and did his best to dispel the notion that each freedman would be given "forty acres and a mule" out of the lands of former masters, he required that labor contracts be registered with the bureau in an effort to ensure fairness. The bureau did some relief work among freed slaves and provided night schools for several thousand. Its most important work was, however, to supervise contracts and protect the freed slaves from unscrupulous employers. Another activity, which generated some controversy, was its intervention in the courts in cases in which freed slaves were involved.

The army also continued to play an active role. Governor Throckmorton contended that President Johnson's proclamation of August 20, 1866, declaring the insurrection in Texas at an end, reestablished the supremacy of civil over military authority. However, with the President's prestige diminishing each day and the strength of the radical Republicans increasing, the governor was able to restore traditional civil government only in part. While the provisional government had been in existence, army officers had exercised extensive power. They continued to exercise a great deal of authority after the inauguration of elected officials.

The governor set to work to make the best of the situation. He sought to restore law and order, to secure the removal of the military from the centers of population to the frontier, to bring an end to the courts of the Freedmen's Bureau, and to limit the jurisdiction of the military courts strictly to military cases. To a limited extent, he succeeded in getting a distribution of the troops for the protection of outlying communities. Less effective, however, were his efforts on behalf of the civil courts. There were in Texas three kinds of courts: the military, which claimed jurisdiction in all cases involving soldiers and federal employees; those established in accordance with the Constitution of 1866, which claimed jurisdiction in all criminal and in most civil cases; and the Freedmen's Bureau, which claimed jurisdiction in all cases relating to the freedmen. The Bureau was helpful in forging the new relationship between the black worker and his or her white employer; furthermore, there were many instances where freedmen would have had little chance for justice in a traditional court proceeding. But there were instances where Bureau agents acted in partisan fashion, sometimes with the support of the military. For instance, a Bureau agent arrested and fined D. L. McGary, editor of the Brenham *Banner*, for unnecessary abuse and ridicule of the Bureau, its wards, and its agents.

Although white Texans frequently condemned the agency, the Freedmen's Bureau operated a system of schools for blacks that had a salutary effect. In January 1866 it had 16 schools attended by 1,041 students, and in June the numbers had increased to 100 schools and 4,447 students. When the Bureau ceased operation in 1870, the black enrollment in schools had grown to 6,499 pupils.

In an age filled with racial tensions and resentment provoked by war and military occupation, violence was to be expected. Between January and June 1867, the Freedmen's Bureau agents reported thirty to forty crimes each month, ordinarily instances of white attacks upon blacks. Gangs of whites in Hoffman County raided black homes to collect any arms that might be found. Outlaws, such as John Wesley Hardin, added to their reputation as "badmen" by killing blacks. Reportedly, another member of an outlaw gang shot to death a young black who refused to stand at attention when he rode by. Indeed, a committee reported in 1868 that 509 whites and 468 blacks had been murdered since the end of the war.

Trouble sometimes developed where federal troops were stationed. For a while, black troops at Victoria controlled the county jail and made it impossible to hold in prison there a freedman or a Union man. Federal soldiers burned Brenham, and neither the soldiers nor their officers were ever brought to justice. Only occasionally was a soldier turned over to civil authorities for trial for violating the laws of the state, and a few Union men, even criminals, received favorable treatment from the troops. Nevertheless, the troops were necessary. Settlers on the frontier demanded more, not fewer, soldiers. Moreover, lawlessness of all types created a need for the protection of military units in other areas.

CONGRESSIONAL RECONSTRUCTION

The radical Republicans in Congress watched the progress of Johnson's reconstruction program with rising resentment and hostility. It was moving too rapidly to suit them; it was turning the state governments of the late Confederacy back into the hands of the former slaveholders; it threatened to place the freed slaves and the ex-Union men at the mercy of ex-rebels; and it would add to the Democratic party a phalanx of 11 states, at least some which would return with a greater representation in Congress than when they seceded. Through pride and failure to comprehend fully the reality of a new era, Southerners had strengthened the cause of the radicals. They had honored prominent leaders of the Confederacy with high office. State legislatures had passed black codes calculated to reduce blacks to serfdom. Southerners had failed to prevent occasional race riots and many acts of lawlessness, and, with the exception of Tennessee, southern states had refused to ratify the Fourteenth Amendment.

In the election of 1866 the radical Republicans gained control of Congress and thus could carry out their own reconstruction program. Ignoring all that had been done by the President and the states, they proposed to place the government of the late Confederate states in the hands of those who professed loyalty to the radical cause, depending largely on white Unionists and the support of blacks. They would disfranchise the people who had always run the government, but whose loyalties were now suspect, and place in control freedmen and Unionists. In short, they proposed to change the basic structure of Southern politics.

The First Reconstruction Act, passed over the President's veto on March 2, 1867, contained the heart of their program. It declared inadequate and illegal the existing governments in the Southern states, divided the South into five military districts, and granted the commanding generals authority superior to state laws and civil officials. The act called for a constitutional convention, the delegates to be elected by voters of both races, exclusive of those disqualified as former rebels. It required that the convention frame and the qualified voters ratify a new constitution that granted blacks suffrage and that otherwise was acceptable to Congress, and it required that the legislature elected under the new constitution should ratify the Fourteenth Amendment.

The commanding generals, armed with the authority to continue with the civil officers as they were or to replace them by their own selections, were quickly appointed. General Philip H. Sheridan, then stationed in New Orleans as commander of the Military Division of the Southwest, was given charge of the Fifth District made up of Louisiana and Texas, and under him General Charles Griffin was made commander of the subdistrict of Texas.

Throckmorton pledged to Sheridan and Griffin his cooperation, but the generals expected more than he was willing to concede. Griffin first became offended with the governor when Throckmorton refused to comply with a request that he pardon the 227 black convicts in the penitentiary. A bureau official had visited the prison and accepted the statement of the prisoners that their offenses were trivial. The radical press and Unionists both sought to undermine Throckmorton's influence. On July 19, Congress passed an act that removed the last doubt as to the power of the commanding generals to remove all civil officers, and on July 30 Sheridan declared Throckmorton "an impediment to reconstruction," removed him, and appointed in his stead ex-Governor E. M. Pease.

Meanwhile, Griffin had brought the civil government completely under his control, using a test oath widely termed the "ironclad oath" to eliminate many from the processes of government. The Reconstruction

Act of March 2 had disfranchised only those persons who were excluded by the Fourteenth Amendment. The Reconstruction Act of March 23 imposed this same restriction more emphatically by requiring the voter to take an oath to the effect that he had never held a state or federal office or taken an oath to support the Constitution of the United States and thereafter engaged in insurrection or rebellion against the Union. Sheridan, with the backing of General Ulysses S. Grant, applied this regulation most rigidly, even after the Attorney General of the United States ruled that the law excluded only those who had taken an oath to support the Constitution of the United States and afterwards had supported the Confederacy. For instance, persons who, without having been required to take the oath, had served in such capacities as mayors of cities, school trustees, or even sextons of cemeteries, and had later taken part in the rebellion were disfranchised. A rule that jurors take the "ironclad" test oath barred men otherwise qualified to serve and threw the courts into confusion. It was in connection with the registration of voters, however, that Sheridan and Griffin were most rigorous in their demands.

Texas was fortunate in the selection of provisional governors. A. J. Hamilton, the first military governor, was a Texas citizen seasoned by years of public service. E. M. Pease was even better prepared. Long a resident of the state, he had served four years as its chief executive. He was, says an early historian of Reconstruction, "the most moderate of all those who had the confidence of the military authorities; and . . . his advice carried weight as Throckmorton's could not."

After Throckmorton's removal came the dismissal of other state and many local officers. On September 15 Griffin died of yellow fever, and his successor, General J. J. Reynolds, removed "rebel officials" in large numbers. In November, General W. S. Hancock succeeded Sheridan as commander of the fifth military district. Hancock, a Democrat and more generous than Sheridan, notified civil officials to return to their normal functions and permitted the registration of about 5,000 additional voters.

When the registration of voters for the election of delegates to a constitutional convention had been completed, the rolls showed about 59,633 white and 49,479 black voters. It was estimated that the number of men disfranchised was not more than 7,500 to 10,000. The Republicans, organized in the Union League and in the Grand Army of the Republic, sought to gain the votes of the freedmen. The Ku Klux Klan, which operated in Texas under various names, by threats, intimidation, and violence sought to destroy the political influence of the blacks and some Unionists.

The election was held in each county seat for five consecutive days, February 10–14, 1868. The law required that a majority of the registered voters had to participate in the election in order to make it effective. The Democrats proposed to stay away from the polls, thereby hoping to defeat the reconstruction program. As some stated, they preferred "Yankee rule to Negro rule." Unfortunately for the plan, some of the Democratic leaders lost confidence in it and at a meeting early in January advised their followers to vote against a convention and for delegates who would oppose black suffrage. The vote was 44,689 (7,757 white and 36,932 black) for the convention and 11,400 (10,622 white and 818 black) against it, the total being a little more than half of the total registration. Thus, the conservatives lost the election and failed to invalidate it.

The convention assembled in Austin on June 1, 1868. Of its 94 members (including four replacements as a result of deaths and resignations), two had served in the constitutional convention in 1845, six in that of 1866, and one in the German National Assembly in Frankfurt. Ten were blacks, including one replacement and George T. Ruby from Galveston, the well-educated, carpetbag president of the Union Leagues in Texas. It has not been possible to identify the exact number of carpetbaggers (Northerners who came South after the war for political office, for economic gains, or to assist freed slaves). Of those whose length of residence is known, 13 had been in Texas three years or less, and only eight of them were true carpetbaggers. It is possible that a few others, whose length of residence is unknown, could be so classed. Thus, the blacks and carpetbaggers together constituted a much smaller proportion of the total than in the reconstruction conventions in other Southern states.

Of the original 90 delegates, no more than 12 were conservatives, including eight to ten Democrats, and 78 were Republicans, irrevocably divided on the major issues. A. J. Hamilton, the leader of the moderate Republicans, had the unwavering support of all the Democrats, and of a number who had been in the army or Congress of the Republic of Texas, in the conventions of 1845 or 1866, or in the Confederate or Union army during the Civil War. Of the radical Republicans, the most prominent in the convention were Edmund Jackson (E. J.) Davis of Corpus Christi, a former judge and the president of the convention, who had organized in South Texas a regiment of Union cavalry and attained the rank of brigadier general; Morgan Hamilton, the wealthy brother of A. J. Hamilton and the military-appointed state comptroller; James P. Newcomb, a pronounced antisecessionist newspaper owner and editor, who had left San Antonio for California at the outbreak of the war; and George T. Ruby, president of the Union Leagues of Texas.

The radicals favored ordinances in favor of disfranchisement of all those who had voluntarily aided or abetted the Confederate States government, the division of the state, and *ab initio*. The first serious debate in the convention was over *ab initio* (a provision that the ordinance of secession was null and void from its passage and that consequently all official acts of the state from that date until congressional reconstruction government was established were null and void). The proposal was defeated, and in its stead a declaration was adopted by a vote of 45 to 28 that validated all acts that were "not in violation of the Constitution and the laws of the United States, or in aid of the rebellion. . . ."

The *ab initio* supporters then set out to delay the restoration of constitutional government in the eastern part of the state and to create a new state or states out of the western section where there were relatively large numbers of Unionists. Their efforts to divide the state provoked the most time-consuming and most bitter debate in the convention.

The convention assumed considerable responsibility beyond the writing of a constitution and spent much time chartering railroads, gathering evidence of lawlessness in East Texas, debating proposals for the sale of a portion of the state to the United States, and dealing with the inappropriate conduct of its own members. With the constitution almost completed, the delegates of all factions decided to delay its completion until after the presidential election—the radicals, because they did not like the constitution as it was being prepared and felt that a Republican victory would strengthen their chances for disfranchisement and division; the moderate Republicans, because they feared that, if the constitution were completed in time, voters in the state might support the Democratic nominee for President of the United States; and the Democrats, because they were opposed to any constitution that might be drafted by the convention and were optimistic that the Democrats would win the election and bring an end to military and Republican rule in Texas. Having delayed the completion of the constitution until it ran out of funds, the convention provided for the collection of a special tax to finance another session and, then, on August 31 recessed until the first Monday in December. During the recess, Ulysses S. Grant, the Republican nominee for President, won an overwhelming victory.

Thus, when the convention reconvened in December, the radicals, convinced that they would have support from Washington, began a determined fight to divide the state. In January 1869 the convention, after refusing to accept a "Constitution of the State of West Texas," voted in favor of division of the state and to send a delegation to Washington to lobby for division. The resolution opposed immediate restoration of eastern Texas to statehood because of excessive violence there against freed slaves and Unionists.

The moderate-conservative coalition gained the ascendancy, however, and on February 3 the delegates approved a constitution for engrossment. Having lost every major controversial issue—*ab initio*, the establishment of a state of West Texas, and disfranchisement—Davis on February 5 and 6 engineered the breakup of the convention before the final vote on the completed document. The A. J. Hamilton faction, however, took control, recovered the records, turned them over to the commanding general, and adjourned the convention on February 8. The constitution as adopted was prepared in final form by a committee of three appointed by the commanding general and signed by 46 delegates, including Davis (by order of the commanding general) and only seven other radicals.

The constitution, as finally adopted, disfranchised only persons disqualified by the Constitution of the United States, and permitted male black suffrage by providing that the right of suffrage should not be affected by "race, color, or former condition." It provided for much centralization of authority. The governor would hold office for four years and would appoint the secretary of state, the attorney general, and the judges of the courts. County courts were abolished. The convention did more for public education than any like body that had preceded it, by providing that all proceeds from the sale of public lands would be added to the permanent school fund and that the available fund would be used for the education of all children from six to 18 years of age, irrespective of race and color. The schools were granted, in addition, proceeds of a poll tax and not less than one-fourth of the revenue from the annual state taxes. All in all, the Constitution of 1869 was not a bad instrument.

Preparation for the vote on ratification and the election of officials produced a flurry of activity. As previously noted, the radicals tried to prevent the final completion of the constitution, and failing, they tried to get President Grant and Congress to reject it. Unsuccessful in this, they did an about-face, endorsed it, and nominated Davis for governor and J. W. Flanagan for lieutenant governor. To oppose the constitution meant defeat, and to join the moderate Republicans would destroy their party. In opposition the moderate Republicans and the Democrats supported A. J. Hamilton as their candidate for governor. The conservatives made a valiant fight, but the odds were against them. Through the Union League the blacks were aligned solidly with the radicals. General J. J. Reynolds, military commander in Texas, stacked the registration boards with Davis men, and many Democrats refused to take part in the election because they believed that Congress would not recognize the new government if Hamilton were elected or because they simply would not vote for any Republican.

The election was held on Tuesday, November 30 and the three days following. There was little violence, but there were many irregularities. General Reynolds never made public the returns (and they have never been found), but the vote that he certified on January 8, 1870, was 39,901 for Davis and 39,092 for Hamilton. Hamilton always believed that he won but was denied victory by a corrupt count; there well may have been fraud on both sides in the election. The constitution was adopted by a huge majority—72,466 as against 4,928. The Republicans elected three congressmen; the fourth Texas congressman, J. C. Conner, a Democrat, was an army officer and carpetbagger.

When Reynolds's alliance with the radicals became known in September 1869, Governor Pease resigned in protest. Reynolds then proceeded to rule the state without a governor until January 8, 1870, when he appointed the successful candidates for state office to the respective offices for which they had been elected to serve as provisional officers until their constitutional terms began. He convened the legislature on February 8. That body promptly ratified the Fourteenth and Fifteenth Amendments and elected Morgan Hamilton and J. W. Flanagan to the United States Senate. On March 30, 1870, President Grant signed the act of Congress admitting Texas senators and representatives; the executive officers of Texas dropped the qualifying title "provisional"; and on April 16, 1870, General Reynolds formally brought military rule to an end by remitting authority to the civil officers.

Texas had been restored to the Union, but for many it was not until four years later when a government was established under the control of Democrats that Reconstruction would be ended.

RADICAL REPUBLICAN HOME RULE

Pursuant to Governor Davis's call, the Twelfth Legislature met in special session from April 26 to August 15, 1870. It was in session twice during 1871, from January 10 to May 31 and from September 12 to December 2. Sixteen of the 30 senators, including two blacks, and 50 of the 90 members

A native of Florida, Edmund Jackson "E. J." Davis moved to Texas in 1838, became a brigadier-general in the Union forces, and returned to Texas after the war to become a Radical Republican leader. After serving one term as governor, he was defeated in his bid for reelection, but he remained active in politics until his death in 1883. (Courtesy Texas State Library)

of the house, including nine blacks, were Davis supporters. Thus, the governor had most of his program enacted into law. In his first message to the lawmakers, Governor Davis stated that the army was not adequately protecting the northern and western frontier against Indian raids and stressed the need for legislation providing for a ranger force for defense. The legislature immediately approved his recommendation for a force of 20 companies, totaling 1,220 men, but, because of insufficient funds and War Department disapproval, the organization never materialized. The legislature then authorized the establishment of companies of minutemen for frontier defense, but they were never very effective.

After providing for the ranger companies, the legislature moved rapidly to enact into law Davis's other recommendations. Five of the measures, called "obnoxious acts" by the Democrats, obviously for political gain, were controversial. Determined, if possible, to suppress the violence and lawlessness in the state, the governor also had urged the creation of a militia system and a state police organization. The militia bill came up for consideration first. A variety of motives influenced the opposition. The Democrats and some Republicans feared such a force would put too much power in the hands of the governor. Railroad lobbyists in search of subsidies hoped to delay passage of the militia bill and to use it as a weapon to force the legislature to appropriate funds for railroad construction.

To prevent a vote on the militia bill, 13 senators left the senate chambers. Without a quorum, no vote could be taken. Subsequently, they were arrested for intentionally breaking a forum. While nine remained under arrest, four of the senators were returned to the senate to make a quorum, and the bill was then approved. The measure provided for the enrollment of all able-bodied males between the ages of 18 and 45 in a state militia under the command of the governor, who was empowered to use it to maintain law and order when local officials and the state police failed to do so. Opponents of the law charged that the arrest of the senators was an act of despotism. Despotism, however, lay not in the arrest, inasmuch as the legislature had the power to compel attendance of its membership to assure a quorum for action, but in holding and denying the right to vote to some and in releasing and allowing the others to vote, an action surely of doubtful propriety. On the other hand, the actions of some of the dissenting senators were apparently less than honorable, for there is considerable evidence to suggest that they were motivated by railroad bribes rather than by lofty principles.

Having passed the militia bill, the legislature, with far less opposition, then enacted into law a companion proposal by Davis for the control of lawlessness. This measure provided for the creation of a state police, consisting of 258 men and officers under the control of the governor, empowered to operate anywhere within the state. All local law officers were to aid the state force when called upon and were subject to removal for hindering the state police in the execution of the laws.

The other three controversial acts of the legislature in the summer of 1870 were unrelated, but each increased the power of the governor. By the so-called Enabling Act, approved on June 28, the legislature authorized the governor to fill offices made vacant by the act readmitting Texas into the Union, including state, district, county, and city. One citizen estimated that Davis appointed, either directly or indirectly, 8,538 temporary or permanent employees as officers. Regardless of the accuracy of this tabulation, the act provided a tremendous amount of patronage. In another act, provision was made for a state printer, an official state journal, and for the printing of public notices and other official matters in a newspaper in each judicial district. This act, although providing for a better informed citizenry, practically assured Davis some support from a subsidized press. The fifth so-called obnoxious act postponed the regular election until November 1872, which for members of Congress should have been held in the fall of 1870 and for state officers in 1871. Supporters argued that the measure made the dates for state and congressional elections coincide; it also extended by an additional year the term of the radical officers elected in 1869.

Of all actions associated with the E. J. Davis administration, those that generated the most controversy pertained to the activities of the state police and the imposition of martial law. In part, the conflict simply reflected the struggle for political power between the conservatives and radical Republicans. Also, the police force unfortunately contained within its ranks some criminals and other persons too weak to exercise authority with restraint. On several occasions they arrested men without justification and instigated or permitted riots. Probably more significant in generating criticism was the practice of using black policemen, who constituted about 40 percent of the force, an action that angered conservative whites. The reputation of the police also suffered when in 1872 its chief, Adjutant General James Davidson, absconded with more than $37,000 in state funds.

Yet, the police force had among its number some renowned lawmen, including L. H. McNelly's Special Force of Rangers. Undoubtedly, the state police rendered valuable service in the interest of law and order. Even the conservative press occasionally praised the men for chasing outlaws and for their dealings with desperate criminals. For the 14-month period that ended on September 17, 1871, the police reported 3,475 arrests; during the same period eight of its men had been killed in the line of duty.

Less widespread, but more severe when it did apply and more unpopular among the majority of conservative whites, was Davis's declaration of martial law. The killing of a citizen by a black policeman had led to an armed insurrection in Limestone and Freestone counties. The governor in the fall of 1871 declared martial law and sent three hundred militia to the region. The cost of occupation was met by a tax of three cents on each one hundred dollars of property valuation in the occupied area. There is some evidence, including a sizeable majority vote in the house of the legislature, that the necessity of martial law in this instance was at least open to question. Davis also declared martial law in Hill and Walker counties. In these two instances, particularly in Hill County, there is considerable evidence to support the wisdom of the governor's decision.

The Twelfth Legislature, apparently in response to strong and possibly unethical pressure from railroad lobbyists, promoted railroad construction. The state was immensely large and without much water transportation. There was very little rail mileage in existence at the end of the war; the population was expanding into new areas rapidly, and having retained its public lands, Texas, rather than the federal government, had to provide its own support to lines within the state. A tabulation of the vote on five railroad bills shows that support was favored by a majority of Democrats and moderate Republicans and opposed by a majority of radical Republicans. The legislators authorized cities to vote bonds as an aid. In a law later declared unconstitutional, they promised to the International Railroad Company, which was to build across the state, 8 percent state bonds to the amount of $10,000 for each mile constructed. Many radicals opposed these grants, and it was over Davis's veto that a similar provisional grant was made to the Southern Pacific and to the Southern Transcontinental Railway. Since the Constitution of 1869 prohibited the legislature from granting lands to railroads, the extensive domain could not be used as a subsidy for construction. This restriction was removed in 1873 by a constitutional amendment, and in later years, a legislature controlled by Democrats substituted land grants for the bond subsidies. Other vetoes by Governor Davis at the time and later substitution of lands for bonds saved the state from being burdened by a huge, long-term debt for railroad construction.

The radicals enacted considerable legislation that was creditable. They designed a constructive program of social and economic legislation for Texas which under more favorable conditions might have been successful. They sought to provide a public road system and levied taxes for that purpose. They enacted a homestead law. They were generous in appropriations to provide state troops to supplement the inadequate frontier defense provided by the federal forces. Theirs was the first administration to envision a genuinely public, free school system. In making attendance compulsory and levying taxes adequate for the maintenance of the schools, they were half a century ahead of their time.

Before it had been completed, the political structure of the radicals showed signs of disintegration. The Republicans had gained control of the state by a slender margin, and their victory was due to the demoralized state of the Democratic opposition. Their power rested mainly on black suffrage, a support that was soon cut away by the persuasion and intimidation of the opposition. Most of their legislative program, whether meritorious or not, was extremely unpopular.

Democrats and conservative Republicans united in attacking the radicals. In September 1871 the representatives of 94 counties met in Austin at a taxpayers' convention to protest the extravagance of the administration. Such men as A. J. Hamilton, Morgan Hamilton, and E. M. Pease united with ex-Confederates to argue that the Davis administration was flagrantly violating the constitution and laws and was bankrupting the state. At a special election in October 1871 (which Davis was pressured into calling because the legislature, in violation of the constitution, had postponed the general election until November 1872), the Democrats elected all four of their candidates for Congress. In 1872 Horace Greeley, the Democratic (and Liberal Republican) nominee for President, outran President Grant in Texas by almost 20,000 votes, and the Democrats again won all the seats in Congress and gained control of the legislature. It was at this election, incidentally, that the voters again chose Austin as the permanent capital.

When it assembled in Austin on January 14, 1873, the Thirteenth Legislature proceeded to repeal the basic laws of the radical program. It began by enacting a new printing law, which withdrew official patronage from radical newspapers. It repealed—over the governor's veto—the police act, limited the power of the governor to declare martial law, and reduced drastically the appointive powers of the governor. It simplified requirements for the registration of voters and provided for precinct voting and one-day elections. The centralized school system of the radicals was reshaped by a law abolishing the board of education and school supervisors and reducing the power of the state superintendent. Before it adjourned, the legislature provided for a general election of state officers for the first Tuesday in December 1873.

The election brought the final test of the strength of the radicals. Davis and R. H. Taylor headed the Republican ticket, running against Richard Coke and R. B. Hubbard, the Democratic nominees. The campaign was hard-fought, with both sides resorting to fraud and intimidation. The Union League threatened blacks who voted the Democratic ticket; the Democrats discouraged black voting; and white men under age voted. Coke's vote was reported as 85,549 to 42,663 for Davis. The other state contests and most county contests were won by the Democrats.

The radicals made their last stand before the courts. They sought to invalidate the election on the ground that it was unconstitutional since, pursuant to the terms of the law passed by the Thirteenth Legislature, the polls were open for one day only while the constitution called for four-day elections. The state supreme court, all members of which had been appointed by Davis, in what became known as the "semicolon court case," upheld their contention. Its decision, however, was ignored by the general public, and Coke and Hubbard were inaugurated late at night on January 15, 1874. Davis appealed to Grant, but the President advised that it would "be prudent as well as right" to accept the verdict of the voters. Davis refused to recognize the new administration, and certain members of the

Thirteenth Legislature sought to organize that body as the constitutional lawmaking agency.

For several days it seemed that bloodshed was inevitable. Davis was supported by some of his state police and black militia. Citizens under such leaders as Henry E. McCulloch and John S. (Rip) Ford, sustained Coke. A local militia company, the Travis Rifles, also took the side of the new governor. At last, after he had received another message from the Attorney General of the United States, stating positively that President Grant would not sustain him against Coke, Davis retired under protest.

EFFECTS OF RECONSTRUCTION

Although Texas did not suffer to the extent of other southern states, the nine years that followed the collapse of the Confederacy proved destructive to the fortunes of many wealthy plantation owners and difficult for smaller landowners and farmers. The war itself had bankrupted numbers of persons; and those who held on to their estates through the war found themselves land-poor, sometimes without sufficient livestock and without slaves to provide labor. Of all the problems, that of securing labor was the greatest on those lands where slaves had once provided it. A new system of labor and land management acceptable to both black and white people had to evolve. In the meantime, thousands of acres lay idle. Land values fell to 20 percent of 1860 prices. Cotton, practically the only money crop, declined in value from 31 cents per pound in 1866 to 17 cents in 1870, and to 13 cents in 1875. The total production of cotton declined from 431,000 bales in 1859 to an average of 343,000 bales for the years from 1866 to 1870, both inclusive.

However, conditions improved in the later years of Reconstruction. Work for wages gave way to leasing or renting, when black labor was involved, and by 1870 the sharecropping system was becoming common. Under this practice, landowners supplied the laborers with all houses and farming equipment and took as their share from one-half to two-thirds of the crop. Improvement in the agricultural situation is reflected in the production of cotton, which by 1873 was exceeding 500,000 bales per year. Following the discovery that cotton would thrive on the rich uplands of North Texas, the increase in acreage was rapid. Immigration stimulated the production of all farm commodities. During this period southern and western Texas became comparatively prosperous from the pouches of gold brought back by drovers who took each year hundreds of thousands of cattle to northern markets. The industrial development of the country is reflected in the railroad mileage, which increased from 395 in 1865 to 1,650 in 1874.

Public indebtedness and taxation had increased during Reconstruction. Money appropriated under the printing act, the police law, the school law, frontier defense, and for the expenses of long legislative sessions amounted to millions. Through state taxes there was raised in 1871 and the three years following nearly $4 million. Besides the state *ad valorem* taxes and other levies, there were large increases in local taxes. In 1871 these combined rates amounted in some instances to as much as $2.17 on $100.00 of valuation, an increase of 1,450 percent over 1866. Meanwhile, it had become necessary to resort to borrowing, and the public debt was increased by more than $2 million. Some of the funds had been spent unwisely, small amounts had been lost through fraud and embezzlement, and the debt would be a burden to future generations. But the need for public expenditures during these troubled times had been real, and most of the money had been spent for good purposes.

Economic losses through the war and Reconstruction were soon overcome, but the effect on political and social institutions was more enduring. Many white voters did not forget their antagonism toward the Republican Party. The Republican Party did not disappear. It took part in elections, occasionally with success, and its members claimed federal jobs in significant numbers. But as a truly effective part of the state political system, the Republican Party offered little after Reconstruction. Whether justified or not, memories of Reconstruction rendered Texas a one-party state controlled by the Democrats for the next century.

For the black people of Texas, Reconstruction was a mixture of success and failure. Blacks achieved some gains—the beginnings of an educational system, land ownership for a few, a degree of civil equality, and some political influence for a time—and they bore the responsibility of freedom as well as anyone might have been expected. But the tide of racial prejudice would have been strong under the best of circumstances, and Reconstruction policies and programs stopped far short of solving the problems of prejudice and discrimination. In the decades to come, segregation, political and economic discrimination, and eventually disfranchisement would become a way of life for the black people of Texas.

SELECTED BIBLIOGRAPHY

There is no definitive work on Reconstruction in Texas. Readers who wish to be familiar with differing interpretations should begin with the following: C. W. Ramsdell, *Reconstruction in Texas;* E. Wallace, *Texas in Turmoil;* Carl H. Moneyhon, *Republicanism in Reconstruction Texas* (Austin, 1980); and James M. Smallwood, *Time of Hope, Time of Despair: Black Texans during Reconstruction* (Port Washington, N.Y., 1981).

Good sketches may be read in S. S. McKay, *Seven Decades of the Texas Constitution in 1876* (Lubbock, 1942); L. J. Wortham, *A History of Texas;* F. W. Johnson, *Texas and Texans;* and O. M. Roberts, *A Political, Legislative, and Judicial History of Texas, 1845–1895.* Excellent biographical studies of participants in the Civil War and

Reconstruction include B. H. Procter, *Not without Honor: The Life of John H. Reagan;* C. Elliot, *Leathercoat: The Life of James W. Throckmorton;* W. J. Hughes, *Rebellious Ranger: Rip Ford and the Old Southwest;* E. Wallace, *Charles DeMorse: Pioneer Editor and Statesman;* J. L. Waller, *Colossal Hamilton of Texas: A Biography of Andrew Jackson Hamilton;* Ernest Wallace, *The Howling of the Coyotes: Reconstruction Efforts to Divide Texas* (College Station, 1979); R. N. Gray, "Edmund J. Davis: Radical Republican and Reconstruction Governor of Texas"; Betty J. Sandlin, "The Texas Reconstruction Constitutional Convention of 1868–1869" (unpublished dissertation, Texas Tech University, Lubbock, 1970).

Other book-length studies are W. C. Nunn, *Texas under the Carpetbaggers* (Austin, 1962); W. C. Nunn, *Escape from Reconstruction* (Fort Worth, 1956); Marion H. Farrow, *The Texas Democrats* (San Antonio, 1944); and D. Richardson, *Texas as Seen in 1870* (Shreveport, 1870).

Of the writings of participants, see O. M. Roberts, "The Experiences of an Unrecognized Senator," *Quarterly of the Texas State Historical Association,* XII, 87–147; John H. Reagan, *Memoirs, with Special Reference to Secession and the Civil War* (W. F. McCaleb, ed., New York, 1906); and A. W. Terrell, *From Texas to Mexico in 1865* (Dallas, 1933).

Valuable specialized studies published as articles include William L. Richter, "Texas Politics and the United States Army, 1866–1867,"*Military History of Texas and the Southwest,* X, 159–186; William L. Richter, "'We Must Rub Out and Begin Anew'; The Army and the Republican Party in Texas Reconstruction," *Civil War History,* XIX, 334–352; Dale A. Somers, "James P. Newcomb: The Making of a Radical," *Southwestern Historical Quarterly,* LXXII, 435–448; W. A. Russ, Jr., "Radical Disfranchisement in Texas," *ibid.,* XXXVIII, 40–52; Louise Horton (ed.), "Samuel Bell Maxey on the Coke-Davis Controversy," *ibid.,* LXXII, 519–525; C. Elliott, "The Freedmen's Bureau in Texas," *ibid.,* LVI, 1–24; George Shelley, "The Semicolon Court of Texas," *ibid.,* XLVIII, 449–468; Billy Bob Lightfoot, "The Negro Exodus from Comanche County, Texas," *ibid.,* LVI, 405–416; O. A. Singletary, "The Texas Militia during Reconstruction," *ibid.,* LX, 23–35; J. R. Norvell, "The Reconstruction Courts of Texas," *ibid.,* LXII, 141–163; and J. E. Ericson, "Delegates to the Texas Constitutional Convention of 1875: A Reappraisal," *Ibid.,* LXVII, 22–27.

For a somewhat different viewpoint of Reconstruction, see Barry A. Crouch and L. J. Schultz, "Crisis in Color: Racial Separation in Texas during Reconstruction," *Civil War History,* XVI, 37–49; Edgar P. Sneed, "A Historiography of Reconstruction in Texas: Some Myths and Problems,"*Southwestern Historical Quarterly,* LXXII, 435–448; Ann Patton Baenziger, "The Texas State Police during Reconstruction: A Reexamination," *ibid.,* LXXII, 470–491; Philip J. Avillo, Jr., "Phantom Radicals: Texas Republicans in Congress, 1870–1873," *ibid.,* LXXVII, 431–444; Allen Hornsby, Jr., "The Freedmen's Bureau Schools in Texas, 1864–1870," *ibid.,* LXXVI, 397–417; and John M. Brockman, "Railroads, Radicals, and the Militia Bill: A New Interpretation of the Quorum-Breaking Incident of 1870," *ibid.,* LXXIII, 105–122; James Smallwood, "Perpetuation of Caste: Black Agricultural Workers in Reconstruction Texas," *Mid-America,* LXI, 5–23, and "Black Education in Reconstruction Texas: The Contribution of the Freedmen's Bureau and Benevolent Societies," *East Texas Historical Journal,* XIX, 17–40; Billy D. Ledbetter, "White Texans' Attitudes Toward the Political Equality of Negroes, 1865–1870," *Phylon,* XL, 253–263; Barry Crouch, "A Spirit of Lawlessness: White Violence, Texas Blacks, 1865–1868," *Journal of Social History* (Winter, 1984), 217–232; and Randolph B. Campbell, "The End of Slavery in Texas: A Research Note," *Southwestern Historical Quarterly*, LXXXVIII, 71–80.

The most essential documents may be found in W. L. Fleming (ed.), *Documentary History of Reconstruction* (2 vols., Cleveland, 1906–1907); H. P. N. Gammel, *The Laws of Texas;* and E. Wallace and D. M. Vigness (eds.), *Documents of Texas History.*

There are many miscellaneous studies pertinent to the period. Some of the most valuable are James A. Baggett, "The Rise and Fall of the Texas Radical, 1867–1883" (unpublished dissertation, North Texas State University, Denton, 1972); Robert W. Shook, "Federal Occupation and Administration of Texas, 1865–1870" (unpublished dissertation, North Texas State University, Denton, 1970); William Lee Richter, "The Army in Texas during Reconstruction" (unpublished dissertation, Louisiana State University, Baton Rouge, 1970); Alwyn Barr, *Black Texans: A History of Negroes in Texas, 1528–1971*; Paul D. Casdorph, *A History of the Republican Party in Texas, 1865–1965* (Austin, 1965); Allen W. Trelease, *White Terror: The Ku Klux Klan Conspiracy and Southern Reconstruction* (New York, 1971); Lucille B. Bullard, *Marion County, Texas, 1860–1870* (Jefferson, Tex., 1965); Traylor Russell, *Carpetbaggers, Scalawags, and Others* (Waco, 1970). The *Texas Almanac* for the years of the Reconstruction period contains a voluminous amount of statistical, factual, and even descriptive information. W. P. Webb has a chapter on the state police in *The Texas Rangers.* Sam Acheson, *35,000 Days in Texas* (New York, 1938), a history of the *Dallas News*, brings out the flavor of the Reconstruction era; John C. McGraw, "The Texas Constitution of 1866" (unpublished dissertation, Texas Technological College, Lubbock, 1959) is an excellent reference. E. Wallace, *Ranald Slidell Mackenzie on the Texas Frontier* (Lubbock, 1965), covers the frontier Indian problem from 1871 to 1879. For an account of E. J. Davis's appeal to the courts, see J. H. Davenport, *The History of the Supreme Court of the State of Texas* (Austin, 1917). Short biographical sketches of the governors of the Reconstruction era are in J. T. DeShields, *They Sat in High Places.*

CHAPTER TWELVE
FROM RECONSTRUCTION TO REFORM 1874–1890

With the election of the Democratic legislature of 1872 and of Governor Coke in 1873, political power came into the secure grasp of those seeking to redeem the state from radical rule. Only the judiciary remained a Republican stronghold, and it proved to be a temporary one. Legislative maneuvering soon removed several district judges, who were replaced with Democrats; a constitutional amendment created a new supreme court with five positions; and within a month after his inauguration, Coke named five Democrats to fill the vacancies.

The triumph of the redeemers initiated more than a decade of conservative government. Reflecting the attitudes shared by most white Texans, these conservative Democrats sought where possible to wipe out the last vestiges of radical rule, the most obvious being the Republican-written Constitution of 1869. Suffering under the miseries of the Panic of 1873 they promoted public economy and retrenchment, sometimes to the point of parsimony, but simultaneously they encouraged the distribution of the public lands and the construction of railroads. Initially preoccupied with the legacies of Reconstruction, such as crime and public indebtedness, they soon found another perplexing challenge. Agrarian unrest, provoked by falling prices, tight credit, and strangling freight rates, would be a persistent problem.

Although the conservative Democrats failed to cope successfully with the problems of unhappy farmers and although their policies otherwise were sometimes shortsighted, the period was not without substantial progress. Certainly, old enmities were being forgotten. When U. S. Grant and Phil Sheridan visited Texas in 1880, they were received cordially, and Sheridan apologized for having once said that if he owned Texas and hell he would "rent out Texas and live in hell." Crime was reduced; personal and property rights were made comparatively secure; railroads were built; industry and agriculture expanded; and finally, the low prices and the business stagnation that followed the Panic of 1873 gave way in the early eighties to a period of temporary prosperity.

THE CONSTITUTIONAL CONVENTION OF 1875

Upon winning control of the legislature in 1872, the Democrats agreed with something approaching unanimity that there must be a new constitution. Critics found the Republican origins of the Constitution of 1869 a sufficient cause to discard it, but they offered more substantial reasons. They wanted elected judges, shorter terms, and fewer courts. Advocating a return to the old law, they sought repeal of the road tax and the maintenance of roads by personal service under overseers in the various communities. They hoped to abolish voter registration regulations and to require that all executive officers be elected to two-year terms. They advocated a biennial legislature with severely limited powers, especially concerning taxation and indebtedness, and a governor with substantially reduced authority.

After an effort to remodel the constitution in 1874 through a legislative commission failed, the legislature, on the advice of Governor Coke, submitted the question of a constitutional convention to the people. On the first Monday in August 1875 the voters approved the convention and elected three delegates from each of the thirty senatorial districts.

Perhaps the evaluation made by the *San Antonio Herald* on the convention delegates who assembled in Austin on September 6, 1875, was as sound as any generalization could be. "We know," observed the newspaper, "that the convention has relatively but a few able men in its composition, but those we deem very able, with sound clear judgment." Certainly the roll of delegates bears impressive testimony that the old Texans were again in the ascendancy. Seventy-five were Democrats, and only 15, including six blacks, were Republicans. Forty-one were farmers, and 29 were lawyers. Eight had participated in the secession convention of 1861; 19 had served in the Texas legislature, two in the Congress of the United States, one in the Confederate Congress, and one in the cabinet of Jefferson Davis. More than a score had held high rank in the Confederate army, and three had been officers in the United States Army. One had served in the constitutional convention of 1845 and another in the convention of 1866, but significantly, none had sat in the convention of 1869.

Among the more distinguished were John S. Ford, noted editor and Texas Ranger; John H. Reagan, postmaster general of the Confederacy and congressman-elect to the United States House of Representatives; Lawrence Sullivan Ross, famed Indian fighter destined to become governor of the state and president of Texas A & M College; Charles DeMorse, gifted editor and ex-Confederate colonel; and Thomas Nugent, who became a leader in the farmers' revolt of the 1890s.

Particularly influential in the convention proceedings was a bloc of 40 or more delegates who were members of the Patrons of Husbandry. This powerful and militant farmers' organization, better known as the Grange, had been introduced into Texas in 1873 by the establishment of a subordinate Grange in Salado in Bell County. Spurred by the Panic of 1873, membership climbed rapidly, until by 1876 the order claimed 45,000 members. Although the Grange as such did not take part in politics, Grangers frequently acted collectively for or against certain issues or candidates. In the convention, constitutional provisions reducing taxes and expenditures, crippling the public school system, prohibiting the state from chartering banks, and restricting corporate and railroad practices reflected the ideals of the Grangers.

From the beginning, the convention manifested a determination to promote measures of economy and retrenchment. Hinting of frugal principles to be incorporated into the fundamental law, the delegates voted themselves only five dollars per day, although members of the legislature had been receiving eight, refused to have the proceedings of the convention printed because of the expense, and even refused to employ a stenographer when they could not secure one for less than ten dollars a day. Surely, few would quarrel with a delegate's remark that "if future State Governments prove burdensome and onerous, it ought not to be the fault of the Convention."

THE CONSTITUTION OF 1876

In keeping with a trend in the making of state constitutions in evidence since the early nineteenth century, the Constitution of 1876 is longer than the fundamental laws that preceded it, and it contains many provisions that the framers of the earlier instruments left to the discretion of the legislatures. It changed the framework of government in several important respects. The legislature was to be composed of two houses, the senate to consist of 31 members and the house of representatives never to exceed 150. The term of senators was reduced from six to four years. In calling for biennial sessions instead of annual sessions, as under the Constitution of 1869, the framers returned to the practice of a long-standing tradition. Lawmakers would receive five dollars a day for the first sixty days of each regular session and two dollars a day thereafter. Like the Constitution of 1845, the new instrument severely limited the powers of the legislature. It was forbidden to incur indebtedness to an amount greater than $200,000, and the maximum tax rate, except for the payment of debt, was set at a low level. An important limitation was the requirement that all property be taxed in proportion to its value. The duration of all offices created by the legislature was two years. A reaction against conditions of the war and reconstruction periods was reflected in the statement that the writ of *habeas corpus* "is a writ of right" that shall never be suspended.

The article describing the executive department provided for seven officers: a governor, lieutenant governor, secretary of state, comptroller, treasurer, commissioner of the land office, and attorney general. All, save the secretary of state, were to be elected by the voters. The maximum salary, that of the governor, was set at $4,000 a year, $1,000 less than he was then receiving. In vain did John H. Reagan, Charles DeMorse, and others plead for higher salaries, contending that such parsimony would, in the long run, prove costly. Terms of the executive officers were fixed at two years, with no prohibition against reelection.

The governor's powers and duties were set forth in considerable detail. He might convene the legislature in special session, call out the militia and declare martial law to suppress insurrection, and fill various vacancies by appointment, subject to approval of the senate by a two-thirds vote. He was given power to veto laws and veto items in appropriation bills, but his veto might be overridden by a two-thirds vote of both houses. It was declared that the governor, as the chief executive of the state, should cause the laws to be "faithfully executed," but the powers granted to him were not equal to such great responsibility. He was given no control over local officers and other elective state executive officers.

The judicial article reflected a reaction against the courts of the Reconstruction era. When the convention met, there were 1,600 undecided cases before the supreme court, and many regarded a number of the judges appointed by Governor Davis to be incompetent. Accordingly, the new constitution provided that all judges be elected by popular vote, with terms of four years for district judges and six years for judges of higher courts. The number of district courts was reduced to 26. Establishing a dual system of appellate courts, the convention provided for a supreme court, with power to review civil cases only, and for a court of appeals, with appellate jurisdiction over all criminal cases and certain classes of civil cases.

Following the leadership of some northern states, the convention forbade consolidation of competing railroads and authorized laws to prevent unjust discrimination and to establish maximum freight and passenger rates but made no provision for a commission with regulatory powers. To promote the construction of new mileage, the legislature might grant public land to railroads up to an amount not in excess of 16 sections for each mile of road constructed. It was forbidden, however, to grant state funds or bonds to railroads. The convention also provided for homestead grants of 160 acres to heads of families and half that amount to single men over 18 years of age.

Suffrage provoked a heated debate in the convention. The most serious contest was over the proposal, supported largely by the East Texas delegates, to make payment of a poll tax a prerequisite for voting, the chief purpose obviously being the indirect disfranchisement of blacks. A substantial majority, including all but one of the Republicans, defeated the move. Otherwise, nobody objected to permitting aliens to vote, if they had resided in the state one year and had declared their intention of becoming citizens.

Women's suffrage produced a brief but bitter scene. In the constitutional convention of 1868 supporters of women's suffrage had made a serious bid for the right of women to vote, but the convention had eventually defeated the move. In 1875 a similar petition was referred to a committee where it provoked an angry denunciation and was never voted out.

More controversial and more affected by demands for economy were provisions regarding public education. Texas had never had a satisfactory public school system, measured even by the standards that prevailed in the nineteenth century. Even now, in the convention some contended that education was a private duty, that no man should be taxed to educate another's child. Supporters of public education overruled that argument, but provisions for education were not as generous as those under the Constitution of 1869. Indeed, possibly the radical Republicans of 1869 had been too ambitious, but surely the conservative Democrats of 1876 were too cautious. The convention authorized the legislature to contribute to the support of the public schools a poll tax of one dollar and not more than one-fourth of the *ad valorem* and occupation taxes. Rejecting the centralization prevailing under the radicals, it abolished the office of state superintendent, eliminated compulsory attendance, established segregated schools, and made no provision for local school taxes. Apparently the delegates saw no inconsistency between these provisions and their declaration that the legislature should "establish and make suitable provisions for the support and maintenance of an efficient system of public free schools." But an aroused *Galveston News* acidly observed that the convention, after "decreeing universal suffrage, had now also decreed universal ignorance."

The convention was more generous with school endowments, a fact that accounts in part for the small support provided for maintenance. It set aside as a perpetual fund all monies, lands, and other property previously granted to the schools and a large portion of the public lands. All told, the land granted amounted to about 42.5 million acres, and the permanent school fund invested in securities at that time was $3,256,970. Largely as a result of the sale of land, oil royalties, and leases, this endowment had grown to more than $4.5 billion by 1986.

To the University of Texas, yet unborn, the convention gave with one hand and took away with the other. By a law of 1858 the school would have been entitled ultimately to about 3.2 million acres, a part of which had already been located and surveyed within the rich domain of North-Central Texas. The delegates repealed this provision and gave the university a million acres of land to be selected from the public domain unappropriated at that time, an exchange very disadvantageous both as to the quantity and the quality of the land. Only additional grants by the legislature and the fortuitous discovery of oil on some of the lands kept the university from suffering severely.

ADOPTION OF THE FUNDAMENTAL LAW

Ratification of the Constitution of 1876 was accomplished without effective opposition but without impressive enthusiasm. Only one delegate expressed hearty approval, declaring that the constitution was "the noblest instrument ever submitted to the verdict of a free people." The six Republicans remaining in the convention joined five Democrats in a vote against adoption, and many delegates were opposed to portions of the document. Nevertheless, by a vote of fifty-three to eleven, the convention adopted the constitution on November 24, 1875. Arrangements had been made previously to submit it to the voters for their approval.

Anticipating some criticism, the convention issued a statement praising its handiwork and explaining that its economies would save the state $1.5 million annually. Significantly, the delegates felt obliged to defend at length the measures on public education, the part of the constitution that had been attacked by the press more severely than any other. The statement pointed to the extravagance of the former school system and the poverty of the state, emphasizing the generous permanent school fund.

Some opposition to ratification did develop. By a vote of 674 to 176, the state Democratic convention evaded endorsement, and the Republican convention denounced the document in a unanimous vote. Opponents claimed that the constitution crippled education; and that in failing to make the payment of a poll tax a prerequisite to voting, the document would surrender to black rule in a large number of counties. However, Governor Coke and much of the state press, together with the powerful

Grange, backed ratification. In a mood for change, the voters probably would have ratified a much poorer instrument. The vote for adoption in a remarkably quiet election was 136,606 to 56,652.

All in all, the constitution complied with public opinion quite faithfully. Biennial sessions of the legislature, low salaries, no registration requirement for voters, precinct voting, abolition of the road tax, a return to the road-working system, a homestead exemption clause, guarantees of a low tax rate, a more economical school system with schools under local control, a less expensive court system, and popular election of officers—all these were popular measures with Texans in 1876.

The constitution, a logical product of its era and a fairly adequate pattern for government for the period in which it was made, was nonetheless an enduring fundamental law with many unfortunate features. Limitations on the powers of the legislature have made necessary many amendments to the original instrument, most of them giving the legislators additional power. Possibly the constitution did not give the governor enough power. It is true that he is regarded as the political leader of the state and that his influence may be very great, but he does not have the power to modify appreciably the policies and practices of other elective officers, and many appointive officers are wholly beyond his control.

Changes to meet the needs of an evolving society have come through amendments submitted to the voters by the assent of two-thirds of the members of each branch of the legislature at a regular session and approved by a majority vote of the electors. Thus, it is state policy to fix in the constitution by amendment the ceilings on taxes, on salaries, and on various expenditures, to define precisely the powers, rights, and prerogatives of various state agencies, and to assume that state legislatures are not to be trusted—all of which makes necessary more and more legislating by the people themselves. Although during the first half-century of the instrument few amendments were added, adoptions have come at an ever-increasing pace in recent times. Of 99 submitted up to September 1928, only 43 were adopted. Up through 1986, however, 443 have been submitted, and of this number, 285 have been approved by the voters, an average of more than two per year since 1876.

Efforts to effect a complete revision have accomplished little. No provision was made in the document for calling another constitutional convention, and legal authorities have generally agreed that this can be done only by the approval of the voters after the question has been submitted to them by a vote of two-thirds of the members of both houses. At different times there has been considerable agitation for a new constitution, but when the question was submitted to the voters in 1919, only nine percent of them were sufficiently interested to express an opinion, and in 1975 voters turned down an extensive revision prepared by the legislature.

POLITICS AND PERSONALITIES, 1874–1890

For nearly a decade and a half following the adoption of the Constitution of 1876, politics were characterized by the same tone of conservatism that prevailed in the convention. Democrats, who won state and local elections with monotonous regularity, differed on various particulars, but most generally agreed that economic retrenchment was more necessary than aggressive reform. Political conflicts focused on the problems of the farmer, and elected officials concentrated on such matters as law enforcement, debt retirement, and disposal of public lands.

Although the composition of the state legislatures varied and the number of black representatives declined thereafter, the legislature elected in 1878 may be viewed as fairly typical of the age. Business and professional men, mostly attorneys, accounted for 64 members, and 44 were farmers or were involved in activities related to farming. More than 90 percent were native-born southerners, 11 were born in Texas, and at least half had served in the Confederate army. Blacks in the delegation numbered five. Nine of the legislators were members of the Grange, and ten formerly had endorsed Whig policies. An overwhelming majority were Democrats, but there were nine Republicans and seven independents.

Throughout the period, the Republican Party, torn by factional quarrels even when in power, continued to deteriorate as an effective political organization. The party elected various local officials, a few state legislators, and occasionally even a congressman, but by and large it found little success at the ballot box. Temporarily, Republican leaders joined with agrarian reform groups in a marriage of convenience to oust the Democrats, but usually they concentrated on establishing their power within the party in order to assure their control over federal patronage in Texas. Factional conflicts of this type were intensified by differences over the role of the blacks in the party. Without the black voters the party faced little but frustration and defeat, but white Republicans found black leadership and control unpalatable, if not totally unacceptable. Nevertheless, after the death of E. J. Davis in the mid 1880s, the most powerful figure in the party was Norris Wright Cuney, a black customs collector in Galveston and one of the most perspicacious politicians of his time.

Cuney's influence reflected the continued activities of blacks in politics. After regaining power, white Democrats evaded the disfranchisement of blacks, feeling that the black vote could be controlled or outnumbered. But in 14 counties located along the Gulf Coast and in East Texas, blacks constituted a majority of the population, and in 13 others they amounted to nearly one-half. Thus, several counties for a time were controlled by a black electorate. Beginning with Harrison County in 1878 and followed subsequently by others, notably Fort Bend County in 1888, white Democrats used organization, intimidation, and other means, sometimes extra-legal, to eliminate these local pockets of black power. But extensive curtailment of black suffrage through sophisticated laws awaited a later day. Meanwhile, blacks participated in politics, often without effectual strength but sometimes holding office. Primarily, they operated in the Republican Party but they also formed a significant portion of the strength of another, the Greenback Party.

The Greenback Party, a threat more serious to Democratic suzerainty than the Republican challenge, was a voice of agrarian discontent calling for various reforms. It was particularly powerful in a West settled recently by poor farmers who had remained poor. Unlike the Grange, which was operated usually within the Democratic Party, the Greenbackers formed their own party. Organized originally in the Midwest as early as 1874 to protest the resumption of the payment of gold for greenbacks (paper money without specie backing), the Greenback party wanted "more money and cheaper money" and argued that a gold monetary standard was deflationary and an undue hardship on debtors, a status common to many farmers. Advertising an intention to protect the poor against bankers and bondholders, the party demanded that the federal government issue more greenbacks as legal tender and redeem all treasury notes and outstanding bonds with such money. In Texas, Greenbackers advocated an income tax, a better school system, a reduction of salaries of state officers, the abolition of useless offices, the regulation of railroads, and various other reforms.

Introduced into Texas in 1877, the party had its first campaign the following year, electing two senators and ten representatives to the legislature and indirectly assisting the election of a number of Republicans. Its strength declined somewhat in the election of 1880, but the Greenbackers regained new hope in 1882 with the arrangement of an independent coalition with the Republicans. The move gave the Democrats their biggest fright of the decade, though Democratic candidates, with only rare exceptions, swept the election on all levels. Efforts to perpetuate the independent coalition through the election of 1884 were only partially successful, and thereafter the coalition and the Greenback Party faded from Texas politics.

Indeed, between 1875 and 1890 major state offices were controlled by a parade of conservative Democrats. Sam Bell Maxey, an "ultra-simon-pure-secession-anti-reconstruction Democrat," was elected to the United States Senate in 1874, to remain there until 1887. The Granger favorite, Governor Coke, was reelected in 1876, only to resign in December of that year to accept the other seat in the United States Senate, where he remained until 1895. When Lieutenant Governor Richard H. Hubbard, a Georgia-born ex-Confederate officer who succeeded Coke as governor, sought reelection on his own in 1878, he found a crowded field. Critics proffered charges impugning Hubbard's integrity and wisdom, while James W. Throckmorton, who had served as governor in the early days of Reconstruction, and W. W. Lang, master of the state Grange, also vied for

Oran M. Roberts: judge, secessionist leader, governor, and professor of law at the University of Texas where he was awarded the title "the Old Alcalde." (University of Texas Library)

the nomination. A deadlocked convention brought about the selection of Oran M. Roberts, an elderly ex-Confederate colonel, then Chief Justice of the Supreme Court and known affectionately as the Old Alcalde. Frugal and legalistic but strong-willed and aggressive, Roberts easily defeated W. H. Hamman, his Greenback opponent, an accomplishment he repeated in 1880, winning over both Hamman and E. J. Davis, the Republican nominee.

When in 1882 Roberts refused suggestions that he accept a third term, the Democratic nomination went instead to Judge John Ireland of Seguin. A native of Kentucky, ex-member of the Know-Nothing Party, and ex-Confederate colonel, Ireland was an intense and intelligent man of integrity, often called "Ox-Cart John" in tribute to his opposition to railroad land grants. His opponent, George W. ("Wash") Jones of Bastrop, was a delightful addition to the political wars. Jones had been a Unionist but had served as a Confederate colonel. A Democratic lieutenant governor in 1866–1867, he had been elected to Congress as an independent in 1878, had won reelection as a Greenbacker in 1880, had welcomed Republican support on all occasions, and was now running again as an independent. If party regularity was not one of Jones's virtues, he was, nonetheless, widely respected for his honesty and engaging oratorical talent. He was awkward but kind, earnest but humorous, and shrewd but forthright. The somewhat colorless Ireland, who wisely declined to speak against him on the same platform after an early debate, won the gubernatorial election, but the contest was the closest of the decade, Ireland receiving 150,891 votes to

Jones's 102,501. In a repeat race in 1884, however, Jones's votes declined
and Ireland's increased substantially.

The practice of electing conservative governors was perpetuated
through the end of the decade. With his campaign directed by railroad
attorney George Clark, a shrewd and successful conservative political manager, Lawrence Sullivan Ross won the nomination from a field of five
candidates and also an easy election in 1886. Agrarian discontent had
increased significantly by 1888, but Ross, not a reactionary but certainly no
reformer, again won by a margin of almost three to one, this time over
Marion Martin, the candidate of an incipient farmers' protest movement.

A number of factors explain the ease with which conservative Democratic elements maintained their political domination. Challenge from outside the party was limited by the lingering memories of Reconstruction and
radical Republican government. Republican factionalism and Democratic
adoption of some agrarian reform programs similarly reenforced the Democratic domination. No doubt, fraud and ballot-box irregularities sometimes accounted for the Democratic victories. Until 1891 the constitution
did not call for voter registration. But even after that date, a voting list in
one county contained the names of several national leaders and Jefferson
Davis! Radical insurgence within the party was controlled to a degree by
nominating practices. Candidates generally were chosen by conventions,
primaries not coming into widespread use until near the end of the century. Politicians already in power often found conventions easily manipulated. Finally, essentially conservative policies, such as promotion of
railroads, frugal expenditures, and low taxes, were attractive to most Texans, even those who wanted more extensive reforms, such as railroad regulation and augmented state services.

PUBLIC POVERTY

Poverty-stricken public finances constantly plagued the government of
Texas during the decade following the adoption of the Constitution of
1876. When Coke was inaugurated governor in January 1874, the state
debt, including some items of doubtful validity, was $3,167,335. The
receipts for that year were not sufficient to meet half of the state's expenditures. Industry and commerce, not yet recovered from the Civil War and
Reconstruction, were prostrated by the Panic of 1873. Taxes already
seemed too burdensome. No new sources of revenue were available, and it
seemed that the only way to balance the budget was to reduce the outlay.

With the cooperation of the legislatures, Governors Coke and Hubbard struggled to reduce expenditures, but their economies were offset by
increased demands on the treasury—funds for buildings for the new agricultural and mechanical college, pensions for veterans of the Texan Revo-

lution, frontier defense, and interest charges. The treasury did not operate on a cash basis until the spring of 1879, by which time the state's indebtedness had increased to approximately $5.5 million.

Taking office in 1879, Governor Roberts insisted that the legislature balance the state's budget at any sacrifice and made several suggestions toward that end. He would refund state bonds and lower the interest rate, reduce the outlay for veterans' pensions, make the penitentiaries self-supporting, and, most extreme of all, lower the appropriation to the public schools from one-fourth to one-fifth of the general revenue. To increase income he would provide for a better system of tax assessment and collection, and in order to hasten the payment of the public debt, he favored sale of the unappropriated public lands to any person in any quantity desired. For his own part, he discontinued the payment of rewards for the arrest of criminals and followed a liberal policy for reprieves and pardons to relieve the crowded prison system.

The legislature responded readily to a part of Governor Roberts's suggestions. It adopted a law offering for sale in any quantity the public domain at 50 cents an acre, one-half the receipts to go to the permanent school fund and the remainder to be applied to the public debt. It passed laws to improve the collection of taxes, to provide fees for government services, and to broaden and increase occupation taxes. Toward reducing expenditures, it lowered substantially the appropriation for the maintenance of the state frontier force. The legislators exceeded the governor's wishes by discontinuing pensions altogether and substituting instead the grant of one section of land to each indigent veteran, an amount later raised to two sections.

But to complete his program of economy, Governor Roberts resorted to the veto. When lawmakers failed to lower the appropriations to the public schools from one-fourth to one-fifth of the general revenue, as he had recommended, the governor vetoed the school item. Sharp criticism was hurled at him, but he stood firmly. At a special session in June 1879 the legislature reenacted the measure, fixing the school appropriation at one-sixth of the general revenue. In 1881, during Roberts's second term, it raised the school appropriation to one-fourth of the general revenue but lowered the tax rate and diverted a part of the public school revenue to the Sam Houston Normal School.

At the end of his administration, the Old Alcalde could report with pride that the public debt had been reduced by more than a million dollars, that the annual interest burden had been cut by a third, and that there was a liberal operating surplus in the treasury. Probably, he found the greatest satisfaction of all in the fact that the *ad valorem* tax rate had been reduced by 40 percent. The achievement was one made at considerable cost. Public lands were disappearing into the hands of speculators, and state services, particularly education, were operating at a minimal level.

John Ireland, who took the oath of office as governor in January 1883, differed from his predecessor in several important matters. He opposed the rapid sale of public lands and favored reserving them to meet the needs of homeseekers in future years. He opposed the state's purchasing its own bonds at high prices in order to hasten the extinction of the debt; he urged a more persistent enforcement of the criminal laws, and he promised to follow a less liberal pardoning policy. In the matter of economy, however, he was disposed to continue the Roberts program. The voters themselves in 1883 broke the spell of public parsimony by approving an amendment to the constitution authorizing special state and local school taxes, but the legislature continued to provide funds only with great reluctance, denying, for example, in 1883 and in 1885 appropriations out of the general revenue for the maintenance of the University of Texas.

Surely, the state finances improved substantially during the 1880s, an accomplishment due in part to the sale of public lands, economies in the government, and more effective tax laws. But, in fact, the state's financial record merely indicated the extraordinary increase in wealth and general prosperity. In many significant areas Texas wealth increased from two to threefold between 1875 and 1890, this growth appropriately reflected on the tax rolls.

Notwithstanding the frugality of the times, slow but evident improvement was made in the physical plants of the state's institutions. The first hospital for the insane had been built in Austin in 1856, and a sister institution was completed in Terrell in 1885. A state orphans' home was

The Texas state capitol, in Austin, constructed between 1883 and 1888, of native granite and financed by an appropriation of 3,050,000 acres of public domain, is an example of classic architectural style. (Southwest Collection, Texas Tech University)

provided in Corsicana in 1887. During the same year the interests of black Texans were recognized in the founding of a school for deaf and blind black youths in Austin. The crowning achievement of the building program is the capitol in Austin, authorized in 1879 and completed in 1888. For this imposing structure of Texas granite, the state exchanged the 3,050,000 acres of land located in the Panhandle that became the famous XIT ranch.

LAW ENFORCEMENT

In respect to government the greatest accomplishment during this period was the victory for law and order. Except in the extreme western part of the state, Indian depredations did not constitute a serious problem after 1875, but there were many other problems. Mexico was in a state of war and confusion, and border troubles were plentiful. Juan Cortina, a folk hero in the eyes of some people but a ruthless murderer in the eyes of others, continued to cause unrest along the lower Rio Grande. The criminal and lawless elements that had become so powerful did not yield readily to the authority of the new government, especially along the western frontier.

Often the spirit of rowdyism and the yearning to establish a reputation as a "tough" caused young men who were not criminals at heart to become so in fact. Thus, certain frontier characters would occasionally "take a town" just to see its inhabitants "hunt cover." More desperate and generally more dangerous was the professional criminal. During the seventies and eighties the far-flung ranch headquarters and isolated cow camps afforded concealment and a measure of protection for numbers of renegades and desperados. In 1876 the adjutant general compiled a list of 3,000 fugitives from justice and noted that other names were arriving in every mail. In his message to the legislature in 1879 Governor Roberts stated that there was "an amount and character of crime and civil wrong entirely unprecedented in this country."

Horse theft, cattle rustling, and stage robbery were the most common crimes. The editor of the *Frontier Echo* (Jacksboro) estimated that there had been 100,000 horses stolen in the state during the three years preceding March 8, 1878, that 750 men were regularly engaged in the business, and that not more than one in ten was even caught and brought to justice. The Northwest Texas Stock Association (which later became the Texas and Southwestern Cattle Raisers' Association), organized in Graham in 1877, devoted considerable effort to suppressing cattle theft, but for several years the results were discouraging, because men of wealth and influence were doing a considerable part of the stealing. Stage robbery became almost an epidemic between 1876 and 1883. On one occasion near Fort Worth in

1876, highwaymen held up a stage, robbed a freighter and a private carriage that came by, and rode away on animals belonging to their victims.

Feuds presented defenders of law and order with one of their most perplexing problems. For instance, in the spring of 1874 feudists in DeWitt County were defying local officers and making it impossible to convict their friends in court. Their method of avoiding conviction was a simple one. They murdered unfavorable witnesses. A bitter feud took place in Mason County in 1875 between the Germans and the Anglo-Americans. Meanwhile, the Horrell and Higgins feud of nearby Lampasas County, which had begun in 1873, grew in intensity. During the chronic quarrel each side committed murders, and the clans were so powerful that local peace officers and even the local courts were helpless to deal with them.

To cope with lawlessness of various types, vigilantes more or less formally organized, were found in almost every community. Such a group at Denison seems to have been quite active; the Hill County vigilantes warned thieves in open letters; and during one week at Fort Griffin in 1878 vigilantes were credited with shooting one man in his jail cell, hanging another, and being responsible for the disappearance of a third.

But of all agencies suppressing crime in Texas, the Texas Rangers were the most effective. From the Gulf to the Panhandle they terrified evildoers and brought a sense of security to the men who obeyed the law. The dauntless Captain L. H. McNelly and his Rangers at least made it possible to hold court in the DeWitt County feuds. Major John B. Jones restored order in the Mason County dispute, though he could not remove the cause of the trouble. In Lampasas County he arrested the leaders of that feud and persuaded them to enter into a peace convenant that temporarily preserved law and order. When Kimble County became notorious as "the worst section of the country there is for men to work in and a better hiding place for rascals than any other part of Texas," the Rangers entered the county and soon arrested 41 men. In 1879 Captain George W. Arrington, a Ranger, was sent with a force to the Panhandle where, working with another great hater of cattle thieves, Charles Goodnight, he played a leading part in bringing first order and then law to the High Plains.

The Rangers were indeed effective, but not everyone held them in high esteem. In South Texas some of the Rangers who rode with great energy and dedication were Mexican-Americans, but other Mexican-Americans claimed that the organization abused and mistreated their people.

Improvement in law enforcement was not left altogether to the peace officers. Court procedure was made more effective. A law of 1876 made it more difficult for the defense in criminal cases to stack the jury with men who were incompetent, venal, or biased. The number of district attorneys was substantially increased in 1879. When cases continued to stack up in the appellate courts, the legislature in 1879 provided for appointed commissioners of appeals to assist the supreme court and court of appeals by deciding certain civil cases in order to clear the way for criminal matters. This plan was continued until 1892, when a system of courts of civil appeals was devised.

THE PUBLIC LANDS

If the establishment of law and order was the state government's greatest accomplishment during this period, the formulation of a wise and far-sighted public land policy may very well have been one of its least satisfactory achivements. In 1876 the state still retained a public domain of 61,258,461 acres. Distribution of these lands brought conflict and confusion and provoked charges of fraud and speculation. In 1881 state officials discovered that railroad land grant commitments exceeded land available for that purpose by 8,000,000 acres. Meanwhile, state policies on sale of school and otherwise unappropriated lands produced a political, if not necessarily an economic, crisis.

Governor Roberts, the Old Alcalde, bore primary responsibility for the crisis. To help defray the cost of public education and to pay the state debts, he persuaded the legislature to pass the so-called Fifty-Cent Law, whereby unappropriated lands could be purchased by anyone for fifty cents an acre in any quantity. The terms allowed the prospective buyer to control the lands for 150 days without paying any part of the purchase price. Receipts from the sale of these unappropriated lands were to be divided equally between the public schools and payment of the state debt. Separate laws provided for sale of school lands at prices of one and two dollars per acre in amounts of up to seven sections per purchaser.

Critics of these land laws declared that they were an open invitation to speculation and fraud, that the heritage of the people was being wasted for an absurdly small return, and that corporations and syndicates would soon own most of the western area of the state. Typical of the critics was the venerable Charles DeMorse who, in indignation over the sacrifice of the public domain, resumed publication of his Clarksville *Standard*. In sympathy with the clamor, the Ireland administration in 1883 put through legislation that established a land board to investigate frauds, terminated the sale of large blocks of land, provided for sale by auction, but for minimum prices of two and three dollars per acre, and offered liberal credit terms to bona fide settlers.

Actually, the damage done by the notorious Fifty-Cent Law was largely indirect. Less than two million acres of land were sold under its provisions, probably because Land Commissioner W. C. Walsh, who objected strenuously to it, blocked many sales by means that were, if not strictly illegal, certainly unanticipated by the legislature. More important, the law depressed land prices to almost giveaway levels. Much of the acreage that fell into the hands of speculators was not purchased directly from the state but from railroads and Confederate veterans and widows at prices of as little as fifteen cents an acre. Furthermore, the law produced little revenue, less than a million dollars.

Modification of the Roberts administration's land policies did not eliminate Ireland's problems with the public domain. Fence cutting, discussed elsewhere, and the leasing of public lands caused trouble throughout the decade. Efforts to achieve true competitive bidding on state-owned, ranchland leases, expected to yield from four to eight cents per acre, resulted in a nasty quarrel involving the land board, the governor, and the ranchers. Suits to force the ranchers to pay the leases and to abandon lands illegally held were of little value. The cases were tried before West Texas cowboy juries controlled by the ranchers.

The state land board was abolished in 1887, and the entire responsibility of administering the public lands was placed on the commissioner of the General Land Office, subject to the approval of the governor in some matters. In an effort to prevent speculation, each purchaser of agricultural land was required to swear that he desired to "purchase the land for a home." It was also specified that he must reside on the land at least six months each year for a period of three years before the state would pass title to him. These provisions were retained in all subsequent legislation, and, according to the 1908 statement of the commissioner of the General Land Office, John J. Terrell, were the occasion of "untold perjury." Notwithstanding the rigid precautions of the law, in western counties the number of sales exceeded greatly the number of settlers. The greater part of the land went into the ownership of the ranchers, whose use of the land necessarily meant that population growth would be small.

If, in a frontier society, acquisition of a population is of highest priority, and if, in depressed circumstances, reasonable revenue from the disposal of the public domain is a logical objective, Texas public land policy between 1876 and 1890 failed to measure up on either count. The failure is particularly strange, considering the preoccupation of the administration with fiscal prudence and the dominance of farmers in the population.

BUILDING THE RAILROADS

Railroad building in Texas began before the Civil War. There was considerable activity in the years immediately after the war, but interest in railroad construction reached new heights and intensity in the 1870s and 1880s. To the Texans of the late nineteenth century, the railroads appeared to be the key to progress and prosperity. Farmers and townspeople alike recognized the necessity of a cheap, fast, and dependable means of marketing, one available apparently only through railroads. Without the market afforded by the rails there would have been little point in mining coal at Thurber or in raising cotton at Sweetwater. Wagon freight rates averaged $1.00 per 100 pounds per 100 miles. With cotton bringing about $35.00 a bale in 1876, wagon freight from North-Central Texas to Galveston would have absorbed more than half of the value of the crop. Rail freight rates, though often discriminatory, were never after 1879 more than 50 cents per 100 pounds per 100 miles and declined more or less consistently from that figure.

Thus, Texans understandably courted the builders of the roads. Citizens of Brenham, for example, were agreeable to a railroad's demand for a right of way through the county and $150,000 in cash. For a time Fort Worth granted bonuses to all railroads building into the city. For the communities already built, the railroad meant population and profit. When the railroad bypassed a community, the town was in almost all instances doomed to a certain and often a swift death.

In addition to the enticements offered by local communities on their own authority, cities and counties, authorized by an 1871 state law, used public resources amounting to more than $2 million to subsidize much of the cost of railroad building. In 1856 a law was enacted authorizing the lending of school funds to railroads to the amount of $6,000 per mile; under this law nearly $2 million was loaned to the railroads. During Reconstruction, from 1869 through 1871, the legislature voted bonds to railroads, but most of these obligations were later paid in land. In fact, by far the greatest bounty to the railroads came from the public lands. From 1854 until 1882, except for the period from 1869 to 1873 when it was prohibited by the constitution, Texas maintained a policy of liberal land grants. In most cases the amount of land given was 16 sections for each mile of road constructed. About 41 railroad companies received state land, first and last, before the repeal of the land-grant act in 1882. The greatest single beneficiary was the Texas and Pacific, which was given 5,167,360 acres. Approximately 32,150,000 acres of the state's public domain were disposed of in this way, an area as large as Alabama.

The wisdom of such generous land grants was, at the time, as it has been since, questionable. Critics have contended that the aid was more generous than necessary, that it caused the building of some lines that were not needed, and that in many instances the land grant actually retarded the development of the country. It must be said, however, that most of the railroads never received any real benefits from their lands. The railroad corporations were undercapitalized; the lands could not be converted into cash; the companies were forced into receivership; and the land was sold at a few cents an acre.

Construction of the bulk of the state's major railroads was accomplished in the span of two decades. Only 11 short railroad lines, with a little less than 500 miles, had been constructed in Texas before the Civil War.

Most of these lines radiated from Houston, and not until 1872 were rail-road connections made with other states. The debacle of the Civil War brought an end to railroad building, and only one line, the Houston and Texas Central, made any progress before the state was readmitted to the Union in 1870. The pace of construction varied in the next two decades, depending primarily on the general prosperity of the state and the avail-ability of subsidies, but by the close of 1890 the state had 8,710 miles of railroads.

The Gulf Coast was soon connected to northern markets, as the Houston and Texas Central built northward through Dallas, while the Missouri, Kansas, and Texas (the Katy) built southward through Indian Territory. Citizens of Dallas hailed the coming of the rails with a buffalo meat barbeque, and a few months later the two roads met in 1872 in a cornfield where Denison now stands. By the early eighties the International and Great Northern Railway, a part of the Gould system, provided service from Longview in East Texas, through Austin and San Antonio, and to Laredo on the Rio Grande, where connections were made with Mexican lines. About the same time, leaders of Galveston, frustrated by yellow fever quarantines imposed almost annually by Houston, built around their

TEXAS RAILROADS

———— Houston and Texas Central

—·—·— Gulf, Colorado, and Santa Fe

—·—·— Fort Worth and Denver City

— — — Texas and Pacific

———— Southern Pacific

+—+—+ International and Great Northern

neighbor to the north, going by way of Richmond toward Fort Worth. By the mid-eighties this railroad was a part of the Atchison, Topeka, and Santa Fe, with connections going in a number of directions.

Two transcontinental roads of particular importance to West Texas were constructed in the eighties. The Galveston, Harrisburg, and San Antonio reached San Antonio in 1877 and six years later connected with the Southern Pacific, which was being built eastward from El Paso. These railroads merged and with others formed the Southern Pacific system.

The Texas and Pacific Railway, organized in 1872 with construction beginning at Longview, reached Fort Worth in 1876. Westward construction resumed in 1880, and two years later the westbound Texas and Pacific met the eastbound Southern Pacific at Sierra Blanca. Here the famous agreement made by C. P. Huntington of the Southern Pacific and Jay Gould of the Texas and Pacific was reached. The two roads publicly agreed to share the lines from Sierra Blanca to El Paso. Other agreements that were kept a secret for many years called for the distribution of traffic and the pooling of receipts between certain lines of the two great systems and promised that neither side would build lines to compete with the other.

Railroad service for Northwest Texas and the Panhandle came with the building of the Fort Worth and Denver City line. Built to Wichita Falls in 1882, the road was extended through Amarillo to Texline in 1888. In 1893 it became a part of the Burlington system.

A CHANGING ECONOMY

In several respects, the economy of Texas changed significantly in the years after the end of the Civil War. In part, the change was a matter of growth, made possible by the building of railroads, population expansion, and new technology. In some respects, however, the changes represented fundamental alterations in the ways the people of Texas earned their living and lived their lives. Agriculture became more of a business enterprise, industry developed, and workers began to organize to protect their interests.

The change in the nature of agriculture in Texas was significant, even revolutionary. In earlier times, a large part of the population were subsistence farmers who lived off of the products of their land, sold little at market, and relied only to a limited extent on a cash economy. By the seventies there was an apparent trend away from such self-sufficiency toward commercialization, wherein the farmer produced for the marketplace and in turn purchased many of his necessities. Although Texans produced a variety of crops for market, cotton dominated the emergence of the commercial agricultural economy. In the late nineteenth century, the average Texan was more familiar with the cotton sack and hoe than with the lariat rope and branding iron; he was a farmer, not a rancher. By 1880 farmers produced a cotton crop valued at about $57,000,000 on slightly less than 2.5 million acres.

Cotton production expanded in the face of innumerable problems and persistent opposition. The vagaries of nature—worms, boll weevils, Johnson grass, root rot, dry weather, wet weather—were enough to try the patience and to test the will of the most determined farmer. Moreover, critics repeatedly questioned the wisdom of expanding production and often the intelligence of the producer. Farm organizations, editors, agricultural colleagues, and self-appointed advisors who volunteered their counsel persistently condemned specialization in general and cotton farming in particular. Diversification, as they used the term—in essence a return to the self-sustaining farm—would ease the burden of the farmer. The cotton farmer paid no heed.

Although some critics argued that ignorance accounted for the cotton farmer's stubborn refusal to restrict his acreage, the reasons were actually more complex and convincing. Prices declined steadily between the 1870s and 1890s, but cotton almost always returned more income per acre than other crops suited to the farmer's labor, land, and machinery resources. Cotton was the most dependable of the southern crops; contrary to popular opinion, it did not exhaust the soil as quickly as many other crops. And the machinery for marketing cotton was more advanced than for other commodities.

Few farmers, whether they raised cotton or other products, found the marketplace and commercial farming an avenue to substantial wealth. Returns fluctuated unpredictably from one year to the next; prices, costs, mortgages, and weather frequently combined to leave the farmer looking anxiously to the "next year" rather than rejoicing in the present one. Theoretically an avenue to a higher standard of living, commercial agriculture often proved to be a relentless cycle of debt and worry.

While Texas farmers turned from subsistence farming to commercial farming, other Texans turned to industry. Although Texas possessed vast natural resources, industry in 1870 was still confined primarily to small shops that seldom supplied a market beyond the immediate community. Industrial workers made up less than one percent of the population. During the next several decades, however, the pace of industrialization quickened, depending mostly on manufacturing related to agriculture and exploitation of basic natural resources.

Processing of agricultural products was one of the major businesses in the late nineteenth century. Into the eighties, flour milling was the leading industry, ranking ahead of lumbering. Meanwhile, the manufacturing of products from cottonseed steadily increased in importance, ranking second in the state's industrial economy in 1900. Meat packing, which began at Victoria in 1868, was soon extended to other communities, and a number of small plants added to the output. A small packing plant was built in Fort Worth in 1884; six years later, the Fort Worth stockyards were opened; and thereafter the packing business in that city expanded rapidly. Textile manufacturing began before the Civil War when a frontier businessman set up a cotton mill in New Braunfels. A plant manufacturing cotton goods was operated in the penitentiary for a number of years during and after the Civil War. Later, plants were established in Dallas, Sherman, and Post, but they remained comparatively unimportant.

One of the early Texas industries was lumbering. With more than twenty million acres of timberland to supply them, pioneers soon started their sawmills turning. Peter Ellis Bean had a sawmill near Nacogdoches in 1829, and there were several in Texas by 1834. With the coming of the railroads after the Civil War, the lumbering business attained huge proportions and by the end of the century was the largest industry in the state. By 1900 Orange and Beaumont had come to be important sawmill centers. Production of Texas mills passed the billion-board-foot total in 1899, and in 1900 the mills of Orange alone were cutting 700,000 feet of lumber a day.

After 1880, mining operations contributed to the industrial economy. Coal deposits existed in many regions of the state, but commercial mining was concentrated in Palo Pinto and Erath counties where Thurber was the center of activity. Oil, the key to the Texas industrial economy in the twentieth century, was not of great significance until after 1900. In 1865 near the town of Saratoga, Edward von Hartin drilled for oil, only to drill the first dry hole in Texas, not the first oil well. A year later Lyne T. Barret completed the first Texas oil well at Oil Springs, a few miles east of Nacogdoches. By 1890 Oil Springs had forty shallow wells, a crude refinery, and a pipeline, but another decade would pass before Texas would truly enter the oil age.

Although industrialization proceeded relatively slowly in Texas during these years, some workers in Texas began to look to unity as a means of protecting and advancing their interests. Sometimes organizations such as the Screwman's Benevolent Association of Galveston, formed originally as a worker's insurance group, evolved into labor unions seeking shorter hours, higher wages, and control of the job. By the 1870s railroad brotherhoods in the state were organizing, and there were scattered militant groups to be found in a few other industries. Until the mid-seventies general public sentiment toward labor unions was either neutral or even perhaps sympathetic. However, primarily because strikes on the railroads during the seventies brought inconvenience to the farmer and the merchant, public opinion had become definitely antilabor by the end of the decade.

In the 1880s the Knights of Labor, a national organization, represented an industrial and a political force of consequence. Claiming 300 locals and 30,000 members in the state, the Knights opened their membership to farmers and allowed blacks to join. Probably the Knights organized the highest percentage of nonfarm laborers ever brought into unions in Texas, perhaps amounting for a short time to 50 percent of the nonfarm workers.

Although officially opposing the use of the strike, the Knights resorted to the weapon on several occasions in Texas. When a shop foreman on the Texas and Pacific Railway controlled by the tycoon, Jay Gould, was fired, the Knights called a strike with about 9,000 men going out. In what was soon known as the Great Southwest Strike of 1886, the conflict between Gould and the Knights developed into open violence. After a clash in Fort Worth over the movement of a freight train in which blood was shed and property destroyed, Governor Ireland ordered the state militiamen and rangers to the area, and the disturbance soon subsided. Meanwhile, Gould's control over the Texas and Pacific had passed into the hands of a federal receiver, and the strike was ruled in contempt of court. Failure of the Great Southwest strike, violence elsewhere in the nation, and poor business operation thereafter brought a rapid decline in the organization. New organizations would take its place, but labor unions would not again play a significant role in Texas until after the turn of the century.

SELECTED BIBLIOGRAPHY

Seth Shepard McKay published several authoritative works on the Constitution of 1876. He wrote *Making the Constitution of 1876* (Philadelphia, 1924); he brought together and edited newspaper accounts of the convention as *Debates of the Texas Constitutional Convention of 1875* (Austin, 1930); and he wrote *Seven Decades of the Texas Constitution* (Lubbock, 1943). See also his "Some Attitudes of West Texas Delegates in the Constitutional Convention of 1875," *West Texas Historical Association Year Book*, V, 100–106. For other studies, see E. Wallace, *Texas in Turmoil;* S. D. Myers, Jr., "Mysticism, Realism, and the Texas Constitution of 1876," *Southwestern Political and Social Science Quarterly*, IX, 166–184; Ralph Smith, "The Grange Movement in Texas, 1873–1900," *Southwestern Historical Quarterly*, XLII, 297–315; J. E. Ericson, "Delegates to the Texas Constitutional Convention of 1875; A Reappraisal," *ibid.*, LXVII, 20–27; and Oscar Walter Roberts, "Richard Coke on Constitution-Making," *ibid.*, LXVIII, 69–75. The constitution with amendments is published and indexed biennially in the *Texas Almanac*.

A comprehensive and reliable general study of the politics of the period is Alwyn Barr, *Reconstruction to Reform: Texas Politics, 1876–1906* (Austin, 1971). See also E. W. Winkler, *Platforms of Political Parties in Texas;* F. R. Lubbock, *Six Decades in Texas;* S. Acheson, *35,000 Days in Texas;* E. Wallace, *Charles DeMorse;* Paul Casdorph, *A History of the Republican Party in Texas, 1865–1965* (Austin, 1965); and his "Norris Wright Cuney and Texas Republican Politics, 1883–1896," *Southwestern Historical Quarterly*, LXVII, 455–464; B. H. Procter, *Not without Honor, the Life of John H. Reagan;* B. M. Jones, *The Search for Maturity* (Austin, 1965); Louise Horton, *Samuel*

Bell Maxey: A Biography (Austin, 1974); and Judith Ann Benner, *Sul Ross: Soldier, Statesman, Educator* (College Station, 1983).

Useful for politics, economics, education, and a variety of other areas is Lawrence D. Rice, *The Negro in Texas, 1874–1900* (Baton Rouge, 1971).

On state finances, the best sources are E. T. Miller, *Financial History of Texas;* A. S. Lang, *Financial History of the Public Lands in Texas;* R. McKitrick, *The Public Land System of Texas, 1823–1910;* and "Memories of a Land Commissioner, W. C. Walsh," *Southwestern Historical Quarterly,* XLIV, 481–497. Also see Thomas L. Miller, *The Public Lands of Texas, 1519–1970* (Norman, Okla., 1972).

Much literature deals with lawlessness in Texas. Some examples are W. C. Holden, "Law and Lawlessness on the Texas Frontier, 1875–1890," *Southwestern Historical Quarterly,* XLIV, 188–203; W. Gard, *Frontier Justice* (Norman, Okla., 1949); C. L. Sonnichsen, *I'll Die Before I'll Run* (New York, 1961); and Jack Martin, *Border Boss: Captain John R. Hughes* (San Antonio, 1942).

For a general study of economic affairs in Texas between 1875 and 1900, see J. Spratt, *The Road to Spindletop.* Other general works of value are Ralph Steen, *Twentieth Century Texas: An Economic and Social History* (Austin, 1942); B. M. Jones, *The Search for Maturity.* Rich in economic information is the *Texas Almanac.* Also see Ralph A. Wooster, "Wealthy Texans, 1870," *Southwestern Historical Quarterly,* LXXIV, 24–35.

The two standard studies on railroads are S. G. Reed, *A History of Texas Railroads* (Houston, 1941); and C. S. Potts, *Railroad Transportation in Texas* (Austin, 1909). See also Ira G. Clark, *Then Came the Railroads* (Norman, Okla., 1958); Vera L. Dugas, "A Duel with Railroads: Houston vs. Galveston, 1866–1881," *East Texas Historical Journal,* II, 118–127; Donald Everett, "San Antonio Welcomes the 'Sunset'—1877," *Southwestern Historical Quarterly,* LXV, 47–60; and Ralph Traxler, Jr., "The Texas and Pacific Railroad Land Grants," *ibid.,* 357–370. A valuable description of the political intrigue on behalf of railroad construction is John M. Brockman, "Railroads, Radicals, and the Militia Bill: A New Interpretation of the Quorum-Breaking Incident of 1870," *Southwestern Historical Quarterly,* LXXXIII, 105–122. Also see William D. Angel, Jr., "Vantage on the Bay: Galveston and the Railroads," *East Texas Historical Journal,* XXII, 3–18, for a good summary of early railroad building.

The evolution of a commercial economy in agriculture and industry is emphasized in J. Spratt, *The Road to Spindletop,* cited above. However, see B. P. Gallaway, "Population Trends in the Western Cross Timbers of Texas, 1890–1960: Economic Change and Social Balance," *Southwestern Historical Quarterly,* LXVII, 376–396; L. Tuffly Ellis, "The Revolutionizing of the Texas Cotton Trade, 1865–1885," *ibid.,* LXXIII, 478–508; Robert A. Cotner, "Nineteenth Century Farmers, Cotton and Prosperity," *ibid.,* LXXIII, 509–521; and Henry C. Dethloff, "Rice Revolution in the Southwest, 1880–1910," *Arkansas Historical Quarterly,* XXIX, 66–75.

For additional information on industry, see V. L. Dugas, "Texas Industry, 1860–1880," *Southwestern Historical Quarterly,* LIX, 151–183; Edwin L. Caldwell, "Highlights of the Development of Manufacturing in Texas, 1900–1960," *ibid.,* LXVIII, 405–431; Dwight F. Henderson, "The Texas Coal Mining Industry," *ibid.,* LXVIII, 207–219; Robert S. Maxwell, "The Pines of Texas: A Study in Lumbering and Public Policy, 1880–1930," *East Texas Historical Journal,* II, 77–86; William R. Johnson, *A Short History of the Sugar Industry in Texas* (Houston, 1961); Mary

Lasswell, *John Henry Kirby: Prince of the Pines* (Austin, 1967); Robert S. Maxwell, "The First Bag Mill: The Beginnings of Commercial Lumbering in Texas," *Southwestern Historical Quarterly*, LXXXVI, 1–30; and John S. Spratt, Jr., *Thurber, Texas: The Life and Death of a Company Coal Town* (Austin, 1986).

Published materials on organized labor are scarce but are growing in number. Pioneering studies have been made by Ruth A. Allen, who has published *Chapters in the History of Organized Labor in Texas* (Austin, 1941); *The Great Southwest Strike* (Austin, 1942); and *East Texas Lumbering Workers, An Economic and Social Picture, 1870–1950* (Austin, 1961). Dealing primarily with an earlier period but useful for later years is James V. Reese, "The Early History of Labor Organization in Texas, 1838–1876," *Southwestern Historical Quarterly*, LXXII, 1–20; more appropriate to this era is his "The Evolution of an Early Texas Union: The Screwmen's Benevolent Association of Galveston, 1866–1891," *ibid.*, LXXV, 158–185.

CHAPTER THIRTEEN
THE ADVANCE
OF THE FRONTIER

In 1860 the frontier, except for some settlements along the Rio Grande near Presidio and El Paso, extended along a line from Henrietta southward through Belknap, Palo Pinto, Brownwood, Kerrville, and Uvalde to Brackettville. During the Civil War there was no farther advance; indeed, in many areas the line retreated eastward, sometimes as much as 100 miles, in response to Indian raids. By 1890, however, there was no true frontier line. At the end of the century, western Texas was the home of 500,000 people, and by the middle of the twentieth century, it contained about one-third of the population of the state. Although many of these people settled within this vast area as a result of the colonizing efforts of railroad and land companies, the overwhelming majority did so on their own initiative, each trusting in his or her own strength and in a kindly Providence as he or she entered the new country.

Stages in the westward movement included the subjugation and removal of the Indians, the expansion of the range-cattle industry, the conversion of the open ranges into big pastures, the advance of the subsistence farmers, the development of commercial farming, and the growth of industry. The latter two, being dependent upon transportation, had to await the building of railroads and highways to get their products to distant markets. Meanwhile, the stubborn contest between the whites and the Indians for possession of the land and the short interlude before the arrival of the railroads, when cattlemen challenged by only a few bold and hardy subsistence farmers held supremacy over the newly won empire of grass, constitute a colorful and significant segment in the history of Texas and the American West.

THE DEFEAT AND REMOVAL OF THE INDIANS

After the collapse of the Confederacy, the state organization for frontier defense gradually ceased operation, and for several months thereafter the western settlers were left without protection. The Indians, soon aware of the situation, scourged the frontier as never before in history, driving the line of settlements eastward in some places by 100 miles. The country west of a line drawn from Gainesville to Fredericksburg was abandoned by all but a few of the most courageous settlers, who moved into stockades. The worst raids were made on moonlit nights, and the soft summer moon

Established in 1867, Fort Griffin was an important link in the chain of military posts along the frontier. Troops from this fort were called on to escort government mail, surveying parties, and cattle drives, and to punish Indians for their forays into white settlements. The town that grew up around the fort attained fame as a headquarters for buffalo hunters, cowboys, and frontier adventurers, but it declined rapidly after the fort was abandoned in 1881. (Texas Highway Department)

became a harbinger of death. Charred rock chimneys stood guard like weird sentries, symbolizing the blasted hopes of pioneers and often marking their nearby graves. A Waco newspaper in April 1866 claimed that not more than one-fifth of the ranches in its vicinity were still occupied, and later that year a large group of citizens in a mass meeting in Denton resolved to abandon their homes unless help arrived before November. Incomplete reports from county judges covering the period from May 1865 to July 1867 showed that 163 persons had been killed by Indians, 43 carried away into captivity, and 24 wounded. These figures did not include Wise and Young counties, whose combined population declined from 3,752 in 1860 to 1,585 in 1870.

Efforts in the fall of 1866 to organize a ranger force to protect the frontier were rejected by Reconstruction military authorities, but a portion of the 4,000 federal troops in Texas were stationed on the frontier. In September a cavalry detachment was sent to Fredericksburg, and by the end of the year federal troops had reoccupied Fort Mason, Fort Duncan, Fort Inge, Fort Clark, and Camp Verde to provide protection against marauding Apaches and bands from Mexico. Within another year several of these posts had been abandoned for more favorable sites, and the remainder of those maintained before the war had been reoccupied, all on a permanent basis. The line ran from Fort Richardson (in Jacksboro) through Griffin (near Albany), Concho (in San Angelo), McKavett (near Menard on the upper San Saba River), and Clark (near Brackettville) to Duncan (in Eagle Pass). An extreme western line was marked by Fort Stockton (near the present town of Fort Stockton), Fort Davis (near the present town of Fort Davis), and Fort Bliss (near El Paso).

The protection afforded by the military was inadequate. The troops were poorly disciplined and too few in number; many officers were unfamiliar with Indian warfare and often were unduly restrained by their superiors; and the policy was strictly defensive—to keep the Indians out of the settlements by scouting maneuvers instead of by attacking their villages. Furthermore, the distance between the posts was too great for the soldiers to prevent the Indians from crossing the line.

In defense of the army, however, it must be said that its delay in establishing permanent posts and in adopting an aggressive policy was partially due to Indian agents who convinced Washington officials that peace could be had by treaty making and the appointment of Quakers as Indian agents. If the Indians could be induced to keep the peace, forts and war would be unnecessary. Consequently, Congress authorized a commission to secure a lasting peace among all the Plains Indians. At Medicine Lodge Creek, Kansas, the commissioners in October 1867 met with the Cheyennes, Arapahoes, Kiowas, Kiowa-Apaches, and Comanches in what seems to have been one of the most colorful councils ever held between Indians and whites in the American West. Satanta, the principal leader of

Kiowa raiding parties into Texas, insisted that western Texas belonged to the Kiowas and Comanches and that he did not want to give up any part of it. Ten Bears, a Comanche chief who realized that the Indians must accept the terms offered by the commissioners or be destroyed, blamed the Texans who had taken his country and pleaded that his people might be allowed to continue their nomadic way of life. They argued in vain. According to the Treaty of Medicine Lodge Creek, the Indians present agreed to accept reservations in the Indian Territory and to cease their depredations. The defiant warriors, nevertheless, continued to raid. Some of the Kiowas and about half of the Comanches refused to move onto the reservation. In fact, the Kwahadi Comanche band was not represented at the Medicine Lodge Creek council and did not recognize the treaty. Later that year a government agent who visited them at present-day Quitaque reported that the band had about 15,000 horses, 300 or 400 mules, and innumerable stolen cattle, and that 18 parties were at the time raiding the Texas frontier.

Nevertheless, President Grant, upon assuming office in 1869, endorsed the peace policy. He appointed as Indian agents Quakers who maintained that in dealing with the Indians kindness and reason would be more effective than force. Quaker Lawrie Tatum, a strong devotee of the peace policy who became the new agent at the Kiowa-Comanche reservation, soon found, however, that his wards would not remain at peace unless compelled by armed force. Unrestrained by troops, the reservation became a sanctuary for restless braves who slipped away to plunder in Texas. Beginning in the fall of 1870, they repeatedly raided the Texas frontier, killing 14 persons during the following spring.

Their most audacious raid was the Salt Creek massacre of May 1871. A band of Kiowas attacked a wagon train between Jacksboro and Fort Griffin, killed or wounded most of the 12 teamsters, and stole the mules. For the Indians the time of the attack proved unfortunate. General of the Army William Tecumseh Sherman, escorted by Randolph B. Marcy, Inspector General of the Army, had passed the site only a few hours before the attack and was in Jacksboro. The two generals were inspecting the frontier to see for themselves if conditions were as bad as had been reported. Marcy thought they were. He noted in his journal that the Indian raiders, unless punished, would soon have the country between Belknap and Jacksboro totally depopulated. By the time a wounded teamster, who had managed to escape and make his way to Jacksboro, had finished with his description of the tragedy, Sherman likewise was convinced that the Indian menace on the Texas frontier had not been exaggerated. The Indian raiders were followed to the reservation where at least one of their leaders (Satanta) was boasting of his exploits. Sherman ordered the arrest of the raiding chiefs. Satanta and Big Tree were brought back to Jacksboro, tried in accordance with the laws of Texas, convicted of murder, and sentenced to be hanged. Governor Davis, however, commuted the sentence to imprisonment, and the chiefs were paroled in August 1873.

As a result of the Salt Creek massacre, the War Department unleashed its troops against the Indians off the reservation where the peace advocates had no authority. To lead the offensive, General Sherman fortunately had transferred to the Texas frontier Colonel Ranald Slidell Mackenzie, regarded by U. S. Grant as the most promising young officer in the army at the end of the Civil War. With his tough Fourth Cavalry regiment, in the autumn of 1871 Mackenzie led an expedition northwest from old Camp Cooper on the Clear Fork of the Brazos to Blanco Canyon, where he harassed the Kwahadi Comanches under Quanah Parker, but was unable to prevent them from escaping unharmed across the High Plains in a heavy snowstorm. In April of the following year at Howard's Well in Crockett County, Indians, apparently Comanches, killed 16 members of a wagon train party and afterwards held off two companies of troops who tried to punish them. In July Mackenzie renewed his campaign. After following two routes across the dangerous and unexplored plains in an effort to catch some cattle thieves, on September 29 he decisively defeated on the North Fork of the Red River, a few miles east of the present town of Lefors, a camp of Comanches who had participated in the attack at Howard's Well. As a result of their defeat and the imprisonment of their captured people, the Comanches and Kiowas remained peaceful for more than a year.

With the Comanches and Kiowas seemingly anxious for peace, General Sherman ordered Mackenzie and his Fourth Cavalry to the Rio Grande border to put a stop to raiding in the area between San Antonio and the Rio Grande by Kickapoo and Apache Indians living in Mexico. By 1873 these Indians, it was estimated, had killed a number of citizens and inflicted damages amounting almost to $50 million. The troops quickly destroyed three of their villages, captured some of the Indians, and established an effective border patrol. By the end of the year, Indian raids along the Rio Grande had ceased, and Mackenzie moved his regiment back to northwestern Texas.

In the spring of 1874, the Indians of the southern plains, led by Quanah Parker, renewed their attacks on the Texas frontier. The new war erupted on June 27, when several hundred Comanche and Cheyenne warriors and perhaps a few Kiowas attacked a buffalo hunters' stockade, known as Adobe Walls, near the present Borger. Superb marksmen among the 28 buffalo hunters in the stockade, armed with their "big fifty" buffalo guns, were more than a match for the Indians. Although repulsed with heavy losses in their initial attack, the Indians were determined to keep white men off their favorite hunting grounds. They again began hitting the isolated settlers along the Texas frontier. When General Sherman learned of the situation, he persuaded President Grant on July 26, 1874, to turn the

Indians, even those on the reservation, over to the military, thus putting an end to the Quaker peace policy.

In August, when the deadline for the Indians to enroll at the agencies had passed, the army moved against the remainder. The majority of the proud and stubborn natives took refuge in the wild canyons and breaks along the eastern edge of the *Llano Estacado*. There they were pursued relentlessly by well-mounted, well-armed, and thoroughly seasoned troops, led for the most part by officers who had learned by experience the way of Indian warfare and, guided by Indian scouts, were able to follow a trail like bloodhounds. Altogether, 46 companies, about 3,000 men, marching in five commands from as many directions, converged on the headstreams of the Red River in the eastern Panhandle of Texas where they found the Indian encampments.

Colonel Nelson A. Miles with 750 men moved southwestward from Camp Supply, Indian Territory, toward Palo Duro Canyon. Opposite the junction of Tule and Palo Duro canyons on August 30, he defeated about 500 Indians, burned their village, and chased those fleeing to the head of Tule Canyon before turning back to scout again the region nearer his supply camp. Major William Price with four companies of cavalry moved from Fort Union, New Mexico, down the Canadian River to join Miles. Near Sweetwater Creek in the eastern Panhandle he won a skirmish with a group of Indians in flight from the reservations. From September to November Lieutenant Colonel John W. Davidson with nine companies of troops searched the country between his Fort Sill base and the main fork of the Red River almost to the Caprock without engaging the Indians in battle, but he returned to the reservation over 300 Comanches who surrendered to him. Simultaneously, Lieutenant Colonel George P. Buell, while scouting up the Red River, destroyed two large Indian villages and a considerable quantity of supplies.

The most effective and dramatic blow to the last bid of the tribes of the southern plains to retain their nomadic way of life, however, was delivered by Mackenzie. After establishing his base at his old supply camp on the upper Brazos River, near the present town of Crosbyton, Mackenzie with about 500 men, including a detachment of Indian scouts, headed northward along the edge of the Caprock for the headstreams of the Red River. After beating off an attack by Comanches at Tule Canyon and marching all night, on September 28 in a daring, almost reckless, display of courage Mackenzie led his men down a narrow path to the bottom of Palo Duro Canyon. Here he defeated five villages of Comanches, Kiowas, and Cheyennes, burned their lodges and huge quantities of supplies needed for survival during the ensuing winter, and captured 1,424 horses and mules.

Flushed from hideouts that their medicine men had assured them could not be found by the blue-coated troopers, many of the Indians sought safety at the waterholes on the *Llano Estacado*. Mackenzie, however, did not intend that they should find safety anywhere except on the reservation. Early in November he surprised and defeated a band of Comanches near the present town of Tahoka. Most of the Indians, however, had gone already or were on their way to the reservation, and the Red River War was over. By June 1875 the remainder had straggled to Fort Sill and surrendered, the last being a large band of Kwahadies led by Quanah Parker. Very few Indians had been killed or taken captive, but left without lodges and supplies or horses to acquire replacements, they could no longer continue their nomadic existence. Thereafter, only a few ever stole away from the reservation to raid in Texas, and the damage they did was negligible.

On the southwestern frontier, from the vicinity of Laredo to the outskirts of El Paso, another five years was to elapse before the Indian problem was settled. In the eastern portion of that section, the Apaches and Kickapoos from Mexico renewed their destructive forays after Mackenzie and his Fourth Cavalry had been removed. To stop the marauding by Indians based in Mexico, Sherman sent Mackenzie to Fort Clark early in 1878. Mackenzie quickly established at strategic sites a number of subposts, reactivated his system of effective border patrol, and in June led an expedition across the Rio Grande in search of the renegade Indians. The reappearance of this aggressive leader on the border influenced Mexican President Porfirio Diaz, who wanted to attract United States capital to Mexico, to assist in the efforts to break up the raiding. Before the end of the year, affairs along the Rio Grande border were "most satisfactory."

Further west, the frontier enjoyed comparative peace in 1875, in part because of a successful scouting expedition led by Lieutenant Colonel William R. Shafter, but the next year Victorio at the head of a band of Apaches from New Mexico began raiding in Texas. In 1879 Victorio left the reservation and from his hideouts at isolated watering places on both sides of the Rio Grande made life and property insecure for all who had dared to settle within or attempted to travel across the Trans-Pecos country. For a time the efforts of federal troops and the Texas Frontier Battalion were ineffective. Benjamin H. Grierson, in command of United States troops, and George W. Baylor, with a contingent of Texas Rangers, cooperated with the commander of a Mexican military force and pursued relentlessly the hostile Apaches on both sides of the international border. In October 1880 Victorio, the last of the troublesome leaders of the Apaches, was cornered and killed by Mexican troops, thereby concluding the elimination of the Indian barrier to the settlement of western Texas.

As during the pre–Civil War years, the defense efforts of the federal government were supplemented by the state. In 1871 the legislature authorized the minute-company plan, which permitted citizens in 24 frontier counties to organize and equip themselves and receive limited pay. The plan, however, was not successful, and in 1874 the state created two organizations of rangers destined to attain renown. The first, the Special Force of Rangers under the command of L. H. McNelly, was sent in the spring of 1875 to the lower Rio Grande where violence was frequent.

Others were involved, but much of the violence centered around the activities of Juan Nepomucino Cortina and his men. Long a popular hero to the Mexican-American and Mexican people of the Rio Grande who looked upon him as a protector of their rights, Cortina was regarded by Anglo-Americans as an outlaw. Although the extent of his activities cannot be determined, Cortina was accused of many crimes and almost daily raids on Mexican and Texan ranches. Captain McNelly moved vigorously in pursuit of the wily Cortina. He soon reported that his men had slain near Brownsville an entire party of 12 cattle thieves, but Cortina was not among them. Later, McNelly crossed the Rio Grande with 30 men, moved against Las Cuevas Ranch, where several hundred bandits and soldiers were established, and recovered some of the stolen cattle. His efforts to capture Cortina were unsuccessful, but shortly thereafter the Mexican army arrested the outlaw leader and removed him from the Rio Grande Valley. McNelly's aggressive and fearless action and the removal of Cortina by Mexican authorities brought a measure of security to several South Texas counties. Thereafter forces of both nations patrolled the border and reduced the lawlessness on both sides of the river. Nevertheless, peace did not come easily. Mexicans and Mexican-Americans continued to remember the Ranger forces with bitterness, contending that the Rangers abused and persecuted their people.

The other famous fighting organization was the Frontier Battalion, commanded by Major John B. Jones, a stern, unassuming, but highly efficient officer. Although created, like the Special Force of Rangers, to deal principally with lawless white men, the Frontier Battalion took the field in time to have an important part in bringing to an end the Comanche and Kiowa raids in Texas. Jones placed his six companies in camps along the frontier in positions calculated to offer maximum protection. From these camps, scouts and patrols were kept constantly on the move to intercept any Indian raiding party that might be trying to make its way into the settlements. At Lost Valley, near the Jack-Young County line, on June 12, 1875, 27 rangers under the command of Jones himself fought 100 well-armed Indians for an entire day. In this instance the Rangers were obliged to send a runner to Fort Richardson (Jacksboro) for aid, but normally they were able to deal successfully with any Indian force they encountered. During the first six months of its existence the Frontier Battalion had 15 engagements with Indians, killed 15 Indians, wounded ten, captured one, followed 28 trails, and recovered livestock valued at $5,000. When the Indian campaigns were over, the Frontier Battalion concentrated its efforts very effectively against lawless white men.

THE BUFFALO SLAUGHTER

Closely associated with the problem of Indian removal and the advance of the Texas frontier was the extermination of the buffalo, or bison. This large, shaggy animal, which roamed the grassy plains in thousands, constituted the Plains Indians' source of existence. In addition to food, clothing, and shelter, buffalo robes provided an important trade commodity. Although 199,870 buffalo robes reached New Orleans in 1828, the peak year, the number of buffalo killed before the end of the Civil War made no apparent reduction in the size of the immense herds nor gave the Indians cause for alarm. Beginning in 1870, however, when experiments showed that buffalo hides could be made into good leather, the demand for hides increased sharply. Buyers gathered at convenient points near the buffalo range and offered good prices for all hides. Hunters, who were superb marksmen, penetrated the plains, beginning near the railroad lines in Kansas, and wrought havoc with the Indians' "cattle."

Having slaughtered most of the buffalo in Kansas, they moved in 1873 from Dodge City to the Panhandle of Texas where they found a massive herd. The attack on their supply post at Adobe Walls in June 1874 only checked their operation for that season. By the end of the year several hunters had taken a long, circuitous route around the Indian country and had entered the range from the east by way of Fort Griffin, near present-day Albany. Before the end of 1875 J. Wright Mooar and his brother John, Joe S. McCombs, and others were hunting in the vicinity of the present towns of Sweetwater, Colorado City, and Haskell. During the 1875–1876 season an estimated fifteen hundred hunters were engaged in their deadly work. The magnitude of their operation is revealed in the volume of business at the supply base. In one day in 1877, the hunters bought at F. E. Conrad's general mercantile store in Fort Griffin, guns and ammunition in the amount of $2,500. Another supply base, Rath City, or Reynolds City, in Stonewall County, had a hide business that that year alone was valued at $100,000. Other bases and camps that became towns included Buffalo Gap, Hide Town (Snyder), and Mobeetie. During two months at the peak of their kill—December 1877 and January 1878—the hunters took at least 100,000 hides from the Texas range. During the following season, however, only a few small herds could be found, and by 1880 the buffaloes were gone.

Frontierspeople long engaged in lively arguments over the comparative effectiveness of the three factors that helped to rid the plains of Indians: the United States Army, the Texas Rangers, and the buffalo hunters. Each made some contribution. The army broke up large-scale resistance to authority; the Rangers made raiding too hazardous for even the most reckless warrior; and the buffalo hunters destroyed the Indians' larder and opened the way for the herds of the cattle ranchers.

THE CATTLE KINGDOM

Before the farmers could establish themselves on the lands vacated after the Civil War by the retreating Indians, except in the Cross Timbers where there was a small supply of timber and water, new inventions and discoveries had to be made. While they impatiently waited for the necessary adaptations, for a relatively short interval of less than three decades, the cattle kingdom rose, flourished, and declined on the free or cheap, but nutritious, grass that covered the plains. Originating in Spanish times, the cattle kingdom eventually spread from Brownsville to Montana. Besides furnishing a large part of the nation's beef supply, Texas cattle stocked the middle and northern plains. The techniques, the lingo, and other aspects of the culture of the cattle kingdom contributed significantly to the history of the West.

When the first soldiers and priests came, they brought along cattle. The Spanish cattle were the progenitors of the wild cattle that in later years were to be found in various parts of the state, and also of the famous longhorns, a type that evolved in southern Texas and came to be known throughout the West. Apparently, cattle brought in from the Old South in the early nineteenth century materially affected the strain of animals on the range. But whether they were the lanky longhorns of South Texas or the better-built, round-barreled "Texas cattle," they were hardy and able to protect themselves. They made fairly good beef when fat and furnished their own transportation to market. Except for roundups at branding time, they were given no attention and needed none.

The open-range cattle industry had its beginnings in South Texas between San Antonio and Brownsville and between Matagorda Bay and Laredo. In climate this region is unsurpassed as a range for cattle that are given practically no care. Some large herds were there during the Spanish era; in 1774 at Goliad, Mission La Bahía Espiritu Santo claimed 15,000 and Mission Rosario 10,000 head. It was during the time of Spanish rule that ranchers developed many of the practices used in raising cattle on the open range. Riders mounted on horseback, or *vaqueros*, tended the herds. The *vaqueros* wore leather coverings or "chaps" to protect their legs from the thorny brush that sometimes covered the land. Their skills as horsemen were highly developed, and they were proficient in their use of ropes or *reatas* to catch cattle whenever necessary. Periodically the *vaqueros* gathered the cattle together in a "roundup," sometimes collecting them in pens or corrals. The cattle were branded with hot irons to indicate the ownership of the rancher. Spanish brands were large designs that sometimes covered one side of the cow.

Anglo-Americans who moved into Texas prior to the Civil War and expanded the cattle industry were already familiar with such practices. In fact, ranchers in southern states from the Carolinas to Louisiana had used most of these procedures for generations. Roundups and branding were practices of long standing, although their brands were much smaller than those used by the Spanish, and Anglo drovers sometimes trailed their herds to market. Anglo-Americans had not relied much on horses, developed roping skills, worn chaps, or ridden with saddles equipped with horns, but otherwise they were already prepared for work on the Texas range.

The ranching industry established during Spanish days expanded during Mexican rule, the Republic, and early statehood. After the retreat of the Mexican army following Santa Anna's defeat at San Jacinto, many Mexicans withdrew from the country between the Nueces and the Rio Grande. However, other Mexican *rancheros* continued to operate large ranches, and Anglo-Americans gradually entered the region. Earlier, mention was made of H. L. Kinney, an adventurous Irish-American from Illinois, who established a trading post at the site of Corpus Christi in 1839 and soon engaged in ranching. Kinney hired a retinue of followers both to work and to fight. The war with Mexico brought a number of prominent Anglo-Americans to this area, among them Captain Mifflin Kenedy and Captain Richard King, who enlarged his initial Santa Gertrudis tract of 75,000 acres into the famous King Ranch of more than a million acres. Many gold seekers on their way to California passed through Corpus Christi and created a limited market for the cattle. The number of cattle increased rapidly, and a few cattlemen prospered, but marauding Indian bands and bandits, and above all, the lack of a good market, limited the growth of the industry. Nevertheless, in 1860 there were an estimated 3,786,433 cattle in Texas, six times as many cattle as people.

Texas cattle were, indeed, much easier to raise than to sell. During the Spanish era they were worth very little and could scarcely be disposed of at any price. Occasionally a herd was driven to Louisiana, notwithstanding the fact that trade with that province was forbidden, and at times dried beef was carried by pack trains to cities in Coahuila. After the Texas Revolution herds were sometimes driven to Louisiana and ranchers shipped cattle in considerable numbers to New Orleans. But cattle were of so little value that many thousands were slain for their hides and tallow.

After the war with Mexico, the range cattle industry spread into the vast prairie region marked today by such cities as Dallas, Fort Worth, and Denton. John Chisum, later the best-known cattleman in New Mexico, owned a herd in Denton County during this period. By 1861 the cattlemen had extended their domain westward, appropriating the best ranges in the Western Cross Timbers, from San Saba County to Clay County. The Civil War halted their westward march, but in 1867, with the reestablishment of a line of military posts, the rangemen began appropriating the Rolling Plains. By 1876 they had reached or passed the one hundredth meridian, from Kimble County in the Edwards Plateau to Childress County in the eastern Panhandle.

Meanwhile, the industry had swung around the High Plains and was well established along the slopes of the Rocky Mountains and the valleys farther west. The career of Charles Goodnight illustrates this movement. Goodnight went to Palo Pinto County in the Cross Timbers of West Texas in 1857. A few years of trail driving, scouting, and ranger service made him one of America's finished plainsmen. With Oliver Loving in 1866 he drove a herd by the Concho-Pecos River route to New Mexico, opening the Pecos (or Goodnight-Loving) Trail. He soon drove herds by this route into Colorado and in 1869 established his home near Pueblo. After business reverses had brought losses and the range had become crowded, Goodnight turned again to Texas. He moved his herd southeastward to the Texas Panhandle. The Comanches, who had formed a barrier against white intrusion into that country, had been driven by the soldiers to a reservation, and Goodnight felt confident that he could successfully deal with any small bands that might slip back to their old haunts. He entered the Palo Duro Canyon in 1876 and in partnership with John Adair, an Irish capitalist, established the JA Ranch.

Goodnight had selected a range with a fairly adequate supply of water. The scarcity of water was a great handicap for the cattlemen. Indeed, the plentiful grass was useless without the control of water. Surface water was impounded in tanks where there were creeks and draws, but for several years after the Indians had been removed, ranchers doubted that the millions of acres of fine grass on the High Plains could ever be grazed because of the lack of water. Fortunately, underneath most of the area lay an ample supply. Before it could be used, however, it was necessary to locate this supply and devise methods for making it available. Wells were drilled as early as 1855, and by the 1880s wells with windmills were providing adequate water supplies and opening lands where there were no creeks or rivers to supply the thirsty cattle.

While solving problems of production, ranchers also developed a solution for marketing problems. Trail driving, used occasionally before the Civil War, began in larger volume and in a somewhat different manner after the war. Before the Civil War a few drovers had proved that trail driving to the railheads in Missouri was practical. Left at the end of the war with very little money and an overabundance of cheap cattle, Texans in great numbers renewed their efforts to reach the affluent markets of the North by means of the long drives. In 1866 an estimated 260,000 cattle were started on the trail for Sedalia and other railroad stations in Missouri from which they could be shipped to eastern markets.

But the Texans met with unforeseen perils. In southern Missouri and eastern Kansas bands of farmers turned them back or broke up their herds, contending that the Texas cattle destroyed their crops and transmitted to their animals the dreaded Texas fever. By following a circuitous route west of the farmers' frontier, some of the herdsmen managed to reach St. Joseph and from there shipped their cattle to Chicago. By mid-

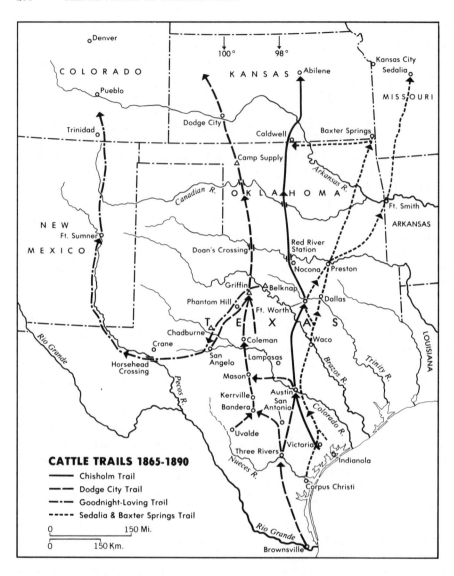

CATTLE TRAILS 1865-1890

—————— Chisholm Trail
— — — Dodge City Trail
—·—·— Goodnight-Loving Trail
- - - - - Sedalia & Baxter Springs Trail

0   150 Mi.

0   150 Km.

summer of the next year, however, the Kansas Pacific Railroad had extended its line beyond the farmers' frontier, and in Abilene, Kansas, herds could reach the railroad without interference.

Each year for more than two decades thereafter, thousands of Texas cattle were driven to railroad stations in Kansas to be shipped to eastern markets. During the first few years of the drives, fortunes varied; but 1874 and the decade following constituted a prosperous era for the cattle owners. A combination of factors created a strong market. Only a part of the cattle driven out of Texas went directly to the slaughter pens. Men soon discovered that the rich grasses of the northern plains would sustain and fatten cattle, and in the cow towns of Kansas, purchasers of stock cattle competed with those who bought for beef. Also, the process of refrigeration, which made it possible to ship dressed beef across the ocean, came into practice in 1875. By 1882 good steers brought five and one-half cents a pound on the Chicago market, at that time the highest price ever paid in the United States. The boom lasted until 1885 when a severe winter, followed by a drought, forced many owners to sell their animals on a market that already was weak, thereby causing the industry to collapse. Thereafter, trail driving declined rapidly. Vexing quarantine regulations and barbed wire fences made it more difficult and more costly each year. Estimates of the number of cattle driven over the trails vary, but the count probably exceeded five million head.

The perils of the trail loom large in the literature of the cattle kingdom. The monotonous fare on the trail; the lonely night guards; the storms with their wind, hail, and lightning; the stampedes when the roar of the 10,000 charging hoofs and the clatter of half as many sharp-pointed horns reminded the rider that his life depended on his surefooted horse; cold wind that chilled men to the marrow and blistering sun that scorched the earth; the swirling water of swollen streams; and the hazards of marauding Indians were experiences that caused many a trail driver to swear that he would quit for good at Abilene, Ellsworth, or Dodge City. Yet when it next came time for the drive, he was usually ready to go again.

Trail driving was economical. Eight, ten, or a dozen men with few supplies and only a small amount of equipment could deliver a herd of 2,000 or more animals from Texas to the railheads in Kansas at a cost per head of 50 to 60 cents, a small fraction of the charge for shipping by rail. Thus, during the later years many herds were driven past Texas railroad stations and on to Kansas to get them as near as possible to eastern markets before shipping by rail.

There were several major cattle trails to the North, each with a number of branches in Texas used by drovers in reaching the main route. The first was the Sedalia Trail, which started near Matagorda Bay and passed through or near Austin, Fort Worth, Denison, and Fort Smith. As a result of unfortunate experiences in Arkansas, the drovers, after crossing the Red River, followed a more westerly course by the Shawnee village to Baxter Springs and around the farmers in eastern Kansas to St. Joseph or to Abilene.

The best-known of the group was the Chisholm Trail, opened in 1867 by, and named for, Jesse Chisholm, a Cherokee Indian trader. It began in South Texas, ran by Austin and Lampasas, passed between Fort Worth and Weatherford, crossed the Red River near present-day Nocona, and ran along or near the ninety-eighth meridian across Indian Territory to Caldwell, Kansas. Here extensions led to Abilene, Wichita, Newton, and other points. As the farmers moved westward, they forced the cattlemen to seek new routes and new shipping termini. For instance, Abilene, Kansas, was the chief shipping point from 1867 through 1871; Wichita to the south and Ellsworth to the west displaced it in 1872; and after 1876 Dodge City received most of the herds on their way to the eastern markets.

The Dodge City or Great Western Trail, formed at Mason by the junction of three important branches that came from the southeast by Lampasas, from the south by San Antonio, and from Bandera to the southwest, led northward through Coleman and Fort Griffin, crossed the Red River near Doan's Store north of Vernon, and then continued in an almost straight line to Dodge City, Kansas. An extension of the trail was used for driving many cattle from Dodge City to stock the vast northern ranges of western Nebraska, Wyoming, and even Montana. Reference has already been made to another major trail farther west that Goodnight and Loving opened in 1866. The Goodnight-Loving (or Pecos) Trail went westward up the Middle Concho, along the Great Comanche War Trail across the waterless stretch to the Pecos River at Horsehead Crossing, and up the Pecos into New Mexico. Within a few years, it had been extended by way of Raton Pass and Denver into Wyoming and Montana.

THE BIG PASTURE COUNTRY

The open-range cattle industry spread with marvelous rapidity; its decline was even more rapid. The crowded ranges, the westward advance of farmers and railroads, the introduction of barbed wire, and the utilization of drilled wells and windmills for obtaining water economically transformed the open range into a country of big pastures. In brief, the open range ceased to exist about 1890 when the ranges had been enclosed by fences.

The very success of the open-range cattle industry led to its destruction. Reports of huge profits attracted eastern and European capitalists as well as many small investors. Numbers of syndicates, such as the Texas Land and Cattle Company, the Matador Land and Cattle Company, the Hansford Cattle Company, the Capitol Syndicate Company, and the Espuela Land and Cattle Company, invested millions in the business. These concerns had the money to buy their lands and to fence them. Furthermore, the ranges soon became crowded. Protracted droughts interspersed by severe blizzards from 1885 through 1887 and quarantine laws of northern states against Texas cattle either decimated many herds or forced owners to sell thousands of gaunt animals, thereby bringing about a disastrous collapse in the cattle market. Fencing seemed to be the logical solution for the problems. Even before barbed wire, which offered a cheap and effective fencing material, had come into use, cattlemen in South Texas were enclosing their better grasslands with smooth wire or with boards.

Fencing was hastened greatly by at least three factors: the extension of railroads into West Texas; the invention and sale of barbed wire; and the discovery of an adequate ground-water supply and the use of windmills to make it available. The network of railroads available in most areas by the 1880s made practicable the importation of fencing material, though some ranches were still more than 100 miles from the nearest line. Within another decade the best range lands had been fenced with barbed wire. J. F. Glidden, a farmer of De Kalb, Illinois, invented barbed wire in 1873. Henry B. Sanborn, a salesman for the Glidden wire and later the founder of Amarillo, at first found it difficult to sell his product in Texas, but by 1880 there were a few barbed wire fences in a number of counties, including Clay and Montague in North Texas and Coleman and Runnels farther westward. Three years later practically all the cattle country of South and Central Texas had been enclosed, and fencing was well under way in the Panhandle and North Texas.

Opposition to fencing swelled with its spread. The first lands to be

In 1987, Texas was still the leading state in the nation in the production of cattle, sheep, and goats. Livestock and their products accounted for more than 50 percent of the agricultural cash income. Shown here, cowboys on the three million acre XIT Ranch that was given as payment for construction of the state capitol, and several Herefords, an improved beef breed. (University of Texas Library)

fenced naturally were those having a supply of surface water. It was soon evident either the fencing movement had to be stopped or else those who did not fence would be ruined. The commissioners court of San Saba County asked the legislature to prohibit by law the building of barbed wire fences; and in 1888 the stockmen's association of Nolan and Fisher counties approved a resolution that the land west of the one hundredth meridian was "fit only for grazing" and that fences should not be allowed. Some men, however, expressed their resentment more violently by cutting the fences. Public sentiment generally supported the fence cutters. In many cases large proprietors had fenced in land that did not belong to them and had closed public roads. Fences displaced many cowboys who had neither the inclination nor training for another kind of work. Rustlers opposed fences because they made theft more difficult. Furthermore, "nesters" and small farmers who pushed ahead into the cattle country might find themselves entirely surrounded by a fence without an outlet or in turn have their own fences cut by those who resented their bold intrusion into the domain of grass. More significantly, the public resented fencing because the movement was led by large cattle companies mostly owned by eastern and foreign capitalists. This sentiment was well expressed by a contemporary newspaper editor, who, after branding fence cutting as an evil, charged it to the fallacious and dangerous policy of the state in selling off its domain in such large tracts, "creating principalities, pashalics, and baronates among a few capitalists and arousing a spirit of agrarianism among the poorer classes."

During 1883 fence cutting occurred in more than half the 171 organized counties of the state. It was most serious along the agricultural frontier, marked by Clay County on the north, Coleman and Brown counties in the center, and Frio and Medina counties farther south. In some areas sentiment was so evenly divided that the local officers and the Texas Rangers were helpless.

To deal with the problem, Governor John Ireland called a special session of the legislature. Early in 1884 it made fence cutting a felony, but required that gates be placed every three miles along a fence. It also made unlawful the enclosing of land not owned or leased. Although in some localities not a fence was left uncut four years later, the legislative enactments, the energetic efforts of a few sheriffs and the Texas Rangers, and a growing public sentiment for law and order combined to put an end, by the close of the decade, to the destructive orgy. The damage to fences has been estimated as high as $20 million, a tremendous financial loss, but even more consequential was the unfavorable publicity that discouraged investments and immigration.

The crowded ranges, the westward advance of farmers and railroads, the introduction of barbed wire, and the utilization of drilled wells and windmills transformed the open ranges into big pastures. In the conversion, some of the cattle companies were faced with the problem of consolidating their holdings. A few had managed to secure compact tracts of land, but many of the large concerns had fenced in land they did not own. They bought a large part of their land from the railroad companies, paying from 25 cents to $1.00 an acre for it. Interspersed with the sections of railroad were alternate sections of school land, which the ranchmen might lease but could not purchase except in small quantities, for the law limited the amount of school land that one person could buy from the state. The ranchmen bought as much school land as possible, but still there was generally land open to settlers in every large pasture. Immigrants in time sought out and purchased or squatted on these lands. The ranchmen ultimately bought out the "nesters," and a number of big, consolidated ranches emerged.

Most famous among them was the King Ranch, which has been previously mentioned. Nearby, Mifflin Kenedy, a former partner of Richard King, established a ranch that encompassed most of Kenedy County. In northwest Texas the JA Ranch, under Goodnight's able direction, by 1887 had 40,000 cattle and 700,000 acres of land under its control. Thomas Sherman Bugbee, who began grazing cattle in the Texas Panhandle in 1876, eventually expanded his Shoe Bar Ranch to 450,000 acres. Within another decade several other very large ranches were operating in the area. The Matador, a Scottish syndicate, at its peak owned 861,000 acres in Texas; the Spur, a British company adjoining the south side of the Matador, obtained a total of 439,972 acres; and the XIT, a Chicago-based syndicate and the largest of the Texas ranches, located the 3,050,000 acres transferred to it for building the state capitol along the border of New Mexico from Hockley County in the south to the Oklahoma line in the north. J. W. Williams, an authority on the subject, listed 19 ranches in 1954

Cattle were introduced into Texas by the Spanish explorers and counted for the principal wealth of the missions. Herds increased during the Civil War when they were neither tended nor thinned. Barbed wire, first available to Texans in quantity in 1879, revolutionized land values and made it possible to open homesteads in frontier plains areas. (University of Texas Library)

with a range of more than 150,000 acres each. The list included the King and Kenedy ranches, the W. T. Waggoner Estate, the West Cattle Company, and the Burnett ranches, all with ranges in excess of 400,000 acres.

On the enclosed pastures, select breeding of animals, impossible under the open-range system, soon came into practice. Durham, Angus, and Hereford cattle replaced the Spanish longhorns, but the Herefords soon dominated. In time the ranchmen began experimenting with crops to supplant their pastures of grass. At first they planted sorghum, then grain sorghum, and eventually wheat on larger and larger farms. In 1985 cattle in Texas numbered 14.1 million, about one-eighth of the total for the entire United States, and the cash receipts from this one commodity amounted to almost half of Texas's revenue derived from agriculture.

HORSES, SHEEP, AND GOATS

Cattle was not the only important product of the ranching industry. For many years in the middle of the nineteenth century, horses were also valuable items for market. "Mustangers" captured and trained wild horses or mustangs and sold them in various locations over the West. In most instances, the mustangers were Mexican *mesteñeros*, who developed considerable skill in this difficult and dangerous work.

Before the Civil War there was a constant demand for horses of all kinds, and mustangs, hardy and spirited animals, were especially prized. Consequently, *mesteñeros* captured large numbers, tamed them, and sold them either to the army or to ranchers. Capturing and training required special skills. Capturing techniques varied, but the *mesteñeros* usually either roped the animal after a long chase or diverted it into a specially constructed pen. Different methods were used in "breaking" or training the mustangs. Sometimes the wilder animals were tied to gentler ones; or in some instances, their legs were hobbled. Occasionally the *mesteñero* simply rode the animal until it decided to accept a rider peacefully.

Mustanging was an important part of the ranching industry until the 1870s. Thereafter, cattle ranching reduced the number of wild horses to the point that few could be found and little profit could be made.

A more permanent part of the ranching industry was the raising of sheep and goats. Sheep, like cattle, were brought to Texas during the early Spanish era and were first raised on a large scale in Texas in the country south of San Antonio. In fact, the sheep industry was confined principally to that region until the 1870s, after which ranchers to the west and north of San Antonio began to acquire large herds. Increasing in the rangelands between Del Rio and San Angelo, the number of sheep in Texas increased several times over between 1870 and 1880.

Mexican-Americans were especially important in the raising of sheep and goats. The shepherds who tended the flocks were usually Mexican-

American *pastores*. Practically all of the shearers who cut the wool off the sheep were *tasinques* of Mexican heritage, and many of them were from Mexico. Mexican-Americans owned some of the sheep ranches, some of them containing herds that numbered in the tens of thousands.

Almost without exception, the sheepmen appeared after the cattlemen had established themselves. This fact, as well as the disposition of sheep to eat the grass so short that a cow could not subsist on it, sometimes made sheep raising unpopular in the cattle country, and sometimes there were clashes and bloodshed between the sheepmen and cattlemen. On the other hand, there were instances where ranchers ran both sheep and cattle.

The rapid growth of the sheep industry is reflected by the fact that in 1870 there were 1,223,000 sheep in Texas, whereas in 1880 there were 6,024,000, a larger number than at any time thereafter until 1930. The number, after declining to less than 2,000,000 in the early twentieth century, increased to nearly 11,000,000 during World War II, making Texas the leading sheep producing state. Since then, however, the number has declined steadily, in 1960 to slightly more than 6,000,000 and in 1970 to less than 4,000,000. In 1984 there were only 1,970,000, but they produced more than $16 million in revenue from wool production.

Angora goats that produce quality mohair were brought to America and to Texas from Turkey in 1849. Goat raising became concentrated chiefly on the Edwards Plateau. In 1984 Texas had 1,450,000 goats, less than half as many as in 1969, which produced more than $48 million in revenue from the sale of mohair.

THE ADVANCE OF THE FARMERS

In 1870 the extreme western line of the farmers' frontier extended from the common border of Montague and Cook counties irregularly to the vicinity of Bandera and thence to the coast a few miles below Corpus Christi, comparatively close to the cattlemen's frontier. But within another decade the cattlemen's frontier had left the farmers' frontier hundreds of miles behind. The cattlemen appropriated the choice watering places and best grasslands, but generally there were not enough persons to form communities and establish local governments. The lawmakers created counties (54 by one act in 1876), and geographers marked them on maps in checkerboard fashion; but the herdsmen generally had to wait for the coming of at least a few farmers before they could secure the 150 signatures required to organize a county. For land records and judicial purposes most of these western counties were attached to older counties to the east until a few farmers arrived to augment the adult male population.

Although they advanced more slowly, the farmers came in far greater numbers than did the cattlemen, and their movement gained momentum after the marauding Plains Indians had been confined to the reservations.

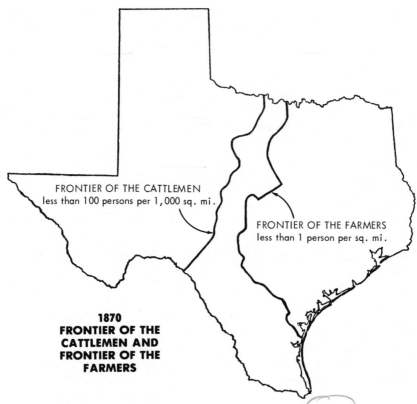

FRONTIER OF THE CATTLEMEN
less than 100 persons per 1,000 sq. mi.

FRONTIER OF THE FARMERS
less than 1 person per sq. mi.

**1870
FRONTIER OF THE
CATTLEMEN AND
FRONTIER OF THE
FARMERS**

An estimated 400,000 immigrants entered Texas in 1876, many of whom went directly to the frontier. At the end of the next year the western line of farms ran from Henrietta in Clay County southward through Archer, Young, Stephens, Comanche, Mills, San Saba, and Mason counties. By 1880 it extended from Vernon through Haskell, Jones, Taylor, Runnels, Coleman, and Mason counties. Within the three-year interval farmers by the thousands had settled within the long, triangular region formed by the Red River and these two lines. The increase in population was phenomenal. Jack County, which had only 694 inhabitants in 1870, had 6,626 in 1880. Taylor County was without white population altogether until about 1874, but by 1880 it was the home of 1,736 persons. Apparently, most of the frontier settlers during the 1870s came from older communities in Texas, but other states, particularly of the Old South, were well represented.

During the late seventies and early eighties several colonies of farmers moved to western Texas, some locating far in advance of the other settlements. The best known included a group of 400 Germans from the vicinity of Indianapolis, who settled in 1878 in Baylor County; Lewis Henry Carhart's Christian Colony, which located in 1879 in the vicinity of the town of

Clarendon; a colony of Quakers from Ohio and Indiana, who, under the leadership of Paris Cox, in 1879 established a settlement on the High Plains in Lubbock and Crosby counties; and a colony of German Catholics from Anderson County, who were induced by the Texas and Pacific Railroad to locate in 1881 at the present-day town of Stanton. Unacquainted with the country, the crops, and the methods of tillage required, and beset by droughts and plagues of grasshoppers, most of these pioneer farmers did not succeed, but their heroic efforts paved the way for others who came later and profited by their experience.

With the coming of railroads in the eighties, the farmers' frontier abruptly ceased its comparatively orderly and solid advancement. No matter where the rails ran, settlers soon followed. The Texas and Pacific Railroad in 1880 overtook the line of settlements in Taylor County. Within a year Abilene, Sweetwater, Colorado City, and Big Spring were flourishing towns, and the better lands in their vicinity were soon occupied by farmers. A terrible drought in the mid-eighties halted the farmers' advance only for its duration; when it broke in 1887, the tillers of the soil arrived in greater numbers than ever. The mainstream of this new wave of settlers followed the Fort Worth and Denver Railroad along the upper Red River valley and across the Texas Panhandle. Almost by the time the line reached Texline on the border of New Mexico in 1888, Quanah, Childress, Memphis, Clarendon, and Amarillo had become service centers for farmers.

By 1890 the farmers had located in numbers throughout the region east of the one hundredth meridian and near the railroads. A decade then passed before there occurred any significant westward advance. A law of 1897 reduced the minimum price of agricultural lands to $1.50 per acre with terms of one-fortieth down and forty years on the balance. A law of 1901 produced some land rushes and conflicts between cattlemen and farmers. However, a more orderly system was created in 1906 by a law requiring competitive sealed bids, a procedure that brought prices as high as $22.00 an acre.

Actually, these land rushes marked the end of the old controversy between the cattlemen and the farmers. As long as there was free grass or land in quantity to lease, the cattlemen opposed the advance of the farmers. But once they had acquired legal possession of their lands, the ranchmen had no reason to oppose the coming of the farmers or of anybody else who would develop the country and increase the value of all land.

The railroads, which inaugurated costly programs aimed at populating the country, probably accomplished more in that direction than all other agencies combined. They had agents in eastern centers who distributed tons of printed materials; some railroads ran exhibition trains; some erected immigrant depots where people might stay while selecting their lands; some established demonstration farms; and with their transportation rates, all favored immigrants. Once settlements were established, the people became enthusiastic about the country, and newspapers sometimes proclaimed its wonders in unrestrained language.

The rush of immigrant farmers into West Texas continued after the turn of the century. Farmers located in the Concho Valley around San Angelo and along the Pecos River around 1900, while the immigration fever spread to the High Plains, where it raged intermittently for decades. The best school and railroad lands passed into the ownership of farmers, and the supply was exhausted early in the century. In 1908 the commissioner of the General Land Office reported that trainloads of prospectors, speculators, and investors were invading western counties of the South Plains. Lands held for the support of asylums were sold by 1920, and practically all surveyed school tracts were sold by 1920. But already ranchmen had begun cutting up their pastures and selling off land in small tracts. Homeseekers were brought in by the trainloads, and land values sometimes increased from 50 to 100 percent within a few months.

While farmers were establishing themselves on the High Plains, others were moving with equal effectiveness against the domain of the ranchers in southern Texas. They practiced both dry farming and irrigation, but irrigation drew in the greater number, especially in the lower Rio Grande valley.

The growth of this region started with the building of the St. Louis, Brownsville, and Mexico Railroad in 1904. Thereafter the production of fruits and vegetables by irrigation increased rapidly, though irregularly. By 1910 a few commercial citrus fruit orchards had been set, and in 1914 it was discovered that by budding grapefruit and oranges on the native orange stock one could produce a tree adapted to the Rio Grande soil and climate. An amendment to the state constitution in 1917 and subsequent liberal acts of the legislature encouraged the organization of irrigation and drainage districts.

Unlike the promoters of the earlier years, the Rio Grande valley sought only the well-to-do or the rich immigrants. In no other area of Texas was the disparity between wealthy landowner and abysmally poor laborer, usually Mexican-American, as apparent as in the valley. Poor people could not purchase these high-priced lands. From North Texas cities agents ran excursion trains of Pullman cars and diners only, frequently making the passengers their guests, without charge for transportation or meals. At times, land sales on a single excursion of this kind aggregated more than a million dollars. Between 1920 and 1930 the population of the lower Rio Grande valley more than doubled.

SELECTED BIBLIOGRAPHY

A general survey of frontier defense and the Indian problem may be found in C. C. Rister, *The Southwestern Frontier;* R. N. Richardson and C. C. Rister, *The Greater Southwest* (Glendale, Calif, 1934); and E. Wallace, *Texas in Turmoil, 1849–1876.*

Major studies devoted primarily to the subject include R. N. Richardson, *The Comanche Barrier;* E. Wallace, *Ranald S. Mackenzie on the Texas Frontier;* W. S. Nye, *Carbine and Lance, The Story of Old Fort Sill* (Norman, Okla., 1937); C. C. Rister, *Fort Griffin on the Texas Frontier* (Norman, Okla., 1956); T. Lindsay Baker and Billy R. Harrison, *Adobe Walls: The History and Archeology of the 1874 Trading Post* (College Station, 1986); J. E. Haley, *Fort Concho and the Texas Frontier* (San Angelo, 1952); W. H. Leckie, *Military Conquest of the Southern Plains* (Norman, Okla., 1963); R. G. Carter, *On the Border with Mackenzie* (New York, 1961); and Dan Thrapp, *The Conquest of Apachería* (Norman, Okla., 1967); Arlan L. Fowler, *The Black Infantrymen in the West, 1869–1891* (Westport, Conn., 1971); R. W. Shook, "Federal Occupation and Administration of Texas, 1865–1870"; Roger N. Conger and others, *Frontier Forts of Texas;* Paul H. Carlson, "William R. Shafter: Military Commander in the American West" (unpublished dissertation, Texas Tech University, Lubbock, 1972); H. Allen Anderson, *Fort Phantom Hill: Outpost on the Clear Fort of the Brazos* (Lubbock, 1976).

Valuable studies of Indian tribes include E. Wallace and E. A. Hoebel, *The Comanches;* M. P. Mayhall, *The Kiowas* (Norman, Okla., 1962); A .M. Gibson, *The Kickapoos: Lords of the Middle Border* (Norman, Okla., 1963); William T. Hagan, *United States-Comanche Relations: The Reservation Years* (New Haven, 1976).

The Indian side of the story is presented by Thomas C. Battey, *The Life and Adventures of a Quaker among the Indians* (Boston, 1875); and W. S. Nye, *Bad Medicine and Good: Tales of the Kiowa* (Norman, Okla., 1962).

Considerable source material dealing with the subject is published in J. M. Day and D. H. Winfrey, *Texas Indian Papers, 1860–1916* (Austin, 1961); E. Wallace, *Ranald S. Mackenzie's Official Correspondence Relating to Texas, 1871–1873* (Lubbock, 1967); E. Wallace, *Ranald S. Mackenzie's Official Correspondence Relating to Texas, 1873–1879* (Lubbock, 1968); Joe E. Taylor (ed.), "The Indian Campaign on the Staked Plains, 1874–1875; Military Correspondence from War Department, Adjutant General's Office, File 2815–1874," *Panhandle–Plains Historical Review,* XXIV, 1–216; XXV, 1–360.

A few of the many articles dealing with specialized phases of the subject are Adrian N. Anderson, "The Last Phase of Colonel Ranald S. Mackenzie's 1874 Campaign against the Comanches," *West Texas Historical Association Year Book,* XL, 71–82; Frank Temple, "Colonel B. H. Grierson's Victorio Campaign," *West Texas Historical Association Year Book,* XXXV, 99–111; E. Wallace and A. N. Anderson, "R. S. Mackenzie and the Kickapoos: The Raid into Mexico in 1873," *Arizona and the West,* VII, 105–126; G. Derek West, "The Battle of Adobe Walls (1874)," *Panhandle-Plains Historical Review,* XXXVI, 1–36; Paul Carlson, " 'Pecos Bill' Shafter: Scouting the Llano Estacado," *Military History of Texas and the Southwest,* XVI, 33–53; Donald Whisenhunt, *Fort Richardson, Outpost on the Texas Frontier* (El Paso, 1968); Ernest R. Archambeau, "The Battle of Lyman's Wagon Train," *Panhandle-Plains Historical Review;* XXXVI, 89–102. For a description of military posts where troops were quartered, see Eugener Graham, "Federal Fort Architecture in Texas during the Nineteenth Century," *Southwestern Historical Quarterly,* LXXX, 165–188.

For the story of the shortest-lived frontier industry, see M. Sandoz, *The Buffalo Hunters* (New York, 1954); W. Gard, *The Great Buffalo Hunt* (New York, 1959); and Charles L. Kenner, *A History of New Mexican-Plains Indian Relations* (Norman, Okla., 1969).

Reading on the ranching industry in Texas should begin with Terry G. Jordan, *Trails to Texas: Southern Roots of Western Cattle Ranching* (Lincoln, 1981), for a thoughtful discussion of the origins of the ranching industry. But also see Jack Jackson, *Los Mesteñeros: Spanish Ranching in Texas, 1721–1821* (College Station, 1986).

Historical literature of the range cattle industry is voluminous. General studies are Ernest S. Osgood, *The Day of the Cattleman* (Minneapolis, 1954); E. E. Dale, *The Range Cattle Industry* (Norman, Okla., 1930); E. E. Dale, *Cow Country* (Norman, Okla., 1942); and James Cox, *The Cattle Industry of Texas and Adjacent Country* (St. Louis, 1895). Bearing especially on Texas is W. C. Holden, *Alkali Trails;* Coleman McCampbell, *The Saga of a Frontier Seaport* (Dallas, 1934); Billy M. Jones, *The Search for Maturity* (Austin, 1965); Robert M. Utley, "The Range Cattle Industry in the Big Bend of Texas," *Southwestern Historical Quarterly*, LXIX, 419–441; Lewis Nordyke, *Cattle Empire* (New York, 1949).

There are several historians of the cattle trails: W. Gard, *The Chisholm Trail* (Norman, Okla., 1954); J. Marvin Hunter and George W. Saunders (eds.), *The Trail Drivers of Texas* (Dallas, 1925); Harry Drago, *Great American Cattle Trails* (New York, 1965); Andy Adams, *The Log of a Cowboy* (Boston, 1931); Emerson Hough, *The Story of the Cowboy* (New York, 1923); Jimmy M. Skaggs, "The Route of the Great Western (Dodge City) Cattle Trail," *West Texas Historical Association Year Book*, XLI, 131–143; Chandler A. Robinson (comp. and ed.), *J. Evetts Haley and the Passing of the Old West* (Austin, 1978).

Ranches and ranchers have been popular subjects for writers. Among the best are Lewis Atherton, *The Cattle Kings* (Bloomington, Ind., 1962); Tom Lea, *The King Ranch* (2 vols., Boston, 1957); William M. Pearce, *The Matador Land and Cattle Company* (Norman, Okla., 1964); J. E. Haley, *The XIT Ranch of Texas* (Chicago, 1929; Norman, Okla., 1953); Cordia Sloan Duke and J. B. Frantz, *6,000 Miles of Fence: Life on the XIT Ranch of Texas* (Austin, 1961); William Timmons, *Twilight on the Range: Recollections of a Latter Cowboy* (Austin, 1962); David J. Murrah, *C. C. Slaughter: Rancher, Banker, Baptist* (Austin, 1981) and *The Pitchfork Land and Cattle Company* (Lubbock, 1983); Frances Mayhugh Holden, *Lambshead Before Interwoven: A Texas Range Chronicle, 1848–1978* (College Station, 1982); Sallie Reynolds Matthews, *Interwoven: A Pioneer Chronicle* (College Station, 1982, reprint of 1936 edition); Jo Ella Powell Exley (ed.), *Texas Tears and Texas Sunshine: Voices of Frontier Women* (College Station, 1985); Sandra Myres, *Westering Women and the Frontier Experience, 1800–1915* (Albuquerque, 1982); Ron Tyler and Bank Langmore, *The Cowboy* (New York, 1975); William W. Savage, Jr. (ed.), *Cowboy Life: Reconstructing an American Myth* (Norman, Okla., 1975); Willie N. Lewis, *Tapadero: The Making of a Cowboy* (Austin, 1972); William Curry Holden, *The Espuela Land and Cattle Company: A Study of a Foreign-Owned Ranch in Texas* (Austin, 1970); J. E. Haley and W. C. Holden, *The Flamboyant Judge: A Biography* (Canyon, 1972); J. E. Haley, *Charles Goodnight, Cowman and Plainsman* (Boston and New York, 1936), an excellent biography; J. E. Haley, *George W. Littlefield, Texan* (Norman, Okla., 1943); W. C. Holden, *Rollie Burns: Or an Account of the Ranching Industry on the South Plains* (Dallas, 1932); J. W. Williams, *The Big Ranch Country* (Wichita Falls, Tex., 1954); Laura V. Hammer, *Short Grass and Longhorns* (Norman, Okla., 1943); L. F. Sheffy, *The Life and Times of Timothy Dwight Hobart, 1855–1953* (Canyon, 1950); L. F. Sheffy, *The Francklyn Land and Cattle Company: A Panhandle Enterprise, 1882–1957* (Austin, 1963); A. Ray Stephens, *The Taft Ranch* (Austin, 1964); Charles Kenner, "John Hittson: Cattle King of West Texas," *West Texas Historical Association Year Book*, XXXVII, 70–81; H. T.

Burton, "A History of the J. A. Ranch," *Southwestern Historical Quarterly*, XXXI, 89–115, 221–260, 325–364; XXXII, 26–66; J. M. Skaggs, "John Thomas Lytle: Cattle Baron," *ibid.*, LXXI, 46–60; David B. Gracy, II, "George Washington Littlefield, Portrait of a Cattleman," *ibid.*, LXVIII, 237–258. For cowboy life and lore, see Ramon Adams, *The Cowman Says It Salty* (Tucson, 1971).

Several other phases of the cattle industry have attracted authors. Some excellent studies in this miscellany are W. P. Webb, *The Great Plains;* Frank S. Hastings, *A Ranchman's Recollections (Chicago, 1921);* R. D. Holt, "The Introduction of Barbed Wire into Texas and the Fence Cutting War," *West Texas Historical Association Year Book*, VI, 65–79; Henry D. McCallum, "Barbed Wire in Texas," *Southwestern Historical Quarterly*, LXI, 207–219; W. C. Holden, "The Problem of Maintaining the Solid Range on the Spur Ranch," *ibid.*, XXXIV, 1–19; T. R. Havins, "The Passing of the Longhorns," *ibid.*, LVI, 51-58; T. R. Havins, "Texas Fever," *ibid.*, LVII, 147–162; J. Fred Rippy, "British Investments in Texas Lands and Livestock," *ibid.*, LVIII, 331–341; W. Gard, "The Impact of the Cattle Trails," *ibid.*, LXXI, 1–6; Lowell H. Harrison, "British Interest in the Panhandle-Plains Area, 1878–1885," *Panhandle Plains Historical Review*, XXXVIII, 1–44; Gene M. Gressley, *Bankers and Cattlemen* (New York, 1966); Jimmy M. Skaggs, *The Cattle Trailing Industry: Between Supply and Demand, 1868–1890* (Lawrence, Kans., 1973); J. B. Frantz and Julian Ernest Choate, *The American Cowboy: The Myth and the Reality* (Norman, Okla., 1955); John I. White, *Git Along Little Dogies: Songs and Songwriters of the American West* (Urbana, Ill., 1975).

The publication of a series of short histories of West Texas ranch families, ed. by Ernest Wallace, is a valuable project of the Ranch Heritage Center, Texas Tech University, Lubbock, Tex.

Two authoritative works on the sheep industry are Edward Norris Wentworth, *America's Sheep Trails* (Ames, Ia., 1948); and Winifred Kupper, *The Golden Hoof: The Story of the Sheep of the Southwest* (New York, 1945); also, see Harold M. Gober, "The Sheep Industry in Sterling County," *West Texas Historical Association Year Book*, XXVII, 32–57. For the correspondence of George W. Kendall, Texas's leading sheep rancher, see H. J. Brown, *Letters from a Texas Sheep Ranch* (Urbana, Ill., 1959).

Preeminent among the accounts of the settlement of West Texas is W. C. Holden, *Alkali Trails;* R. N. Richardson, *The Frontier of Northwest Texas, 1846 to 1876;* B. M. Jones, *The Search for Maturity;* Robert Lee Hunt, *A History of Farmer Movements in the Southwest, 1873–1925* (College Station, 1935); Francis W. Rathjen, *The Texas Panhandle Frontier* (Austin, 1975). Other writings dealing with various phases of the subject are Mrs. S. C. Miller, *Sixty Years in the Nueces Valley, 1870–1930* (San Antonio, 1930); Stuart McGregor, "Migrations of Population in Texas" (reprinted from the *Dallas News), Bunker's Monthly*, September, 1929, 271–279; R. C. Crane, "Early Days in Fisher County," *West Texas Historical Association Year Book*, VI, 124–169; Walter B. Stephens, *Through Texas* (reprint of a series of letters published in the *St. Louis Globe Democrat*, 1892); Mary L. Cox, *History of Hale County, Texas* (Plainview, 1937); Willie N. Lewis, *Between Sun and Sod: An Informal History of the Texas Panhandle* (College Station, 1977); Nellie W. Spikes and Temple Ann Ellis, *A History of Crosby County* (San Antonio, 1952); David B. Gracy, *Littlefield Lands: Colonization of the Texas Plains, 1912–1920* (Austin, 1968); Vernon G. Spence, *Judge Legett of Abilene: A Texas Frontier Profile* (College Station, 1977); and Kathryn Duff, *Abilene on the Catclaw* (Abilene, 1970; Clayton W. Williams, *Texas' Last Frontier: Fort Stockton and the Trans-Pecos,*

1861–1895 (College Station, 1982); Wayne R. Austerman, *Sharps Rifles and Spanish Mules: The San Antonio–El Paso Mail 1851–1881* (College Station, 1985); and C. C. Rister, *Southern Plainsmen.* See also W. C. Holden, "Experimental Agriculture on the Spur Ranch, 1885–1904," *Southwestern Social Quarterly,* XII, 16–23; and Riley E. Baker, "Water Development as an Important Factor in the Utilization of the High Plains," *ibid.,* XXXIV, 31–34. For southern Texas, see J. Lee Stambaugh, *The Lower Rio Grande Valley of Texas* (San Antonio, 1954). On the public land system, see A. S. Lang, *Financial History of the Public Lands in Texas;* and R. D. Holt, "School Land Rushes in West Texas," *West Texas Historical Association Year Book,* X, 42–57. An account of the transition from ranch to farm is found in D. B. Gracy, II, *Littlefield Lands: Colonization on the Texas Plains, 1912–1920* (Austin, 1968). The effects of drought are portrayed in Richard King, *Wagons East: The Drought of 1886* (Austin, 1965).

CHAPTER FOURTEEN
IN THE AGE
OF REFORM
1890–1910

The conservative and frugal policies of the years immediately after Reconstruction were not acceptable to many Texans. Often desperately poor and convinced that their plight was both unfair and unjustified, they began as early as the 1870s to seek, without success, government intervention to improve their circumstances. Economic conditions improved somewhat in the 1880s, but the level of dissatisfaction seemed to increase.

By 1890 the demands for reform in political and economic affairs could no longer be ignored or rejected. Texans in the next two decades adopted laws regulating business, expanding education, reforming the electoral system, and making other changes designed to meet the needs of the emerging modern society. In the nineties the primary impetus for reform was the unhappy farmer. Seeking the elimination of economic inequities and the expansion of political democracy, the more militant agrarian radicals organized a third party, the People's or Populist party, while other reformers sought similar goals within the Democratic party.

With the decline of agrarian protest, sentiment for reform subsided temporarily, only to be revived after 1900 with the spirit of the progressive movement. Progressivism of the new century was not merely a renewal of agrarian protest. The strength of the movement was broader, with more emphasis on the role of businessmen, teachers, and professional people, and on new organizations such as the State Federation of Labor and the

Texas Local Option Association. The goals were more complex. Business regulation continued to be a primary objective, but progressives also stressed humanitarian reforms, reorganization of municipal government, expansion of education, and other changes affecting not only the rural but also the urban population. In many ways, it was as much an attitude as it was a program. In short, progressivism reflected the growing importance of industrialization and urbanization. Nevertheless, twentieth-century Texas progressivism preserved a strong rural influence. Many of the goals and some of the leadership of former years were the same; moreover, a new agrarian organization, the Farmers' Union, was one of the more effective reform pressure groups.

Reform, however, was not the only element determining the course of politics during these years. Except for the Populist challenge, most political conflicts took place within the Democratic party. In the one-party structure, personal and factional rivalry sometimes disregarded ideology for the sake of political expediency, forming alignments not particularly related to the matter of progressive change.

THE PRELUDE TO REFORM

During the first two decades following the Civil War, the prevailing attitude in Texas toward big business was friendly. We have seen that the Constitution of 1876, though framed by a convention controlled by farmers, contained no provisions hostile to organized wealth. It is true that the Grange and the Greenback party repeatedly criticized the Democratic administration, contending that it was too generous toward corporations and that it failed to control them, but the dominant party continued with its program of encouragement of business with a minimum of regulatory measures. The demand for regulation increased, however, and during the later eighties the number of malcontents grew rapidly.

As in former years, the center of dissatisfaction was among the farmers; this group, let it be remembered, constituted a majority of the people. Since the Civil War the ills of the farmer had been many and real. The price of cotton, the great money crop of Texas, declined from 31 cents a pound in 1865 to less than five cents in 1898. It seemed that the more the farmers made, the less they had. The supply of money in circulation, limited anyway, seemed unreasonably diminished when the Coinage Act of 1873 eliminated subsequent coinage of silver into money. Meanwhile, taxes and interest charges on mortgages seldom diminished, and the cost of many other articles the farmer had to buy increased from year to year. It was easy for him to believe that the corporation that held a mortgage on his farm charged him exorbitant interest; that the railroads were overcharging him for hauling his crops; and that the middlemen were appropriating too much for services, some of which he deemed unnecessary.

Amid the disintegration of the first farmers' movement, the Grange and the Greenback party, arose a second, the Farmers' Alliance. The Farmers' Alliance was founded in Texas in about 1875 and was reorganized in 1879. In 1887 it became a national organization, and soon its strength was estimated at from one to three million members. At a state meeting in Cleburne in 1886, the alliance set forth a political program in a series of "demands." After a preamble that referred to "the shameful abuses that the industrial classes are now suffering at the hands of arrogant capitalists and powerful corporations," the program "demanded," among other measures, that the public school lands be sold only in small grants to actual settlers; that railroad property be assessed at its full value; and that an effective interstate commerce law be enacted. Two years later the alliance called for an antitrust law as well as more effective regulation of railroad rates.

The alliance and, to a lesser extent, the Knights of Labor affected the pronouncements of the Democratic party. The party's platform, as it was framed in 1886, called for the sale of land "in tracts of reasonable size" to bona fide settlers only, favored laws correcting various abuses practiced by the railroads, and most extreme of all, contained a plank that stockholders of a corporation be made liable, within limits, for the debts of the corporation. In 1888 the Democratic convention adopted a stronger plank on railway regulation and called for an antitrust law. Then, two years later the Democratic candidate for governor, running on a platform calling for the abolishment of the national banking system, free coinage of silver, and a state railway commission, received the endorsement of the alliance. All these proposals were the essence of the alliance. At last, the agrarian reformers had triumphed; they felt that they had captured the Democratic party.

Meanwhile, certain Texans worked hard for reforms in the national government. In Congress, Roger Q. Mills, chairman of the Committee on Ways and Means, proposed a tariff reform measure that was passed in the House of Representatives in 1888 and became the Democratic manifesto in the national campaign of that year. More successful as a national reformer was the veteran John H. Reagan, who, as a member of the Senate in 1887, was coauthor of the Interstate Commerce Act, which marked the beginning of federal regulation of railroads.

Prohibition was another active reform movement of the period. Introduced into Texas in about 1870 were the United Friends of Temperance and its juvenile society, the Bands of Hope, whose members pledged total abstinence from drink and sought to cultivate public sentiment against the liquor traffic. In 1882 the Women's Christian Temperance Union, which grew rapidly in the state, entered the campaign for prohibition with great fervor. Meanwhile, the Grange had declared against the sale of intoxicating liquor, and the Greenback Party had denounced the Democrats for failing to submit the question to the voters. After dodging the issue as long as possible, the legislature submitted to the voters in 1887 an amendment that would replace the local option law of 1876 with state-wide prohibition. With both the prohibitionists and their opponents orga-nized, the campaign was heated and bitter, but the amendment was defeated in the election of August 1887 by a vote of 220,627 to 129,270. For the next 24 years the forces of moral reform could not muster strength enough to force another prohibition election, but they steadfastly refused to allow the issue to die. Meanwhile, reform was accomplished in a variety of other areas.

REFORM TRIUMPHANT: JAMES STEPHEN HOGG

For more than a decade, James Stephen Hogg was instrumental in deter-mining the tone of the Texas government. First elected to state office in 1886 as attorney general in the administration of Lawrence Sullivan Ross, Hogg stood in striking contrast to the conservative governor. Thirty-five years old, son of a Texas statesman and Confederate brigadier, and left an orphan at 12, Hogg had grown to manhood in his native East Texas during the Reconstruction era. He had not passed the intermediate grades when he left Peyton Irving's school in Tyler in 1866. Unaided, he made his way at such jobs as he could secure. Years as a typesetter and printer furnished the background for a sympathetic understanding of the problems of the common people. After serving as prosecuting attorney and spending a few years in private law practice, Hogg was elected attorney general. He real-ized that the dominant question in Texas was the regulation of corpora-tions. On that issue he soon appropriated the center of the political stage and was elected governor in 1890 on a platform promising correction of the abuses of big business.

Men who knew him were never indifferent to Jim Hogg. Corporation lawyers soon learned that he was a dangerous antagonist, and as a stump campaigner he had few equals. He knew the mind of the common man and how to appeal to it with fluent speech and expressive vernacular. News-papers of the opposition charged that his frequent "by gatlings" (his near-est approach to profanity) and the earthy epithets he hurled at his enemies "were offensive to the ladies who honored him with their presence," but the ladies and all others continued to go to hear him. First and last he was a commoner. In the scant shade of a picnic arbor he could hold crowds for hours while he berated the railroads and denounced discrimination against farmers. When the heat became severe he would doff his coat, fling off his suspenders, and periodically gulp water from a pitcher or a bucket. His public record was punctuated with incidents that made good news and kept him ever in the public eye. When the Southern Pacific Railroad in 1894 deliberately stranded 700 marchers of Coxey's Army at a West Texas des-

James S. Hogg earned a reputation as champion of the people's rights when he served as attorney general and governor of Texas during the last quarter of the nineteenth century, the period when big business was being brought under public control. (University of Texas Library)

ert station, a Hogg ultimatum defying the awesome corporate power forced the railroad to convey the men across the state.

After he became attorney general in 1887, Hogg first directed his efforts against certain insurance companies that were operating in unlawful fashion. Attorney General Hogg drove about forty of these from the state and compelled certain others to pay taxes and to obey the laws.

Hogg also contributed to the passage of antitrust measures. There had long been a widespread conviction that monopolies or "trusts" conspired to fix prices and to eliminate competition. Farmers' organizations complained of the "cotton-bagging" trust, there were charges that the packers constituted a "beef combine," and there was much resentment against land corporations. Agitation on the subject in Congress, moreover, inspired legislation on the state level. Hogg assisted in framing the Texas law. Enacted on March 30, 1889, it was the second antitrust law in the nation, preceded by four weeks by a similar law in Kansas. With labor and farm organizations exempted, the law carried heavy penalties against combinations of any kind for the purpose of restricting trade, fixing prices, or limiting production. The law was extended in 1895 to apply to insurance companies, and subsequent changes in 1899, 1903, and 1907 added to the severity and effectiveness of antitrust regulation.

Hogg's greatest efforts were directed toward regulation of the railroads. The article on railroads in the Constitution of 1876 declared railroads to be public highways and common carriers, authorized the legislature to pass laws to "correct abuses, and prevent unjust discrimination and extortion" in rates and fares, required the railroads to maintain offices where their books were to be open to inspection, forbade the consolidation of competing lines, and authorized the legislature to set by law reasonable maximum rates. The power over the railroads reserved by the state was altogether adequate, except that it did not provide for their regulation by a commission. Under its rate-making authority, the legislature in 1879 set the maximum freight rate, and in 1882 passenger fares were reduced from five to three cents per mile. These regulations were not adequate, however, and apparently little effort had been made to enforce some of them prior to Hogg's administration as attorney general. He found various abuses and proceeded against the railroads with such vigor that he was charged with trying to drive capital from the state. He compelled one railroad that had ceased to operate to revive and continue its service. He forced the dissolution of the Texas Traffic Association, a pool through which nine railroads with headquarters outside the state were controlling all Texas lines save one. Through various suits and official actions he reduced the control that certain out-of-state corporations had over the Texas railroads and compelled the Texas railroads to reestablish their general offices in the state.

The best efforts of Attorney General Hogg were not sufficient, however, to secure effective railroad regulation. Realizing this, Hogg worked aggressively while he was attorney general to secure the enactment of a railroad commission law and while he was governor to sustain the power of the commission after it had been established. Since the constitutionality of such a measure was in doubt, the legislature in 1889 gave up the idea of establishing a commission by law and submitted to the voters a constitutional amendment that would settle all questions as to the legality of such an agency.

At once the commission amendment became a leading political issue. An organization of businessmen, known as the State Freight Rate Convention, endorsed it and the Farmers' Alliance favored it. In his campaign for governor in 1890, Hogg championed it with the zeal of a crusader. He showed by a series of comparisons and contrasts how unreasonable certain of the Texas rates were, how lumber, for instance, could be shipped from the East Texas forests to Nebraska more cheaply than to Dallas. The opponents of the commission rallied behind Gustave Cooke of Houston, but the Democratic convention nominated Hogg by an overwhelming vote. The convention also endorsed the railroad commission, and the voters adopted the amendment in the November election.

Acting under the leadership of Hogg, the legislature in April 1891 set up a commission with the power to make classifications and to fix rates and fares. As originally established, the commission was to consist of three members appointed by the governor, but by constitutional amendment, which became effective in 1894, the commission was made elective. John H. Reagan resigned his seat in the United States Senate to accept the chairmanship.

The commission enjoyed a measure of success. It secured the reduction of freight rates and claimed credit for the increase of milling and manufacturing in the state and for saving a million dollars on the shipment of cotton in two seasons. The railroads, however, contending that the rates were confiscatory, brought suits in 1892 to restrain the commission from enforcing its orders, and for nearly two years the commission was impotent. The long fight in the courts ended in victory for the state, and in July 1894 the body again took up the work of rate regulation.

While litigation over rate regulation was under way, the commission acquired additional authority. Realizing that the question of rates was inseparably linked with that of railroad capitalization, Governor Hogg pointed out that the railroads were increasing their obligations on an average of $30 million annually without making any improvements of consequence. Since they would endeavor to maintain rates high enough to pay interest and dividends on this increased capitalization, the increase was, in effect, a charge against the shippers of the state. To correct this evil, the legislature, at Hogg's behest, passed a law in 1893 authorizing the railroad commission to ascertain the value of all property and franchises belonging to each railroad and to regulate and control the issue of securities. The law proved especially effective in enabling the commission to hold down the capitalization of new railroads.

Meanwhile, a bitter political controversy had raged over the railroad commission issue. In the gubernatorial campaign in 1892, the railroads and most leading newspapers supported George Clark of Waco, a railroad attorney. Clark had opposed the commission amendment in 1890 as "wrong in principle, undemocratic and unrepublican"; its only function, he said, was to harass the railroads. Now he accepted the commission as an established fact but insisted that it should be conservative, completely democratic, and elective, and that the law should be liberalized to permit the railroads to appeal to the courts. Hogg defended the commission and attacked his opponent with all of the tactics of the versatile stump speaker that he was. At the famous "Street Car Barn Convention" in Houston in August 1892, the Democrats divided, one group nominating Hogg, the other Clark; and in the autumn the warring factions continued their campaign before the voters. Although one wing of the Republican party supported Clark, Hogg was reelected by a substantial majority.

Other reforms of the Hogg administration, or "Hogg laws" as they were often termed, affected a variety of issues. In response to Governor Hogg's urgent plea, the legislature in 1891 passed a law prohibiting foreigners from owning lands in Texas. The supreme court declared it unconstitutional on a technicality, and in the following year the legislature enacted another alien land law. Another law, which became effective in

1893, prohibited the organization of corporations for the special purpose of dealing in lands and required that such corporations already in existence dispose of their lands within 15 years. All other corporations were required to sell within 15 years all land not necessary to enable them to carry on their business. The law was easily contravened and failed to accomplish its purpose. Otherwise, Hogg promoted prison reform, the establishment of a board of pardon advisors, extension of the school term from four to six months, additional revenue for the University of Texas, and a law forcing railroads to segregate facilities for blacks and whites.

Leaving office in 1895, Hogg spent the final decade of his life amassing a fortune, though he did not abandon his interest in public affairs. His zeal as a reformer perhaps diminished somewhat; indeed, his wealth came in large measure from the interests he had sought as a reformer to control. Nevertheless, the position of James Stephen Hogg as the symbol of Texas reform remained deservedly unshaken.

THE CHALLENGE OF POPULISM

Reforms either promised or accomplished by Governor Hogg and the Democrats quieted for a time criticism from the Farmers' Alliance, but the Democrats did not go far enough to suit the more militant of the agrarian radicals. Government ownership of railroads and similar proposals found little sympathy among Democratic leaders. Governor Hogg even refused to name a leader of the Farmers' Alliance to the newly created railroad commission. Moreover, Hogg and his followers in the Democratic Party refused to endorse the favorite program of the Texas Alliance, a subtreasury plan whereby the general government would make loans to farmers directly, at a nominal rate of interest with farm produce as collateral. In fact, the Democratic leaders in 1891 read out of the party those alliance men who supported the subtreasury plan.

Thus, disenchanted with Hogg and snubbed by the Democrats, the Farmers' Alliance evolved, before the elections of 1892, in effect and purpose into a new third party, the People's or Populist Party. It was organized not only in Texas but in other states as well by similar dissident groups. The People's Party grew rapidly. When the Democratic convention chose Grover Cleveland, the conservative sound-money champion, as its standard bearer in 1892, many of the Democratic faithful were alienated along national lines. The hard times of the early nineties, reinforced by the economic catastrophe of the Panic of 1893, fed the discontent, enlisting thousands of small farmers in the Populist cause. With this formidable strength, the Populists contested each election in Texas for several years, their rivalry with the Democrats at times comparable in bitterness to that of Reconstruction days.

The list of reforms supported by the Populists was lengthy and comprehensive. Some were adopted from earlier reform movements, others from the Democrats, and some were Populist innovations. Demands of the People's Party emphasized government regulation of business, public ownership of railroads, free coinage of silver, abolition of the national banking system, and establishment of the subtreasury system. The Populists supported laws to improve the status of the laborer and to implement a graduated income tax. To further democracy, they advocated direct election of United States Senators and other federal officers, limiting all officeholders to two terms, and the use of referendum and recall. But Texas Populists, perhaps for political expediency, did not take up the cause of women's suffrage and statewide prohibition.

Populism, however, was more than a platform of an organization; it was also an attitude, a crusade, the determined effort of those who felt oppressed to use the machinery of government to ameliorate their miseries. In a very real sense an example of class consciousness in politics, the Populists at times oversimplified their problems and their solutions, but the problems were real and the solutions were not without merit. It was a rural movement; almost half of the leaders in Texas were farmers. Strongest among the poorer farmers of East- and West-Central Texas and among some laboring groups, Populism had little attraction for most business and professional men. Its greatest appeal was to the alienated, to those who felt that they could no longer depend on traditional institutions to protect their interests and to advance their cause.

Basing their program on doctrines of economic and political equality, the Populists struck telling blows at various abuses of the prevailing order. Seventy-five weekly newspapers, among them the *Southern Mercury*, printed in Dallas, carried the gospel of Populism to every part of the state. A corps of stump speakers, led by a few men of superior ability, for example, Thomas L. Nugent, Jerome Kearby, T. P. Gore (who later represented Oklahoma in the United States Senate), and James H. ("Cyclone") Davis, served as ardent evangelists of the new gospel. Many of their leaders were Protestant preachers, who not only appropriated the camp meeting, the hymns, and the religious fervor of the pioneer churches, but took from the Bible many of their utterances and arguments.

As the campaigns became more and more acrimonious, Populists and Democrats resorted to various political tricks. The People's Party made a strong bid for the black voters, many of whom were naturally attracted by doctrines suited to their interests. Leaders of both parties, however, sometimes purchased the services of white and black men who were influential in controlling the black vote and distributed among the black voters many petty bribes. If the Democrats were a little less active and successful in their appeals to the black voter, they were as guilty as the Populists of using corrupt practices to control the Mexican-American vote in South Texas.

Although the Populists did not gain control of the state government, they had some success at the ballot box. The party's maximum strength in the legislature came immediately after the election of 1894, when it had 22 of the 128 members in the lower house and two senators. In the gubernatorial campaign of 1894, Populist Thomas Nugent received nearly one-third of the vote. Two years later Jerome Kearby, aided by the Republicans, threatened Democratic supremacy more seriously than had any candidate since Reconstruction. Kearby polled 238,692 votes to 298,528 for Governor Charles A. Culberson, the Democratic incumbent. More successful in local campaigns, the Populists elected large numbers of county and precinct officers.

After 1896 the Populist party faded quickly from Texas and national politics. With William Jennings Bryan as their standard bearer, the Democrats on the national level had sealed the doom of the third party by appropriating its chief plank, free coinage of silver, and a number of other proposals that the Grange, the Greenback Party, the Farmers' Alliance, and the People's Party had advocated over the years. Moreover, the wave of prosperity that appeared in Texas near the turn of the century did much to silence the voices of discontent.

While successfully meeting the challenge of Populism, the Democratic administration had cautiously perpetuated the reform programs of Governor Hogg. Between 1895 and 1899 Governor Charles Culberson, former attorney general and son of a well-known United States congressman, signed laws regulating primary elections, strengthening antitrust regulations, adding to the authority of the railroad commission, improving the judicial system, setting aside school lands for a black university, and modifying the collection of delinquent taxes. He occasionally thwarted efforts toward corporate consolidation in the state. In a dramatic move he called a special session of the legislature to outlaw prizefighting in Texas. But primarily for fiscal reasons, Culberson vetoed a number of measures, many of them furthering the cause of reform. Neither an enthusiast nor an opponent of reform, his administration thus was a logical transition from the preceding reform-minded regime of Governor Hogg to the relatively conservative era that followed.

REFORM QUIESCENT: SAYERS AND LANHAM

Although the reform impulse was not entirely absent, the years between 1898 and 1906 reflected a noticeable lack of strife and a tone of conservatism. With the Populists fading and the Republicans quarreling, Democratic rule was virtually unchallenged. In the Democratic party much of the tumult usually associated with gubernatorial politics was eliminated by the shrewd and efficient manipulations of Colonel Edward M. House, a well-to-do planter and railroad builder who made politics his avocation and surpassed the professionals in it. A veteran of the electoral wars who had helped reelect Hogg in 1892 and had directed Culberson's campaigns in 1894 and 1896, House skillfully guided the campaigns of governors Joseph Sayers (1899–1903) and Samuel Willis Tucker Lanham (1903–1907). House, unknown to most Texans, was not a leader of a political machine in the usual sense, but relying on careful, thorough organization and the assistance of a few intimate and powerful friends, he exerted a degree of influence without parallel in Texas politics.

In part, the leadership of governors Sayers and Lanham was responsible for the resurgence of conservatism. Both were genteel, high-minded men; both were ex-Confederates, the last to serve as chief executive of the state; and both had rendered their previous public service mainly in Congress. Both brought to the office mature judgment and high idealism but little imagination; by temperament and training, neither was a zealous crusader for change.

But other forces contributed to the decline of progressive fervor. The conservative mood was a natural reaction to the agitation and drive of the Hogg era, and the Spanish-American War diverted the attention of many Texans. Moreover, an attitude more favorable toward business prevailed. Oil discoveries, including the fabulous Spindletop, excited the hopes of Texans and enticed a welcome flow of capital to the state. Other industries, such as the lumbering companies of East Texas, nearing their peak level of production, bolstered the state's economy. Indicating the growing importance of the commercial community, the proportion of farmer members of the legislature declined from about one-half in the early nineties to about one-third after 1900. Political leaders, such as Colonel House, though surely not subservient to corporate interests, nevertheless did not harbor the suspicious convictions about business common among the agrarian rebels of the nineties. Texas remained a rural land, but the industrial age was fast approaching.

Despite the conservative temper of the times, some worthwhile reforms were accomplished. The legislature adopted several laws protecting labor. An 1899 statute exempted organized labor from antitrust regulations; in 1901 the legislature outlawed the use of blacklists to control union organization and the use of company script that could be spent only at company stores. In 1903, laws limiting the hours of railroad employees and requiring certain safety measures on street railways were passed. The same year the first Texas law regulating child labor was adopted. Unfortunately, enforcement of labor laws was often weak and erratic.

A state banking system, prohibited for many years by the Constitution of 1876, was established during the Lanham administration. In 1904 the voters ratified a constitutional amendment permitting the state to charter banks, and the legislature of the following year established a commission of insurance and banking. Directed by Thomas M. Love, a native of Missouri and a progressive politician of Dallas, the commission supervised the chartering of more than 500 banks during the next five years.

Tax reform, sought unsuccessfully during the Sayers administration, was partially accomplished in the second Lanham term. The general property tax had provided the greater part of the state's revenue, and valuations had not kept pace with the increasing demands. Railroad properties, for example, were evidently undervalued; the greater portion of intangible properties escaped taxation. In response to Governor Lanham's request, the legislature in 1905 raised taxes on intangible assets of railroads and certain other industries. Laws providing for franchise taxes and levies on gross receipts of express companies, sleeping-car companies, pipelines, and similar concerns also were adopted.

Guided by a peculiar mixture of progressive and reactionary goals, the legislature reorganized the state's election system. Prior to 1903, party candidates in some counties were nominated by primaries and in others by conventions. In either case, abuses were widespread. Unscrupulous party officials sometimes failed to give adequate notice of impending conventions; occasionally the meetings were at places and under conditions that made it impossible or impractical for the rank and file of voters to attend. Relying on proxies and other devices, corporation attorneys and other special interests wielded an undue influence. Dates of party primaries were sometimes manipulated to the advantage of particular candidates; ballot-box frauds were common.

There were many abuses in the primary and general elections. Although the constitution authorized the legislature to provide for punishing fraud and preserving the integrity of the ballot, little had been done to eliminate such practices as the purchase of votes, extravagant campaign expenditures, and dishonest election returns. In 1895 the legislature passed a law that regulated primary elections in those counties where they were held, but it was inadequate. The law was changed in 1897 and again two years later, but it did not attack the abuses prevalent in that day. Registration of voters was assured, however, by the constitutional amendment adopted in 1902, which made a poll tax receipt or exemption certificate mandatory for voting.

During the Lanham years the legislature took hold of the problem in earnest. Two laws, named after Judge Alexander W. Terrell, their author, affected both primaries and general elections. The first became effective in 1903, and the second, repealing the first and passed in 1905, constitutes the foundation of Texas election laws to this day. The first law did not make the primary election mandatory, but permitted a political party to determine for itself whether it would nominate its candidates by a primary or a convention. The most important features of the second and more comprehensive law may be stated thus:

(1) It set forth in great detail who would be permitted to vote both in primary and general elections;

(2) It required candidates to file within ten days after a primary or general election itemized statements of expenditures;

(3) It made mandatory a primary for parties that polled at the last general election 100,000 or more votes (the Democratic party);

(4) It set forth detailed regulations for the governance of parties and required that primaries be held on the fourth Saturday in July;

(5) It provided that county and precinct nominees be determined by the results of the primary, but that the county committee might call a second primary, the voters to make their choice from the two leading candidates;

(6) It required that nominees for state and district offices still be chosen by conventions.

Subsequent legislation modified these rules. In 1907 a law required that, in all cases, the candidate receiving the highest number of votes be declared the nominee. Thus, the primary election had come to be the nominating agency; party conventions were mere canvassing bodies. A 1913 law provided for a second primary in which the voters would select one of the two candidates receiving the most votes, if no candidate for the United States Senate received a majority in the first contest. In 1918 this provision was extended to all state and district contests and made optional in county races.

Although the electoral reforms made at the turn of the century eliminated many abuses, the changes, in some respects, were made at the expense of democracy. The poll tax discouraged poor people of all kinds from voting, but blacks generally fared worse than others. Inspired by a long-standing fear of black suffrage, which was reinforced by the events of the Populist years and the rising tide of racial antagonism prevalent near the end of the century, white politicians deliberately sought to eliminate the black voter from politics. By the early 1900s most Democratic primaries, which were usually tantamount to elections, were open only to white voters. For the next several decades, blacks would be denied an effective voice in the politics of the state. Not until the Supreme Court of the United States in 1944 ruled white primaries unconstitutional and in 1966 the poll tax unconstitutional was the black voter assured of his or her place at the polls. Progressive electoral reform, indeed, progressive reforms in general, did little to improve the lives of black people.

Public welfare services and education, which perhaps needed improvement even more than the electoral system, received some attention during the Sayers and Lanham years. Limited improvements were made in education. The Pasteur Institute for the prevention of rabies was organized in 1903, and the Abilene State Hospital for epileptics began receiving patients in 1904.

During this period the state continued its war against the trusts. More stringent antitrust acts were passed in 1899 and 1903, and state attorneys successfully prosecuted a number of violators. Indeed, the Texas antitrust policy was more severe than that of the federal government. Of the 110 prosecutions brought under the Texas statutes up to 1915, 84 were settled by compromise with penalties exacted in 74, totaling $3,324,766. In comparison, federal antitrust laws in effect during about the same period of time brought 187 prosecutions with fines or penalties in 33 cases, amounting to only $548,881.

The most famous Texas antitrust case involved the Waters-Pierce Oil Company, a Missouri corporation with Standard Oil affiliations. In 1897 the attorney general brought suit for violations of the Texas antitrust act. A verdict revoking the firm's permit to do business in the state was upheld by the United States Supreme Court in 1900. Then, claiming that it had reorganized and had severed all ties with the Standard Oil combine, the company secured a new Texas license, though not without the objections of some Texans such as Jim Hogg, who questioned the sincerity of the Waters-Pierce officials. Subsequently, a suit brought by the state of Missouri in 1905 revealed that a majority of the stock of the company, though registered in the name of an individual, actually belonged to the Standard Oil Company. Acting quickly, the state of Texas sought and obtained a judgment for ouster and penalties of $1,623,900. When the decision was affirmed by the court of last resort, the corporation paid a fine amounting to $1,808,483.30, the largest ever collected by the state, and the properties of the firm were sold at auction.

Meanwhile, the case had provoked an even greater controversy— Baileyism. While a candidate for the United States Senate in 1900, Congressman Joseph Weldon Bailey, ignoring the possible conflict of interest, urged Governor Sayers and the state attorney general to allow Waters-Pierce to return to the state. Though he did not receive a fee for this service, he was employed by Henry Clay Pierce in other matters. Furthermore, he had borrowed $5,000 dollars from Pierce, who, unknown to Bailey, had placed the note on company records.

Almost immediately some questioned the propriety of Bailey's intervention, but not until new investigations in 1905 and 1906 publicly disclosed the relationship between the senator and the oilman did the state divide into angry camps of pro- and anti-Bailey men. Though Bailey was unopposed for reelection in the Democratic primary of 1906, critics argued that the legislature should ignore the primary and refuse to return him to the Senate. Bailey, in response, contended that the whole affair was a conspiracy to deprive the nation of his great services.

By a vote of 108 to 39, the legislature reelected the senator, but meanwhile, a legislative investigating committee was studying the ethics of the colorful figure. The Texas senate, taking the affair out of the hands of its committee, quickly exonerated him, but the house committee was divided in its report. Not satisfied with this victory, Senator Bailey announced that he would make the selection of the Texas delegation to the Democratic National Convention in 1908 a test of his strength; none but Bailey men would go to the convention. Both the Bailey and the anti-Bailey forces waged a contest with heat and rancor that has rarely been equaled in the annals of Texas politics. By an overwhelming vote Bailey and his slate of delegates won. Nevertheless, differences still rankled, and no doubt the controversy would have flared up again in 1912 if Bailey had not voluntarily retired to private life.

THE REVIVAL OF REFORM: THOMAS M. CAMPBELL

A definite swing away from conservatism was apparent in the gubernatorial contest of 1906. For the first time in more than a decade, Colonel House refused an active role in the contest, and none of the candidates had a decided advantage. Each of the four major contenders favored a war on the trusts, an antilobby law, tax reform, and generous support for the state's institutions. Emerging the victor from a rather evenly divided race was a lawyer from Palestine, Thomas M. Campbell. Generally regarded as the most progressive of the candidates, Campbell had the endorsement of ex-Governor Hogg, who had voiced repeatedly his dissatisfaction with the attitude of the Sayers and Lanham administration toward big business, and the last-minute support of Senator Bailey. Armed with the support of farmers, labor, and various others, Campbell energetically promoted tax reform, insurance regulation, improvements in education, additional laws protecting labor, and a number of other changes. Though sentiment for reform declined in his second term and he was unable to perpetuate the control of progressives beyond his own administration, nonetheless in large measure he justified the confidence of Hogg.

Powerful interest groups contributed to the vigorous program of reform. The State Federation of Labor, which met for the first time in 1898, claimed 158 unions and more than 9,000 members by 1906. The Farmers' Union, organized in 1902, claimed 100,000 members by 1906. Sometimes working together, these organizations lobbied for laws protecting workers, for compulsory school attendance, for free textbooks, and for laws against child and convict labor. The Texas Federation of Women's Clubs, with 5,000 members, worked hard on behalf of better schools, pure food and drug laws, improved legal rights for Texas women, and more libraries.

Tax reform, begun under Lanham, continued in the Campbell years. Most important was a 1907 "full rendition law" requiring that property be rendered for taxation at its "reasonable cash market value." This law also created an automatic tax board consisting, as amended in 1909, of the governor, comptroller, and treasurer, and gave to the board the power to set the tax rate for general revenue and school purposes within the constitutional limits. The full rendition law very nearly doubled the value of property on the tax rolls, but it also provoked anguished protests, not only from corporate interests but also from land-owning farmers.

Other aspects of Campbell's fiscal program were similarly somewhat controversial. The governor's plea for an income tax had little success; he did obtain a light inheritance tax, but it produced more complaints than revenue. In the interest of economy he vetoed appropriations in 1909 to the amount of $1.7 million; some items were for badly needed improvements. At the end of his administration, the automatic tax board lowered the tax rate to an unrealistic level, leaving a deficit of nearly a million dollars for the next governor. Moreover, it should be noted that the laws of the Lanham and Campbell period did not shift the tax burden extensively. The general property tax continued to produce the greater part of the state's operating revenue, and real estate continued to bear approximately two-thirds of the tax burden placed on property. Not until the coming of the automobile and the development of the oil industry did Texas succeed in placing a larger share of the burden on natural resources and on the production and exchange of goods.

Regulation of insurance companies was a signal accomplishment. Comprehensive codes for life, health, accident, home, and fire insurance were adopted. Furthermore, the Robertson Insurance Law, enacted in 1907, required life insurance companies to invest in Texas securities at least 75 percent of their reserves set aside for insurance policies on the lives of Texas citizens. When they failed to defeat the bill, 21 insurance companies withdrew from the state, contending that its requirements were harsh and unreasonable. As a matter of fact, other states had similar requirements; furthermore, of the $40 million in reserves held by the companies, less than $1 million had been invested in Texas. Some of the companies returned after the commissioner of insurance and banking modified certain regulations. Others continued with great persistence to work for the repeal or the modification of the law, but it was not repealed until 1963.

In a related area, in 1909 the state established an insurance program protecting funds deposited in state banks. A few bank failures during the panic of 1907 had centered public attention on the need of greater protection for small depositors. For a number of years the plan worked quite successfully, but numerous failures in the early 1920s put a heavy strain on the system, and it was abolished in 1927.

Reforms in municipal government, a prominent feature of progressive change elsewhere, were most noticeable during the Campbell administration. The commission system of government, first used in Galveston in 1901, was encouraged by the governor, who approved 13 city charters containing the plan. Although demands for similar practices on the state level accomplished nothing, practically every city charter issued under Campbell provided for more direct democracy through the use of the initiative, referendum, and recall.

A number of other progressive measures were adopted. Campbell, who had consistently advocated greater regulation of corporations, signed a law in 1907 strengthening antitrust restrictions. Several laws improving conditions for labor were passed, and the legislature created the state medical board and the state board of health. Significant improvements, particularly in the area of financing, were made in education. Campbell also approved laws giving towns of populations of 2,000 or more power to regulate utilities, restrict free passes by railroads, promote pure food, and prohibit nepotism in state administration, as well as laws against lobbying and several acts for the improvement of roads.

Prison reform was the last major change of the Campbell administration. Texas prisons had long been a problem, in many respects a disgrace. In 1871 Texas tried the prison-lease system, under which the state leased the penitentiary to private individuals. The lessees were to employ the convicts in any way they wished, subject only to the mandates of state inspectors, who were supposed to see that the prisoners were not abused and that the prison property was not damaged. This was perhaps the worst system practiced in modern times. The death rate of convicts doubled, and the number of escapes per year more than tripled. The lease was terminated in 1876, but the lease system was not abolished until 1883.

In 1883 the state completed a new prison at Rusk and adopted a new plan for administering the penal system. Known as the contract-lease system, it was better than the old lease plan but far from satisfactory. Under the new arrangement the state retained control of the prison and prisoners, but leased to private operators the shops within the penitentiary walls and also hired out gangs of convicts to railroad construction foremen, planters, and others. The Huntsville industries were not successful, and an iron industry at the Rusk prison proved to be a white elephant. Meanwhile, intelligent people were coming to realize that as long as the labor of convicts was used to promote the interests of private capitalists, abuses would exist. Thus, the Texas prison system began operating its own farms, without plan or design, but prison farming would present its own set of problems. Complaints about prison conditions were heard from time to time, but no significant action was taken for many years.

Spurred by a series of newspaper articles in 1908 and 1909 and charges made in the gubernatorial campaign of 1910, Campbell called a special session of the legislature after the election. An investigating committee of state senators and representatives had found conditions in the state penal system intolerable. Convicts had been shot or whipped to death for trivial offenses; women prisoners had been abused; and the sanitation was abominable. The financial affairs of the system were in such confusion that it was impossible to audit the books.

Acting on the recommendation of the committee, the legislature abolished the contract-lease system whereby the services of convicts were sold to different private employers. Management of the system was placed under the direction of three commissioners appointed by the governor. Stripes were to be abolished except for the worst class of prisoners, sanitation and medical service improved, and each convict paid ten cents a day for his or her labor.

With the close of the Campbell administration shortly after the enactment of these prison reforms, the progressive movement in Texas was, in many respects, nearing an end. Prohibition, absorbing much of the energy of Texans after 1908, would dominate the election of 1910 and political affairs for sometime thereafter. But the progressives in countless ways had already turned the services of government to the benefit of the many rather than the few. In Texas, as elsewhere, they had not succeeded in every instance in their quest of reform. Despite the laws calling for corporate regulation, giant corporations would grow larger and more powerful. Nevertheless, the more obvious abuses had been eliminated, and the most pressing needs had been met.

SELECTED BIBLIOGRAPHY

General studies dealing with these years are Alwyn Barr, *Reconstruction to Reform: Texas Politics, 1876–1906;* S. Acheson, *35,000 Days in Texas;* B. M. Jones, *Search for Maturity;* and S. S. McKay, and O. B. Faulk, *Texas after Spindletop.*

Very useful are the biographies of figures active in the era. For James S. Hogg, see Robert C. Cotner (ed.), *Addresses and State Papers of James Stephen Hogg* (Austin, 1951) and *James Stephen Hogg, A Biography* (Austin, 1959); and H. P. Gambrell, "James Stephen Hogg; Statesman or Demagogue?" *Southwest Review,* XIII, 338–366. See also B. H. Proctor, *Not without Honor: The Life of John H. Reagan;* C. Nugent, *Life Work of Thomas L. Nugent* (Stephenville, Tex., 1896); Wayne Alvord, "T. L. Nugent, Texas Populist," *Southwestern Historical Quarterly,* LVII, 65–81; S. Acheson, *Joe Bailey: The Last Democrat* (New York, 1932); R. N. Richardson, *Colonel Edward M. House: The Texas Years, 1858–1912* (Abilene, 1964); Janet Schmelzer, "Thomas M. Campbell: Progressive Governor of Texas," *Red River Valley Historical Review,* III, 52–64; and Pollyana B. Hughes and Elizabeth B. Harrison, "Charles A. Culberson: Not a Shadow of Hogg," *East Texas Historical Journal,* XI, 41–52.

Concerning reforms, on railroad regulation there are M. M. Crane, "Recollections of the Establishment of the Texas Railroad Commission," *Southwestern Historical Quarterly,* L, 478–486; Robert L. Peterson, "Jay Gould and the Railroad Commission of Texas," *ibid.,* LVIII, 422–432; and J. R. Norvell, "The Railroad Commission of Texas: Its Origin and History," *ibid.,* LXVIII, 465–480. The standard work on trust legislation is Tom Finty, Jr., *Anti-trust Legislation in Texas* (Dallas and Galveston, Tex., 1916). See also O. D. Weeks, "The Texas Direct

Primary System," *Southwestern Social Science Quarterly, XIII, 95–120; E. T. Miller, A Financial History of Texas:* and *The Report of the Prisons Investigating Committee* [first special session of the Thirty-third Legislature] (Austin, 1910). Difficult to classify but a reminder that Texans were concerned about things other than politics and economics is Charles Carver, *Brann the Iconoclast* (Austin, 1957). For reforms in local government, see Bradley R. Rice, "The Galveston Plan of City Government by Commission: The Birth of a Progressive Idea," *Southwestern Historical Quarterly,* LXVIII, 365–408; and Paul E. Isaac, "Municipal Reform in Beaumont, Texas 1902–1909," *ibid.,* LXVIII, 409–430. There is a historical sketch of the Texas penitentiaries by Carl Rosenquist in the *Handbook of Texas,* II, 411–413. See also C. S. Potts, "The Convict Labor System in Texas," *Annals of the American Academy of Political and Social Science,* XXI.

On politics and political parties, see Roscoe C. Martin, *The People's Party in Texas* (Austin, 1933); Ralph Smith, "The Farmers Alliance in Texas," *Southwestern Historical Quarterly,* XLVIII, 346–369; E. W. Winkler, *Platforms of Political Parties in Texas;* and S. S. McKay, *Texas Politics, 1906–1944* (Lubbock, 1952). A number of studies in recent years have examined the role of the farmer. See Lawrence Goodwyn, *Democratic Promise: The Populist Movement in America* (New York, 1976); Robert C. McMath, Jr., *Populist Vanguard: A History of the Southern Farmers Alliance* (Chapel Hill, N.C., 1975); James R. Green, *Grass-roots Socialism: Radical Movements in the Southwest, 1895–1943* (Baton Rouge, 1978) and "Tenant Farmer Discontent and Socialist Protest in Texas, 1901–1917," *Southwestern Historical Quarterly,* LXXXI, 133–154; Graham Adams, Jr., "Agrarian Discontent in Progressive Texas," *East Texas Historical Journal,* VIII, 24–28; Robert Saunders, "Southern Populists and the Negro, 1893–1895," *Journal of Negro History,* LIV, 240–261; Evan Anders, *Boss Rule in South Texas: The Progressive Era* (Austin, 1982); "Boss Rule and Constituent Interests: South Texas Politics During the Progressive Era," *Southwestern Historical Quarterly,* LXXXIV, 269–292; and "The Origins of the Parr Machine in Duval County, Texas," LXXXV, 119–138.

Particularly valuable is a number of manuscripts in various libraries. Bob Holcomb's study of Joe Bailey is in the library of Texas Tech University, and in the library of the University of Wisconsin is James Tinsley's work on the Progressive movement in Texas. In the University of Texas library are Charles Chamberlain, on A. W. Terrell; George P. Huckaby, on Oscar B. Colquitt; R. L. Peterson, on the Railroad Commission; R. L. Wagner, on Charles Culberson; and H. L. Crow, on the Texas penal system.

CHAPTER FIFTEEN
LIFE AT THE TURN
OF THE CENTURY

Life in the twentieth century began with tragedy for Texas when the century opened with a massive hurricane. With the storm came death and destruction, but otherwise the picture of the state was one of progress. More than three million people made their home in Texas in 1900. The number had increased fivefold since the Civil War, and an added indication of the growth of the state was the fact that slightly more than one-fourth of the population had been born in other states. Almost 200,000 had been born in foreign countries; large non-Anglo cultural groups included blacks, Mexican-Americans, and Germans, and there were a number of other cultural backgrounds represented.

Lifestyles reflected not only the diverse cultural backgrounds but also a rapidly changing pattern of living. For decades Texans had depended primarily on the land for their living and most still did in 1900. Cities were growing, however, and the effects of industrialization were noticeable, particularly in the cities, and in rural Texas as well. On the other hand, the literature and art tended to reflect the past, especially the more heroic and romantic past.

THE GALVESTON FLOOD

Texans experienced a tragic natural disaster in the first year of the twentieth century. In a day before adequate warning devices were available, a gigantic tropical hurricane swept inland over Galveston Island on September 8, 1900. The magnitude of the storm and the destruction it brought almost defied description. The storm raged for more than 12 hours, with winds of more than 120 miles per hour and tidal waves that completely covered the land. No completely accurate count of the fatalities was ever made, but estimates of 6,000 were commonly heard and many placed the count much higher. When the waters receded, the city was in ruins, with thousands of people left homeless.

Galvestonians were determined to rebuild. The Red Cross provided first aid and emergency care for the survivors. From throughout Texas and the nation people sent food and supplies, and the state government allowed the city to retain taxes for use in rebuilding and organized committees to raise money for supplies. But it was the determination of the people of Galveston that was most important in rebuilding the city. Within a short time they had reorganized their city government, and within five years they had built a sea wall on the Gulf side of the island. The wall, 17 feet high and more than 7 miles long, successfully protected the city from storms that struck in 1909, 1915, and 1961.

LIFE ON THE FARMS AND IN THE TOWNS

Approximately 80 percent of the population lived in rural areas in 1900, with about six out of every ten workers directly involved in agriculture. Horses and mules still provided most of the power; the age of the tractor would not come until the 1920s. But here and there were seen huge steam tractors, and threshing machines, reapers, and new types of plows and riding cultivators were commonplace.

Work patterns on farms had changed little from pioneer days. The farm family was a relatively tight, cohesive unit, and all shared in the work. Daylight to dark was the schedule, with some planting, plowing, and cultivating, while others chopped weeds and tended the livestock. Harvest season demanded the efforts of everyone; many youngsters could not attend school until the cotton crop was at the gin.

In the towns, work schedules were not usually as demanding. Family income in urban areas generally was provided by a business or by the employment of the father, though employment of women was becoming more and more common. In smaller communities where opportunities were available, young people living in towns found summer jobs on nearby farms.

Living conveniences were a mixture of old and new. Farm homes were usually small, warmed by fireplaces or iron heaters with coal or wood cookstoves and kerosene lamps for light. City homes ranged from the simple to the elegant, but often offered little more in the way of conveniences than did the farm homes. Although gas and electricity were available in the larger cities before 1900, many homes had neither, depending on ice deliveries for food refrigeration or doing without. The revolution in living conditions produced by electricity was not widespread until the 1920s.

Nevertheless, before the turn of the century the services and conveniences associated with urban life were available in the Texas cities. By 1900 all cities had telephone exchanges, and practically all were linked by telegraph systems. The electric light and power industry was not quite as advanced. Galveston had a power plant in the early 1880s and other cities soon had electric service, but the power these plants generated was insignificant in comparison with the output of our own day. The production of power was a local industry until about 1913, when the Texas Power and Light Company constructed a transmission line from Waco to Fort Worth and Dallas. Soon various small concerns were consolidated, and outlying communities were supplied by high-voltage transmission lines radiating from huge plants.

Travel was slow and difficult for both rural and urban Texans at the turn of the century, though the period was one of transition, and transportation methods were improving. Long-distance travel by railroad was relatively comfortable and safe, but most travel was for short distances for which railroads were either unavailable or impractical. For many families, wagons and buggies were the only choice. There were no paved roads and few bridges; the roads were poorly kept, dusty in dry weather and muddy in wet. A twenty-mile journey required the better part of a day.

In the cities, street construction and maintenance were major problems. Large cities by the end of the century had begun paving the main thoroughfares; Houston, for example, had paved 26 miles. Brick was commonly used, though other materials, even wood, were also tried. Streetcars and trolleys powered by electricity appeared by 1890 and were available in the larger cities by 1900.

Two other new inventions hailed the opening years of the twentieth century. In about 1900 the first automobiles were seen in Texas, and the success of the machines was apparent within a short time. Houston was the home of 80 automobiles by 1905 and had already experienced a fatal automobile accident. The state recognized the automobile in 1907 with the adoption of an 18 mile-per-hour speed limit. Airplanes attracted attention by 1910, but mostly as a curiosity. Air shows demonstrated the machines in

San Antonio and Houston and eventually in most other cities, but airplanes were rare until World War I introduced military aviation to the state.

URBANIZATION

Although most Texans still lived in rural areas at the turn of the century, city life was becoming more common. In 1870 only 6.7 percent of the people lived in incorporated urban areas with a population of 2,500 or more. By 1900, urban incorporated centers contained 17.1 percent of the population. The appearance of urban centers is even more impressive when the growth of individual cities is considered. In 1870, only two towns, Galveston with a population of 13,818 and San Antonio with 12,256, contained more than 10,000 people. Houston counted slightly more than 9,000; Dallas had an estimated 3,000; and Fort Worth was a village of about 500. By 1900, 11 towns claimed more than 10,000 people. San Antonio was the largest city with 53,321, followed by Houston, Dallas, Galveston, and Fort Worth.

Other factors were involved, but transportation facilities accounted for much of the growth of these population islands before 1900. Houston, Dallas, and Fort Worth exploited their strategic locations in the railroad

Parker County Courthouse, Weatherford. Such structures, built near the turn of the twentieth century, generally on the town square, added a touch of elegance to many Texas county seats and represent rather well the preferred architectural style for the public buildings of that period.

network to become leading market centers. Similarly, cities that lost their advantage in the transportation system either grew slowly, remained stagnant, or declined. Jefferson, once connected to the sea by way of Caddo Lake and the Red River, was a busy port town of more than 4,000 in 1870. When clearing debris reduced the level of the lake to a point at which commercial navigation could not be sustained and railroads opened up competitive markets elsewhere, Jefferson's population declined by more than one-fourth.

Oil brought spectacular growth after the turn of the century. Beaumont, a sleepy lumber town of 9,000 people, grew to more than 50,000 within a few months after the discovery of oil at Spindletop a few miles to the south. Often such population growth was only temporary, housed in tent cities and troubled by lawlessness and disease, but oil and related industries promised a more permanent impact on the lives of twentieth-century Texans.

OIL AND THE EMERGENCE OF AN INDUSTRIAL ECONOMY

Until 1901 oil did not play a major role in the Texas economy or lifestyle. Commercial oil production and exploration increased considerably in the 1890s, with Corsicana in Navarro County as the site of most of the activity. By 1898 there were more than 300 wells in the Corsicana field and an operating refinery, but the wells were small and the project attracted little national interest.

The discovery of oil on January 10, 1901, on Spindletop Hill south of Beaumont was a different matter. The well, drilled by Captain Anthony F. Lucas, began spewing oil more than 100 feet in the air. Before it was finally capped, the gusher roared out with nearly one-half million barrels of oil, and a new age in Texas was at hand. At least two giant oil companies and many smaller ones were born out of the profits of the Spindletop boom; oilmen began to search for discoveries in other parts of the state; and refining and marketing operations were soon providing jobs and profits for Texans.

More discoveries came quickly. By 1903 there were fields opened at Sour Lake, Saratoga, and Batson. The following year oilmen discovered a large field north of Houston in the community of Humble. Meanwhile, the first fields were opened near Wichita Falls in North Texas, and by 1912 the search for oil had moved into North-Central Texas.

Closely associated with oil production was that of natural gas. Corsicana and Marshall were the first towns to secure natural gas distribution systems. In 1910 a pipeline was completed to supply Fort Worth and Dallas. Various other towns and cities secured this service during the next 15 years, though the gas companies encountered many difficulties, chief of which was that of securing a dependable supply of gas.

Also allied with oil production were the refining and manufacturing of various petroleum products. The first refineries were small, crude units built in the 1890s, but major companies began constructing large operations soon after the discovery of Spindletop. By 1919 there were 43 refineries in the state.

In the oil industry, as well as in other Texas industries, there was a trend toward consolidation evident by the turn of the century. In some respects the early Texas oil booms in the twentieth century challenged the near-monopoly held elsewhere by the Standard Oil combination. But out of Spindletop and subsequent discoveries came similar gigantic oil companies such as Gulf, Texaco, Exxon, and Mobil. Big business in Texas, however, was not just limited to big oil companies. In the last decades of the nineteenth century, the number of flour mills declined by about 50 percent, but production increased about sixfold. Like the grasslands of West Texas, the timberlands of East Texas came to be owned by comparatively few people. After 1879 timberlands (which had been set aside for the schools) could be bought in small quantities at five dollars an acre. Soon capitalists of vision, among them H. J. Lutcher, G. B. Moore, and John H. Kirby, made heavy investments that later brought them large fortunes. The Kirby Lumber Company, chartered in 1901 as the first multimillion-dollar industrial corporation in the state, dominated the lumber business from its formation.

LEISURE-TIME LIVING

Even when survival was more uncertain, Texans found opportunities for amusement and entertainment, and these opportunities became more frequent as Texas entered the twentieth century. Visiting with neighbors remained an important social activity, especially on Sunday afternoons. Church socials, the general store, cotton gin offices, sewing circles, and community parties provided many occasions for people to meet and relax together. Children were often a part of these affairs, taking advantage of them to play marbles, various ball games, and other games. Dancing, one of the most important social diversions throughout the nineteenth century, declined somewhat, primarily because many church groups strongly opposed it.

Holidays were important, especially the Fourth of July and Christmas. Texans often celebrated the Fourth with community picnics and parties, but Christmas was more of an occasion for family gatherings. Among black people, June 19 was a day for celebrating their emancipation from slavery, and Mexican-Americans celebrated two national holidays of Mexico, Cinco de Mayo and Diez y Seis de Septiembre. Less often celebrated, but not entirely ignored, were Thanksgiving and Easter.

Sports, though not nearly as important to the culture as they would become later in the twentieth century, were popular. Horse racing, the most popular sport throughout the nineteenth century, continued to attract large crowds. In 1887 the Texas League of Professional Baseball Clubs was organized, and in the 1890s Texas schoolboys began to play football. A Galveston dock hand, Jack Johnson, won the heavyweight boxing championship of the world in 1908 and held the title until 1915.

Music, theater, and shows provided diversions for many. Sometimes local talent put on the plays or shows, but there were many traveling groups, some with national reputations. At one time or another there appeared on Texas billboards the name of almost every distinguished actor or actress who played in the United States during the late nineteenth and the early twentieth centuries. Among these were Joseph Jefferson, noted for his portrayal of Rip Van Winkle; Edwin Booth, renowned Shakespearean actor; and Sarah Bernhardt, the greatest actress of her generation. Others were Richard Mansfield, Maude Adams, and Ethel Barrymore. Larger towns and many of the smaller ones built theaters for the performing arts in which operas, plays, concerts, and minstrel shows were performed on a more or less regular basis. An opera house was opened in Galveston in 1871, one in Dallas two years after, and others soon followed. Many communities organized bands, some had singing societies; and in Mexican-American communities there were often string orchestras. The traveling circus was a popular show of the time, and in Texas it was the Mollie Bailey Circus. Replete with tigers and elephants, acrobats and clowns, the circus of Mollie Bailey began its tour of Texas about 1880 and lasted for nearly thirty years. Shortly after the turn of the new century, motion pictures were shown in Texas for the first time. The event attracted statewide attention and interest, but Texans would not attend the movies in large numbers on a regular basis until the 1920s.

HEALTH AND MEDICAL CARE

Disease was a dreaded and frequent occurrence in Texas homes at the turn of the century. Cholera, typhoid, diptheria, and occasionally smallpox epidemics swept the state from time to time. Malaria was common along the coast, and yellow fever was not unknown. Children's diseases, such as measles, whooping cough, mumps, and chicken pox afflicted most families sooner or later.

Professional medical care was limited and often not particularly good. Physicians were few in number and only large towns had hospitals. For a time the state suffered from an abundance of "quack" medical schools that offered quick but poor and improper training. The Medical Association of Texas, organized in 1853, became more active near the end of the century and made the establishment of standards for the training of physicians one of its primary goals. Toward the end of the century, medical care improved somewhat. By 1900 there were several competent medical schools, the best-known of these being the University of Texas Medical School located in Galveston.

Texans often relied on their own resources when disease struck. Neighborhood women, in particular, acted as midwives and sometimes treated the sick. Few of them had formal medical training, but in many instances there was no other care available. Mexican-Americans often turned to a curandero when confronted with illness. Curanderos, who used herbs and folk medicine in their treatments, were generally given high respect in their communities, and some attracted patients from distant parts of the country. Home remedies were the favorite approach of many families. In the spring, a mixture of sassafras tea, sulfur, and molasses paved the way for a healthy year. Castor oil, quinine, and calomel were also frequently used as home medicines.

RELIGION

By the turn of the century, religion in Texas had changed somewhat from what it was at mid-century. At the time of the Civil War, the Methodist church, with more than 400 churches and more than 30,000 members, was easily the largest denomination in the state. The Baptists, who claimed more than 500 congregations but fewer members than the Methodists, were second, and the Presbyterians, Disciples of Christ, Episcopalians, and Catholics were all considerably smaller in number. By 1906, Baptists, with about 33 percent of the state's church-going public, had surpassed the Methodists who now accounted for about 27 percent. Catholics, armed with large numbers of German, Polish, Czechoslavakian, and Mexican immigrants, were not far behind, while the Disciples of Christ, Presbyterians, Lutherans, Episcopalians, and a number of smaller denominations accounted for the remainder.

Black people were responsible for much of the growth of the Baptists. Although there was some debate among white Baptists over whether to accept blacks as members of predominantly white churches, black Baptists for the most part ignored the controversy and proceeded to organize black churches. After the first black Baptist church was organized in Galveston in 1865, others quickly followed. By 1890 there were 111,138 black Baptists, while black Methodists numbered only 42,214.

Whether black or white, Baptist or Methodist, or in some instances, other denominations, Texas churches were active in many issues at the time of turn of the century. The prohibition movement, long-present but growing in intensity, was a major concern. A prominent churchman, who proclaimed in 1900 that the tavern was "greatest curse" of the nation, expressed the views of many Texans. The success of the prohibitionists in the next two decades would be due to a considerable degree to the efforts of Baptists, Methodists, and certain other denominations. Horse racing and, to some extent dancing, also came under church scrutiny and disfavor, and where sentiment was strong, they either disappeared altogether or were severely curtailed as community activities.

Not all religious groups held such views. In parts of the state where German, Czech, Polish, and Mexican heritage was strong, sentiment for prohibition was almost nonexistent, and dancing and horse racing encountered little criticism. Often these groups were Catholic in their religious affiliation, but there were smaller denominations that held similar views. Inasmuch as these issues were frequently debated in the context of morality, the conflict between supporters and opponents often took the form of religious controversy as well as secular arguments. Nevertheless, the role of religion in Texas culture at the turn of the century was strong, perhaps stronger than it had ever been.

EDUCATION

As Texans entered the final quarter of the nineteenth century, they organized their first public high school, but the state still did not have a public school system worthy of the name. Land was set aside for support of public education during the Republic and early statehood, but few schools were established and no system was created. During Reconstruction the Republican government created a system, potentially well-supported, but most of this effort was undone by the Constitution of 1876. At the same time, the legislature in 1876 adopted a "community school system" that had no boundaries, no means of acquiring and controlling property, and no assurance that it would be continued from one year to the next. It was, in fact, no system at all. Governor O. M. Robert's veto of the school appropriation bill in 1879 reduced the meager expenditures authorized by the constitution even more.

Public sentiment in the 1880s, however, demanded that the schools of Texas be given a more predictable share of public revenues, a necessary move before a public school system could be assured. Among the leaders who promoted an interest in public education were O. N. Hollingsworth, secretary of the state board of education, who initiated *The Texas Journal of Education*; Dr. Ashbel Smith, a friend of education since the days of Mirabeau B. Lamar; R. C. Burleson, president of Waco University; and William Carey Crane, president of Baylor University. Their efforts were evident in a constitutional amendment adopted in 1883 during the Ireland administration that provided for a limited amount of support from the state and allowed district voters to vote a small local tax.

The following year witnessed the complete rewriting of the school law and a major step toward the development of a true public school system. The law of 1884 provided for an elective state superintendent of instruction and placed schools under the immediate supervision of county judges. It provided that most counties should be divided into school districts with the privilege of voting local taxes. It extended the scholastic age to include the years from 8 through 16; it required that teachers hold certificates; and it prescribed a system of registers and reports.

Progress under the new system was slow. Immigration and a high birth rate caused the scholastic population to increase more rapidly than the available school fund. The law of 1884 tended to place a significant part of the responsibility for supporting public schools on local taxes, and the people were frequently indisposed to vote local school taxes. Thus, country schools remained poor and inefficient, with improvement confined largely to the cities and towns.

More progress was made in the years of reform around the turn of the century. During the Hogg administration a law extended the school term from four to six months. The legislature in 1901 authorized the state board of education to invest the permanent school fund in bonds issued to fund the construction of school buildings. Many communities organized independent school districts (free of county control), and by 1904 about 90 percent had begun to collect local taxes for school purposes.

Unfortunately, country schools, most of which were organized as common school districts under county control, lagged far behind urban programs. Primarily because of conditions in rural schools, Texas in 1901–1902 ranked from twenty-eighth to forty-second among the states of the nation, according to the various tests that were used at the time to determine the adequacy of the school system. In 1900, towns and cities spent $8.35 for the education of each child; the country schools spent only $4.97. The average term of 162 days in town and city schools was almost twice the average of 98 days found in rural areas. A strange and unreasonable restriction in the constitution limited the taxing authority of country districts to less than one-half of that of independent school districts. Adding to the tragedy of inadequate rural schools was the fact that they served more than three-fourths of the school-age population.

Progressive reformers during the Campbell administration continued to work to improve the schools. Organized in 1907, the Conference for Education in Texas struggled to awaken people to the needs of the schools. Its work was reinforced and extended by the state's Department of Education, the Congress of Mothers, parent-teacher associations, and other agencies. In 1908 the friends of school improvement made certain distinct gains. Noteworthy was the constitutional amendment that permitted common school districts to use funds derived from taxation for the equipment of buildings. During the first year after this and other amendments were put into operation, local taxation in rural districts increased by 35 percent. Local taxation, in fact, between 1905 and 1910 increased by 153 percent. Texas, nevertheless, continued to lag behind many other states in the availability of educational opportunities, but by the end of the first decade of the new century, the educational foundations of the state were firmly in place.

While establishing a system of public schools, Texans also created a system to provide higher education in the last quarter of the nineteenth century. The first institution of higher learning supported by public funds was the Agricultural and Mechanical College, established near Bryan in 1876. It is a land-grant college, now named Texas A & M University, and owes its origin to the Morrill Bill passed by Congress in 1862, by which Texas received 180,000 acres of land to establish a college for the study of agricultural and mechanical arts. Texas accepted the offer in 1866, but the school was not opened until 1876, just after the constitutional convention declared that it would be a branch of the University of Texas. A school for black youths under the management of the board of regents of the Agricultural and Mechanical College was established in 1876. At that time no black students sought training in agriculture, and in 1879 the school was reestablished as Prairie View Normal School. It was not until 1899 that agricultural and industrial departments were added for both boys and girls. Sam Houston Normal Institute at Huntsville had its beginning in 1879 when the state matched a donation of $6,000, and the citizens of Huntsville made available the campus formerly used by Austin College there.

Although there was considerable interest in the matter, the founding of the University of Texas was delayed for some years. During the Republic, 50 leagues of land were set aside for the endowment of two universities. A bill establishing the University of Texas was passed in 1858, but the Civil War and subsequent problems postponed the project for another 20 years. The Constitution of 1876 granted a million acres of land to the university and its branches but contained no provisions to compel the actual organization of the school. The State Teachers' Association, organized in 1878 under the presidency of Dr. William Carey Crane, was instrumental in developing sentiment for establishing the university. At a meeting of the association in 1880, a committee was appointed to present to Governor O. M. Roberts a plan for organizing the school. The governor sent the report of the committee to the legislature with his endorsement; the legislature carried out the plan substantially in the law approved March 30, 1881, providing for the establishment of the school. In an election the voters selected Austin as the site for the main university and Galveston for the medical branch. The main university was opened in 1883 and its medical branch in 1887.

WOMEN AT THE TURN OF THE CENTURY

In 1900 slightly less than half—about 48 percent—of the population of Texas were women. Reflecting the change from a frontier society to that of a more civilized one, the population of women was increasing at a rate more rapid than that of men, but women would not outnumber men in the state for some years.

Although the women of Texas enjoyed more rights than those of many other states, Texas women were less than equal in their legal rights in comparison with men. Not only were women denied the right to vote, but they also were limited in their rights to conduct business. Because of the heritage of Spanish civil law, a woman could own and convey property, make contracts, and sue or be sued. However, if she was married, a woman's property was subject to the management of her husband, even if the property was hers before marriage. She could not dispose of property without her husband's consent, but her husband could do so, unless the property involved was the family homestead. A husband was required by law to support his wife and was liable for any debts she might incur, while under some circumstances wives were not responsible for their own debts. Single women generally retained more rights than married women, inasmuch as they were legally responsible for their own acts and could legally manage their own property.

Educational opportunities for Texas women of the late nineteenth century were available but limited. By 1890 female students outnumbered males, but few females attended college. The Texas Women's Council, however, stressed improvement in vocational education for girls, and there were other organizations working to improve educational opportunities for women. Business colleges and trade schools appeared, and many of these institutions encouraged the enrollment of women, claiming that many jobs in business were available for women. More traditional forms of women's education persisted, however. Some colleges, such as Baylor University, began to offer courses equal in difficulty to those of men, but often education for women beyond basics in reading and writing were taught at a lower level or consisted of learning the social graces or studying the arts.

At the turn of the century most Texas women followed the role of wife, mother, or homemaker as their career. The percentage of women who married outnumbered that of men. Women tended to marry earlier in life, often to older men, and frequently were widowed at a young age. Divorce was rare. In 1890 slightly more than two percent of the female population were divorced.

In 1890, approximately eight percent (86,015) of the women of Texas were involved in occupations outside the home. Almost half of this number were in occupations related to agriculture, holding jobs as laborers, farmers, planters, or ranchers. The next largest number, 37,210, worked as domestic or personal servants. The remainder of the female work force was scattered among a wide variety of occupations. Among approximately 6,000 women employed in the professions, about 75 percent were teachers. In addition, there were writers and journalists, librarians and ministers, lawyers and physicians, merchants and clerks, seamstresses and copyists, and even gamblers and outlaws. No women held jobs as sailors in 1890, but two claimed to be locomotive engineers.

Organizations to improve conditions for women and for society in general were numerous at the turn of the century. Suffrage and temperance were the most common goals, accounting for a large number of the organizations and for most of the membership. But there were many other women's groups. Literary clubs were organized in small towns and large, with one reported in Clarendon in 1885 and one in Houston the same year. By the 1890s, Houston women had organized the City Federation of Women's Clubs, and in 1897 Waco was the scene of the organization of the Texas Federation of Women's Clubs.

In Belton, women's organizations took an unusual turn with the formation of a women's communal society. The moving spirit for the group, often referred to as the "sanctificationists," was Martha McWhirter, a longtime Belton resident who claimed to have had a vision. Some of the women who gathered together with Martha McWhirter were divorced; others were not, but all were determined to live free, without male support or domination. As the years passed, the group grew in number and prospered, primarily from profits earned in the operation of a hotel, and some of the controversy associated with the early days of the organization faded away. In 1889 the group left Texas, selling their property and moving to Washington, D.C.

THE ETHNIC GROUPS

Blacks and Mexican-Americans, with about 25 percent of the population, accounted for the majority of the non-Anglo cultures in Texas at the turn of the century. But there was a constant flow of immigrants, especially from Europe, and cultural diversity was one of the most notable features of the state.

Blacks in Texas numbered 620,722 in 1900, or approximately 20 percent of the total population. The ratio of blacks to the general population had declined from nearly one black to three whites at the beginning of the Civil War, but the number was more than twice that of 1860. Most—about 80 percent—lived on farms, and about 90 percent lived in the eastern parts of the state. Houston, with blacks amounting to one-third of its population, contained the largest number of urban blacks, with Austin, Dallas, Waco, and Galveston also containing substantial numbers.

Although some were ranchers and cowboys, most blacks who lived on the land were cotton farmers. About 25 percent of the black farmers owned their own land; the remainder were tenants, mostly sharecroppers and usually very poor. Even when the black farmer owned his own land, his situation was often insecure. In 1910 the average value of a black farmer's holdings was about one-fifth the value of a white farmer's.

Urban blacks accounted for about 25 percent of the nonfarm work force at the turn of the century. The greater number held jobs as laborers, and a significant number were employed as domestic or personal servants. Together, these occupations accounted for 80 percent of the black urban workers. Less than five percent entered the professions, and an even smaller number were craftsmen. Most black professionals were either teachers or ministers, but Texas in 1900 claimed the largest number of black physicians in the nation, 136. The ratio of black people in the crafts, however, was smaller in Texas than commonly found in other states.

Wages for black workers were low. Apparently, black and white workers who performed the same job were generally paid at the same rate; discrimination occurred in the assignment of the jobs. Wages paid in 1910 ranged from a low 30 cents a day for hotel workers to a maximum of ten dollars per day for certain jobs in mills, but the average pay seems to have

One of the major industries of Texas at the turn of the century, lumbering depended on black workers for a large proportion of its work force.

been about two dollars daily. Black women received substantially lower wages than did the black men. In fact, women, whether black or white, generally were paid lower wages, even when the tasks performed were the same as those of men.

Black workers assumed contradictory roles in the development of labor unions in Texas. In the lumber, railroad, and shipping industries in which labor unions were most often formed, there were large numbers of black workers, and many were involved in the organization of unions. On the other hand, the use of black workers as strikebreakers in labor disputes was not uncommon.

Businesses owned by blacks were few in number and generally quite small. Often operated by the entire family, the business was usually a grocery store, restaurant, tavern, blacksmith shop, or some other type of service agency, and was ordinarily confined to providing for the needs of the black community. However, there were several black insurance companies, most of them connected with black fraternal groups, and there were at least eight black banks in business in the early twentieth century.

Provisions for education of blacks, segregated in their schools by the Constitution of 1876, were inadequate. Black education in Texas for a time compared favorably with that of other southern states, and illiteracy declined from more than 75 percent in 1880 to less than 40 percent in 1900. By 1900, however, Texas ranked fifth among southern states in the enrollment of black students and daily attendance and third in the number of black teachers. There were a number of able black leaders, such as R. L. Smith, a graduate of Atlanta University and an aide to Booker T. Washington, who diligently sought educational gains, and some white leaders recognized the merit of the cause. But often the white community was either disinterested or openly unsympathetic. Generally, black schools labored under the burden of inadequate financial resources and poorly trained personnel. Until the nineties, laws required that funds be divided equitably between white and black schools, but violations of the rule were not unknown. Complaints that many black teachers were deficient in training were often heard. Yet, significant improvement of black faculties could scarcely have been expected. As late as 1900, secondary training for blacks in Texas was not only inadequate, it was practically nonexistent, with only 19 black high schools in the state. A black student in Texas seeking an education during these years could likely learn the rudiments of reading and writing, but he or she probably would find little opportunity beyond those humble beginnings.

All in all, the situation of black Texans at the turn of the century suggests a mixture of regression and progress. Economically, black Texans were at a disadvantage when compared with their white neighbors. Poverty was common among white Texans, but black people were even poorer. Education for blacks was not equal to that offered whites, and from the 1890s forward, the discrepancy became even greater. The effectiveness of black people in politics declined in the decade before the end of the century and would decline further in the years to come. Mortality rates for black people were much higher than those for white people, probably influenced by an inadequate diet and lower quality of medical care. Segregation and violence, long a part of life in the black community, continued. In a 21-year period ending in 1903, 199 blacks were lynched; 171 were lynched during the next 24 years.

But despite the problems and the inequities, there was also substantial evidence of progress. In 1900, black Texans were only 35 years removed from slavery. During those years, a number of capable black leaders had emerged, illiteracy had been reduced, and sufficient capital had been acquired to enable some to buy land and others to establish businesses. Perhaps of most significance to the future was the formation of literally dozens, possibly hundreds, of black organizations of all types. Some were religious; others were political. A large number were fraternal, and there were many primarily concerned with social affairs. Perhaps most important were the chapters of the National Association for the Advancement of Colored People (NAACP), the first chapter in Texas formed in Houston in 1912. But all were ultimately concerned with the improvement of the black community. These organizations would provide an ongoing level of leadership in the twentieth century.

Much smaller than the black population, but a major ethnic minority were the Mexican-American people. At the turn of the century, natives of Mexico living in Texas numbered about 70,000 and were the largest group of foreign-born. The number of people of Mexican heritage was many times larger, with some families able to trace their origins back to the days of the Spanish. Well into the twentieth century, 60 percent of the landowners in Cameron, Starr, and Zapata counties were descendants of the original land-grant recipients. Other Mexican-Americans were recent arrivals, for increasing agricultural production in South Texas attracted workers from Mexico during the 1890s. In 1910, Mexican-Americans made up slightly less than six percent of the population, but revolution in Mexico increased the immigration thereafter. Most lived in South Texas and along the Rio Grande. San Antonio was the largest urban center for Mexican-Americans, and there were many in El Paso and other towns along the Rio Grande; but other cities, particularly Houston, would prove attractive in the years following the turn of the century.

Mexican-Americans, whether descendants of old settlers or recent immigrants, often found life in Texas difficult. Prejudice, poverty, and discrimination were common problems. Sometimes signs declaring "No Mexicans Allowed" were posted in restaurants and other public businesses. In some towns Mexican-Americans could live only in certain areas, and generally only low-paying and physically tiring jobs were available to the Mexican-American worker. Language was sometimes a barrier, for many Mexican-Americans retained the use of Spanish, the language of their heritage. Since schools normally allowed only English to be spoken, Mexican-American students who spoke only Spanish often dropped out at an early age. Nevertheless, Mexican-Americans were not an illiterate people, and by the 1890s several Mexican-American newspapers were being published on a more or less regular basis for the benefit of Spanish-speaking Texans.

Poverty was a problem almost always present. Although some Mexican-Americans entered professions such as law, medicine, or teaching, and others owned ranches or businesses, most were laborers in the towns, on the roads or railroads, or more frequently, on the land. Often they were *vaqueros*, who took care of cattle or sheep, or workers in the cotton and vegetable fields of South Texas. Some owned the land on which they worked, but most did not and received meager pay for their efforts.

To cope with their poverty, Mexican-Americans used imagination and ingenuity. They frequently depended on inexpensive and readily available materials provided by nature. Where it was appropriate, they built their homes out of sun-dried brick or adobe. Where this was not feasible, they built *jacales*, sturdy and simple houses made from straw, mesquite, and other available materials that cost little or perhaps nothing. Their clothing was simple and colorful, but practical for their way of life, as was their food, which was inexpensive but in keeping with their Mexican heritage.

For help in times of unusual adversity, Mexican-Americans often formed *mutualistas*, organizations that provided financial assistance in times of death or sickness or other crisis. The *mutualistas*, active in most of the communities of South Texas, also raised funds to help Mexican-Americans to preserve their Mexican heritage and to meet the general needs of their community.

In the late nineteenth century, Mexican-Americans exercised only limited influence on state politics, but often they assumed a major role in local politics if the Mexican-American population was large. On the state level only three Mexican-Americans were elected to the legislature in the period between 1865 and 1900. One of these was Santos Benavides, mayor of Laredo, a brigadier general in the Civil War, and three times a member of the Texas legislature. In some instances economic pressure or open coercion were used to prevent Mexican-American voters from going to the polls, but frequently voting was allowed, and the vote was controlled to the advantage of local political bosses. Some of the political bosses were Anglos, but others were Mexican-Americans. Manuel Guerra of Rio Grande City was the most powerful politician in Starr County for many years. Although most of the political leadership, whether Anglo or Mexican-American, was quite conservative, sometimes Mexican-American leaders were successful in efforts to correct abuses. When San Pedro Park in San Antonio was closed to Mexican-American people in the 1880s, protests forced its reopening. In later years protests against economic discrimination led to the organization of a number of labor unions made up primarily of Mexican-American workers. These unions participated in victories won in a streetcar strike in 1901, in a coal mining strike in 1903, and in a railroad strike in 1906.

Somewhat smaller in number but generally more prosperous were the Germans, Czechs, Poles, and Scandinavians. In 1900 almost 50,000 Texans had been born in Germany, and people of German heritage made up the majority of the population of several counties. Large German communities existed in Houston, Galveston, and San Antonio. More German immigrants arrived in Texas in the late nineteenth century than in the years before the Civil War. In most instances the newcomers settled in communities established by Germans before the war, with Austin, Fayette, Lee, and Washington counties receiving large numbers. Attracted primarily by the lure of cotton-growing lands, German settlers were scattered in isolated communities, known as "folk islands," over Central and West Texas in the late nineteenth and early twentieth centuries. German settlers tended to retain their cultural heritage to a marked degree. Often German was spoken in the daily routine, church services, and occasionally in the schools. There were a number of German newspapers. Foods, holidays, architecture, and other customs made the distinctly German culture quite visible.

Immigrants from Czechoslovakia, then Bohemia and Moravia, made their way to inland areas. Fayette County was a favorite destination, but some chose other locations, usually in communities where the German population was large. Polish settlements founded before the Civil War similarly grew with the new immigration, until, by the early 1900s, there were some 17,000 people of Polish heritage in Texas. Smaller numbers of Swedes joined the tide of settlers, mostly locating near Austin in Travis and Williamson counties.

People from most of the European countries and from some in Asia made their home in Texas during these years. Nederland in Jefferson County was founded by immigrants from the Netherlands. Galveston became the home of a colony of Yugoslavians who made their living by fishing; San Antonio was selected to be the home of a group of Lebanese; and there were sizable numbers of English, Irish, and Italians who settled in the towns and cities. Smaller number of immigrants came from Belgium, Denmark, France, Hungary, Norway, Russia, Scotland, Switzerland, and Wales. By 1900 almost 1,000 Chinese lived in Texas, and a small number of Japanese had settled along the Rio Grande.

LITERATURE AND THE ARTS

The last third of the nineteenth century witnessed a substantial increase in Texas writings and some improvements in quality, and these achievements carried over into the early twentieth century. The best works pertained to adventure. Some were reminiscences dealing largely with the time of the Texan Revolution and early statehood and were of genuine historical value. Z. N. Morrell, a pioneer Baptist preacher who came to Texas in 1836, wrote *Flowers and Fruits of the Wilderness*, a lively narrative of his long career on the frontier. Similarly, in his reminiscences of *Fifty Years in Texas*, John J. Linn gave much information about the Texan Revolution. Equally interesting is Noah Smithwick's *The Evolution of a State*. John C. Duval's *Early Times in Texas* was a classic. An earlier book of his, just as meritorious, was *The Adventures of Big Foot Wallace*, a biography of a famous Ranger who had come to Texas in 1836 to avenge the death of his brother killed in Goliad. Containing less adventure, but associated with a broader scene, were Francis R. Lubbock's *Six Decades in Texas* and John H. Reagan's *Memoirs*. Cowper Brann wrote and published in the 1890s, first in Austin and later in Waco, the newspaper *Iconoclast*, in which he purported to combat hypocrisy, intolerance, and other evils.

During this period, books of travel were relatively less important than they had been earlier. However, *On a Mexican Mustang through Texas*, by Alex E. Sweet and J. Armory Knox, two newspapermen, is notable. Their writing shows the influence of Mark Twain. N. A. Taylor's *The Coming Empire or Two Thousand Miles in Texas on Horseback* contains less satire and is more trustworthy and dependable than the book by Sweet and Knox.

Since the frontier era did not close in Texas until nearly the end of the nineteenth century, for two decades and more following the Civil War, men who sought adventure of the hardest frontier style did not have to leave the state to find it. Thus, authors continued to write of contemporary experiences, of the exploits of an early period, or of both. J. W. Wilbarger filled a fat volume entitled *Indian Depredations of Texas* with accounts of border tragedies. This book was a precursor of James T. DeShield's *Border Wars of Texas*, published in the twentieth century. Neither book made much effort to present the Indian side of the story. N. A. Jennings, a New York newspaperman who came to Texas and served with the Rangers on the frontier in the eighties, wrote of some of his own experiences in *A Texas Ranger*. In 1886 Charles A. Siringo, a real cowboy who could interest readers, published his *Texas Cowboy or Fifteen Years on the Hurricane Deck* of a *Spanish Pony*. As a paperback thriller, its sale ran into many thousands, and it pointed the way for many other writers who have, since that day, dealt with similar themes in books, in fact or fiction.

By no means did all Texas literature of adventure in the period deal with legitimate enterprise or with men on the side of the law. The "bad man" theme was popular. The later frontier period brought forth Henry C. Fuller's *The Adventure of Bill Longly*, the story of a notorious killer. Sam Bass, a train robber, who, since his death has been memorialized as the Robin Hood of Texas, was the subject of a biography published anonymously in 1878. The gruesome record of John Wesley Hardin was written by himself. W. M. Walton wrote *The Life and Adventures of Ben Thompson,* sometime city marshal of Austin and noted for fights in which he was not always enforcing the law.

Many poems were written during this period, but few of them bear evidence of talent. John P. Sjolander, a Swedish-American, has been called the "greatest pioneer poet of the Southwest." Crude but genuine and destined to endure was William Lawrence (Larry) Chittenden's "Cowboy Christmas Ball." Sam H. Dixon compiled and edited *Poets and Poetry of Texas*, and Francis L. Allen published a collection known as *Lone Star Ballads.*

The late nineteenth century was also characterized by many works of fiction. Although few of these had any enduring value, there were some notable exceptions. Mrs. Molley E. Moore Davis, the wife of a New Orleans editor, began her writing in Texas, and her best work had a Texas setting. *Under the Man-Fig,* probably her best-known novel, dealt with the destructive effects of gossip in a small town. William Sidney Porter, known as O. Henry, came to Texas from his native North Carolina in 1882. Two years on a ranch in La Salle County and a decade in Austin, where he held and lost various jobs, supplied much of the experience and setting for the literary work that made him one of the great short story writers of all time. His collection of stories, *Heart of the West*, published during the first decade of the twentieth century, is based almost wholly on Texas scenes.

Historical writing in Texas took a major step forward in 1897 when the Texas State Historical Association was organized. The association began the publication of the *Quarterly of the Texas State Historical Association*, which in 1912 became *The Southwestern Historical Quarterly*. George Pierce Garrison and Herbert E. Bolton contributed much to the success of this publication, and, under the editorship of Eugene C. Barker, which lasted a quarter of a century, it came to be recognized as an important historical journal.

Garrison and Bolton were the vanguard of a group of outstanding Texas historians who were active in the early decades of the twentieth century. In his *Texas, a Contest of Civilizations*, Garrison brought to bear on the subject years of research and historical training. Bolton, a noted scholar of the Spanish Southwest, published some studies pertaining to Texas, among them *Texas in the Middle-Eighteenth Century* and *Athanase de Mézières and the Louisiana-Texas Frontier*. A contemporary, Charles W. Ramsdell, earned a place among the authorities on the Old South and the Civil War. Barker's studies on the Austins remain the standard work, and his scholarly articles filled several volumes. Later in the period, relatively lengthy histories of Texas were written by Louis J. Wortham and Clarence R. Wharton.

Among the well-known artists of the period was H. A. McArdle, whose pictures, "Battle of San Jacinto" and "Dawn of the Alamo," attracted

Elisabet Ney——beautiful, talented, and willful—— learned sculpture in Munich and Berlin where she cast busts of such famous men as Schopenhauer, Garibaldi, and King William I of Prussia. She moved to the United States with her British husband in 1870 and settled in Texas two years later. Unhappy on a remote plantation, she received commissions from the state for busts of Stephen Austin and Sam Houston that enabled her to move to a studio in Austin. One of her best works, a statue of General Albert Sidney Johnston, is now in the state cemetery, but it was her last work, a statue of Lady Macbeth, that won her the fame she enjoyed. (E. C. Barker History Center, University of Texas)

much attention when they were hung in the state capitol. A contemporary of McArdle was William H. Huddle, whose "Surrender of Santa Anna" also hangs in the state capitol. Robert Jenkins Onderdonk left some superior portraits and paintings of scenes in the vicinity of Dallas and San Antonio. His son, Julian, who died in 1922 at the age of 40, was probably Texas's most distinguished painter. Of particular note were his landscape scenes, especially "Dawn on the Hills."

In Texas sculpture one name stood supreme—Elisabet Ney. Ney came to the state with her husband, Dr. Edmund Montgomery, in 1870, from her native Bavaria where she had already attained fame. Best-known to Texans were her statues of Stephen F. Austin, Sam Houston, and Albert Sidney Johnston. Of higher quality, however, were her imaginative works: for example, the group that she called *Sursum*, now in the Chicago Art Institute, and her statue of Lady Macbeth, now in the National Gallery in

Washington, D.C. After Miss Ney's death, her studio in Austin became a museum and a shrine for Texas artists and art lovers.

In the early decades of the twentieth century, Texas musicians contributed to the cultural development of the state. Born in Germany and trained in Europe, Carl Venth had already earned fame when he moved to Texas in 1909, and he contributed much to the musical growth of the state thereafter. The cultural diversity of Texas was otherwise particularly influential in the music of this period. Many of the familiar ballads and folk songs heard reflected the culture of the Mexican-American people. Scott Joplin, son of a slave and born in Texarkana, took part in the development of ragtime music, wrote an opera, and composed other songs. Active in the popularization of jazz were Blind Lemon Jefferson and Huddie ("Leadbelly") Ledbetter. Born in Ballinger in 1895, David W. Guion took the folk music of the Indian, the black, and the cowboy and presented them in popular form.

SELECTED BIBLIOGRAPHY

There are a number of autobiographical studies that tell much about life at the turn of the century. See Edward Everett Dale, *The Cross Timbers* (Austin, 1966); Bertha McKee Dobie, *Growing Up in Texas* (Austin, 1972); Drury B. Alexander, *Texas Homes of the Nineteenth Century* (Austin, 1966); Adah Robertson Hadlock, *My Life in the Southwest* (ed. Kenneth A. Goldblatt, El Paso, 1969); C. C. White and Ada Moreland Holland, *No Quittin' Sense* (Austin, 1969); and Robert W. Richmond, ed., "Letter from Wise County, Texas," *The American West*, IX, 42–47. See also Catherine Ikard Carrow, "Amusements of Men and Women in Texas in the 1880s," *West Texas Historical Association Year Book*, XXXV, 77–96; Calvin Dickerson, "Collegiate Life in Nineteenth Century Texas," *Texana*, VII, 313–321; Jim Tom Barton, *Eighter from Decatur: Growing Up in North Texas* (College Station, 1980). A readable and comprehensive discussion of the Galveston flood is available in Herbert M. Mason, Jr., *Death from the Sea: Our Greatest Natural Disaster, the Galveston Hurricane of 1900* (New York, 1972). For information on medical care, see P. I. Nixon, *A History of the Texas Medical Association;* and B. M. Jones, *Health Seekers in the Southwest, 1817–1900.*

Increased interest in urban studies is evident in the availability of city histories. *Houston: A History and Guide* (Houston, 1942), compiled by the Federal Writers' Program of the Works Projects Administration in the state of Texas, is useful, but see also for a more specialized aspect of the city, Marilyn Sibley, *The Port of Houston* (Austin, 1968). For twentieth century developments, see James Howard, *Big D Is for Dallas* (Dallas, 1957). A superior study is Lawrence Graves (ed.), *History of Lubbock* (Lubbock, 1962). Also see Dan E. Kilgore, "Corpus Christi: A Quarter Century of Development, 1900–1925," *Southwestern Historical Quarterly*, LXXV, 435–443; Roger N. Conger, "Waco: Cotton and Culture on the Brazos," *ibid.*, LXXV, 54–60; and Keith L. Bryant, Jr., "Arthur E. Stilwell and the Founding of Port Arthur: A Case of Entrepreneurial Error," *ibid.*, LXXV, 19–40. Among the longer studies are

Robert L. Martin, *The City Moves West: Economic and Industrial Growth in Central West Texas* (Austin, 1969); David G. McComb, *Houston: The Bayou City* (Austin, 1969). Donald E. Everett, *San Antonio: the Flavor of Its Past* (San Antonio, 1975); A. C. Greene, *A Place Called Dallas: The Pioneering Years of a Continuing Metropolis* (Dallas, 1975); Katherine Hart and others, *Austin and Travis County: A Pictorial History, 1839–1939* (Austin, 1975); Leonard Sanders, *How Fort Worth Became the Texasmost City, 1849–1920* (College Station, 1986); and John S. Garner, "The Saga of a Railroad Town: Calvert, Texas, 1868–1918," *Southwestern Historical Quarterly*, LXXXV, 139–160; and David G. McComb, *Galveston: A History* (Austin, 1985).

Considering the importance of the industry, the large number of studies on oil is to be expected. C. C. Rister's *Oil! Titan of the Southwest* (Norman, Okla., 1949) is the standard general work, and a colorful account of the first important discovery in Texas is William A. Owens, "Gusher at Spindletop," *American Heritage*, IX, 34ff. Those seeking additional sources should consult Walter Rundell, Jr., "Texas Petroleum History: A Selective Annotated Bibliography," *Southwestern Historical Quarterly*, LXVII, 267–278, which lists and describes more than 60 studies. See also Walter Rundell, Jr., *Early Texas Oil Photographic History, 1866–1936* (College Station, 1977); and John O. King, *Joseph Stephen Cullinan: A Study of Leadership in the Texas Petroleum Industry, 1897–1937* (Nashville, 1970). Considering economic matters generally is J. S. Spratt, *The Road to Spindletop* (Dallas, 1955).

Additional information on women in Texas is available in Lawrence W. Neff, *The Legal Status of Women in Texas* (Dallas, 1895); James M. Day and others, *Women of Texas* (Waco, 1972); Emily Jones Shelton, "Lizzie E. Johnson: A Cattle Queen of Texas," *Southwestern Historical Quarterly*, LVIII, 315–348; Evelyn M. Carrington, ed., *Women in Early Texas* (Austin, 1975); Elizabeth York Enstam, "The Frontier Woman As City Worker: Women's Occupations in Dallas, Texas, 1856–1880," *East Texas Historical Journal*, XVIII, 12–28; Ann Fears Crawford and Crystal Sasse Ragsdale, *Women in Texas: Their Lives, Their Experiences, Their Accomplishments* (Burnet, 1982); Mary S. Cunningham, *The Women's Club of El Paso: Its First Thirty Years* (El Paso, 1978); Francis Edward Abernethy (ed.), *Legendary Ladies of Texas* (Dallas, 1981); and Jayne A. Sokolow and Mary Ann Lamanna, "Women and Utopia: The Woman's Commonwealth of Belton, Texas," *Southwestern Historical Quarterly*, LXXXVII, 371–392.

Life for black Texans at the turn of the century is described thoroughly in Lawrence Rice, *The Negro in Texas, 1874–1900;* and in Alwyn Barr, *Black Texans.* There is an abundance of literature dealing with specialized topics: See John D. Weaver, *The Brownsville Raid* (New York, 1970); Alwyn Barr, "Occupational and Geographic Mobility in San Antonio, 1870–1900," *Social Science Quarterly*, LI, 396–403; and Mason Brewer, *Negro Legislators of Texas and Their Descendants* (Austin, 1970). Also invaluable is the manuscript of Bruce Glasrud in the Texas Tech library, "Black Texans, 1900–1930: A History"; and that of William J. Brophy, "The Black Texan, 1900–1950: A Quantitative History," in the library of Vanderbilt University. Additional studies are: Alwyn Barr and Robert A. Calvert (eds.), *Black Leaders: Texans For Their Times* (Austin, 1981); Bruce Glasrud, "Enforcing White Supremacy in Texas, 1900–1910," *Red River Valley Historical Review*, IV, 65–74; James M. Sorelle, "The 'Waco Horror': The Lynching of Jesse Washington," *Southwestern Historical Quarterly*, LXXXVI, 517–536; and Randy Roberts, "Galveston's Jack Johnson: Flourishing in the Dark," *ibid.*, LXXXVII, 37–56.

Useful as a starting point for additional study on Mexican-American history is Juan Gómez-Quinones and Luis Leobardo Arrayo, "On the State of Chicano History: Observations on Its Development, Interpretations, and Theory," *Western Historical Quarterly*, VII, 155–185. Also see Paul S. Taylor, *An American-Mexican Frontier: Nueces County, Texas* (Chapel Hill, N.C., 1934); Pauline R. Kibbe, *Latin Americans in Texas* (Albuquerque, 1946); William Madsen, *The Mexican-Americans of South Texas* (New York, 1964); Arnulfo D. Trejo, *The Chicanos As We See Ourselves* (Tucson, 1979); Clifford Alan Perkins, *Border Patrol: With the U.S. Immigration Service on the Mexican Boundary, 1910–1954* (ed. C. L. Sonnichsen, El Paso, 1978); Lawrence A. Cardoso "Labor Emigration to the Southwest, 1916 to 1920; Mexican Attitudes and Policy," *Southwestern Historical Quarterly*, LXXIX, 400–416; Rodolfo O. de la Garza, et. al., (eds.), *The Mexican-American Experience: An Interdisciplinary Anthology* (Austin, 1985); Robert J. Rosenbaum, *Mexicano Resistance in the Southwest: The Sacred Right of Self Preservation* (Austin, 1981); Arnoldo DeLeon, *The Tejano Community, 1836–1900* (Albuquerque, 1982); and *They Called Them Greasers: Anglo Attitudes Towards Mexicans in Texas, 1821–1900* (Austin, 1983).

For information on other ethnic groups, see Terry G. Jordan, "The German Settlement of Texas after 1865," *Southwestern Historical Quarterly*, LXXIII, 193–212; Edward J. M. Rhoads, "The Chinese in Texas," *ibid.*, LXXXI, 1–36; and T. Lindsey Baker, *The First Polish Americans: Silesian Settlements in Texas* (College Station, 1979). The Institute of Texan Cultures has published some studies on individual ethnic groups which are useful introductory materials.

On the history of education, see F. Eby, *The Development of Education in Texas;* and C. E. Evans, *The Story of Texas Schools.* In this connection see also H. Y. Benedict, *A Source Book Relating to the University of Texas* (Austin, 1917); George Sessions Perry, *The Story of Texas A & M* (New York, 1951); William Hooper, Jr., "Governor Edmund J. Davis, Ezra Cornell and the A & M College of Texas," *Southwestern Historical Quarterly*, LXXVIII, 307–312; W. J. Battle, "A Concise History of the University of Texas, 1883–1950," *ibid.*, LIV, 391–411; George P. Garrison, "The First Twenty-five Years of the University of Texas," *ibid.*, LX, 106–117; and E. Bruce Thompson, "William Carey Crane and Texas Education," *ibid.*, LVIII, 405–421; and Roger A. Griffin, "To Establish a University of the First Class," *ibid.*, LXXXVI, 135–160.

The most valuable sources for the literature of this period are Martin Shockley, ed., *Southwest Writers' Anthology* (Austin, 1967); Mabel Major and others, *Southwest Heritage: A Literary History* (Albuquerque, 1948); and J. Frank Dobie, *Life and Literature of the Southwest* (rev. ed., Dallas, 1973), and "The Southwest, a Cultural Inventory," *Saturday Review of Literature*, May 16, 1942.

For the fine arts, see Pauline Pinckney, *Texas Artists of the Nineteenth Century* (Austin, 1967); Lota M. Spell, *Music in Texas* (Austin, 1938); and Cecilia Steinfeldt, *The Onderdonks: A Family of Texas Painters* (San Antonio, 1976).

CHAPTER SIXTEEN
CRUSADES AND
COMPLACENCY
1910–1930

Both crusades and complacency characterized Texas politics in the score of years between the progressive era and the Great Depression. Many Texans joined the crusade for Prohibition with enthusiasm; practically all supported the great crusade of the First World War; and not a few endorsed the reactionary crusading of the Ku Klux Klan. It was, moreover, an age of social, technological, and economic change. Yet, in some respects it was an era of complacency. Particularly in the twenties, politics was largely the story of governors who sought reforms, reforms that were mainly moderate, reasonable, and generally needed, but which indifferent legislators and a still more indifferent electorate would not accept. Prohibition, a world war, the impeachment of a governor, and the rise of a hooded tyranny contributed diversity. But basic problems associated with the rapid pace of industrialization and urbanization and a corresponding decline in the role of agriculture provided an element of continuity.

OSCAR BRANCH COLQUITT

Having the support of most of the opponents of Prohibition in the Democratic gubernatorial primary of 1910, Railroad Commissioner Oscar Branch Colquitt captured 40 percent of the vote, the nomination, and subsequently the general election. A former Hogg man, the governor nevertheless was generally regarded as the most conservative man in the race. Most assuredly, he was not a crusader and received the support of some corporate interests. Once in office, his record, in part, fulfilled conservative expectations. He attempted to block some labor legislation, vetoed a city charter providing for initiative and referendum, denounced direct democracy as "socialistic, un-American," curbed appropriations for higher education, and frowned on the introduction of free textbooks in the public schools.

Yet the Colquitt years were not without progressive achievements. Additional penal reforms were adopted, two hospitals for tuberculosis patients were authorized and one was established; and a training school for delinquent girls was founded. Crude but well-aimed was a law permitting counties to provide poor houses and poor farms for indigents. There were laws regulating child labor, promoting factory safety, and limiting the hours of women workers. Most important was the workmen's compensation act requiring that persons employed in most industries be insured against accidents and setting forth rules for compensation in case of injury.

An old vexing problem returned during the Colquitt administration. Provoked by a series of Mexican revolutions beginning in 1910, violence erupted along the Rio Grande, and rumors of a Mexican insurrection in the United States were heard. Ill will and confusion persisted on the border until long after the First World War. An investigating committee of the United States Senate reported that, between November 1910 and October 1919, 500 Americans lost their lives in the Mexican troubles; of these, 62 civilians and 64 soldiers were killed along the American side of the river. Governor Colquitt twice sent state troops to the Rio Grande; they were soon supplanted by federal soldiers. A thousand Texas Rangers stationed along the border afforded a measure of protection, but violence did not cease until several months after the close of the war. Following a sweeping legislative investigation in which it was charged that the Rangers had maltreated peaceful Mexican-American citizens of the United States, a law of March 31, 1919 reduced the force to four regular companies of 17 men each.

Less dramatic than rumored insurrection but certainly serious were the state's financial problems during the Colquitt years. When the outgoing administration set tax rates too low, Governor Colquitt inherited a deficit of nearly a million dollars. A rising cost of living necessitated an increase in salaries. New departments, new institutions, and repairs on buildings at the older institutions required heavier outlays. Various calamities, especially a fire at the Agricultural and Mechanical College, augmented the normal expenses. The penitentiary seemed the most hopeless of all state institutions, requiring the state legislature in 1913 to authorize additional funds to pay debts, make repairs, and add improvements. Reelected in 1912 without much difficulty, Colquitt during his second administration vetoed some appropriations, but even then it was necessary to raise the state tax rate. State expenditures, in fact, more than doubled between 1903 and 1914.

PROHIBITION: THE TRIUMPH OF A MORAL CRUSADE

Although discouraged temporarily by their severe defeat in 1887, prohibitionists soon renewed their fight, directing their efforts mainly toward local option. The Texas Local Option Association was organized in Dallas in 1903, and in 1907 the Anti-Saloon League entered Texas. To meet their challenge, the powerful Texas Brewers' Association raised more than $2 million between 1902 and 1911, by assessment of its members. In 1907 the Retail Liquor Dealers' Association was organized, its members pledging themselves to obey all laws as the only way to stop the march of prohibition. Nevertheless, through the extension of local option, the prohibitionists gained ground steadily. During the nineties they drove the saloons out of most of North and West Texas, and in the following decade they began to make inroads into South and Southeast Texas. The constitutional amendment of 1902 requiring a poll tax for voting was regarded as a victory for the prohibitionists. Encouraged by their triumph, prohibitionists turned their aims toward a statewide ban, only to encounter among some of its former opponents a strange and new enthusiasm for local option.

By 1908 prohibition had become the all-absorbing political issue. In fact, from the primary campaign of 1908 when the question of statewide prohibition was again submitted to the voter until the First World War, there were in effect two Democratic parties in Texas, one prohibitionist, the other antiprohibitionist. True, there was no formal division; there was only one set of party committees, and there was only one Democratic primary. But the factions were so pronounced that every prominent leader was forced to join one side or the other, and the great rank and file of voters took their places in the respective camps to fight one another with greater vehemence than Democrat had ever fought Republican since the time of E. J. Davis.

The forces were evenly matched. In the primary election of 1908 the prohibitionists won by a slender margin, but the brewery interests were able to defeat the submission of a constitutional amendment by the legislature. When the entire question was fought out again in the primary election of 1910, the prohibitionists again committed the party to submission. In the selection of candidates, however, they were not so successful. Better organized than their opponents, the antiprohibitionists centered their votes on Colquitt, who was elected by a large plurality over three opponents, two of them ardent prohibitionists who split the votes. Thus, in its primary the Democratic party called for a prohibition amendment and at the same time made sure of the election of an antiprohibitionist governor.

When the legislature submitted the prohibition amendment to the voters and designated July 22, 1911, as the day for the election, the two factions aligned themselves for another desperate contest. With great fervor, lay leaders and ministers campaigned for the cause, while Governor Colquitt joined others in opposition. By a close vote, 237,096 for to 237,393 against, statewide prohibition again failed.

Although they kept up the fight, the prohibitionists in Texas made little headway for some time. However, suits filed by Attorney General B. F. Looney in 1915 revealed that brewers had violated the state's antitrust laws and had illegally used funds in elections. Then came the impeachment of Governor James Ferguson in 1917 and evidence indicating that the brewers had shown him favors. Moreover, Prohibition became a patriotic issue, a measure with which to win World War I. Women, long a strong voice in the movement, renewed their efforts with the formation of the Texas Woman's Anti-Vice Committee, particularly concerned with conditions for servicemen. A law which became effective on April 15, 1918 forbade the sale of liquor within ten miles of any place where troops were quartered. Shortly thereafter, a statewide law closed all saloons. Then, beginning July 1, 1919, a federal law prohibiting the sale of intoxicating liquor anywhere in the nation went into effect, and on January 16, 1920, the Eighteenth Amendment to the United States Constitution made Prohibition a national policy. Meanwhile, the legislature of Texas had ratified the Eighteenth Amendment, and on May 24, 1919, the voters of Texas had adopted a prohibition amendment to the state constitution by a vote of 188,982 to 130,907. Traces of the rift caused by the issue would linger nearly as long as the experiment. But other national and state issues had already diverted the interest of both voter and politician alike.

THE BIRTH OF FERGUSONISM

In 1914 there appeared in Texas politics a man destined to stir the emotions of the people for a generation. Rising from poverty and a meager formal education, by 1914 James E. Ferguson was a successful banker at the Temple State Bank, lawyer, and businessman, but he was a virtual unknown in state politics. Yet, Ferguson, who was often referred to as "Farmer Jim," was twice elected governor, serving from January 1915 to September 1917. Through his wife, Governor Miriam A. ("Ma") Ferguson, he guided many policies of the state when she served as governor from January 1925 to January 1927 and again from January 1933 to January 1935. In addition to his successful campaigns, he was an unsuccessful candidate for governor in 1918, for President of the United States in 1920, and for the United States Senate in 1922. Besides the years when she was elected, Mrs. Ferguson ran for governor in 1926, 1930, and 1940. Meaning different things to different people, "Fergusonism" became a familiar term to the Texas voter. Critics angrily denounced the Fergusons as unprincipled demagogues, but to their loyal supporters they were undaunted crusaders seeking justice for the oppressed.

Believing that the majority of Texans were tired of the prohibition controversy, Ferguson announced as a candidate for governor in the primary of 1914 with the declaration that he would hold aloof from both prohibition political factions and make this campaign on other and more important issues. Although he posed as a businessman's candidate, the principal plank in Ferguson's platform appealed to tenant farmers. For many decades tenantry in Texas had been increasing. In 1880, 37 percent of all farms were operated by tenants; in 1900 the percentage had increased to 59; and in 1910 it was 62.6 percent. While their number had increased, the lot of tenants was growing harder and their outlook more discouraging. The time-honored custom of the landlords taking a rental of one-fourth of the cotton and one-third of most other crops was not being followed uniformly in Texas. In the richer farmland regions the practice of charging higher rentals, or the customary one-third and one-fourth plus a money bonus, was increasing. Ferguson proposed to fix by law farm rentals at one-third and one-fourth and to make a higher rate illegal. He opened his campaign in Blum, Hill County, a tenant community. Of the 155 speeches that he delivered before the primary election, only ten were made in towns and cities. In the primary he defeated Thomas H. Ball of Houston, who was supported by the prohibition wing of the party. In November he was elected governor with little opposition.

Ferguson's first administration was characterized by harmony and an imposing list of constructive laws. Of the 160 general laws enacted during the regular session of the Thirty-fourth Legislature in 1915, the governor vetoed only five. Ferguson was easily reelected in 1916, and the first five months of his second administration witnessed a continuation of a constructive legislative program. The governor's rental plank was readily enacted into law in 1915. Apparently never rigidly enforced, however, the law was declared unconstitutional in 1921. Interesting and indicative of a new era was a law setting automobile speed limits at 15 miles an hour in towns and 18 miles an hour in the country. More significant and, in view of subsequent developments, more incongruous, were a number of laws substantially improving educational services.

Governor Ferguson's popularity declined during his second administration, but he still had a large following both in the legislature and among the rank and file of voters. In March 1917 the house of representatives investigated charges of irregular conduct on the part of the governor and discovered some questionable transactions; the committee, nevertheless, recommended that the charges be dropped. The regular session of the legislature completed its work and adjourned, but developments soon indicated that the governor would not be allowed to finish his second term.

Although charges of corruption and incompetence were leveled at Ferguson, both friend and foe have usually agreed that he would not have been impeached if he had not antagonized the alumni of the University of Texas. The governor's quarrel with the university began as early as 1915 when he attempted to dictate to Acting President W. J. Battle the interpretation of the appropriation law for the school. In the following year he apparently became piqued because he was not consulted by the regents in their selection of a president for the university. Later, he demanded that the regents dismiss President Robert E. Vinson and several other faculty members, threatening to veto the entire university appropriation if they did not. The regents supported by the powerful alumni association, refused to yield. The governor was not bluffing; in June 1917, just after the legislature had adjourned, he vetoed the appropriation. Although the attorney general declared the veto void on a technicality, the fight between Ferguson and the university was then eclipsed by a movement to impeach the governor.

Another Ferguson foe appeared as impeachment proceedings began. The Texas Equal Suffrage Association looked upon the governor as a man of questionable morality and an obvious opponent of women's suffrage. Led by Minnie Fisher Cunningham, the association's president who went to Austin for the contest, the suffragists enthusiastically urged that the cause not be abandoned.

Responding to rising sentiment for impeachment proceedings, on July 23 the speaker of the house issued a call for a special legislative session. He had no constitutional authority for such an act, but Governor Ferguson made the session legal by issuing a call after it became evident that the legislature was going to meet anyway. When the legislature convened, the house impeached the governor on 21 articles. On September 24 the senate convicted Ferguson on ten charges. The most serious counts held that Governor Ferguson had appropriated for his own use certain state funds; that he was guilty of irregularities in connection with deposits of public funds in the Temple State Bank, of which he was a stockholder; and that during his campaign in 1916 he had secured currency in the amount of $156,500 from unknown sources. It was discovered later that most of this money had been borrowed from the brewing interests and apparently had never been repaid. The court of impeachment removed Governor Ferguson from office and prohibited him from holding office in Texas again, a restriction that would yield strange developments in later years.

Despite the ban on his holding office, Ferguson returned to the political wars the following year, contesting Will P. Hobby, the lieutenant governor who had taken his position after his impeachment, for the Democratic gubernatorial nomination. Ferguson campaigned with enthusiasm, venting his ire on the University of Texas in particular. One professor of the school, he declared, had devoted two years to an attempt to grow wool on the back of an armadillo. Faculty members were "educated fools," "butterfly chasers," and "two-bit thieves"; crooks and grafters controlled the school's administration. Governor Hobby was a "political accident." Hobby won the nomination with a comfortable margin of almost 70 percent of the vote. But the state had not heard the last of Farmer Jim Ferguson.

TEXAS IN THE FIRST WORLD WAR

The impeachment of a governor in Texas took place in the midst of a titanic military contest in Europe that was shaking the foundations of civilization. When German submarines took the lives of United States citizens, Texans, along with other Americans, became aroused. When Congress declared war on Germany on April 6, 1917, sentiment in Texas in support of the measure was overwhelming.

Politics determined that Texans would play a prominent role in the world conflict that dominated the second term of President Woodrow Wilson. It was the Texas delegation in the Democratic National Convention in Baltimore in 1912, the "immortal forty," that voted for Wilson first and last and possibly assured his nomination. Later Wilson appointed Thomas Watt Gregory, of Austin, as attorney general and David F. Houston, a former Texan, as secretary of agriculture. Albert Sidney Burleson, of Austin, served as postmaster general and during the war directed government operation of the nation's telephone and telegraph systems. Colonel E. M. House was for some time probably the president's most trusted and important private counselor and personal representative. Thomas Love of Dallas served as assistant secretary of the treasury, and many other Texans held positions of great honor.

Within the state the military demands of war were quite apparent. Thousands of soldiers trained in four large camps (McArthur in Waco, Logan in Houston, Travis in San Antonio, and Bowie in Fort Worth) and in officers' training schools in Leon Springs and Kelly Field. A number of aviation schools scattered over the state provided many citizens with their first view of an airplane. Almost one million Texans registered for military service. Through the selective service law and voluntary enlistment, 197,389 served in the army, navy, and marine corps, with only a few opposing or evading the draft. Women made their contribution to the services, providing 449 nurses. Of those Texans in the armed services, more than 5,000 lost their lives.

At home the state council of defense sought to make the resources of Texas available for the war effort. Its work was distributed among major committees. Cooperating with it were 240 county councils and approximately 15,000 community councils. The services of these committees were placed at the disposal of the directors of various drives for Liberty Loans and support of the Red Cross. These committees also assisted in promoting wholesome recreation for the soldiers and in doing various other things to add to the comfort of the troops and to improve their morale. The publicity committee of the council directed war information, kept available a staff of "four-minute men" for various campaigns, distributed pamphlets, urged the conservation of food, and remained on the alert for disloyal acts and utterances. After the war, the council aided returning soldiers in securing employment.

Independent of the council of defense but cooperating with it was the Federal Food Administration in Texas. Its first campaign in the fall of 1917, which aimed at getting housewives to sign cards agreeing to conserve flour, sugar, fats, and meats, was not so successful as had been expected. Then the emphasis was shifted from the homes to the merchants, and each dealer was requested to conform to the "fifty-fifty" rule which required the sale of one pound of wheat substitute for every pound of wheat flour. From April 15 to June 15, 1918, a "wheat fast" was imposed on Texas, during which period no flour was shipped into the state. Thus, some Texans found themselves eating corn bread even for breakfast.

Industry expanded during the war. Shipbuilding yards and factories producing goods for the war effort were located in various cities, particularly along the coast. New oilfields located at Ranger, Desdemona, and Breckinridge in West-Central Texas brought boom town conditions to those areas and added to the supply of petroleum necessary for the armies and the civilian population. Unemployment declined to almost nothing.

The war effected a number of other significant changes. Inflation brought a soaring cost of living not always matched by a comparable increase in incomes, though farm prices generally advanced. A permanent change was the rapid increase in public expenditures, expenditures that failed to decline when the war ended. In 1913, the government of Texas spent approximately $13 million for all purposes; by 1919, this amount had increased to $27 million. Still another change was in the role of women who provided a major part of the additional labor force needed for the war effort. Often they worked in voluntary agencies, but some took jobs formerly reserved for men, such as in law enforcement, real estate sales, and labor union management.

Wartime also saw the triumph of the women's suffrage movement. Organized in 1903, the Texas Woman Suffrage Association gradually gained strength and narrowly missed securing legislative approval of a constitutional amendment granting women's suffrage in 1915. The suffragists resumed their battle in the legislature in 1917, only to see the impeachment of the governor intervene. But in a special session in 1918, the legislature adopted a law granting partial suffrage, in that it permitted women to vote in all primary elections. That same year several women were elected to posts in local governments, and Annie Webb Blanton won a race for the state superintendent of education. Voters in 1919 turned down a state constitutional amendment granting women's suffrage, but the cause was triumphant anyway, inasmuch as the decision would be made nationally. Another special session of the legislature in June 1919 ratified the Nineteenth Amendment to the Constitution of the United States, Texas being the ninth state in the union and the first in the South to give its approval.

Racial tensions grew during the period, though black Texans gave their support to the war effort. Approximately 25 percent of the soldiers from Texas were black, and blacks took part in Liberty Loan drives, supported the Red Cross, and otherwise demonstrated their patriotism. But a mob lynched a black man at Huntsville who was accused of evading the draft, and before the turmoil was ended, six members of his family were also dead. When rioting broke out in Houston in August 1917, 17 people were killed, and there were other instances of racial violence scattered throughout the war.

Predictable but regrettable was a spirit of fear, intolerance, and enforced conformity. Following the example set by the general government, the state legislature in a special session in 1918 enacted a drastic law to promote loyalty. To utter criticisms of the United States government, its flag, its officers, soldiers' uniforms, or to question the wisdom of the entrance or continuance of the United States in the war was an offense punishable by fine and imprisonment. The election law was changed to deny the ballot to foreign-born persons not naturalized. It was required that all classes in the public schools—the study of foreign language excepted—be conducted in English; that all schools devote at least ten minutes each day to the teaching of patriotism; and that the United States flag be displayed from a flagpole in every school yard. The law of 1923 requiring that the Constitution of the United States and that of Texas be taught in all public schools and that all teachers be citizens of the United States was, beyond a doubt, a belated product of the war mood.

Sometimes there were excesses of superpatriotism, which ranged from the absurd to the tragic. In keeping with the spirit of the times was a legislative investigating committee's recommendation that all recent books and periodicals in the state library extolling the greatness of Germany be immediately destroyed or securely boxed and put out of the way. Governor Hobby in 1919 vetoed the appropriation for the German department of the University of Texas, observing that elimination of such courses would promote purer Americanism. In some communities the obsession for conformity led to terror. "Influential and esteemed" citizens of a central Texas town, for example, flogged six of their neighbors who declined to join the American Red Cross. A newspaper editor in a nearby community endorsed the action, remarking that "whipping may convert some, while others are beyond conversion and should be shot." Texans found that crusading may beget intolerance.

THE POLITICS OF COMPLACENCY

"You are assembled here in a new era. You have problems to deal with that concern a new age." Thus did Governor William P. Hobby, in a message to the legislature in 1919, evaluate the importance of that time and occasion. Two years later, in the midst of a brief financial depression, Governor Pat M. Neff expressed a similar feeling in language even more startling: "We are pioneering today," he said to the legislature, "amid the rocks and reefs and whirlpools of the most disturbed and uncertain financial ocean the world has ever known. These are testing times. The affairs of men are shifting. Things are abnormal. The world is at a turning point in civilization...."

Indeed, the sense of change was very pronounced in the postwar years. Most Texans seemed to feel that with the defeat of Germany and the triumph of democracy, time had turned a page and begun a new chapter. The old order had passed, and a new era had come bringing sharp changes in the affairs of people and nations. In a sense this was true; it was the dawn of a great boom. As men went from the army and navy back to civilian life, they were easily absorbed by industry. The depression of 1920 was short lived, and Texas shared the general prosperity that soon returned. New plants were erected for the manufacturing and processing of goods, land values doubled, millions were invested in public utilities, and thousands of new oil wells belched forth their black gold. The great state highway system was constructed, destined to be used by an ever-increasing number of foreign and Texan-owned cars. New colleges were built, and thousands of youths crowded into all the institutions of higher learning; the public school system grew larger and more creditable each year. Prices of farm commodities lagged behind those enjoyed by industry, but bountiful crops tended to offset the price handicap. Texas was prosperous during the "mad decade," and people paid no heed to timid prophets here and there who told them that ahead were lean years that would devour the fat ones.

Thus, the decade following the close of the First World War did constitute a new era for business and industry, but in politics and political institutions there was little to distinguish it from the years that preceded it. A few new government agencies were added and some of the old ones were enlarged, but there was little suggestive of the "new era" that Governor Hobby thought he saw ahead. In many respects, the governor recognized the political demands of the emerging industrial and urban society. But a reluctant legislature and a complacent electorate refused to respond.

Complacency in politics was apparent even before the end of the war. In February 1918 a legislative investigating committee made a report suggesting various changes in the state government, but nothing except the eventual creation of the state board of control as a budget agency came out of the report. After the war Governor Hobby advocated more aid for education, a civil service commission, judicial reform, and state aid for home buyers, but only some educational improvements were made. The question of a constitutional convention was submitted to the voters in 1919 and defeated as voters rejected 10 out of 13 constitutional amendments. Caught by the spell of the new era, the legislature might propose changes, but the people disposed of them in their own way.

Proclaiming a new democracy, Pat M. Neff entered the race for governor in 1919, subject to the action of the Democratic primary in the following year. The dignified and devout Waco lawyer knew Texas politics firsthand, for he had served as speaker of the house of representatives in 1903 and 1904. His chief opponent in the Democratic primary was Joe Bailey, who returned to politics after eight years of retirement to base his campaign largely on opposition to the Wilson administration, women's suffrage, and most of the trends in government that had appeared during the last decade. Neff championed the great causes Bailey opposed, and he also favored a graduated land tax and other proposals that scandalized the staunch champions of the old Democratic party. Bailey led in the first primary, but in the runoff Neff won by a majority of 79,376. In spite of opposition from organized labor, Neff was renominated and reelected in 1922.

The new democracy was triumphant, but the people were not ready for any drastic changes. Through various messages to the legislature, Governor Neff advocated a number of reform measures and got practically nowhere. Rejected were changes in the state administrative system, a constitutional convention, and more laws to combat what Neff called the worst "crime wave" in the history of Texas. Neff, however, did his part to keep prisoners in the penitentiary. He disbanded the board of pardons, made his own investigations, and granted very few pardons. In this respect his administration was in striking contrast to those of Hobby and the Fergusons.

Otherwise, some permanent improvements were made. Governor Neff, an ardent champion of good roads, must be given a share of credit for the expansion and improvement of the highway system. Similarly, he used his influence effectively to promote the conservation of natural resources. The state park system had its beginning in 1923 with the creation of a nonsalaried park board. A harsh comment on the lack of foresight of those who had gone before is the fact that the state of Texas, which once had owned millions of acres of land, was obliged to solicit donations of a few hundred acres here and there so that its people might have access to recreational facilities.

THE KU KLUX KLAN AND THE RETURN OF FERGUSONISM

In 1921 there appeared in Texas an organization that remained the subject of controversy for several years. The Ku Klux Klan had its beginning near Atlanta, Georgia, in about 1915, taking the name of the organization of Reconstruction days and making white supremacy one of its slogans. It was, however, more akin to the various nativist movements that have arisen among the American people from time to time than it was to the original Ku Klux Klan of Reconstruction. In fact, the activities of the Klan in Texas were, as much as anything else, an effort to impose social and moral conformity on a society in rapid transition from the farm to the city. The Klan made little headway until after the First World War, when various conditions combined to promote its spread. The nation had been made aware of the presence of millions of foreign-born persons, commonly called "hyphenated Americans," whose loyalty had been impeached, in many cases unjustly, and after the war there arose sharp resentment toward everybody and everything foreign. Protestant in sympathy, the Klan was distinctly anti-Catholic and anti-Jewish. It declared war on crime and corrupt officials, a phase of its program that appealed to thousands of men who had little sympathy for its racial and religious intolerance. It gained its maximum growth in Texas during 1921 and 1922, at a time when Governor Neff (not in sympathy with the Klan) was writing and speaking against the "greatest crime wave" in Texas history and giving credence to the estimate that "not ten percent of those who violated the law were arrested, and not half of those who are arrested are convicted." The Klan went further, assuming for itself the responsibility of protecting "virtuous womanhood," "premarital chastity," "marital fidelity," "respect for parental authority," and "abstinence from alcoholic beverages."

Covertly, the Klan entered politics and soon its power was felt in almost every community. In 1922 it gained control of many local offices and participated in the campaign for the United States Senate. That year several candidates sought to succeed United States Senator Charles A. Culberson, who had served continuously since 1899 but was prevented by poor health from making an active campaign. The strongest contenders were Earle B. Mayfield, member of the Texas railroad commission, and James E. Ferguson, who had left the Democrats in 1920 to run for President of the United States on his own American party ticket but returned to the Democratic party two years later. Mayfield admitted that he had belonged to the Klan, and it was generally understood that he was supported by it, whereas Ferguson attacked the organization severely. Mayfield received the nomination, and disgruntled Democrats, uniting with the Republicans behind George E. B. Peddy, a Houston attorney, failed to defeat him in the general election.

In the election of 1924 the Klan played an even more important part by supporting Judge Felix D. Robertson of Dallas. His opponent, James E. Ferguson, disqualified from holding the governorship by the terms of his impeachment in 1917, entered the race through his wife, Miriam A. Ferguson. Robertson and Mrs. Ferguson survived the first primary, and the race became the keenest the state had seen in many years. The Klan was powerful but it had already lost ground. In their zeal to impose moral conformity, the Klansmen had frequently taken the law into their own hands. From many communities came reports of hooded men, working by night, serving as their own sheriff, judge, and jury, and flogging persons, driving them from their communities, or otherwise terrifying them. The Klan denied its connection with most of these outrages, but its masked parades and secret conclaves had inspired many of them. In the primary Mrs. Ferguson defeated Robertson by nearly 100,000 votes. Another minority of the Democratic party was now dissatisfied, and this group united with the Republicans in an effort to defeat Mrs. Ferguson in the general election. The bolters supported George C. Butte, dean of the University of Texas law school. Mrs. Ferguson defeated him by more than 100,000 votes to become the first woman governor of Texas.

During this second era of Fergusonism (1925–1927), reform took a holiday. James E. Ferguson, who determined the policies his wife followed, was disposed to pursue a conservative course. No drastic proposals appeared in the governor's messages, and no outstanding laws were enacted. Ferguson's liberal pardoning policy—2,000 acts of executive clemency, counting furloughs and extensions, during 20 months—evoked much gossip and unfavorable comment. An investigating committee found that most of the governor's pardons were issued on the recommendation of her husband, some of them before the beneficiaries reached the prison. The chief attack by the enemies of the administration was, however, aimed at the highway commission, a body composed completely of Ferguson appointees and dominated by the former governor who sat with it whenever important matters were up for consideration. It was alleged that favoritism, rather than the best interests of the state, was the determining factor in awarding contracts for the construction of roads. Several contracts were canceled as the result of suits brought by Attorney General Dan Moody, who became the chief antagonist of the Fergusons.

A crusader for reform, Dan Moody entered the campaign for governor in 1926 against Mrs. Ferguson. The Fergusons were confident, but the attorney general was able to defeat her by a substantial majority to become the next governor of the state.

MOODY'S REFORM PROGRAM

In Dan Moody the friends of reform had an able spokesman. Although he was the youngest governor who ever served Texas (elected at the age of 33), he had been seasoned by experience as a local prosecutor and by two years as attorney general. As district attorney in Williamson County, Moody had attained a statewide reputation for his vigorous prosecution of certain members of the Ku Klux Klan who had committed acts of violence, a distinction that brought him the office of attorney general.

He proposed a broad reform program that represented in the main the best ideals of the progressive forces of the day. He advocated a number of measures calling for important changes in the constitution and state laws. He supported a change in the constitution to permit the legislature to enact new laws on taxation. He proposed that the judiciary article of the constitution be rewritten so as to raise the number of justices of the supreme court from three to nine. He would give the governor power to appoint the important executive officers who were not elected under the Constitution of 1876. With these appeals Moody was no more successful than his predecessors who advocated the same or similar reforms, and the governor's most earnest and persistent plea for a civil service law was similarly rejected.

The perennial problem of prisons and prison management demanded attention during this period. The prison population was growing, the system was difficult to manage, and costs were climbing. Pursuant to the recommendation of Governor Moody, who favored a centralized system with fewer farming and more industrial projects, the legislature created a centralization commission to make a study of the Texas system and those of other states and to formulate a plan that would settle the vexing problem. The commission report resulted in a compromise measure that fell far short of the complete reorganization and concentration that the governor and other champions of reform had advocated. However, a previous legislature had created a governing body of nine members to select and employ a manager to be in charge of the entire system and to be responsible to the board. After Lee Simmons, a Sherman businessman, was appointed manager in 1930, the prison system thereafter showed marked improvement.

In the election of 1928, for the first time in history the interest in the contest for the presidential electoral vote in Texas was keener than the interest in state and local races. Governor Moody received a majority vote in the first primary, over Louis J. Wardlaw, who was supported by the

Fergusons. But early in the year the presidential candidacy of Governor Alfred E. Smith of New York, a Catholic and an outspoken opponent of prohibition, threatened the unity of Texas Democrats. The Republicans also were, as usual, divided. The "Harmony Democrats" chose Governor Moody as their leader and at the state convention prevailed against the "Constitutional Democrats" led by Thomas Love, who sought to instruct the state delegation against Smith. After Smith was nominated at the national convention in Houston, the anti-Smith forces organized to do battle with the regular Democrats. Most of the party leaders stayed with the regular organization, but they were not able to match the strength of the bolters who united with the major Republican faction in a campaign for Herbert Hoover that resembled the prohibition crusades of other years. Hoover's plurality was 26,000; he was the first Republican to receive an electoral vote in Texas. It has been said that the chief issue in the campaign of 1928 were "the three P's"—Prosperity, Prohibition, and Prejudice. In this election, Tom Connally defeated Earle B. Mayfield for the United States Senate.

Moody's first term was, perhaps, the most prosperous period the state had ever known. But during the last year of his administration, the state began to feel the pinch of the Depression and panic that had begun in 1929 with the collapse of the stock market and had since spread to all parts of the nation. The brunt of the Depression, however, was born by the Sterling and Ferguson administrations (1931–1935).

AN EXPANDING ECONOMY

The sense of change evident in many aspects of Texan life in the twenties was particularly noteworthy in matters of technology. In urban areas conveniences such as electrical appliances and lights and plumbing facilities became commonplace, and occasionally a radio was seen. In rural areas living conveniences changed little, inasmuch as electricity was rarely available, and indoor plumbing was the exception rather than the rule. However, the number of farm tractors tripled, signaling the acceleration of the mechanical revolution in agriculture.

Both farm and city shared in the growth of the automobile industry. The number of automobiles in Texas rose more than 500 percent during the decade, to the point which by 1929 there was an automobile for every 4.3 Texans. Apparent everywhere was the economic impact of the automobile, but there were also many social consequences. By the end of the decade, many smaller towns were losing population, and some of the churches and businesses within them were disappearing as the automobile made long distance travel practical. Another consequence, somewhat more intangible, was the belief of some that the morality of the people was declining and that the automobile bore much of the responsibility.

It was a period of rapid population growth and mobility within the population of the state. With an increase in population from 4,663,228 to 5,824,715, Texas enjoyed one of the most rapid growth rates in the union. Rural Texas gained only nine percent in population, while urban Texas increased 58 percent. Between 1920 and 1930, the rural farm inhabitants declined from about 48 percent of the population to 40 percent. All cities of more than 25,000—and there were sixteen of them—grew at an average rate of 61 percent. Smaller cities generally grew in a similar manner, but not quite as consistently, some with notably high rates of increase and a few even showing a decline. In 1930 Houston, Dallas, and San Antonio each contained between 200,000 and 300,000, together more than 10 percent of the state's total population.

Petroleum and transportation accounted for much of the urban growth after the turn of the century, especially during the twenties. Railroads, largely in place by the beginning of the twentieth century, continued to influence the development of certain inland cities. Along the coast, the development of a system of deep-water ports combined with comprehensive rail systems to spur the growth of other cities. The natural ports of Texas, even in the days of light sailing craft and small steamers, had never been adequate. As early as 1883 a project was begun to deepen the channel of Galveston Port. By the early twentieth century a 25-foot channel had been provided, and by 1927 it had been increased to 35 feet. For many years Galveston ranked second only to New York in exports and was the

The Houston Ship Channel has contributed much to the development of the City of Houston and the prosperity of the state. It has enabled Houston to become one of the major ports of the world. (Courtesy Houston Chamber of Commerce)

greatest cotton-shipping port in the world. By 1910 the Sabine and Neches system and the ports of Freeport, Port Aransas, and Houston had been improved. The development of the Houston Ship Channel, linking the city with the Gulf of Mexico, began in 1899, but it was not until 1925 that a 55-mile channel 30 feet deep and costing more than $14,000,000 truly opened the age of ocean-going traffic for Houston. Within a short period of time, Houston became the leading port in Texas and the second or third largest in the nation.

Oil similarly brought spectacular growth. Port Arthur expanded from fewer than 1,000 in 1900 to 50,000 in 1930. In West Texas oil discoveries during the twenties actually built towns such as Pampa, Borger, McCamey, and Wink, and substantially added to the populations of Amarillo, Abilene, San Angelo, and others.

While growing, Texas cities often acquired a distinct character and identity. San Antonio, perpetuating its early pattern of expansion, retained its military installations and historic sites and sustained a steady growth rate but a somewhat leisurely atmosphere. Dallas became a financial and mercantile center, widely known for its cultural achievements and aspirations. Fort Worth, generally regarded as a city of the west, developed an extensive livestock market and packing facilities, as well as the sobriquet of "Cowtown." Houston, perhaps because of its more varied economy and sprawling explosive growth, could not be given only one label. In all these cities and in a host of smaller ones could be found substantial evidence of the ubiquitous oil industry.

During the twenties oilmen made significant oil discoveries at various places over the state. Geologists believed that a geological fault line extending from Corsicana and Mexia on the north to a point south of Luling to the southwest contained oil. Their theory was confirmed with the discovery of the Mexia field in 1921 and the Luling field a short time thereafter. By 1922 oil fields were producing in South Texas with discoveries located in Jim Hogg, Webb, Duval, and Zapata counties, and before the decade ended, Starr and Brooks counties joined the list of producers.

One of the largest areas of oil production opened in the twenties with the development of the first fields in the Permian Basin, an area that extends from Tom Green County on the east to Culberson county on the west, and from Crockett County on the south to Lubbock County on the north. Commercial production was opened near Colorado City in 1920, but the boom period began with the discovery of Santa Rita near Big Lake in 1923. This discovery, soon followed by many others over the basin, brought wealth not only to the oilmen who opened the fields, but also to the University of Texas and A&M University, owners of some of the land where many of the fields were developed.

In the Panhandle gas production was opened in 1918, and in 1926 the first Panhandle oil boom began with the discovery of a 10,000 barrel per day well near the small community of Borger.

Network of iron and steel. Beginning in the 1920s, Texas led the nation in oil production, and it still has a large share of the nation's oil and gas reserves. Oil field machinery like that pictured here is a familiar sight in many parts of the state. (Texas Highway Department)

Oil refining and chemical manufacturing utilizing petroleum products likewise expanded rapidly during the 1920s. Large refineries and chemical plants, usually located in coastal areas where port facilities were available, took advantage of the ever increasing volume of petroleum production to produce refined oil products and chemicals that were shipped to points all around the nation, indeed, around the world. However, while oil was rapidly becoming the dominant factor in the Texas industrial economy, the manufacturing and processing of agricultural products continued to be important. Their value, as late as 1929, exceeded the value of refined petroleum goods produced in Texas refineries.

Although industrial production increased in the twenties, organized labor, ordinarily associated with the development of industrialization, did not fare particularly well. In fact, labor unions were more influential at the beginning of the century than they were at the end of the twenties. From about 1890 to about 1915, a strong, militant labor organization, the United Mine Workers, struggled with some success in the coal mines of Erath and Palo Pinto counties to improve the poor pay and pitiful working conditions that prevailed. At its peak, soon after 1900, 4,000 miners belonged to the union, but membership declined thereafter and almost disappeared altogether during the twenties. Oil workers in the Gulf Coast oil fields were organized by the American Federation of Labor in 1905. For a time in the first decades of the new century, the Texas State Federation of Labor grew in size and influence, attaining 783 organizations with 50,000 members by 1920, but thereafter it also declined. To some extent, the decline was caused by the open-shop campaign pursued by business interests and chambers of commerce and to the unfriendly open-port law of 1920, enforced vigorously by state officials. Bad union management, including ill-advised strikes, may also have contributed to the decline. By 1927, membership in the state federation had declined to 25,000.

Efforts of farmers to organize to protect their interests similarly enjoyed only limited success. In 1902 ten Rains County farmers laid the foundation of the Farmers' Educational and Cooperative Union of America. Better known as the Farmers' Union, the organization exercised some influence for a time, but declined on the eve of World War I. Two farm groups were formed in the 1920s. The Farm-Labor Union, which limited its membership to "dirt farmers," grew rapidly for a time but declined rapidly after 1925. The Farm Bureau Federation, however, fared better. It grew out of a national base, and though it experienced some difficult years in the late twenties, it survived to become an influential, if somewhat conservative, voice of Texas agriculture.

LIFE IN THE TWENTIES

The twenties are often remembered as a flamboyant age, replete with "flappers," raccoon coats, speakeasies, real estate promotions, bathtub gin and bootleggers, gangsters, and the Charleston. The image is probably greatly exaggerated for the nation as a whole; certainly it is exaggerated for Texas. But there were social changes evident in the life of the people, some that were viewed as wholesome and desirable, but others that many considered to be evidence of decadence and immorality.

Whether or not immorality increased during the decade is debatable, but certainly there was a great deal of concern about the matter. Parents, preachers, school authorities, social workers, editors, and others condemned the behavior of society. Concern was frequently expressed over immodest dress, modern dances, smoking, drinking, lewd movies, midnight joy riding, the rising crime rate, and an increasing traffic in narcotics. In addition to the automobile, the movies were often held accountable for the altered pattern of behavior. Surely, the movies were an important part of life in the twenties. By 1920 Texans were spending more than $24 million a year for movie tickets, an average per capita attendance of more than 20 movies per year.

Efforts to regulate morality took many forms. In some instances the violent and lawless methods of the Ku Klux Klan were used to punish suspected evildoers, but more lawful and less violent methods generally prevailed. A number of cities established movie censor boards; other cities passed ordinances prohibiting questionable behavior. One ordinance seems to have banned flirting; there were laws regulating the type and extent of clothing worn by bathers and prohibiting the showing of movies on Sunday. A law was proposed, though never passed, even limiting the height of a woman's shoe heel to one inch. Toward the end of the decade such efforts to regulate behavior tended to diminish.

The changing character of society was reflected in the status of the family. Texans married at a rate generally higher than the national average, but by 1929 the divorce rate in Texas was one of the highest in the nation and had more than doubled since 1916. At the same time, the size of the average family grew smaller, declining from 4.6 in 1920 to 3.5 in 1930; urban families were even smaller. On a more positive note, the employment of children declined rapidly. Whereas in 1910 more than 40 percent of the boys in Texas were employed, only slightly more than 7 percent of all children were employed in 1930. Compulsory school attendance laws, child labor regulations, and a growing urban population likely accounted for the decline.

Conditions for women suggested some significant changes during the decade. The total proportion of women in the population who worked outside the home rose only slightly, but the nature of their employment changed a great deal, as farm employment declined and more found urban jobs. The number of married women who worked increased almost two-thirds throughout the state, even more in larger cities during the decade. More and more women engaged in political activity, and by 1929 three women held seats in the state legislature. But the quest for equality still had a distance to go. Wages for women were generally one-half or less than those paid to men. Efforts were made to secure legal equality for women, particularly with respect to laws regarding property management and marriage rights, but to no avail.

Although the decade opened with a considerable amount of violence and oppression, conditions for black people improved in subsequent years. The number of black people in the population increased, though more blacks left the state than moved into it. Similarly, there was a movement of black people from rural to urban areas. The violence of earlier years, which had often ended in lynching, almost ceased, and a significant, if temporary, victory in the ongoing battle for the right to vote was won in 1927 when the United States Supreme Court ruled that the legislature could not, by state law, establish a white primary.

Even against the obstacle of political complacency, the educational system of Texas made substantial progress during these years. To be sure, by most criteria that could be used to evaluate the public schools, Texas continued to lag behind the national norms. But through constitutional reforms, added local responsibility, expanded resources, and consolidation, public education came nearer than previously to meeting the needs of a modern society. The creation of new institutions of higher learning and the dramatic growth of older ones were additional evidence of a maturing educational structure.

The legislature on the eve of the twenties took several steps toward providing educational opportunities. In 1915 the legislature approved a special appropriation for rural schools, provided that the rural district itself maintained a certain level of taxation. The measure had the effect of greatly stimulating the levying of local school taxes in rural districts where they were most needed. Legislatures continued the practice until 1949 when more fundamental reforms were made. Ferguson's administration also gave the state a compulsory school attendance law, which went into effect in the fall of 1916. In 1918 a constitutional amendment authorizing free textbooks was adopted; at the same time the constitutional maximum for the state school tax was raised; and in 1920 the voters entirely abolished the limit on the tax rate that communities might levy for school purposes. Yet, these measures, and even more generous expenditures in the early twenties, did not lift the Texas school system from its low rank when compared with other states. A survey of the schools, authorized in 1923, revealed deficiencies and brought forth a number of recommendations, most of which the legislators and voters did not see fit to adopt. But a number of changes in education in the twenties did take place.

Consolidation of schools was an apparent trend. The building of a state highway system and the improvements of other roads during this period made it possible for communities to take advantage of a law of 1914 that permitted the consolidation of schools whenever a majority of the voters of two or more districts favored it. A 1925 law permitted trustees to make consolidations under certain conditions, and with the decision to provide transportation at public expense for students who lived at a distance, the beginning of the end of the "little red schoolhouse" was at hand. By 1930, 1,530 consolidations had been made.

A second trend noticeable in the public schools was in the matter of curriculum changes. Especially in the urban schools, the influence of so-called progressivism was felt, as some educators insisted that schools must go beyond traditional teaching and prepare the students for life in a wide

The lack of a public school system was one of the grievances listed in the Texas Declaration of Independence, and the Constitution of the Republic of Texas stipulated that Congress provide such a system. Despite the support of President Mirabeau B. Lamar and Governors E. M. Pease and James S. Hogg, among others, the Texas public education system was relatively poor, and the one-room school house was still very common in 1914 (the date of the photograph). Not until the automobile was in general use was it possible for widely separated families to send their children to larger and better-equipped schools that offered more specialized education. (E. C. Barker History Center, University of Texas)

Dewey

variety of ways. With the movement came changes in teaching methodology, school health programs, comprehensive student testing programs, and an expansion of vocation training, especially in courses related to business. In another curriculum matter there was an ongoing effort to prohibit by law the teaching of evolution. Beginning in 1923, critics of the theory of evolution fought the battle regularly in each session of the legislature until 1929, but no law was ever passed.

With the pattern of segregation as rigid as ever, black schools, already far behind those for white students, failed to share equally in the educational gains. Between 1905 and 1930 the salaries of white teachers in rural areas increased $8.98 per scholastic; salaries of black teachers per student increased 16 cents. In 1929 black teachers received about $120.00. Blacks constituted approximately one-third of the scholastic population of East Texas, but more than 97 percent of the high schools of East Texas were for whites only. Nevertheless, progress was made. By 1930 the illiteracy rate for black people had declined to 13.4 percent.

During these years the junior college movement, associated with Texas since its infancy, expanded rapidly. In 1897 the Baptist state convention established a correlated system of higher educational institutions, with Baylor University and Mary Hardin-Baylor College as senior schools and Howard Payne College, Rusk College, and Decatur Baptist College as two-year institutions. Other denominations entered the field, establishing by 1920 a number of church-controlled junior colleges. About the same time the state created junior colleges in Stephenville and Arlington, and with the founding of El Paso Junior College in 1920, Texas cities had begun to provide junior colleges.

Four-year colleges and universities also grew in number and size. During the early decades of the twentieth century, the state established a college for women in Denton and acquired, founded, or authorized normal schools in Canyon, Commerce, Kingsville, and Alpine. In 1923 the state normal schools were made into teachers' colleges. The same legislature authorized the establishment of Texas Technological College in Lubbock, thus meeting the demand for a university pressed by citizens of that area for many years.

The twenties saw the most rapid growth the state colleges had known. Each year brought additional thousands of students to tax the facilities of the already overcrowded institutions. In fact, student enrollment grew about 150 percent during the decade. To solve the space problem temporarily, the University of Texas erected flimsy wooden structures dubbed "shacks" by the students. In a sense, the shacks symbolized the position of education in Texas at this point. Progress had been made, and the need for improvement had been recognized, but there remained much to do.

SELECTED BIBLIOGRAPHY

General studies on this period are R. Steen in F. C. Adams (ed.), *Texas Democracy* (4 vols., Austin, 1937); S. S. McKay, *Texas Politics, 1906–1944;* Lewis L. Gould, *Progressives and Prohibitionists: Texas Democrats in the Wilson Era* (Austin, 1973); Lewis L. Gould, "Progressives and Prohibitionists: Texas Democratic Politics, 1911–1921," *Southwestern Historical Quarterly,* LXXV, 5–18; S. Acheson, *35,000 Days in Texas,* and *Joe Bailey: The Last Democrat;* R. Steen, *Twentieth Century Texas; An Economic and Social History;* and S. S. McKay and O. B. Faulk, *Texas after Spindletop.* Of particular value is Norman D. Brown, *Hood, Bonnet, and Little Brown Jug: Texas Politics, 1921–1928* (College Station, 1984).

Much writing has been done on border troubles of this period. See Don M. Coerver and Linda B. Hall, *Texas and the Mexican Revolution: A Study in State and National Border Policy, 1910–1920* (San Antonio, 1985); Clifford Alan Perkins, *Border Patrol: With the U.S. Immigration Service on the Mexican Boundary 1910–1954* (El Paso, 1978); C. C. Cumberland, "Border Raids in the Lower Rio Grande Valley, 1915," *Southwestern Historical Quarterly,* LVII, 285–311; Charles H. Harris III, and Louis R. Sadler, "The 1911 Reyes Conspiracy: The Texas Side," *ibid.,* LXXXIII, 325–348; Charles H. Harris III and Louis R. Sadler, "The Plan of San Diego and the Mexican-United States War Crisis of 1916: A Reexamination," *Hispanic-Amer-*

ican Historical Review, LVIII, 381–408; Frederick Katz, "Pancho Villa and the Attack on Columbus, New Mexico," *The American Historical Review*, LXXXIII, 101–130; Craig Smyser, "The Columbus Raid," *Southwest Review*, LXVIII, 78–84; and W. P. Webb, *The Texas Rangers*. A different viewpoint of the Rangers is found in Julian Samora, et. al., *Gunpowder Justice: A Reassessment of the Texas Rangers* (South Bend, 1979).

For special studies on the Fergusons, see Lewis J. Gould, "The University Becomes Politicized: The War With Jim Ferguson, 1915–1918," *Southwestern Historical Quarterly*, LXXXVI, 255–276; R. Steen, "The Ferguson War on the University of Texas," *Southwestern Social Science Quarterly*, XXXV, 356–362; Ouida Ferguson Nalle, *The Fergusons of Texas* (San Antonio, 1946); H. G. James, "The Removal of Governor Ferguson of Texas by Impeachment," *National Municipal Review*, VI, 725–726; W. F. McCaleb, "The Impeachment of a Governor," *American Political Science Review*, XII, 111–115; and Octavia F. Rogan, "Texas Legislation, 1925," *Southwestern Political and Social Science Quarterly*, VI, 167–168. Useful also is the manuscript of Jack Lynn Calbert on the Fergusons, located in the library of Indiana University.

Activities of two other governors are described in James Clark, *The Tactful Texan: Governor W. P. Hobby* (New York, 1958); and in Emma M. Shirley, *The Administration of Pat M. Neff, Governor of Texas, 1921–1925* (Waco, 1938). Also see S. A. MacCorkle, "The Pardoning Power in Texas," *Southwestern Social Science Quarterly*, XV, 218–228; and O. D. Weeks, "The Election of 1928," *ibid.*, IX, 337–348.

Texas's part in the First World War is treated, inadequately, in Army and Navy History Company, *History of Texas World War Heroes* (Dallas, 1919). For the operation of the draft law, see *Second Report of the Provost Marshal General to the Secretary of War* (Washington, D.C., Government Printing Office, 1919). See also James W. Pohl, "Slayden's Defeat: A Texas Congressman Loses Bid as Wilson's Secretary of War," *Military History of Texas and the Southwest* (1972); William E. Nicholas, "World War I and Academic Dissent in Texas," *Arizona and the West*, XIV, 215–230; and Robert V. Haynes, *A Night of Violence: The Houston Riot of 1917* (Baton Rouge, 1976).

For additional reading on other crusades, see H. A. Ivey, *Rum on the Run in Texas* (Dallas, 1910), biased but of value; Elizabeth A. Taylor, "The Woman Suffrage Movement in Texas," *Journal of Southern History*, XVIII, 194–215; Charles C. Alexander, *Crusade for Conformity: The Ku Klux Klan in Texas, 1920–1930* (Houston, 1962); and John Carroll Eudy, "The Vote and Lone Star Women: Minnie Fisher Cunningham and the Texas Equal Suffrage Association," *East Texas Historical Journal, XIV, 52–57*.

Texas's place on the national scene is touched upon in Arthur Link, "The Wilson Movement in Texas, 1910–1912," *Southwestern Historical Quarterly*, XLVIII, 169–185; Lewis L. Gould, "Theodore Roosevelt, William Howard Taft, and the Disputed Delegates in 1912; Texas as a Test Case," *ibid.*, 33–56; Dewey Grantham, "Texas Congressional Leaders and the New Freedom, 1913–1917," *ibid.*, LIII, 35–48; R. N. Richardson, *Colonel Edward M. House: The Texas Years, 1858–1912;* W. P. Webb and Terrell Webb (eds.), *Washington Wife: Journal of Ellen Maury Slayden from 1897–1919* (New York, 1962); Lee N. Allen, "The Democratic Presidential Primary Election of 1924 in Texas," *Southwestern Historical Quarterly*, LXI, 474–493; Tom Connally and Alfred Steinberg, *My Name Is Tom Connally* (New York, 1954); and Bascom M. Timmons, *Garner of Texas; A Personal History* (New York, 1948).

For oil and industrialization, see C. C. Rister's *Oil! Titan of the Southwest* and a list of more than 60 titles found in Walter Rundell, Jr., "Texas Petroleum History: A Selective Annotated Bibliography," *Southwestern Historical Quarterly*, LXVII, 267–278. See also David F. Prindle, "Oil and the Permanent University Fund: The Early Years," *ibid.*, LXXXVI, 277–298. Kenneth Ragsdale, *Quicksilver: Terlingua and the Chisos Mining Company* (College Station, 1976) tells the story of a unique Texas industry, and George T. Morgan's "The Gospel of Wealth Goes South: John Henry Kirby and Labor's Struggle for Self-Determination, 1901–1916," *Southwestern Historical Quarterly*, LXXV, 186–197, explains well the problems of unions in twentieth-century Texas.

Social, cultural, and ethnic affairs in the 1920s are studied in Lynn Ray Musslewhite, "Texas in the 1920's: A History of Social Change," a manuscript in the Texas Tech University Library. See also Alwyn Barr, *Black Texans;* Mary Beth Rogers, et. al., *We Can Fly: Stories of Katherine Stinson and Other Gutsy Women* (Austin, 1983), Arnoldo DeLeon, *San Angeleñnos: Mexican-Americans in San Angelo, Texas,* (San Angelo, 1985); James J. Thompson, Jr., *Tried as by Fire: Southern Baptists and the Religious Controversies of the 1920's* (Macon, Ga., 1982), and Charles R. Wilson, "Morons, Monkeys, and Morality: Reactions to the Scopes Trial in Texas," *East Texas Historical Journal*, XII, 51–63.

CHAPTER SEVENTEEN
THE GREAT DEPRESSION
1930–1941

In the early autumn of 1929, after a long period of soaring prices, the New York stock market turned downward. On October 23 a sharp drop precipitated much selling, and on the next day panic seized the exchanges of the nation as the stock market crashed. Although Texans suffered their share of losses in the stock market crash, their immediate injuries were not as great as those that followed later. Prices fell, business volume declined, unemployment rose, the number of bankruptcies increased, and with the closing of all banks in March 1933, the Great Depression reached every farm and hamlet in the land.

"Prosperity is just around the corner" came to be a trite, sorry joke. President Herbert Hoover, who was unduly optimistic, thought for a time that local relief agencies could supply adequate aid to those in need, but toward the end of his term, he advocated stronger measures. In 1933 newly inaugurated President Franklin D. Roosevelt announced his "New Deal." His positive action in dealing with the bank crisis and his assurance that the general government would apply its vast resources toward relief and recovery restored a measure of confidence, but it did not bring the nation out of the financial doldrums. Meanwhile, state and local governments tried to survive and to offer a degree of assistance in the troubled times.

Progress toward recovery was uneven until midsummer 1935; henceforth improvement was rapid until the autumn of 1937, when a recession that continued through much of the following year wiped out a considerable part of the gain. Not until the gigantic defense program of 1940-1941 stimulated demands for labor and goods did the economic society attain "recovery," and even then many thousands of workers continued to be unemployed.

The times were difficult, but the decade was not without positive achievements. Conservation of natural resources received more attention than ever before, and cultural achievements were rich and varied.

TEXANS IN HARD TIMES

Although Texans apparently fared somewhat better than people in some other areas, the Depression brought worry and concern to most people, and to others it brought suffering, even desperation. An unemployment census taken in 1933 showed that 105,045 families, representing 7.1 percent of the population, were on relief. The next year there were 246,819 relief cases, representing a million people, or about 13 percent of the population. Building construction came almost to a standstill. Cotton, which sold for 18 cents a pound in 1928, dropped to five cents in 1932. East Texas oil, which was selling for 60 cents a barrel in 1930, fell to 5 cents a barrel; steak sold for 18 cents per pound; milk sometimes cost as little as 4 or 5 cents a quart; and hamburgers cost a nickel.

These statistics, though grim, tell only a part of the story, for even though the prices were meager, many could not afford them. In one West Texas town a citizens' relief association killed, dressed, and stored wild rabbits to be distributed to those in need. The demand soon exceeded the supply. Aransas Pass businessmen donated tons of fish to feed the poor and hungry people of Dallas. Soup kitchens and bread lines appeared in most towns of any size. Many farm laborers and tenants, dispirited and broken, gathered in towns and cities, hoping either to share in direct relief or to draw small wages on public works projects. Merchants, manufacturers, and shopowners laid off workers, adding to the ranks of the unemployed.

In many cases relatives and friends helped for a while and local charity organizations did the best they could, but all such efforts proved to be inadequate. Thousands of individuals and not a few families took to the highways, hitchhiking from place to place. Many were without funds, and persons living near the roads were often compelled either to give them food or turn them away hungry. Swarms of unfortunate people sought protection in abandoned buildings, caves, dugouts, and shanties made of discarded boxes.

Some groups suffered more than others in the Depression. The unemployment rate for black people was approximately twice that for the white population, and sometimes relief agencies refused to aid blacks or otherwise discriminated against them. In San Antonio the dependence of Mexican-American people on relief seems to have been in line with that of the general population. In 1933, however, the percentage of Mexican-Americans receiving aid exceeded all other groups. Some returned to Mexico, apparently because of the hard times they encountered in Texas.

Schools and local governments shared in the hard times. In Houston in 1932 one-half of the street lights were turned off because money to pay for the electricity was not available. Beaumont in 1934 reduced funds for the city library to almost nothing and for the city schools by almost one-half. Street lights were turned off altogether. School teachers in San Antonio whose husbands earned at least $2,000 per year were not rehired. The severity of the budget cuts varied from city to city and from school district to school district, but few, if any, escaped altogether. Even churches suffered from the Depression. Other factors were involved, especially the automobile, but financial problems played a large role in the decline of the number of churches by almost 4,000 during the period between 1926 and 1936.

Texans' reactions to the Depression varied but were not greatly different from reactions elsewhere in the nation. At first, most seemed to believe that there was no cause for worry. By 1930 there was still a considerable amount of optimism, but some were beginning to question the future. From 1931 on, the existence of the crisis was generally accepted and the search for solutions intensified.

On the whole, the solutions supported were of a moderate kind. There were "Buy Now" campaigns, "Give-a-Job" and "Share-the-Work" programs, and most widely discussed of all, a "Back-to-the-Farm" movement. Some worried about socialism or communism, and many believed that capitalism was threatened. But there is little to indicate that revolution or rebellion was a serious possibility. There were demonstrations by the unemployed such as those in Houston in 1930 and in Beamont in 1931, but these were orderly and peaceable. Sheep shearers in San Angelo and pecan shellers in San Antonio, both desperately poor Mexican-American groups, struck for higher wages. There was some violence, but not of the scale found in labor disputes elsewhere in the nation.

Violence of another kind, however, did afflict the countryside of Texas from time to time. Perhaps to some degree a holdover from the lawless side of Prohibition, or perhaps a reflection of the unsettled conditions of the Depression, notorious and outrageous criminals occasionally killed and robbed on a grand scale, apparently relishing the publicity. Of these, none were more flagrant in their disregard for human life and decency than Bonnie Parker and Clyde Barrow. This pair terrorized large areas of Texas from 1932 until they were finally shot to death in 1934 in an ambush in neighboring Louisiana.

THE POLITICS OF POVERTY, 1930–1935

The gubernatorial campaign of 1930 sustains the exaggerated statement that the Democratic party in Texas chooses its candidate for governor by lottery. Twelve persons filed for that office, and it seemed that of a half-dozen or more any two might have qualified for the second primary. Governor Moody supported Ross Sterling of Houston, who was completing his fourth year as chairman of the highway commission. James E. Ferguson, as usual, was in the race through the candidacy of his wife. In the first primary, Mrs. Ferguson led the ticket and Sterling ran next to her. After a bitter contest preceding the second primary, Sterling was nominated by a majority of about 100,000. His chief claim to the office was the promise of "a business administration to meet the demands of a growing State, by a successful business man." In the general election he defeated without difficulty the Republican nominee.

During Sterling's administration (January 1931 to January 1933), emergency followed emergency, and one crisis had not passed before another appeared in the offing. Taxes were in arrears; state income fell off sharply; expenditures were nearly as high as ever; and Sterling was obliged to use the veto often and to call special sessions repeatedly.

Governor Sterling worked faithfully and brought to bear on public affairs the rich experience of a varied business career, but the times bred discontent and in 1932 the voters were ready for a change. Sensing the dissatisfaction, James E. Ferguson again entered the contest. In supporting his wife's campaign he said to the voters: "Two years ago you got the best governor money could buy, this year you have an opportunity to get the best governor patriotism can give you." He added that when his wife was governor he would "be on hand picking up chips and bring in water for mama." He charged that Sterling had wasted state highway funds; he attacked him for invoking martial law in the East Texas oilfields; and he proposed certain drastic changes in state taxes. Former Governor Moody and other prominent Texans worked diligently for Sterling, but in the second primary Mrs. Ferguson beat him by a few hundred votes out of a total of nearly a million.

The Forty-third Legislature, which convened in January 1933, found that the Depression was aggravating old problems and creating new ones. Governor Ferguson recommended a sales tax of three percent, but the legislature, like its successors until 1961, refused to adopt such a measure. Despite budget economies, the administration found it difficult to make ends meet, and municipalities and school districts everywhere were impoverished. The urgent need for more revenue accounted in part for a measure, enacted as a rider on an appropriation bill in 1933, making betting on horse racing legal. Texas joined in ratifying the Twenty-first Amendment to the Constitution of the United States, which ended national Prohibition on December 5, 1933. Then the Forty-fourth Legislature submitted an amendment repealing state prohibition, and the voters ratified it in August 1935.

It is difficult to evaluate objectively Mrs. Ferguson's second administration. Relations between the legislature and the executive were not harmonious, as lawmakers distrusted the governor and her husband. The return of the Fergusons' policy of liberal pardons and paroles for state prisoners was attacked from various quarters. It must be said, however, that the administration was economical and apparently met with much greater public approval than did Mrs. Ferguson's first administration as governor.

In the election of 1934 Texas voters were not confronted directly by "Fergusonism" for the first time since 1914, as Governor Ferguson did not seek reelection. Nominated and elected was James V. Allred of Wichita Falls, who was completing his second term as attorney general. Although his platform was more conservative than those of his opponents, Allred was relatively liberal and is sometimes referred to as "Texas's last liberal governor." All candidates favored, or at least refused to oppose, old age pensions, an issue that would dominate Texas politics for the remainder of the decade.

By the beginning of Governor Allred's term, January 1935, the New Deal relief program was well under way and President Roosevelt's plans for national social security had been announced. The governor urged "planned recovery" for Texas, and to that end a Texas planning board was established for a period of four years. It set out to prepare a comprehensive program for the construction and utilization of the resources of the state. No fewer than a dozen boards and commissions were created by the legislature to aid in carrying out projects associated with the program of relief and security in its various forms.

RELIEF, RECOVERY, AND REFORM

As the Depression deepened, it soon became evident that private relief organizations and antiquated public agencies, such as poor farms, could not care for the increasing number of persons who had no means of support. Governor Sterling in 1931 suggested public works as a means of providing indirect relief, but of greater immediate value was his committee for the relief of unemployment.

Meanwhile, the federal government had attacked the problem in a program calling for billions of dollars for direct relief and work relief, much of which was to be spent through state and local agencies. There were two means of approach: the first by making grants to the states for general relief, and the second by carrying out a works program that would serve the double purpose of relieving unemployment and "priming the pumps" of business and industry. The first aid was extended late in 1932 under a law authorizing the lending of Federal Reconstruction Finance Corporation (RFC) funds to state and local bodies for relief activities. Through various state and local agencies, both public and private, these funds were used to provide work on different projects, supposedly of public value. The RFC insisted that the state should share with the federal government the burden of relief. The legislature accordingly submitted to the voters a constitutional amendment to authorize the issuance of bonds not to exceed $20 million for the relief of unemployment. Issued from time to time, the last of these "bread bonds" were sold during the Allred administration. The legislature also established a Texas relief commission as a coordinating and administrative organization through which the various agencies worked. County relief boards were provided to make plans for roads and other public improvements through which needy persons might be given employment.

The Federal Emergency Relief Administration, the first major New Deal relief agency, provided the states with funds for both direct relief and work relief. Through this agency and through the RFC, which continued to provide funds, Texas received approximately $50 million for the aid of its destitute in 1933 and 1934. Unfortunately, the number of persons calling for relief did not diminish.

While these agencies were meeting the pressing needs of the people who had neither property nor jobs, a broader program of government spending was launched that was designed both to furnish employment and to revive business and industry. From 1933 through 1938 the Civilian Conservation Corps employed about 110,000 men and war veterans. The National Youth Administration, directed for a time in Texas by Lyndon B. Johnson, was established in 1935 to administer a program of assistance to young people. Under the National Industrial Recovery Act, the Federal Emergency Administration of Public Works (PWA) organized and coordinated a gigantic system of public building. The RFC loaned funds both to private business establishments and to construction firms for the purpose of financing public and public-guaranteed projects. In May 1935 work relief was coordinated in a Works Progress Administration, which made possible construction and rehabilitation of all kinds of public property and provided hundreds of white-collar jobs. The various works programs left some results of enduring value in Texas. For instance, PWA alone listed in its "physical accomplishments" up to 1939, 510 public buildings, 998.7 miles of new highway pavement, and improvements in 135 parks and playgrounds.

For the calendar years 1933 through 1936 the national government supplied through various agencies $10,667,379,186 for relief and works programs. Of this sum $351,023,546, or about 3.03 percent, was spent in work programs in Texas. During the same period, state and local funds used for relief and work programs in Texas amounted to $80,268,595. Expenditures continued with some variations but without any substantial decrease. General relief functions were transferred from the Texas Relief Commission to the Welfare Department in September 1939, and during the following four years the administration of general relief cost $1,300,000. For the sound of mind and able-bodied, war industry ended the need for aid from the state.

More permanent reform to cope with the problems of the needy came with the adoption of the National Social Security Act in August 1935. This law provided support for the elderly either through pensions supplied by state and federal taxes (old age pensions) or through funds provided jointly by employee and employer contributions (social security). The law, which also provided assistance to other groups in need, has been amended a number of times over the years.

INDUSTRY, OIL, AND TRANSPORTATION

The Depression that brought uncertainty and worry to so many Texans brought stagnation or even retrenchment to some areas of the state's industrial economy, though not to all. Spurred by business organizations, such as the Texas Manufacturing Association and regional chambers of commerce, manufacturing expanded slowly and steadily in the early decades of the twentieth century. By 1929 industry in Texas employed more than 150,000 people and contributed almost a half-billion dollars annually to the economy. With the onslaught of the Depression, almost 30 percent of these factories disappeared by 1933, and with them disappeared almost 40,000 jobs and more than $225 million of annual production. By 1932 some industries declined to about one-third of their normal level of activity. Not until 1939 would conditions return to the level of ten years earlier.

Chemicals, petrochemicals, and oil refining were the most prosperous of Texas industries during the Depression. Using a sulfate process, a large paper mill that made paper out of yellow pine began production in a plant near Houston in 1937. The production of alkalies, used in the manufacture of a wide variety of items ranging from stockings to soap, began in a Corpus Christi plant in 1934. Oil refining, in particular, expanded. By 1939 more than 80 percent of the state's oil production was processed in Texas refineries, and volume had almost doubled during the Depression decade.

Oil, in fact, became more and more a mainstay of the state's economy

Texas farmers used "sleds" and other devices to reduce the use of hand labor in cotton production, but cotton farming remained heavily dependent on migrant workers until after World War II. (Courtesy of The University of Texas at Austin, Archives)

in the 1930s. With Texas leading the petroleum-producing states of the nation after 1928, oil production generally edged upward until 1937. Production was increased greatly in the 1930s through the discovery of the East Texas field by Columbus Marion ("Dad") Joiner, a veteran wildcatter. Other discoveries after 1930, though not so sensational, added to the supply. A slowdown in pipeline construction during the Depression temporarily impeded the growth of the natural gas industry, but over the decade it, too, expanded.

Transportation, in some ways, suffered from the impact of the Depression. Railroad construction had continued at a slow pace in the early decades of the twentieth century. Mostly, the construction consisted of feeder roads or extensions of trunk lines, with only a few projects of major proportions between 1910 and 1930. In 1932, however, railroad mileage in Texas reached its peak of 17,000 miles and began a slow decline. Electric railroads, which came into use earlier in the twentieth century, similarly began to disappear in the thirties.

Possibly the Depression slowed, but certainly it did not stop, Texans' growing dependence on the automobile and the highway. Automobiles became commonplace in the twenties and continued to grow in numbers in the thirties in spite of the hard times. While the population increased about 10 percent, motor vehicle registration grew almost 25 percent between 1929 and 1939.

With the coming of the automobile came the demand for good roads, a demand that would not truly be answered until the 1930s. Until 1907, roads were built and maintained, or not maintained, by the counties, using the personal labor of local citizens who contributed their time. After 1907, counties could vote for bonds and build roads, but the state could not. In

1916 a limited amount of federal aid became available, and the next year the state set aside a small fund for roads under the supervision of a newly created state highway department. But as late as 1923 Governor Neff was quite correct in claiming that there were not a hundred miles of continuously good roads in the state. Texas had no highway system worthy of the name.

Reform and success came with the reorganization of the Texas Highway Commission through laws enacted in 1923 and 1925 and with energetic and efficient management during the Moody years. Under capable leadership and with sufficient funding from gasoline taxes and federal sources, the state by 1932 began to develop a highway system worthy of pride. In a decade not noted for tangible progress, the number of miles of paved roads in Texas more than tripled.

Although progress was slow and came mostly in the second half of the decade, labor unions gained in numbers and power in the Depression. During the 1920s, labor unions declined somewhat, hampered by determined opposition from management, the competition of company unions, and even a bit by lethargy. With the advent of the Depression, workers were more inclined to turn to unions in search of security, and the federal government lent a friendly hand. The organization of workers especially made headway among oil, chemical, and refinery workers after the Congress of Industrial Organizations (CIO) launched a campaign along the Gulf Coast. In addition to efforts directly affecting workers, unions regularly took stands on public issues. Organized labor aided in the repeal of Prohibition and secured favorable amendments to the Texas eight-hour law. It helped in delaying the adoption of a general sales tax and worked to secure a law prohibiting the sale of prison-made goods.

AGRICULTURE IN THE DEPRESSION

Despite disasters, such as floods and price fluctuations, the early years of the twentieth century were relatively prosperous ones for Texas farmers. Growing cities and the consequent enlargement of markets brought to them an affluence greater than they had ever known. Sharp price breaks were temporary and prices soon recovered. The value of Texas farms more than doubled between 1910 and 1920. The twenties were more difficult. Mechanization aided production, but prices declined, and the value of Texas farms fell slightly. On the national level Congress passed several acts intended to assist the troubled farmer, but these had little effect.

The Depression years, often coinciding with drought, threatened disaster. For the farmer, prosperity was out of the question, and survival was often in doubt. The Roosevelt administration attacked the problem with the most elaborate farm program in history. In fact, it made relief for agriculture a cornerstone for the entire New Deal structure. At the heart of the plan was a concept known as parity—that is, a fair price. Prices for farm products would provide farmers with the purchasing power they had had in the years immediately preceding World War I.

To accomplish this goal, Congress passed the Agriculture Adjustment Act of 1933, commonly called the "Triple A," under which farmers received payments for taking land out of cultivation and for producing small numbers of livestock. Texas growers received more than $44 million under the program, income desperately needed, for low prices were combining with a major drought to bring many perilously close to bankruptcy. The Agriculture Adjustment Act was declared unconstitutional in 1936, but other legislation was passed limiting acreage and providing payments to assure the farmer of at least a portion of parity.

Other New Deal farm programs expanded credit facilities for farmers. This additional credit enabled many farmers to hold onto their homes, when otherwise they would have lost them through foreclosure. Limited in scope but of particular value to low-income farmers was the Farmers Home Administration. It lent money for purchasing livestock, fertilizer, and a small number of farms.

Pumpjacks, derricks, and oil tanks were famillar sights in many Texas counties by the 1930's. (Courtesy of The University of Texas at Austin, Archives)

The New Deal farm program was a popular program with most Texas farmers. In the election of 1936, one West Texas town almost totally dependent on agriculture voted for Roosevelt by a margin of eight to one, and this type of support was general across the state. For many, only the government payments enabled them to hold onto their lands.

But the New Deal programs did not solve the problems of Texas agriculture. The value of Texas farms declined 28 percent during the Depression decade. Texans talked a great deal about going "back to the farm," and there were a few experiments in rural resettlement. But the actual movement of the population was in the other direction. While the total population of the state increased, the number of Texans living on farms declined. Forty percent of the population lived on farms in 1930; only one-third of the population did so by 1940.

CONSERVATION

In the Depression decade, conservation programs intended to preserve the state's natural resources made considerable headway. Soil, timber, water, and petroleum—all exhaustible resources—were affected by programs either begun or expanded in the midst of the Great Depression.

A survey by the Soil Conservation Service of the United States Department of Agriculture reported that about three-fourths of the area of Texas suffered from soil erosion. A few people had recognized the gravity of the problem at an early date, long before the 1930s. In Newton County a farmer constructed a farm terrace in 1882, and other East Texas farmers imitated his practices. The Farmers Cooperative Demonstration Work, now known as the Extension Service, began to educate farmers on the dangers of soil erosion as early as 1910. The United States Soil Conservation Service, created by the Department of Agriculture in 1935, began to apply to the problem the vast resources placed at its command, and the Agricultural and Mechanical College of Texas cooperated with it. Texans generally complied enthusiastically with the Soil Conservation and Allotment Act of 1935 under which farmers of wheat, corn, cotton, and tobacco received government grants for leaving part of their land idle and practicing measures that would conserve the soil. In order that Texas might get the maximum benefit from the federal agencies, the legislature in 1939 passed a state soil conservation law under which landowners may, by their own vote, establish soil conservation districts, and today nearly all of the state has been organized into such districts.

Although there is very little virgin timber left, the more than ten million acres of forest land in eastern Texas represent one of the state's greatest natural resources. Very little was done by way of conserving the timberlands until the Texas Forest Service was created in 1913 and placed under the direction of the Agricultural and Mechanical College. In the following year federal cooperative aid for fire prevention was secured and a skeleton organization was established. Demonstration and research facilities were provided in 1924 when the state acquired its first forest. Later, forest nurseries and research laboratories were established.

But again, it was in the 1930s that a major step was taken in the development of forests in Texas. Pursuant to an invitation extended by the legislature in 1935, the federal government began to purchase forest lands. By 1980, the national forests in the state represented a total of almost 700,000 acres.

Water is another resource of Texas that has long affected the movement of population and the comfort and prosperity of the people. Abundant springs and running streams made the settlement of East Texas easy, but in many parts of Central and West Texas settlement was retarded because of the difficulty of securing water. It will be recalled that the High Plains were not appropriated until well drills and windmills tapped the bountiful veins of underground water.

The problem of flood control and of the equitable distribution for irrigation, municipal supply, and industry brought about the enactment of a number of laws pertaining to the surface waters of Texas. Coincidental with the beginning of the Depression, the oldest large Texas conservation district was created. This was the Brazos River Conservation and Reclamation District, created with generous powers for conserving and exploiting the waters of the entire Brazos River watershed. A similarly large and independently powerful water district was the Lower Colorado River Authority (LCRA). In the Depression years LCRA began the construction of a series of dams along the Colorado River that formed the reservoirs now known as the Highland Lakes. Other river systems in the state were developed in a similar manner. Anticipating some problems of a later day, the legislature in 1932 passed the Wagstaff-Woodward Law, which placed the claims of cities to water ahead of all other interests.

Conservation of oil, which became a reality and attracted the most attention in the 1930s, was actually an old idea, dating back to the time of the Spanish. Under the Spanish and Mexican law, title to minerals remained with the state when land was deeded to individuals, and the Republic of Texas and the state of Texas pursued this policy until adoption of the Constitution of 1866. This constitution and subsequent ones provided that minerals and land were released with the sale of the land by the state. More modifications of the policy followed, until the Relinquishment Act of 1919 gave landowners fifteen-sixteenths of the oil and gas found under the land and retained one-sixteenth of the minerals for the benefits of public funds, particularly for the public schools.

The first Texas law to regulate the production of oil and gas was enacted in 1899, just four years after the first commercial production of petroleum in Corsicana. It required that water be cased off from oil-bearing formations, that abandoned wells be plugged, and that gas not be permitted to escape. More adequate efforts at regulation followed the adoption of the constitutional amendment of 1917, which greatly enlarged the control of the legislature over natural resources. The pipeline law of 1917 was enacted, providing for the organization of the oil and gas division of the Railroad Commission, with power to supervise common carrier pipelines and to regulate their rates. Two years later the oil and gas conservation law was enacted. Under its terms, the Railroad Commission issued regulations calculated to prevent waste in the production of oil and gas, and after some delay the rules were enforced through agents and supervisors. Work was confined chiefly to requiring drilling reports of operators, to preventing injury to oil and gas formations by permitting water seepage, and to preventing drilling a well too close to a property line or to another well.

But it was overproduction and collapsing markets that truly brought regulation to the Texas oil industry and led oil operators to turn to the Railroad Commission for aid. At first the commission assisted in making voluntary agreements to limit production, but after trying this method for some three years, the commission in 1930 held a hearing and issued an order limiting the production of the state to a certain number of barrels each day. The order was attacked in the courts on the contention that it was not designed to prevent the waste of oil but to fix the price. It was, however, upheld by the Travis County district court.

Meanwhile, there came a flood of oil from the newly discovered East Texas field. The commission was slow in asserting its authority in the new field, and when it did so, many operators either ignored its orders or resisted with suits in the federal courts. Thus, there was inaugurated a train of litigation over oil production that seemed interminable. During three special sessions the legislature gave much time to the problem. Rules made by the Railroad Commission were modified and repealed repeatedly, and the decisions of the courts were not consistent. For a period in 1931, many wells were opened completely. The production amounted to one-third of the nation's requirements, and the price declined to a few cents a barrel. Then Governor Sterling placed the field under martial law, sent in the National Guard, and controlled production until February 1931, when a three-judge federal court ruled that he was acting without authority.

The cause of conservation was strengthened when the federal government, first by an executive decree and later by an act of Congress, prohibited the shipping of illegally produced oil across state boundaries. The state laws were improved; the courts became more sympathetic to regulation; and the plan of proration set forth in the order of the Railroad Commission in April 1933 was finally upheld by the federal courts. At last proration had become a reality. The purpose of the practice of proration, claimed a senior member of the Railroad Commission, was to leave in the earth "the least possible amount of oil never to be recovered by man." Production limits, however, were generally restricted to the level that would supply the market demand but not result in an oversupply that might depress prices unduly. Later compacts to regulate production were made with other oil-producing states, and although claims were again made that these agreements were not "for the purpose of stabilizing or fixing the price" of petroleum products, market demand was a major factor in determining production quotas.

LITERATURE AND THE ARTS IN THE DEPRESSION

Although the times were hard, jobs were scarce, and life was often inse-cure, the age of the Great Depression in Texas brought forth a number of outstanding accomplishments in literature and the arts. The Texas Institute of Letters, organized in 1936 in keeping with the observance of the centennial of Texas independence, came to be an effective agency in encouraging writing and improving its quality. Perhaps J. Frank Dobie gave it its watch word when he wrote: "Great literature transcends its native land, but there is none that I know of that ignores its own soil. All great literature plumbs and soars to the elementals. Texas authors need not be antiquarians; in the rich soil of the novel there has not been even a furrow plowed."

Dobie was one of a trio long linked with the Texas Institute of Letters who constituted what is perhaps the nearest thing to a school of writers that Texas has known. The others were Roy Bedicheck, a naturalist, and Walter Prescott Webb, an historian. The range of Frank Dobie's writings was remarkably broad: cowboys and the cattle industry, folklore, and themes of nature. His publication of *A Vaquero of the Brush Country* in 1929 was soon followed by *Coronado's Children, Tales of Lost Mines, Buried Treasure in the Southwest, Tongues of Monte,* and others. Bedicheck twice won awards for his *Karankawa Country* and *Adventures with a Texas Naturalist.* Webb wrote con-vincingly on such diverse subjects as *The Great Plains* and *The Texas Rangers,* and later his *Divided We Stand* and *The Great Frontier* would receive national acclaim.

The tradition of scholarly historical writing continued in the Depres-sion years. C. C. Rister and R. N. Richardson published studies on the Indian frontier of the late nineteenth century; J. Evetts Haley and W. C. Holden wrote on the same period but turned their attention more to the settlement of western areas and the development of the ranching industry.

Carlos Castaneda began his seven-volume study of the Catholic heritage in Texas, which would require more than twenty years to complete. Julia Kathryn Garrett featured the filibusters and short-lived Texas Republic in her *Green Flag over Texas*. Twentieth century Texas began to attract some writers, as evidenced in S. S. McKay's studies on twentieth century politics and Sam Acheson's biography of the colorful Texas senator, Joe Bailey.

Folklore attracted the attention of a number of creative artists. J. Mason Brewer in prose and Huddie ("Leadbelly") Ledbetter in song captured many of the folk stories and songs of the black people of Texas. Another collector of folklore was John A. Lomax, who began his work in an earlier decade but continued to collect ballads throughout the 1930s.

Texas writers of fiction produced works that received national recognition. Of these, Katherine Ann Porter was the most widely known. A prolific writer, she published stories with a variety of settings, including some within Texas. *The Leaning Tower and Other Stories*, *The Days Before*, and *Ship of Fools* are her better-known books. Dorothy Scarborough and George Sessions Perry, writing about life in rural Texas in a realistic style, described the struggle for survival in a land where nature often turned harsh, relentless, and unrewarding.

New types of media offered opportunities for creativity. Texas contributed a number of stars to the motion picture industry. Among the actors were Tom Mix, Joan Crawford, Ginger Rogers, Mary Martin, and Gene Autry; and achieving fame as directors were King Vidor and Howard Hughes. Radio, which was little more than a curiosity in Texas during the 1920s, was of great value to the aspiring artists of the 1930s. During the Depression decade several network chains were organized, and by the end of the decade, Texas was well-covered by radio stations. An important feature of radio programming was hillbilly music, later to achieve a kind of respectability as country music. Ernest Tubb and Bob Wills began their music careers in Texas, as did Leonard Slye, who became better known as Roy Rogers; and there were many others.

THE POLITICS OF RECOVERY

The Allred administration, which took office in 1935, faced many problems, the most difficult of which was that of old age assistance, more commonly referred to as old age pensions. The constitutional amendment establishing the pension program was vague, not specifying the amounts to be paid or the standards for determining who should receive them. Furthermore, the amendment made no provision for raising additional funds necessary to meet the payments. Pension questions occupied much of the regular sessions of the legislature and led to the calling of several special sessions, but the problems persisted. Applications for aid quickly climbed to more than 80,000; the legislature voted more funds and made conditions for receiving pensions more difficult, but by June 1937 more than 125,000 aged Texans were receiving pensions. At that time the legislature conducted an investigation of the old age assistance commission, and it was evident that the subject of pensions was in politics.

Pensions and taxation, subjects necessarily linked together, drew sharp attention in the gubernatorial campaign of 1936 when Allred sought reelection. Texans had heard a great deal of Huey Long's "share of the wealth" program in Louisiana; they were well-acquainted with Dr. Francis E. Townsend's plan to pay a pension of $200 a month to most persons past 60 years of age; and Father Charles E. Coughlin's National Union for Social Justice was then active. The candidates accordingly leaned toward a more generous pension policy. Governor Allred, who advocated pensions for the aged needy only and but few new taxes, was more conservative than his opponents; and the fact that he was nominated in the first primary by receiving more votes than his four opponents combined indicates that the Texas voters were still in a conservative mood.

The governor was obliged, nevertheless, to appeal to the Forty-fifth Legislature, which convened in January 1937, for additional revenue. Colleges, public schools, and almost all state institutions and agencies needed more money. The voters had, moreover, authorized worker's compensation for state employees, had planned a teachers' retirement fund, and, apparently, would soon authorize the state to care for the needy blind and for dependent children.

Allred proposed to raise most of the additional revenue by an increase in all taxes on oil, gas, and sulfur. The legislature refused to increase taxes, and in keeping with the spirit of the times, it showed a weakness for imposing new burdens on the general revenue fund without providing additional income. In appropriating it was as bold as a lion; in taxing, as timid as a lamb.

Some decisions made earlier in the decade brought more problems to the Allred years. An urgent need for revenue accounted in part for a measure, enacted in 1933, making betting on horse racing legal. The act, denounced in the pulpits of the state and by many editors and businessmen, was repealed in 1937 by a special session of the legislature called by Governor Allred for that purpose.

The return of legalized liquor similarly brought problems. When voters in August 1935 repealed the state prohibition amendment, they rejected a plan for state liquor sales. Shortly thereafter, the legislature provided for taxing and licensing dealers, prohibited the sale of hard liquor by the drink, provided for local option elections, and placed the administration of the traffic under a liquor control board. Soon there were complaints of violations by dealers, especially of the provision of selling liquor by the drink, and for years thereafter each legislature had to deal with the question in one or more of its phases. The status of liquor in counties and cities that were dry at the time that state prohibition was enacted in 1919 was not affected by the repeal of the amendment, and local option again became an issue in many communities. Revenue from the sale of liquor was of substantial aid in paying social security obligations.

Pursuant to a mandate of the voters in a constitutional amendment in 1932, Texas celebrated in 1936 the one hundredth anniversary of its independence. The state appropriated $3 million for the use of the centennial commission and the United States government matched it with an equal amount. The WPA also made contributions. The public funds were divided between the main exposition at Dallas and various other historical and commemorative projects in different communities. A considerable part of the money was spent in erecting numerous monuments to historical personages and placing markers at historic sites.

In the Texas gubernatorial race of 1938, politics and showmanship combined to produce one of the most spectacular campaigns in the state's history. Among the 13 candidates there were a number of veteran campaigners, but it was W. Lee O'Daniel, a flour-milling company executive and salesman of Fort Worth, who attracted the most attention. About a month before the election it became evident that he was reaching more people than all other candidates combined.

O'Daniel was a familar name to most Texans. For several years he had conducted a noonday radio program, replete with a hillbilly band, humor, and homely advice. "Please pass the biscuits, Pappy," and "The Light Crust Dough Boys are 'On the Air'" were words heard by thousands each week. Many thought that O'Daniel's candidacy was only a device to sell more flour, and perhaps it was, at least at first, but he soon became a serious contender. He applied to the race the same tactics he had used in selling flour by radio: a bit of country music interspersed with comments and an occasional short, informal speech filled with blasts at "professional politicans." Whether it was the promise of a businesslike administration, the castigation of professional politicans, the music, the candidate's homely philosophy, or the promise of pensions that drew the votes has not been determined; it is only known that for the first time since the Texas primary law was adopted did a candidate for governor, making his first race, poll more than half of the votes.

From the beginning, O'Daniel was a controversial figure in politics. His admirers were as loyal as had been those of the Fergusons and accepted O'Daniel as the spokesman for the ordinary citizen who had long been victimized by the people in power. His critics were equally determined in their opposition. Many of them looked upon O'Daniel as someone who was more foolish and naive than he was wicked, an innocent who had strayed into politics. Actually, O'Daniel was neither a crusader for the ordinary people nor an innocent. He was a shrewd and tough businessman, a superb actor, and a successful salesman who was one of the early politicians in Texas who hired and relied upon a public relations firm. He was often inconsistent and had the ability to be so without alarming his supporters, but he did have some convictions that never wavered. For example, he was a dedicated enemy of organized labor.

O'Daniel's performance as a governor left much to be desired. His campaign promise to give a pension to every old person was pared down to a proposal to give only to needy persons past 65 years of age an amount sufficient to raise their income to $30 a month. Similarly, the governor soon abandoned the hope, often expressed to the voters, that the new taxes would not be necessary and proposed to the legislature that an enlarged pension program be financed by a tax of 1.6 percent on all transactions. The lawmakers dubbed the proposal a sales tax (anathema in Texas at that time) and attacked it bitterly. The affair widened the breach already existing between the governor and the legislature. The legislature liberalized pensions but failed to provide additional revenue, and the problem became even more vexing. In spite of vetoes the deficit in the general fund continued to increase.

Six candidates challenged O'Daniel's bid for reelection in 1940. Although they attacked his record and his plan for raising revenue, his opponents did not directly attack his proposal for more liberal pensions. Texas had developed a "share-the-wealth" movement of its own, and the candidates did not dare to resist it. O'Daniel was renominated by an overwhelming vote and reelected in November 1940.

Like the lawmaking bodies that had preceded it for a decade, the Forty-seventh Legislature, which convened in January 1941, found that the problem of taxation was its chief worry. It could not, like its predecessor, take up the question, debate it, and drop it. The general fund, which supplied most of the agencies, showed a deficit of $25 million. There were predictions that Texas would be deprived of all federal pension money unless it raised more funds to meet the increasing demand of its own liberal pension laws. The teachers' retirement payments had not been matched by the state; the electorate demanded that it care for its destitute children and the blind. After extended debate there was passed and given executive approval an omnibus tax bill calculated to bring $22 million in additional revenue annually. Approximately one-half of the amount was to come from increased taxes on the production of oil and gas and the remainder from a variety of sources. This measure doubled the old age pension income but did not quiet the agitation over pensions.

When a seat in the United States Senate was made vacant by the death of Morris Sheppard in 1941, the governor appointed as his successor, until an election could be held, Andrew Jackson Houston, the 87-year-old son of the hero of the Battle of San Jacinto. Houston got to Washington but did not live to complete his short appointive term. Meanwhile, several candidates entered the senatorial race, one of the last being Governor O'Daniel.

Although O'Daniel was elected to finish out Sheppard's term, his prestige was seriously impaired, for he had defeated by only a few hundred votes Congressman Lyndon B. Johnson, an "old friend" of President Roosevelt. In the Democratic primaries of 1942 he defeated ex-Governors Dan Moody and James V. Allred, after a hard-fought campaign in which it was charged that O'Daniel had failed to support adequately President Roosevelt's defense and war policies.

With the election of O'Daniel to the United States Senate, Lieutenant Governor Coke R. Stevenson, formerly a speaker of the house, was inaugurated governor in August 1941. Stevenson's term coincided with the years of World War II, and this, coupled with Stevenson's strong conservative beliefs, would mean that his years in the governorship would see little change in state government, services, and programs. However, the state highway system was given additional funding early in Stevenson's administration.

During the 1930s the influence of Texans in the national government became greater than ever before. John Nance Garner, who had served continuously in the House of Representatives since he first took the oath of office before Speaker Joe Cannon in 1903, was elected Speaker in 1931. In the year following he was nominated and elected Vice-President and was reelected in 1936. In presiding over the Senate, his great personal influence and broad acquaintance with legislative tactics were brought to bear on most of the measures that made up the New Deal. A movement was launched to nominate him for President in 1940, but the movement declined as it became increasingly evident that President Roosevelt would again accept the nomination.

There were other influential Texans in Washington. Jesse Jones of Houston was chairman of the RFC from 1933 to 1939. In 1939 he was appointed administrator of the powerful Federal Loan Agency and in 1940 was appointed secretary of commerce. In 1933 Texans held the chairmanships of six major committees in the House of Representatives. Sam Rayburn of Bonham became majority leader and later Speaker of the House of Representatives. Morris Sheppard, mostly remembered for his work on behalf of national Prohibition, promoted President Roosevelt's New Deal in the Senate until his death in 1941. The other senator, Tom Connally, became chairman of the Committee on Foreign Relations and was a staunch spokesman for the administration in the enactment of the gigantic defense program and the war measures of the 1940s.

SELECTED BIBLIOGRAPHY

General accounts of the Depression include the writings of S. S. McKay and O. B. Faulk, *Texas after Spindletop;* Robert C. Cotner (ed.), *Texas Cities and the Great Depression* (Austin, 1973); the manuscript of Donald Whisenhunt, "Texas in the

Depression, 1929–1933: A Study of Public Reaction," in the library of Texas Tech University, and Donald Whisenhunt (ed.), *The Depression in the Southwest* (Port Washington, N.Y., 1980). Very useful is Julia Blackwelder, *Women of the Depression: Caste and Culture in San Antonio, 1929–1939* (College Station, 1984). For political affairs toward the end of the decade, George Green, *The Establishment in Texas Politics, The Primitive Years, 1938–1957* (Westport, Conn., 1979), is invaluable.

The annual reports of the Texas Department of Human Resources give the most complete accounts of the aid given by the state to certain classes of citizens. The *Annual Report* for 1949 is especially useful for the period preceding that date. On federal aid during the Depression years, see F. A. Williams, *Federal Aid for Relief* (New York, 1939). On Texas relief, see Booth Mooney, "925,000 Texans Getting Government Aid," *Texas Weekly*, November 11, 1939, pp. 6–7. Also see William R. Johnson, "Rural Rehabilitation in the New Deal: The Ropesville Project," *Southwestern Historical Quarterly*, LXXIX, 279–295.

On national affairs, see Bascom Timmons, *Jesse H. Jones* (New York, 1956), and *Garner of Texas* (New York, 1948); C. D. Dorough, *Mr. Sam, A Biography of Samuel T. Rayburn* (New York, 1962); Lionel Patenaude, "Garner, Sumners, and Connally: The Defeat of the Roosevelt Court Bill in 1937," *Southwestern Historical Quarterly*, LXXIV, 136–151, and "The Garner Vote Switch to Roosevelt: 1932 Democratic Convention," *ibid.*, LXXIX, 189–204; and Richard B. Henderson, *Maury Maverick: A Political Biography* (Austin, 1970).

The best general reference on industrial development is the *Texas Almanac.* The *Texas Business Review,* published monthly by the Bureau of Business Research, The University of Texas, Austin, is invaluable. Especially useful are Edwin J. Foscue, "The Pulp and Paper Industry of East Texas," April 1967, pp. 105–109; Stanley A. Arbingast, "Notes on the Industrialization of Texas: Synthetic Rubber," September 1952, pp. 16–17; and Robert D. Maxwell and Robert D. Baker, *Sawdust Empire: The Texas Lumber Industry, 1830–1940* (College Station, 1983). On the history of oil, good references are C. C. Rister, *Oil! Titan of the Southwest,* comprehensive and authoritative; W. Gard, *The First Hundred Years of Oil and Gas* (Dallas, 1966); Craig Thompson, *Since Spindletop* (Pittsburgh, 1951); Henrietta M. Larson, *History of Humble Oil and Refining Company* (New York, 1959); Alfred M. Leeston, John A. Chrichton, and John C. Jacobs, *The Dynamic Natural Gas Industry* (Norman, Okla., 1963). Jack Donahue, *Wildcatter: The Story of Michel T. Halbouty and the Search for Oil* (New York, 1979); and Walter Rundell, Jr., *Oil in West Texas and New Mexico: A Pictorial History of the Permian Basin* (College Station, 1982). *Texas Highways,* official journal of the Texas Highway Department, Austin, and *Texas Parade,* published in Austin monthly with the endorsement of the Texas Good Roads Association, are rich sources of information on Texas roads. On railroads, see Everett L. DeGolyer, Jr., "The Railroads: The End of An Era," *Southwestern Historical Quarterly*, LXXIII, 356–364.

Considerable writing has been done on conservation efforts. The beginning of demonstration work in Texas is related in H. R. Southworth, "The Later Years of Seaman A. Knapp," *West Texas Historical Association Year Book,* X, 88–104. A satisfactory account of the New Deal farm program is given in Henry Bamford Parkes and Vincent V. Carosso, *Recent America, Book II* (New York, 1963). See also *Agricultural Research in Texas since 1888* (College Station, 1956). For an account of soil conservation, the *Annual Reports* of the Agricultural Extension Service, Texas A. & M.

University, are most useful. On water conservation, floods, and droughts, much has been written in recent years. Among the best sources are W. P. Webb, *More Water for Texas* (Austin, 1954); and Robert Lee Lowry, *Surface Water Resources in Texas* (Austin, 1958). The long and involved history of the conservation of oil in Texas is dealt with by R. E. Hardwicke, *Legal History of Conservation of Oil in Texas,* Maurice Cheek, *Legal History of Conservation of Gas in Texas* (Mineral Law Section, American Bar Association, 1938); and David F. Prindle, *Petroleum Politics and the Texas Railroad Commission* (Austin, 1981). Brief studies are James P. Hart, "Oil, the Courts, and the Railroad Commission," *Southwestern Historical Quarterly,* XLIV, 303–320; and David F. Prindle, "The Texas Railroad Commission and the Elimination of the Flaring of Natural Gas, 1930–1949," *ibid.,* LXXXIV, 293–308. Concerning the East Texas oil field, see Ruel McDaniel, *Some Ran Hot* (Dallas, 1939). The work of the Texas Railroad Commission is brought out in J. A. Clark's *Three Stars for the Colonel* [Ernest O. Thompson] (New York, 1957).

Texas writers are discussed in Mabel Major and others, *Southwest Heritage: A Literary History;* J. Frank Dobie, *Life and Literature of the Southwest;* Ronnie Dugger (ed.), *Three Men in Texas: Bedicheck, Webb, and Dobie* (Austin, 1967); and Lon Tinkle, *An American Original: The Life of J. Frank Dobie* (Boston, 1978). Also, see the publications of the Texas Folklore Society. Country music is featured in two studies: Bill C. Malone, *Country Music U.S.A.; A Fifty-Year History* (Austin, 1968); and Charles R. Townsend, *San Antonio Rose: The Life and Music of Bob Wills* (Urbana, Ill., 1976).

CHAPTER EIGHTEEN
WAR AND
READJUSTMENT
1941–1959

On December 7, 1941, the armed forces of Japan attacked Pearl Harbor and drew the United States into the global war that had started in Europe in September 1939 when England and France resisted the German dictator Adolph Hitler. For months the nation had been moving toward hostilities: Congress, short of declaring war, had appropriated funds for a two-ocean navy, had enacted the first peace-time conscription law in American history, and had aided the enemies of Hitler and Benito Mussolini of Italy through almost every agency.

The government of Texas and the people loyally supported the national war effort. In keeping with its traditions, the state's men and women responded to the call to arms. Its oil kept ships, trucks, tanks, and planes moving against the enemy, and its industries were strengthened and harnessed for the cause of freedom. Everybody was needed in the war effort, and the people loyally did their part. Soon the rate of industrial activity was the highest ever known, and the total income surpassed all previous records. In spite of the many heartbreaking experiences of war, material prosperity generally prevailed, and after the victory was won, the problems of postwar readjustment were made easier by expanding industry, high prices for farm commodities, and a generous federal policy of providing schooling or on-the-job training for veterans. As in most of the rest of the nation, the Texas economy continued to expand; full employment, high wages, and high prices emphasized the abundance of the period.

Prosperity did not bring tranquility to the state, however. Farmers protested that they were not sharing fairly in the general abundance and called for greater freedom in their farming practices or for more controls, as their interest and points of view varied. Labor unions chafed at restraints and penalties they considered unfair and grew stronger regardless of them. The public school system, growing costlier each year and declining in efficiency, was completely reorganized. There were pleas, fervent and often repeated, for better care of children; the friends of the needy aged were not reconciled to the aid accorded them; and the blind and the crippled had their champions. During the war and the decade that followed, minority groups, though not as vocal as they would become in the sixties, began to express their demands for equality of treatment and for expansion of opportunity.

PUBLIC AFFAIRS DURING THE WAR YEARS

Public affairs in the state reflected the conditions of wartime. Although Governor Coke Stevenson was critical of the rationing program, he sought to promote the war effort. He called for rigid economy in all agencies of government and entered into a no-strike covenant with organized labor that prevented work stoppages in Texas. Attorney General Gerald Mann announced that the strict Texas antitrust laws would not be enforced against concerns seriously engaging in production. In its session of 1943 the legislature cut appropriations to most state agencies and reduced substantially expenditures for senior colleges, which were then short of faculty and students.

As the war proceeded, various federal agencies brought their efforts to bear on the people. The War Manpower Commission in Texas, with some 12 regional directors, sought to see that all qualified people were employed and that those deferred from military service worked at essential jobs. The National Office of Price Administration, in charge of rationing and price ceilings, used the staff and pupils of the public schools to implement sugar rationing. Later, rationing was extended to meats, fats (including butter), canned goods, coffee, shoes, and gasoline. One state agency, the powerful Railroad Commission, in charge of the production of from 40 percent to 50 percent of the nation's gas and oil, occupied a strategic position in the nation's war effort. It was effective and managed to cooperate with Harold L. Ickes, secretary of the interior and petroleum administrator for war.

In spite of the "freezing" of rents, salaries, and wages and the restraints on prices, the cost of living rose moderately during the war; but since almost every employable person was busy, family incomes increased significantly, and the rank and file of people were in relatively good circumstances.

For the most part, Texans at home accepted the problems of wartime with a minimum of complaints. They collected scrap iron and grew "victory gardens." They bought war bonds and gave to the Red Cross. They practiced blackout and air raid alerts, and generally they complied with the restrictions of rationing, although hoarding certainly was not an unknown practice. Occasionally the tensions of race mixed with the tensions of wartime to produce a crisis. Rioting in Beaumont in mid-June 1943 lasted for 20 hours until national guardsmen, local police, and Rangers restored peace. From time to time there were complaints about the stationing of black servicemen in the state, and often they were subjected to discrimination. A signal of the future, however, was the establishment of a civilian and military committee in Houston, charged with the responsibility of ending the mistreatment of black soldiers and lowering the tensions of the community.

It was during the war years that the cleavage between Texas conservative and liberal Democrats developed fully, with race having a significant influence in that development. The opponents of President Franklin Roosevelt and the New Deal were in evidence as a minority group in 1936. The candidacy of the staunch Texas Democrat, John Nance Garner, for president held the factions together in 1940, but President Roosevelt's determination to seek a third term prevented the Garner-for-President movement from reaching far beyond Texas. Added to their objections to Roosevelt and the New Deal, the conservative Texas Democrats had a grievance against the Supreme Court in 1944: namely, its decision in *Smith v. Allwright* (321 U.S. 649) that the Texas Democratic party's rule excluding blacks from its primaries violated the Fifteenth Amendment. When the conservatives in control of the Texas convention sought to make a party test of opposition to the Supreme Court's decision, the convention split, and the conservatives, organized later as "Texas Regulars," made a futile effort against the Franklin Roosevelt–Harry Truman presidential ticket.

These factional contests had their repercussions in the state Democratic executive committee and to a limited extent in the legislature. Texas's war governor, Coke R. Stevenson, a conservative Democrat, managed to stay aloof from them. He was easily reelected in 1944.

For the Forty-ninth Legislature, which assembled in January 1945, the problem of state finance was delightfully simple. Income had outrun expenditures so far that a $12 million deficit had been eliminated by economies and increased revenues and had been changed to a surplus. Appropriations surpassed those of any preceding legislature in history; much of the surplus was distributed to the schools.

Before the legislature adjourned on June 5, 1945, it was evident that the war's end was near. Thousands of veterans had returned home and tens of thousands would follow them. Texas laws allowed them free voting privileges, the renewal of drivers' licenses without examination, and the privilege of attending state colleges without charge. Already the federal G.I. Bill of Rights was in effect, providing aid for schooling or training, and these privileges were later extended to veterans of post World War II service. Texas voters ratified an amendment to the constitution authorizing bonds for the purchase by the state of land to be sold to veterans. The program has since been extended from time to time. These bonds were the Texas answer to the urge for a blanket state bonus to veterans.

The tang of change was in the air. For the new day the old constitution seemed inadequate in many respects. Bales of proposed constitutional amendments were submitted to each legislature after World War II. In the Forty-ninth Legislature, 84 proposals were introduced and eight were submitted to the voters (not including one proposing a constitutional convention). The voters approved amendments extending benefits to veterans, raising to nine the number of Supreme Court justices, and raising the ceiling on social welfare payments.

TEXAS AND TEXANS IN THE WAR

Long before the day of Pearl Harbor, Texas was a huge training field for the armed forces. The first peace-time draft in American history went into effect on October 16, 1940, when 17 million Americans registered. Of the state army organizations transferred to federal service, the Thirty-sixth Division and the Fifty-sixth Cavalry Brigade were all-Texas units. Texas posts became headquarters of importance. San Antonio, long a soldier's center, was, during a considerable part of the war, the headquarters of the Third Army, which trained men from Arizona to Florida. It was also the headquarters for the Fourth Army, which prepared men for overseas combat service in nine states. The Eighth Service Command, serving as the operating agency for army forces in Texas and adjoining states, had its headquarters in Dallas. For a period the army had as many as 15 training posts in Texas and 21 prisoner-of-war camps. For defense of the Gulf Coast and Mexican border areas, the Southern Defense Command, with its headquarters at Fort Sam Houston, was maintained during most of the war.

Texas became the most active training region in the nation for airmen. Randolph Field, Kelly Field, and Brooks Field, all near San Antonio, were enlarged; Ellington Field near Houston was rebuilt; and additional air fields were established in Wichita Falls, San Angelo, Lubbock, Midland, San Marcos, Amarillo, and other cities. The national headquarters of the

American Air Force Training Command was in Fort Worth, a command that at its peak strength in January 1944 had more than a million men and women under its jurisdiction.

It is estimated that one and a quarter million men and women in all branches of the service were trained in Texas, among them more than 20 combat army divisions. Probably as many as three-quarters of a million Texans, including 12,000 women, served in all branches of the armed forces. Of these about a fourth were in the Navy, Marine Corps, and Coast Guard combined. More than 8,000 Texas women served in the Women's Army Corps (WAC), about 4,200 in the Women Accepted for Voluntary Emergency Service (WAVES), and others in the women's division of the Coast Guard (SPARS) and the Marines.

The Selective Service Act of September 1940, applicable to men between the ages of 21 and 36, was extended after the United States entered the war to include all men between the ages of 18 and 45. Secretary of the Navy Frank Knox stated in December 1942 that Texas was contributing a larger percentage of men to the fighting forces than any other state, a circumstance perhaps caused by the fact that the great majority of Texans were acquainted with the history of their state.

Texas organizations came to be known around the world. The Thirty-sixth Division, a Texan force, sent to Java an organization whose epic experiences caused it to be known as the Lost Battalion. The division landed at Salerno, Italy, the first American force to enter Europe, and in 400 days of combat advanced through Italy, France, Germany, and into Austria. Texas also had a special claim on the Ninetieth (Texas-Oklahoma) Division, the 112th Cavalry Regiment, the 144th Infantry Regiment in the Pacific theater, and the Second Infantry Division and the First Cavalry Division in the European theater.

Wherever they went Texans seemed to have been very much in evidence. The Thirty-sixth Division carried the Texas flag and often displayed it. Where Texas troops were congregated, natives sometimes spoke of the "Texas army." Many Texans were recognized for valor as well as for enthusiasm. Lieutenant Audie Murphy of Farmersville became the "most decorated" soldier of World War II. The Congressional Medal of Honor went to him and some 29 other Texans. Six Texans received the Navy's Medal of Honor, among them Commander Samuel D. Dealey, killed in action, and known as the "most decorated man in the Navy."

Many military officers of renown were Texans or had once called Texas home. Oveta Culp Hobby was director of the Women's Army Corps. The state could claim at least 12 admirals and 155 generals, among them Chester W. Nimitz, commander-in-chief of the Pacific Fleet, and Dwight David Eisenhower, Supreme Allied Commander in Europe. Texans fought on every front and paid their share of war's cruel toll. Their war dead for all branches of the service amounted to 23,022. The seriously wounded and permanently injured numbered many more.

THE JESTER YEARS

As the gubernatorial campaign of 1946 began to take shape, Homer Price Rainey, former president of the University of Texas who had been dismissed from that post after a long, bitter controversy with the board of regents, seemed to be the strongest of a long slate of candidates. Railroad Commissioner Beauford Jester however was nominated in the run-off primary. Although Jester had the support of the conservative element of the party, his middle-of-the-road course prevented an open breach with the liberals.

Like his predecessors in office, Governor Jester emphatically opposed any new taxes. Still, the expanding economy and general prosperity that prevailed placed the executive in the happy position of being able to recommend substantial increases in appropriations without being obliged to suggest new sources of revenue. In his "Report to the People" by radio in 1949, the chief executive could point to the doubling of appropriations for hospitals and orphanages and the opening of several other institutions that provided care for the unfortunate. Under the constitutional amendment limiting appropriations to anticipated revenue, which had become effective in 1945, the comptroller refused to certify a number of appropriations made near the end of the session.

Labor unions became the focus of attention in the postwar years. In 1947 a veritable shower of laws regulating unions came to Governor Jester, some of which he had advocated. Chief of these were:

(1) The check-off of the workers' union dues, to be paid directly to the union, was forbidden, except by the assent of the worker;
(2) The "right to work" law made it unlawful to require union membership of any employee;
(3) Picketing was rigidly regulated and mass picketing outlawed;
(4) Strikes by public employees were forbidden;
(5) Secondary strikes, picketing, and boycotts were forbidden;
(6) The picketing of utilities was prohibited;
(7) Labor unions were brought under trust-law regulations.

This was the year also that Congress passed the Labor-Management Relations Act (Taft-Hartley Law), which made substantial changes in the body of federal law regarding labor. Even this was not the end. In 1951 a law was enacted that provided beyond the shadow of a doubt that there be no closed shops in Texas—no sort of labor agreement could require that workers belong to a union.

On the national scene, many conservative Texas Democrats opposed President Truman (who became President upon the death of Franklin Roosevelt in April, 1945) as they had opposed Roosevelt. Indeed, with Truman they associated the Fair Employment Practice Committee, the

CIO Political Action Committee, and other features and groups that they had consistently opposed. Governor Jester worked for harmony, however, and there was no party division when the Democratic National Convention nominated Truman in 1948. The number of those who supported the Republican and Dixiecrat tickets evidently was not large.

Jester was reelected without having to campaign. For the United States Senate seat, vacated by O'Daniel, who did not seek reelection in 1948, Congressman Lyndon B. Johnson opposed former Governor Coke R. Stevenson, in a contest close, acrimonious, and undecided until a federal court ordered Johnson's name placed on the ballot as the Democratic nominee.

In the longest session the state had known, from January 11 to July 6, 1949, the Fifty-first Legislature enacted many laws, some of them probably of enduring value. In an effort to improve the pitiable conditions in the institutions for the mentally ill, it created the Board for Texas State Hospi-

Beauford H. Jester (left) was elected governor of Texas in 1946 and again in 1948. He died in office in 1949. Here he is shown with Harry Truman and a fellow Texan, John Nance Garner. In a close national election, 750,000 Texans voted for Truman and 280,000 for his Republican opponent, Thomas E. Dewey. Garner was Vice-President from 1933 to 1941. (E. C. Barker History center, University of Texas)

tals and Special Schools and gave it supervision over state mental hospitals and state schools for handicapped children. A Youth Development Council was set up to take charge of schools for juvenile offenders. The body enacted an antilynching law, adopted a controversial basic science law that set forth minimum requirements for all persons in medical and health work and provided for the licensing of chiropractors.

During this session, state appropriations for the biennium, when supplemented by various federal grants, came to a billion dollars, so the session was the first to be called a "billion-dollar legislature." Like its predecessors, the body refused to vote new taxes, and in order to keep expenditures within the limits of income, Governor Jester vetoed second-year appropriations for state hospitals and special schools. Two of its measures were far reaching in effect: the modernization of the state prison system and the reorganization of the state public school system through the Gilmer-Aiken school laws.

Because of limitations brought about by the war and its aftermath, the Texas prison system, never a high-ranking one, had deteriorated rapidly. The growth of the prison population—a gain of 1,000, or 29 percent in 1946 over the preceding year—added greatly to all problems. The board secured O. B. Ellis, an experienced prison administrator, who drew up the Ellis plan for rehabilitating the system. In 1949 the legislature appropriated $4.29 million for improvements; subsequent legislatures continued to improve the system. In 1957 the name was changed to the State Department of Corrections. The prison population continued to grow, necessitating the periodic enlargement and improvement of the plants.

Reorganization of the state public school system was the result of three far-reaching laws sponsored by Representative Claude Gilmer and Senator A. M. Aiken and representing some badly needed reforms. By the end of World War II most school systems in the state had added a twelfth year to their programs. Broadening of the curriculum was a process that had been going on for many years, but one that had accelerated in the postwar year, with added emphasis on vocational subjects, music, and the other fine arts. Most problems centered on funding. Despite enormous increases in appropriations, Texas schools remained near the bottom of the scale of state school systems.

The Gilmer-Aiken laws reorganized state school administration, established a system of minimum standards for programs, and altered the manner in which state funds for education were distributed. One law created an elective board of education with the power to appoint a commissioner and to supervise the Texas Education Agency. Another law required that all persons of school age be given a minimum of nine months of schooling each year, under teachers who met certain minimum training requirements, and in an environment conforming to certain standards. The third law established an intricate formula whereby schools were to be supported by state and local funds, with larger amounts of state aid to be given to poor districts.

Some wholesome effects of the new system were soon in evidence. It eliminated many hundreds of inoperative or "dormant" school districts, and it helped to improve school attendance. It placed a premium on academic training and thereby stimulated thousands of teachers to get more schooling. It provided a means for enforcing minimum salary schedules, and it removed much of the political pressure on the distribution of funds.

SHIVERS AND THE INTERPLAY OF NATIONAL AND STATE ISSUES

When on July 11, 1949, Governor Jester died of a heart attack, Lieutenant Governor Allan Shivers succeeded to the office. Shivers was just 41, but ten years in the state senate and two as lieutenant governor had seasoned him. A called session of the legislature in 1950 was made necessary by the failure of the body to complete appropriations for the second year of the biennium.

The governor called for additional taxes as the only way of meeting the demands for increased expenditures. "If we are going to appropriate in the spring," he said, "we must tax in the winter." Shivers pleaded for large appropriations to hospitals to improve old plants and add new. Too many mentally ill people were in jails because of inadequate hospital space. The legislature followed with relatively generous appropriations for the operations of state hospitals and increased taxes slightly.

The next legislature, the fifty-second, meeting in 1951, found that still more taxes were needed. Two agencies worked on the budget for that year: the Board of Control, as it had been accustomed to do for some years, and the Legislative Budget Board, or Council, created by the preceding legislature from its own members. All agreed that additional revenue must be found, and again levies in the Omnibus Bill of 1941 were raised, and a gathering tax on natural gas pipelines was added. Unfortunately the courts later declared this tax unconstitutional, as being in effect a state levy on interstate commerce, and the natural gas interests avoided their equitable share of taxation.

This legislature enacted the first redistricting law in 30 years. Another act, which was the object of much criticism, was the safety inspection and driver responsibility law designed to force unsafe cars off the road and also to give the public a modicum of assurance that drivers were responsible for the damage they might do to others.

More and more the political stage in Texas came to be appropriated by national and international issues and by state-federal relationships. President Truman continued to decline in the esteem of conservative Texas

Democrats. Charges of corrupt practice and the infiltration of Communism were hurled at his administration. There was also much criticism of his policies in the Korean War. But it was Truman's tidelands policies that aroused the most criticism in Texans.

The tidelands were areas under the sea but closely adjacent to the coast and believed to be rich in oil deposits. Early opinions held almost unanimously that the state owned the tidelands, until Secretary of the Interior Harold Ickes formally challenged the claim in 1937. In August 1947, the Supreme Court of the United States held that the state of California did not have the right to exploit its tidelands through oil leases and other means because the federal government had "paramount right and power" over this domain. In 1950 the Court by a vote of four to three (two not voting) handed down a similar decision against Texas. It was a heavy blow, for these lands were being leased for oil and gas development, and nearly $10 million in lease bonuses had been received.

President Truman vetoed an act of Congress in 1946 recognizing the rights of the states to lease these lands, and when a similar act was submitted to him in 1952, he vetoed that also. By way of completing the account of these lands, it may be stated that on May 22, 1953, President Eisenhower signed a quit-claim bill, restoring the tidelands to state ownership and extending ownership to "historic limits." For Texas and the west coast of Florida, where the rule of Spanish law still prevailed, "historic limits" meant three Spanish leagues or about ten and a half miles.

For many Texans the subject of the tidelands became a prime factor in the presidential election of 1952. The Democratic party split that year. The liberal wing bolted; the conservatives led by Shivers kept control of the party organization and refused to support Governor Adlai Stevenson, the Democratic nominee for President, after Stevenson had indicated no sympathy for the claims of the states to the tidelands. That year Texas Republicans also had a breach between the forces supporting Senator Robert A. Taft for President and those supporting General Dwight D. Eisenhower. Later the factions united, joined with the conservative Democrats, and carried the state for Eisenhower. Two million Texans voted that November, the greatest turnout to the polls the state had known. Eisenhower carried the state by a majority of over 100,000, winning the second Republican victory in Texas within a quarter of a century. Shivers was easily renominated that year over his chief opponent, the liberal judge Ralph Yarborough. Most of the Texas state offices were not sought by Republicans in 1952; by a system of "cross filing" they placed in their columns on the ballot the names of the Democratic nominees. That year Attorney General Price Daniel defeated Congressman Lindly Beckworth, a pro-Truman or liberal Democrat, for the United States Senate seat of Tom Connally, who withdrew from the race.

With the support of the conservative Democrats, Shivers, in a campaign for his third full term as governor, defeated Ralph Yarborough again in 1954 in an acrimonious contest that was settled by the second primary. Yarborough awaited the renewal of the contest in 1956.

CRUSADES AND SCANDALS: POLITICS OF THE FIFTIES

In the turmoil of the sixties and seventies, some observers have looked back to the fifties with the nostalgic conviction that the decade was tranquil and complacent, with scarcely a conflict in sight to mar the peace of the day. Actually, the fifties were neither tranquil nor complacent. A Communist "scare" began the decade; black and Mexican-American groups turned to the courts and to other means to claim their rights; and in the second half of the decade, insurance and land scandals alarmed voters and threatened many political careers.

Tensions and frustrations in foreign affairs and fears of subversion at home resulted in a sensational and sometimes less than responsible search for Communists, Socialists, and their sympathizers. Texas shared in this "Red Scare," often termed McCarthyism in keeping with the activities of Wisconsin Senator Joseph McCarthy. McCarthy dominated the headlines of the day with indiscriminate charges of Communism levied against a wide variety of people. In Texas his supporters included right-wing extremists, who were prepared to believe almost anything about almost anybody and who made similar charges, and more moderate groups whose fear of subversion may or may not have been justified but certainly was real.

Except for the legislative requirement of loyalty oaths for public employees, "Red Scare" politics had little effect on state affairs, but in local politics the issue often dominated. Agitated interests demanded that libraries be purged of books sympathetic to Communism, that educators suspected of Socialist tendencies be fired, and that speakers of dubious loyalty be silenced. Such groups were particularly active in larger cities such as Houston, San Antonio, and Dallas, but smaller communities also experienced their crusades. One Communist among the approximately 65,000 school teachers of Texas was discovered and discharged, but not much else was accomplished. By the mid-fifties most of the more extreme evidences of the fear had disappeared, though the ubiquitous loyalty oaths would linger in government agencies and public schools for many years to come.

In two areas, suffrage and school desegregation, black people in the fifties made significant progress toward the attainment of their civil rights. The right to vote came more easily than did the integration of the schools. Most significant was the Supreme Court decision of 1944 in *Smith* v. *Allwright*, a Texas case, which outlawed the white primary. Later court decisions applied the rule to local primaries, and thus the principal device whereby blacks were denied an effective voice in politics was removed. Some resistance by white citizens lingered, but black voters became more numerous in the late 1940s. By 1958 more than one-third of the potential black voters of the state were registered; in comparison, almost one-half of the potential white voters were registered. In some areas of the state, however, as much as 70 percent of the eligible black population registered to vote.

Integration of the state's schools was another matter; much was accomplished, but progress was slow and often painful. Again, Supreme Court decisions played a crucial role. Ruling in *Sweatt* v. *Painter* in 1950, the Court directed the University of Texas to admit a black man, H. M. Sweatt, to its law school, thus opening to blacks the graduate and professional schools of the university. Far more sweeping was the decision in *Brown* v. *Board of Education of Topeka* in 1954. Basing its opinion squarely on the Fourteenth Amendment, which guarantees to all persons the equal protection of the laws, the Court held that even if the schools that were maintained by the state for blacks were in every respect just as good as those for whites, segregation itself deprived the children of the minority group of equal educational opportunities and added: "We conclude that in the field of public education the doctrine of separate but equal has no place." The Court indicated a willingness to move slowly in applying its doctrine and left the approach to the lower federal courts.

Reaction to the decision divided along racial lines in Texas. Polls reflected a four-to-one opposition in the white community and a two-to-one support in the black community. Tensions began to build. In the 1954 election Governor Shivers left little doubt of his opposition to the decision, though his stand was not as adamant as that of some southern leaders. In the July 1956 Democratic primary certain segregation issues were submitted on the ballot. A large majority of voters favored stronger laws against intermarriage between whites and blacks, laws exempting white students from attending integrated schools, and interposition by the state to avoid the effects of certain Supreme Court decisions. Here and there in the fall of 1956 there were threats of violence as the schools opened in September. Happily, the serious disturbances were few, though some did occur. In Mansfield near Fort Worth, attempts of black students to attend the local school pursuant to a federal court order brought a threat of mob action, and Governor Shivers sent in state Rangers to restore order. No violence occurred, but the black students were not allowed to enroll. Integration proceeded peacefully in some other districts, with more than 120 carrying out at least some integration by the 1957 school term.

Integration of colleges generated less opposition. A mob of outsiders sought to prevent blacks from entering Lamar State College of Technology in Beaumont in 1956, but without success, though a similar mob had succeeded in their efforts the previous year at Texarkana Junior College. By 1958 approximately two-thirds of the colleges and universities of Texas had integrated their classes.

Opposition to integration did not die easily. Early in 1957 the legislature passed a law making mandatory the assent of the voters of any school district before the races could be mixed in the schools. The penalty provided was the withdrawal of all state aid for the district. Before the year ended, another law was enacted providing for the closing of any public school at which troops, either federal or state, were stationed. But legislation against integration and disapproval of it in many communities only delayed it. Its proponents appealed to the federal courts, and federal judges, by the authority of the Supreme Court of the United States, uniformly ordered school districts to present plans for desegregation. Governor Price Daniel, elected in 1956, made no effort to interpose state authority against the federal agencies charged with carrying out the judicial decrees.

Mexican-American people also made progress in the 1950s in their struggle for equal civil rights. Although not subjected to the legal discrimination common against black people, Mexican-Americans in Texas frequently were denied opportunities and rights extended to other people in the state. Organized efforts to combat such discrimination began early in the century and picked up momentum after World War I. In 1921 a group known as the Orden Hijos de America was formed to help Mexican-Americans secure the rights enjoyed by other citizens. The League of Latin-American Citizens, eventually to be known as LULAC, was formed in 1927 and continued the struggle. After World War II, a Mexican-American veterans' group, the American G. I. Forum, became very active, promoting poll tax drive payments, the establishment of scholarships, and otherwise encouraging political involvement. In 1948 a court decision ruled segregation of Mexican-Americans in the public schools to be unconstitutional, and three years later another decision outlawed the exclusion of Mexican-Americans from juries. Mexican-Americans became considerably more active in politics during the decade of the fifties, and in 1956 San Antonio voters elected Henry B. Gonzales to the state senate, the first Mexican-American in the Texas senate in modern times. Gonzales eventually won a seat in Congress.

Otherwise in public affairs, taxation, spending, administrative reorganization, and scandals occupied the legislature. The Fifty-third Legislature in 1953 held out against a tax increase but saw a voted teachers' pay raise voided for lack of funds. Two years later the legislature established new state commissions to supervise state building construction and higher education; terms of county officials were lengthened; and state employee and teacher retirement systems were improved. This term saw the legislature finally accept the necessity for more taxes, with increases of $100 million applied to certain specialized sales taxes.

But it was insurance, not taxes, that captured the headlines in 1955 and for the next two years. Texas insurance laws were lax and long had left the way open for fly-by-night promoters and operators. Failures of insurance companies, never uncommon, became more frequent after World War II. In 1955, Lieutenant Governor Ben Ramsey reminded the lawmakers that during the last ten years 86 Texas insurance companies failed, largely because of an inadequate insurance code. The legislature enacted 22 laws on the subject, providing for more effective regulation generally and placing the sale of insurance stock under the board of insurance commissioners.

Failure continued, however—among them the United Services Trust and Guaranty Company, a concern that controlled some 74 insurance and finance companies in 22 states and Alaska—and in 1957 the lawmakers complied with the governor's request that he be authorized to appoint an entirely new insurance commission. The legislature also passed 16 laws designed to improve the insurance situation in the state. Meanwhile, Texas insurance companies were subjected to an audit, and more than a hundred were denied, temporarily or permanently, permits to continue in business. Among other things, investigations of the failures brought before the public an unwholesome relationship between certain Texas lawmakers and some corporations. For instance, nine members of the Texas senate had received legal fees or other income from the United Services Trust and Guaranty Company.

Babe Dedrikson Zaharias, born and reared in Texas, for more than two decades was recognized as one of the outstanding athletes in American sports history. After breaking four world records in track and field and winning acclaim in the 1932 Olympics, she went on to master a number of sports. She became a golf champion in the 1930s and continued to win tournaments in the post-World War II years.

In the midst of the furor over insurance, politics continued, and the line of cleavage in the Texas Democratic party between conservative and liberal elements intensified. The liberals, those loyal to the national organization, controlled the Democratic state presidential convention in 1956, but Governor Shivers again refused to support Stevenson, the Democratic nominee, and threw his strength to Eisenhower. Eisenhower and Nixon carried the state by a majority about twice that of four years before. This year Senator Price Daniel became a candidate for governor, running against Ralph Yarborough and a field of other candidates. Yarborough had the support of organized labor and a majority of the liberal Democrats. In the contest he charged Daniel, along with Shivers, with responsibility for certain irregularities of the veterans' land board, of which Daniel and Shivers were ex-officio members when Daniel was attorney general. The $100 million program, by which the state purchased land for resale to veterans, was placed under the direction of a veterans' land board, composed of the commissioner of the General Land Office, the governor, and the attorney general. Reports of irregularities and frauds in the work of the commission brought investigations by grand juries and senate and house committees. Bascom Giles, commissioner of the General Land Office, who had just been elected to his ninth term, was sent to the penitentiary for six years on charges of misrepresentation and perjury. By a small margin, Daniel defeated Yarborough for governor in a second primary; then over a slate of opponents Yarborough was elected to the United States Senate to take the seat Daniel had vacated to become governor.

The Fifty-fifth Legislature in 1957 worked under trying conditions. It was brought out that many legislators were employed more or less regularly by corporations, some of which maintained very active lobbies in Austin. Charges of bribery were hurled freely, and one representative who resigned in the face of the charge was convicted in court. The legislature adopted annual budgets of well beyond a billion dollars, and voters approved constitutional amendments liberalizing retirement benefits for state employees and increasing the state's share in pensions to the aged.

The final years of the fifties offered hope to liberal Democrats and disappointment to aspiring Republicans. Encouraged by the election of Ralph Yarborough to the Senate, liberal Democrats under the leadership of Mrs. R. D. ("Frankie") Randolph of Houston, a Democratic national committeewoman, and Jerry Holleman, president of the Texas A.F.L.–C.I.O., and others organized the "Democrats of Texas" (DOT). Outstanding among a list of demands they made of the party were the abolition of the poll tax, greater liberal representation in party affairs, and loyalty to the national Democratic party. Joined by other liberals in 1958, the DOT gave Yarborough a decisive victory over his conservative opponent, William A. Blakley (charged with being the candidate of big business), in the Democratic senatorial primary. Yarborough was elected in November.

In contrast, Governor Price Daniel, generally regarded as a moderate conservative, was continued in office by a generous margin, and he dominated the Democratic state convention. Republican hopes for victory after Eisenhower's large margin in 1956 did not materialize. The party elected only one congressman in 1958, Bruce Alger of Dallas.

As the decade drew to a close, the outstanding feature in Democratic circles was the bid for the presidency by Lyndon Baines Johnson, the Texan who was now majority leader in the United States Senate and who had the endorsements of Sam Rayburn, the powerful Speaker of the House of Representatives, and of Governor Price Daniel. To promote Johnson's candidacy, the legislature moved the party primaries up to May and changed the convention system so that Senator Johnson's name could appear on the ballot as the incumbent candidate for senator, while on the same day precinct conventions could endorse him for the presidency.

SELECTED BIBLIOGRAPHY

Fighting by Texans in World War II is related in *The Infantry Journal,* March 1944, an account of the Thirty-Sixth Division (Paris, France, 1944); and in "The Thirty-Sixth Division at Salerno," by Major James E. Taylor, *Southwestern Historical Quarterly,* XLVIII, 281–285. Also see Robert L. Wagner, *The Texas Army: A History of the Thirty-Sixth Division in the Italian Campaign* (Austin, 1972); Fred L. Walker, "The 36th was a Great Fighting Division;" Robert L. Wagner, "The Odyssey of a Texas Citizen Soldier," *Southwestern Historical Quarterly,* LXXII, 40–87; and Philip Ardery, *Bomber Pilot: A Memoir of World War II* (Lexington, Ky., 1978).

Politics of the era are considered in George Norris Green, *The Establishment in Texas Politics;* James R. Soukup, Clifton McCleskey, and Harry Holloway, *Party and Factional Division in Texas* (Austin, 1964); Sam Kinch and Stuart Long, *Allan Shivers: The Pied Piper of Texas Politics* (Austin, 1974); Rowland Evans and Robert Novak, *Lyndon B. Johnson: The Exercise of Power* (New York, 1966); Anthony Champagne, *Congressman Sam Rayburn* (New Brunswick, 1984); and Irvin M. May, Jr., *Marvin Jones* (College Station, 1980). For accounts of the tidelands and the issues involved, see Ernest R. Bartley, *The Tidelands Oil Controversy* (Austin, 1953). The post-World War II Red Scare is discussed by Don E. Carleton, *Red Scare! Right-Wing Hysteria, Fifties Fanaticism, and Their Legacy in Texas* (Austin, 1985); and "McCarthyism in Houston: The George Ebey Affair," *Southwestern Historical Quarterly,* LXXX, 163–176. A political and economic issue of the time is discussed by Johnny M. McCain, "Texas and the Mexican Labor Question, 1942–1947," *Southwestern Historical Quarterly,* LXXXV, 45–64.

Some sources on education in Texas are C. E. Evans, *The Story of Texas Schools* (Austin, 1955); James T. Taylor, "Gilmer-Aiken Program and State Finances," *East Texas,* January 1950, p. 9; Texas Research League, *Texas Public Schools under the Minimum Foundation Program, An Evaluation, 1949–1954.* Delightful reading is Joe B. Frantz, *The Forty-Acre Follies* (Austin, 1983).

In connection with scandals in insurance, see: The Texas Legislative Council,

"Insolvency in the Texas Insurance Industry; Insurance, Texas' Frauds and Failures," *Time*, May 31, 1954, p. 64; "Those Texas Scandals," *The Saturday Evening Post*, November 12, 1955, pp. 19ff; D. B. Hardeman, "Shivers of Texas: A Tragedy in Three Acts," *Harpers*, November 1956, pp. 50–56; and Ronnie Dugger, "What Corrupted Texas?" *Harpers*, March 1957, pp. 58–78.

On developments in black history, Alwyn Barr, *Black Texans*, is very useful and reliable, but also see Norman V. Bartley, *The Rise of Massive Resistance: Race and Politics in the South During the 1950's* (Baton Rouge, 1969); Darlene Clark Hine, "The Elusive Ballot: The Black Struggle against the Texas Democratic White Primary, 1932–1945," *Southwestern Historical Quarterly*, LXXXI, 371–392; "Blacks and the Destruction of the Democratic White Primary, 1935‹944," *Journal of Negro History*, LXII, 43–59; *Black Victory: The Rise and Fall of the White Primary in Texas* (Millwood, New York, 1979); Michael Gillette, "The Rise of the NAACP in Texas," *Southwestern Historical Quarterly*, LXXXI, 393–416; and "Blacks Challenge the White University," *ibid.*, LXXXVI, 321–344.

CHAPTER NINETEEN
REFORM, REACTION, AND REPUBLICANS

Although Texas politics of the fifties were seldom dull or tranquil, the following decades were even more eventful. Tragic violence marred the sixties, and charges of scandal and corruption brought efforts at reform in the early seventies. Minority interests continued their search for equality, justice, power, and position throughout the period. Much of the attention focused on two groups, blacks and Mexican-Americans, whose efforts of the fifties had resulted in significant change, and others joined the struggle. Women's organizations, youth groups, native Americans, the handicapped, and others grew more active and in some instances more effective in their activities.

Protest and dissent became much more visible. Several cities and a number of college campuses witnessed marches, gatherings, and various other manifestations of dissatisfaction with the "establishment." The aims of the protesters were sometimes poorly defined, but calls for more freedom, more democracy, and more equal treatment seemed to be paramount. Charges of brutality were made against law enforcement officers at times. There were accusations of discrimination, bribery, and embezzlement made against officers in high places and in low, and some of the charges were sustained.

In the eighties much of the open conflict associated with the search for civil rights disappeared, and seldom did a story about scandal in politics create a stir. But there were, nevertheless, an abundance of political issues. Public education reform, obvious and long needed, received some attention. But more was given to matters of money, when an economic recession bringing unemployment, bankruptcies, and budget deficits posed a challenge to the people of the state and their political system.

Developments within and between the political parties reflected the public issues. Within the Democratic party, factionalism persisted throughout the period, and toward the end of the seventies the election of a Republican governor, the first since Reconstruction, brought speculation about a possible new era. But careful observers tempered their speculation with caution. In some respects it appeared that politics were becoming more polarized, with both liberal Democrats and conservative Republicans gaining power, but this was far from certain. Exciting events in considerable number brought interest to the period, but no clear theme emerged to show the way for the prophet of the future.

THE ELECTION OF 1960

Texas politics in 1960, rarely simple in the post-World War II years, were more complicated than usual. In his race for a third term as governor, Price Daniel easily defeated his more conservative Democratic opponent, Jack Cox, and was elected in November with little opposition. Liberal Democrats gained a few seats in the legislature. The complicating element in the election was the dual candidacy of Senator Lyndon B. Johnson. Johnson had hopes of securing the Democratic presidential nomination, but he had no intention of giving up his Senate seat should he fail in his presidential bid.

The Senate race was much closer than the contest over the governorship. Republican hopes rested on a young teacher at Midwestern University, John Tower. Johnson's vote of 1,306,625 was sufficient to win reelection, but Tower's vote was surprisingly large. Resentment by some voters of Johnson's dual candidacy may account in part for the small margin, but Republican strength was also increasing.

Although there was discontent, the Democratic party in Texas generally supported Senator Johnson's bid for the presidential nomination. With little opposition the state convention chose a delegation pledged to Johnson. The DOT (now calling themselves the Democrats of Texas Clubs) made an unsuccessful fight, not directly against Johnson's candidacy, but in an effort to require all state convention delegates to make an individual written pledge that they would support all Democratic candidates in the election of 1960. This was clearly an effort to put an end to party bolting,

The second United States President born in Texas (Dwight D. Eisenhower was the first), Lyndon Baines Johnson made his home state the base for a long and distinguished political career. Elected to Congress in 1937, to the Senate in 1948, to the vice-presidency in 1960, he became president when John F. Kennedy was assassinated and was elected for the next term in 1964. The University of Texas awarded him a degree as a distinguished American statesman as well as the state's most illustrious citizen of the day. After deciding not to seek reelection, Johnson returned to Texas in 1969 where he lived quietly until his death in 1973. (E. C. Barker History center, University of Texas)

such as had occurred in 1952 and 1956. However, only a general loyalty resolution could be passed through the convention.

Senator Johnson campaigned energetically for the Democratic presidential nomination, traveling more than 30,000 miles. He relied heavily on the political strength and prestige of his supporter, Texas Speaker of the House Sam Rayburn, and his supporters emphasized his experience in government, his leadership so well-proven in the Senate, and the youth and inexperience of his leading opponent, Senator John F. Kennedy of Massachusetts.

When the Democratic National Convention met in Los Angeles in 1960, the Johnson campaign for the presidency ended quickly. Johnson got only 409 delegate votes, mainly from the South, and Kennedy was nominated on the first ballot. Kennedy then appealed to Johnson to become the vice-presidential candidate for the party. Johnson agreed, a decision that puzzled many who were his followers and alarmed others who were not. On one hand, many Texans were disgruntled with the strong civil rights plank in the national party platform, and, on the other, many liberals were dissatisfied with Johnson. Party discord at home in Texas was apparent in the Democratic state convention held in September. The Texans supported the state's right-to-work law (disliked by organized labor) and the oil depletion allowance (which reduced the federal income tax on oil production) and generally advocated state rights.

Relative harmony prevailed among the Republicans. The state party organization centered its efforts on carrying Texas for the national Republican ticket, headed by Vice-President Richard M. Nixon with Henry Cabot Lodge, III, as his running mate. Republican efforts were supported by some conservative Democrats, such as Allan Shivers, who campaigned for Nixon and Lodge.

Texas was a pivotal state, with 24 electoral votes, and an electorate divided rather evenly. Both parties had strong organizations in the state, and neither candidate ignored Texas. There was a record vote in November, with the Kennedy-Johnson ticket carrying Texas by a narrow margin of 24,019 votes. The Democratic margin on the national level also was exceedingly close. By slightly more than 100,000 votes, Kennedy and Johnson were elected.

Despite their losses in the election of 1960, Texas Republicans were encouraged. Nixon and Lodge had polled the greatest Republican vote in Texas in history. Party workers set out immediately to increase their strength in the state legislature and in Congress. In a special election held in 1961 to fill the Senate seat vacated by Lyndon Johnson, Republican John Tower defeated a conservative Democrat, William A. Blakley. The victory was evidence of the growth of the Republican party, though the liberal Democrats' refusal to support their conservative candidate likely contributed to the Republican cause. In 1962 the Republicans gained a second congressman and several house seats in the legislature, six of them from Dallas districts.

The election of the governor in 1962 offered additional evidence of a growing Republican party. In the Democratic party there were a number of candidates for the nomination. Price Daniel sought a fourth term; Houston attorney Don Yarborough represented the liberal faction of the party; John B. Connally, who had close ties with Lyndon Johnson, claimed support from both conservatives and moderates; and there were others. Connally suffered to some extent from charges that he was running as the "Johnson candidate," but he won the Democratic nomination in a run-off with Yarborough, possibly because his promise to appoint black executives won some support from black voters. In the general election in the fall he defeated Jack Cox, a conservative Democrat turned Republican, but Cox polled almost 46 percent of the vote.

These and a few other victories raised high hopes in Republican ranks, but dissension soon appeared to plague the party in Texas. Many conservative Democrats were joining the party, which may help to explain a noticeable tendency toward the extreme right. The conservative political philosophy of Republican Senator Barry Goldwater of Arizona, coupled with his opposition to federal intervention in the race issue, gave him a large following in Texas. Goldwater's nomination as the Republican candidate for President in 1964 marked the ascendancy of conservative Republicanism in the nation, and conservative Texas followed him with enthusiasm. Many Republicans were loath to support him, however, and he had no appeal for some of the Democrats who were getting into the habit of voting for Republican candidates for President.

JOHNSON AND CONNALLY

Tragedy in Texas on November 22, 1963, profoundly affected the course of public affairs in Texas, indeed in the world. While the people of Dallas and of the state were receiving President John Kennedy with enthusiastic hospitality, a hidden assassin shot and killed him and seriously wounded Governor Connally, who was riding with him. Within two hours after the death of President Kennedy, Lyndon Baines Johnson, a native Texan, took the oath of office that made him President of the United States.

Through the prestige of the presidency, Johnson was able to suppress to a degree the factionalism in Texas Democratic ranks for a period, but the relationship between Senator Ralph Yarborough, Texas's most prominent liberal Democrat, and Governor Connally was cool. There were differences in ideology, and both sought to control the Democratic party in Texas. With President Johnson in office, Governor Connally had a clear advantage, for his ties to the President were close. In the Democratic primaries of 1964 the influence of the President, working through and with Governor Connally, prevailed. Connally was easily nominated and elected governor for another term and defeated his Republican opponent, George Bush. Connally's control of the Democratic state convention was complete, and the delegation was sent to the national convention in Atlantic City with instructions to "put forth every effort" to secure Johnson's nomination. Johnson was nominated with ease.

Although the Republican candidate Barry Goldwater visited Texas six times during the campaign, and Republicans worked hard otherwise, Johnson's strength proved invincible. Even former Governor Shivers supported the Johnson ticket. Out of a record vote of 2.558 million, the Republicans received less than a million votes.

A determined leader in his first term, Governor Connally gained additional strength in his dealings with the legislature upon his reelection in 1964. State finances, usually a major problem for both governor and legislature, were not as much of an issue during these years. After much wrangling between liberals who wanted additional taxes on business, and conservatives, who favored some form of a sales tax, the legislature earlier in 1961 had adopted a sales tax and some other levies. Governor Daniel, who opposed a sales tax, did not sign the law establishing it, but he allowed it to become law. The sales tax, with some additional levies adopted during

Connally's first term, gave the state a firm financial base. When additional funds were needed, the sales tax was increased. Consequently, Governor Connally was free to concentrate on other issues in his administration.

Putting great emphasis on the need for long-range planning, Connally encouraged the legislature in the enactment of an impressive legislative program. New intergovernmental planning agencies, which coordinated the efforts of counties, cities, schools, and other political subdivisions, were created. The legislature established a state Fine Arts Commission. Constitutional amendments liberalizing the state welfare program, expanding teacher retirement programs, increasing building funds for state colleges, and authorizing student loans were adopted. A 25 member committee to make a study of education beyond the high school level was appointed, and its recommendation led to the strengthening of the Texas Commission on Higher Education, which acts as a coordinator for colleges and universities. The governor sought to provide greater appropriations for the colleges, and to offer greater facilities for vocational training generally. The University of Houston was made a state university, and Angelo State College in San Angelo and Pan American College in Edinburg were made senior colleges.

Two changes in the electoral process during these years had far-reaching implications. In compliance with the mandates of federal judicial decrees, the legislature redistricted the state, drawing new boundaries for the election of members of the state legislature and for the house of representatives. Most agreed that redistricting would diminish the influence of rural areas in the government, but while some thought that the Republicans would benefit from the changes, others believed that liberal politicians would gain an advantage. In another issue, federal courts ruled in 1966 that the poll tax voting requirement (which Texans had consistently refused to change) was unconstitutional, whereupon the legislature enacted a law eliminating the poll tax. Over the objection of many liberals, the legislature included a provision in the law requiring that voters register annually. Whatever the long-range consequences of these changes might have been, the immediate impact on statewide office holding was limited. In the election of 1966 Governor Connally, who had kept his promise to appoint black executives, was elected overwhelmingly for a third term, and other conservative candidates fared well.

Although Governor Connally was successful in securing the enactment of much of his program, he was not successful in all instances. The legislature refused to license the sale of liquor by the drink or to license betting on horse races, nor would it submit to the voters the question of a convention to revise the state's constitution. Voters refused to approve constitutional amendments giving the governor a four-year term and providing for annual legislative sessions.

The outlook of Texas politics was changed greatly in 1968 when both Governor Connally and President Johnson announced that they would not seek reelection. Half a score of candidates sought the Democratic nomination for governor, and nearly two million voters took part in the primary. Lieutenant Governor Preston Smith, a conservative, and Don Yarborough, a well-known liberal, entered the run-off. Yarborough advocated a minimum wage of $1.25, a state poverty corps, and increased state aid to the aged, to the disabled, and to dependent children. Some of Smith's billboards read, "Continue Conservative Government."

Results were disappointing to the liberals. The "new voters" they had counted on either did not vote or had fragmented their strength. Smith's vote was 756,909 against Yarborough's 620,726. In November Smith defeated the Republican nominee, Paul Eggars, with a comfortable margin.

Led by Governor Connally, the conservative Democratic forces controlled the state presidential convention and sent to the national convention in Chicago a delegation of 104 instructed to support the governor as a favorite-son candidate. In Chicago the Texas liberals unsuccessfully contested the seating of the regular delegation. Vice-President Hubert Humphrey won the nomination on the first ballot.

Texas Republicans united by supporting Richard Nixon and his running mate, Spiro T. Agnew, who were nominated at the national convention in Miami. George C. Wallace, former governor of Alabama, headed the new American party in the contest. The Democrats carried Texas by a close vote, and, by an even narrower margin, Nixon and Agnew carried the nation. Wallace's vote in Texas and in the nation was relatively small.

THE SEARCH FOR CIVIL RIGHTS

The civil rights movement, building upon the gains of the fifties, added momentum thereafter. The right to vote was relatively secure and legally, segregation was supposedly a policy of the past, but discrimination and socioeconomic inequities persisted. Across the nation, minority groups formed organizations and launched campaigns to correct the problems. Texas, with about one-third of its population made up of two major ethnic minorities, was the scene of much of the activity.

Although their interests were not dissimilar, there was rarely much cooperation between the two groups. Black minorities concentrated their activities in urban areas, particularly in Houston and Dallas, and although there were a number of new black organizations formed, the long-established NAACP remained the most important. Among Mexican-American peoples, a wide variety of organizations, many of them formed in the 1960s and 1970s, reflected basic differences over the proper approach for solving the problems of discrimination and inequality. Some called themselves Chicanos, asserting the distinctiveness of their culture and rejecting that of the Anglos. Some Chicanos, though not all, were militant in their demands and in effect advocated a form of separatism. Other Mexican-Americans rejected both the name Chicano and the idea of militancy, preferring to work "within the system or establishment."

Both minorities launched concerted campaigns to secure the election of their people to important offices, particularly to the legislature. In 1961 only two members of the state senate and five members of the house of representatives were Mexican-Americans, and no member of the legislature was from the black community. With the support of a number of organizations on both the state and the local level, minority candidates entered more contests, and the number of minority office-holders in the legislature moved steadily upward. By 1985 the Texas house of representatives included 13 blacks and 19 Mexican-Americans. Four Mexican-Americans and one black served in the senate. One black and four Mexican-Americans held posts in the United States Congress. During this period Houston voters elected a black woman, Barbara Jordan, to the state senate, where she served with distinction between 1967 and 1971. Subsequently she won election to the United States Congress where her abilities attracted national attention.

Local politics also felt the impact of the civil rights movement. In a dramatic and hostile contest in South Texas in 1963, Mexican-American activists won control of the Crystal City town government. The election focused on racial discrimination, and victory encouraged similar efforts elsewhere, especially in communities where the Mexican-American population was either in a majority or was quite large. By 1980 almost 1,000 Mexican-Americans held public offices in local government. Black politicians on the local level were less successful. In 1970 there were 42 black officeholders in the state, and while the number increased thereafter, it remained small.

Mexican-American political activism on the local level led to the organization of a new political party, La Raza Unida. The party was an outgrowth of the Mexican-American Youth Organization (MAYO), formed in 1967 with José Angel Gutierrez as its leader. For a time the party appeared to have prospects of at least some success. Party leaders contributed to Chicano victories in Crystal City and in other local elections, and in the 1972 gubernatorial race, La Raza candidate Ramsey Muniz polled more than 200,000 votes. But the defection of liberal supporters who tired of one-issue politics, the lack of organization, the inherent difficulties faced by any third party, and the 1976 conviction of the party's gubernatorial candidate on a charge of conspiracy to distribute marijuana brought hard times in the late seventies.

A major issue throughout the period was the strained and often hostile relations between law enforcement officials and minority groups. Blacks and Mexican-Americans had long claimed that they were often subjected to harassment, brutality, and other forms of unfair treatment by police and other law officers. The rise of activism, with demonstrations and protest meetings, offered more opportunities for conflict, and a number of confrontations occurred. On the campus of Texas Southern University in May 1967, rumors of trouble and a gathering crowd of black students led to violence involving the students and the Houston police. Rocks and bottles were thrown; shots were fired; and a state of siege existed around one of the dormitories for several hours. Before order could be restored, a policeman was shot to death. Three years later in the summer of 1970 there was another shootout resulting in a fatality between the Houston police and a radical black group. Violent incidents took place in Midland in 1968, in Lubbock in 1971, and there were others. Frequently, charges were made that the police resorted to undue force in making arrests and were too quick in the use of their guns. In an effort to add minorities to the police force and thereby lessen the tensions, Houston adopted a special recruiting program in 1971, and other cities followed with similar programs. Special police-community relations councils were established in a number of cities. Still, the problems and charges persisted. Between 1975 and 1978 there were more than 30 official charges of alleged police brutality, and in at least two Houston cases, policemen were convicted on serious charges.

Much of the enthusiasm and energy of the civil rights crusade of the sixties and early seventies centered on the student protest movement, which brought tensions and unrest to college campuses all across the nation. Underlying the movement was a broad reaction against the unpopular war in Vietnam, but civil rights was also an important goal. Texas students on a number of college campuses took part in these protests. In some instances these were the result of traveling student activist organizers, such as those associated with the Student Nonviolent Coordinating Committee (SNCC). In other instances the demonstrations were altogether the product of local talent. Rarely did the protests assume threatening proportions, except for the tragic affair on the campus of Texas Southern University, but many college administrators had some anxious moments before the momentum of the movement waned in the early seventies.

A completely fair and sound evaluation of the effects of the student protest movement cannot be easily made. No doubt, the demonstrations and the enthusiasm of the students focused attention on the issue of civil rights. However, the movement offered relatively few solutions beyond a host of platitudes, and the fears and frustrations of public reaction may well have hindered the development of solutions.

Women—no longer a minority in the state since they outnumbered men as of the 1960 census and thereafter—but certainly a group subjected to discrimination and unequal treatment—joined the search for civil rights. The National Organization for Women (NOW), which formed in 1966, soon after had chapters in Texas. In 1971 women's rights workers met in Austin to organize the Texas Women's Political Caucus (TWPC), and shortly thereafter the group organized a successful campaign to secure legislative ratification of the proposed Twenty-seventh Amendment to the United States Constitution, the Equal Rights Amendment. The TWPC promoted greater involvement of women in politics, urging more to seek public office and to take more active roles in party affairs. The cause of women in politics was assisted in 1972 by the gubernatorial candidacy of Frances ("Sissy") Farenthold, who ran a strong, though unsuccessful, race. Women have since been gaining more influence in Texas politics, though progress has been painfully slow. By 1985 about five percent of the elected officials in Texas were women; one member of the state senate was a woman, and 15 women were in the house of representatives. Moreover, women have held increasingly influential posts in both Republican and Democratic party organizations.

SMITH, SHARPSTOWN, AND BRISCOE

While the struggle for civil rights provided some interest and excitement in the final years of the sixties, political affairs in Texas were generally quiet. In style, appearance, and background, Governor Smith was unlike the colorful and aggressive John Connally. Less than dynamic, the governor was not even very articulate, but over a long political career he patiently learned the system, cultivated his supporters, and took advantage of the opportunities that came his way. Rural and small-town voters were his primary strength. Leadership in the legislature was strong but closely tied to business and financial interests and not particularly sympathetic to reform or change. Speaker Gus Mutscher ruled the house of representatives with a firm hand, and Lieutenant Governor Ben Barnes's rule over the senate was almost as complete. Barnes was an able, pragmatic leader, and many regarded him as the politician with the most promising future.

Smith in his first term presented a legislative program that received only limited support. He proposed more funds for vocational education, two new medical schools, higher pay for legislators, a relatively small increase in taxes, and a lower voting age. He supported a comprehensive program to provide additional water supplies, primarily for western areas of the state. Somewhat surprisingly, he endorsed a state minimum wage. The legislature approved increased spending for vocational and medical schools and adopted a state minimum wage. But voters rejected the water plan, and the legislature turned down the governor's proposals for additional taxes.

In the election of 1970, attention focused not on the governor's race but on the contest for the Senate seat held by liberal Ralph Yarborough. Yarborough, who had first been elected in a special election but had won reelection to two regular terms, faced a difficult task. Conservative business and financial leaders in the Democratic party generally supported Lloyd Bentsen of Houston. The primary campaign, which was vigorous and somewhat bitter, ended in victory for Bentsen, who then defeated Republican George Bush in the general elections. Party emphasis on the Senate race perhaps affected Governor Smith's campaign for reelection. Smith defeated Paul Eggars, his Republican opponent of the previous election, but his margin of victory declined. Smith received 57 percent of the vote in 1968 but only 53 percent in 1970. In the election, voters gave their approval to a constitutional amendment making the sale of liquor by the drink permissible.

Scandals and charges of corruption dominated state affairs during Smith's second term. In January 1971 the Federal Securities and Exchange Commission filed charges in federal court against a number of Texas businessmen, alleging illegal manipulation in the sale of securities. Although the original charges did not name any politicians currently holding office, subsequent disclosures did, and charges of scandal, fraud, and bribery were soon heard throughout the state. The affair was complicated, but the essence of it was the allegation that high-ranking officials were given opportunities to profit in stock transactions in which prices were illegally manipulated in order to assure their profits. Frank Sharp, a prominent Houston banker, allegedly organized the scheme. He hoped to secure special legislation that would allow his troubled banking empire to evade the supervision and regulation of the Federal Deposit Insurance Corporation. The politicians involved were expected to see that the legislation desired by Sharp became law.

Several state officers did speculate in the stock, using funds loaned to them by Sharp's bank. Governor Smith and a close associate, Speaker of the House Gus Mutscher and two of his aides, and two other representatives quickly amassed profits that amounted to more than $300,000. The legislation was introduced in a special legislative session in August 1969 and with the strong support of Mutscher, it passed both houses of the legislature. But Governor Smith, who had allowed the measure to be considered in the special session, vetoed it.

The consequences of the so-called Sharpstown case were many. After a Travis County grand jury indicted Mutscher and two associates in September 1971, an Abilene jury convicted the trio on charges of conspiracy and bribery the following March. Within the house of representatives a strange collection of liberals, conservatives, mavericks, and members otherwise unclassified, all known collectively as the "Dirty Thirty," led a fight not only to oust the embattled speaker but also to change the rules so that no future speaker could exercise so much power.

The call for reform was strong and not entirely unanswered. The next legislature after Sharpstown, the sixty-third, adopted seven reform bills. The legislation established new rules for regulating lobbying, required financial reports from officeholders, laid down rules for opening public meetings and records, and tightened regulations on campaign financing. Much support developed for a comprehensive revision of the constitution.

The immediate impact of the scandal was felt in the elections of 1972. It was not a good year for incumbents. Less than half of the members of the house of representatives and of the senate returned to take their seats in the next legislature. Among the losers was Gus Mutscher, who sought reelection despite his conviction. Members of the "Dirty Thirty" who had challenged the power of the speaker fared somewhat better, especially those who sought reelection rather than new offices. Many factors contributed to the large turnover in the legislature, particularly the effects of newly installed single-member districting, but observers gave the Sharpstown scandal much of the credit.

Several candidates entered the race for governor. Smith, who had profited from the stock deals but who had not been charged with a crime, campaigned for a third term. Other major candidates included Lieutenant Governor Ben Barnes, Representative Frances Farenthold, who was one of the "Dirty Thirty," and Dolph Briscoe, who was a wealthy South Texas landowner. Smith ran a distant fourth and Barnes fared little better. Probably Sharpstown accounted for their poor showing, though there was little or nothing to connect Barnes with the affair. Briscoe, enjoying the support of business and financial interests, in a run-off defeated Representative Farenthold, generally regarded as the candidate of the liberals.

The general election saw triumph for Briscoe, but the vote was close. Briscoe polled slightly more than 100,000 votes over his Republican opponent, Henry Grover, winning with only 47 percent of the vote. The La Raza Unida candidate, Ramsey Muniz, received six percent of the vote, and had he received very much more, the election might well have fallen to the Republicans. On the national level Republicans did well in Texas. President Richard Nixon, in his contest with Democrat George McGovern, received 65 percent of the vote and carried 246 counties. Republican Senator John Tower also won reelection.

The election of Briscoe brought little in the way of change to Texas politics. Briscoe, who had little active experience in political office except for a brief period in the legislature during the fifties, was less than aggressive in his new post. Indeed, he seemed to enjoy being governor but to care little about performing the functions of the office. Although some regarded the governor as a leader of limited political ability, he was not entirely lacking in such skills. While maintaining a conservative reputation and the support of business and financial interests, he also maintained good relations with organized labor and much of the Mexican-American electorate.

"No new taxes," law enforcement, constitutional revision, school finances, and, toward the end of the period, tax revision were the issues of the Briscoe years. Constitutional revision, however, though one of the more important issues, received scant attention from the governor. In fact, he eventually announced his opposition to the effort. Perhaps heard more often than any other during the six years was the governor's promise of "no new taxes." It was a promise well kept, though lack of increased tax levels was not necessarily an indication of frugal public spending. The state budget almost doubled during the Briscoe years, but revenues from existing taxation more than kept pace with the needs. Public school finances was the most persistent budget problem of the period. Solutions adopted were only makeshift and tended in many instances to shift the tax burden from the state treasury to local districts. The legislature spent considerable time on law enforcement legislation, eventually adopting a new criminal code, several anticrime bills, and an act restoring the death penalty.

In the final year of his tenure, after he had lost his primary bid for renomination, the governor called a special legislative session to enact a program of tax relief. The legislature increased inheritance tax exemptions, repealed the sales tax on utilities, and adopted a constitutional amendment, later approved by the voters, that reduced property taxes levied primarily on the local level.

CONSTITUTIONAL REVISION

Voters in an atmosphere sympathetic to reform in 1972 approved an amendment to the constitution authorizing the legislature to meet in a convention in January 1974. In the interim a 37-member constitutional revision committee prepared recommendations calling for a new, shorter, and more general constitution. The committee suggested annual legislative sessions, more power for the governor, reorganization of the judicial system, and other extensive changes.

With Speaker of the House Price Daniel, Jr. as its presiding officer, the legislative constitutional convention met as planned in January 1974. After much debate and compromise, the convention completed an 11-article constitution in July. Though government reforms were not as extensive as those proposed by the commission, the document did provide for many changes. However, the convention refused, by a three-vote margin, to approve its own work, and the document was not presented to the voters. The controversy over a "right-to-work" provision, the dissatisfaction of some members who wanted more drastic reforms, the opposition of those who wanted fewer reforms, and the opposition of those who wanted no new constitution at all accounted for the defeat.

The following legislature which met in 1975 revived the constitutional revision issue. Eight proposed amendments were drafted, and these in effect amounted to a new constitution and were similar to the constitution prepared the previous year. The legislature adopted the amendments and presented them to the voters in the November elections. But interest in reform was waning; certain groups were adamantly opposed; the governor belatedly announced his opposition; and the voters rejected constitutional revision by a margin of three to one.

A REPUBLICAN GOVERNOR—A NEW ERA?

The 1978 elections in Texas provided more than the usual number of political surprises. Governor Briscoe announced for a third term, not an unusual move except that election would mean ten years in office since the governorship became a four-year term in 1974. His opponent for the nomination was John Hill, the attorney general, who was considered by most to be moderately liberal. Supported enthusiastically by the state's teachers who were attracted by Hill's stand on education, the attorney general defeated Briscoe in the Democratic primary. Other factors contributing to Briscoe's defeat included his less-than-aggressive style of leadership, defection of some labor and Mexican-American support, and the reluctance of some voters to have the same governor for ten years.

In the Republican party the contest for the nomination was between Ray Hutchinson, a highly respected and able long-time party leader, and William Clements, a wealthy and outspoken Dallas oilman. Relying on an effective, well-financed publicity campaign, Clements won the nomination.

To the surprise of most, he also won the election. By a very narrow margin and with less than 50 percent of the vote, Clements defeated Hill to become the first Republican governor elected in Texas in more than a century. Political observers offered many explanations in analyzing the victory. Voter turnout was light; many conservative Democrats voted Republican; Hill supporters were overconfident; and Clements's campaign, which spent more than seven million dollars on the primary and general elections, was better financed than Hill's. To these may be added the fact that Clement's campaign not only was well-financed, it was also shrewdly effective in its appeal to a conservatively inclined Texas electorate. Republican strength in the legislature increased slightly, claiming 23 members in the house of representatives and four in the senate.

Governor Clement's first term of office offered many contrasts to that of his predecessor, Dolph Briscoe. Energetic and aggressive, the new governor had an opinion on nearly all issues and a willingness to express it. If he had a goal more important than any other, it was the reduction of state expenditures. During the campaign he had frequently complained about the excessive expenses of state government, particularly about unnecessary state employees, and had promised to reduce the number of state workers by thousands and to cut the cost of government by millions. In pursuit of that objective, the governor's office required state agencies to prepare elaborate reports explaining the work of the agency and defending employment needs. The program of reports and related studies continued throughout the term, but there was little decrease in the number of state workers, while salary costs increased considerably. However, the campaign on behalf of frugality was not altogether a failure. The population of Texas increased more than ten percent during the governor's term, but the number of state employees remained relatively stable. Moreover, while salaries of state workers increased, inflation more than offset the increase.

Legislative accomplishments under the Republican governor were creditable but not impressive. The relationship between the Democratic legislature and the governor could best be described as proper and polite but cautious and skeptical as well. In the first session, the governor offered a host of proposals, and some were adopted, but most were rejected. The most important accomplishments of the session included the passage of a new public school finance law and the adoption of a more uniform program for the taxation of property. Both of these laws were primarily the work of leaders within the legislature. In the second session of the governor's term, the legislature adopted, with the strong support of the governor, a series of laws strengthening the state's power in dealing with crime, particularly the traffic in narcotics. Well-intentioned but generating an endless stream of paperwork for teachers was legislation that required revision of the curriculum of the public schools and a more structured system of classroom teaching.

As the elections of 1982 approached, many observers expected Governor Clements's reelection, confirming the establishment of two-party politics in Texas. For the most part, the state was exceptionally prosperous, enjoying the benefits of an oil boom of unprecedented proportions, and early polls showed the governor with a comfortable lead. Although the accomplishments of his administration were not especially notable, the governor and his office were singularly free of any hint of scandal. Republican Ronald Reagan in his campaign for President in 1980 had won the vote of Texas by a large margin, and Clements's campaign fund amounted to millions of dollars.

But the prophets who hailed the establishment of two-party government in Texas were wrong. Democrats won most of the contests across the state, and in the race for governor, Attorney General Mark White won with 53% of the vote. Despite an expenditure of more than $12 million, Clements lost by more than 200,000 votes.

Several factors seemed to account for the outcome of the election. In some instances, voters may have been alienated by the governor's abrasive manner. Public school teachers, in particular, believed that Clements's administration had done little for them or for education. Mexican-Americans voted in large numbers, and usually for White; rural Texans, who tended to support the Democratic cause, turned out in greater numbers, as did black voters. Overall, the vote was substantially larger in 1982 than in 1978.

The election of Mark White as governor in 1982 brought into office a seasoned veteran of Texas politics. A graduate of Baylor University and political associate of former governor Dolph Briscoe, White had developed his skill as a politician, while establishing a broad base of support among the local party faithful across the state. A familiar face at party banquets, barbeques, receptions, and fund-raisings, he had patiently established himself as a loyal servant of the party. His principles and goals, however, were not as well-known. Many liberals regarded him as a conservative tool of business interests, while many conservatives considered him to be a liberal masquerading as an advocate of conservative government. Others expected him to perform in much the same manner as some governors of the recent past, enjoying the fruits of office and otherwise doing little.

Perhaps reflecting his political skills, White managed to respond to many different interest groups in the state. In keeping with the practices of all governors after the time of John Connally, he frequently repeated the cry of "no new taxes" (even though as late as 1986, Texas ranked forty-first in the nation in the level of state and local taxation). Although he ordinarily rewarded party loyalists in matters of appointments to boards and agencies, he also took care to see that minorities and women were given some of the appointments. Fulfilling a campaign promise, he appointed a consumer representative to the Public Utility Commission, and there were indications that utility rate increase requests received closer and less sympathetic scrutiny than under previous administrations.

It was, however, education and budgets that occupied most of the administration's attention. In the campaign of 1982 White had sought the support of the state's public school teachers, promising to promote the improvement of education and teacher salaries. The necessity for both was evident in a contemporary report published by the U. S. Secretary of Education, which observed that Texas ranked forty-second among all states in the percentage of students who graduated from high school, next to last in the percentage of per capita income spent on public education, and below national averages in standardized test scores, teacher-pupil ratios, and teacher salaries. White reacted to the report with the appointment of a select committee on public education headed by Dallas millionaire and industrialist, H. Ross Perot. After many months of hearings and study, the committee prepared a list of ten reform recommendations, which in turn were submitted to a special session of the legislature in June 1984.

The Educational Reform Act (House Bill 72) passed by the legislature and signed into law on July 2, 1984, was long (228 pages) and complex. Among its most important provisions was the reorganization of the state board of education, requirements for competency testing for pupils, teachers, and administrators, a requirement that students must be passing all subjects to participate in extracurricular activities ("no pass, no play"), a broad and significant salary increase for teachers, and an arrangement for merit pay that was both complicated and unusual.

While students, teachers, parents, and the general public were trying to understand House Bill 72, the state became mired in budgetary problems that were at first troublesome, then serious, and ultimately, critical. The problem actually developed over a period of several years. Throughout the 1970s and early 1980s, state expenditures increased, but revenue generated by a high level of economic activity and inflation increased at a more rapid rate. Political leaders were able to maintain the popular slogan of "no new taxes," and at the same time more or less to fund the needs of state government. But beginning in 1983, the economic recession which had already been prevalent in many other parts of the nation for several years began to be a problem in Texas. Oil prices, which had risen to more than $35 per barrel, began to decline; oil companies reduced their expenditures; and unemployment increased steadily. Agricultural income fell, and economic chaos in Mexico generated hard times along the Texas border. Meanwhile, education reforms required more funds; court orders demanded substantial and costly expansion of the state prison system; and the highly prized highway system of the state was rapidly deteriorating.

The 1984 special session of the legislature, which enacted the education reform bill, dealt with the budget problem to some extent. An act expanded the base of the sales tax and increased the rate slightly, with the additional revenue to be used in part for education and in part for support of the highway system. At the same time, motor vehicle fuel taxes and certain other related taxes were increased. No further taxes were added in 1985, but it was evident that the budget was balanced precariously, if at all, and that any additional decline in the economy of the state would mean a deficit (prohibited by the constitution).

Beginning in the spring of 1986, oil prices, which had been maintained at high levels by a foreign cartel, declined precipitously, eventually reaching a point as low as $10 per barrel. The result was disaster for the already badly damaged oil industry, overextended financial institutions, and thousands of Texas workers. But it was also a disaster for state government. By the end of the spring, the comptroller was forecasting a budget deficit of several billion dollars. After considerable delay, perhaps because it was an election year, Governor White called a special session of the legislature. Divided and unhappy, the legislature debated for weeks before finally agreeing upon a compromise. Legislation was passed that postponed obligations, increased taxes temporarily, moved funds from special accounts to the general revenue fund, revoked employee salary increases, and reduced expenditures wherever possible. The measure did little more than allow the state to limp along until the regular session met in January, 1987, after the elections.

In the midst of the budget crisis, the 1986 elections were held and Governor Mark White and ex-governor William Clements renewed their contest for the governor's office. The campaign was spirited and ill-tempered, with each candidate spending millions on television and other media. From the early stages of the campaign, polls showed Clements with a comfortable lead, and although the margin declined somewhat, the polls were accurate. Clements, who lost by 230,000 votes in 1982, won in 1986 by almost the same number. For the second time since Reconstruction, Texans elected a Republican governor.

Reasons for the Clements victory were many, albeit sometimes contradictory. To some degree, the education reforms of 1984, an achievement of considerable merit, were responsible. Teachers, who had worked diligently for White in 1982, in many instances turned against him in 1986. Although he was, more than anyone else, responsible for substantial salary increases in public education, teachers held the governor accountable for the despised competency test (TECAT) that they had recently been forced to take. Curiously, legislative leaders, who were far more responsible for the competency test requirement than White, were reelected easily. "No pass, no play" unquestionably alienated some voters who considered victory at the Friday night football games more important than education. And others resented the modest tax increases necessary to fund the reforms.

Economic hard times was an important factor. Many Texans were unemployed, others feared that they would soon lose their jobs, and many businesses struggled daily just to keep their doors open. Governor White, after some delay, had spoken out in favor of tax increases to meet the budget deficit; increased taxes, never welcome in Texas, were even more unpopular in hard times. Clements, whose program to meet the crisis remained unclear even after months of campaigning, seemed to have convinced the voters that he had the solution in hand.

It was, however, White's most conspicuous talent, the skill of a politician, that failed him in the election. In most areas where Democratic voters dominated, the turnout dropped, while in Republican areas, voters went to the polls in numbers larger than in 1982. In rural East Texas and Hispanic South Texas, both traditional Democratic strongholds, voters in significant numbers stayed at home, and in the upper Texas coast where union support remained loyal, White's vote was 36,000 less than in 1982. On the other hand, voter turnout increased in Austin and Dallas suburbs, and most of the increase supported the Republican candidate. For whatever reason, White's failure to generate voter enthusiasm, even in his own party, was evident.

To a considerable extent, the elections of 1986 failed to answer the question of whether or not Texas was at last a two- party state. Republicans added only one seat in the house of representatives, and Democrats won all four of the open positions in the senate. In the race for governor, the outcome more likely represented a rejection of the incumbent than a vote for Republicanism. Certainly, Republican fortunes had improved considerably since World War II. Although Republican candidates once had polled only five to ten percent of the vote, as Texans went to the polls in the eighties, Republicans in statewide races could ordinarily expect a respectable vote, generally in excess of 40 percent. Success beyond that level remained uncertain, dependent upon the various issues of particular elections. One-party domination seemed to be a thing of the past, but the future of two-party politics remained uncertain.

THE NEW FEDERALISM

If political trends within the state were not exactly clear in the seventies and eighties, another development in government was quite obvious. The role of the national government in the lives of Texans was ever more a larger and larger one. Although activities of the federal government have always been important in the state, extensive involvement came with the programs of the New Deal. More programs and more regulations were added after World War II, and the sixties and seventies saw even more. Other aspects were involved, but regulatory functions and financial support were the two primary areas of federal activity.

A number of agencies carried on investigations to determine compliance with federal law and judicial decrees. Many of these stemmed from the civil rights legislation of the sixties, with added emphasis toward the end of the seventies on protection of the handicapped and the elderly. Acting under the authority of the Voting Rights Act of 1965, as amended in 1975, the Civil Rights Division of the Justice Department supervised certain election practices and approved or disapproved any changes in voting procedures. Minority rights, however, by no means accounted for all of the federal regulatory action in the state. Exercising a degree of control over private industry and public activities were two powerful agencies, the

Environmental Protection Agency (EPA) and the Occupational Safety and Health Administration (OSHA). And there were others.

Federal courts similarly have become more active. Often the controversies centered on alleged violations of civil rights, but the issues were many and varied. By the end of the seventies a significant number of school districts in the state were functioning under federal court orders calling for busing or some other method to accelerate the pace of integration. Indeed, in many school districts the school attorney was a vital part of the organization, and integration was not always the issue. Tuition for aliens, students' rights, teachers' rights, bilingual education, and other controversies kept the schools in the courtrooms.

Financial support was the other area in which the federal government loomed large in Texas. In 1984 the federal government provided about 14 percent of the money used by the public schools of Texas. Although the level of support had declined somewhat from that of the seventies, federal funds in the mid-eighties provided more than 20 percent of the monies spent by the state government. In addition, there were large sums parceled out through special grants to cities and other governmental units.

The desirability of federal regulation is a matter of personal values, to be determined in large measure by political ideologies and the degree to which one is affected for good or for bad. Supporters argue necessity and justice, but critics claim that, at best, harm is more often done than good.

Federal financial contributions were likely to be more generally welcomed, though not in all instances. State government in Texas provided in the eighties only a minimal level of state services in terms of money, spending at a rate of less than 80 percent of the national average. But even so, the costs were high. Welfare costs in 1984, administered primarily through the Texas Department of Human Resources, required more than 16 percent of the state's budget, but federal funds supplied about 60 percent of the need. More than 30 percent of the monies spent on highways and transportation came from federal sources. These two areas, together with education, accounted for about three-fourths of the federal monies spent in the state.

SELECTED BIBLIOGRAPHY

George Green, *The Establishment in Texas Politics,* surveys briefly the politics of the sixties and seventies, but no general study of the period in depth has been published. One aspect, however, has been thoroughly studied: For information on the bank bill scandals, consult Sam Kinch, Jr., and Ben Proctor, *Texas under a Cloud* (Austin, 1972); Charles Deaton, *The Year They Threw the Rascals Out* (Austin, 1973); Jimmy Banks, *Money, Marbles, and Chalk: The Wondrous World of Texas Politics* (Austin, 1971); and Harvey Katz, *Shadow on the Alamo: New Heroes Fight Old Corruption in Texas Politics* (Garden City, N.Y., 1972). On a later crisis of lesser proportions, see

Robert Heard, *The Miracle of the Killer Bees: 12 Senators Who Changed Texas Politics* (Austin, 1981). Rowland Evans and Robert Novak, *Lyndon B. Johnson: The Exercise of Power;* and Ann Fears Crawford and Jack Keever, *John B. Connally: A Portrait in Power* (Austin, 1973), focus on two of the prominent figures of the period. See also, E. V. Nemeyer, Jr., "Personal Diplomacy: Lyndon B. Johnson and Mexico, 1963–1968," *Southwestern Historical Quarterly,* XC, 159–186. For a look at the rise of the Republican party, see Roger M. Olien, *From Token to Triumph: The Texas Republicans Since 1920* (Dallas, 1982).

For interesting and not always predictable articles on Texas politics, read those found in the *Texas Monthly.* Also useful, but predictable, are those of the *Texas Observer.* The lobby, often charged with exercising undue influence in Texas politics, is described and discussed in Lee Clark, "May the Lobby Hold You in the Palm of Its Hand," *Texas Observer,* May 24, 1968 pp. 1–3; and in several studies in the *Texas Monthly,* July 1973. The *Texas Journal of Political Studies* is a valuable source for contemporary politics.

Literature on minorities and their politics is becoming more available in recent years. Alwyn Barr, *Black Texans,* provides material up to 1971. Matt S. Meir and Feliciano Rivera, *The Chicanos: A History of Mexican Americans* (New York, 1972) is a useful general study. Typical of more specialized studies are John Stapler Shockley, *Chicano Revolt in a Texas Town* (Notre Dame, Ind., 1974); and Robert W. Talbert, "Poll Tax Repeal in Texas: A Three Year Individual Performance Evaluation," *Journal of Politics,* XXXVI, 1050–1056. See also David W. Brady and Kent L. Tedin, "Religion and Political Ideology in the Anti-ERA Movement," *Social Science Quarterly,* LVI, 464–475; and Jan Meadows, "Woman against Herself," *Texas Parade,* March 1975, pp. 29–33.

CHAPTER TWENTY
IN THE AGE OF ATOMS
AND SPACE

Dramatic change, highlighted by the use of atomic power and human flight in space, characterized the economic, scientific, and social development of the United States in the years after World War II. Economic, social, and cultural change in Texas in these years depended only to a limited extent on space and perhaps even less on atomic power, but these were, nonetheless, years of change in which Texas economically and socially experienced a transformation of almost revolutionary proportions.

Industrialization and urbanization, trends long apparent in Texas, accelerated in the years following World War II. In 1983 an estimated three percent of the population or less depended on farms and ranches directly for their income; eight out of ten Texans lived in urban areas; and about one-half of the people were concentrated in the Dallas-Fort Worth, Houston, and San Antonio areas. For most, living was no longer a matter of wide-open spaces and the smell of the earth, but rather an environment of housing developments, freeways, and shopping centers.

These were the most obvious changes, but there were many others. Though requiring the efforts of a relatively small portion of the population, agriculture by no means assumed an unimportant role. Social and cultural institutions grew in number and scope and added their contributions to the postwar world, as did many individuals in the arts and liter-

Nuclear power, once thought to be an important part of the solution to the energy needs of Texas, has not yet proven to be the answer. However, the construction of some plants has been started. This one is the South Texas Project Unit 1, under construction in Matagorda County and jointly owned by Houston Lighting and Power Co., Central Power and Light Co., and the cities of San Antonio and Austin. The other nuclear plant in the state is the Comanche Peak Project, being built near Glen Rose by Texas Utilities Co.

ature. The population grew, in part because of the attraction offered by the appeal of the so-called sunbelt. Economically and otherwise, the roles of women and minorities in the society were altered.

Until the early eighties, Texans generally prospered, some at unprecedented levels, but a decline in oil prices, which began in 1983 and accelerated in 1986, combined to bring the state's economy to recession levels by mid-decade. For the first time since the Great Depression, Texans questioned their future and that of their state.

THE ECONOMY

Although the role of agriculture declined in the years after World War II, farming and ranching remained an important part of the postwar economy. Agricultural production, in terms of monetary value, increased fourfold between 1954 and 1983, with livestock providing about two-thirds and field crops one-third of the income. Cotton continued to be the most valuable field crop—though displaced temporarily in 1975 by grain sorghums—but by a wide margin cattle was the most valuable single product. With only a small portion of the population living on farms, the influence of agriculture has declined significantly over the years; but it appears that the voice of agriculture in the state has remained substantially stronger than the number of farmers indicates that it would likely be.

Production levels remained stable, but high interest rates and fuel costs and declining commodity prices in the mid-eighties brought many farmers to the point of bankruptcy and others to sell their lands. Thus, the practice of consolidation that has characterized Texas agriculture in the twentieth-century continues, with no end in sight.

By any measure, industry grew vigorously in the years after World War II. Employment in manufacturing more than tripled between 1947 and 1982, rising to more than one million workers, and the increased value added to goods by manufacturing was even more impressive, amounting to more than $30 billion annually. Oil refining, chemicals, and petrochemicals, all important in the thirties, continued to dominate in the eighties, but electronics, aerospace components, and other high-technology items were also important. The aircraft industry, located in the Dallas-Fort Worth area during World War II, continued production thereafter, and electronics plants were built nearby in later years. In the late seventies and early eighties, a number of plants manufacturing computers and related items were located in Austin and San Antonio, as "high-tech" became a familiar phrase to most Texans. Oil and chemical refining concentrated in locations along the coast, with many plants being established in the Beaumont-Port Arthur and the Houston-Baytown-Texas City areas. The manufacture of oil-field equipment became a major industry in Houston.

Oil production rose more or less steadily after World War II, reaching a peak of slightly more than 1.3 million barrels in 1972. That year the Railroad Commission abandoned its practice, in effect since 1933, of restricting production. Nevertheless, declining reserves and weakening wells brought lowered production, so that in 1984 less than 900 million barrels were pumped. Prices, however, remained high until 1983, and the oil industry prospered and contributed to the general prosperity of the state. In 1983 the petroleum industry employed 350,553 people; at the same time, oil and gas production provided slightly more than 20 percent of the tax revenue available to finance state government.

Developments beginning in 1983 demonstrated well the dependence of Texas and Texans on oil. World-wide overproduction of petroleum and conservation measures led to a surplus of petroleum products and consequent decline in prices for the next three years. And, in the spring of 1986, the cartel of foreign oil producers, which had attempted to maintain oil prices at high levels collapsed, thus allowing prices to decline from about $30 per barrel to as little as $10.

The 1986 collapse only added to the troubles of Texas oilmen. Drilling activities had been declining steadily since 1983; refinery runs and the production of oil field equipment were similarly significantly reduced, and employment moved steadily lower. Analysts reported early in 1987 that more than 100,000 jobs in the Texas oil industry had disappeared since 1982. Thousands of highly trained geologists and technicians were unemployed, while factories which once produced oilfield equipment stood empty and refineries operated at minimum levels or closed their gates. While other parts of the nation enjoyed at least moderate prosperity, Texas in the mid-eighties suffered the consequences of economic recession.

Although affected somewhat by the recession of the eighties, transportation in the postwar years reflected the growth of the population and the economy. Motor vehicle registration rose from 2,192,654 in 1947 to 13,491,236 in 1983, a rate of growth approximately five times greater than the rise in population. Only California had more automobiles on the highways. Commercial air passenger service began in the state in 1928, with schedules connecting Dallas with San Antonio and Fort Worth with Galveston. Growth was modest during the years of the Depression, but military aviation in World War II built interest and support. Air travel rapidly expanded in postwar years, and between 1957 and 1983 the number of people traveling by air each year increased tenfold. At the same time rail travel dwindled to almost nothing, and miles of railroad track continued their decline, falling to 12,942 in 1983. However, railroad freight tonnage increased almost 50 percent during the postwar years, and railroading in Texas continued to be profitable.

Organized labor shared in the economic growth of the postwar years, for, despite a barrage of laws regulating unions passed in the late 1940s and early 1950s, labor gained strength and membership. Unification of the American Federation of Labor (AFL) and the Congress of Industrial Organizations (CIO) in 1957 brought a larger role in politics. Labor's voice in state politics was heard more often, and in local politics of certain areas it was a voice that could not be ignored. Oil refining and chemical industries were, in most instances, unionized, as were most of the construction trades. In the seventies there were a number of instances in which public employees formed unions or similar organizations. However, in the eighties union membership was apparently declining slightly. Among the reasons given for the decline was the continued existence of the "right-to-work" law, long opposed by organized labor, but the decline of unionized industries such as chemical manufacturing and oil refining also contributed.

CHURCHES, SCHOOLS, AND SOCIETIES

The growth of Texas churches has generally kept pace with the population. In 1890, church members represented 30.3 percent of the population, and by 1916 they had increased to 40 percent. In 1980 a membership of almost eight million was reported, but the number was probably higher, inasmuch as not all churches reported their members and some counts were incomplete. The Baptist bodies led, with more than three million members; Roman Catholics numbered more than two million; and United Methodists counted almost one million. The Church of Christ, Disciples of Christ, Presbyterians, Protestant Episcopal, and Lutheran denominations were represented by large numbers, and there were many others.

Notwithstanding certain distinct differences, the larger Protestant bodies have had many characteristics in common. They have maintained Sunday schools and auxiliary organizations for young people. Certain churches have had special organizations for men, and most of them have had one or more organizations for women. Almost without exception they have emphasized the importance of maintaining a zealous and active laity to aid a ministry that was better trained and better paid than any ministry that had preceded it. Although the state has taken over much of the burden that the churches once bore alone, the churches still carry on extensive work in education, child care, and the maintenance of hospitals.

Public education in Texas benefited significantly from the adoption of the Gilmer-Aiken program, shortly after the end of World War II. State leadership in the fifties worked in various ways to emphasize productive living and citizenship. After the Russians placed satellites in orbit in 1957, there was a persistent demand for more study and more effective teaching in the schools, from kindergarten through the university level.

Later years saw added emphasis on special programs. Programs for the instruction of handicapped children reached a substantial number of the less fortunate young, and programs to assist educationally deprived children were established in many communities. Bilingual education received special attention in the seventies. Toward the end of the decade, declining scores on verbal and mathematical achievement tests generated widespread concern and gave rise to a "back-to-basics" movement.

The educational reforms of the eighties were, in fact, the consequence of such concerns. The reforms encompassed in House Bill 72 passed by a special session of legislature in 1984 were many and complex, emphasizing competency testing, increased salaries for educators, and expanded resources. At the heart of the program was a commitment to the ideal that quality education was fundamentally necessary to the success and happiness of individuals and society. But the reforms were expensive, cumbersome, and often conflicted with long-standing, almost sacred, institutions such as athletics. Whether or not the reforms will survive in the face of determined opponents and tight budgets remains a question as the state enters the second half of the decade of the eighties. In keeping with a long tradition in Texas, politicians continue to talk about the value of education, but in keeping with another long tradition, there is a reluctance to provide the necessary funds.

In higher education the years after World War II have been a period of steady growth. The growth rate was especially high in the seventies, with student enrollment almost doubling and the addition of 36 new units of higher education. By 1980 more than 150 institutions in the state provided opportunities for those seeking education beyond the high school. Public-supported senior colleges numbered 24 in 1984, and there were 49 public community colleges and a number of educational centers. Specialized training was offered by seven medical schools, two dental schools, allied health units, a technical institute, and a maritime academy.

Private institutions, most with church connections, numbered 43 in 1986. Rice University was noted for its educational excellence. Largest of a number of Baptist institutions was Baylor University, and Southern Methodist University, established in 1915, was the largest of nine Methodist schools. The Presbyterians had Austin College and Trinity University; the Church of Christ had Abilene Christian College and several smaller schools; the Disciples of Christ maintained Texas Christian University; and Saint Mary's University was the largest Catholic school. Even though their proportion of the enrollment has declined in recent years, the private and denominational schools are still important to Texas higher education, providing in 1986 education for one out of every nine students. In addition to their emphasis on religious training, several of these schools do outstanding work in music, drama, and the other fine arts.

Lodges, clubs, and societies, some with roots that extend far back into pioneer times, have continued to form an important sector of Texas's social and cultural institutions since World War II. The Masonic orders, active in the early nineteenth century, located lodges in practically every city and town in the state. Among other strong organizations are the Odd Fellows, the Knights of Pythias, and the Woodmen. These and other lodges have provided a measure of security for their members and have contributed to the general welfare through the maintenance of homes, orphanages, and hospitals.

Service clubs have assumed a more important role over the years. First to be established in Texas was the Rotary Club, founded in Dallas in 1911. During the First World War the Lions, an organization dedicated to community service, was founded. It has one or more clubs in practically every town and city in the state. Other organizations with similar purposes are Kiwanis, Optimists International, and Exchange Clubs.

Veteran's organizations have exercised considerable influence in the state. The American Legion, formed first in 1919 by veterans of the First World War, have constructed buildings, provided facilities for recreation, and carried on various programs of community improvement. The American G. I. Forum, a veterans' group formed by Mexican-Americans, has taken an active stand in many state and local matters. The Veterans of

Foreign Wars, an organization with purposes similar to the American Legion, has had rapid growth in Texas.

Of particular value in promoting adult education has been the Texas Federation of Women's Clubs. In earlier years the organization played a major role in the establishment of public libraries across the state. In addition to its library work, the federation promoted legislation in the interest of rural education, compulsory school laws, the protection of women and children in industry, and Texas heritage.

Indeed, Texans are confirmed "joiners." Apparently everyone belongs to at least one organization, and the average for adults of middle and higher incomes is surely three or more. There are hundreds and hundreds of organizations in the state. There is the Texas State Teachers' Association, a powerful group that long has wielded great influence in legislation. Similar organizations of strength are the state bar and the state medical association. There are also learned societies, such as the Texas Academy of Science and the Texas Philosophical Society, which was founded during the republic and revived in 1936. There are three geological societies and six organizations of engineers, one statewide historical association and half a dozen regional ones. There are organizations as unrelated as barbers and cattle raisers, Indians and skeet shooters, veterans and Zionists. These provide outlets for the innumerable interests and emotions of the people and are channels of communication and cooperation. More perhaps than any other source, they reveal the nature of our civilization. They are the institutions of a free people and could not thrive except in an atmosphere of freedom.

LITERATURE AND THE ARTS

Since World War II the literature of Texas has grown in volume, richness, and diversity. The traditional topics of earlier years have continued to attract the interest of both writers and readers. Ernest Wallace and E. Adamson Hoebel dealt with both history and ethnology in *The Comanches, Lords of the South Plains*; Mildred P. Mayhall published a historical study of the Kiowas; Charles L. Sonnichsen wrote on the Mescalero Apaches; and W. W. Newcomb surveyed the entire subject in *The Indians of Texas*. In Ernest Wallace's *Ranald S. Mackenzie*, the story of Texas's last great Indian war is well told. J. Evetts Haley, W. C. Holden, J. W. Williams, Tom Lea, Wayne Gard, and others have added to the literature on the cattle industry.

A number of biographies have appeared. Llerena Friend published the authoritative *Sam Houston, The Great Designer*. Ernest Wallace's *Charles DeMorse, Pioneer Editor and Statesman*, Ben Proctor's *Not without Honor* (about John H. Reagan), Joe B. Frantz's *Gail Borden, Dairyman to a Nation*, Alvy King's *Louis T. Wigfall*, and Robert C. Cotner's *James Stephen Hogg* deal with prominent nineteenth-century figures. The lives of more recent Texans are portrayed in R. N. Richardson's *Colonel House: The Texas Years*, John O. King's *Joseph Stephen Cullen: A Study in Leadership in the Texas Petroleum Industry, 1897–1937*, T. Dwight Donough's *Mr. Sam* (about Sam Rayburn), Rowland Evans and Robert Novak, *Lyndon B. Johnson: The Exercise of Power*, and Ann Fears Crawford and Jack Keever, *John B. Connally: Portrait in Power*.

Interpretative writing on Texas and Texans has increased greatly during the last quarter-century. Some are autobiographical and at times, sympathetic, but more often they are critical. William A. Owens has produced several works, among them *This Stubborn Soil*. Edward Everett Dale's *The Cross Timbers*, Bertha McKee Dobie's *Growing Up in Texas*, and C. C. White's *No Quittin' Sense* emphasize the rural heritage of the state. Somewhat more critical are Willie Morris's *North Toward Home* and David Nevin's *The Texans: What They Are—and Why*. In his *Big Country, Texas*, Donald Day has sought to explain the country and its institutions through history, politics, and folklore. Joseph Leach in *The Typical Texan: Biography of an American Myth* has sought to find in history, novels, and biography a true account of Texan character. Frank Goodwyn's *Lone Star Land: Twentieth Century in Perspective* deals with the social changes Texas has known in the light of its culture, geography, and history. T. R. Fehrenbach's *Lone Star* offers some interesting insights into the forces that have molded the state. The cowboy, a type inseparably linked with Texas, is appraised by Joe B. Frantz and Julian Earnest Choate in *The American Cowboy: The Myth and the Reality*.

In fiction during the middle decades of the twentieth century, Texas novelists were writing on an increasingly varied list of subjects. In *Wetback*, Claud Garner attacked the injustice often done to Mexican immigrants who crossed the Rio Grande unlawfully. William A. Owen's *Walking on Borrowed Land* is a plea for better understanding between the races, David Westheimer, in *Summer on the War*, deals with the humor and tragedy of a family in a summer colony near Houston. Madison Cooper's *Sironia, Texas* discusses the intimate affairs of the people of a town. In the *Brave Bulls*, Tom Lea treats the interplay of courage and fear in the mind of a matador hero. In *Hound Dog Man*, Fred Gipson took a boy and his dogs through commonplace experiences in a style suggestive of Mark Twain and Booth Tarkington. Loula Grace Erdman's *The Years of the Locusts*, a story of farm people, won a prize of $10,000 from a national publisher. Larry McMurtry's *Lonesome Dove* is a powerful account of personal relationships on a cattle drive. In keeping with the spirit of the age, his novel, *The Last Picture Show*, set in a fictional Panhandle oil-field and ranching community, is a critical portrayal of personalities limited by a provincial environment. In a similar vein, Garland Roark wrote of the skullduggery of two East Texas oil promoters in *Drill a Crooked Hole*. *North to Yesterday*, a tragicomic novel about a cattle drive written by Robert Flynn, won an award from the Texas Institute of Letters. James A. Michener's *Texas*, a novel which covers the history of Texas from the time of the arrival of the Spanish, tells its story in a way that is both sympathetic and critical.

In folklore, the pioneering works of John Lomax, John Mason Brewer, and J. Frank Dobie have endured and been joined by others. *Adventures of a Ballad Hunter* by Lomax won a Texas Institute of Letters Award in 1947. J. Mason Brewer's collections of folklore dealing with the lives of black people, recorded in *The Word on the Brazos, Aunt Dicey*, and others, continue to be read. One of the first Mexican-American folklorists to be published was Jovita Gonzales, and adding to her contributions have been the works of Americo Paredes. His study of the *corrido* (Mexican-American folk ballad) is particularly noteworthy. "With His Pistol in His Hand," a study of Gregorio Cortez, is probably his most popular work. Moody Boatwright and William Owens have collected many tales that offer much about the culture of the state.

Societies and journals have done much to preserve the literature of Texas. Vital to the preservation of folklore is the work of the Texas Folklore Society, which over the years has published a large number of volumes. Of the two outstanding literary magazines in the state, the oldest is the *Southwest Review*, founded in Austin in 1915 and later moved to Dallas, where it is sponsored by Southern Methodist University. The quality of its articles is high, and it is a worthy exponent of the life and literature of the state. In 1958 the *Texas Quarterly* was established by members of the faculty of the University of Texas. It carries a wide range of narratives, biographies, poems, and art and provides an outlet for a number of talented writers. Through the pages of these journals much of the poetry of recent times has been preserved and made available to readers.

Interest in the theater dates at least back to the days of the Texas republic and has grown in the twentieth century. In 1909 the Curtain Club was organized at the University of Texas, and after the First World War the little theater became a community project in most towns and cities. Of such organizations, the oldest and best-known in Texas is one in Dallas, founded in 1921. Professional drama presented in the Alley Theater in Houston and in the Dallas Theater Center has won national recognition since World War II.

In twentieth-century music Texas has made some substantial contributions. Dallas, Houston, San Antonio have major symphony orchestras, and interest in ballet has increased significantly in recent years. Beaumont, Dallas, Fort Worth, Houston, and San Antonio maintain opera groups. Since World War II there has been an unprecedented development of music education through the Interscholastic League. North Texas State University and the University of Texas are known nationally for their excellent music programs, and other universities have developed similarly.

Affecting a larger proportion of the population was the growth of country and western and rock music, or combinations thereof. Drawing on the foundations made popular in the thirties by musicians such as Bob Wills and Ernest Tubb, music once termed "hillbilly" by some evolved into western and then into country music. The change was more than a matter of names. Lyrics, emphasis, and instrumentations were altered, although many of the basic themes remained the same. In the sixties, seventies, and eighties, elements of rock were added, to produce a combination termed by some as "progressive country."

Austin became a prominent center for country and western musicians. Willie Nelson, a Texan who abandoned Nashville to return to his home state, perhaps won the most acclaim, but there were many others. On occasion large festivals or "picnics" were held where literally tens of thousands gathered for all-day concerts.

Rock music also attracted a large following in the postwar years. An early pioneer in the development of rock and roll was a Texan, Buddy Holly, whose promising career was cut short in a tragic plane crash. Janis Joplin of Port Arthur, in a brief but hectic career, won national fame for her versions of rock and roll. Touring rock groups regularly attracted large audiences, mostly youth, and in every city and hamlet, rock groups of widely varying abilities were formed. Especially in the late sixties, rock was often viewed as a part of the social protest movement attractive to those who questioned the values of contemporary society, but in the seventies and eighties, more seem to be attracted to rock because they enjoyed listening to it or playing it.

Widespread interest in art in Texas may be measured from the organization in 1911 of the Texas Fine Arts Association. During recent years this interest has grown. Most large Texas cities and many smaller ones have art museums. Also, the colleges have art departments, and art is an increasingly popular subject in the public schools. Over the years the state has produced many fine artists, and some have gained national acclaim. Porfirio Salinas is known for his paintings of the Texas hill country, particularly for scenes featuring bluebonnets. Another artist is José Cisneros, who is noted for his pen-and-ink illustrations.

Thus, in many ways, the cultural progress of Texas in modern times has kept pace with the economic growth of the state. In literature, drama, music, and the arts, Texans have brought enrichment to their lives and to the nation.

THE PEOPLE

In the eighties, Texans celebrated the tricentennial of settlement by peoples other than native Americans (and also the sesquicentennial of the Texas Revolution). It was in 1682 that the Spanish friars established their

The 1980 Dallas skyline. (Courtesy Dallas Chamber of Commerce)

first settlement in Texas, the mission of Corpus Christi de la Ysleta, located a few miles east of the modern city of El Paso. Three centuries have brought great changes in the land that is Texas and changes also—perhaps even more dramatic—in the people who inhabit the land.

Estimates in 1986 placed the population at 16,682,000, third highest in the nation, and more than double that of Texas in 1940. The growth rate was higher than the national average in the early 1970s and much higher at the end of the decade, but it declined in the early eighties, and at mid-decade, was scarcely increasing at all. Women have outnumbered men since 1960, but the female-male ratio remains lower than the national average. The bulk of the population lives in the 28 Metropolitan Statistical Areas (MSA) and Primary Metropolitan Statistical Areas (PMSA), but in the seventies rural areas began to increase in population once more. Because of a declining birth rate, Texas was increasingly dependent upon migration for its population growth. Among the many ethnic groups that made up the population in 1980, "Anglos" represented 66 percent; blacks 12 percent; people speaking Spanish as a native language or with a Spanish surname, 21 percent; and two percent were other nonwhites. The distribution of ethnic minorities within the population has spread in some respects, and grown more centralized in others. Mexican-Americans remained the dominant ethnic group in South Texas, but whereas they were at one time concentrated in that area, by 1980 they lived in every county and in large numbers in Dallas, Fort Worth, and Houston. Two counties, Dallas and Harris, contained about 45 percent of the black population.

Perhaps the most striking change of recent decades has been the altered role of ethnic minorities and women within the society. As progress has been made in the direction of political equality, so has progress been made in social and economic areas. Blacks and Mexican-Americans, once almost automatically relegated to low-paying, common-labor jobs, today hold responsible and influential posts in industry, business, the professions, and government. Sports and cultural areas similarly have been strengthened by the contributions of the minorities.

Women have assumed a more visible role. In the late seventies and early eighties, women were elected mayors in San Antonio, Austin, and Houston. A Texas woman was appointed as the United States ambassador to Great Britain, and another served for several years as the president of the University of Texas. More and more, women sought employment outside of the home, and in the 1980s women made up approximately one-third of the work force. In a variety of ways, the women of Texas struggled for equality and the expansion of opportunities. Regularly, women's groups appeared at state public-school textbook hearings to ensure that a fair image of women and their role was presented to the school children of the state. With the support of grants from a variety of sources, the Texas Foundation for Women's Resources has conducted extensive research and compiled publications and films to present more accurately the role of Texas women in history. Toward the end of the seventies, the National Organization of Women held its national convention in Houston, attended by thousands. Noticeable at the convention was some disagreement over both methods and goals, and this has been apparent in other ways. A group of Texas women, sometimes called the "Pink Ladies," has campaigned tirelessly to secure the repeal of the legislature's ratification of the ERA amendment to the Constitution. But older organizations, such as the League of Women Voters (with more than 40 chapters), the Texas Women's Political Caucus, and the Texas chapter of NOW, have been joined by new organizations, Texas Women for the Eighties and the Governor's Commission on Women, to work on causes of particular concern to women.

To a considerable extent, the progress of minorities and women in Texas has come through the use of federal regulation. Laws passed primarily in the sixties and administered through federal agencies sought to ensure an open society and an end to ethnic and sexual discrimination. On occasion the courts have taken a role. But even without the regulation of law, opportunities have become more abundant and open discrimination more rare.

Total equality for ethnic minorities and women remains a goal, however, not a reality. The proportion of Mexican-Americans, blacks, and women who hold low-paying, lower-status jobs continues to be much higher than that of Anglo males. Among state government employees, for example, in 1976 approximately 37 percent of Anglo males held higher-paying jobs, while slightly less than four percent of black and Mexican-American women held such jobs. But the proportion of Mexican-Americans, blacks, and women employed was substantially higher than it had been a decade earlier.

Progress for minorities, even though not completely satisfactory, was in many respects typical of Texas in the 1970's. It was a decade of optimism, prosperity, pride, almost unlimited faith in the future. In some ways it was an occasion for pride that was not always justified. In 1970 Texans could claim that its people had completed an average of 11.7 years of school. But this was slightly less than the achievement for the nation. Approximately 30 percent had not gone beyond the eighth grade, and three percent had not completed the first grade. On the other hand, more than 22 percent had attended college. There was the stereotype of the fabulously wealthy Texan who flaunted his or her money, and there always seemed to be enough of that sort around to perpetuate the image. Indeed, one of the most popular television programs aired in the late seventies (and in the eighties) was a fictional account of a rich Texas family whose outrageous wealth was exceeded only by its outrageous behavior. Certainly, there was much wealth in the state—enough to support the Astrodome, two professional football teams, two major league baseball clubs, a long list of leisure-time activities, and considerable luxurious living. But for the population as a whole, per capita income was only $6,827 in 1977, even with the impact of inflation. In 1976 the state ranked twenty-fifth in the nation, slightly less than the national average in these terms. Disparities in per capita income were striking. In some communities in the Rio Grande Valley, income was only a little more than a third of what it was in the city of Midland located in the West Texas oilfields. But, justified or not, the image of prosperity, success, and optimism persisted as the seventies turned into the eighties.

In the mid-eighties, much of that optimism and confidence was not to be found. The economic recession, precipitated by many factors but particularly by hard times in the oil industry, left at times more than ten percent of the work force unemployed, the state budget with a shortfall in the billions, and the owners of businesses wondering if there was any hope of continued operations. But the troubles of the eighties were more than just a matter of money. For the first time in many decades, perhaps since the Great Depression, Texans were questioning the future, and with some doubt about it. Few expected the oil industry to return to its former status, and there was little agreement on what might replace it. Some economic experts talked knowledgeably about diversification, others advocated the advantages of "high-tech," and all seemed to agree that education was a part of the solution. Prophets of gloom were few, but the confidence of the past was notably absent.

As the people of Texas entered their fourth century of modern civilization, many of the problems that had prevailed throughout the previous three were no more. Indian wars, starvation, and back-breaking physical labor were no longer a part of the struggle for survival. For practically all, the standard of living was at least comfortable, though certainly much higher for some than for others.

But the challenges of the future were obvious in the eighties. City life had brought new comforts and conveniences, but posed problems in the form of congestion, cultural conflicts, transportation, and pollution. The energy crisis presented by declining petroleum reserves added to the uncertainties in a variety of ways. Sometimes ignored, but perhaps the most serious problem of all for a large part of the state, was the declining supply of water reserves.

In one way or another, Texas has resolved its problems of an earlier day. A free, prosperous, and contented life depends upon its ability to solve those of the present and of the future. Ultimately, the outcome depends upon the people.

SELECTED BIBLIOGRAPHY

For information on contemporary industry and business in Texas, *The Texas Almanac* is indispensible, and the *Texas Business Review* is quite valuable. Another excellent source is the issue of *Newsweek* dated December 12, 1977, which features articles on a variety of aspects in Texas but especially considers economic affairs. See also John A. Burghort, "Trends in Population Growth in Texas," *National Business Review*," June 1978, pp. 112–114. Useful is Mary Ann Norman, *The Texas Economy Since World War II* (Boston, 1983). Looking at economic affairs in a somewhat different way, see Paul F. Lambert and Kenny A. Franks (eds.), *Voices from the Oil Fields* (Norman, OK., 1984); Roger M. Olien and Diana David Olien, *Oil Booms: Social Changes in Five Texas Towns* (Lincoln, Neb., 1982); and Mamie Sypert Burns, *This I Can Leave You: A Woman's Days on the Pitchfork Ranch* (College Station, 1986). Studies of railroads that include the postwar period are Charles Zlatkovich, *Texas Railroads: A Record of Construction and Abandonment* (Austin, 1981); and Don L. Hofsommer, *The Southern Pacific 1901–1985* (College Station, 1986).

References on minorities may be found in the bibliography of the previous chapter; in addition see Vernon M. Briggs, Jr., and others, *The Chicano Worker* (Austin, 1977); Manuel A. Machado, Jr., *Listen Chicano! An Informal History of the Mexican-American* (Chicago, 1979); Shirley Achor, *Mexican-Americans in a Dallas Barrio* (Tucson, 1979); F. Arturo Rosales, "Mexicans in Houston: The Struggle to Survive, 1908–1975," *The Houston Review*, III, 224–248; and Terry Jordan, "A Century and a Half of Ethnic Change in Texas, 1836–1986," *Southwestern Historical Quarterly*, LXXXIX, 385–422.

Art is discussed in Al Lowman, *Painting Arts in Texas* (Austin, 1975). Harold V. Ratliff surveys Texas sports in "A History of Sports in Texas with a Unique Philosophy," *Proceedings of the Philosophical Society of Texas* (1968). John W. Story writes on religion in "Texan Baptist Leadership, the Social Gospel and Race, 1954–1968," *Southwestern Historical Quarterly*, LXXXIII, 29–46 and *Texas Baptist Leadership and Social Christianity, 1900–1980* (College Station, 1986). William T. Pilkington surveys Texas writing in *Imaging Texas: The Literature of the Lone Star State* (Boston, 1981); but also see Lon Tinkle, *An American Original: The Life of J. Frank Dobie* (Boston, 1978). For a look at art, politics, and the media, see Ben Sargent, *Texas Statehouse Blues: The Editorial Cartoons of Ben Sargent* (Austin, 1980). Country music is discussed in *The Texas Monthly* and in a number of other contemporary publications, sometimes in depth. Hubert Rouseel has written *The Houston Symphony Orchestra 1913–1971* (Austin, 1972).

APPENDIX

GOVERNORS OF TEXAS[1]

1691–1692	Domingo Terán de los Ríos
1693–1716	Texas unoccupied but included in Coahuila
1716–1719	Martían de Alarcón appointed governor of Texas on December 7, 1716. (On August 5, 1716, he had been appointed governor of Coahuila.)
1719–1722	The Marqués de San Miguél de Aguayo, governor of Coahuila and Texas
1722–1726	Fernando Pérez e Almazán
1727–1730	Melchor de Media Villa y Ascona
1730–	Juan Antonio Bustillo y Zevallos
1734–	Manuel de Sandoval
1736–1737	Carlos Benites Franquis de Lugo
1737–	Fernández de Jáuregui y Urrutia, govenor of Nuevo León, governor extraordinary and *visitador*
1737–1740	Prudencio de Orobio y Bazterra (*governor ad interim*)
1741–1743	Tomás Felipe Wintuisen

[1]The list of governors holding office before the Texan Revolution is based on Herbert E. Bolton, *Guide to Materials for the History of the United States in the Principal Archives of Mexico* (Washington, D.C., 1913) pp. 478, 479. Bolton makes the statement that "there are some imperfections in the results, in spite of care, for the materials for compiling a correct list are still mainly unprinted." In a few instances information made available subsequent to the publication of Bolton's study has removed doubt as to the terms of governors.

1743–1744	Justo Boneo y Morales
1744–1748	Francisco García Larios (*governor ad interim*)
1748–1750	Pedro del Barrio Junco y Espriella
1751–1759	Jacinto de Barrios yJáuregui. Barrios was appointed governor of Coahuila in 1757, but was retained in Texas until 1759 to complete a task.
1759–1766	Angel de Martos y Navarrete
1767–1770	Hugo Oconór (*governor ad interim*)
1770–1778	The Baron de Ripperdá
1778–1786	Domingo Cabello
1786	Bernardo Bonavía was appointed July 8, but apparently did not serve.
1787–1790	Rafael Martínez Pachecho appointed February 27; his removal was approved October 18, 1790.
1788	The office of governor was ordered suppressed and the province put under a presidial captain.
1790–1799?	Manuel Muñoz
1798(?)	Josef Irigoyen, apparently appointed but did not serve.
1800(?)–1805	Juan Bautista de Elguezábal
1805–1810	Antonio Cordero y Bustamante
1810–1813	Manuel de Salcedo
1811(Jan. 22– March 2)	Juan Bautista Casas (revolutionary governor)
1814–1818	Christóbal Domínguez
1817–	Ignacio Pérez and Manuel Pardo (*governors ad interim*)
1817–1822	Antonio Martínez
1822–1823	José Felix Trespalacios
1823(?)–1824	Luciano García

GOVERNORS OF COAHUILA AND TEXAS

1824–1826	Rafael Gonzáles
1826–1827	Victor Blanco
1827–1831	José María Viesca
1831–1832	José María Letona
1832–1833	Juan Martín de Beramendi
1834–1835	Juan José Elguezábal
1835–	Agustín Viesca
1835–	Ramón Eca y Músquiz

PROVISIONAL GOVERNORS DURING THE TEXAN REVOLUTION[2]

Nov. 14, 1835–March 1, 1836	Henry Smith
Jan. 11, 1836–March 1, 1836	James W. Robinson[3]

[2]This list of Texas chief executives is taken in part from the *Texas Almanac*, 1936, p. 317. Later information courtesy Ray Barrera, Secretary of State.

[3]Robinson was elected by the council after Smith had been deposed and the office of governor declared vacant by the council. Thereafter both men claimed the right to exercise the executive authority.

PRESIDENTS OF THE REPUBLIC OF TEXAS

March 17, 1836–Oct. 22, 1836	David G. Burnet
Oct. 22, 1836–Dec. 10, 1838	Sam Houston
Dec. 10, 1838–Dec. 13, 1841	Mirabeau B. Lamar
Dec. 13, 1841–Dec. 9, 1844	Sam Houston
Dec. 9, 1844–Feb. 19, 1846	Anson Jones

GOVERNORS AFTER ANNEXATION

Feb. 19, 1846–Dec. 21, 1847	J. Pinckney Henderson
May 19, 1846–Nov.—, 1846	A. C. Horton[4]
Dec. 21, 1847–Dec. 21, 1849	George T. Wood
Dec. 21, 1849–Nov. 23, 1853	P. Hansborough Bell
Nov. 23, 1853–Dec. 21, 1853	J.W. Henderson[5]
Dec. 21, 1853–Dec. 21, 1857	Elisha M. Pease
Dec. 21, 1857–Dec. 21, 1859	Hardin R. Runnels
Dec. 21, 1859–March 16, 1861	Sam Houston[6]
March 16, 1861–Nov. 7, 1861	Edward Clark
Nov. 7, 1861–Nov. 5, 1863	Francis R. Lubbock
Nov. 5, 1863–June 17, 1865	Pendleton Murrah[7]
July 21, 1865–Aug. 9, 1866	Andrew J. Hamilton (provisional)
Aug. 9, 1866–Aug. 8, 1867	James W. Throckmorton[8]
Aug. 8, 1867–Sept. 30, 1869	Elisha M. Pease
Jan. 8, 1870–Jan. 15, 1874	Edmund J. Davis[9]
Jan. 15, 1874–Dec. 1, 1876	Richard Coke[10]
Dec. 1, 1876–Jan. 21, 1879	Richard B. Hubbard
Jan. 21, 1879–Jan. 16, 1883	Oran M. Roberts
Jan. 16, 1883–Jan. 18, 1887	John Ireland
Jan. 18, 1887–Jan. 20, 1891	Lawrence Sullivan Ross
Jan. 20, 1891–Jan. 15, 1895	James S. Hogg
Jan. 15, 1895–Jan. 17, 1899	Charles A. Culberson
Jan. 17, 1899–Jan. 20, 1903	Joseph D. Sayers
Jan. 20, 1903–Jan. 15, 1907	S.W.T. Lanham
Jan. 15, 1907–Jan. 19, 1911	Thomas M. Campbell
Jan. 19, 1911–Jan. 19, 1915	Oscar Branch Colquitt
Jan. 19, 1915–Aug. 25, 1917	James E. Ferguson (impeached)
Aug. 25, 1917–Jan. 18, 1921	William P. Hobby

[4]Lieutenant Governor Horton served as governor while Governor Henderson was away commanding troops in the war with Mexico.

[5]Lieutenant Governor Henderson became governor when Governor Bell resigned to take his seat in Congress, to which he had been elected.

[6]Houston refused to take the oath of allegiance to the Confederacy and was deposed. He was succeeded by Lieutenant Governor Edward Clark.

[7]Murrah's administration was terminated by the fall of the Confederacy. Murrah retired to Mexico, and for a period, May-June, 1865, Lieutenant Governor Fletcher S. Stockdale was acting governor.

[8]Throckmorton was removed by the military. Pease, the provisional governor who succeeded him, resigned September 30, 1869.

[9]Davis was appointed provisional governor after he had been elected governor.

[10]Coke resigned to enter the United States Senate and was succeeded by Lieutenant Governor Hubbard.

Jan. 18, 1921–Jan. 20, 1925	Pat M. Neff
Jan. 20, 1925–Jan. 17, 1927	Miram A. Ferguson
Jan. 17, 1927–Jan. 20, 1931	Dan Moody
Jan. 20, 1931–Jan. 17, 1933	Ross S. Sterling
Jan. 17, 1933–Jan. 15, 1935	Miriam A. Ferguson
Jan. 15, 1935–Jan. 17, 1939	James V. Allred
Jan. 17, 1939-Aug. 4, 1941	W. Lee O'Daniel (resigned to enter U.S. Senate)
Aug. 4, 1941–Jan. 21, 1947	Coke R. Stevenson
Jan. 21, 1947–July 11, 1949	Beauford H. Jester (died)
July 11, 1949–Jan. 15, 1957	Allan Shivers
Jan. 15, 1957–Jan. 15, 1963	Price Daniel
Jan. 15, 1963–Jan. 21, 1969	John Connally
Jan. 21, 1969–Jan. 16, 1973	Preston Smith
Jan. 16, 1973–Jan. 16, 1979	Dolph Briscoe
Jan. 16, 1979–Jan. 18, 1983	William Clements
Jan. 18, 1983–Jan. 20, 1987	Mark White
Jan. 20, 1987–	William Clements

UNITED STATES SENATORS

Houston Succession

Feb. 21, 1846-March 4, 1859	Sam Houston
March 4, 1859–July 11, 1861	John Hemphill[11]
Feb. 22, 1870–March 3, 1877	Morgan C. Hamilton
March 3, 1877–March 3, 1895	Richard Coke
March 3, 1895–March, 3, 1901	Horace Chilton
March 3, 1901–Jan. 8, 1913	Joseph W. Bailey (resigned)
Jan. 8, 1913–Feb. 3, 1913	R.M. Johnson (filled vacancy on appointment)
Feb. 13, 1913–April 9, 1941	Morris Sheppard (died)
April 21, 1941–June 26, 1941	Andrew Jackson Houston (died)
Aug. 4, 1941–Jan. 3, 1949	W. Lee O'Daniel
Jan. 3, 1949–Jan. 20, 1961	Lyndon B. Johnson
Jan. 20, 1961–June 15, 1961	William A. Blakley
June 15, 1961–Jan. 21, 1985	John G. Tower
Jan. 21, 1985–	Phil Gramm

Rusk Succession

Feb. 21, 1846–July 29, 1857	Thomas J. Rusk (died)
Nov. 9, 1857–June 4, 1858	J. Pinckney Henderson (died)
Sept. 29, 1858–Dec. 5, 1859	Matthias Ward (filled vacancy on appointment)
1859–1861	Louis T. Wigfall
Feb. 22, 1870–March 3, 1875	James W. Flanagan
March 3, 1875–March, 3, 1887	Samuel B. Maxey

[11]Succession was broken by the secession of Texas. Louis T. Wigfall and W.S. Oldham represented Texas in the Confederate Senate. On August 21, 1866, the Texas legislature elected David G. Burnet and Oran M. Roberts to the United States Senate, but they were not allowed to take their seats.

March 3, 1887–June 10, 1891	John H. Reagan (resigned)
Dec. 7, 1891–March 30, 1892	Horace Chilton (filled vacancy on appointment)
March 30, 1892–March 3, 1899	Roger Q. Mills
March 3, 1899–March 4, 1923	Charles A. Culberson
March 4, 1923–March 4, 1929	Earle B. Mayfield
March 4, 1929–Jan. 3, 1953	Tom Connally
Jan. 3, 1953–Jan. 15, 1957	Price Daniel (resigned to become governor)
Jan. 13, 1957–April 19, 1957	William A. Blakley
April 19, 1957–Jan. 12, 1971	Ralph W. Yarborough
Jan. 12, 1971–	Lloyd Bentsen

INDEX

TEXAS

⊙ County seat.   ‡ Population of metropolitan area.   ■ Name not shown on map.

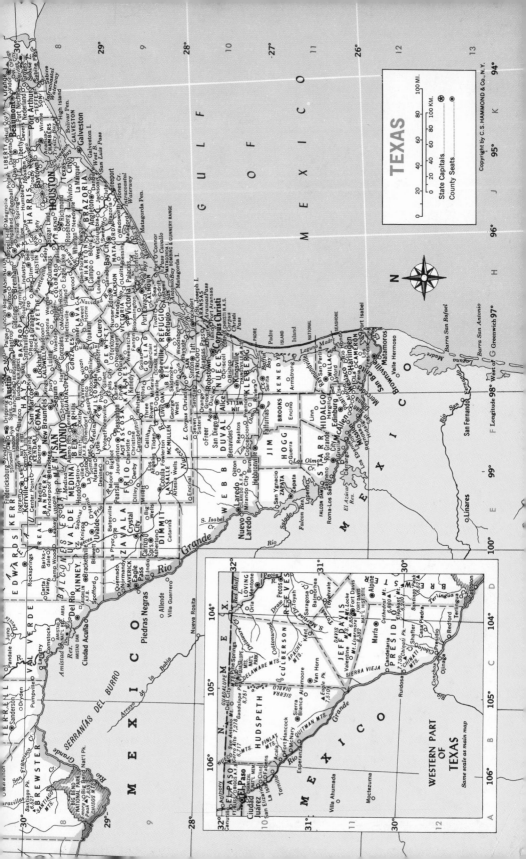

TEXAS

State Capitals ⊛
County Seats ⊙

Copyright by C. S. HAMMOND & Co., N.Y.

0 20 40 60 80 100 MI.
0 20 40 60 80 100 KM.

GULF OF MEXICO

MEXICO

WESTERN PART OF TEXAS
Same scale as main map